High-Performance Client/Server

Chris Loosley

Frank Douglas

D1410618

WILEY COMPUTER PUBLISHING

John Wiley & Sons, Inc.

New York ▲ Chichester ▲ Weinheim ▲ Brisbane ▲ Singapore ▲ Toronto

For Cynthia, who made it possible.—CL

To Jane, Jer, and Kate. Thanks.—FD

Publisher: Robert Ipsen
Editor: Robert M. Elliott
Managing Editor: Brian Snapp
Text Design & Composition: Impressions Book and Journal Services, Inc.

Designations used by companies to distinguish their products are often claimed as trademarks. In all instances where John Wiley & Sons, Inc., is aware of a claim, the product names appear in initial capital or ALL CAPITAL LETTERS. Readers, however, should contact the appropriate companies for more complete information regarding trademarks and registration.

This book is printed on acid-free paper. ♾

This publication is designed to provide accurate and authoritative information in regard to the subject matter covered. It is sold with the understanding that the publisher is not engaged in rendering legal, accounting, or other professional services. If legal advice or other expert assistance is required, the services of a competent professional person should be sought.

Library of Congress Cataloging-in-Publication Data:

Loosley, Chris, 1945–
    High-performance client/server / Chris Loosley, Frank Douglas.
      p. cm.
    "Wiley Computer Publishing."
    Includes index.
    ISBN 0-471-16269-8 (pbk. : alk. paper)
    1. Client/server computing.   2. High performance computing.
I. Douglas, Frank, 1942– . II. Title.
QA76.9.C55L66   1997
005.2′76—dc21   97-21747
                                   CIP

Printed in the United States of America.

10 9 8 7 6 5 4 3 2 1

Contents

3   Performance Fundamentals 41

PART II   Process 83

4   Software Performance Engineering 85

Foreword

Over the past decade, client/server computing has had a considerable impact on all aspects of the design, development, and deployment of enterprise computing systems. It has enabled corporations to move away from the monolithic centralized development of the '80s, to a new modular and flexible architecture that allows application processing to be distributed across a network of systems. This flexibility permits data to be stored, and processing to be done, on central, local, or departmental computers, based on performance, cost and security requirements. Stand-alone desktop computers and workstations can also to be connected into a client/server network, supporting access to existing centralized systems and new distributed ones.

Client/server computing enables the use of low-cost hardware and software, increases local autonomy and ownership of data, and offers better performance and higher availability. It is used to build many different types of application, from corporate distributed OLTP and data warehousing applications, to departmental and groupware systems. These applications often involve a wide range of different hardware and software—powerful parallel processing machines, departmental servers, desktop systems, or even network computers. Some people argue that the advent of Internet/Intranet and Web technology signals the demise of client/server, but closer examination shows that this technology is just another form of client/server computing. In fact many organizations are interested in connecting new Web-based applications to existing client/server systems. Client/server, therefore, is likely to be with us for some time to come, and will be used for developing an ever-increasing set of complex and interconnected applications.

Early implementers of client/server applications were focused primarily on fast application development, and on the cost savings provided by the use of cheaper hardware and software. The first client/server systems paid little attention to good architecture design, systems management, or even performance. Experience has shown that designers and developers ignore these issues at their peril. A sound application architecture that focuses on providing good performance is crucial to the success of a client/server development project.

There are many books on client/server, but few focus on designing for performance, especially when discussing the building of enterprise-level applications. To cover such a topic in a book requires an extensive background in large enterprise systems and in associated performance issues and design techniques. It also requires detailed knowledge of the many different types of client/applications being deployed by organizations today. I have known Chris Loosley, the author of *High-Performance Client/Server*, for over twenty years, and I cannot think of anyone more experienced or more suited to writing a book on this topic. *High-Performance Client/Server* offers in-depth and unparalleled information about building enterprise client/server applications, and has to be essential reading for IT specialists who are concerned with the development and deployment of high-performance client/server systems.

—Colin J. White
President DataBase Associates International, Inc., and InfoIT, Inc.
August, 1997

Acknowledgments

"To write it, it took three months; to conceive it—three minutes; to collect the data in it—all my life."

F. Scott Fitzgerald

This book is about software architecture and design, with a special emphasis on the performance aspects. Because this subject has been a lifelong interest of mine, many people have helped to inspire and clarify the thoughts I have finally collected together here.

It all began with my parents, Ron and Rose Loosley. Rose was self-educated with the aid of BBC Radio and the public library; she gave me an inquiring mind and a love of books. Ron was an architect, until the war interrupted his apprenticeship in 1939. The struggle to raise a family in post-war Britain temporarily redirected his energies into farming, but architecture was ever his calling. I never thought to follow in his professional footsteps, but it turns out that I did anyway, although it took me about 25 years to recognize it.

It was not until the late 1980s, when I was working on CASE and modeling tools, that I made a clear mental connection between architecture and software engineering. In their different ways, Charlie Bachman's ideas about modeling languages and John Zachman's inspired presentations about information systems architectures each helped to focus my thoughts. I saw then that most software design tasks did not require huge amounts of invention. The right solution is usually obtained by applying a few key design principles and assembling a few fairly standard components in a particular way. In 1992, I wrote in my notes, "In the business world, good software design is the ultimate marriage of theory and practice, of elegance and function, of technology and the needs of people who have a job to do. Just like good architecture, in fact."

Recently, I discovered that this very idea had given birth to a *patterns movement,* a new community within our profession that seeks to apply the ideas of the architect Christopher Alexander, whose seminal work, *A Pattern Lan-*

guage[1] was published in 1977. Interestingly, Alexander's ideas about the value of pattern languages have found far more favor with the proponents of object-oriented programming than with the members of his own profession.[2]

Similarly, my father had no way of knowing at the time just how much his love of architecture was preparing me for a career in software engineering. Yet I grew up observing his eye for balance and simplicity, his desire always to blend the functional and artistic elements into a solution that "feels right," and his willingness to care about all the small details of that solution. A career in software engineering has shown me that these are essential qualities in the field of software architecture and design too, and I am sure that I find these ideas to be familiar and natural because I learned them firsthand from Dad.

At the time, however, my own love was mathematical problems and puzzles—an early interest that was nurtured by my grade school teacher, Miss Annie Morgan. Eventually this led me to the Pure Mathematics and Statistics Departments of the University College of Wales, Aberystwyth, where Professor Dennis V. Lindley taught us how to reason logically about random events. I was fortunate to have such a good teacher; Lindley's own tutor had been M. P. Meshenberg, who had been taught by Markov himself, the Russian mathematician who gave his name to the field of random (or *Markovian*) phenomena.

Even more interesting was the brand-new course in computer science. The college had the latest IBM 1620, a 2000-word machine (about 8K bytes)—a small slice of silicon today packs far more computing power than a room full of relays and transistors did in 1964. But Peter J. H. King taught me to program it in FORTRAN, which in turn launched me into a career with IBM.

In 1972 or 1973, in my early days at IBM, I received some very practical career guidance. It was dispensed late one night by a more experienced systems engineer whose name I do not even remember. Sitting by the printer in the IBM computer room in Croydon, pausing between rounds of debugging, he told me that the secret to a successful and enjoyable career was always to keep "the three Ps" in your job: *Programming*, *Performance*, and *Presentations*. I followed his advice, and it worked well for me; in many ways, this book is the result. Maybe my anonymous mentor will come forward to receive the credit.

Now the names I *do* remember:

▶ First, from my years in the UK before 1978: Gordon Smith at The Freshwater Group; Phil Hoffman and Ian Finch at IBM's Finance Branch in the City of

---

[1]Christopher Alexander, *A Pattern Language* (New York, NY: Oxford University Press, 1977).
[2]Richard P. Gabriel, *Patterns of Software: Tales from the Software Community* (New York, NY: Oxford University Press, 1996).

London; Phil Stapleton at Banker's Trust; Ian Tyson at Fodens; Paolo Bruni, Mike Burman, Harry Hill, and Ron Kliesch during a temporary assignment to IBM's Palo Alto Development Center to benchmark the first release of IMS/VS; Brian Cookson, Harry DeBrett, Dave Schofield, and Pete Russell at the IBM UK Systems Center; and Sally Hoffman at IBM's Education Center.

▶ Next, from my time at IBM's Santa Teresa Laboratory in the USA between 1978 and 1987: Valdo Androsciani, Juan Benavides, Marilyn Bohl, Ted Codd, Jack Duey, Mike Golding, Don Haderle, Mike Hatch, Ed Lassettre, Earl Libby, Tony Lukes, Prem Mehra, Evelyn Miller, Roger Miller, Bob Ojala, Akira Shibamiya, Angelo Sironi, Christian Skalberg, Lionel Smith, Phil Teale, Mike Tucker, Norris van den Berg, Shelly Weinberg, Sharon Weinberg, and Pat Worthington.

▶ Finally, from my time with Bachman Information Systems and DataBase Associates since 1987: Nagraj Alur, Tim Andrews, Arnie Barnett, Charlie Bachman, Chris Date, Larry English, Greg Faust, Mike Ferguson, Chris Gane, Paul Hessinger, Cynthia Holladay, Phil Jones, Dick Manasseri, Giovanni Modica, Alex Mimo, Casey Quayle, Alec Ramsay, David Stodder, Jeff Tash, Linda Thorsen, Colin White, Paul Winsberg, and John Zachman.

In their different ways, each one of these people either helped me to better understand how computer systems work, provided a larger vision or framework that I could fit that knowledge into, or supplied a forum for me to practice organizing and communicating ideas to others. I am grateful to all those I have named, and to countless others I have met along the way.

I would particularly like to thank Bob Elliott, my editor at Wiley, who insisted that I should write a book, and helped me get started and keep moving forward. Later, Brian Calandra and Brian Snapp at Wiley dealt patiently with me (authors can be difficult at times) as I struggled to organize and complete all the necessary details.

A special thanks is due to Cynthia Holladay, to whom this book is dedicated, whose unflagging enthusiasm and tireless labor for the cause of software performance engineering launched the Bachman WindTunnel project and was an inspiration to me and to everyone else connected with it. She has supported me throughout in every possible way.

Finally, thanks to my children, Hunter Bryn and Anwen Heather, for their patience and encouragement during my seemingly endless months at the computer. They have no plans to follow in my footsteps, but . . .

Contributors

I wish to acknowledge several authors and speakers whose original contributions of either written material or the recordings of conference presentations have evolved into sections or chapters of the book. They are, approximately in chapter order:

Alex Mimo, for helping me organize the first draft of the book, and for asking many insightful and difficult questions that kept me on my toes.

Linda Thorsen, for her work while we were at Bachman converting my spoken presentations arguing the case for software performance engineering into coherent material that could eventually be published. Many of those ideas survived to form the core of Chapter 1.

Paul Winsberg, for his original contributions to Chapter 2 on the subject of client/server architecture and for his invaluable help in clarifying and refining the presentation of the ideas in Chapter 4.

Tom Cushing, for his contributions to the ideas in Table 4.3, for the capsule in Chapter 5 on application profiles, and for the insight on caching that bears his name in Chapter 14.

Neal Nelson, for his generous assistance with the material on benchmarking in Chapter 6 during a time when his own schedule was especially hectic.

Nagraj Alur, Mike Ferguson, Dan Graham, and Colin White, for their presentations and InfoDB articles on parallelism that provided the foundation for much of Chapter 13.

John Kneiling, for the presentations and InfoDB articles that provided the groundwork for the sections on application-level communication protocols and message-oriented middleware in Chapter 15 and the messaging case study in Chapter 17.

Charles Brett of Spectum Reports Inc. (*www.interalpha.net/middlewarespectra/*), for free access to back issues of *MiddlewareSpectra*, invaluable during the production of Chapter 15, and for his timely advice and insights while I was wrestling with the arguments and conclusions of Chapter 16.

David Linthicum, for stepping in at short notice and producing a solid and usable draft of Chapter 18.

Nagraj Alur, for his presentation on data replication that provided the foundation for Chapter 21. The transcription of Nagraj's talk was particularly enjoyable, containing many amusing references to *pier-to-pier replication* and other technological innovations previously unknown to me.

Sid Adelman, for his original contribution to the capsule on "The Cost Effective Data Warehouse" that appears in Chapter 21.

David Stodder, editor of *Database Programming & Design,* for giving me permission to reuse material that I originally wrote for articles or columns published in that magazine.

Three collaborators deserve special recognition:

Frank Douglas, my coauthor, for staying with the project despite being under tremendous time pressure. After volunteering originally to write Chapter 22 on transaction management, Frank was not only forced to condense his encyclopedic knowledge of that subject into a single chapter, he eventually wrote the early drafts of Chapters 2 and 4, several sections that ended up in Part IV of the book, and Chapters 20 and 21 in their entirety.

George Peters, for creating all but the final drafts of both the Performance-Oriented Glossary and the Index of Guidelines by Subject Area. Through the generous contribution of his time, George converted these two sections from a desirable goal into a reality, and their final form is largely due to his efforts.

Jan Wright, my editorial assistant, who joined the project at a time when it was floundering, and got it moving again. Jan read literally every word in the book at least twice, and most chapters many more times as we produced, revised, reworked, edited, re-edited, and reorganized the numerous drafts. In the process, she made endless improvements in the clarity and consistency of the text. I doubt if I would ever have finished without her persistent, cheerful, patient assistance.

Needless to say, I am responsible for the final text, including any errors it may contain.

—Chris Loosley
Aptos, California
July 11th, 1997

I would like to extend my thanks to Chris Loosley for his help, cheer, strength, and exciting concepts. I would never have traveled this road without his guidance.

—Frank Douglas

Introduction

"What's the use of a book," thought Alice, "without pictures or conversations?"

Lewis Carroll

With all the books available today on client/server technology, you may wonder why we would write yet another. The short answer is this: By and large, our industry devotes far too much shelf space to the bells and whistles of the latest technology, and not nearly enough to solid practical guidance on how to use that technology effectively to solve business problems. Our aim is to redress the balance, particularly in the area of application performance.

In today's world of visual programming, rapid development, and out-of-the-box solutions, software vendors offer a bewildering array of new products and promises, producing a neverending flood of information in books and magazines, on the Internet, and at conferences, seminars, and trade shows. Unless you employ a batallion of research assistants, it is impossible to keep up to date. But one thing remains constant: to be effective, software applications must meet business performance objectives.

In fact, our main reason for writing the book is that we see performance as a fundamental cornerstone of application quality. At the same time, we also know that performance is one area of software design that is frequently misunderstood, forgotten, ignored, or postponed, often with disastrous results. Yet we cannot hope to achieve and maintain acceptable levels of performance by simply tuning the code or tweaking the computing environment—it requires an integrated approach that spans all phases of the system life cycle. And client/server technology does nothing to diminish this need; rather, it reinforces it by offering many new possibilities for performance problems.

From the beginning, therefore, we have had three aims for the book:

1. To explain clearly the five performance factors and the six basic principles of all performance-related thinking.
2. To draw conclusions and give guidelines that show how to apply those principles systematically to design, develop, and deploy effective applications for the distributed enterprise.
3. To do so using language and examples that are understandable and interesting to any professional working with today's information technologies.

The following sections elaborate on these goals. After a short section defining our audience, we explain in more detail what we really mean by *client/ server*. Next we explain what *high performance* means (and does not mean) in that context, and finally we explain the structure of the book.

Do You Need This Book?

This book is written for anyone who works with information technology in a distributed enterprise and wants applications that deliver acceptable performance. It is not just for the performance specialist, if such a person even exists in the overworked, downsized MIS departments that use information technology today.

Do you already have client/server applications whose response times are erratic or unacceptable? Or are you about to design, develop, maintain, or manage a software application that must:

▶ Support a very important business process?
▶ Meet defined response time goals?
▶ Handle a high volume of business transactions?
▶ Process very large databases?
▶ Update small shared tables, or tables with small indexes?
▶ Support multiple users who often process common subsets of data?
▶ Update data at multiple locations within a single unit of work?
▶ Update data that is also used by other performance sensitive applications?
▶ Manipulate data that resides at one or more remote locations?

If you answered yes to one of these ten questions, then we believe that you will find this book useful. If you scored more than 2, don't put this book down—you are the reader we have in mind.

Our list of 10 questions may seem to be a fairly inclusive one. In our view, that just goes to prove how important performance really is. When you think about it, do you really have *any* applications whose performance does not matter at all? Saying that application response time is not important is a bit like saying that you don't care how fast your car goes—as long as it doesn't take you three hours to drive to work in the morning.

What Do We Mean by *Client/Server*?

Although it began as a fairly precise description of one style of distributed processing, the term *client/server* has now acquired many meanings, some more technical, others more related to business reengineering. For a few years in the early 1990s, the DBMS vendors hijacked the term, equating it with a two-tier database server architecture. It is a tribute to the success of their marketing efforts that many people still think of client/server computing in that way. But as we explain in more detail in Chapter 2, this is not what we mean by *client/server*. In fact, the relatively simple LAN-based computing environments that served as a platform for two-tier client/server databases were just one step along a path that leads to distributed information systems operating enterprise-wide.

Enterprises are moving along this path because of changes in the business environment. Some of these changes are intended to deal with perceived problems in their existing information systems, for example:

▶ Self-contained "stovepipe" applications that do not support initiatives across business areas.
▶ Centralized management information systems (MIS) departments that control decisions about how and when new applications are developed and are often perceived as overly bureaucratic and unresponsive to new business needs.
▶ Developers with centralized computing backgrounds and skills who are primarily concerned with technical problems, sometimes to the exclusion of business issues.

More important, however, is the widespread attempt to apply new computing technology in pursuit of better business processes—to stay competitive, or to become more efficient or profitable. Many such initiatives involve changes in the way an enterprise conducts business. There is an increased focus on the importance of the customer, and consequently on the information resources and services that are required to support interactions with customers. A common example is the goal of creating a business process that offers the customer a "single point of contact" with the enterprise—a goal that imposes significant information-processing requirements.

The collective term for these efforts to integrate and align information resources with business needs is Business Process Reengineering (BPR), and the client/server model has become a standard feature of the BPR movement.[1] In contrast to the perceived restrictions and limitations of centralized computing, the client/server model represents flexibility and responsiveness to fluid business conditions. It does not even matter that this analysis oversimplifies the issues enormously and glosses over the technical and management challenges of distributed computing, or that aggressive marketing to business leaders by the vendors of distributed computing technology is one of the forces that has propelled client/server architectures into their current preeminent role.

The plain fact is that business reasons are driving the move toward distributed systems—despite the general consensus that these systems are difficult to build and expensive to maintain. They are being built because the modern enterprise is already distributed, and needs a distributed information system to support it.

This is what we mean by *enterprise client/server*. So when we use the term *client/server,* unless we specifically refer to a two-tier implementation, we are usually intending it to be read in its most inclusive sense, in which it is synonymous with the combination of *enterprise systems*, *information processing*, and *distributed computing.*

What Do We Mean by *High Performance*?

Despite its title—*High-Performance Client/Server*—this is *not* a book about high-performance computing.

Taken at face value, this disclaimer may seem to be almost an oxymoron. But the real problem is in our industry's use of terminology—the term *high-performance computing* has come to mean both *more,* and *less,* than the simple sum of its parts might imply. It actually has a more precise meaning than one might suspect, having become largely synonymous with what was once called *supercomputing*—the design of hardware and software to perform large numbers of computations very quickly. But *more* precision means, of course, that *less* is included. To equate *high-performance computing* with *supercomputing* is to exclude many important aspects of performance in the realm of *enterprise information processing.*

To clarify our point, Table I.1 summarizes the fundamentally different perspectives of high-performance computing and enterprise information processing.

---

[1] One of the most readable tutorials on this subject is David Vaskevitch's Client/Server Strategies: A Survival Guide for Corporate Reengineers (Foster City, CA: IDG Books Worldwide, 2nd Edition, 1995).

Table I.1	**Perspectives of Two Computing Genres**	
	High-Performance Computing	**Enterprise Information Processing**
Workload type	Massive computations	Massive amounts of data
Purpose	Answers to problems	Access to information
Program duration	Long-running programs	Short transactions
User population	Small, relatively homogeneous	Large, relatively diverse
Response objective	Minimize program run times	Meet business transaction goals

Grand Challenges

One reason for this particular quirk of terminology is the 1987 executive order entitled "A Research and Development Strategy for High Performance Computing." This government-approved definition of "grand challenge" problems states that:

> A grand challenge is a fundamental problem in science or engineering, with broad application, whose solution would be enabled by the application of the high-performance computing that could become available in the near future. Examples of grand challenges are: (1) computational fluid dynamics for the design of hypersonic aircraft, . . . (2) electronic structure calculations for the design of new materials, . . . (3) plasma dynamics for fusion energy technology, . . . (4) calculations to understand the fundamental condensed matter theory, . . . (5) symbolic computations including speech recognition, . . ."[2]

Because these problems are deemed important enough to attract government funding, *high-performance computing* holds great interest for the research community. An Internet search is likely to produce over 30,000 references, the bulk of which appear to have academic connections.

In high-performance computing, the key resource is the *processor*. Research focuses on techniques for speeding up processor operations and optimizing the way the software uses the processor(s). Thanks to the definition of a grand

---

[2]Executive Office of the President, Office of Science and Technology Policy, A Research and Development Strategy for High Performance Computing (November 1987).

challenge as a problem that cannot be tackled with existing computers, work on high-performance computing necessarily revolves around subdividing a massive computational problem into many smaller, relatively independent chunks that can be parceled out to a network of independent processors. It focuses on the design of high-speed computers employing parallel processors, and on techniques of writing and compiling *very large programs* to exploit that parallel hardware to its maximum potential.

In the realm of enterprise information processing, on the other hand, the key resource is the *data*. There are good reasons why this has been called "the information age." Today, a company's success can hinge on the quality of its data and the timeliness of its information retrieval. Few modern corporations could survive for long without their data, which is stockpiled in files and databases of every size, shape, and format throughout the enterprise. Every day this mountain of data grows even larger, with millions (maybe even billions) of dollars being devoted each year to its care and maintenance.

Today's enterprise systems must accommodate this continual growth. When information systems grow, performance issues arise along six distinct dimensions:

1. **Very large databases:** Transactions, queries and reports must work with progressively larger and more complex operational and decision support databases.
2. **Complex stored objects:** Originally, databases stored relatively short alphanumeric business records; increasingly they must store graphics, voice, and video information too.
3. **Massive user populations:** Progressively more users need online access to business information.
4. **Very high transaction rates:** Very high transaction processing rates can occur, especially at peak business periods when responsiveness is critical to the profitability of the business.
5. **Sophisticated data analysis:** Traditional transaction processing recorded relatively simple business events. Now online systems must support progressively more complex data analysis.
6. **Enterprise-wide networks:** Linking departmental level local-area networks (LANs) with corporate wide-area networks (WANs) creates ever more complex enterprise networks.

Our goal in this book is to provide you with the analytical tools and the software design principles to create systems that will not be overwhelmed by this kind of growth. Good design anticipates the effects of business growth on performance, and accommodates it gracefully.

To sum up, our primary concerns in this book are:

▶ How should we organize massive amounts of business information to support the computing needs of a distributed enterprise?
▶ How can we provide timely access to that information for what is typically a very large number of relatively small programs?

In contrast to high-performance computing, with its emphasis on *processing*, our primary concerns will be highly scalable architectural frameworks and design techniques for *maintaining, locating, relocating, relating, organizing, summarizing,* and *displaying the right data* as quickly as necessary to meet the needs of some (larger) business process. We might even call this "the grand challenge of enterprise information processing."

Naturally, there is some overlap with high-performance computing, mostly in the areas of code tuning and the general principles of parallelism (which we discuss in Chapters 8 and 13 respectively). But we feel that it is important to establish our fundamental perspective at the outset: we are *data bigots* at heart! So if your interests run to massively parallel algorithms or TeraFLOPS, look elsewhere.[3] We will bore you with talk of high transaction volumes and Terabytes.

Finally, to avoid all this terminological confusion we thought about calling the book "Designing and Developing Information Processing Applications that Perform Acceptably in an Enterprise-Wide Distributed Computing Environment," but our editor, Bob Elliott, vetoed it. So the book you hold in your hand is *High-Performance Client/Server*—a nice, snappy title with a four-page explanation of what it means.

How the Book Is Organized

Perhaps the best way to explain the book is to review its contents. . . .

Parts and Chapters

The book contains 22 chapters and related reference material, arranged in six parts as follows:

Part I: Foundations   As the name suggests, the material in Part I is intended to serve as a firm foundation for the remainder of the book:

---

[3]For a comprehensive, readable (and inexpensive) introduction, we recommend Kevin Dowd's High Performance Computing (Sebastopol, CA: O'Reilly & Associates, 1993).

▶ **Chapter 1**, *Connections*, is a relatively short chapter explaining the motivation for the book, and elaborating on the themes that we touched upon in the opening paragraphs of this Introduction. It concludes with a checklist of potential performance factors that points forward to later chapters.

▶ **Chapter 2**, *Enterprise Client/Server*, describes the evolution of client/server architectures, introduces the subject of client/server middleware, and reviews some of the challenges of client/server development. It is intended to provide sufficient foundation for the discussions of performance that follow in Parts II and III of the book, without delving into the details of middleware choices or the architectural conclusions that will appear later in Part IV.

▶ **Chapter 3**, *Performance Fundamentals*, is a tutorial on performance from an application, system, and organizational perspective. It explains the fundamental factors that determine all software performance and how they are interconnected, concluding with *Nagraj's Law of Tuning Choices*. For readers with a performance background, this material will be an overview; for others, we hope it explains what performance is all about without getting too technical.

Part II: Process   In the second part of the book, we focus on the process of achieving and maintaining acceptable performance:

▶ **Chapter 4**, *Software Performance Engineering*, explains how we can create applications and manage their performance using the systematic approach of *software engineering with performance in mind,* or SPE for short. We identify the ten fundamental activities that together comprise SPE, the performance life cycle that every application goes through, and the various ways of approaching that life cycle. We conclude with an extensive discussion of service level management and other organizational issues, and the roles various members of the organization play in managing performance.

▶ **Chapter 5**, *Software Performance Engineering Activities*, deals with performance management "from soup to nuts," stepping in detail through eight of the ten SPE activities identified in Chapter 4. Beginning with setting performance objectives and identifying key business factors that will affect performance, the discussion works its way through application design, development, and deployment to end with the ongoing task of capacity planning.

▶ **Chapter 6**, *Predicting Future Performance*, is devoted to the ninth of the ten SPE activities. It deals with the general principles of modeling and prediction, and covers the techniques of analytic modeling, simulation, and benchmarking in detail.

Part III: Principles   The tenth and final SPE activity is "evaluating application, database, and system design alternatives," or more concisely, "design." We devote the third part of the book to this topic:

▶ **Chapters 7**, *SPE Design Principles and Techniques*, introduces the subject of design, explains how performance as a design goal fits into the larger subject of software engineering, and sets the stage for the subsequent discussions of the six SPE design principles.

 The succeeding chapters discuss these six principles in detail. These chapters have a common structure (for this purpose, we may regard Chapters 11 and 12 logically as one). First we introduce and explain the principle, then we illustrate how it applies to a variety of design issues, drawing conclusions and making design recommendations. Our goal throughout is to avoid general discussions that do not lead to a firm conclusion about how to apply the principle.

▶ **Chapter 8,** *The Workload Principle*, deals with minimizing the total processing load.

▶ **Chapter 9**, *The Efficiency Principle*, deals with maximizing the ratio of useful work to overhead.

▶ **Chapter 10**, *The Locality Principle*, deals with grouping components based on their usage. Also, marking the approximate mid-point of the book, this chapter includes a lighthearted case study, featuring the tireless efforts of the performance sleuth, "Joe Tuna," and an assorted cast of familiar (?) characters.

▶ **Chapter 11**, *The Sharing Principle*, deals with sharing resources without creating bottlenecks.

▶ **Chapter 12**, *The Sharing Principle: Shared Databases*, discusses how *The Sharing Principle* applies particularly to shared databases.

▶ **Chapter 13**, *The Parallelism Principle*, deals with exploiting opportunities for parallel processing.

▶ **Chapter 14**, *The Trade-off Principle*, provides the concluding framework that ties the design principles together. It deals with the need to make tradeoffs among workloads, computing resources, and the SPE design principles themselves, showing that in any design situation the principles must always be interpreted within the context of a particular performance perspective and a specific set of performance objectives.

Part IV: Applications Part IV is the climax of the book. Applying the ideas and principles we have been developing in the preceding chapters, we now draw conclusions about the best way to approach the architecture and design of systems for the distributed enterprise. Where necessary, we also point ahead to the more detailed analyses of client/server technologies that appear in Part V of the book.

▶ **Chapter 15**, *Middleware and Performance*, continues the discussion of client/server middleware first introduced in Chapter 2. It explains how application-level communication protocols affect performance and compares and contrasts

RPCs, synchronous and asynchronous messaging, distributed databases, distributed objects, and distributed transaction monitors—always with performance issues in mind. This analysis provides the point of departure for the next chapter.

▶ **Chapter 16**, *Architecture for High Performance*, draws upon many previous arguments and conclusions to make a case for abandoning the single synchronous transaction paradigm. We argue that the most important technologies in the complex environment of the distributed enterprise will be those that let us implement applications as multitransaction workflow, using decoupled components and transactional messaging. The chapter concludes with a discussion of architectural and design patterns, and a summary of the key design guidelines drawn from previous chapters.

▶ **Chapter 17**, *Design for High Performance*, continues our analysis to the next level of detail—how to design a distributed application. We discuss data placement, multiphase updating of replicated data, the design of multiphase applications, and the issue of how to control and coordinate the parts of a multiphase transaction. We follow this with a reference model for client/server response time and a simple technique for estimating the likely response times of distributed applications based on their complexity.

Part V: Technologies   This part of the book provides supporting material for the earlier design discussions, and more detailed investigations of key technologies. Although these chapters all turned out differently in the end, the general framework for these chapters was as follows: introduce the technology, explain when and how it is useful, explain its performance characteristics, discuss examples of its use, and suggest performance-related usage guidelines. The subjects are:

▶ **Chapter 18**, *Performance Tools*, provides an overview of application development tools, performance modeling and load testing tools, and performance monitors.

▶ **Chapter 19**, *Using DBMS Technology,* discusses database design and the crucial (and paradoxical) role of the relational database optimizer. The chapter concludes with a recommended 10-step design process.

▶ **Chapter 20,** *Using Data Replication*, deals with the particular performance issues that arise when we wish to create and maintain multiple copies of databases at separate locations.

▶ **Chapter 21**, *Using Data Warehousing*, addresses the performance issues involved in designing, maintaining, and using special-purpose read-only databases for decision support.

▶ **Chapter 22**, *Using Transaction Managers and Transaction Monitors,* focuses on the particular performance issues and benefits of transaction management in a distributed environment.

Part VI: Resources   This part of the book contains useful reference material.

▶ *A Performance-Oriented Glossary* collects together many terms defined and used in the book. The glossary contains many internal cross-references to related terms, indicated in bold type, in addition to references to the chapters where the glossary entries first appear.
▶ *An Index of Guidelines by Subject Area* is an index of all the guidelines grouped according to various topics. Some guidelines are listed under more than one subject area. Guidelines are a special feature of the book; they can be found in most chapters.

Guidelines

Guidelines are presented throughout the book; most design discussions include at least one guideline summarizing the most important conclusion(s) or recommendation(s). Not every item of information identified as a *Guideline* is strictly prescriptive in nature. Rather than invent a variety of distinctly formatted elements to record hints, tips, conclusions, notes, and so on, we felt it was simpler to use a single graphic element to record all key conclusions, recommendations, principles, rules, or laws.

Within each chapter, the guidelines are highlighted and numbered sequentially for ease of reference. For example, here is the first guideline in Chapter 5:

Guideline **5.1**	**Determine business factors early**

Business factors form the context for the other SPE activities—identify them early in the development process. When working on functional requirement for a system, also establish when and how often it will be used, and how its intended usage is related to business factors.

As the example shows, the guideline itself follows directly below the title. The "tabs" in the upper-lefthand corner make it easy to flip through the book and find the guideline by its corresponding number. This numbering scheme allows any guideline, once defined, to be cross-referenced (see Guideline 5.1). There are more than 250 guidelines in the book; all of which are sorted and grouped in *An Index of Guidelines by Subject Area.*

In Chapters 16 and 17 only, we repeat many guidelines identified and explained earlier in the book. This is because the material in those chapters draws on the earlier discussions about the design principles to arrive at larger conclusions about client/server architecture and design. The repeated Guidelines appear with their respective numbers in the margin and the title italicized.

Capsules

Most chapters contain sections that are formatted like this one. We call these "capsules." Capsules contain interesting ancillary material that illustrates or supplements the main text, but is not strictly essential to the main flow or argument being presented in the chapter.

Products

The central focus of the book is on design principles, which remain constant, rather than on particular client/server products, which evolve and change continually. However, we do mention many specific products, as examples of a particular class of technology, or to illustrate a design conclusion. We have tried to make sure that any information about specific products is correct and up to date, but we cannot guarantee its accuracy. In most cases when we mention products, we include a Web site or other reference.

Bibliography

In addition to the occasional reference within the text, references are presented in two places. Each chapter includes numerous footnotes, each found on the page of the reference, and some chapters also contain a capsule listing a small library of recommended reference works on a particular topic. Our preference is to place bibliographic references in context in this way, because we feel that they are more likely to be used there. Therefore, we chose not to collect all the references into a single combined bibliography for the book.

Pictures and Conversations

There are even some of these, although maybe not of the kind that would have interested Alice.

PART I

Foundations

CHAPTER 1

Connections

"All things are connected."

Seattle, Chief of the Dwamish, Suquamish, and allied tribes

In This Chapter . . .

Performance
The Risks of Ignoring Client/Server Performance
Technology: A Vision of Unlimited Capacity
Client/Server: A Vision of Unlimited Scalability
Connections: Performance Variables
Client/Server Performance: The Earlier the Better

Designing high-performance client/server systems is all about *making the right connections.* Some of the key connections we explore in this book are:

▶ How the principles of performance connect directly to the well-established foundations and principles of software engineering.
▶ How interconnected application components can operate efficiently in the world of workstations, workgroup servers, and enterprise servers, connected by LANs and WANs.
▶ How achieving performance in a distributed enterprise depends on connecting the application design to the business process it supports.
▶ How middleware can connect together the separate parts of enterprise systems, yet still allow them to operate independently.

This chapter was going to be called "Themes" because in it we introduce the major themes of the book: *performance, software performance engineering,* and *enterprise client/server technology.* But as we wrote the book, we realized that our true concern is not just the individual themes—in fact, more comprehensive books are available in every area. Rather, our goal is to reveal the connection between performance and software architecture and design by explaining the *connections* among all the themes.

It took us only about a year to reach this conclusion. Making the right connections is the key to understanding.

Performance

In the world of information systems, performance is much like diet and physical fitness. Everyone agrees it's important to eat *properly* and exercise *regularly.* The complications begin when we try to determine exactly what constitutes "properly" and "regularly." Arnold Allen, an authority on performance modeling and capacity planning, writes that for computer systems, "*. . . performance means the same thing that performance means in other contexts, that is, . . . 'How well is the computer system doing the work it is supposed to do?'* "[1]

This is a good definition because it highlights the subjective nature of computer performance. In fact, how we view performance depends entirely on our viewpoint and our expectations. What *is* the computer system *supposed to do,* and how do we judge whether that is being done *well?* Like diet and fitness, performance is a very individual matter.

While individual users only care about the performance of their own work, systems professionals are like community health care professionals. They serve the entire population of computer users and aim to increase the overall efficiency of the computing system. Because these two views often conflict, achieving harmony involves a delicate balancing act.

We explore these ideas in Chapter 3 which is devoted to *Performance Fundamentals.* There we expand on these topics:

▶ People's roles and their perspectives on performance
▶ The significance of various measures of response time
▶ Throughput and related performance measures
▶ The fundamental computing resources from which systems are assembled

But for now, let's return to our analogy of diet and fitness . . .

Software Performance Engineering

Another interesting similarity between software performance and physical fitness is that, even when everyone agrees on the goals and knows "the right

---

[1]Arnold Allen, *Introduction to Computer Performance Analysis with Mathematica* (Cambridge, MA: Academic Press, 1994), 1.

thing to do," few people actually do anything systematic about it. So, as the years go by, we gradually get slower and fatter. Exactly the same thing happens to software. Even worse, whereas the fitness and fine-tuning of our youth wears down only slowly, information systems are prone to be overweight and lethargic from day one.

But there is a remedy. As a runner and a software engineer, I know from experience that, when we apply ourselves diligently to the task, we can accomplish surprising improvements. This is true in the field of human endeavor, and it's true for software and systems—even in a complex client/server environment. The task for today's information systems professionals is to create the infrastructure and systems to deliver accurate, timely information to the people who need it. To accomplish this, we must:

▶ First understand the factors that affect performance
▶ Set clear goals, defining acceptable system performance in our particular environment
▶ Take action to realize those expectations, by the way we design and develop systems
▶ Manage and maintain acceptable performance levels by monitoring and tuning

In this book, our goal is to explain how to apply this simple prescription to the complex and confusing technology of client/server computing in the distributed enterprise. This systematic approach is called *Software Performance Engineering,* which is the subject of Chapters 4, 5, and 6. Those chapters address:

▶ Performance and the software development process
▶ Performance and the organization
▶ Service-level management and service-level agreements
▶ The performance management process
▶ The 10 basic software performance engineering activities

Is Performance Really Important?

As a customer waiting in line to be served, how often have you heard a clerk complain that "the computer is really slow today"? And when that happens, how do you feel? If you're like me, you probably don't immediately volunteer the information that you are a computer professional yourself. Perhaps this reaction has both a conscious and a subconscious element. Consciously, we may prefer to avoid presenting ourselves as handy targets for the clerk's frustration. But subconsciously, it is also difficult to be proud of a profession whose products are so frequently judged by their real users to be seriously lacking in quality.

Performance is an integral element of quality. In today's competitive business environment, to achieve service objectives, systems must perform better than ever before. Consider how critical application performance is to the success of these applications:

▶ A stockbroker receives a call from a client looking for advice about which stock to sell. To do her job well, the broker needs to retrieve quickly not just the current stock prices, but also the client's recent portfolio history and complete financial profile. Ideally, she wants to run "what-if" scenarios as they're talking. If she can't do this promptly, then she will have to call the client back later, by which time stock prices may have changed.

▶ A couple arrives at the airport in Paris an hour before their flight is scheduled to depart for Amsterdam. They have confirmed reservations to Amsterdam, continuing on to London the next day. The flights are already paid for, but they need the airline agent to issue the tickets and boarding passes. The agent painstakingly reads the information from the reservation system and enters it manually, item by item, into the ticketing system. For each item, she presses the Enter key and waits for the system to respond. But the system is mysteriously unresponsive; the couple nervously watches the minutes go by. Finally giving up, the agent summons a second agent. Together they write out four tickets by hand. Finally, they rush the couple down to the gate, only to discover that the plane has already pushed back for departure. After more delay, the couple is given another ticket on another airline—for the next day.

The first example is an imaginary one, but the second actually happened to me. (Note: Perhaps one of the few perks of authorship is having the opportunity to record your best airline stories for posterity.) The poorly performing system had two directly related consequences. First, the delay in our arrival inconvenienced a client who was waiting at the airport in Amsterdam to take us to dinner. Second, being accustomed to the routine efficiency of my preferred airline's ticketing system, I vowed on the spot to avoid this particular competitor until it upgraded its information systems.

In our view, achieving acceptable performance is not an "option," it is a fundamental cornerstone of application quality. Of course, as Figure 1.1 shows, performance is not the only consideration in software design—we must balance many goals including function, user interface, time-to-deliver, cost, and performance.

In our rush to embrace the new technologies of distributed computing and put them into the service of the business enterprise, application performance is often forgotten or ignored during design, and addressed only at the very end of the process. Rapid application development tools and methods focus develop-

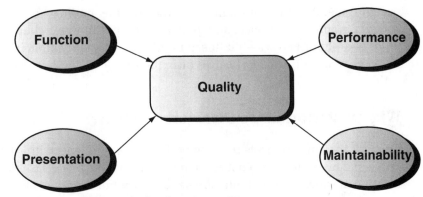

FIGURE 1.1   The elements of software quality.

ers' attention on the user's interaction and the screen's appearance while ignoring the resource demands and the ultimate performance of the running application. But the underlying client/server technology does not actually eliminate performance problems. Instead, it creates a wider variety of potential bottlenecks, posing a new challenge for developers and for the organizations they support.

The Risks of Ignoring Client/Server Performance

The biggest risk companies face by ignoring performance issues during application design is that these bottlenecks will not surface until the application is deployed and transaction and data volumes begin to rise toward their expected production levels. At this point, it is extremely difficult, if not impossible, to redesign a client/server application without a lot of pain and inconvenience for both developers and users.

Can you imagine an automobile manufacturer designing and building a new car in this way? Suppose Honda or Ferrari were to design a new car, then wait until the first model rolled off the production line to determine how fast it went. On finding that it couldn't go more than 35 miles an hour, the manufacturer would have to send it back to the engineering department for major changes. Putting in a bigger engine might require a change in the shape of the engine compartment, which would require new body work, which would trigger a need for a new interior design. In short, it would face all kinds of expensive reengineering and significant delays in its ability to deliver the car.

Of course, manufacturers don't build cars this way—the design process weighs all the elements: form and function, cost and performance. In software engineering, as with automotive engineering, performance should be a central design issue. An application may use the latest technology, have a nice, user-friendly graphical interface, and even all the right function, but—much like a 35-mile-an-hour Ferrari—if it doesn't perform acceptably, then it will frustrate its users and be a constant cause of irritation and complaints in the organization.

Why Do Performance Disasters Happen?

From all accounts, projects run into performance problems with such regularity that very few readers have not encountered a performance disaster in their organization at some point in their careers. Industry publications often print stories of important projects gone bad—of companies that lost millions of dollars because of a critical application that, at the last minute, proved unworkable.

Why does this happen so often? First, let's list two things that are usually **not** the cause:

► **Incompetence.**   Although some projects fail for this reason, for many projects with good people, good managers, good methods, and good ideas, performance was the Achilles' heel. In the more visible disasters, it is often the case that the most skilled and experienced people had been chosen for the project because of its size and importance.

► **Lack of tools.**   Once again, a lot of tools are available. For distributed systems, the coverage is not nearly as complete as it is in a mainframe environment, but systematic development methods can always compensate for missing tools—it just takes a bit longer.

Typically, the designers of failed applications built them in good faith, believing they were workable. The tragedy is not that performance problems arose, but that *they were discovered too late to be fixed because the organizations involved did not focus on performance during development.*

When software is designed without regard for its performance, is it any wonder that it frequently does not perform according to expectations? Sometimes, the shortfall is so great that the whole project is canceled, senior management looks for someone to blame, and things can get rather unpleasant. Occasionally, a failed project leads to lawsuits and is featured on the front page of the trade press. But most disasters are quietly buried and soon forgotten, except perhaps by those individuals unlucky enough to be singled out for blame.

We say "unlucky" because, in our experience, the real reasons are endemic in the software development culture. To overcome them, it takes the kind of systematic approaches to performance management that we describe later in Chapter 4—practices that are, sadly, in short supply in many development projects. Arnold Allen[2] lists some reasons managers often use to justify taking a "seat-of-the-pants" approach to performance management:

▶ We are too busy fighting fires.
▶ We don't have the budget.
▶ Computers are so cheap that we don't have to plan.

The many projects that have failed for reasons of performance are surely testimony to the weaknesses of these arguments.

The problems, however, are not solely with management. The vast majority of developers typically approach design as if an application's performance is unrelated to its functional design. If they think about performance at all, they may take the view that focusing on performance will demand "special coding tricks" that will make the code harder to maintain. More often, they assume that performance is "someone else's problem." Widespread misconceptions are that we can always "fix it later"; we can either "tune the software" or "buy a bigger box."

There are solid technical reasons why these assumptions are usually mistaken; these will become apparent later in the book. But for software engineers working to deliver a lot of new function on a tight schedule, the idea of fixing performance problems later is a particularly appealing one. And unfortunately, it is an idea that is fostered by the rampant optimism that pervades the industry.

Technology: A Vision of Unlimited Capacity

Some optimists take the view that the relentless march of technological improvement will soon render performance issues redundant. As evidence, they often point to Moore's Law,[3] which suggests that CPU speed doubles about every 18 months. Memory sizes and speeds follow a similar pattern. This surprising rate of progress spans the past 20 years, as miniaturization packs ever more circuits into silicon chips. According to the engineers, we can expect this trend to continue for another 20 years.

At the same time, communications technologies are rapidly growing in penetration and power. Driven by the explosive growth of Internet technology, formerly separate islands of computing are becoming networked enterprises.

---

[2]Allen, *Introduction,* 4.
[3]Actually, this "law" is an empirical observation. In 1965, the late Gordon Moore, a founder of Intel Corporation, predicted that microprocessor complexity (and power) would double every two years—a prediction that turned out to be surprisingly accurate. In recent years, the rate has even accelerated.

LAN technology has gone from 4Mb/s to 10Mb/s and is now moving toward 100Mb/s, while standards are being developed that will allow future WANs to support speeds up to 2400 times faster than the typical 64Kb/s available today. Industry analysts like to make bold projections of the unlimited possibilities for computing in the coming *post-scarcity* environment.

This enticing vision of unlimited computing power has encouraged some people to conclude that advances in hardware alone will be sufficient to overcome any concerns about software performance. While this is probably a comforting thought for all those people who never understood performance in the first place, it is a risky position to take if you are responsible for the success of a mission-critical application.

So, if you really believe that tomorrow's high-speed hardware will guarantee your application's responsiveness, then return this book to the shelf. Get the latest distributed objects technology and start coding that neural net application. Look for patterns in the 2000 tables that—spread across 10 business systems in 25 locations—collectively comprise the database for your enterprise.

On the other hand, perhaps you are more like us. We are doubters. Of course, no one can truly know the future, but we can, at least, learn from the past. And since we have already experienced 20 years of this phenomenal rate of growth in computing power, why do we still have huge performance problems today? How will the next 20 years be any different? We suspect that those making optimistic projections have forgotten a crucial variable in their performance models: growth in demand.

In 1677, Benedict Spinoza observed that *nature abhors a vacuum.*[4] Almost 300 years later (in 1957), Cyril Northcote Parkinson coined his famous law, *Work expands to fill the time available for its completion.*[5] This idea has its parallels in many other areas of life—for example, freeway traffic expands to fill the lanes available, our spending expands to match or exceed our income. Economists talk of "pent-up demand" and note how demand expands to match the supply of a scarce commodity.

After 25 years of experience in the computer industry, we cannot avoid the conclusion that software and hardware enjoy a similar relationship. Have you noticed that, no matter how much more disk space you get, your new software promptly eats up half of it, and your files soon fill up the remainder? In our opinion, for every amazing new increase in capacity the hardware engineers can produce, there will be armies of software engineers with new ways to con-

---

[4]Benedict Spinoza, Essex [1671] *Pt. I, Proposition 15: note; Everyman Edition,* translated by Andrew Boyle.

[5]Cyril Northcote Parkinson, *Parkinson's Law* [1957], Chapter 1; as quoted in Bartlett's Familiar Quotations, 15 edition (Boston, MA: Little, Brown & Co., 1980).

sume it. The bottom line is this: *Software workloads expand to consume the available computing capacity.*

As far as we are concerned, the vision of unlimited capacity will always be just that—a vision, not a reality.

Client/Server: A Vision of Unlimited Scalability

Another seductive vision suggests that when we move our applications into a client/server environment, performance becomes less of a design issue. "*The new flexible, scalable application architectures,*" this argument holds, "*will let us address any performance problem by simply moving parts of the processing to faster hardware.*"

Actually, years of experience with high-performance transaction systems tell us that the opposite is true because the problems typically arise not in the individual system components, but in the links between components. The more we distribute the components of our applications, the more opportunities there are to create performance problems.

In the world of monolithic mainframe applications, it is not wise to ignore performance issues during development. A block of data stored together can be retrieved together, but data split into separate tables must be joined back together by the DBMS—which will only perform well if we have designed and built the right indexes. The mainframe environment, however, can also be a forgiving one. When we break an application into separate software components or modules, the precise location of the module boundaries may have little effect on performance. Every module is processed by the same machine, and any communication between modules happens at processor speed.

The client/server environment is actually much less tolerant of poor software design, especially in the area of application and database partitioning or modularization. Distributing application and data components among several processors introduces network delays into the performance equation. In fact, the division of work between client and server, and the communication traffic between them, may now turn out to be the dominant factor in that equation.

Although it's true that in the past, most stories of performance disasters concerned large mainframe-based systems, that's mainly because organizations have only just begun to focus on high performance in the client/server environment. In the world of *departmental client/server systems,* workloads are typically relatively low in volume, the network in question is almost always a LAN, and the nature of the applications (decision support, for one example) is such that performance is rarely critical anyway.

But as enterprises begin interconnecting their central processing operations and their departmental LANs, they create the more complex "*three-tier*" *distributed environments* involving both LAN and WAN technologies. We describe this evolution in more detail in Chapter 2. Applications must now be specifically designed to use both the local and remote servers; if they are not, performance issues quickly rise to the top.

To sum up, far from being a boon to performance, the very concept of distribution is fundamentally opposed to the core technique of performance, namely bringing together components that need to be used together. If we could somehow record all our enterprise data and programs on a single chip and connect that chip to everyone's desktop with fiber-optic cables, the only remaining performance worry would be pathologically bad programming algorithms.

In fact, the continued existence of distributed systems is evidence that we have not yet reached the goal of unlimited computing capacity that future hardware developments were supposed to deliver. If we had sufficiently powerful multiprocessors and sufficiently fast wide area network technology to connect them to every user, then why would any organization ever want to employ distributed computing? Designing applications to meet performance goals is already hard, and distributing them just complicates things further.

Enterprise Client/Server

Whereas most of the early client/server systems were built for departmental or decision-support applications, many organizations are now building mission-critical systems with client/server technology. These are operational systems. As such, they are expected to deliver a high degree of data integrity, a high level of availability, and predictable performance. High-volume transaction processing is the norm.

When we consider applying client/server technologies to mission-critical applications, performance soon emerges as a vital area of concern. In a distributed environment, many components can contribute to an application's overall performance:

▶ An enterprise network may comprise many subnetworks having a wide variety of speeds.
▶ In addition to central enterprise servers, the network may connect many distributed servers, each with its own disk devices, and many different sized processors and disks from which to choose.

In such an environment, design issues arise that do not exist when all data is stored and processed by a single central computer. To distribute data and processes, we must decide:

▶ How to divide up the data and where to store the database fragments or partitions. This is usually called *data distribution, partitioning, fragmentation,* or *declustering.*

▶ How to maintain consistency among the values of interrelated (or duplicate) data items stored in databases on different computers. This involves *transaction processing* and may involve *distributed database* or *data replication* technology.

▶ How to divide the application logic and where to process the components. This is usually called *application partitioning.*

▶ How to bring together some particular subset of the data and a process that needs to work on it. This is called *data shipping* when we move the data or *function shipping* when we move a process to its target data.

▶ How separate processes or process components running on different computers will interact. The general term for this area is *interprocess communication,* or *IPC.* The technology that supports IPC is some class of *middleware.*

Upon reading this list and considering all its implications, you may wish to turn to another chapter, or possibly even another book altogether. In fact, if reading this list makes you decide to reconsider your plan to distribute your key business applications, then we will have succeeded. It is not easy to do distributed processing well—it is much easier to do it badly. The combination of networks, servers of varying sizes, middleware, database management systems, and operating systems software, all making differing demands on hardware and software resources, can lead to a bewildering assortment of possible performance bottlenecks.

Unless you are willing to reexamine your business processes and redesign your computing architecture accordingly, we can almost guarantee that your attempts at enterprise-wide distributed processing will be painful.

Others with more courage and sound business reasons for distributed processing will find that we discuss all these issues, and many more, some in more detail than others, but always within a performance-oriented framework. So if you are already heading down the enticing path of distributed computing, perhaps even past the point of no return, we aim to give you the roadmaps you need. We begin with a checklist of potential performance factors.

Connections: Performance Variables

In an enterprise client/server environment, many factors can influence application performance. In Chapter 3, we explain in more detail how the performance of any application depends on the interaction of the five major classes of performance-related factors shown in Figure 1.2. Briefly, these classes are:

► Business factors (BF)
► Application logic (AL)
► The data or database (DB)
► The software platform (SW)
► The hardware environment (HW)

We conclude our introduction to client/server performance with an extensive checklist of potential performance factors. Table 1.1 lists these factors, showing which of the five classes they are related to, using the two-character abbreviations (BF, AL, DB, SW, HW) noted above. Where appropriate, the table also shows which chapter(s) in the book discuss each performance factor. For some factors, two classes are marked because the factor represents a connection between two (or more) classes. For example:

► Application partitioning is related to both application logic and the hardware environment.
► Table size is related to data and to business variables.
► Database access paths are related to application logic, data, and the software platform.

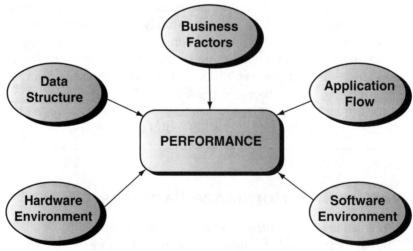

FIGURE 1.2   Key performance variables.

Table 1.1 **A Checklist of Potential Performance Factors**

Performance Factor	Class(es)	Chapter Reference(s)
1. Average/peak business transaction volumes	BF	5
2. Number of customers, orders, etc.	BF	5
3. Application logic	AL	16, 17
4. Use of processor, storage, network resources	AL, HW	3
5. Relationship to business variables, potential business growth	BF, AL	5, 6
6. Application architectures	AL, HW	16
7. Partitioning a single application between client and server	AL, HW	16, 17
8. Partitioning an application across servers	AL, HW	16, 17
9. Current database size	DB, BF	19
10. Current table sizes	DB, BF	19
11. Impact of business growth on data	DB, BF	19
12. Database design	DB	19
13. Normalization, denormalization, and multitable joins	DB, AL, SW	9, 19
14. Database locking	DB, AL, SW	12
15. Indexing, clustering, partitioning	DB	19
16. DBMS access path	AL, SW, DB	19
17. Logical versus physical I/O differences	AL, SW, DB	6
18. DBMS buffering or caching	AL, SW, DB, HW	14, 19
19. Query result set sizes	AL, DB, BF	19, 21
20. Copy management applications	DB, HW, SW	20, 21
21. DBMS-controlled replication	DB, HW, SW	20
22. Data refresh volumes	DB, HW, SW, BF	20, 21
23. DBMS and OS platform	SW	19
24. DBMS tuning choices	DB, SW	19
25. Operating system tuning options	SW	5, 19
26. Middleware	AL, SW	15
27. Access to legacy data via gateways	AL, SW	19
28. Transaction monitors	AL, SW	22
29. Message queuing middleware	AL, SW	15
30. DBMS/hardware compatibility	SW, HW	19
31. Support for parallel processing	SW, HW	13
32. Hardware platform	HW	3, 13
33. Processor speed	HW	3, 11, 14
34. DASD speed, capacity	HW	3, 11

Table 1.1   **A Checklist of Potential Performance Factors (*Cont'd*)**

Performance Factor	Class(es)	Chapter Reference(s)
35. LAN performance	HW	3, 11
36. WAN performance	HW	3, 11
37. Impact of other workloads	AL, HW	11
38. Effect of background work on servers and network	AL, HW	11
39. Impact of network traffic for client table initializations	AL, HW	11
40. Separating applications across servers	AL, HW	13

Client/Server Performance: The Earlier the Better

As organizations reengineer legacy systems to serve the needs of new business processes, as they integrate multiple systems into an enterprise network that links many LAN-based servers, as they find new applications that must be built or old ones that must be modified, it becomes critical to consider performance early.

In a large, shared computer system that handles a variety of different workloads, the performance measures for those workloads are always interrelated. We must always be ready to make trade-offs. Performance objectives for different applications vie with one another and with other goals such as cost, function, and development time, for priority. We discuss these issues in more detail in Chapter 5.

When computing resources are shared among many applications, rarely can we optimize one aspect of performance for one application without affecting another adversely in some way. Ideally, we want to know in advance how an application will perform so that we can make relatively painless midcourse corrections early in the application development life cycle. In Chapter 14, *The Trade-off Principle,* we focus on design trade-offs we must make among hardware and software resources to achieve an optimal design.

Software performance engineering can range from just a little thinking ahead to more elaborate modeling, sensitivity analysis and prediction. Informal methods are sometimes adequate for small projects. But the bigger the project and the greater its complexity, the bigger the risk and the greater the need for careful planning. In Part II, we discuss how we can incorporate performance analysis and performance management into the earliest stages of the application development process, and we revisit performance issues at each subsequent stage.

Unexpected performance problems expose the enterprise, at best, to inefficiencies in the business and, at worst, to failure of mission-critical business practices—an inability to sell or deliver core products or services. An early investment in performance planning will pay off in an application that minimizes cost, maximizes return on investment, and delivers the performance users need to meet their business goals.

CHAPTER 2

Enterprise Client/Server

"Great wits are sure to madness near allied,
And thin partitions do their bounds divide."

John Dryden

In This Chapter . . .

The Evolution of Distributed Systems
Challenging the Gartner Model
Client/Server Technology
Client/Server Performance Management Challenges
Achieving Performance: The Design Problem
Conclusions
Client/Server Computing Bibliography

The history of computing might be described as a succession of eras, each era being defined by the most popular technology or buzzword at the time. On the surface, the industry sometimes appears to be lurching from one technology fad to the next, driven largely by marketing hyperbole. For example, the 1980s witnessed the era of relational databases, the AI/expert systems era, and the CASE (computer-aided software engineering) era. These were followed in the 1990s by the client/server era and the Internet/intranet era. Tomorrow, according to some, the object-oriented era will finally arrive.

But behind the inscrutable facades of jargon there are no revolutions, as the enthusiasts like to claim, only the steady pace of technological evolution. Several interrelated forces are at work: A constant flow of *hardware* improvements drives the evolution of *systems software,* which, in turn, forces our *application development techniques and tools* to evolve. In each of these three areas, evolutionary developments build on the foundations previously established.

Client/server computing is a good example. Stripped to its essentials, client/server computing is simply a powerful extension of the fundamental idea of modular programming. It extends the concept of modular programming to the distributed environment by recognizing that those modules do not have to be executed on a single platform. This extension leads to the following fundamental characteristics of a client/server architecture:

▶ Systems are created by assembling independent components, each of which contributes unique, specialized functions to the system as a whole. In the simplest arrangement, *client* components interact with users and with *servers* that manage various computing resources. In more sophisticated arrangements, some servers can also be clients of other servers.

▶ Clients and servers can use hardware and software uniquely suited to the required functions. In particular, front-end and back-end systems normally require computing resources that differ in type and power. Database management systems can employ hardware specifically designed for queries, while graphics functions can employ memory and computing resources that can generate and display intricate diagrams.

Colin White writes that the "benefit of client/server computing is the availability of hardware servers that scale from a small uni-processor machine to a massively parallel machine containing hundreds, possibly thousands of processors. Corporations can now match the computing power of the server to the job at hand. If a server runs out of capacity, the old server can simply be replaced by a larger one. This change can be made without affecting existing client workstation users or the tools they employ. This provides not only scalability, but also flexibility in handling hardware growth as compared with central mainframes where an upgrade is a major undertaking that is both costly and time consuming."[1]

All these statements can be true, with the right level of attention to client/server systems and application design. But poor design can ruin this utopian vision, making upgrades every bit as painful, time-consuming, and costly as installing a new mainframe. Our goal in this book is to help you make good on the promises of high-performance, scalable client/server systems.

The Evolution of Distributed Systems

Systems in which a client sends a request to a module and receives some type of service did not appear magically from nowhere when distributed computing

---

[1]Colin White, "Supporting High-Performance DSS Applications," *InfoDB* 8(2) (1994), 27.

became popular. The simple client/server model, often referred to as a two-*tier* model, is frequently associated with small LAN-based distributed systems. But architecturally, it owes much of its origins to software engineering principles developed for traditional, centralized mainframe systems.

Traditional Mainframe Systems

Modular programming and the organization of modules into logical groupings, or layers, has long been a standard practice in the design of complex mainframe software. As we explain in more detail in Chapter 7, *SPE Design Principles and Techniques,* layering is good design practice. No matter what the target environment, specialization of function within distinct layers encourages designers to keep similar functions closely aligned, from both a functional and a performance viewpoint.

For example, if we examine the structure of a database management system such as IBM's DB2, we find that it is implemented as a set of well-defined layers:

▶ Applications communicate with a layer (called the *relational data services,* or RDS) that understands the SQL language, including a relational optimizer that can determine how to access tables and indexes to satisfy any SQL data request.
▶ The RDS communicates with a data manager layer that understands how to navigate table and index structures.
▶ Below that is a buffer manager layer that keeps track of where any data or index page is actually located.
▶ The buffer manager stores pages in its memory buffers by invoking yet more layers of disk access methods (VSAM) and operating system functions to read the data from disk.

As we see in Figure 2.1, examples of layering can also be found in other places:

▶ Inside mainframe transaction monitor software like CICS or IMS/TM
▶ In the architecture of large information management systems as a whole—shown here in the common three-tier arrangement of transaction monitor, application program, and DBMS

As the left side of Figure 2.1 indicates, many poorly designed applications consist of a mass of "spaghetti code." (We even wrote some ourselves—they did not teach computer science when we began our programming careers in the mid 1960s!) But larger, better architected applications incorporated modularization concepts.

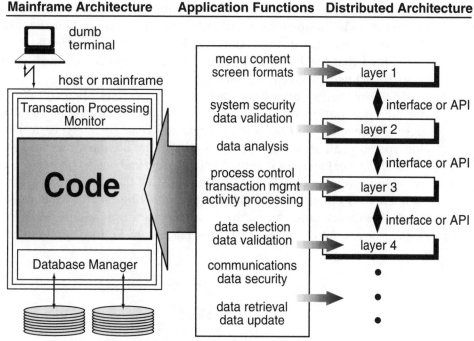

Mainframe Architecture   Application Functions   Distributed Architecture

FIGURE 2.1   Functional layering in traditional and distributed systems.

Distributed Systems and Layering

The technique of "layering" software is not unique to distributed architecture. Distributed systems impose a more stringent requirement to build the software using a layered architecture because layering provides one basis for geographic distribution. To put it simply, it's very difficult to move layers around if they haven't been constructed in the first place, if they've been designed badly, or if they lack well-defined interfaces.

There are now some fairly well-established concepts for determining what goes into the various layers of a distributed application. An early contributor to this subject was Alex Berson.[2] He divided the application into three components:

▶ Presentation functions
▶ Business logic functions
▶ Data management functions

[2]Alex Berson, *Client/Server Architecture* (New York, NY: McGraw-Hill, 1992), 202.

An alternate version of this idea was published by the Gartner Group; it received more widespread recognition.[3] Dividing the central business functions layer into presentation logic and data logic components, the Gartner Group concluded that the functions required in a distributed application could be constructed using the four logical layers shown in Figure 2.2.

In this model, we use off-the-shelf products, such as Microsoft Windows 95, for the *Presentation Manager* and a DBMS, such as Oracle, for the *Data Manager*. We develop the *Presentation Logic* and *Data Logic* layers in the middle, incorporating all necessary application logic *and* business rules.

The Gartner Group next considered the physical design question "Where do we split the application?" That is, assuming that the application will be implemented in a client/server environment involving two computers—a "front-end" client workstation and a "back-end" server—how should we map the four logical layers onto these two physical platforms? Following the same path as

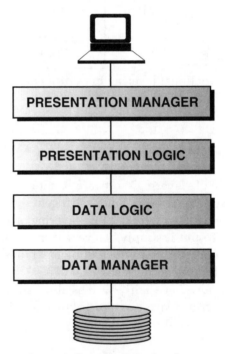

FIGURE 2.2   The Gartner Group's four application layers.

[3]The Gartner Group *(charon.gartner.com),* a company based in Stamford, CT that specializes in research and analysis of IT industry developments and trends.

Berson. In this way, the Gartner Group produced five distribution models with essentially the same names as those used by Berson, but with a simpler structure because of the absence of the business logic layer. These were:

▶ Distributed Presentation
▶ Remote Presentation
▶ Distributed Logic
▶ Remote Data Access
▶ Distributed Database

The Gartner Group model, expressed using a diagram similar to Figure 2.3, quickly became the de facto standard for representing the concept of application distribution models. By 1993, 9 out of every 10 presentations on client/server development started with a version of Figure 2.3. For more detail, see the capsule, "The Gartner Group Distribution Model."

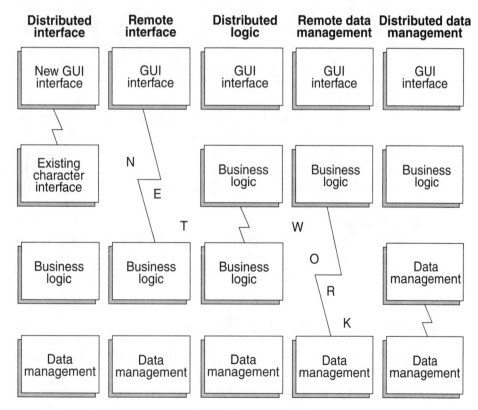

FIGURE 2.3   The Gartner Group Distribution Model.

The Gartner Group Distribution Model

In the Gartner Group's model for distributed applications, five possible modes of distribution were identified.

▶ **Distributed Presentation.**   In this model, only the presentation management function is shared between the server and the client; everything else remains on the server. This model usually applies to the technique known as screen-scraping, in which a GUI is placed in front of an existing character-based interface, to migrate a legacy application into an environment having graphical workstations.

▶ **Remote Presentation.**   In this model, the Presentation Manager resides entirely on the workstation; everything else—the presentation logic, data logic, and data manager—resides on the server. The two most well-known examples of this model are the X Window System, in which the clients are *OSF/Motif* applications, and the World Wide Web, where the clients are Web browsers.

▶ **Distributed Logic.**   In this model, we split the application between the presentation logic and data logic components. All presentation management activities take place on the workstation; all data management takes place on the server.

▶ **Remote Data Access.**   In this model, presentation management and data logic all reside on the client; only the database manager resides on the remote server. This model is offered by client/server database technology such as DB2 Common Server, Informix, Oracle, and Sybase. Because of the widespread adoption of development tools like PowerBuilder and SQL Windows, this model is very common in departmental LAN-based client/server environments.

▶ **Distributed Database.**   In this model, portions of the database reside on the client and portions on the server. The DBMS manages the communication involved. Although some limited implementations of this model are available, they are not in widespread use.

Challenging the Gartner Model

The Gartner Group model, despite its attractive symmetry, did not really present the issues properly. In an article published in 1993 in *Database Programming & Design*,[4] Paul Winsberg pointed out the following flaws:

---

[4]Paul Winsberg, *Database Programming & Design* 6(7) (1993).

▶ Distributed processing is not distributed data.
▶ Some designs are more equal than others.
▶ Enterprise and workgroup systems are different.

Explaining these flaws in his article, Winsberg reemphasized the importance of Berson's business logic layer and, in the process, developed a new, improved model of client/server computing. We summarize his points in the following sections.

Distributed Processing Is Not Distributed Data

The fifth design in the Gartner Group model, distributed database, splits the database itself. Data sits in several physical locations, managed by a distributed database system that presents a single logical image to the application. Winsberg points out that this design is fundamentally different from the other four:

▶ It describes distributed data, while the others describe distributed processing. In other words, the fifth design is orthogonal to the first four—it can be used in combination with any of them. The Gartner model incorrectly implies that this design is an alternative to the other four.
▶ Distributed data is usually managed by a distributed database system and consequently it is completely transparent to the developer. The other four designs are not.

For these reasons, the distributed database design does not belong in the model. It is certainly a legitimate issue for client/server design, but it should be considered separately.

Some Designs Are More Equal Than Others

Addressing the physical partitioning of the application layers into client and server, Winsberg concluded that there are really only *three* basic physical designs—remote presentation, remote data access, and distributed logic, as shown in Figure 2.4.

Remote Presentation.   In *remote presentation,* both presentation and data logic are on the server. The presentation manager remains on the client; it has limited screen control functions but not much else.

Remote presentation has one important advantage—it is easy to build and administer because all code is on one central machine. However, it usually suffers from poor performance. The network is between presentation manager and presentation logic, an extremely busy interface, so it is heavily loaded. The

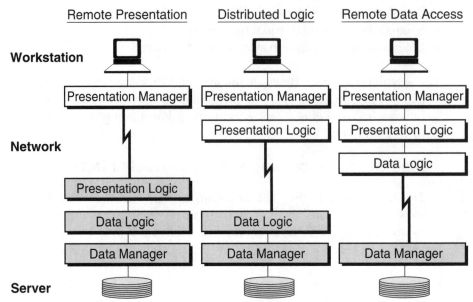

FIGURE 2.4   Winsberg's three distribution models.

server also suffers heavy processing loads because it runs both presentation and data logic. Since both network and server are shared resources in a client/server system, these loads degrade performance of the system as a whole. We discuss these issues in more detail in later chapters.

Overall, the disadvantages of remote presentation usually outweigh the advantages. For this reason, remote presentation is not widely used today.

Remote Data Access.   In *remote data access,* both presentation and data logic are on the client. As we explain in more detail later in the book, this design also has performance problems. The interface between data logic and data manager is busy with SQL calls and result sets, so the network is a bottleneck, as it is in remote presentation.

Remote data access also has data integrity problems. Transactions are coded on the client rather than on the server. Since the client is usually less secure than the server, this design gives less control over sensitive database updates. If the network fails while a transaction is in progress, the transaction must be rolled back.

For these reasons, remote data access is also of limited utility. It is good for read-only applications, like decision support, where data integrity is not an issue. It is often used as a transitional step from centralized to distributed computing, as a company's skills and technology gradually mature.

Distributed Logic.   For most operational applications of a commercial nature, *distributed logic* is usually best. It solves all the problems of the other designs. Each message between client and server is a complete *transaction,* so the network load is relatively low. Presentation logic is on the client, thereby reducing the load on the server. Database integrity is managed entirely on the (relatively) secure server.

The main disadvantage of distributed logic is that development and administration are divided across two machines. In an Internet or intranet environment, however, Web-based architectures help with this problem. Presentation logic is stored on the Web server, downloaded in the form of an *applet,* and executed on the client. This helps to explain the interest in network computers.

In the rest of the book, when we discuss the performance aspects of two-tier client/server architectures, we'll frame our discussion in terms of Winsberg's three physical distribution models: *Remote Presentation, Distributed Logic,* and *Remote Data Access.*

Enterprise and Workgroup Systems Are Different

Winsberg's third critique dealt with the growing interest in client/server systems for the enterprise. In simple client/server applications for small workgroups or departments, there are usually two physical software layers. Figure 2.5 shows a typical example of such a system.

One layer consists primarily of presentation logic and the other, data logic. *Presentation logic* includes screen management functions, application control functions, data validation, and handling of user error messages. It also converts data from SQL views to graphs, bar charts, or some other display. *Data logic* contains SQL statements, transaction logic (when to commit and roll back), database error message handling, and so on. It includes both read and write queries.

These two layers of logic are sandwiched between a *presentation manager,* like Windows 95, and a *data manager,* like Oracle or DB2. The presentation and data manager layers are commercial products purchased from software vendors. In this respect, they are quite different from the two logic layers, which you must code the hard way.

Interfaces to the presentation manager and the data manager are defined by industry standards (like SQL) and the software vendors of those products. So in a two-tier system, the only interface the developer must define is the one between presentation logic and data logic. When we are building the application, these two central layers and the logical interface between them are the subject of all our design and development efforts.

Applications that support the entire enterprise usually have a more complex structure, as shown in Figure 2.6. They usually have several user interfaces, each with a different presentation logic layer. They also access several

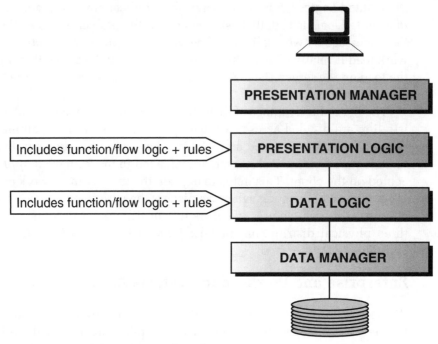

FIGURE 2.5   Logical structure of workgroup system.

databases, often stored by different data managers running on different machines. In other words, many presentation logic layers must communicate with many data logic layers.

In this situation, adding a third layer of logic that manages communications between presentation and data logic is a good idea. It accepts transactions from presentation logic, decomposes them into local components, and directs each component to the correct data logic layer. It also performs a variety of calculations and manipulations that are not appropriate elsewhere, such as complex statistical analysis. Collectively, we'll call this type of processing *application logic.*

It would be tempting to conclude that adding an application or business logic layer neatly resolves all questions of how and where to enforce business rules. Unfortunately, although many business rules will end up in the central layer, others don't fit well in any single layer. Enforcing these business rules usually requires cooperation among the layers. We discuss this in more detail in Chapter 17, *Design for High Performance.*

Terminology for application logic varies somewhat. It is sometimes called *control logic, business logic,* or *function logic.* The point is that an enterprise system usually has three kinds of logic—presentation, application, and data—

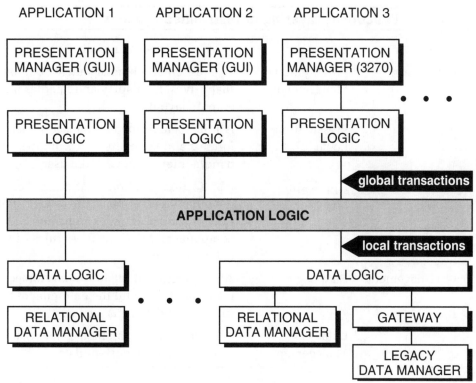

FIGURE 2.6   Logical structure of an enterprise application.

implemented in many physical layers. The Gartner Group model does not account for complex enterprise systems.

The Five Logical Layers of an Application.   Summarizing Winsberg's analysis, we obtain the five logical layers shown in Table 2.1. The table also shows that (as Berson originally argued) the layers divide application functions into three distinct areas, namely the *user interface,* the *application logic,* and the *data management.*

Client/Server Technology

Up to this point, our discussion has centered on the logical view of distributed application architectures. We now turn our attention to the physical aspects. As we explained in the introduction, this is a book about architecture and design, and not really about products; products are forever changing their form to meet our needs. On the other hand, products turn architectural concepts into real systems.

Table 2.1   **Functional Layering of Distributed Systems**

Functional Area	Layer Name	Layer Function
User Interface	Presentation Management	The presentation management component that drives the display and handles all graphic layout.
	Presentation Logic	All the logic needed to manage screen formats and the content of windows, and to handle interaction with the user.
Application Logic	Application Logic	Application functions that do not belong in the other layers—the business logic and the flow of control among application components. Many business rules can be enforced here.
Data Management	Data Logic	All the logic that relates to the storage and retrieval of data and the enforcing of business rules about data consistency.
	Database Management	All storage, retrieval, management, and recovery of all persistent data.

In theory, there have always been many ways to distribute the logical layers of an application. In practice, new architectural models become popular only as technology evolves to support them. Using our five layers as a framework, Figure 2.7 illustrates how distributed computing evolution over the last ten years or so:

▶ At the outset, simple remote presentation systems relied upon a central processor host or mainframe arrangement with dumb terminals.
▶ As the intelligence in the terminals increased, graphical user interface (GUI) functions were added to remote presentation systems. More importantly, the increase in terminal intelligence enabled developers to move some presentation logic from the central host to the workstation.
▶ The development of X-terminals and MOTIF made further expansion of the presentation logic possible, followed by more intelligent presentation styles.
▶ The early client/server databases such as Sybase, Informix, and Oracle provided only data management functions. All other functionality resided at the workstation. This type of arrangement represented pure remote data access.
▶ Gradually, however, the client/server database products began to move some of the workstation functionality (e.g., stored procedures, triggers, and other database processing) to the server.

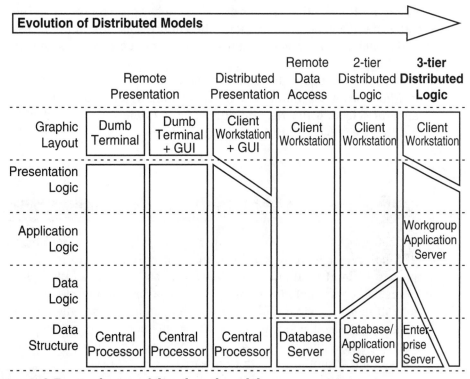

FIGURE 2.7 Evolution of distributed models.

▶ Two-tier distributed logic gradually evolved into our representation of three-tier distributed logic.

A key factor in this evolutionary process has been the growing availability and sophistication of client/server middleware products—the "bricks and mortar" of software construction.

An Introduction to Middleware

Any time we split an application into components and place those components on separate computers, we must provide a way for them to communicate. *Middleware* is a general term for all the software components that allow us to connect separate layers or components into complete distributed systems. As such, it is often referred to as the slash (/) in client/server. Since the slash can have a different meaning depending on the distribution model, it turns out (not surprisingly) that we need different kinds of middleware to implement each of the different physical models we have been discussing. Unheard of before the 1990s, client/server middleware has grown rapidly in the past several years. We must now evaluate a bewildering assortment of messaging software, gateways, interfaces, request brokers, queue managers, and transaction monitors.

For more thoughts about middleware and a key reference, see the capsule on *Middleware Essentials.* For now, we simply want to establish the importance of selecting the right middleware; we defer all detailed discussion of middleware choices until Chapter 15, *Middleware and Performance.*

Middleware Essentials

A category of system software that has largely been defined by *what it is not,* rather than by *what it is,* middleware is hard to pin down. Like a people without a country, middleware is software without a place to call home. Other familiar classes of software have been around long enough to establish their domains; middleware is left scrambling for the bits of IT territory no one else has occupied. If software is not in some other recognizable category (an application program, a DBMS, a development tool, or an operating system) then it must be middleware.

In a very real sense, *middleware is client/server computing* because middleware provides the language through which clients and servers communicate. Just as our command of language determines what we can say or even think, the nature and sophistication of its middleware determines a system's capacity to function and perform acceptably. So choosing the right middleware and using it in the most effective way are vitally important.

Most explanations of middleware contain several new acronyms per sentence and little in the way of a common framework for organizing and understanding this amorphous mass of software. Ill-defined and ill-named, middleware is hard to love or even to get excited about—that is, perhaps, unless you are Orfali, Harkey, and Edwards, authors of *The Essential Client/Server Survival Guide,* a comprehensive guide to client/server technology.[5] The bulk of its almost 700 pages is devoted to highly readable discussions of middleware concepts, products, capabilities, and trends.

We give this book our whole-hearted endorsement. It has authoritative coverage of all aspects of middleware and plenty of detail for most readers. To reuse a familiar advertising slogan: *If it's not in here, it probably doesn't exist!*

[5] Robert Orfali, Dan Harkey, and Jeri Edwards, *The Essential Client/Server Survival Guide, 2nd edition* (New York: John Wiley & Sons, 1996).

Enterprise Client/Server: A Complex Environment

This is a book about performance, yet functionality and interoperability of components have dominated our discussion thus far. We have yet to confront the choices that we must face to get the various components to work correctly together.

The three-tier physical arrangement (Figure 2.8) requires us to make choices about hardware, software, and operating systems. Once we have designed the logical layers, if we are going to address the issue of performance, we need to distribute the layers to geographic locations and assign them to specific processors having specific operating systems. We need to introduce a new dimension to the discussion of client/server design: *performance.*

Client/Server Performance Management Challenges

There is a paradox in client/server computing. The process of grouping related components—which is critical to achieving good performance—is almost completely opposed to the separation of components introduced by distributed systems. Separation creates the need to communicate and synchronize. Communication and synchronization introduce processing overheads and delays. A well-managed, high-speed LAN environment can mask these delays, but, in the WAN-connected enterprise, unplanned communication overheads can easily dominate the performance equation. It is not surprising, therefore, that designing

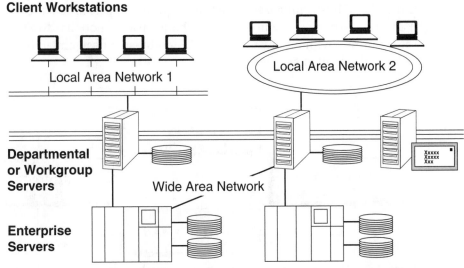

FIGURE 2.8   Distributed three-tier system.

systems and applications to exhibit good performance is more difficult in a distributed world than it ever was when all data and processing were centralized.

To understand more about how and where these difficulties arise, we need to introduce the performance life cycle. These are the four fundamental activities we must perform to produce and operate systems that perform well, namely: *design, predict, build,* and *monitor* (Figure 2.9). We examine all these activities in more detail in Part II of the book, but in the following paragraphs we list some of the reasons why each one is harder in the client/server environment.

More Difficult to Design

There are a number of reasons why designing distributed systems is harder:

▶ Distributed applications often have more complex functionality than centralized applications, and they are built from many diverse components as well. Applications are also more closely tied to business strategies, which influence designers to avoid purely "technical" solutions.
▶ Multitier architectures provide a nearly limitless set of choices for where we locate functions, data, and the processing. Any time we increase the number of choices, we increase opportunities to make mistakes.
▶ More data sharing occurs. We are trying to leverage a costly investment in the corporate information resource in as many different ways and as many different places as possible.
▶ Distributed systems also involve moving more data between locations. This introduces new capacity planning requirements to the design process. It also introduces subtle timing issues that the application design must resolve.
▶ In addition to choices about locations, there are also more hardware and software choices—without any established, step-by-step design methodology for building distributed systems.

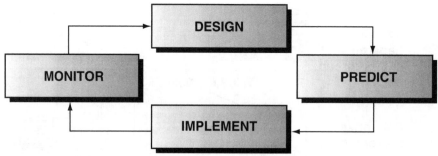

FIGURE 2.9 Fundamental performance life cycle.

▶ Building distributed systems involves a lot of invention—we make up the rules as we go along. One reason for this approach is that relatively few designers have built enough systems to have developed good rules of thumb.

We discuss some specifics of the design problem in more detail later in this chapter.

More Difficult to Project Performance

Predicting performance is yet another challenge arising from the distributed system. We cannot use simple modeling tools, nor can we build simple models. The system consists of components that can interact in surprising ways and that can introduce hidden problems that undermine performance.

Add to this the fact that modeling methodology isn't well developed for this type of complex system. Instead of a slow, careful design and modeling process, current development practice places its emphasis on rapid application development and prototyping, an approach that actively discourages developers from analyzing the system-wide consequences of the elements being developed.

One more fact makes it to difficult predict performance. There are no standard benchmarks, regardless of what the industry press would have us believe. Reliable, relevant benchmarks could contribute some elements to a performance model. Clearly, the lack of standard benchmarks and modeling methodology contributes to problems in predicting performance in a distributed systems environment.

Finally, the workload changes when the application is distributed. This makes prediction even more difficult. Even if we are familiar with the behavior of a service running in a centralized environment, that application is significantly different in a distributed environment. In reality, when we distribute an application, we never implement it in precisely the same way as it ran in the centralized, host environment. That fact alone makes prediction extremely difficult.

More Difficult to Build

There are many sources of difficulties in building distributed systems. For example, the design may use components that do not work well together. Industry "standards" such as SQL should prevent this kind of incompatibility, but they are not really standard across different DBMS products. The enhanced functionality that makes one product particularly attractive frequently introduces a major deviation from the standard. In addition to incompatible components, distributed system software has been unusually prone to defects, adding a dimension of unreliability to the other difficulties.

The methods employed in designing, building, and implementing a distributed application further compound the difficulties. Client/server systems are frequently built using RAD techniques that stress incremental delivery of system elements. There is minimal design before iterative construction begins. And, developers in this environment are relatively inexperienced with the tools and the environment. In the grip of urgency, without systematic design models, these relatively inexperienced developers are likely to make performance mistakes without realizing it.

More Difficult to Monitor and Tune

Actually, the client/server environment provides a lot of tuning opportunities. Every component has its own particular configuration parameters. But if we are going to do more than "tweak" the system, we must measure the effects of our actions. It is difficult enough to fit the choices for each component to the choices made for every other component. This difficulty is compounded by the need to do this harmonization while "blindfolded."

Measuring performance is particularly difficult in a client/server environment. We must overcome four basic sources of difficulty in collecting the measurements we need to tune the system:

▶ **Diversified software platforms.**   Different systems generate different measures and present them in different formats. The process of measurement itself becomes subject to interoperability limitations and translation requirements. Major development effort to get "clean" measurements isn't likely in most projects.

▶ **Hard-to-correlate data monitored on different components.**   Software doesn't pass around enough tokens to allow an inference that a change on one processor is related to something that happened previously on another one. Analysis becomes much more difficult without direct evidence for cause and effect.

▶ **System clocks may not be synchronized on different platforms.**   Having to reconcile possible inconsistencies in the clocks makes it hard to work with elapsed times. All sorts of fancy footwork may be needed to determine how long something actually took when part of the information is measured on one processor and part on another one.

We discuss all these issues in more detail in Chapter 5, *Software Performance Engineering Activities*.

Achieving Performance: The Design Problem

We have looked at some of the forces that have made client/server systems essential to the current business environment. We have also surveyed some of the obstacles facing the software engineer trying to manage performance systematically. It is now time to think about the advantages a distributed system might offer to the designer. To rephrase the old joke about real estate, *there are three factors affecting distributed performance: location, location, and location.*

Performance is all about grouping. Layered architecture provides a framework for designing good performance into a system by grouping functions, then by placing those functions at the right place in the distributed environment. Table 2.2 shows how a designer needs to concentrate on logical attributes of performance, then on the physical character of the system. The logical design sets the stage for the physical. Grouping sets the basis for most of the design decisions we must make later. If the logical grouping of functions is wrong, the physical options will be restricted. In the final analysis, it is the physical choices that determine performance: location, location, and location.

The point is, it is absolutely critical to design the layers correctly. A distributed system requires a more complex design than does a centralized system. Incorrect structure and design of the layers in a centralized environment might result in extra overhead, but since everything happens at instruction speed, the overhead is inconsequential. The distributed environment is much less forgiving. If the logical software design doesn't provide for tight cohesion and minimal coupling between the layers, the system can generate a large volume of communication back and forth between the layers—and at network speeds that are generally much slower than instructions.

Partitioning and Performance

Logical structure of the layers is the first step toward achieving performance in the client/server environment; the second is the need for physical distribution

---

Table 2.2 **Performance Design Goals**

Component	Logical Design Goals	Physical Design Goals
Layers	Maximize cohesion within layers	Optimize performance of each layer
Links	Minimize coupling between layers	Optimize performance of each link

of the functions and services, that is, mapping the logical layers onto physical processors, then optimizing the performance of each layer and each link between the processors.

In the early days of distributed computing, many developers believed that performance could be improved by upgrading processors. Unfortunately, the early software designed specifically for the distributed environment demonstrates the flaw in this belief. We can't always scale up every part of the system. If we divide the separate layers incorrectly, heavy traffic usually occurs on the links between the layers. Often, system performance problems are rooted in excessive communication among the layers rather than in the individual layers themselves. In this case, scaling up the performance of the individual layers does nothing to resolve the actual problem and very little to relieve it. It is im-

Case Study: A Tale of Two Cities

An example of a scaling problem is provided by an associate, **F**, who was retained by a financial institution in London to diagnose a problem with a client/server system database. The financial trading application was taking minutes to display its screens and to receive information. The IS personnel in London couldn't understand why the application was running so slowly. No performance problems had been observed when it was implemented at the New York headquarters. Management had been so pleased with the application that they decided to distribute it to London, and they expected it to work just as well there.

Upon investigation, **F** found that the application development package and the tool used to develop the application created a system in which all the business rules required by the user interface were enforced by the DBMS. First, tables of valid user input values were stored in the database. Next, stored database procedures were used to run validity checks of user input against those stored values. Whenever a user pressed Enter on the screen, a stored procedure was invoked to retrieve information from a table to check that the value entered was valid for that particular field. **F** discovered that almost every user entry in the front end invoked at least one such business rule requiring database access.

There is nothing inherently wrong with a style of design involving table-driven validation of user input. The problem in this case concerned the physical distribution of the elements. The design worked fine when the user workstations and the database server enforcing the business rules were all connected to the same LAN in the New York office. But it created major problems when the server was in New York and the clients were in London!

portant to remember that we need to design the layers properly, then deal with optimization. Logical errors usually cannot be fixed with more computing or communicating power.

Guideline 2.1 — Logical layering mistakes cannot be easily resolved at the physical level

The logical design for a distributed software application should ensure maximum cohesion within layers and minimum coupling between the layers while the physical design should maximize the performance of each layer and each link between layers. Effective physical design depends on having a sound logical design to optimize.

This is an example of a departmental client/server application design that is simply not scalable to the enterprise environment. Running a stored procedure to check something on the server every time the user presses Enter on the client may be fine within a departmental LAN, but it is not likely to deliver satisfactory and consistent performance in a distributed enterprise—especially when the enterprise network includes satellite links between some clients and the database server.

To resolve the problem, **F** suggested installing a separate server in London and replicating the validity tables to London—essentially changing the design of the application from a two-tier implementation to a three-tier implementation. But this required an effort to redesign the application rather than tune it. This downloading proposal also raised many basic questions about the volatility of the validity checking data and the most efficient way to maintain replicated versions of the tables in London. These are the kinds of questions that must be resolved before an application can be scaled from a single-site implementation to a full, three-tier, geographically distributed system.

The conclusion: It's easy to develop small systems that don't scale well, particularly when we move from two-tier systems to three-tier systems. To enable successful scalability and distribution, we must first consider the performance of each layer and each link between layers separately, then look at how the system comprising those layers and links behaves when it is stressed by the demands of real workloads.

Today, no one would expect to create a good distributed application simply by slicing an old mainframe application down the middle. Similarly, we cannot expect to produce a good three-tier application by scattering the components of a two-tier application across the enterprise. Enterprise client/server computing demands careful thought.

Conclusions

This chapter is intended as a brief introduction to client/server computing and some of the key challenges of achieving acceptable client/server performance. After looking at performance in more detail in Chapter 3, we return to the subject of software performance engineering (SPE) in Chapters 4 through 6. Chapters 7 through 14 focus on the SPE design principles in detail, and Chapters 15, 16, and 17 apply those principles to the architecture and design of enterprise client/server applications.

Client/Server Computing Bibliography

Baker, Richard H. *Networking the Enterprise* (New York: McGraw-Hill, 1994).

Bakman, Alex. *How to Deliver Client/Server Applications That Work* (Greenwich, CT: Manning Publications, 1995).

Boar, Bernard. *Implementing Client/Server Computing* (New York: McGraw-Hill, 1993).

Orfali, Robert and Harkey Dan. *Client/Server Survival Guide* (New York: Van Nostrand Reinhold, 1994, 1996).

Orfali, Robert and Harkey Dan. *Client/Server Survival Guide with OS/2* (New York: Van Nostrand Reinhold, 1994).

Renaud, Paul E. *Introduction to Client/Server Systems* (New York: John Wiley and Sons 1993).

Schank, Jeffry D. *(Novell's Guide to) Client-Server Applications and Architectures* (San Jose, CA: Novell Press/Sybex, 1994).

Vaskevitch, David. *Client/Server Strategies: A Survival Guide for Corporate Engineers* (2nd ed.) (Foster City, CA: IDG Books Worldwide, 1995).

Vaughn, Larry T. *Client/Server System Design and Implementation* (New York: McGraw-Hill, 1994).

CHAPTER 3

Performance Fundamentals

"Many things difficult to design prove easy to performance."

—Samuel Johnson

"Many things easy to design prove difficult to performance."

—Chris Loosley

In This Chapter . . .

The Elements of Performance
Performance Perspectives
Response Time
The Psychology of User Response Time
Throughput, Workload, and Related Measures
The Fundamental System Resources
The Application-Resource Usage Matrix
Why a System Runs Slowly

In our experience, almost every software developer has some acquaintance with performance concepts, but most are reluctant to claim any real expertise. Although we might think that everyone understands the words *software performance,* when we probe a little deeper, we find that people's intuitive notions of their meaning are quite diverse. To some, software performance is an arcane science, the domain of mathematicians and computer science graduates with Ph.D.s in queuing theory (a mistaken perception). Others believe that to pursue software performance means to seek blazing speed at the expense of everything else (incorrect again). Because of such misconceptions, performance has been largely ignored by the vast majority of people who develop software.

Actually, performance for software means much the same as it does elsewhere: *getting the work done, on time.*

To get acceptable performance from any computer system, client/server or otherwise, we must first understand how computer systems are designed and developed. We devote the next 15 chapters to these subjects. Our goal in this chapter is to review the basics—to set down the foundation of performance concepts and terminology on which later chapters will build.

For some readers, what follows may be familiar. Nonetheless, even if you have worked in this area before, we encourage you at least to review this chapter quickly, if only to compare your own viewpoint and terminology with our presentation. As you will see, there are many different perspectives on performance at both the managerial and technical levels; yours will probably depend on your role and responsibilities. If we are to reach a shared understanding, we must begin from shared assumptions.

The Elements of Performance

When our systems don't perform the way we would like them to, we tend to look for the one tuning change that will fix "the problem." Responding to this need, many articles about performance take the cookbook approach. "*Ninety-five ways to soup up your widgets,*" the trade-magazine covers proclaim boldly. Yet rather than just trying to learn a checklist of tuning techniques, we should first grasp the foundations of performance. Remembering a few simple, general principles can be every bit as effective as following long lists of suggestions for optimizing different software products. Applying the basic principles of performance can save us time and effort in two ways: It can help us avoid costly mistakes when we build our systems and avoid wasting time later with unproductive tuning experiments.

At the most fundamental level, almost everything we ever need to know about the performance of any computer system can be described in terms of just five simple concepts:

▶ Workload
▶ Response time
▶ Throughput
▶ Resource utilization
▶ Resource service time

When a computer system (comprising a set of **computing resources**— processors, storage devices, network links, and so on) is applied to the task of processing a given **workload, response times** and **throughput** are external measures that describe the observed performance. **Resource utilizations** and **resource service times** describe how the computer system behaves internally, providing the technical explanation for the externally observed performance characteristics.

At the simplest level, **response time** is a measure of how long it takes to finish some task; there are many ways to measure response time depending on how we plan to use the results. We'll discuss this concept in more detail a little farther into this chapter, but the key point we want to make here is that *we should always make sure we understand exactly what is included, and what is not included, in any quoted response time figure.*

Throughput, on the other hand, is a measure of the amount of work a component or a system performs as a whole or a measure of the rate at which a particular workload (or subset) is being processed. Once again, of course, this definition hides quite a few complexities that arise once we set out to actually measure throughput in the real world. In practice, the measured throughput reported for any system depends crucially on (a) how the system is configured, (b) the precise workload mix being processed, and (c) how the results are computed.

Guideline 3.1	**The law of measurements**

The law of measurements

The result of any measurement will depend on what is measured, how the measurement is done, and how the results are computed.

We call this *the law of measurements.* This self-explanatory law may seem rather silly at first. But it is amazing how often and easily we can be misled by software measurements whose authors, sometimes deliberately, omit from their report of the results crucial details about the measured hardware and software environment, the exact workload used, the measurement methodology and its accuracy, or the methods used to compute the final results from the observed data.

As Benjamin Disraeli said, long before the modern computing era ever began, "*There are three kinds of lies: lies, damned lies, and statistics.*"[1] Notice the sequence! Lies disguised as detailed measurements can be especially beguiling.

Performance Perspectives

When we move to the next level of detail, we find that there are several sides to performance, including:

---

[1] Benjamin Disraeli, as quoted in *The Concise Oxford Dictionary of Quotations, 2nd edition* (Oxford, UK: Oxford University Press, 1981), 87.

▶ Application processing speed, or response time, or batch processing time
▶ Timely access to important business data via query tools
▶ Minimizing the utilization levels of hardware devices, like the processor (or CPU), disk storage, or networks
▶ Maximizing workload throughput or minimizing the overall costs of a computing environment
▶ Maximizing the system's capacity to support the needs of the business—a large population of users or a growing volume of transactions
▶ Creating a scalable computing system that can grow incrementally to accommodate growth in business volumes, without requiring a major overhaul

Figure 3.1 illustrates these aspects of performance graphically. Viewed in isolation, each one expresses a potentially important software development goal. But in the real world of enterprise systems, our personal roles and responsibilities determine how we view performance and which performance goals we care about the most. For example:

▶ End users don't want to sit and wait for the computer system to give them information, so response time is at the top of their list of priorities.
▶ System programmers or database administrators often have significant amounts of processing that must be done in a limited batch window, and they are therefore concerned with elapsed time for longer running programs.

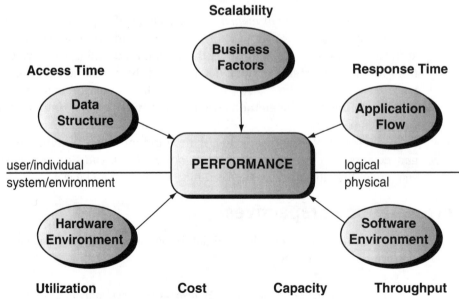

FIGURE 3.1   Performance factors and measures.

▶ Department managers approving a budget or chief financial officers looking at overall expenditures generally focus on what gets the job done at the lowest cost.

▶ Information systems managers may be most concerned with high throughput for database transactions or with supporting the maximum number of users on the network because they want to get the most from existing hardware and software resources.

Clearly, these different views of performance give rise to different goals for improving performance. For most organizations, these various performance perspectives can be generalized into three categories: the application perspective, the system perspective, and the organization perspective. We now discuss each of these in more detail.

Individual/User/Application Perspective

The first view of performance is concerned with a single application or a group of applications.

An individual user is typically concerned with how long it will take to get a segment of work completed—whether that work is a single transaction that executes in less than a second, a database query that runs for minutes, or a batch job that runs for several hours.

Similarly, *an application development team* seeks to satisfy specific business goals and user requirements. Apart from supplying all the right functions, typical software development goals include creating an application that is easy to use, easy to maintain and support, and efficient:

▶ If interactive application performance is an important goal, the team must aim to get transactions and database queries through the system quickly and reliably and to make information available to the users who need it in a timely fashion.

▶ Reporting applications must be flexible and responsive to the business's need for timely information.

▶ If some transactions are to be processed in batches, developers must be concerned with minimizing the resources needed to process each transaction in the batch, so that all of the batched work can be completed within the processing windows available.

Whether we refer to this perspective as the *individual, user,* or *application view* of performance, it always centers around the *elapsed time* or *response time* of a unit of work. In performance terms, software effectiveness for people with this perspective is measured by the following criteria:

▶ For transaction processing: transactions per second, response time
▶ For batch processing: elapsed time, CPU time per transaction
▶ For query processing: query response time

Community/Systems/Environment Perspective

For a system manager, the question of "how long will the job take?" doesn't address the issues. The system manager is concerned with optimizing performance for *all* of the users—a task that is significantly more complex than optimizing performance for a single user or application, and one that must view the system from a "*community*" perspective. Typical concerns are:

▶ Can our computing resources satisfy the needs of all the users?
▶ Can we complete the month-end processing requirements on time?
▶ If more users or new applications are added, what effect will the increase have on the existing set of shared resources?

For systems professionals in an enterprise computing environment, the primary challenge is not to optimize the performance of a single application, but that of an entire system or processor complex, which typically serves a diverse mix of applications and business areas. Quality of performance is measured in terms of *throughput* and *capacity* levels and depends on the *utilization* levels of *shared resources* like databases, hardware, and networks. Key performance goals are:

▶ Minimizing the impact of new work on scarce system resources
▶ Maximizing throughput using existing hardware and software resources
▶ Maximizing the system's capacity to support connected or concurrent users
▶ Balancing competing demands from different application areas

Availability is also important because shared resources affect many areas of the business, and—even though this is not true in the strictly technical sense—users often *perceive* system failures and excessive amounts of down time as being "poor performance."

Organizational Perspective

The organizational perspective combines the concerns of the systems and applications perspectives. It takes a wider view, focusing on the costs and benefits of systems in the context of overall organizational goals, applying business priorities when making trade-offs among individual perspectives. We sometimes use the term "enterprise computing" to convey the organizational perspective and the infrastructure needed to support it.

Taking an organizational perspective on performance involves balancing the performance needs of individuals and of the community—for example, by integrating the application-processing activities of two departments that use similar information to eliminate duplication and improve overall efficiency.

To balance the individual perspective with the system perspective, we must make trade-offs. As we explain a little later in this chapter, improving throughput and reducing response times are opposing performance goals. When pursued to their fullest extent, they will eventually come into conflict. That is, of course, one of the reasons why performance is interesting, why it is a technically challenging subject—it requires us to make trade-offs and choices.

As we shall see in later chapters, as systems become ever more complex and as departmental networks are interconnected to form an enterprise computing infrastructure, narrowly focused performance approaches are at best suboptimal, if not altogether ineffective. Distributed computing environments do offer design choices and possibilities for trade-offs not previously available in the traditional host-based computing—but, to take advantage of them, we must move beyond the narrow concerns of separate business applications. When enterprise computing is distributed, the business enterprise and the flow of business information are one and the same thing. *To respond, performance therefore must be a team effort incorporating all perspectives, reaching out across application and departmental boundaries.*

In Chapter 4, we discuss the implications of this conclusion for the software development life cycle and the process of performance management.

Response Time

In general, the term *response time* refers to the time required to process a single unit of work. It is more commonly applied to interactive applications—online transactions or queries—because it records the time between the instant a request is made and the computer's *response* to that request. In the same vein, a *responsive* system or application is one that *responds* to requests quickly—that is, it has a short response time.

For batch processing, we generally prefer the term *elapsed time,* signifying the amount of time that *elapsed* on the clock while the work was being processed. Sometimes *clock time* is actually used. Colloquially, this is sometimes even called "wall clock time"—partly because you really can use a wall clock to measure the performance of some long-running batch jobs, but more to emphasize the distinction from the *CPU time* or *processor time* of a batch program.

We discuss the CPU and its significance in more detail a little later in this chapter, but for more background on the concept of CPU time, read the capsule *Time Waits for No One,* later in this chapter.

Although it affects performance, users do not experience CPU time directly; it is a measure of invisible events that happen "under the covers." Users are generally concerned only with response time, an altogether more tangible and observable quantity. Although it may seem like a simple concept ("*How long does it take?*"), response time is actually more complex than it seems at first.

Response time, because it is primarily an *external* measure of performance, conceals a great deal about the *internal* software processes that make up the application, but these processes are also important to an understanding of performance. In fact, when we focus on particular performance issues, our interests may center on one of several aspects of response time:

▶ **Minimum** response time
▶ **Internal** response time
▶ **Effective** response time
▶ **Complete** response time

To illustrate the differences among these four response time measures, we will use an example of a hypothetical (but typical) SQL application, of the kind that might be built using a client/server database product like DB2, Informix, Microsoft SQL Server, Oracle, or Sybase SQL Server.

A Response Time Example

Suppose that a user interacts with a database application, which, in turn, invokes a stored procedure on the database server to retrieve a set of results. For this example, the major components of interest are illustrated in Figure 3.2. (Incidentally, note that the figure, because it illustrates the generic functions of the client/server database environment, shows character set translation of results as occurring on both the client and server. This happens because it *can* be done on either side. But in any particular DBMS, it is only necessary on one of the two sides.)

Table 3.1 describes a prototypical application flow. As the application executes, a sequence of interactions takes place among the components of the system, each of which contributes in some way to the delay that the user experiences between initiating the request for service and viewing the DBMS's response to the query.

Numerous variations in that sequence are possible, depending on whether the application employs dynamic SQL or a stored procedure, whether the user

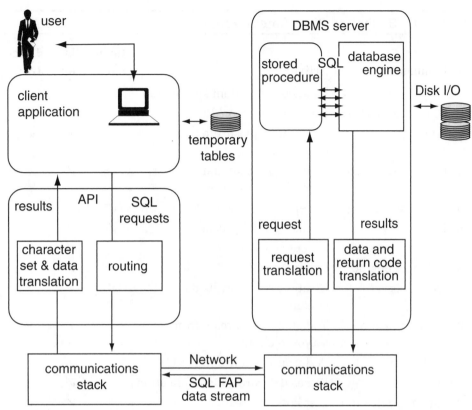

FIGURE 3.2   Typical client/server database components.

executes a stored procedure directly by name or from an application using an RPC mechanism, whether the application uses cursors or not, and so on. Those details, although important in practice, are incidental to our purpose here. The point is that each activity in the sequence requires some time to complete and, therefore, contributes to the response time.

Now suppose we had a performance monitoring or tracing tool capable of timing and recording each step separately for the sample application. It would report times for a series of events. In Table 3.1 we summarize the entire application flow, showing how each component in the flow would contribute to the four different response time measures. Next we discuss some of the concepts illustrated by the table.

Sample Application Flow.   (1) The **user** interacts with the **client application,** which (2) passes an SQL *execute* request, together with a parameter string

Table 3.1   **Response Time Components**

No.	Component	Activity	Inter-nal	Min-imum	Effec-tive	Com-plete
1	User	Interacts with client application				✓
2	Client application	Passes request to API		✓	✓	✓
3	API	Converts request into data stream		✓	✓	✓
4	Communications	Transfers data stream from client to server		✓	✓	✓
5	DBMS server	Accepts data stream	✓	✓	✓	✓
6	DBMS server	Invokes stored procedure	✓	✓	✓	✓
7	Stored procedure	Executes SQL calls	✓	✓	✓	✓
8	Database engine	Extracts results	✓	✓	✓	✓
9	DBMS server	Creates initial results data stream	✓	✓	✓	✓
10	Communications	Transfers data stream from server to client		✓	✓	✓
11	DBMS server	Performs asynchronous I/O				
12	API	Passes data stream to application		✓	✓	✓
13	Client application	Displays first results		✓	✓	✓
14	API	Handles acknowledgment			✓	✓
15	Client application	Prompts user			✓	✓
16	Communications	Transfers data stream from client to server				✓
17	DBMS server	Creates final results data stream	✓			✓
18	Communications	Transfers data stream from server to client				✓
19	API	Passes data stream to application				✓
20	Client application	Acknowledges receipt of data				✓
21	API	Handles acknowledgment				
22	Communications	Transfers data stream from server to client				
23	DBMS server	Frees up DBMS server resources				

specifying what work the application wants to do, to the client-side **DBMS API** layer. The **API** software (3) converts the SQL request and parameters into a data stream to be shipped to the server using the native formats and protocols (FAPs) of the particular DBMS. Then (4) the various components of the **communications stack** on the client machine send the data stream across the **network** to the server, where it is received and passed on by the **communications stack** on the server machine. The **DBMS server** software (5) accepts the input data stream and extracts the execute request and parameters. It then (6) locates the stored procedure (optimizing or compiling it if a compiled copy is not already available in a server cache) and invokes it, passing along the application's parameters. The **stored procedure** (7) executes a series of **SQL calls** to the **DBMS server database engine,** which (8) performs query-related disk I/O operations to retrieve or update the appropriate database records, inserting all the result rows into a temporary table ready to be passed back to the server side API.

When the stored procedure completes, (9) the **DBMS server** converts the first block of results into a data stream to be shipped to the client and, (10) reversing the input sequence, the **communications subsystem** (stacks and network) returns the data stream to the client. Meanwhile, the **DBMS server** (11) executes asynchronous background I/O operations to free up dirty buffers.

On the client, (12) the **API** software converts the data stream into results to be passed to the **client application,** which (13) displays the first part of the results, (14) acknowledges successful receipt of the first block of data from the API, and (15) issues a new prompt to the user.

The **API** software ships the acknowledgment via the **communications subsystem** (16) back to the **DBMS server,** which (17) converts another block of results into a data stream to be (18) shipped to the client by the communications subsystem. In our example, this will also be the final block of results, for obvious reasons. In practice, there could be many more.

The **API** software (19) passes more rows to the **client application,** which (20) acknowledges successful receipt of the final block of data, again invoking the sequence of (21) **API** and (22) **communications subsystem.** Finally, (23) the **DBMS server** receives the acknowledgment and frees up the temporary table and any other resources associated with this client request.

Individual Response Time Measures

Minimum response time is the response time outside a particular component, that is, the time a requester is inactive between issuing a request and the return of the first character of the response to that request. To make the meaning clear, this could also be referred to as the *observed* response time or the *external* response time for a particular component, as in the next sentence. In the example, we show the external response time for the client application program.

Internal response time is the inverse of minimum response time for a server component, that is, the response time viewed from *inside* a particular system component, from the time it receives a request until the time it returns the response. In the example, the DBMS server is used to illustrate the concept of internal response time because activity by the DBMS server runs over multiple steps in the flow (rows 5–9). The second DBMS server interaction (row 17) may or may not be considered part of the same internal response time for this transaction, depending on the context. With multiple-stage interactions, the stages might be discussed separately or considered as a single unit of work with a *total internal response time.* There are no strong conventions in this area—it all depends on the application logic and which performance measures make sense.

Effective response time is the time that elapses before a user is free to interact with the system, even if the response to the initial request is not yet complete. This quantity is also referred to as *time to prompt. It is perhaps the most important of all response time statistics because it directly measures the delay a user experiences.* In the example, we have shown the user prompt following the initial batch of output (row 15). In a simpler version of the application, we could equally well have kept the user waiting until the completion of the final batch of output (row 19). It is not uncommon when designing applications in a distributed information system to have this kind of choice; clearly, the design decision will play an important role in determining the user's view of system responsiveness.

Complete response time includes *all* the time between the start of a task and the complete return of the response set. First, it includes all the time it takes the user to interact with the system and create the initial request for processing. Also, assuming that the application's requirements were properly determined, then someone really does want to use all the output, at least some of the time. And in those situations, the time it takes to return all the results is important.

Asynchronous events are activities that, although they consume system resources, do not actually extend anyone's response time *directly.* In the example, activities such as updating the database tables (row 11) or releasing temporarily associated resources after the transaction completes (rows 21–23) are not included in any response time measure because they occur in parallel with the main line activities whose response time the user experiences. This is an important consideration for application design, one that we revisit in more detail in Chapter 13, *The Parallelism Principle* (see the section, *Level 2: Workflow Parallelism*).

Note that asynchronous activities are certainly not completely free, and they may well contribute *indirectly* to the server components of response time. Depending on the overall workload and the server's scheduling policies, if the server's shared resources are busy processing asynchronous work, they are not readily available to handle other activities that do contribute directly to some-one's view of response time.

The Psychology of User Response Time

As we remarked at the beginning of this chapter, *performance* does not mean *blazing speed.* It means *an acceptable level of responsiveness* when people use the system in the course of their work. Performance is acceptable as long as the system is fast enough to let users do their jobs without imposing unnatural de-lays. Occasionally, a job actually does demand blazing speed, but this isn't usu-ally the case. Indeed, most users care far more about slowness than they do about blazing speed! A better statement of the goals of performance would be *avoiding slowness,* not *achieving blazing speed.*

Perceived Response Time

This insight is particularly significant when we turn our attention from *indi-vidual measures* of response time to *response time distributions.* Two ques-tions arise. How should we summarize the response time characteristics of a program or an application? And how should we reflect the existence of varia-tions in the distribution of response times?

For reporting purposes, if we need to summarize a set of response times, it may be more useful to find the *median* of the response time distribution, rather than the simple arithmetic mean, or average, The median is that value that bi-sects the distribution, with one-half of the values falling above it and one-half below it. As such, it is less influenced by the existence of a few long response times that would drive up the mean significantly.

On the other hand, because of the importance of avoiding slowness, users are generally more concerned with deviations from average response time than they are with the average itself. If, for example, an application has an average re-sponse time of 8 seconds, but individual response times vary between 1 second and 20 seconds, users are likely to complain about the occasional long delays.

According to Arnold Allen in *Introduction to Computer Performance Analysis with Mathematica*, in the folklore of capacity planning the *perceived value* of the average response time is not the *median,* but the *90th percentile value* of the response time distribution, the value that is greater than 90 percent of all observed response times.[2] For example, if response time has an expo-nential distribution, which is typical, then the 90th percentile value will be

---

[2]Arnold Allen, *Introduction to Computer Performance Analysis with Mathematica* (Cambridge, MA: Academic Press, 1994), 10.

2.3 times the average value. Thus, if a user has experienced a long series of exponentially distributed response times with an average value of 2 seconds, that person will perceive an average response time of 4.6 seconds! Even though only 1 out of 10 responses actually exceeds 4.6 seconds, the long response times make a bigger impression on the memory than the 9 out of 10 that are smaller. We all seem to remember bad news more clearly than good news!

Finally, the time required to submit the initial request also contributes to perceived response time. If the user interface does not support the natural flow of business actions, users cannot possibly perform their jobs efficiently. This makes the whole system inefficient. Conversely, we can make significant improvements in the user's perception of a system's performance by streamlining the user interface without even touching the rest of the application's code. We discuss this subject in more detail in Chapter 10, *The Locality Principle.*

Guideline 3.2 — **Perceived response time**

The perceived response time is the amount of time that a user *perceives* a task to take. It is disproportionately influenced by the longest response times. One rule of thumb is that the perceived value of average response time is the 90th percentile value of the response time distribution.

The time required to submit the initial request also contributes to perceived response time. Streamlining the user interface can make significant improvements in the user's perception of a system's performance.

Tuning Response Times

The concept of perceived response time has important consequences for our tuning efforts. Because users are generally more aware of response time variations than they are of minimal improvements in average response time, when we tune a system it is usually best to focus first on minimizing response time variability, ignoring the average response time until we've reduced or eliminated the variability.

Guideline 3.3 — **Reduce response time variations first**

Users are far more sensitive to response time variations than they are to small improvements in average response time. Therefore, when we tune a system, we should focus on minimizing response time variability, ignoring the average response time until we've reduced or eliminated the variability.

Once we've eliminated the worst of the response times variations, then we can focus on reducing the average. Unfortunately, because of the significance of the longer response times, our efforts may go largely unnoticed at first. Studies indicate that *users are not generally aware of response time improvements of less than 20 percent.* The system appears to be more responsive and users begin to notice improvements when response times shrink by 30 to 40 percent.

Smart designers, recognizing users' sensitivity to response time variations, have been known to smooth the introduction of new systems and counter the creation of artificially high user expectations by deliberately *slowing down* response times during a project's early stages. Timer-based delays built into the application code compensate for the short response times produced by the initially small databases and relatively light system usage. The artificial delay is phased out later as the system grows to handle its intended volumes of data and users, gradually replaced by the real transaction response time of the loaded system. The users, meanwhile, remain happy with the system, perceiving no degradation in response time as the volumes grow to production levels.

Guideline 3.4	**Avoid response time variations in new applications**

Slowing down response times during a project's early stages can smooth the introduction of new systems. Artificial delays in the application code can counterbalance the short response times produced by the initially small databases and relatively light system usage. These delays can be phased out later as the system grows, keeping response times largely unchanged.

Throughput, Workload, and Related Measures

While response time is a measure of the amount of time needed to do work, throughput is a measure of the amount of work that can be done in a certain amount of time. So the throughput of a computer system is the average rate at which the system completes jobs in an interval of time. As a measure of productivity and overall efficiency, throughput is generally of more concern to company management than to end users. Also, because it deals with system-wide performance, in a client/server environment throughput is a measure of performance that is primarily used for *servers,* whereas response time relates primarily to the view of performance as seen by the user or *client.*

To calculate throughput, we divide the number of jobs or transactions completed by the amount of time that it took to complete them. We may, for example, measure the throughput rate for an order-entry application by number of orders that are processed in an hour. For transaction-processing systems, we

Time Waits for No One

"Time keeps on slippin', slippin', slippin', into the future . . ."—Steve Miller

When analyzing performance information, computer systems profession-als need to create a clear distinction between the actual elapsed time to complete a process and its "CPU time" or "processor time"—a useful statistic reported by certain classes of software performance monitoring tools.

The CPU time of a process is the total time the computer actually spends executing instructions for that process. In the multitasking environment sup-ported by all server operating systems, tasks proceed through a succession of small chunks of service from the processor. When a task pauses during pro-cessing to wait for interruptions like disk or network I/Os to complete, the clock on the wall keeps on ticking, but the processor moves on to handle other tasks or even waits, if no tasks are ready for processing.

Therefore, the accumulated CPU time of a typical process is much smaller than its total elapsed time.

typically measure throughput in transactions per second (TPS) or transactions per minute (TPM).

Throughput is not a measure of an application; it is a measure of the ability of a particular set of computing resources to process a given workload. And be-cause it is a system measure, many system-related factors affect it (recall the five factors shown in Figure 3.1), including the overall mix of transaction types in the workload, the application complexity, the layout of data on disk, specifi-cations of the host computer, the degree of hardware and software parallelism, and the amount of processing in the system software and middleware.

Therefore, for any particular throughput statistic to be useful, all these vari-ables must be known. Notably, the application workload must be well defined and fairly uniform. It does not make much sense to say that throughput is 10 transactions per second if every transaction is an unknown quantity.

It is also difficult to make meaningful statements about the throughput of a system that handles a very diverse workload. In Table 3.2, we define eight funda-mentally different types of applications, based on two workload characteristics:

▶ On the vertical dimension, the amount of data being processed. This can be a single business object, a group of related business objects, a collection of unre-lated business objects, or an entire file, table, or database.
▶ On the horizontal dimension, whether the processing involves modifying stored data or simply reading it.

Table 3.2 **Eight Different Workload Types**

	CREATE or UPDATE	RETRIEVE
Single business object	Business transaction	Business inquiry
Group of related objects	Object update	Object inquiry
Object collection	Batch data entry	Ad hoc query
Entire database	Batch update process	Batch report

When we design systems, we must consider which of these workload types we need to support. Any statement about the (projected or measured) throughput of a workload comprising a mix of the eight types will be impossible to interpret unless the statement is accompanied by a precise definition of the different workload components and their relative frequencies. This is one motivation for defining standard throughput benchmarks, which we discuss at the end of this section.

User Population Supported

Because adding users generates more work, the size of the **user population** a system can support is a measure of performance that is related to throughput. It isn't synonymous with throughput, however, because it's obviously much easier to support 100 transactions per minute from a population of 20 users than it is to support the same level of processing from a population of 1000 users. This is because each user places an additional load on the system, so a system that can support 20 users comfortably may well be completely swamped by 1000 users. This fact has a direct bearing on the relevance of throughput benchmarks conducted by software vendors for marketing purposes, as we discuss in Chapter 6, *Predicting Future Performance.*

Tuning for Response Time or Throughput

When tuning, we can opt to improve response time for the individual users or for throughput for the system or for both. Frequently, when we improve throughput, response times actually slow for some users, depending on how we increased the throughput. For example, on a system with a population of 200 users, workload-balancing activities aimed at optimizing a system's ability to handle concurrent work may increase throughput so that all 200 users will *collectively* get more work done, but no one user will necessarily experience a faster response time.

Alternatively, if we have a situation in which only one job is running on the system and the CPU is constantly waiting for its I/O requests to finish, we can start another job that needs only the CPU to run without affecting the performance of the first job. In this case, we've increased system throughput—completing two jobs instead of one—without affecting the performance of the first job at all. We'll discuss the relationship of throughput to system resources in more detail later in this chapter.

Some tuning actions do improve *both* response times and throughput:

▶ Resource bottlenecks lower throughput and extend response times. More processes complete more quickly when the necessary resources (i.e., the processor, disks, network, or whatever) are readily available. So if we speed up a device, we can often improve both the response time and the throughput because all tasks using that device will complete their work faster.

▶ Similarly, if we redistribute the workload to reduce the load on a shared device, we typically achieve better response time because waiting times decrease if fewer people are using the device and better throughput occurs because of the workload redistribution.

▶ Finally, the most effective way to improve both throughput and response time is to tune the workload to reduce the demand for system resources. To put it simply, *do less work.*

We'll discuss resources and their effect on performance in more detail later in the chapter; the main point here is that we can affect performance by regulating the work that devices perform.

The Performance of Batch Processing

For batch processing, the concept of performance involves elements of both throughput and response time. We can measure batch performance in terms of *throughput, average job turnaround time,* and completion within a *batch window.*

▶ **Throughput.**   The amount of work that the system completes in a given period of time. Throughput measures are particularly important for batch jobs that handle large numbers of individual items, like recording payments or creating invoices.

▶ **Average job turnaround time.**   The interval between the instant that the computer system reads the batch program (or "job") and the instant that it completes program execution.

▶ **Batch window completion.**   Important for organizations that must run a collection of batch jobs within an allotted amount of time—a window in which the job stream must be started and finished.

These measures are interrelated. For example, consider a nightly suite of 15 database extract and replication programs that must replicate 1.5 million database rows daily. If the extracted data is to be current the next day, the replication process cannot begin until all the normal daily database processing has been completed. Suppose the programs are run at the national headquarters of a U.S. company that is based in Aptos, California, where normal work continues until midnight (PST). Processing must be completed in time to distribute the replicated data to the remote locations in New York and update the local databases for the start of business there, at 6:00 A.M. (EST).

In this example, suppose the company uses a four-way multiprocessor capable of running up to four database extract streams in parallel. Then the performance goals for this system are:

▶ A batch window of three hours (from 12:00 midnight PST until 6:00 A.M. EST)
▶ An average job turnaround time of 48 minutes (3 hours × 4 processors / 15 jobs)
▶ Average throughput rates of 5 extract jobs per hour and about 35 extracted rows per second per job (100,000 rows per job / 48 × 60 seconds per job)

When planning large-scale projects involving batch processing, simple calculations like these are invaluable in setting expectations and in providing goals for the remainder of the development process. We discuss performance prediction in more detail in Chapter 6, *Predicting Future Performance.*

Throughput Benchmarks

A benchmark is a standard workload, or the process of setting up, running, and measuring such a workload, for the purpose of comparing hardware or software performance. Traditional benchmark tests such as Livermore Loops, Linpack, Whetstones, and Dhrystones were designed to test specific types of performance (e.g., scalar and vector floating-point, basic arithmetic, or nonnumeric processing) in specific environments, typically small and midsized computers. Of more interest and relevance to our subject matter, an industry-wide organization, Transaction Processing Performance Council (TPC), introduced a benchmark suite that is intended to support throughput comparison across hardware configurations and database servers. We discuss this subject in more detail in Chapter 6.

Guideline 3.5	To measure throughput, use a benchmark workload

A benchmark is a standard workload, or the process of setting up, running, and measuring such a workload, for the purpose of comparing hardware or software performance.

Related Quality Measures: *Cost* and *Availability*

Cost and availability are important measures of software quality, but they are related only indirectly to performance.

Cost per Transaction

The cost per transaction is a financial measure of a system's effectiveness that is generally more significant to capacity planning and chargeback than to software performance engineering. Theoretically, *cost per transaction* is a metric that can be used to compare overall operating costs between applications, database servers, or hardware platforms.

Cost itself is an elusive quality. In theory, for a *dedicated system* with *uniform transactions,* we could calculate the cost per transaction, by summing all the costs associated with an application and dividing by the total number of transactions and queries for the life of the application. Unfortunately, we rarely encounter such a situation. In real life, systems are shared, and workloads include a wide mix of transactions of all shapes and sizes.

In such an environment, apportioning the true total cost for any workload subset is not easy. And it gets harder as we add more components to the system. As workloads move from monolithic mainframes to networked systems of processors, isolating the true cost of anything becomes next to impossible.

Even if we could compute the cost of the computing resources, the true total cost of processing any workload includes much more than just running the hardware and software environment. There are many other administrative and management costs associated with database and system administration—all of which contribute substantially to the true total costs. And because these costs differ enormously across computing environments, it is also very difficult to compare costs of different implementations of the same function and to weigh cost as a factor against other measures of quality.

Although these complications limit the value of cost per transaction as a engineering or design measure, there are some business situations in which software performance is crucial because the viability of an application is directly related to its overall computing costs, or to the cost per transaction.

When Cost and Performance Are Synonymous

Organizations whose core business depends on handling very large transaction or batch-processing workloads must usually dedicate multiple processors to the task. In this type of environment, tuning the processing cost per transaction through SPE techniques can directly affect the number (or size) of processors required to handle the total workload, thereby having a direct effect on company profits. Since it's easier to compute the total cost of anything if it requires a dedicated processor, the trend away from large shared mainframes to smaller, dedicated, distributed processors can actually make it easier to compute cost for some workloads.

For example, consider any company that sells a business service (like volume billing or mailing-list processing) for which the principal variable cost is the information processing involved. Rarely is it possible for the service provider to pass the direct processing costs to the client through chargeback methods; more often, it must negotiate a fixed rate per business transaction handled. Once the rate is fixed, performance tuning directly increases the net profitability of that application for the service provider. Alternatively, if performance is not strictly controlled, the provider risks incurring a loss on the service.

In these cases, *cost per transaction* and *transaction performance* are closely related concepts.

Availability

Availability is another "performance" measure that is of great interest to user departments. Availability is generally defined as the percentage of scheduled system time in which the computer is actually available to perform useful work. As such, it is an important measure for describing the stability of a system. We usually measure availability in terms of the mean time to failure (MTTF) and define a failure as any reason that the system is not available during normal operating hours.

Technically speaking, availability is not a performance issue at all; it is a software (or hardware) quality issue. Performance and availability are orthogonal issues. You would not call a London taxicab a high-performance vehicle just because it runs for 300,000 miles without ever breaking down. Conversely, for broken software or a car that will not start, performance measures are irrelevant.

However, while availability is not actually a measure of performance, it certainly has an effect on performance. Unstable systems often have specific effects on performance in addition to the other consequences of system failure. For example, instability affects the average processing time of large batch workloads because of the possibility of failures during processing. Also, additional processing is inevitable as users try to catch up with their work following a period of down time, thereby creating artificial peaks in the distribution of work, leading to higher system utilization levels and longer response times. Highly available systems, on the other hand, usually invest in redundant hardware and software and impose a need for careful design that often benefits performance. In this case, availability (and any improved performance) is traded for cost.

The Fundamental System Resources

The one performance perspective we have not really discussed in any detail yet is the **computer's view of performance**. It is a view that is likely to occupy more of the system professional's time than any other because it is the view from which we must try to correct many performance problems. And, in the computer's view, all performance issues are essentially resource contention issues.

Distributed computer systems incorporate four fundamental types of devices: **CPUs**, computer **memory**, **disk storage**, and **networks**, although the last two may be also referred to jointly as the **I/O subsystem**. Figure 3.3 illustrates the basic

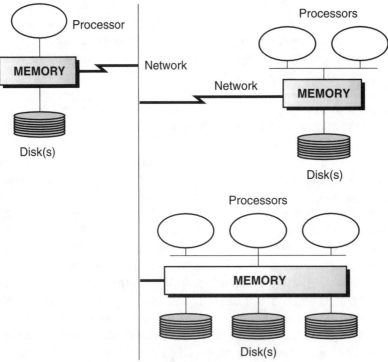

FIGURE **3.3**   Basic structure of a computer system.

structure of a computer system that comprises these devices. Because the devices interact with one another, and because most application workloads use all four types to varying degrees, it is often difficult to identify the specific causes of performance problems. But a thorough understanding of the role played by each device is invaluable to identifying and diagnosing performance problems.

Resource Utilization

The term *resource utilization* normally means *the level of use of a particular system component.* It is sometimes also used to mean the resource requirement of a process: the level of demand for a particular resource that is characteristic of the process. Because the latter usage is less common, we will use the unambiguous term *resource requirement* instead.

Although each resource works differently, in very general terms, resources are either busy (in use) or idle (available for use), and we can compute their utilization levels accordingly. For example, if a CPU is busy processing instructions for a total of 54 seconds during a single minute and is available for the remaining 6 seconds, its utilization during that interval is 54/60, or 90 percent.

Latency.   All computing resources share another important performance characteristic—*latency*—which sounds obscure, but actually is just a technical term for *delay* or *response time.* In other words, no device is infinitely fast; so whenever a process uses any computing device, it incurs some delay. Often, there are two distinct components to this delay: a fixed overhead per request and a variable delay that depends on the size of the request. In fact, this is a general characteristic of all computing that we discuss in Chapter 9, *The Efficiency Principle.*

In practice, the term *latency* is usually applied to devices other than the CPU—that is, memory and I/O devices—because they are slower than the CPU, and therefore they delay processing.

Estimating Waiting Times for Resources

Like tellers in the bank, many computing resources are shared. And when a shared system resource such as a processor or disk on a database server is busy handling work for one client application, it is unavailable to process other requests from other clients. They must wait in a queue for service.

Before we proceed further with this discussion, let's introduce some terminology:

▶ The average time a process spends using (or being served by) a resource is known as the average *holding time,* or *processing time* for that resource.

▶ The higher the percentage of time that a resource is in use, the longer each queued request must wait for its turn. This *wait time* or *waiting time* may also be referred to as the *queuing time,* or the *scheduling time.*

▶ The sum of the wait time and the holding time is the *service time* of the resource. This formula, of course, applies both to an individual request for service, and to the long-term average values of wait time, holding time, and service time for a given workload.

The service time of a shared device grows exponentially as its utilization level increases. This fact is captured in a simple formula that can be used to estimate the average waiting time at a shared device:

$$\text{waiting time estimate} = \frac{(\text{processing time} \times \text{utilization})}{(100 - \text{utilization})}$$

where processing time is the time it takes for a device to satisfy a request once it is available, and utilization is expressed as a percentage.

Notice that as device utilization approaches 100 percent, the estimated waiting time increases rapidly, because the divisor (100 − utilization) in the formula approaches zero. And if the device is 100 percent busy, the waiting time is infinite—an estimate that exactly corresponds with our experience when we try to download files from busy Web sites in the middle of the day.

On a more optimistic note, suppose the average data access time for a disk device is 10ms and the disk is 60 percent busy. Then an estimate of the waiting time is 10ms − 60/40, or 15ms, producing a total service time of 25ms for the device (15ms waiting plus 10ms processing). This formula is based on some statistical assumptions that are beyond the scope of this introduction; however, it is usually a safe method of obtaining a rough estimate for the service time of any shared resource. We discuss this subject further in the section *Shared Resources* in Chapter 11.

Resource Bottlenecks

We are probably all much too familiar with bottlenecks. Even if, by some miracle, we've managed to avoid bottlenecks in our computer systems, we've certainly encountered them in banks, in supermarket checkout lines, and on the highway. The concept is the same in all cases—too much of something—whether it is data, people, or cars, trying to pass through an overloaded resource: a disk, server, checkout counter, traffic light, or toll booth. The results are generally much the same also; frustration builds as performance slows. In computer systems, we use the term *resource bottleneck* to refer to a device or server that is overloaded.

Although the term *bottleneck* is used loosely to describe any slow or heavily loaded device or server, strictly speaking, there is only one *bottleneck device* in any system. It is the first device to saturate (i.e., to reach 100 percent of its capacity) as the workload volumes increase. In a client/server system, we can define the *bottleneck server* as the first server to saturate. As predicted by the estimated waiting time formula we presented earlier, the presence of a saturated resource causes a dramatic increase in both response times and queue lengths. Assuming for the moment that we cannot tune the applications, then the first and only rule of system-level performance tuning is: *Find the biggest bottleneck and eliminate it.* Then do it again, recursively, until performance is acceptable.

Bottlenecks, of course, depend on workload—different workloads have different effects on the same computer system. Some types of workloads, particularly those associated with scientific computing applications, are said to be CPU bound, which refers to the fact that the CPU is the bottleneck device. Business-oriented application workloads, because of their emphasis on information processing, tend to form bottlenecks in the I/O subsystem, saturating a heavily used disk or a slow network link.

As the workload mix changes during the day, so too do the bottlenecks. We are generally most concerned with the bottlenecks that occur during the peak processing hours. That is when the workload places the greatest demand on system resources and also when the most users are affected by processing delays. When it comes to bottlenecks, computers are just like commuters.

Guideline 3.6	**The first rule of system tuning: Find the biggest bottleneck and eliminate it.**

A device that is too busy to keep up with all of its requests for service becomes a bottleneck in the flow of work through the system, limiting throughput and extending response times. If we cannot tune the applications, then the first and only goal of system-level tuning should be to locate the biggest bottleneck (there always is one) and remove it. Then do it again, recursively.

The Processor or CPU

The *processor* or central processing unit (*CPU*) is the heart of the computer system. It handles all processing of program instructions for all applications, performs computations, and moves data around within the computer. Modern software, especially that running on servers with multitasking operating systems, makes many concurrent demands for service from the CPU. Ideally, the operating system is able to allocate the CPU resource to handle the workload demands adequately, but eventually, if there is enough work to process, the CPU can become a bottleneck.

In the enterprise client/server environment, even though users are likely to blame the "slow" CPU for performance problems, the fault is more often located elsewhere. So before we rush out to buy a faster processor, we must understand how the CPU interacts with the memory and I/O subsystems. As indicated in Figure 3.3, the CPU generally acts as the traffic cop for the other devices—moving data to and from memory, reading and writing data from disks, or sending and receiving data from networks.

If we are truly experiencing CPU contention, it is probably caused by trying to process too many programs concurrently. It generally does not mean that the system is short of memory or that it can't do disk I/O fast enough. In a typical configuration, we cannot tie up the processor with I/O activity alone.

Although the CPU gets involved in sending and receiving data from the I/O devices, it operates at speeds that are orders of magnitude faster, as illustrated by the sample device speeds shown in Table 3.4, later in this chapter. When the system is slow because of I/O problems, the chances are that the CPU is actually idle most of the time. So installing a faster processor won't actually make the applications run any faster. Indeed, the new, faster CPU will now spend even more time sitting idle.

CPU Utilization.   A high CPU utilization level doesn't necessarily signal a performance problem. It may simply mean that the CPU is being used to its fullest potential. Think of the CPU as a furnace, where instructions are the fuel. To maximize the heat output from the furnace, we must keep it constantly supplied with fuel. The CPU is the fastest device in the whole system, and we want to keep it working at full tilt to maximize throughput and minimize response times. Any hiccup in the supply line means a temporary loss of efficiency that can never be recovered. As long as the transaction throughput is high and remains proportional to CPU utilization, a high CPU utilization rate normally means that the system is well tuned and working efficiently.

The warning signal occurs when transaction throughput does not keep pace with CPU utilization. In this case, the CPU is probably overloaded and is wasting its processing cycles "thrashing"—typically diverting cycles to internal housekeeping chores such as *memory management,* which we discuss in the next section, *The Memory Subsystem.* In this situation, CPU utilization rises, throughput drops, and response times increase.

In online systems with hundreds of users, sometimes these situations are transient, brought on by natural peaks in the arrival and distribution of work. As the peak in demand subsides, the system returns to a more efficient state. But if transaction response times increase to unacceptable levels and if CPU utilization remains high, then we must investigate further to determine if the processor is overloaded. If so, some form of workload balancing may be required; we discuss this subject in more detail in Chapter 11, *The Sharing Principle,* and in Part IV of the book.

> | Guideline 3.7 | **Monitor high CPU utilization** |
>
> High CPU utilization alone does not indicate a problem. But if transaction throughput does not rise and fall proportionately with CPU utilization. CPU time is probably being devoted to overhead processing of some kind. Investigate CPU usage to find where the wasted CPU cycles are being spent.

The Memory Subsystem

The computer's random access memory (*RAM*), or more simply *memory,* holds the transient information used by the CPU. The operating system and its associated status information, program instructions, program data, and I/O buffers—whatever the CPU is currently working on—resides in the computer memory.

When active processes require more memory than is physically available on the machine, the operating system begins **paging**—moving inactive parts of active processes to disk in order to reclaim some pages of physical (real) memory. For more details, see the capsule, *Squeezing a Quart into a Pint Pot.*

Under a virtual operating system, paging is normal. It is a very useful mechanism that allows software developers a great deal of freedom to design software without undue concern for the physical execution environment. As is often the case, though, we can get too much of a good thing. Because paging uses the CPU and I/O devices, system performance can slow dramatically if the paging rate gets too high.

Operating systems generally provide detailed statistics about memory management activity. When we see consistently high paging rates, it generally indicates that memory utilization is (or is becoming) a problem. The solutions are to limit the number of concurrent tasks, to tune the programs to tighten up their patterns of reference to memory locations, or to add more memory. While the last solution may be the most expensive, it is often the simplest and most effective way to fix a memory utilization problem.

> | Guideline 3.8 | **Tune for high memory utilization** |
>
> High paging rates indicate that memory utilization is (or is becoming) a problem. The solution is to limit the number of concurrent tasks, to tune the programs to tighten up their patterns of reference, or to add more memory. In this situation, adding more memory will almost always improve performance.

Squeezing a Quart into a Pint Pot

In most modern computer systems, memory is managed as a collection of small elements called *pages* or *page frames,* typically 2K or 4K in size. The operating system, meanwhile, supports a mechanism known as *virtual memory,* which allows programs to use more memory than the amount actually available (the *real* memory) on the computer. In effect, this works by substituting disk space—typically referred to as a *swap* disk, swap space, or swap area—for the shortfall in real memory.

When the operating system needs to allocate memory for use by a process, it first looks for any unused pages in real memory. If none is available, it must select pages that are being used by other active processes. Although memory management systems vary somewhat, most use a least-recently-used (LRU) algorithm to select pages that can be copied out to disk to free memory for other processes.

Locating pages and copying them to disk require CPU cycles and, therefore, have an effect on CPU utilization. Once the CPU has identified pages to swap out, it copies the old data from those pages to a dedicated disk. Later, if the pages sent to the swap disk are referenced by the program, they must be brought back into memory, whereupon the paging activity must be repeated if the system does not have unused pages available.

Because paging requires I/O operations, it is much slower than simply executing instructions, and can have a noticeable effect on response times. The

The I/O Subsystem

In an enterprise client/server system, the disks and networks are vital to overall system performance. As we show later in Table 3.4, these devices are orders of magnitude slower than the CPU or the time it takes to read data from memory. Yet corporate information, which is measured in gigabytes (if not terabytes), must be stored on disks and shipped across the networks of our distributed enterprises. So it is crucial that we focus on the likely performance of the I/O subsystem at all stages of development.

Disk I/O.   Disks are magnetically coated rotating platters that can store gigabytes of data in readily available formats. The average time to read *any* piece of data from a rotating magnetic disk is determined by three factors:

▶ **Seek time.**   The time for the read/write head to move laterally to the correct location on the magnetic surface, typically about 10ms.

total amount of paging activity that takes place on any computer depends on three factors:

► The number of processes running concurrently
► The ratio of the total virtual pages used by those processes to the size of the computer's real memory
► The pattern of memory references by those processes

As the demand for memory increases, so too does the paging rate and the associated CPU and I/O activity to support it. When the activity builds to the point at which the CPU is almost solely occupied with shuffling pages around, with barely any time for useful work, the system is said to be "thrashing."

Thrashing is the computer's equivalent of a traffic jam. When there is so much traffic that it fills up all the lanes on the highway, everything stops. To get things flowing again, we need to open another lane or limit the traffic. When a system is thrashing, paradoxically, we can get more work done by slowing down the arrival of new work. Like the metering lights that control the number of cars on the freeway, any scheme that limits the system to fewer concurrent programs will lessen the demand for pages, lower the overhead of paging, and speed work through the system.

The alternative, of course, is to buy more hardware—adding another memory lane would be a sure way to keep those programs strolling along.

► **Rotational delay.** The time for the start of the data to rotate to the position of the read/write head. If the disk spins at 3600 RPM, this is about 8.3ms for the average delay of one-half a revolution of the disk. At 7200 RPM, the average delay comes close to 4ms.

► **Data transfer time.** The time to read the data stored on the disk, usually at 1 to 10MB per second. A 4K block of data (like a memory page) can be transferred in between 0.4 and 4.0ms.

Combining these estimates the typical latency for a single 4K block is between 15ms and 23ms. If we have no other information, 20ms per disk I/O is a safe estimate, before we add any waiting time due to contention. When multiple blocks are read at random, we can simply multiply this estimate by the number of blocks to be read. For example, 100 4K blocks (1MB in all) might take 2 seconds.

However, if we read a large block of data sequentially, we can get much better performance because we do not incur the repeated seek and rotational delay times. A single 4MB block of sequential data might take as little as 414ms (10ms seek time, 4ms rotational delay, plus 400ms to read the data at 10MB per second).

This improvement highlights the performance advantages of reading large sequential blocks of data, as opposed to many smaller blocks organized randomly. The ability that random access disks give us to read many separate data items at random is a useful one, and one that that gives us a lot of freedom in how we design databases and applications. But if performance is crucial, reading large sequential blocks of data is still much faster.

Guideline 3.9	**Random versus sequential risk performance**

Disks allow applications to read many separate data items at random, without noticeable performance differences. But if performance is crucial, reading large sequential blocks of data is much faster.

Disk Striping and RAID.   To speed up disk response times even more, disk devices employ the technique of disk striping. *Striping* involves spreading a sequence of data across many disks so that every disk in the sequence can (if it makes sense for a particular data request) be read in parallel. **RAID** (which stands for redundant array of *inexpensive,* or *independent,* disks—both versions appear in the literature) devices employ this technique, as do multiprocessing database servers. We discuss these subjects in more detail in Chapter 13, *The Parallelism Principle.*

Using the striping technique, in the previous example a bank of eight disks might be striped so that 32K goes to the first disk, 32K to the second, and so on up to 8 × 32K; and after that the process would begin at disk 1 again. For our hypothetical 4MB transfer, this approach would lower the estimated transfer time into the region of 50ms (4MB/8, or 0.5MB, at 10MB per second), which, in turn, drops the total service time for the example to less than 70ms—a big improvement over the previous 414ms.

On the other hand, notice that striping does not help with random accesses unless we can invoke several random reads in parallel to the striped data that previously would have been processed in sequence. Because of this, it is important to understand what disk drive vendors mean when they quote average data access times. Vendors of RAID devices often quote average access times of a few milliseconds, but these times assume the maximum degree of parallelism when reading.

Combining RAID with caching[3] can offer the possibility of even lower average access times. For the right application, the performance gains can be astonishing. But once again, not all applications can achieve the RAID vendors'

---

[3]For example, see Seek Systems *Adaptive RAID* at *www.seek.com.*

quoted performance numbers, usually because of random data access patterns or because of the *skimming effect* of higher level cache(s). We discuss caching in detail in Chapter 14, *The Trade-off Principle.*

Guideline 3.10	**Disk striping**

Disk striping can lower the response time of large data requests, provided multiple disks can be read in parallel. It may make no difference to the performance of small random reads.

Performance of Local versus Remote Disks.   I/O subsystem issues become considerably more complex in distributed environments.

First, let's clarify some terminology. *Local* and *remote* are relative terms— their meaning changes according to the context. A working definition in most computing contexts seems to be that local means "as near as possible for this type of component" and remote means anything farther away. When we talk about local and remote *disks,* the local disk is the one attached to the processor in question; the remote disk is attached to another processor. On the other hand, when we talk about local and remote *servers,* for a client workstation a local server is connected to the LAN, whereas a remote server is at another location. This shifting context can be a bit confusing when we discuss a process running on a client workstation, for which a *remote disk* is attached to a *local server.* We will try to avoid any ambiguity by making the context clear.

When a client process queries a local disk, the disk driver simply passes a call to the disk controller, which returns the requested data. When it makes the same type of query to a disk on a server, however, the data request must be passed *in both directions* through the series of layers illustrated in Figure 3.4.

Obviously, compared with local disk access, reading data from a disk on a network server involves a significant amount of overhead. Even though the network transmission delay is probably the largest of the overhead components, each layer of software between the client application and the data access on the server introduces some overhead. In addition to the processing overheads, there will normally be some contention with other users for the network and the server because these are both shared devices. In a busy system, the extra wait times may be the largest components of the remote disk access time.

It is always important to limit disk I/O activity to optimize application performance. But if the disk in question is located on a server, then this guideline is even more important because of the significantly longer access times involved. Reading 30 blocks of data from a local disk may well take a second, but the same amount of data read from a remote disk is unlikely to take less than 3 seconds and could easily take more than 10 seconds when the network and server are both busy with other work.

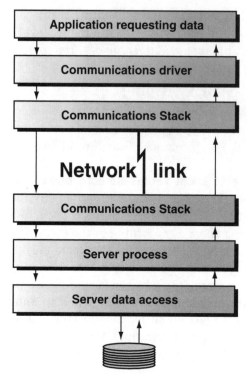

FIGURE **3.4**   Reading from a remote disk.

<table>
<tr><td>Guideline
3.11</td><td>**Local vs. remote disks**</td></tr>
</table>

Guideline 3.11   Local vs. remote disks

It is always important to limit disk I/O activity to optimize application performance. But if the disk in question is located on a server, then this guideline is even more important because of the significantly longer access times involved.

Network I/O.   When we don't want to get bogged down in unnecessary detail, it is often convenient (by analogy with a disk I/O event) to refer to "a network I/O event" or "the latency of a network." However, these handy logical concepts defy precise definition.

We might think of a network input or output "event" as what happens from the time a program passes a read or write command to some other software component (typically some form of middleware) until it receives a response. But, as we noted earlier in our *Response Time Example* (see Figure 3.2), that event actually comprises a large number of smaller events, many of which are not strictly in the network at all, but involve software components running on computers connected by the network.

In Chapter 15, we discuss the roles of middleware and communications software in more detail (see the section *Communicating Processes* and Figure 15.2 in *The OSI Reference Model*). But in summary, the problem with defining "a network I/O event" is knowing what to include in it. In complex distributed systems, the boundaries between application processing, middleware, the communications stack, and network devices are blurry. In fact, this is exactly the same reason why *middleware* is so hard to define, a subject we also discuss in Chapter 15 in the capsule, *Defining Middleware.*

Network Bandwidth and Latency.   What about *bandwidth,* the most widely quoted measure of network performance? Bandwidth is the *capacity* of a network component to transmit data—in other words, its throughput. It is determined by the transmission medium and the protocol in use, and can range from 9.6 Kbits/sec for a typical PC modem all the way up to 10 Gbits/sec for high-performance switching backplanes. The problem is that the available bandwidth in a network is usually a lot less than we might expect, because:

▶ Network throughput is determined by the slowest link in a long chain of components on the route connecting the communicating machines.
▶ Because of overhead traffic (message headers, acknowledgments, and so on), a lot more data than the original message is actually transmitted.
▶ With synchronous communications protocols like Ethernet, all networked devices contend for the same bus. Collisions between data packets cause retransmission overheads.

So, we cannot predict a network's *latency* (its response time, or message transmission time) just by knowing its rated speed. Actual network performance depends on many factors, chief of which are:

▶ The network *communications protocols* (Ethernet, SDLC, ISDN, TCP/IP, SPX/IPX, LU6.2, etc.).
▶ The speed of the *network interface cards* connecting the communicating computers to the network.
▶ The *transmission medium* (twisted pair, coaxial cable, fiber-optic cable, wireless).
▶ The network *topology,* and possibly, how it is partitioned into *subnets.*
▶ Transmission delays (*latency*) caused by the length of *the route* connecting the source and destination of a message.
▶ Additional latency introduced by intermediate *switching devices* like *hubs, routers, gateways,* and *bridges* on that route.
▶ Overheads introduced by *protocol conversion* and *protocol encapsulation* as message traffic moves from one portion of the network to another.

▶ *Contention* with other competing *network traffic.*
▶ Delays and *contention* caused by *device errors* in the network.

We discuss many of these issues in more detail in the section *Shared Networks* in Chapter 11, *The Sharing Principle.*

Guideline 3.12	Network performance involves much more than bandwidth

The rated bandwidth of its slowest component supplies only an upper bound for a network's performance. A long list of hardware and software factors determine the actual time to transmit a data packet across a network.

The Hierarchy of Computing Resources

Table 3.3 shows the typical hierarchy of computing resources in a distributed client/server environment, organized by relative speed with the fastest resources at the top.

Because all device access times are relatively small, it may be hard to visualize the differences among them. So to illustrate the wide range of speeds involved, the right-hand column equates 10 nanoseconds with 1 second.

We have also included estimates for the time to access a remote disk with various server machines. These were computed by taking the time for a disk access (25ms) and adding 2ms for metropolitan area network (MAN) or high

Table 3.3   **The Hierarchy of Computing Resources**

Device Type	Typical Service Time	Relative to 1 second
High-speed processor buffer	10 nanoseconds	1 second
Random access memory	60 nanoseconds	~6 seconds
Procedure call	1 microsecond	~2 minutes
Expanded memory	25 microseconds	~1 hour
Local RPC	100 microseconds	~4 hours
Solid-state disk	1 millisecond	~1 day
Cached disk	10 milliseconds	~12 days
Magnetic disk	25 milliseconds	~4 weeks
Disk via MAN/high-speed LAN server	27 milliseconds	~1 month
Disk via typical LAN server	35–50 milliseconds	~6–8 weeks
Disk via typical WAN server	1–2 seconds	~3–6 years
Mountable disk/tape	3–15 seconds	~10–15 years

speed LAN, 10–25ms for a typical LAN, and 500ms–1sec for a typical WAN. These estimates are intended to cover the time to execute the appropriate (RPC) instructions, transmit the request across the network, dispatch a process on the server, and transmit the response—including all network device latencies.

Note the following:

▶ Many different technologies are used for processors, storage, and communications devices. This is a typical list, not an exhaustive one.
▶ The table does not include devices that are not normally under the control of an application designer, such as high-speed cache memories or I/O channels.
▶ Every class of computer hardware is available in a very wide range of speeds, and service times also depend on the size of the request, so the service time column provides only typical values.

The point here is that in any organization, a developer must work with a set of computing resources that form a hierarchy similar to this one. Because of the vast differences in the speeds of the various devices, *caching* is one of the most widely used techniques to improve software and hardware performance. We discuss caching in detail in Chapter 14, *The Trade-off Principle.*

The Application–Resource Usage Matrix

We began this chapter by introducing the elements of performance—the five fundamental performance concepts of *workload, response time, throughput, resource utilizations,* and *resource service times.* Now that we have described these concepts in some detail, we can review the relationships among them.

These relationships are best illustrated using a tool that is very useful for recording performance-related data: an *application-resource usage matrix.* Figure 3.5 is a conceptual illustration of the components of such a matrix.

In the matrix, the **workload,** consisting of a set of **applications,** is listed vertically on the left, one application per row. In practice, a row of the matrix may be devoted to any application or group of applications having similar processing characteristics. System **resources** are listed horizontally, one per column of the matrix. A column may be devoted to a *logical resource* like an object, a table, or a database, or to a *physical resource* like a processor, a disk device, or a network link.

The central matrix (shaded in Figure 3.5) describes how the set of applications shown on the left uses the set of resources represented by the columns. At the intersection of a row and a column, a cell records the use of a particular resource by a particular application. In the illustration, the usage statistics are shown as $U_a \ldots U_z$.

Knowing this information is the key to understanding performance.

Workload	Resource Usage Pattern						
	#1	#2	#3	#4	#5	#6	#7
Application 1	U_a		U_b			U_c	
Application 2	U_d	U_e		U_f			
Application 3	U_g	U_h					U_i
Application 4	U_j		U_k		U_l	U_m	
Application 5	U_n	U_o		U_p			
Application 6	U_g				U_r		U_s
Application 7	U_t		U_u		U_v	U_w	
Application 8			U_y	U_z			

FIGURE 3.5   The application-resource usage matrix.

Using the Matrix

We can use various flavors of the application-resource usage matrix during many phases of the development process. Depending on the purpose of a particular matrix, the cells may contain qualitative or quantitative information. Cell values can represent application usage patterns, unit costs for each application, projected future resource utilizations for a particular workload mix, or current utilization levels observed by using a performance-monitoring tool. For example:

▶ During data analysis or database design, a logical analysis tool called a *CRUD matrix* is often used to record how a particular application manipulates a set of data resources. The resources may be tables, or individual data items, or columns. At first, the cells simply record whether the application performs create (*C*), read (*R*), update (*U*), or delete (*D*) operations against the data resource. Later, the frequencies of each type of activity can be recorded, too.
▶ During physical design for a distributed database environment, each column in the matrix could represent a database table or a distinct, logical subset of a table. Each row could contain statistics summarizing the projected level of data manipulation activity against those tables, for all work originating from a particular geographical location. Using techniques known as *affinity analysis,* this data can then be used to help select an optimal strategy for data distribution.

Extending the Matrix

As development progresses, the matrix can be extended to record more information, as illustrated by Figure 3.6, a more elaborate version of Figure 3.5. To obtain the extended matrix:

Workload Type	Workload Mix	Resource Service Times and Utilizations							Response Times
		#1	#2	#3	#4	#5	#6	#7	
		s_1	s_2	s_3	s_4	s_5	s_6	s_7	
Application 1	f_1	U_a		U_b			U_c		rt_1
Application 2	f_2	U_d	U_e		U_f				rt_2
Application 3	f_3	U_g	U_h					U_i	rt_3
Application 4	f_4	U_j		U_k		U_l	U_m		rt_4
Application 5	f_5	U_n	U_o		U_p				rt_5
Application 6	f_6	U_q				U_r		U_s	rt_6
Application 7	f_7	U_t		U_u		U_v	U_w		rt_7
Application 8	f_8	U_x			U_y	U_z			rt_8
Totals	**Throughput**	ru_1	ru_2	ru_3	ru_4	ru_5	ru_6	ru_7	

FIGURE 3.6 Extended application-resource usage matrix.

▶ A measure of frequency or **throughput** is associated with each application; we show it as the set of values $f_1 \ldots f_8$ in the second column, labeled *workload mix.* In a matrix used for a logical analysis task during the early phases of the development process, frequency information may not be available for new workloads. For any kind of numerical performance analysis, however, relative frequency information is vital.

▶ From the information in the second column, we can compute the **total throughput** for the set of applications recorded in the matrix. We show it as the total, at the base of the column.

▶ For physical resources, we may be able to record information about **resource service times,** shown in the figure as an additional row containing values $s_1 \ldots s_7$.

▶ When the central matrix is populated, we can compute summary statistics along both its dimensions.

▶ Summing columns of numerical cell values produces **total resource utilizations** for each resource ($ru_1 \ldots ru_7$ in the figure), for the application workloads represented in the matrix. If all workloads are represented in the matrix, then the resource whose sum is closest to 100 percent of its capacity is the **bottleneck** (or will be, when the application frequencies reach those recorded in the table).

▶ Given sufficient data about the resources, applying the mathematical techniques known as queuing theory to the data in each row can produce estimates of **application response times,** shown as $rt_1 \ldots rt_8$ in the figure. We discuss queuing theory in more detail in Chapter 6.

A Unifying View of Performance.   Early in our discussion of performance, we summarized three perspectives on the subject. The application-resource matrix provides the unifying framework for these various perspectives: Its rows represent the *application* or *user* view of performance, its columns represent the focus of those with a *system* or *community* view, and to look at the entire matrix is to embrace the larger, *organizational* concerns.

As we shall see in later chapters, because it integrates all three perspectives, the matrix is a simple but powerful tool for organizing and analyzing performance information. A tool for structuring our thought processes, it helps us to uncover the relationships underlying performance information. Even if our knowledge is incomplete, knowing some cells of the matrix can help us to compute or infer others and so aid in problem isolation.

> Guideline
> **3.13**   **The application–resource usage matrix**
> An application-resource usage matrix describes how a set of applications uses a set of computer resources. Knowing this information is the key to understanding the performance of those applications and how to tune either the applications or the resources.
>
> Given application frequencies, the matrix can yield useful insights into likely causes of performance problems in the areas of resource capacity or application response time.

Why a System Runs Slowly

We now use the concepts embodied in the extended application-resource usage matrix (Figure 3.6) to introduce the subject of performance tuning. Conceptually, tracking the performance of a system involves periodically observing its application-resource usage matrix. If performance worsens, we can tell from the two sets of totals in the matrix whether it is an application problem (indicated by longer response times) or a system problem (indicated by higher resource utilizations and resource bottlenecks). Examining the matrix also indicates the source of the problem since it shows the workload frequencies and the resource utilizations.

But while the conceptual framework of the application-resource usage matrix helps us to think about the components of system performance, it certainly does not reveal everything about the task of solving real performance problems. We now consider some real-world issues of problem diagnosis and removal.

Assuming that our expectations of the system's performance were realistic to begin with, then the reason a system's performance slows down is usually because a mismatch between the amount of work to be done and the computing resources available has created a resource contention problem. That is, different parts of the workload are contending (competing) for the same resource(s). As in everyday situations like waiting in the checkout line at the supermarket or driving to work during the rush hour, contention for a common resource introduces delays.

Two types of mismatch between a workload and the computing resources can occur:

▶ We allocated the resources to the workload inefficiently.
▶ There is too just much work, or viewed another way, we have insufficient resources to handle the work.

Performance specialists make their living solving the first class of problem, looking for more resource-efficient ways to get the same amount of work done. As long as there is some spare capacity in some computing resource somewhere, we can usually find a way to realign the workload to better match the available resources. The managerial and technical practices we use in this endeavor are collectively known as **software performance engineering (SPE).** The principles of SPE, and their application to the design of efficient and acceptable distributed (client/server) systems for the enterprise, are the central topic of this book. In Part II, we provide a comprehensive overview of SPE practice.

When there are insufficient computing resources to handle the workload, people's view of the problem ("too much work" or "not enough computing resources") tends to be a subjective one, depending on where they sit in the organization. But either way, when this situation arises, the actions required to improve performance are likely to be painful for someone. To avoid this trauma, organizations whose business depends on having sufficient computing capacity spend a lot of time and money on **capacity planning**—tracking evolving workloads and planning hardware acquisitions to match. Although we do touch on it, capacity planning is not the main focus of this book. We discuss capacity planning in a little more detail in Chapter 5.

Tackling Performance Problems

Up to this point, our explanation of performance problems has been largely theoretical in that it ignores the practical difficulty of *determining the cause* of any performance problem. In practice, it usually takes a mixture of business politics and technical insights to determine which of the possible interpretations of any problem is the "right" one. And, of course, agreeing on the cause is the essential first step in improving performance. Once we agree, we can decide on a course of action that will improve the match between workload and computing resources.

When determining the cause, we are often working in a large gray area between the two classes of performance problems. Frequently, what appears at first sight to be a *capacity* problem turns out, on closer inspection, to be amenable to a *performance engineering* solution.

The reason for this gray area is partly technical: Initially, it *is* difficult to know whether performance can be improved by tuning to remove some bottleneck in the software. Diagnosing bottlenecks and finding a way to remove them usually take time and analysis. But there is also a nontechnical reason that is just as important: *cost.* Even though tuning a system certainly does take time and money, it may well cost much less than the alternative of buying faster hardware. So organizations usually have a strong incentive to tackle capacity problems using tuning methods before resorting to hardware upgrades.

In this respect, the relationship between the workload and the available computing resources is similar to that between expenditure and income, in which spare capacity is like cash in the bank. Consider:

▶ If we want to fly to the Bahamas for a week but don't have enough in the bank, it does not necessarily mean that we must first resign from our current job in favor of a new one with a larger paycheck or even that we must go out and borrow some money. We can usually figure out how to make room for the extra expense by examining our current spending carefully and then making judicious spending cuts. Our current lifestyle may be affected, but only in a relatively minor way.

▶ On the other hand, if for some reason we decide to buy a mansion in the Bahamas and fly there once a month, then we'll certainly need to find more cash or make substantial cuts in our other commitments, or both.

▶ Before we sign the contract, we probably ought to reconsider whether we actually need that mansion. There may be a much less expensive way to get away from it all, or we may prefer to spend our money on something more urgent.

Priorities and Choices.   In software engineering, as in other walks of life, we generally look for ways to eke out our existing resources before spending money. When pressured, we look carefully at our use of those resources to see if everything we are doing is really necessary. By far, the best and fastest way to improve performance is to stop doing work that does not need to be done. As Peter Drucker wrote in 1963, "There is surely nothing so useless as doing with great efficiency what should not be done at all."[4]

In theory, from the perspective of system resources, there is a straightforward solution to all resource contention problems: Buy more of whatever re-

---

[4]Peter Drucker, *The Practice of Management* (New York, NY: Harper & Row, 1963), 48.

source you lack. That is, buy more memory; buy faster disk storage devices or disk controllers; buy fatter, faster communication paths; buy a bigger processor or more computers. But—even supposing it were feasible, which is not always the case—this is an expensive and, therefore, a painful way to solve performance problems.

In practice, although we can usually solve most problems by throwing more money at them, that approach is typically not the *first* choice, but the *last* resort after we have satisfied ourselves that other, less expensive methods will not work. The first rule of performance tuning is to get the most out of the existing hardware and software.

Guideline **3.14**	**Nagraj's law of tuning choices**

When faced with a performance problem, adopt the logical sequence of tuning activities that my colleague Nagraj Alur of DataBase Associates likes to describe as follows:

▶ **Do less work.**   By far the best and fastest way to improve performance is to stop doing work that does not need to be done.

▶ **Make the best use of what you have.**   Tune the hardware and software environment (operating system, middleware, DBMS, and so on) to make it match the workload better; tune (and possibly redesign) the applications to cut out any unneeded processing.

▶ **Steal from Peter to pay Paul.**   Make trade-offs between subsets of the overall workload to improve the performance of one at the expense of another.

▶ **Water down the requirements.**   Revisit the performance requirements to see whether the business can actually tolerate poorer performance for some application(s). This may be preferable to the final option.

▶ **Throw money at the problem.**   Buy more memory; buy faster storage devices, faster disk controllers, faster communication paths; buy a bigger processor; or buy more computers.

Of course, there is a limit to what can be achieved by tuning, and the law of diminishing returns does apply. After a while, we find that it simply is not cost-effective to search for smaller and smaller incremental performance improvements. When we finally conclude that we cannot squeeze a quart of workload into a pint-sized system and that an upgrade is the only solution, our previous investment in performance tuning will pay off. We will know exactly how the system should be upgraded—we will know whether we need more memory, faster disks, a faster network, or a bigger processor.

These are subjects we shall revisit in more detail later in the book:

▶ We explain why a systematic performance management process must include setting performance objectives and weighing those objectives against other software engineering goals, including costs and service levels (Chapters 4 and 5).
▶ We describe how we can apply SPE design principles to make the best use of our processing resources (Chapters 7 through 13).
▶ We discuss the important role that trade-offs play in all aspects of performance management and design (Chapters 5 and 14).

PART II

Process

CHAPTER 4

Software Performance Engineering

"There's never enough time to get it right, but there's always enough money to do it over."

Anonymous (contributed by George Peters)

In This Chapter . . .

What Is Software Engineering?
Software Performance Engineering
The Software Development Process
The Performance Life Cycle
Performance and the Organization
SPE Conclusions

What Is Software Engineering?

Engineering, according to the dictionary, is "the planning, designing, construction, or management of machinery . . ." Although this definition does not refer strictly to software engineering, it exactly captures the meaning intended. Over the last 20 years, programming professionals have observed many parallels between software engineering and civil or mechanical engineering. As a result, we now accept that creating a large software system can be every bit as complex as building a bridge or manufacturing an airplane, and must be managed just as carefully.

Consequently, we acknowledge that the work of building quality into software cannot be carried out haphazardly or left to chance or luck; like civil or mechanical engineering, it must be a controlled and systematic process, and it must be a forward-looking process. Can you imagine an engineer who starts thinking about quality after the bridge is built or when the first cars roll off the production line?

It is in this context that we must approach the subject of software performance. Like function, ease of use, and maintainability, performance is an indispensable element of software quality. Unfortunately, performance has often been the poor relation of the software engineering process, forgotten and ignored. In fact, many software developers regard performance as "someone else's job" or an issue to be dealt with "later" (if at all!). Not surprisingly, projects in which the earlier phases are skimped in a desire to "crank out some code" are usually the ones that end up needing the most rework and maintenance later.

Software Performance Engineering

The idea that *prevention is better than a cure* is certainly not a new one. But in the demanding world of corporate information systems, there has long been an *application backlog.* The imperative for the software developer has been new function, not better performance. While there have always been software vendors and developers who prized performance and software efficiency, the majority preferred to *build it first and tune it later.* Unfortunately, as some companies have discovered—much to their regret—if you design and build *poor performance* into a system, correcting the problems can be next to impossible without a complete rewrite and a lot of unpleasant political repercussions.

Software performance engineering takes the opposite approach. It is best summarized by the opening paragraph of Connie U. Smith's definitive book, *Performance Engineering of Software Systems:*

> Software performance engineering (SPE) is a method for constructing software systems to meet performance objectives. The process begins early in the software life cycle and uses quantitative methods to identify satisfactory designs and to eliminate those that are likely to have unacceptable performance, before developers invest significant time in implementation. SPE continues through the detailed design, coding, and testing stages to predict and manage the performance of the evolving software and to monitor and report actual performance against specifications and predictions. SPE methods cover performance data collection, quantitative analysis techniques, prediction strategies, management of uncertainties, data presentation and tracking, model verification and validation, critical success factors, and performance design principles.[1]

---

[1]Connie U. Smith, *Performance Engineering of Software Systems* (Reading, MA: Addison-Wesley, 1990), 1.

There are many motivations for SPE. Some people are concerned primarily with application performance and with building efficient software and systems to support business processes. Others are more involved with capacity concerns—tuning the systems to resolve existing problems or to claw back some extra capacity to accommodate growth. Yet others have a financial motive—seeking to postpone the expense of new hardware or displacing hardware to cut costs. Whatever the reasons or interests, adopting SPE will always involve performing many activities. The 10 fundamental activities of SPE are as follows:

1. **Identify** sensitivity of the application design to key business factors (forecast, analyze)
2. **Specify** business priorities and performance objectives (establish, agree, decide, set)
3. **Evaluate** application, database, and system design alternatives (design)
4. **Summarize** application performance profiles (profile, characterize)
5. **Predict** performance on the target platform (project, estimate, model)
6. **Monitor** ongoing software performance (measure, observe)
7. **Analyze** observed performance data (review)
8. **Confirm** performance expectations (verify, validate, corroborate)
9. **Tune** application or system performance (optimize)
10. **Manage** ongoing system capacity (plan capacity)

To emphasize the fact that each item in the list represents a separate and distinct sphere of activity, we have chosen to name them using ten distinct verbs. In some cases, when an alternate verb is available with a similar or related meaning, we list that too. (There is considerable confusion and overlap in the terminology, so we cannot promise to select everyone's favorite term for every concept, but we will at least attempt to avoid ambiguity.)

Although the order of the activities corresponds roughly with the order of the phases of a software development process, we do not intend to imply that these SPE activities constitute a sequential development methodology. Nor do they correspond directly to individual phases of a development life cycle—typically, several SPE activities take place in parallel over several phases of the development process. Rarely do we simply complete one SPE activity and move on to the next. Rather, our focus evolves gradually as we work through the development process, as the emphasis and level of effort constantly shift among the SPE activities as development progresses.

The activities are interrelated, connected by the common ground of performance. Usually, the information developed while carrying out one SPE activity at one stage helps us understand how best to tackle a different SPE activity in a later stage. For example, *summarizing* the performance profile of an application

---

Table 4.1   **Ten Fundamental SPE Activities**

SPE Components	Performance-Related Activities
Identify sensitivity of the application design to key business factors.	*Key business factors* are the business quantities that most affect the processing load placed on the system. They are statistics like *number of customers, new orders per day,* or *peak hour sales.* The key to successful SPE is to understand the relationship between these quantities and the computing applications.
Specify business needs and priorities.	To manage performance, we must set *quantifiable, measurable performance objectives,* then design with those objectives in mind, project to see whether we can meet them, monitor to see whether we are meeting them, and tune against them.
Evaluate application, database, and system design alternatives.	In addition to the normal functional goals of creating applications to support business processes, the design activity must address performance goals. This includes creating an overall architecture that permits growth, using shared resources efficiently, and meeting application response time objectives.
Summarize application performance profiles.	An *application performance profile* is a collection of information about the performance characteristics of an application. Knowing the performance characteristics of an application or a workload mix is an essential prerequisite to other SPE activities like performance modeling, problem diagnosis, and tuning.

---

helps us to *predict* its performance or to decide how best to *monitor* it once it's running.

Table 4.1 defines the 10 fundamental SPE activities. In Chapters 5 and 6, we discuss each of these activities in more detail.

The Software Development Process

In this section, our goal is to clarify what we mean by the *software development life cycle (SDLC)* or the *software development process.* This is quite important for two reasons: first, because it provides the context for our discussion of SPE and, second, because there are so many different models of the software development process and people tend to hold religious positions as to which is the "right" one.

Table 4.1   **Ten Fundamental SPE Activities (*Cont'd.*)**

Predict performance on the target platform.	All design involves prediction, if only implicitly. Explicit prediction techniques range from following simple rules of thumb, through mathematical analysis and simulation, to full-scale benchmarks.
Monitor ongoing software performance.	There are many tools for performance monitoring. We can measure response time at the user interface, operating system and subsystem behavior, database activity, network traffic, and the performance of hardware devices.
Analyze and review observed performance data.	Systematic monitoring allows us to understand the normal operation of the system, observe relationships among performance variables, detect trends, and identify performance problems and their likely causes.
Confirm performance expectations.	Formal monitoring tools and informal monitoring by users are complementary techniques for confirming that application performance meets defined objectives.
Tune application or system performance.	After the application has been built, tuning involves making adjustments to improve some aspect of the application's performance. There is a limit to what can be achieved by tuning because not all performance problems can be addressed easily after the system is operational.
Manage ongoing system capacity.	Capacity planning encompasses the planning and management activities required to deliver sufficient computing capacity to maintain acceptable performance as workloads grow and change.

Let's begin with a simple definition. The life cycle defines a ". . . set of phases that a software product undergoes from concept on to retirement. . . ."[2] There are many models of the software development life cycle, but all involve working through a set of distinct development *tasks.* Older development models typically assign each task to a development *phase,* then step through the phases in an invariant sequence. In more recent models, a relatively flexible group of interconnected tasks can be executed in almost any order, within an independent collection of phases. Another important aspect of any life-cycle model is that it defines the essential *activities* within each phase, along with the critical success factors for those activities. Development *methodologies* address the practical details of

---

[2]C. Baudoin and G. Hollowell, *Realizing the Object-Oriented Life Cycle* (Upper Saddle River, NJ: Prentice-Hall, 1996).

implementing the process, suggesting tools, responsibilities, and deliverables, and sometimes providing ways to tailor the various phases and their sequence of execution.

Life-cycle models and methodologies come and go with the regularity of spring fashions. Over the years, the life cycle has been defined, refined, undefined, and redefined. It has been a *Meta Life Cycle,* an *Object Life Cycle, Information Engineering,* a *Macro Process,* a *Framework,* a *Waterfall, Sashimi,* a *Spiral,* or a *Scrum.* Yet, despite this variety, all life-cycle models share a common set of core activities.

To illustrate this, Table 4.2 compares three very different life-cycle models: from left to right, the Zachman framework, information engineering, and Grady Booch's macro process. There are many differences in terminology and methodology:

▶ Zachman's terminology deals with the things that we produce during the development process; it is independent of any development methodology.
▶ Information engineering reflects the stages of information systems development and assumes a rigid top-down approach to development.
▶ Booch addresses object-oriented development and advocates an iterative approach, in which the output of the initial design work is an executable architecture, which is then evolved into a fully functional system by further iterations of analysis, design, and implementation.

In fact, these life cycles have a great deal in common. As Table 4.2 indicates, the difference between them is as much a matter of terminology as of sub-

Table 4.2   **A Comparison of Life-Cycle Models**

Zachman Framework	Information Engineering	Booch's Macro Process	Generic Tasks
Objectives/Scope	Information strategy planning	Conceptualization	*Planning*
Business model	Business area analysis	Analysis/Evolution	*Analysis*
Information system	Business system design	Design/Evolution	*Schematic design*
Technology model	Technical design		*Technical design*
Detailed	Construction	Implementation	*Construction*
n/a	Transition	Evolution	*Deployment*
Functioning system	Production	Maintenance	*Production*

stance. The phases in each row of the table all have a similar purpose, reflected in the generic names listed on the right. We'll call this the **generic development process.**

The Generic Development Process

The generic development process has seven phases:

▶ In the **planning** phase, we identify the major functions of our business. We also identify *subject areas,* or broad areas of related business data, and correlate them with business functions. We often prioritize business functions and subject areas for implementation as software systems and databases and consider whether to build or buy each system.

▶ The **analysis** phase documents the requirements for a particular business function or subject area. This documentation captures user requirements in text and graphics, such as entity-relationship and data flow diagrams. Analysis does not specify the technology or structure of the system—it specifies *what* the system must do, not *how* it is done.

▶ **Schematic design** develops the structure of the system at a high level. At this point, we usually know our technology, such as relational database or object-oriented programming language, but not specific products. If the system is client/server, for example, we may specify the software layers or partitions. If the system is particularly large and complex, we may specify subsystems. Often, schematic design specifies software procedures or classes and relates them to each other in a structure chart or message diagram. This phase is sometimes called *logical design.*

▶ **Technical design,** sometimes called *physical design,* extends the work of schematic design for specific products. If we are using relational database technology, for example, we design for a specific relational product such as DB2 or Oracle. Consequently, this phase determines characteristics that vary from one product to another, such as indexes, locking size, and tablespaces.

▶ In principle, the main work of **construction** is quite simple—writing code. Since code is based on the technical design, most important decisions have already been made. Nevertheless, construction is usually the most time-consuming and labor-intensive phase because of the tremendous complexity and detail of most software systems.

▶ **Deployment** includes a myriad of tasks related to installation, such as loading old data to the new system, training users, and establishing a help desk. Often an older system runs in parallel with the new system for a limited period of time as a "failsafe" measure. Deployment is complete when the new system is operating normally.

▶ **Production** is the daily operation of the system in support of routine business activity. Unlike the first six phases, production continues indefinitely. However earlier phases are usually revisited in parallel with production as we maintain and enhance the system. For example, we may revise our analysis, extend the technical design, or modify some of the code. This results in a new version of the system, which moves through deployment and into production and eventually replaces earlier versions.

No matter what development model we adopt, we must carry out all these tasks sooner or later. In a waterfall or top-down approach, we complete each phase in one pass and then move on to the next. In an iterative methodology, we cycle through phases repeatedly, beginning with a prototype and ending with a complete system. For the purposes of our discussion of SPE, the sequence of phases is a secondary concern. *No matter which life-cycle model or methodology is adopted, we can assume that it involves our generic phases.*

Therefore, we can use this generic development process as a framework for our discussion of SPE activities, without getting sidetracked by religious debates about methodology or terminology.

The Development Process Is Cumulative

Our generic model highlights the cumulative nature of software development. Entities and relationships from the analysis phase are the basis of tables and keys in schematic design. Procedure modules and interfaces of technical design are the starting point for code in the construction phase. By the time we reach deployment, the system itself is complete, and we develop procedures for administration, training, and support.

In other words, the detail and complexity of the system grows rapidly as development moves forward. For this reason, it is expensive to change the results of one phase once we have moved on to the next. Adding a new relationship during analysis, for example, is easy—a few changes to an entity-relationship diagram are sufficient. It is harder during technical design—we must revise tables, indexes, tablespaces, and perhaps even views, as well as the original analysis diagrams. It is extremely costly during deployment or production because we must modify any code, user manuals, and design documents that are affected by the new relationship.

Figure 4.1 shows the cost of changing an analysis document during the later phases of development. The dollar amounts are hypothetical but representa-

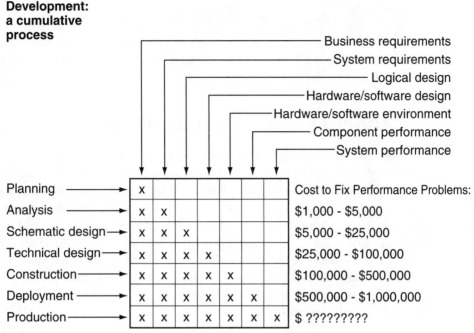

FIGURE 4.1   Development is a cumulative process.

tive of a typical change. They apply whether the change is the result of an error, omission, or enhancement to the system.

As a result, developers naturally try to avoid fundamental design changes late in the life cycle. It is easier to *patch* the system—that is, to write code that is inconsistent with system design. Patches save time and money in the short term, but they increase system complexity and compromise its design. In the long run, this approach usually costs much more than design revisions.

These arguments are particularly significant for performance. If we disregard performance during analysis and design, we face either costly design revisions or short-sighted performance patches. Occasionally, a relatively simple change like adding extra indexes is all that's needed; more often, we are forced to buy more hardware or rework parts of the code. These two alternatives are costly, time-consuming, or both. In some cases, meeting performance goals may be impossible by *any* means once transaction volume and database size are at production levels.

What we're really talking about is developing with performance in mind. In fact, that's our definition of software performance engineering: *software engineering with performance in mind.* It's not much different from normal software engineering; it just adds performance as a consistently important attribute of a system.

> **Guideline 4.1**
>
> ### Address performance early
>
> Addressing performance early in the life cycle saves development dollars, helps keep projects on schedule, and produces higher-quality software.

SPE Activities versus Development Phases

Figure 4.2 shows specific activities associated with each of the generic development phases. As the figure indicates, these activities are not necessarily confined to a specific phase of the development process, nor do we necessarily complete them in sequential order. In fact, most of the activities occur during several phases of the development life cycle. But we must carry out every activity at some point during development to attain acceptable performance.

During the *planning* phase we should ask if any performance objectives are critical to business success, and we should determine which business functions affect those objectives. We must also identify performance requirements in *analysis,* asking questions like:

▶ Which system components have the highest performance requirements?
▶ What are the relative priorities of different transactions?

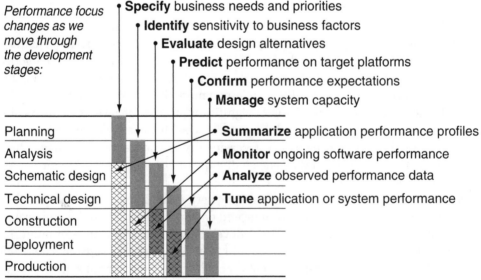

FIGURE 4.2   SPE activities versus development phases.

▶ What is the response objective of key system components?
▶ How frequently will each key component run?
▶ How does application behavior depend on business factors like sales volume and database size?

Because analysis identifies performance-critical processes, design can focus on achieving performance goals. In *schematic* and *technical design,* we also make concrete predictions of actual performance measures such as throughput and transaction response times. During *construction,* we measure the performance of critical components and validate previous predictions, adjusting our performance estimates or design decisions as necessary.

At *deployment,* we calibrate our performance predictions based on actual observations, although we must allow for differences in the eventual production environment. Transaction rates, data volumes, and competition for system resources from other applications are common examples of factors that may change between deployment and production. When the system is in *production,* it runs at peak levels and competes with other applications for resources. We now monitor its actual performance against previous predictions and track its impact on overall performance of the system as part of a larger exercise in capacity planning.

Proactive Performance Management

As the development process unfolds, the focus of performance engineering gradually shifts. During planning and analysis, the primary concern is identifying business needs and priorities. In design, the focus shifts to choosing alternative solutions and predicting their impact on performance. When the system goes into production, validating predictions and managing capacity are most important. In short, as we see in Figure 4.3, the emphasis shifts from estimates and projections in the early phases to monitoring and tuning in the later phases.

These shifts suggests a **proactive** style of performance management, a systematic approach that identifies and resolves performance problems before they occur. In proactive performance management, we establish performance *objectives* during planning and analysis, and we compare these with performance *predictions* made during design. During production, we *monitor* the system to verify that it meets our objectives. Compare this with a **reactive** approach, in which we consider performance only after users actually report problems.

The proactive approach offers several advantages over the reactive approach:

▶ Development costs are lower because we fix performance problems earlier in the process.

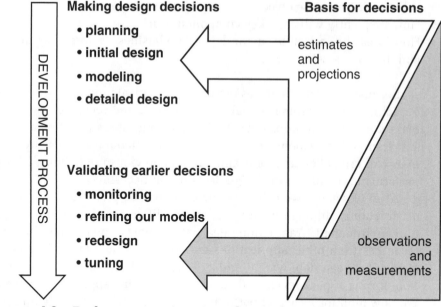

FIGURE 4.3   Performance engineering: The emphasis shifts.

▶ The risk of a performance crisis is reduced.
▶ We maximize our system resources because we make informed trade-offs among competing priorities.

We expect an application to perform well when it is first deployed and to continue to perform well as workloads grow and change, the system is enhanced, and technology improves. Keeping ahead of the problems is the only practical way to do this. Ultimately, proactive performance management helps us to deliver applications that meet the needs of the business, now and in the future.

Guideline 4.2	**Be proactive**

Be proactive
Proactive performance management involves modifying the applications, the hardware and software environment, and even staff assignments to meet defined performance objectives.

The Performance Life Cycle

In one sense, three of our performance engineering activities—*evaluating* or *designing, predicting,* and *monitoring*—are more fundamental than the other seven. One way or another, we always carry out these three activities whenever we develop a system. We must also *implement* our design as code. In its simplest form then, this **basic performance life cycle** is a recurring loop of the four activities shown in Figure 4.4.

This cycle is unavoidable, whether we are building new software or changing existing applications. It occurs either by accident or by design:

▶ We must have some idea about what we want to build before we begin—this is *design.*
▶ Most of us believe we will build a good product—in other words, we make implicit or explicit *predictions* about performance.
▶ Next, we build the system—that's *implementation.*
▶ Sooner or later, someone will *monitor* the system—if we don't do it systematically, our users will do it for us.

Most developers follow a **traditional performance life cycle** (Figure 4.5), which takes a casual approach to prediction and monitoring. Performance predictions are unplanned and undocumented, an intuitive part of design. Monitoring is also informal and often left to the users. Developers monitor the system only when forced to by political pressure, often originating with dissatisfied users.

The traditional performance life cycle is characterized by a reactive approach to performance management. Despite its obvious disadvantages, it is the norm in most organizations.

Recently, several incremental approaches to software development have become popular, such as *prototyping* and *rapid application development* (RAD). Strictly speaking, these approaches are not at all comparable. Some are comprehensive development methodologies while others are limited techniques or development styles. Nevertheless, they share a common philosophy—an emphasis

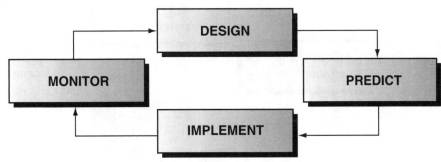

FIGURE 4.4   The basic performance life cycle.

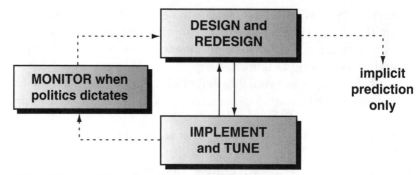

FIGURE **4.5**   The traditional performance life cycle.

on design, implementation, and testing. In these approaches, monitoring is an explicit, formal part of testing. Performance predictions are often overlooked, however, as in the traditional life cycle. This is the **prototyping performance life cycle** illustrated in Figure 4.6.

Iterative approaches offer distinct benefits. Incomplete versions of the system are tested early and often; this improves our understanding of business requirements and reduces the risk of runaway development projects. Ultimately, the iterative approach results in quality software and satisfied users.

There is a downside to this approach, however. When compared with the development environment, *production* data and transactions volumes are much higher, and machine and network configurations are quite different. As a result, performance may suffer when the complete system moves into production. In the jargon of the industry, the system may not *scale up* to production loads.

In the **model-driven performance life cycle,** we document models of our system during analysis and design. A **model** is a (more or less) formal representation of the system in text or diagrams. With a documented model of our

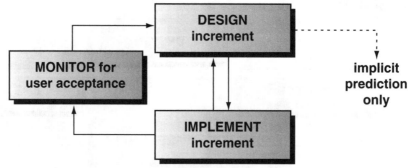

FIGURE **4.6**   The prototyping performance life cycle.

design, it is relatively easy to make predictions—we apply an algorithm that computes performance estimates from the model. The algorithm may be crude or sophisticated, depending on the complexity of the system and severity of our performance requirements. It may be computed automatically if the model is available on computer media or manually.

A model encourages frequent performance estimates alternating with design activity. In other words, there is a feedback loop within the larger life cycle, as we can see in Figure 4.7. Feedback loops between design and prediction, or between implementation and monitoring, are sometimes called **continuous quality improvement.**

Model-driven performance management has several advantages:

▶ It provides a framework for the actions throughout the life cycle. Development is disciplined and coordinated, not ad hoc.
▶ The model provides a common representation of the system, a *lingua franca* for designers, programmers, database administrators, and capacity planners. This commonality facilitates communication and helps to establish satisfactory performance levels.
▶ We can avoid costly redesigns and fixes by diagnosing trouble spots before we actually implement our application or place it into production.

Unfortunately, the model-driven approach is the exception, not the rule. It requires a high level of technical sophistication and management discipline, absent in most information systems organizations. Furthermore, it takes time and money to document and maintain the model. As a practical matter, the model-driven approach may not be appropriate for small systems with few users.

Science fiction writers are fond of a plot in which characters discover that they are repeating the same scene, action for action and word for word. The

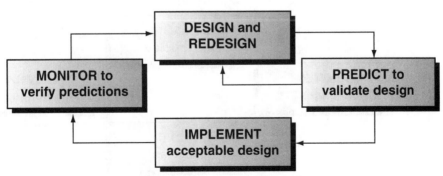

FIGURE 4.7   The model-driven performance life cycle.

characters find that they are fictional, forced to repeat their actions as the writer revises the details of the story. Sound familiar? In the world of information systems, these characters might be developers working in a **user-driven performance life cycle** (Figure 4.8).

Actually, Figure 4.8 isn't entirely accurate. In reality, there is *no* arrow connecting *Are Users Complaining?* to *Relax* because users are *always* complaining. *Relax* is like a mirage on the horizon; we can never get to it! No matter how hard we try, we hear the same complaints and make the same promises. We repeat this costly cycle forever.

The cure for this illness, as we see in Figure 4.9, is proactive performance management based on explicitly defined objectives. Simply stated, to manage performance, we must:

▶ Set performance goals
▶ Design systems that will achieve our goals
▶ Project performance to confirm that we can meet our goals
▶ Monitor the actual performance against our goals
▶ Tune our systems to achieve our goals

As we have seen, these approaches identify and resolve many problems before they occur. They reduce the number and severity of user complaints. Unfortunately, we cannot always be proactive—sooner or later, the unexpected happens, performance suffers, and users begin to complain. In short, we must be reactive from time to time.

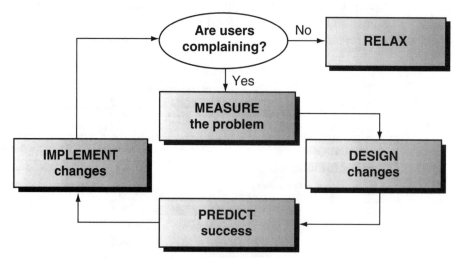

FIGURE 4.8   User-driven performance life cycle.

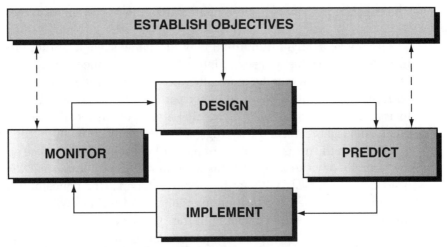

FIGURE 4.9   Proactive performance management.

> **Guideline 4.3**   **Be proactive and responsive**
>
> Even with the most proactive style of performance management, we can't eliminate all problems. Circumstances beyond our control can introduce new bottlenecks and inevitable performance fluctuations. Even though we actively anticipate and avoid problems wherever we can, we should also be prepared to respond to unexpected problems promptly. The ideal performance management style then is to be both **proactive** and **responsive.**

Performance and the Organization

Many individuals must collaborate to achieve satisfactory performance:

► The user community is the basis of performance measures.
► The business analyst identifies performance requirements for each business process.
► The application designer must ensure that program structure supports these requirements.
► The programmer writes code that implements these structures.
► The database administrator designs and tunes the database for satisfactory performance.
► Network administrators, operating system administrators, and other specialists monitor and tune systems software and hardware.

▶ The capacity planner reviews overall utilization of system resources.

Of course, a single individual may discharge several of these responsibilities. Nevertheless, as we see in Figure 4.10, performance management involves at least four or five people, more often dozens, working in several different departments and groups. With so many participants, no one individual is likely to assume overall responsibility, which almost always leads to reactive performance management. As the saying goes, "too many cooks spoil the broth."

Although the decisions and actions of all participants *influence* performance, few actually have an explicit focus on application performance. Often, software users deal exclusively with application developers, who concentrate on meeting user requests for new application functions—on time and within budget. Developers typically have no contact with the systems specialists and capacity planners who focus not on application performance, but on how to apply computing technology within the enterprise and on overall hardware capacity concerns.

This problem is compounded by poor communication:

▶ Business analysts often speak and think in terms data and process models.
▶ The programmer speaks the language of COBOL or C, of loops and procedure calls and global variables.

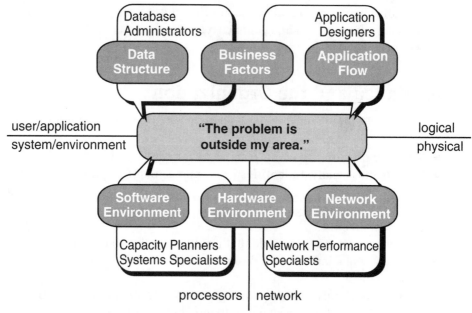

FIGURE 4.10   Who's responsible for performance?

- The database administrator works with indexes, lock sizes, buffer pools, and access paths.
- Software developers know a lot about how applications behave, but they view the network as a black box.
- Network designers understand network performance in great detail, but they view applications as a black box.
- Network administrators talk about packets and protocols, nodes and bandwidth.

We have a proverbial tower of Babel! Since it's difficult for the participants to communicate, it's unlikely we can set and achieve realistic performance goals.

Service-Level Management

The remedy for the lack of communication and its ensuing confusion is called **service-level management.** With this approach, a *team* takes overall responsibility for performance. The team is drawn from many different departments, regardless of established reporting lines, and includes all individuals who participate in our 10 performance engineering activities. In simple terms, service-level management applies *matrix management* principles to the problem of performance.

Guideline 4.4	**Service-level management**

Service-level management is the process of coming to a common understanding about performance on an organizational level.

This team reaches a common understanding of the business factors that drive the need for a certain level of performance. They adopt a methodology for performance management and assign specific tasks to individuals. Many of these individuals are official team members, but some are drawn from the organization at large. In other words, the team is responsible for *managing* the performance effort but not necessarily for carrying out all 10 activities.

The team must also establish a common language. One solution to this problem is to focus on the **business transaction.** The user community understands a transaction as a basic business event, like entering an order or enrolling a student in a class. Application developers can relate a business transaction to a set of application processes or software transactions. Database administrators understand a software transaction as a series of database interactions ending with a COMMIT or ROLLBACK statement. Network administrators might view a business transaction as a *natural forecasting unit* that allows them to project the volumes of data moving across the network at various times of the day, week, or month.

Getting to Know Each Other

The table below describes the major "players" in a typical client/server environment, all of whom affect and are affected by performance issues. While some of our descriptions are tongue in cheek, they do reflect some stereotypical attitudes—attitudes that can sometimes hinder communication among the various roles. And, effective communication, which involves sharing ideas and observations, is a necessary part of successful performance management.

People We Know and Love

Application Users	Bought the application. Need the application. Fiendishly clever at finding ways around limitations and restrictions that keep them from doing their jobs. Responsible for all the work done by the application—one way or another. Use business terminology and misuse computing acronyms. And do not like to be referred to as "the users."
Operating System Administrator	Makes the system work. Responsible for everything about the hardware and the operating system software, including such things as the amount of shared memory and the relative priorities for processes. Does not understand that *your* project is important. Probably a good person to take to lunch, if he or she has time for lunch.
Network Administrator	Often gets the blame for problems. Responsible for ensuring that all the three-letter acronyms fit together. Very technical, but becoming more like the old time doctor in a buggy. Often seen at the desk of someone working frantically to have the mail package actually send e-mail.
Database Administrator (DBA)	Once considered a cushy job, now a chaotic mix of resource managers, bitmap indexes, heterogeneous locking protocols, optimizer anomalies, and irate users who can't access their own information and get angry every time they hear the word "user." Still has to worry about buffer sizes, index fragmentation, disk

striping, and database backup and recovery. Be nice to a DBA today.

Often expected to tune applications after they are developed. When showing application developers problems revealed by trace data, DBAs tend to carry themselves with an air of "this evidence confirms what I thought was going on all along."

Application Developers	Actually many types. These folks devise standards, write programs, and developer user dialogs or screens. They are responsible for many of the performance characteristics of an application, even when most of the work is done by modules from the class library.
	They actually enjoy building good programs, but their culture is built around the specter of the "*3 A.M. phone call.*" They seem to savor a sense of impending doom even as they build.
	When examining trace data produced by DBAs, application developers are always surprised to see how much I/O their programs actually do, and they marvel at the performance inefficiencies that "someone before them" has coded into these programs.
System Operator	Carries out specific responsibilities. Watches the system and can regulate the load on it. Intervenes during emergencies. Cancels you off the system if you hog resources. Generally feels unappreciated.

In an amusing *Computerworld* article about communication problems in our profession, Dennis Vanvick proposed that IS managers and user managers each take a short quiz, to "reveal the depths of understanding—or misunderstanding—between users and IS."[3] In the one-week user reeducation camp for low-scoring IS managers, all acronyms would be banned. In the parallel camp for user managers with low IS scores, acronyms would be the only means of communication.

Perhaps Vanvick's suggestions could be usefully extended to include all the other participants in the world of corporate information systems.

---

[3]Dennis Vanvick, "Getting to Know U(sers)," *Computerworld* (January 27, 1992), 103–107.

If all team members accept this concept, they can communicate more easily. They might develop a list of transactions and, for each transaction, determine the peak transaction volume and acceptable response time.

Of course, a common language is useless if team members don't talk to one another. To this end, the team must establish procedures for ongoing communication. One obvious approach is periodic team meetings. Other techniques include regular bulletins, a problem-tracking system, and performance reviews.

Service-Level Agreements.   The team generally produces a document called a service-level agreement, or SLA for short. This document defines measures of performance, satisfactory performance levels, and individual roles and responsibilities.

A service-level agreement is not simply a record created and stored away with the specifications of the application. It is a contract among all involved parties that defines for everyone the objectives that the project is striving to meet. It is a living document shared by project participants, changing over time as business requirements change, processing volumes fluctuate, priorities are reset, and so on.

To formulate useful service-level agreements, the organization must draw on the user's needs, the application designer's and developer's knowledge of the system, and the capacity planner's knowledge of the hardware and software behavior of the chosen platforms.

> **Guideline 4.5   The service-level agreement**
> A service-level agreement is a contract among all involved parties to meet an agreed objective. Effective service-level agreements draw on the user's needs, on the application designer's and developer's knowledge of the system, and on the capacity planner's knowledge of the hardware and software behavior of the chosen platforms.

Compromises and Trade-offs.   Service-level objectives are part of requirements—what the business needs from the application to meet important goals. Yet the process of creating a service-level agreement may be highly political since performance is always a delicate balance of business needs, computing resources, and development costs.

Software development is a world of trade-offs. We can very quickly produce an application that has poor performance. Or we can take much longer to produce an application with great performance. We can provide less function but get a better service level, or we can provide more function with a lower service level and a higher development cost.

Creating a service-level agreement forces the team to start making those trade-offs right at the beginning—long before we get to the more technical kinds of trade-offs involved in software design. All participants must recognize these trade-offs and agree to them.

The Management Sponsor.   We cannot over-emphasize the importance of obtaining a **high-level management sponsor.** Although SPE is primarily a technical discipline emphasizing prevention, it also involves political issues. Because performance issues touch so many different areas of the enterprise, disputes about service levels often lead to *turf wars* among departments. The process stalls when everyone involved says "the problem is not in my area."

Guideline 4.6   Create a service-level management function

Create a service-level management function that formulates, negotiates, and maintains service-level agreements. The participants include users, application developers, and capacity planners. Working together to meet common organizational goals, they must be willing to compromise between service level and other software engineering goals, including functionality, time to build, and cost.

One major obstacle to successful SPE is the fact that we must invest time and resources early in the development process, with no immediate and **visible return** on that investment. The benefits come later, in more efficient systems that cut equipment costs and reduce the staff costs that would be generated by performance problems, tuning, and rework. But many lower-level development managers adopt a cavalier attitude toward performance, saying in effect, "There won't be any problems, and even if there are, someone else will have to fix them."

Service-level management is designed to solve this problem by establishing *common* ownership of the performance and service-level issues, and a common way of thinking about performance and business-oriented performance goals. But it helps to have a high-level management sponsor who participates, at least occasionally, and helps resolve conflicts.

Unfortunately, it is often hard to sell management on the benefits of SPE until they have experienced the costs of not having it. Often, because of the prevalence of the cavalier attitudes we mentioned earlier, SPE practices are adopted only in the wake of a performance crisis. For the management sponsor, SPE may be a form of insurance against a repeat of previous problems. When good service levels are essential to a sponsor's political success, performance issues become a lot more visible. Developers and lower-level management are far more likely to treat performance seriously when they know that senior management will not tolerate systems that do not perform properly.

| Guideline 4.7 | **Service-level management needs a high-level management sponsor** |

Performance issues touch many different areas of the enterprise. The SPE process stalls when everyone involved says "the problem is not in my area." Having a high-level management sponsor who participates, at least occasionally, and helps resolve conflicts is essential.

What's in a Service-Level Agreement?

For a service-level agreement to work well in practice, there must be a clear understanding between the users and the suppliers of the computing services. This is best promoted by a comprehensive agreement spelling everything out in unambiguous language.

A brief survey of the literature produced the following checklist for the content of such an agreement.

The parties
► Organizations making the agreement
► People representing the organizations
► Date of the agreement

Prologue
► *Intent* of the agreement
► *Assumptions* about business conditions that form the context for the agreement
► *Process* for revising the agreement if business conditions change
► *Commitments of the parties* to cooperate as necessary for success

Service details
► *Service* to be provided
► *Volume* of demand for service over time
► *Timeliness* requirements for the service
► *Accuracy* requirements
► *Availability* of the service required
► *Reliability* of the service provided
► *Limitations* to the service that are acceptable

Measurement procedures
► How service levels will be *measured*
► How *compliance* with the agreement will be *scored*
► How the service level and compliance levels will be *reported*

Benefits of Service-Level Management. Adopting a formal service-level management approach based on SLAs enhances both the development and the performance management processes. Arnold Allen describes several benefits:

▶ **Expectations are set.** Both the suppliers and consumers of computing resources can agree on expected workloads and performance goals.

Financial terms
▶ *Compensation* for providing the service
▶ *Refunds* or *discounts* tied to lower levels of service
▶ *Additional compensation* for superior service levels or extra volumes
▶ Method of resolving *disputes*
Duration
▶ Renegotiation date of the agreement
▶ How the contract will be terminated
The definition of all the terms used in the agreement

Not all items in the list are relevant to all situations; the list can be tailored as appropriate. For example, agreements between departments of a corporation may contain no direct financial terms. On the other hand, there may be indirect financial terms involving a commitment of people or computing resources by the departments involved.

References

Browning, T. *Capacity Planning for Computer Systems* (Cambridge MA, Academic Press, 1995).

Duncombe, B. "Managing Your Way to Effective Service Level Agreements," *Capacity Management Review* (December 1992). The *Capacity Management Review* (formerly *EDP Performance Review*), is a monthly newsletter on managing computer performance. It is published by the Institute for Computer Capacity Management, Demand Technology, 1020 Eighth Avenue South, Suite 6, Naples, FL 34102. Telephone (941) 261-8945 or online at *demandtech.com*.

Miller, G. W. *Service Level Agreements: Good Fences Make Good Neighbors,* (Computer Measurement Group, 1987), 553–560. The Computer Measurement Group (CMG), an organization for computer performance professionals, holds its annual conference each December, and publishes the quarterly journal, *CMG Transactions*. Local CMG chapters usually meet monthly. Contact CMG at 414 Plaza Drive, Suite 209, Westmont, IL 60559. Telephone (708) 655-1812 or online at *www.cmg.bc.edu*.

▶ **A dialog is created.** SLAs promote dialog between user departments and computer systems management. Two-way communication helps system management understand their customers' needs and lets users know the problems IS management faces.

▶ **Reviews are normal.** User management can review existing service levels and change the service objectives based on the needs of the business.

▶ **Capacity planning is integrated.** Capacity planners obtain a systematic way to review current and planned workload levels. Existing capacity plans can be factored into the SLA process, and planned business growth can be used to schedule hardware purchases.

▶ **Budgeting is more realistic.** IS management obtains input to use when budgeting for resources, services, and new technology.

▶ **Resources are applied to the problem.** Less energy is wasted debating the definition of "good" or "bad" performance, freeing more resources for cooperative problem solving.

▶ **Normal operation is understood.** Embracing SLAs means thinking about performance before it becomes an issue. When diagnosing problems, it helps a great deal to know what a healthy system looked like. We discuss this further in Chapter 5, in the section *Analyzing Observed Performance Data*.[4]

Guideline 4.8	**Service-level agreements regulate political pressure**

Since performance always involves trade-offs, political forces ultimately determine all performance goals and tuning actions. Unless our activities are driven by previously agreed goals, our attention to performance will inevitably be driven instead by the day-to-day complaints of our most vocal end users. Embracing service-level agreements replaces arguments about problems with planning for solutions.

Performance Management Tools

Because of the complex interplay between the computer system and application components, specialized performance management tools are essential. There are tools for every conceivable purpose. Some are highly specialized

---

[4]Arnold Allen, *Introduction to Computer Performance Analysis with Mathematica* (Cambridge, MA: Academic Press, 1994), 11–14.

while others offer a wide range of features and utilities. Each helps us to collect and analyze information about a distinct aspect of performance.

We can classify performance management tools in four broad categories:

▶ A **catalog** is a database of system parameters and configurations. It records information about tables, columns, keys, network configurations, computer memory, buffer pool size, block size, and so on. Catalogs usually have many utilities for viewing, updating, and managing this information.

▶ A **monitor** tracks part or all of a computer system as it executes in real time. There are many types of monitors—some trace the execution of a computer program line by line, while others track database events or network messages. Most monitors record trace data in a file or database for subsequent statistical analysis. Some can play back the recorded data and display a graphical animation of system behavior.

▶ **Profilers** analyze and display the structure of some component of the system. **Database profilers** include utilities like EXPLAIN in DB2 and Showplan in Sybase. These products display the access path that the database optimizer has selected for a query. **Application profilers** analyze or display the structure of a program. Some profilers depict the relationships *between* program modules as a structure chart. Others look *inside* a program module and analyze its flow and its pattern of using system resources.

▶ A **history tool** is a database of performance statistics, which are indexed by date, time, application class, and system resources. Indexing allows the performance manager to select performance statistics and summarize them in a variety of ways. For example, we might summarize response time by transaction, by day, for the previous week. We might report transaction volumes by machine, by hour.

The terms *profiler* and *history tool* are not standard industry jargon. Unfortunately, there are no good names for these categories, so we must make up our own.

We have described these categories in terms of the *functions* they perform. We can also understand the categories in terms of the type of *data* they collect and report on:

▶ Catalogs collect data on system configurations.
▶ Monitors assess the dynamic behavior of the system.
▶ Profilers assess the static structure of an application or query.
▶ History tools collect summary performance statistics over an extended period of time.

Figure 4.11 relates these categories to the 10 SPE activities that they support. Monitors, for example, help with *monitoring, analyzing, validating,* and

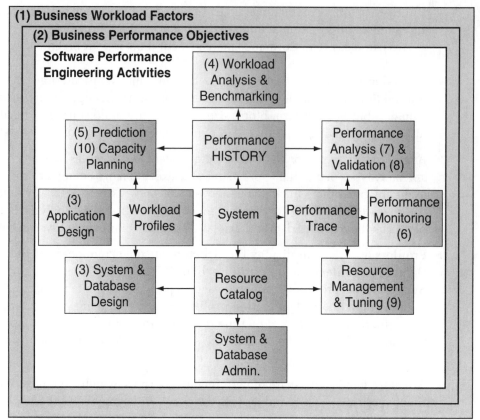

FIGURE **4.11**   Performance management tools.

tuning. The first two activities, *determining* workload factors and *identifying* performance objectives, provide the context and goals for performing all the activities and using all the tools.

Like performance management itself, selecting tools should be proactive. The service-level management team should review tools in all 4 categories and all 10 activities. The team should try to acquire tools that work together and cover as many activities as feasible.

We'll discuss performance management tools in greater detail in Chapter 18.

The Centering Principle

Centering is a vital management technique. The Centering Principle has been expressed in many forms:

▶ Dennis Shasha's first principle of database tuning is: *Think globally, focus lo-cally.*[5] This seems to be the most general statement of the underlying idea.

▶ Connie Smith's sixth SPE principle applies this idea to design and tuning. It says: *Identify the dominant workload functions and minimize their processing.*[6]

▶ The well-known Pareto principle, commonly known as the *80/20 rule,* is: *Focus on that 20 percent of the problem that will return 80 percent of the benefits.*[7]

▶ The first rule of system tuning (see Guideline 3.6) is: *Always work on the biggest bottleneck.*

Applying the Centering Principle reminds management and developers alike to focus on the most performance-critical components of the highest priority, highest volume, most performance-critical applications.

As developers, we tend to believe that if we make our code nicer in some abstract way—cleaner, more modularized, or more elegant, for example—people will like the result more. For example:

▶ *"IS Professionals enjoy their power to create software works of art."*[8]

▶ *"Programmers . . . tend to look at the world through code colored glasses."*[9]

Of course, this view of the world is quite unrelated to reality. Although it is common for developers to spend most of their time focusing on the most difficult aspects of a coding task—trying to simplify the solution or make their code more elegant—this work is not usually the most important to performance. The real performance issues are usually on another path entirely—in code that is actually quite simple. The most frequently executed code is rarely the most complex, and there is no systematic correlation between elegant code and good performance.

The Centering Principle reminds us to think about both the development process and the software we develop from a performance point of view and to *focus on those parts that will have the greatest impact on performance.* This rule is particularly useful in a distributed environment since we have more components to think about.

---

[5]Dennis E. Shasha, *Database Tuning: A Principled Approach* (Upper Saddle River, NJ: Prentice-Hall, 1992), 2.
[6]Smith, *Performance Engineering,* 56.
[7]Steve McConnell, *Code Complete* (Redmond, WA: Microsoft Press, 1993), 682.
[8]Kirk Arnett and Terry Obert, "IS Professionals Enjoy Their Power to Create Software Works of Art," *Datamation* (March 15, 1995).
[9]McConnell, *Code Complete,* 676.

Guideline 4.9	**The Centering Principle**
	Think globally, focus locally.

Applying the Centering Principle reminds management and developers alike to focus on the most performance-critical components of the highest priority, highest volume, most performance-critical applications, to focus on the main-line execution path, and to tune the most critical resource first.

The performance of a client/server environment depends on many parts; to create an acceptable application we must consider the entire system, not just one part. Then we apply the Pareto principle. We focus on the 20 percent of applications that are executed 80 percent of the time and within those, on the critical 20 percent of components where tuning will produce 80 percent of the benefit.

If we don't apply the Centering Principle to everything we do, we can waste a lot of effort refining the design of components that are rarely used or that are not performance critical.

Before leaving this subject, we should set the record straight on one aspect of the Centering Principle. In his interesting book, *Tog on Software Design,* Bruce Tognazzini[10] criticizes the use of the 80/20 rule by software vendors. According to Tog, vendors use the 80/20 rule to justify shipping products that are only 80 percent complete. This is quite a different version of the 80/20 rule from the one we espouse. In all cases, we view the 80/20 rule as a mechanism for *selecting the next action,* not one for *deciding when to stop* an activity. In the world of SPE, we stop when we have met the performance objectives, and not before.

SPE Conclusions

As we have seen, we must establish objectives before we design, and we must address performance throughout the development life cycle. This is the performance engineering approach to application development. Embracing this approach allows us to:

▶ Identify applications for which performance is a critical success factor
▶ Develop performance models that expose the sensitivity of the application to business factors
▶ Consider performance early in the life cycle and refine our understanding as the project evolves
▶ Determine what levels of service each group of users requires and allocate resources according to real business needs

---

[10]Bruce Tognazzini, *Tog on Software Design* (Reading, MA: Addison-Wesley, 1996), 153.

▶ Understand the organizational roles that must participate in performance management and mold them into an effective team

▶ Select the tools and techniques that are best for each project and phase

As long as people play different roles in the enterprise, technical solutions alone cannot eliminate conflicts. Performance engineering is not just a matter of technical issues:

▶ **Business awareness** identifies the basic performance requirements.

▶ **Good communication** is essential to achieving these requirements. Encouraging communication among the constituencies can help to ensure good performance for all of them.

▶ **Politics** often plays a role in balancing user needs against computing resources and in assigning staff with the appropriate technical skills.

▶ **Management skills** are important to form cohesive teams of performance specialists.

We emphasize the technical aspects of performance, but we must not overlook these critical *soft skills.*

CHAPTER 5

Software Performance Engineering Activities

"You can always tune it later, but the results are never as good."

Connie Smith

In This Chapter . . .

Identifying Key Business Factors
Identifying Business Priorities and Performance Objectives
Evaluating Application, Database, and System Design Alternatives
Summarizing Application Performance Profiles
Predicting Performance on the Target Platform
The Information Systems Life Cycle
Monitoring Ongoing Software Performance
Analyzing Observed Performance Data
Confirming Performance Expectations
Tuning Application or System Performance
Managing Ongoing System Capacity
Conclusions

One of the most difficult aspects of software performance is its unpredictability. Of course, there are always cynical software users who expect performance problems in every new system. There are equally optimistic developers who never give performance a thought. But most of the time, no one really knows what to expect, at least until a system has been in production for a while.

The goal of SPE is to change that unpredictability by pursuing the idea that *knowledge is power.* Being proactive in software performance engineering means taking the necessary steps to *know* our software's performance characteristics. Instead of worrying about potential performance problems lurking like undiscovered bugs, we must make performance an explicit component of software and systems design. Then we can have the security of knowing and understanding not just *how* our software works, but also *how fast*. Figure 5.1 summarizes five aspects of this knowledge:

▶ Knowing the key **business factors** and how they relate to application volumes
▶ Knowing what's important and where to focus our design efforts (**centering**)
▶ Knowing what performance should be and setting **objectives**
▶ Knowing the workload characteristics (**profiling**)
▶ Knowing what performance will be (**predicting**)

We discussed the importance of *focus* or *centering* in Chapter 4. In the sections that follow, we examine the other aspects of the proactive approach.

In Chapter 4 we introduced the 10 fundamental activities of SPE. They were listed in Table 4.1. In the first part of this chapter, we focus on the first four of these activities (highlighted on the left side of Figure 5.2), which are predominantly *forward looking* in nature. They are:

▶ **Identify** the sensitivity of the application design to key business factors.
▶ **Specify** business priorities and performance objectives.

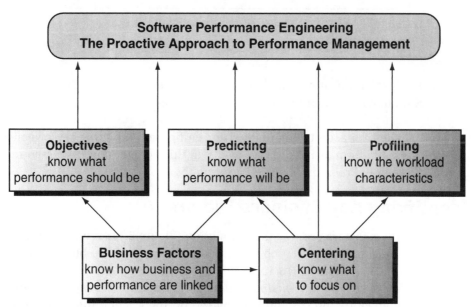

FIGURE 5.1   Goals of proactive performance management.

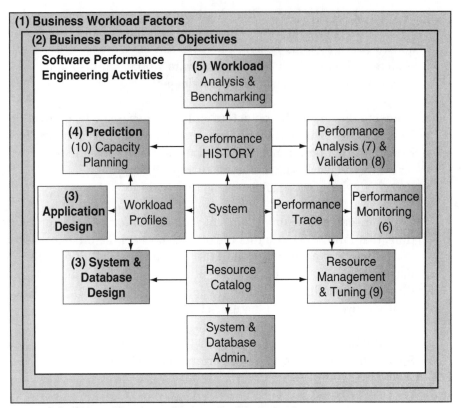

FIGURE 5.2   The five forward-looking SPE activities.

▶ **Evaluate** application, database, and system design alternatives.
▶ **Summarize** application performance profiles.

The fifth activity highlighted in the figure, predicting performance on the target platform, is introduced briefly in this chapter and discussed in detail in Chapter 6, *Predicting Future Performance.*

Identifying Key Business Factors

Business factors provide the foundation (Figure 5.1) on which other key activities—centering, setting objectives, and predicting—are built, and the context (Figure 5.2) for all SPE activities.

What are the *key business factors?* They are the business quantities that most affect the processing load placed on the system. Information processing needs depend on statistics like these:

- ▶ Number of customers
- ▶ Number of customer inquiries per day
- ▶ Number of orders per hour, per day, per month
- ▶ Peak hour sales
- ▶ Number of telephone salespersons
- ▶ Schedule of times open for business
- ▶ Date when a new line of business will be introduced
- ▶ Rate of growth by business area by month
- ▶ Economic indicators and external variables

Basic Concepts and Terminology

We call these *business factors,* but they also have several other names in the literature. Sometimes they are called *business drivers* because they drive application-processing volumes and databases sizes, and so drive the performance of the whole system. They are also called *business elements,* or *business element drivers,* and *natural forecasting units*—the latter because they permit workload forecasting based on statistics that arise naturally within the business. In the world of capacity planning, natural forecasting units are often known by their acronym, NFUs.

Types of Business Factors.   **Business volumes** include such things as numbers of customers, numbers of transactions, and sizes of files and databases. Tracking the relationship of computing workloads to these kinds of statistical factors helps us define current resource requirements and project how growth in business demand will affect performance.

Business events identify performance requirements imposed by irregularities in the business and expected cyclic fluctuations. Knowing these allows us to prepare for their processing effect on key resources during peak periods. For example, a seasonal business may expect to handle 80 percent of its annual volume during a six-week period. Another handles 80 percent of its business during a three-hour period every business day, leading to a quite different design requirement.

System events identify significant changes in the way the information systems are configured or the way business volumes are handled. For example, system events might include a schedule for moving part of a workload or several departments to a new processor or a plan for a staged introduction of a major new application.

In the Application-Resource Usage Matrix.   In Chapter 3, we introduced the concept of the *application-resource usage matrix* (illustrated by Table 3.5 and Table 5.2).

The second column of the matrix (labeled *workload mix*) records the *frequency* or *throughput* of each application. If we need to construct a matrix during forward-looking activities like design or prediction, when measurement data is limited, then business factors are one source for the information in the second column.

Locating the Key Business Factors

To uncover business factors, we must move outside the narrow confines of computing into the wider world of the business served by the computing applications. In that world, we find many projections of future business activity—*budgets, staffing plans, manufacturing schedules, sales forecasts, marketing plans,* and *special promotions.* Although they are estimates, these are the best starting points.

The key to successful SPE is to understand the relationship between these quantities and the computing applications. This understanding cannot be obtained easily—it requires trial and error, tracking, and refinement. Application users generally have little idea what the relationship is because they do not really care about how the computer systems work. But when systematic service-level management is an organizational goal, it is possible to develop an overall model of business activity that uses and tracks these factors so that the effects of changes are understood.

Guideline 5.1	**Determine business factors early**

Business factors form the context for the other SPE activities—identify them early in the development process. When working on functional requirement for a system, also establish when and how often it will be used and how its intended usage is related to business factors.

Direct and Indirect Relationships.   Even though a business factor (like *orders per day*) may measure the activity in a certain area of the business, assuming that it is directly reflected in the volume of application processing is a mistake. Sometimes there is an *indirect* relationship because of buffering by manual systems or by other computer systems. To understand the relationship, we must observe the *business workflow.*

When business transactions are entered interactively into a central computer system as they occur, the relevant business factor drives processing volumes directly. But business events are often recorded manually on business forms, in mobile computers, or in feeder systems at remote locations. In these situations, the total volume of processing at the central system is still driven by the business factors, but the schedule of processing is not. The schedule may be a fixed one, in which all recent business activity is entered in batches and processed the same day. Batch processing is typical for systems involving receipt of payments, for example, because the recipient usually wants to get the money into the bank promptly. For other systems, a more flexible processing schedule may allow work to be delayed one or more days.

For data entry from manual business forms, processing rates may be driven by staffing levels at the location(s) handling the forms. In that case, other factors quite unrelated to the particular application can slow the manual data-entry process. Peaks in the distribution of business activity may be smoothed out. Peaks in business activity may even produce a decrease in processing, as people overloaded with other work defer data entry until things settle down to normal again.

Many clerical activities involve a fixed work rate per employee. The corresponding computer transaction rates depend on the number of staff assigned to the task. In these situations, processing requirements are only partly affected by fluctuations in business volumes; the more important business factor is the staffing level. A related phenomenon occurs when new systems are introduced in controlled phases—processing volumes increase predictably as each new batch of users is brought online.

Projecting Peak Processing Loads. It is vital that we understand these smoothing mechanisms because being able to predict peak processing volumes is usually far more important than knowing total daily or weekly volumes. Peak arrival rates generate peak resource utilization levels, which, in turn cause peaks in response times. We discuss this concept further in Chapter 6, *Predicting Future Performance,* and in Chapter 11, *The Sharing Principle.*

Overall processing volumes, while an essential element of capacity planning, are not nearly as significant for performance as the sizes and duration of peaks. The amount of time that a user *perceives* a task to take is most strongly influenced by the longest response times—the ones that occur during peak periods.

Recall the discussion of *perceived response time* in Chapter 3. One rule of thumb is that the perceived value of average response time is the 90th percentile value of the response time distribution. If 10 percent of all processing

Guideline 5.2	**Processing plans determine perceived performance**

Predict and track the sizes and duration of peaks in processing demand. Peak processing maximizes resource utilizations and response times. Performance during peaks strongly influences perceived response times.

occurs during peaks, a user's entire perception of response time could be determined by the system's responsiveness during those peaks.

Identifying Business Priorities and Performance Objectives

"Our plans miscarry because they have no aim. When a man does not know what harbor he is making for, no wind is the right wind."

Seneca

In performance management, as in the rest of life, the first step in getting what you want is knowing what you want. Management requires a purpose, a target; we cannot manage anything effectively unless we have a goal. Even when we know that performance is an important aspect of an application, unless specific objectives are quantified and recorded as absolute requirements, it is difficult, if not impossible, to evaluate and manage performance.

As Figure 5.2 illustrates, objectives must be derived from business requirements and must provide the framework for all subsequent SPE activities. For example:

▶ Should we spend time trying to improve application performance during design and development? How do we know if (or when) the design is good enough?
▶ Why tune the production environment if applications are meeting business needs?
▶ If we tune systems performance, when should we stop? How fast is fast enough?
▶ When monitoring a system's behavior, what conditions might be symptoms of performance problems?

Without performance goals that we can measure, we have no way to answer these questions. In fact, *unless we have an objective, we can never have a performance problem.* We will never know exactly what level of performance is optimal and what constitutes a problem. To manage performance then, we need to set *quantifiable, measurable performance objectives,* then design with those objectives in mind, project to see whether we can meet them, monitor to see whether we are meeting them, and tune against them (see Figure 5.3).

Relevance to Client/Server Computing

The practice of setting objectives has always been a vital element of SPE. But it's even more relevant when we build distributed applications—not only be-

> *Unless we have an objective, we can never have a performance problem.*

Objectives are essential to enable all other aspects of performance management. To manage performance, we must set *quantifiable, measurable performance objectives,* then design with those objectives in mind, project to see whether we can meet them, monitor to see whether we are meeting them, and tune against them.

cause of their added complexity (as we discussed in Chapter 2), but also because of the changed political climate. Depending on a central IS organization that did not respond adequately to users' real needs was a factor that led many user departments to invest in their own computing resources. This trend eventually fueled the move to enterprise client/server computing.

Today, large organizations are realizing that not everything can be distributed. If information is to be shared across the organization, some degree of centralization and cooperation is essential. Of course, computing will never return to the fully centralized model either, but we can learn from our industry's previous mistakes. It is widely accepted today that the way to create *effective* applications is to involve users in the development process. Let's not forget that performance is one aspect of application function that *every single user* cares about. During the earliest stages of development, when we work with users to

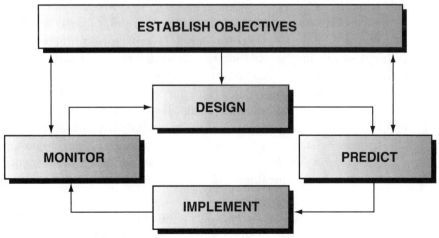

FIGURE 5.3 Objectives define performance.

define and refine application *function*, we should also establish specific *performance* goals that will drive our subsequent design decisions.

Guideline 5.4	Encourage users to define performance objectives

During the earliest stages of development, when we work with users to define and refine application function, we should also establish specific performance goals that will drive our subsequent design decisions.

Trade Off Individual, Community, and Enterprise Goals

In any enterprise that makes extensive use of computers to run its business, achieving good performance means different things to different people. In Chapter 3, we discussed how people's roles and responsibilities determine their view of performance. Added to that, existing computer resources and budgets always impose limits—an ideal world of instantaneous, simultaneous read and update access to all corporate data by all users is simply not technologically feasible. Therefore, organizations must *balance* the performance needs of individual applications and their users with those of the community or system as a whole. This process always involves making trade-offs.

A given set of computing resources can always be arranged to increase responsiveness for one particular application if we are willing to sacrifice overall capacity by removing all potentially competing work. Of course, this is rarely an option; most large computing systems are intended to be shared. Designing systems involves striking a balance between increasing responsiveness for particular subsets of the workload and maximizing the system's overall capacity to process work.

Enterprise goals, like delivery dates for a new application function, are also a factor. A simple implementation will be available sooner, but it may not perform well. Poor performance may cost us business or may drive up other costs. On the other hand, if we wait for a more complex solution with better performance, we may lose so much business that the application is no longer profitable. Factors like *reliability, data integrity, portability, reusability, and ease of maintenance* also have associated costs that vie with performance for development dollars.

There are no standard solutions. When establishing performance goals, we must resolve many questions that involve balancing business priorities:

▶ What mix of update transactions, decision support queries, reporting, and other types of application processing does the database server typically handle? Are current performance levels acceptable, and how will additional work affect the current balance?

▶ Is our top priority to maximize throughput for certain transaction types, to minimize response time for specific applications, or achieve some optimal balance between the two?

▶ Are we willing to trade processing speed of business update transactions for database availability to users submitting ad hoc queries or throughput of other applications?

▶ Are we willing to trade currency of shared data or a lag in data consistency among locations for more efficient update processing?

▶ What is the budget (or schedule) for upgrading our computing resources with faster processors, disks, or network links? Are we willing to trade increased costs for improved performance? Is that technically feasible?

▶ What is the deadline for delivering the new application function? Are we willing to trade a quicker, simpler implementation for reduced performance levels? Would we prefer better performance but a later delivery date?

Answering questions like these can help us set realistic performance goals given our mix of applications and computing environment. See Chapter 14, *The Trade-off Principle,* for a discussion of technical trade-offs in design.

Guideline 5.5	Objectives must balance individual, community, and enterprise goals

An ideal world of instantaneous, simultaneous read and update access to all corporate data by all users is not technologically feasible. When setting objectives, we must strike a balance between:

▶ The need for responsiveness in particular subsets of the workload
▶ The need to maximize overall throughput given the resources available
▶ The cost of implementing computing solutions to business problems
▶ The time to deliver those solutions

See Figure 5.4.

What Are Performance Objectives?

Performance objectives must be explicitly stated. Generic objectives (like *reduce CPU, minimize elapsed time, increase throughput,* or *increase responsiveness*) are useful only as general guidelines to be applied to all development activity. Like the concepts of *family values* or *United Nations,* they sound good but do not really mean anything until they are made more specific.

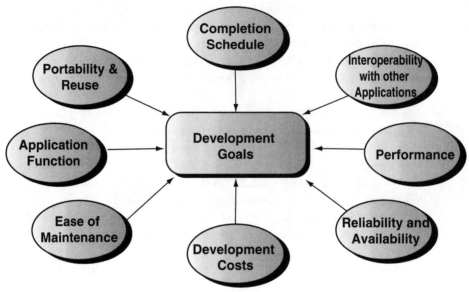

FIGURE 5.4   Balancing conflicting goals.

There are four criteria for good performance objectives: They must be *realistic, reasonable, quantifiable,* and *measurable.*

▶ **Realistic** objectives are ones that *can* be achieved with the right technology and a sensible design. Suppose we set out to develop a new application that will retrieve 10,000 pieces of data at random from a database of several gigabytes. If the intended user requires a subsecond response time, we know immediately that we're going to have a performance problem, no matter what technology we use. There is no technical platform that will give us that kind of performance.

Guideline 5.6	**Never accept impossible performance objectives**

Like impossible development deadlines, no matter what the political pressure, impossible performance objectives must be identified as early as possible. Usually, once the problem is acknowledged, a different combination of business processes and computing applications can be found to meet the needs of the business.

▶ **Reasonable** objectives follow, directly or indirectly, from the business requirements and constraints on an application, and they are justified by the needs of the business. An application's response time objective should be determined by the business process the application supports; not every business process requires subsecond response times. Also, there is a relationship between performance and function. Too often, when new applications are specified, people throw in all kinds of requirements that would be *nice to have.* As we discuss in Chapter 8, in the section *Minimizing Unit Costs,* those extra features are usually the ones that kill performance.

▶ **Quantifiable** objectives are expressed in numerical terms, as an amount, rate, or percentage (see the examples that follow).

▶ **Measurable** objectives can be observed and tracked so that we can confirm that we're actually meeting our objectives. Like objectives for costs or development schedules, performance objectives help us measure how well we are doing at each stage of a development project. We discuss this aspect further in the section *Monitoring Ongoing Software Performance.*

   If the application team defines explicit objectives while the application is being analyzed and designed, we can then measure how well that application is meeting its objectives. Here are some examples of specific, measurable application performance objectives:

▶ Ninety-five percent of *GenerateOrderNumber* requests should have a subsecond response time.
▶ Ninety percent of *AccountStatus* transactions must take no more than five seconds each to complete.
▶ A user should never experience more than a seven-second delay without some system response.

   Here are some examples of *throughput objectives, for online or batch systems:*

▶ The clerk must be able to enter up to 20 orders per hour.
▶ The server must process 100,000 credit inquiry transactions in an eight-hour day.
▶ The overall system needs to process more than 10 million transactions during an eight-hour batch window.

   Here are some examples of *resource usage objectives:*

▶ We need to optimize the processing power we already have on the desktop before we buy any more machines.
▶ This application should not use more than 30 percent of the processor capacity.
▶ One goal of this distributed application is to free up 25 percent of the mainframe capacity.

The following are examples of *elapsed time objectives:*

▶ It must be possible to perform this task in less than two minutes, or else manual methods will be more efficient.
▶ The workstation database refresh should complete in two hours.
▶ Daily summary processing must be completed between 9 P.M. and 8 A.M.

Here are examples of *cost objectives:*

▶ The cost per 1000 transactions must not exceed *x*.
▶ When we deploy this application, the cost of each clerk's workstation must not exceed *y*.

Service-Level Management

When a formal performance management process is adopted by an organization, it may also be called **service-level management.** The performance objectives agreed on may be referred to as **service-level objectives** because they define organizational goals for the level of service to be provided to external or internal customers of the information systems.

Once a technical approach to the application has been discussed and accepted, business objectives can be transformed into specific system performance objectives that are attached to particular parts of the application. Ideally, those performance objectives can be formally documented in a **service-level agreement.**

Chapter 4 contains a more detailed discussion of *service-level management* and *service-level agreements.*

Evaluating Application, Database, and System Design Alternatives

In addition to the normal functional goals of creating applications to support business processes, the design activity must address these performance goals:

▶ **Acceptable performance.** This involves creating a design that meets the defined performance objectives.

▶ **Efficiency.** The best solution is one that conserves resources for other applications, now and in the future.

▶ **Scalability.** As we pointed out in the introduction to the book, today's enterprise systems must accommodate growth. And when information systems grow, performance issues arise along six distinct dimensions; these are shown in Table 5.1. Good design anticipates the effects of business growth on perfor-

Table 5.1 **Six Dimensions of Growth**

Growth Area	Characteristics
Databases	Transactions, queries, and reports must work with progressively larger and more complex operational and decision-support databases.
Stored objects	Originally, databases stored relatively short alphanumeric business records; increasingly they must store graphics, voice, and video information, too.
User populations	Progressively more users need online access to business information.
Transaction rates	Very high transaction-processing rates can occur, especially at peak business periods when responsiveness is critical to the profitability of the business.
Data analysis	Traditional transaction processing recorded relatively simple business events. Now, online systems must support progressively more complex data analysis.
Networks	Linking department-level local area networks with corporate wide area networks creates ever more complex enterprise networks.

mance. Will the design still provide acceptable performance when the number of transactions or users doubles, or increases five-fold, or the database grows to 10 times its current size?

To simplify our discussions of performance, we often consider one of these dimensions separately from the others. In any real enterprise, some correlations will normally exist among these four effects (for example, complex networks typically host large client populations, and a high transaction rate generally implies a large client population). However, such relationships are not essential.

▶ **Limits to growth.** Design must identify the critical components or potential bottlenecks and include a plan for removing them as the business grows.

Part III of this book provides a complete discussion of design and SPE design principles.

Summarizing Application Performance Profiles

"In the kingdom of the blind, the one-eyed man is king."

Anonymous

An *application performance profile* is simply a collection of information about the performance characteristics of an application.

To explain further, we revisit the concept of the *application-resource usage matrix*, originally introduced as Figure 3.6 in Chapter 3. Figure 5.5 is a reminder of its general form. The information recorded in the matrix describes how the set of applications (the rows) uses the set of resources (the columns). Each cell at the intersection of a row and column records the use of a particular resource by a particular application.

A row of the matrix describes the resource usage pattern for an application or a group of applications with similar processing characteristics. As such, each row of the application-resource usage matrix is an example of an application performance profile. This is not to say, however, that the two concepts are identical—some performance profiles may record *more* than just *resource utilization* data. For example, a detailed profile of a database application may contain database access path information for a set of SQL requests—a level of detail that has no natural home in the matrix.

It can be argued that, since the matrix is simply a framework for organizing ideas, it may appear that we could associate access path information for an ap-

Workload Type	Workload Mix	Resource Service Times and Utilizations							Response Times
		#1	#2	#3	#4	#5	#6	#7	
		s_1	s_2	s_3	s_4	s_5	s_6	s_7	
Application 1	f_1	U_a		U_b			U_c		rt_1
Application 2	f_2	U_d	U_e		U_f				rt_2
Application 3	f_3	U_g	U_h					U_i	rt_3
Application 4	f_4	U_j		U_k		U_l	U_m		rt_4
Application 5	f_5	U_n	U_o		U_p				rt_5
Application 6	f_6	U_q			U_r		U_s		rt_6
Application 7	f_7	U_t		U_u		U_v	U_w		rt_7
Application 8	f_8	U_x			U_y	U_z			rt_8
Totals	**Throughput**	ru_1	ru_2	ru_3	ru_4	ru_5	ru_6	ru_7	

FIGURE 5.5   Application performance profiles.

plication with the cells in a row. But a complex access path that involves several tables and indexes on several different physical devices does not belong naturally in any single cell of the matrix. Therefore, we prefer to confine our use of the matrix as a way to express the simpler concept of *net resource usage by application.* So in the DBMS access path example, the matrix represents the *result* of executing the access path against the database, but not the application or database logic involved. As we will see a bit later, the view of the world captured in the matrix is ideal for performance modeling.

> **Guideline 5.7** **Application performance profiles**
>
> An *application performance profile* is a collection of information about the performance characteristics of an application. Each row of the application-resource usage matrix is a simple example of an application performance profile; however, some performance profiles may record more than just resource utilization data.

Workload Characterization

Knowing the performance characteristics of an application or a workload mix is an essential prerequisite to other SPE activities like performance modeling, problem diagnosis, and tuning.

We can collect application performance profiles to characterize a workload at three distinct levels of detail: *workload, application area,* and *transaction type:*

▶ Using the *workload* approach, we view all work as a single, standard (or homogeneous) workload consisting of some level of CPU and I/O activity against all devices—either per user per minute or per transaction.

▶ The obvious extension of the single workload approach is to break up the work into major *application areas* and develop a standard profile to represent each.

▶ The normal—and most natural—approach is to characterize the workload as individual business *transaction types* or as groups of transactions that are each truly homogeneous. The major challenge of this approach is the data analysis required to separate out the workload profiles for each transaction group.

In Chapter 6, in the context of performance modeling, we discuss these three levels in more detail.

Will the Real Application Profile Please Stand Up?

Consultant Tom Cushing offers the following 10 laws of application performance profiles, based on his many years of experience in the field of SPE.[1]

1. Typically, a single application program comprises many user functions (corresponding to distinct business transactions). When response times vary "all over the place" for a given system transaction, the different response times can usually be mapped to the corresponding business transactions.
2. Everyone, everywhere in the world, will tell you that he or she (or "others in my organization") knows the exact I/O requirements for each business transaction.
3. The reality is that no one, in any organization, anywhere in the world, has even the remotest clue to the actual I/O requirements for a business transaction.
4. When pressed for specific I/O requirements for business transactions, application managers quickly direct you to someone else who is "a little closer" to the application code. (Managers deal, after all, at a management level and are, therefore, "more removed from the code.")
5. When pressed for more specific I/O requirements for business transactions, application programmers usually start to make things up, impatiently producing "best guesses" to "satisfy this requirement," so that they can "get on with their real work." These best guesses turn out to be deplorably inadequate.
6. It is not possible for anyone, anywhere in the world, to determine I/O requirements for application programs in his or her lifetime by looking at existing application code. This is a major show-stopper for predictive performance modeling.

[1]Thomas Cushing, Advanced Computer Services, Inc. Telephone (203) 457-0600 or online at teushing@cshore.com.

Predicting Performance on the Target Platform

All design must involve some performance prediction, if only implicitly—no one does design with the idea that the result will perform poorly. To enhance our designs, it is important that we develop techniques for predicting performance explicitly early in the development process.

7. Trace facilities can be used to capture the actual I/O requirements for application programs.
8. Trace data always reveals more I/O statements in an application than anyone ever thought. Most business applications contain two kinds of statements:
    ▶**Duplicate I/O statements.** These are created as a normal part of the development and maintenance process and are rarely cleaned up.
    ▶**Unproductive I/O statements** (for example, returning "NOT FOUND" status codes). Typically these statements result from choosing the wrong defaults in a coding technique (for example, always "checking for duplicates" before inserting a new row in a table even though the input always contains unique key values).
9. Every application manager thinks that you can "just put the applications in a model and look at the results."
10. Application programmers themselves cannot build performance models using the current tools on the market. Given enough time and tenacity, DBAs could probably work with the application developers to build a small performance model. DBAs, although tenacious, usually do not have any time.

Cushing concludes that the key to successful SPE is a development process that incorporates:

▶ Systematic tracing using realistic workloads to capture the real I/O requirements of application programs
▶ Systematic extraction and summarization processes to transform trace data into application performance profiles that can be used in a performance model
▶ An iterative performance modeling and feedback loop that drives the optimal designs back into the developing applications.

We discuss modeling tools in Chapter 18.

This is illustrated in Figure 5.6. We can't begin to measure things until we get to the deployment and production stages of the development process. Once we can make observations and measurements, our knowledge can improve quickly, but before that, any information about performance must come from estimates or projections.

We discuss a number of explicit prediction techniques—ranging from following simple rules of thumb, through mathematical analysis and simulation,

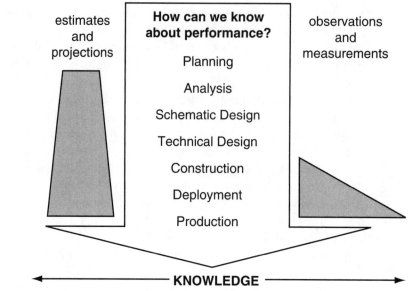

estimates and projections

How can we know about performance?

observations and measurements

Planning

Analysis

Schematic Design

Technical Design

Construction

Deployment

Production

◄──────── **KNOWLEDGE** ────────►

FIGURE 5.6   How can we know about performance?

to full-scale benchmarks—in detail in Chapter 6, *Predicting Future Performance.*

The Information Systems Life Cycle

To frame our discussion for the second half of this chapter, we introduce a different view of the SPE activities. Whereas our previous frameworks (Figures 4.11 and 5.1) emphasized the nature of the different SPE activities, Figure 5.7 deals with the relationships among them, within the performance management process. It is an elaboration of Figures 4.4 through 4.9, introduced in Chapter 4.

We particularly like this figure because it shows both the principal SPE activities and the most important relationships among them. We can think of it as the *information systems life cycle* because all major systems go through all of these stages, either formally or informally.

To summarize our earlier discussion, starting at the upper-left corner of the figure, every new application should begin with **objectives.** First, if we don't define what *acceptable* performance is, we can never recognize a performance problem after the application is installed. Second, when we move on to the next stage—**design**—we won't know if our design is good enough unless we have a target—a defined objective—to shoot for. Next, design involves making **projections,** either explicitly or implicitly, and only when we're satisfied that

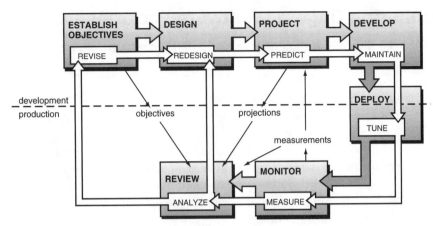

FIGURE 5.7   The information systems life cycle.

our design will meet the user's needs can we move on to complete **development** and **deploy** the application in a production environment.

Once the application is in production, it becomes the focus of an ongoing maintenance cycle. To keep performance and service levels under control, we **monitor** its actual behavior, **reviewing** the results regularly to confirm that we are meeting the objectives and projections we established earlier. Notice that when we hit a performance problem, Figure 5.6 shows how we then move from the cycle described by the large outer boxes to the inner cycle of smaller boxes. We then follow *the same cycle of SPE activities* as before, except with a specific, problem-oriented focus. After we **analyze** the problem and isolate the cause, we may need to **revise** our objectives. Ideally, we can take action to **redesign, predict, maintain, tune,** and **measure** the effects of our changes, always with the goal of returning to the regular cycle of monitoring, reviewing, and ongoing **capacity management.**

This maintenance cycle involves the remaining five SPE activities—those not highlighted on the right side of Figure 5.2. They are:

▶ **Monitor** ongoing software performance.
▶ **Analyze** observed performance data.
▶ **Confirm** performance expectations.
▶ **Tune** application or system performance.
▶ **Manage** ongoing system capacity.

In the next five sections, we discuss each of these SPE activities in more detail.

Monitoring Ongoing Software Performance

"A single measurement is worth more than a thousand expert opinions."

Nagraj Alur

Before we embark on our discussion of *systematic* performance monitoring, we should note the enormous value of *informal* monitoring, of the kind that can be done by software developers and users.

Later, in the section *Responsive Performance Management,* we discuss monitoring by users. But why even wait until the system is seen by its ultimate users? If we truly are *"developing with performance in mind,"* developers can be an invaluable source of performance data at a much earlier stage, because they must test their code.

Developers typically work in an artificial environment, so that the performance they experience is not representative of the real world. But one of the most effective ways to encourage developers to pay attention to performance is to require testing against copies of production data, rather than the tiny databases developers might otherwise use. When performance is poor even during routine testing, conscientious developers will usually investigate and, more than likely, fix the problems. So the more closely the test environment resembles the real production system in both its size and content, the less likely we are to be surprised by performance problems later.

> **Guideline 5.8 Use production data for testing**
>
> Require developers to test against copies of production data, not tiny test database. The more closely the test environment resembles the real production system in both size and content the less likely we are to be surprised by performance problems later.

Systematic Monitoring

The need for ongoing performance measurement may seem obvious. Unfortunately, doing so is not as simple as it may appear. An enterprise client/server system is composed of many independent, cooperating components, as we see in Figure 5.8. Describing the behavior of such a system is like peeling the layers of an onion:

▶ At the outermost layer are business transactions. This is what the system is designed to support, and it is really the only thing the user sees and cares about.

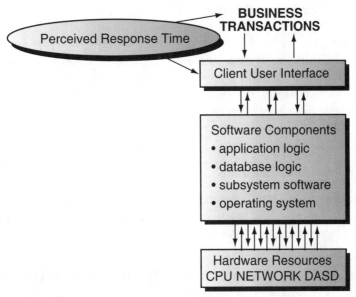

FIGURE 5.8   Areas for monitoring.

▶ Executing the business transaction typically requires one or more interactions with the client user interface. As we discussed in Chapter 3, the user's perception of performance depends on the response time for these interactions.

▶ Underlying the user interface are many layers of software components: application logic, middleware, DBMSs, communications subsystems, and operating systems.

▶ Underneath the software, all of those layers interact with the various hardware resources.

A multitude of measurement tools—also called *performance monitors*—are available to reveal and track the various layers. Unfortunately, not all layers are equally visible to measurement tools. The four fundamental problems that we discuss in the following sections complicate the performance monitoring task for all large systems:

▶ Impact of monitoring
▶ Multiple data sources
▶ Uncorrelated data
▶ Missing information

Impact of Monitoring

If we tried to trace everything that goes on in a large computer system, we would slow the system to a crawl, fill up every available storage device with trace data, and need hours to analyze the data and summarize our findings. And after all that, the results would be practically useless because the system was not operating normally during the monitoring process.[2]

This extreme example illustrates what we might call the *Uncertainty Principle of Software Performance* (modeled on Heisenberg's Uncertainty Principle of quantum mechanics), which is that *the act of measuring any system changes its performance.* In fact, any systematic tracing of all but the most infrequent events can seriously degrade performance. For example, turning on a typical debugging trace that records every intermodule call can easily double or triple the number of program instructions executed if that trace is written to external media.

Guideline 5.9	**The uncertainty principle of software performance**

The act of measuring any system changes its performance. The more detailed the measurement the greater its impact on performance. Detailed tracing should therefore be minimized—reserved for occasional problem analysis only.

Don't Make a Problem Worse.   Because turning on software traces always slows down the software being traced, the middle of a performance crisis is the worst possible time to collect detailed performance data. Using a detailed monitoring tool to debug a performance problem actually compounds the problem—the more detailed the trace, the greater the impact.

Ideally, we hope to solve problems quickly using the absolute minimum of data collection. To accomplish this, we must already have data available about the normal state of the system, recent trends in performance, and any recent changes that may be important.

Even when monitoring tools are available, we must be careful how we use them. As with other aspects of SPE, the optimal strategy for monitoring is a proactive one. We recommend a systematic, three-level monitoring scheme:

---

[2]*Instruction tracing* tools do exist. A software harness completely surrounds the program of interest, passing its instructions to the computer, one at a time, and recording the outcome of literally every instruction executed by a program. This process typically extends the normal execution time by a factor of about 100. These tools are used by software vendors to measure and optimize complex systems software and were routinely used in the DB2 Performance department during my years at IBM.

► **Level 1: Continuous, low-cost exception monitoring.** Periodically sample statistics that are already maintained by software components for exception conditions. The goal of this level is to detect unexpected performance changes without starting special traces or affecting normal processing.

► **Level 2: Regular, targeted performance tracking.** Monitor key performance indicators for a representative cross-section of performance-critical applications. Do this at least weekly, during selected time periods that represent both peak and average workload conditions. Monitor and record response times, processor utilizations, and other critical resource utilizations. Track the level of these key indicators over time, treating them as early warning signals indicating impending performance problems.

► **Level 3: Occasional, focused performance audit.** Occasionally, focus attention on a single performance-critical application, a single software component, or a single processor. Create a profile, and analyze carefully to determine if tuning is appropriate. Compare with previous profiles to detect changes, hidden problems, and potential problems as workload volumes increase.

Guideline 5.10 **Three-level monitoring strategy**

We recommend adopting a strategy of systematic monitoring comprising three levels of detail.

Level 1: Continuous, low-cost exception monitoring
Level 2: Regular, targeted performance tracking
Level 3: Occasional, focused performance audit

To isolate the source of a specific problem, we may need to supplement the routine three-level monitoring scheme with additional detailed measurements.

Multiple Data Sources

We always hope to isolate a problem with minimal fuss, ideally by using data already available from regular monitoring. This is not always possible. Often, to isolate the source of the problem, we must take additional detailed measurements. Depending on the problem, the areas to monitor may include:

► Resource utilization levels
► Database activity rates
► Locking statistics
► CPU utilization

▶ Memory management
▶ I/O rates at the server
▶ Retransmission requirements between the client and the server
▶ Extreme variations in wait time for service at a single server

Progressively increasing the sensitivity of measurements in these areas often helps to pinpoint the cause of a problem. These detailed measurements supplement the routine three-level monitoring scheme.

We usually have to use several different tools to find out what's happening in any system. Some tools measure response time at the user interface; some measure different parts of the various subsystems, particularly the DBMS (generally the best instrumented of the subsystem components); some are network monitors; and some monitoring tools inside operating systems measure the work processed and the performance of hardware devices.

The choice of available tools differs, largely depending on the software environment. We discuss monitoring tools in a bit more detail in Chapter 18, *Using Performance Tools.*

Uncorrelated Information

To turn *data* from performance monitors into useful *information* about application performance, we must be able to tie it together—interrelating the results of the various monitoring activities and tools. Unless we can do this, we can gather lots of measurement data but still have difficulty knowing, for any particular application, where a problem may lie. In practice, when several independent monitoring tools collect and record data separately, it is extremely difficult—sometimes impossible—to correlate the information.

We've always needed to relate the different types of measurement data to obtain meaningful results, but the advent of distributed computing—with its multiple components—complicates the situation enormously because:

▶ Client/server monitoring tools are generally less sophisticated, and the information they gather is less complete.
▶ The plethora of hardware and software platforms creates more data sources to correlate.
▶ Clock differences between processors make it difficult to relate data items based on timestamps.
▶ In a client/server environment, many interactions between software components do not communicate the identifying tokens that would permit a subsequent performance monitoring process to identify every recorded event properly.

This last problem is particularly difficult to overcome. If we collect and analyze data from a single component without knowing the application context for that data, we cannot possibly tell if any application has a performance problem. It's much like standing on a bridge over the freeway watching the cars going by underneath and trying to figure out which driver is late for an appointment. We're in the wrong place. All we can see is whether things are flowing smoothly where we are looking. Similarly, we can never detect or analyze application-related performance problems by monitoring separate components in a distributed system.

Guideline 5.11	**Monitoring components cannot reveal response time problems**

In a distributed computing environment, there are many tools for monitoring component performance. These tools, although useful, do not usually help us investigate response time problems.

Six Dimensions of Performance Data.   In an ideal world, the information provided by monitoring tools would explain the way the layers in Figure 5.8 interact for each application and would report the information in a format based on the application-resource usage matrix (recall Figures 3.5, 3.6, and 5.5). These two frameworks together provide the three principal dimensions of interest for all performance information: *applications, resources,* and *software components.* If every item of performance data collected was associated with these three dimensions, then we would be able to produce the following useful reports:

▶ **Resources used by applications.** A summary of resource usage by application, corresponding to the rows of the usage matrix.

▶ **Resources used by applications by software component.** A further breakdown of the previous information, showing usage within each layer of Figure 5.8.

▶ **Resources used by software component.** A summary of the previous information, showing the resources used with each layer of Figure 5.8.

▶ **Software components used by application.** A breakdown of the time spent by applications interacting with other system components.

▶ **Application summary.** A summary of all application response times.

▶ **Software component summary.** A summary of each software component, showing usage statistics as appropriate for that component.

▶ **Resource usage summary.** A summary of all resources, showing utilization levels, service times, and waiting times.

All these summaries are created by grouping information by application type or class—whatever groupings we choose for the rows of the application-resource usage matrix. Sometimes we need to go one level deeper, to investigate individual instances of computer transactions or individual users. Therefore, we need performance monitors that can record the additional dimensions of *transaction instance* and *user-id.* The final dimension of interest is *time,* so that we can track event durations and report on activity by time period. To sum up, we list the six dimensions of interest for all performance measurements:

- ▶ Time
- ▶ User identifier
- ▶ Transaction instance
- ▶ Application name, type, class, or group
- ▶ Software component or subsystem
- ▶ Hardware resource

If all data collected by performance monitors recorded these six dimensions, it would be a relatively simple matter to correlate and summarize the data, analyze it, and identify the source of any problem in any computer system. Unfortunately, few if any tools capture all six dimensions, which leads to the correlation and analysis problems mentioned earlier. As we noted, there are two main reasons for these deficiencies, namely that the software does not maintain all the information required and that the monitoring tools do not record all the information available.

Missing Information

Tool capabilities vary greatly from platform to platform. But rarely do the tools capture all the information we need to understand performance and diagnose the source of problems. In summary, though, in any given client/server environment we can probably obtain data about *some* application event occurrences, *some* software component behavior, and *some* hardware resource usage and delays.

These deficiencies lead to a practical guideline for client/server monitoring—the Instrumentation Principle—which we summarize in the next section. The capsule *A Performance Monitoring Checklist* suggests some questions to ask during the planning stages of new application development.

The Instrumentation Principle.   In her book, Connie Smith reminds us to *"Instrument systems as you build them, to enable measurement and analysis of work load scenarios, resource requirements, and performance goal achieve-*

ment."[3] In other words, unless we can measure an application's performance, we will never know whether to tune it, when to tune it, how to tune it, or when to stop tuning it. Our shorter version of Smith's guideline is *"Make sure you can measure it."*

Guideline 5.12	The Instrumentation Principle: *Make sure you can measure it*

Instrument systems as you build them, to enable measurement and analysis of work load scenarios, resource requirements, and performance goal achievement.

Unless we can measure an application's performance, we will never know whether to tune it, when to tune it, how to tune it, or when to stop tuning it.

Because of the limitations of monitoring tools in the distributed environment, often the only way to find out where response time goes in a distributed application is to *build response time monitoring into the application itself.* When a distributed application is critical to the business, we must plan for performance monitoring and, if necessary, write a few extra lines of code to take some timestamps at key points in the processing and record them for later analysis. This extra code can pay huge dividends later when we need to pinpoint the location of unexplained delays.

Illustrating this guideline is the experience of application developers working for a commercial bank based in New York. Their currency trading applications must move large sums of money between London, New York, Hong Kong, and Tokyo. Communications delays can prove very expensive when international exchange rates change rapidly. To ensure that they could pinpoint the cause of any application delays, the developers built monitoring capabilities into the distributed applications. Whenever a global variable was set on, applications began monitoring their own performance. This capability proved invaluable in tracking down the location of delays in a multitier application spanning three continents.

Guideline 5.13	Build response time monitoring into the application itself

If the performance of a distributed application is critical to the business, consider writing code to take timestamps at key points in the processing and record them for later analysis.

---

[3]Connie U. Smith, *Performance Engineering of Software Systems* (Reading, MA: Addison-Wesley, 1990), 59.

Monitor Standard Applications

Standard applications are programs whose behavior and workload are known. In a sense, they are benchmark programs because they perform a similar function to the standard benchmarks, which we discuss in detail in Chapter 6. Benchmarks, however, are normally used to measure system capacity and throughput; standard applications are designed to measure a system's responsiveness.

In an enterprise client/server system, as we discussed in Chapter 2 (recall Figure 2.8), many components contribute to performance. These include LANs, workgroup servers, workgroup DBMSs, WAN connections, enterprise servers, and enterprise DBMSs. Standard applications are programs specifically designed to test the responsiveness of these various components individually.

The characteristics of a standard program are:

▶ Has a known fixed workload
▶ Runs in the normal production environment
▶ Runs against the production databases
▶ Is instrumented to record response time

Using existing applications, we can quickly develop a suite of standard programs that perform various levels of activity, such as "minimal," "small," "typical," and "heavy." For example:

▶ A *minimal* workload might involve a request to a remote server that returns without doing any database activity, allowing us to monitor the communication delay.
▶ A *small* workload might retrieve a single database record using an index.
▶ A *typical* workload would be one that matched the performance profile for a certain application class.
▶ A *large* workload might do a table scan of a large table or retrieve a large amount of data.

When service-level agreements exist, these definitions can be tailored to match defined workloads. One element of the ideal service-level agreement (see Chapter 4) is the definition of how service levels will be verified. A standard application with a known workload is an obvious candidate.

Developing and Using Standard Applications.   As a matter of course, developers and testers create test cases to validate aspects of their code. With a little more planning, standard applications can be created during development and used during testing and deployment to verify that an application meets its performance goals. Once they have been created, standard applications can be incorporated into the suite of tools available for performance monitoring.

Using a load-testing tool (like those we discuss in Chapter 18), we can create a script that runs a suite of standard applications, measures their response times, and summarizes the results. Given a sufficiently comprehensive suite of standard applications, this report would serve as a system-wide summary of response time performance. Also, we can use the individual programs interactively when we need to investigate specific response time concerns and isolate the location of performance problems.

Guideline 5.14	**Create and monitor standard applications**

Standard applications are programs whose behavior and workload are known. They can be used individually to investigate and isolate the location of performance problems. A suite of standard applications can be used to summarize system-wide response time performance.

A Performance Monitoring Checklist

When we're building a distributed computing system, we can't assume that appropriate monitoring software will be available. To plan for the SPE monitoring activity, we suggest using the following questions—contributed by Dr. Thomas E. Bell of Rivendell Consultants[4]—as a checklist:

1. What kinds of performance data are available on implemented systems similar to the one that we're going to build?
2. What kinds of performance data collection will be available to measure against our service-level objectives?
3. What tools are available for measuring and improving the performance of the resulting system?
4. What performance monitoring is built into the proposed DBMS?
5. What performance monitoring is built into the transaction monitor (if we're going to use one)?
6. How will performance measurements be made across processors, given that clocks are not identical? How will we correlated the results?

---

[4]Thomas E. Bell, Rivendell Consultants, 2921 Via Pacheco, Palos Verdes Estates, CA 90274. Telephone (310) 377-5541.

Analyzing Observed Performance Data

Embracing SPE means thinking about performance before it becomes an issue. When a performance problem hits us, we can certainly measure the system, but what symptoms should we look for? Unlike the human body (98.6 degrees) or a Jeep (check the manual), the normal operation of complex computer systems is not a well-documented standard. Unless we measure and record its temperature regularly, we have little idea of how the system's components behave when everything is normal. When diagnosing problems, it helps a lot to know what a healthy system looks like.

Normal versus Abnormal Statistics

Mike Loukides, discussing UNIX performance tuning, writes:

> All too often systems run for months without anyone looking to see what the I/O system or memory is doing. Sooner or later a crisis appears and everyone starts worrying about performance. *vmstat* shows that you are paging, *iostat* shows that your disk load looks unbalanced, and so on. But you are missing one crucial piece of information: you have no idea what the system looks like when it is running normally and, therefore, you don't really know what any of these statistics mean. Maybe your system is paging all the time but for some reason it hasn't been a problem; maybe your disk workload has always been unbalanced.[5]

Guideline 5.15	**Monitor when performance is normal**

The key to analyzing a mass of performance data is to look for the changes. Therefore, monitor the system when it is operating normally. Otherwise, when a problem occurs you will not be able to interpret the data.

Trend Analysis.   If we implement the three-level monitoring scheme that we recommended earlier, we can spot many impending performance problems by observing trends in the trace data collected. For this, the most useful monitoring is not the occasional massive audit (level 3) or the exception report (level 1). These may be more fun, but the endless, boring, routine tracking of level 2 trace data is almost always the most effective in highlighting performance is-

---

[5]Michael Loukides, *System Performance Tuning* (Sebastapol, CA: O'Reilly & Associates, 1990), 10.

sues. If we have chosen the right statistics to monitor, we can expect to see relationships among the measured variables and trends over time. Even the absence of any obvious pattern in the data is interesting and useful information because it tells us that important variables that affect performance are *not* being monitored.

Typically, these patterns appear only after the application has been running in its target environment with production volumes for an extended period of time. Tracking performance variables over an extended period of time may not be the most exciting work, but someone's got to do it.

Guideline 5.16	**Look for trends in monitored data**

Look for trends in monitored data

If we have chosen the right statistics to monitor, we can expect to see relationships among the measured variables and trends over time. The absence of an obvious pattern indicates that variables important to performance are *not* being monitored.

Cause and Effect.   Having considered the importance of knowing what normal operation looks like and the presence of trends, we now turn our attention to abnormal conditions. How does performance suddenly become "abnormal"? Of course, the answer is, it doesn't—at least, not on its own. Performance does not change for no reason; there is always an external cause. To solve the problem, we must find the cause—usually *more of something.* Look for things like:

▶ Increased processing volumes
▶ More data in the database
▶ More users
▶ A new application competing for resources
▶ Increased competition from existing applications on the same processor
▶ Increased interference from printers on the network

Growth is not always sudden or dramatic. The system may gradually reach a point where memory size, processor speed, I/O processing, and communications overhead are interacting in a way that was not predicted when an earlier

Newton's first law of performance

The graph of performance continues in a straight line unless the force of some external event causes it to change. Sudden workload growth can produce sudden changes in performance; gradual growth tends to produce a corresponding gradual decline in performance levels.

performance model was evaluated. Regular monitoring should reveal a corresponding gradual decline in performance levels.

If nothing in the workload grew noticeably, then the explanation must be that some component of the application or its environment became less efficient. Typical examples of environmental changes that create performance problems are:

▶ A new version of the application, or a fix to critical application routines, is installed, changing the way hardware or middleware resources are used.

▶ A database or index becomes sufficiently disorganized that normally efficient processing is seriously degraded. (We discuss this further in Chapter 19, *Using DBMS Technology.*)

▶ Previously matched software components become mismatched when system software is upgraded. For example, a new version of server DBMS software may handle certain types of requests differently, and previous default settings used by the client may need to be changed accordingly.

▶ Changes to system software parameters (like cache sizes or scheduling priorities) affect the performance of some applications directly. Alternatively, changes in the environment can invalidate the previous settings of system parameters. For example, when a new application is added to the system, server buffers—previously tuned to match a low rate of requests—are now overloaded, causing excessive queuing of requests to disk.

▶ Changes in the hardware or software environment can consume resources previously available. For example, new applications, users, or devices may be suddenly dumping large volumes of data into the network.

▶ A network device may develop a fault that reduces the effective bandwidth of the network. (We discuss this further in Chapter 11, *The Sharing Principle.*)

The ideal performance management process is one that tracks all such external changes because they are the source of most performance problems. Knowing what changed is often the key to understanding the problem; not knowing what changed is a serious impediment to problem diagnosis. Usually, the prime suspect is the application itself.

Guideline 5.18 **Monitor external changes**

Always keep track of external changes; they are the source of most performance problems. Knowing what changed is often the key to understanding the problem; not knowing what changed is a serious impediment to problem diagnosis.

Responsive Performance Management

Encountering problems such as these can be a little humbling if we've been practicing SPE diligently, but the reality is that no reasonable SPE process can anticipate every possible change. So when problems arise, we must react—but in a planned way. We call this not *reactive,* but *responsive* performance management. Our goal is to regain control, following a three-step plan:

1. Locate the problem.
2. Fix the problem.
3. Restore the prior cycle of proactive performance management.

Involve the Users.   Monitoring should not be confined to performance tools alone. *Users* are a valuable source of performance-related data. Users often report the first symptoms of an unexpected performance problem. They interact with the system more than anyone else, and when they can't get their work done on time, they are the first to notice.

Users are also very sensitive to change and frequently notice fluctuations in performance that periodic monitoring can easily miss. They probably can't provide an exact statement of what is happening, especially at the beginning of the slippage. They may only complain that their job is getting harder or that they are missing deadlines. But these firsthand reports represent the best hope for finding and stopping an unexpected performance problem before it becomes serious.

Look for the two most common types of performance changes that users perceive:

▶ Systematic response time increases. Actually, what may have increased is the *variation* in response times, creating a more noticeable gulf between average and long response times, but users' perceptions are strongly influenced by the top 20 percent of the response time distribution. There may even be an absolute decrease in transaction throughput, but this is rarely perceived as such by a user because the consequence for a *particular* user is that a *particular* process is taking longer to complete.
▶ The system sometimes fails to finish scheduled work according to the business schedule. This is generally an intermittent problem, typically caused by overloads at peak times. But if it creates an embarrassing situation, users will soon start complaining about performance. Another variant of this is long-running database queries that "never finish." Normally, the user gives up and cancels the query.

If we adopt a service-level management approach, there should be a way to use this kind of qualitative data before it turns into a flood of complaints.

▶ First, by having staff with the skills to listen to a user's problems, we maintain user satisfaction. The goal of SPE is to involve the user as early as possible and stay out of the reactive cycle in which all fixes are a response to complaints.

▶ Second, when someone calls to say "something is wrong" the user generally does not need to be encouraged to describe the problem as he or she sees it. Recording this information is the best starting point for many problems; it generally helps us to focus both our initial investigation of what changed and any exploratory performance measurements.

▶ Finally, if in following up on user observations, we find that our routine performance tracking (level 2 in the three-level monitoring scheme) did not detect a problem, we can refine our subsequent monitoring program accordingly.

In summary, responsive performance management is both politically wise and practical.

Guideline 5.19	**Listen to users**

Users are a valuable source of performance-related data. They can often report the first symptoms of an unexpected performance problem and may notice fluctuations that our periodic monitoring has missed.

Confirming Performance Expectations

The reason for gathering and reviewing performance data is to confirm that we are meeting the performance expectations of computer users. But who is "the user"?

Once, that question was easy to answer. The computer was devoted to business use, and everyone else had to make do with minimum resources. The "user" got to use the computer, and everyone else didn't. Not so long ago, programmers compiled their programs overnight, and system administrators were kept away from the system until it crashed or until something had to be changed.

No longer—we are all users now. We compete for resources to support complex integrated development environments, documentation tools, *sniffers, simulators, debuggers,* and a host of project planning, administrative, and management tools. The fact that we can isolate our resource consumption so that business usage is not adversely affected is a measure of the value of client/server systems.

Users make performance. Application design, database design, and network design *allow* performance under certain defined conditions and (ideally) even *predict* something about performance as those conditions change. But users make *actual* performance by using the system in the course of their work, winning recognition for success or approbation for failure.

The problems arise when a user's work involves running massive multivariate statistical analyses of sales data every morning at 10:30, gobbling up all the CPU and I/O resources in the system while we are struggling to process the peak season's catalog orders and store them in the sales database. In these situations, espousing SPE principles alone does not make for acceptable performance—cooperation is essential.

Performance Management for User-Driven Workloads

SPE is founded on twin beliefs:

▶ We can minimize the risks of a performance crisis by knowing as much as possible about our workload in advance.
▶ We can work cooperatively to manage the load on our shared computing resources.

When users select their own tools or submit database queries using query tools, we cannot possibly know the exact workload in advance. Through an ongoing program of service-level management, we can have an idea of *how many users* will be using the query tools and *what types of queries* they are likely to run. Often, what at first are unplanned ("*ad hoc*") queries are later institutionalized as standard ("*canned*") queries that are run regularly, becoming—in effect—routine reporting applications with a known frequency and performance profile. In general, although we can't always set quantifiable performance objectives, through a cooperative process we can find out a lot about workloads and about users' needs and expectations.

Managing performance in this type of environment involves a combination of four approaches: *education, billing, isolation,* and *resource limits.* We discuss each of these in the sections that follow.

Education.   Users today are quite computer literate. Any computer user who knows enough to use a query or a reporting tool can also be taught the facts of life about table sizes, indexes, joins, and response time. We do not suggest that everyone should become database design experts or understand the workings of SQL query optimizers. With even a little education, though, users can help themselves and others get better performance. We recommend basic performance classes for all end users whose actions can actually affect the performance of shared systems.

Billing (or Chargeback).   Computers, like lunches, are not free; they are relatively expensive to purchase and maintain. When computing resources are shared among several departments, some accountability is appropriate. Department managers should have a line item in their budgets for their share of the computing resource, and IS organizations should have a method for tracking usage by department and allocating costs accordingly.

In a complex client/server environment, this is not easy to do in a rigorous way, and we certainly do not advocate trying to gather precise data about every CPU cycle or disk I/O consumed by every user. But for most organizations, precision is not essential here. There simply needs to be an agreed-on formula for dividing the total computing costs based on resource usage. A service-level management program that promotes this level of accountability raises everyone's awareness of the relationships among business workloads, computer usage, and performance, and it greatly reduces the risks of performance surprises.

Separate Resources.   In a client/server environment, many potential performance conflicts can be addressed by shifting certain workloads to dedicated processors. When possible, this is certainly the least complicated solution, both politically and technically, because it eliminates all the debates that arise from conflicting demands for shared resources. It can, however, introduce new problems of data sharing and data replication (which we discuss in Chapter 20).

In general, dividing work among parallel servers is an example of the Parallelism Principle, which we discuss in some detail in Chapter 13.

Enforced Resource Limits and Governors.   Not all work can have its own dedicated server. To help us manage the allocation of shared computing resources among competing workloads of differing sizes and priorities, many operating systems and DBMSs support *service classes*—logical groupings of work that will receive a defined level of service. Typically, we assign short programs and ones with a high business priority to the service classes having the higher scheduling priorities. Sophisticated schedulers can automatically lower the priority of programs that run for a long time, which is a reasonable tactic provided the program is not holding onto database locks that other programs need. We discuss this issue in more detail in Chapter 12, *Database Locking.*

Resource governors take an even more radical approach—if a process exceeds its resource allocation, it is canceled. This technique, which sounds somewhat draconian, can actually be very effective *when it is combined with the right type of support.*

Mistakes are common in environments where users have access to large databases using interactive query tools. For example, accidentally omitting the join predicate from a query produces a Cartesian product of the tables involved, something no normal database user ever wants to see. The idea is to have the governor act as an initial screening mechanism, catching mistakes and badly designed queries to prevent any unnecessary processing. If the query contains an obvious mistake, the user can correct the problem immediately and resubmit the query. If the query actually seems correct to the user, he or she must then have access to a specialist who can review it. The specialist can either suggest a more efficient coding technique or assign the user to a service class that permits the work to be processed.

Working Together.   We emphasize that these approaches will work in today's client/server environments only if there is open communication between users and systems administrators within a cooperative framework of service-level management. Ultimately, the users determine the tactics available to resolve potential performance issues.

Because of the flexibility of operating system services, it is difficult for a system administrator to impose resource limits and enforce them by changing system settings. If one server restricts access, another may allow it—and offer a route to the first server that can inherit the permission. Users will always find ways to circumvent even enterprise-wide limits if such circumvention is important enough to their jobs.

The goal of SPE is to direct all of this creativity toward producing a better performing system by involving all parties, including users, in monitoring performance and suggesting more efficient ways to get the job done.

Guideline 5.20   **Manage user-driven workloads**

When users select their own tools or submit database queries using query tools, we cannot possibly know the exact workload in advance. In this type of environment:

▶ **Education** helps users to improve their own application performance.
▶ **Billing** focuses management attention on the costs of shared resources, encouraging efficiency.
▶ **Isolation** limits large workloads by providing dedicated resources.
▶ **Resource** limits and governors prevent user mistakes from consuming excessive resources.

These approaches will work in today's client/server environments only if there is open communication between users and systems administrators within a cooperative framework of service-level management.

Staying on the Right Side of Your Server

This amusing piece of advice to users appears in the performance manual of one relational DBMS product:

> *As an end user, pay attention to performance and report problems to your (DBMS) administrator promptly. You should be courteous when you schedule large, decision support queries and request as few resources as possible to get your work done.*

The first item of advice appears to be unnecessary—it is like General Motors telling car buyers to "call your local service station promptly if your car won't start in the morning." Users cannot avoid paying attention to performance.

We wonder how many users have followed the second item. Perhaps the company in question (or its DBMS) attracts a particularly courteous type of user. But we have been working with relational databases since the late '70s, and our experience has been that long-running queries do not respond any better to courtesy than they do to verbal abuse. Physical abuse, on the other hand, like pounding uncontrollably on the keyboard or hurling the monitor through the window, can seriously degrade response times.

In a related development, we predict that the same company will soon implement a set of recently proposed server-friendly extensions to SQL, which we understand are currently under consideration for adoption as a variant of ANSI standard SQL V57. When all else fails, frustrated SQL users may wish to try rewriting their queries using these extensions.

Space does not permit us to describe the proposal in full, but complete documentation is available on the Web site *www.ansisql57.po.lite.* For the in-

Tuning Application or System Performance

Technically, there is little difference between *design* and *tuning.* Therefore, this section is a short one since we devote Chapters 7 through 14 to design. Tuning is simply a constrained version of the design process; the constraints are as follows:

► Tuning is usually a more focused activity because it is almost always done in response to a particular problem.
► The design choices available during a tuning exercise are typically limited to a subset of those once available during the original design process.

Beyond having to observe the constraints, these differences do not materially affect the design process that we adopt during tuning. The most significant

terested reader, the following example should give the flavor of these language extensions:

```
PLEASE
SELECT (LASTNAME, FIRSTNAME, DEPARTMENT, SALARY)
FROM EMPLOYEE
WHERE SALARY > 50000
IF PROCESSOR AVAILABLE
ORDER BY LASTNAME, FIRSTNAME;
```

Optional syntax permits alternatives for IF PROCESSOR AVAILABLE, including "IF TIME PERMITS" and "IF YOU ARE NOT TOO BUSY". A variant being considered by the OMG allows the syntax "IF YOU DO NOT OBJECT" to be substituted where appropriate.

In his latest book on the SQL standard[6], Chris Date reviews the proposed OMG version of specification at length. His analysis highlights areas where the proposal "lacks precision and orthogonality," concluding that ". . . in fact, it lacks everything."

Perhaps the lesson here is that long queries will at least *appear* to run faster when users maintain a calm and courteous demeanor. Remember the old programmer's saying: "The watched query never responds."[7]

---

[6]C.J. Date with Hugh Darwen, *A Guide to the SQL Standard, 4th ed.* (Reading, MA: Addison-Wesley, 1997).

[7]Despite its many varieties, SQL has not yet reached version 57. The new server-friendly SQL extensions, the web site at www.ansisq157.po.lite, the OMG variant, and Chris Date's purported analysis and comments are, to the best of our knowledge, entirely fictitious. At least, they do not appear in reference 6. But be courteous anyway.

---

difference is that there is often a limit to what can be achieved by tuning changes because not all performance problems can be addressed easily after the system is operational.

In some cases, the available choices are not even sufficient for the problem. Perhaps the most common example of this is database tuning. Because DBMSs come with lots of tuning options, database administrators are frequently expected to understand the applications and the environment and to somehow work performance magic by tuning the database structures. Typically in these situations, the results are less than ideal—as Connie Smith put it: "*You can always tune it later, but the results are never as good.*"[8]

---

[8]Smith, *Performance Engineering*, 6.

One aspect of tuning that is worthy of note, however, is the significance of the Centering Principle, which we introduced in Chapter 4, and resource bottlenecks, which we discussed in Chapter 3.

The Centering Principle and Tuning

The Centering Principle is all about knowing what to focus on to achieve our goals. Applying the Centering Principle to the task of *tuning* a system produces this very simple guideline: *Find the biggest bottleneck and fix it.* Then repeat the process: Find the biggest bottleneck and fix it, and so on. When we introduced this guideline earlier (as *Guideline 3.6* in Chapter 3), we called it *the first rule of system tuning.*

Every piece of software has a bottleneck somewhere. Of course, to apply this guideline we must first find out where the bottleneck is, which is why we need good monitoring tools. If we fix something that isn't the bottleneck, it may help another application, but it won't improve the performance of the one we're trying to tune.

Ultimately, our goal in tuning should always be to make the processor the bottleneck because the processor is the fastest device in the system. With this approach, the software will perform as fast as it possibly can. After that, we must focus on reducing the instructions to be processed if we want to make it go even faster.

Guideline 5.21	**Make the CPU the bottleneck**

When tuning, our goal should always be to make the CPU the bottleneck because it is the fastest device in the system. After that, if we want to make the software run even faster, we must focus on reducing the instructions to be processed.

Problems with Processing Peaks.   Applying the Centering Principle also means knowing which applications are the performance-critical ones and which components of the system are the most heavily exercised. This is why we emphasized the importance of monitoring during peak periods of processing. Performance problems almost always show up first during peak periods.

In the worst cases, response time peaks may even limit the arrival rate artificially because users are not able to work as quickly as they like. In these situations, tuning the system to remove bottlenecks and reduce response times may simply result in a higher transaction rates, reflecting the pent-up demand.

Ideally, systems should be designed so that peaks in the demand are submitted from other computer systems, during a time when no human users are waiting for responses at a workstation. Then the system can be tuned for overall throughput, not individual transaction response time.

Even if peak processing loads can be handled today without performance problems, volumes grow continually in most systems. A useful rule of thumb is: *Today's peak is tomorrow's average.* Tracking and tuning performance at peak processing levels are the most effective ways to prepare for future processing requirements.

Guideline 5.22	**Today's peak is tomorrow's average**

Today's peak is tomorrow's average

In most systems processing volumes grow continually. Tracking and tuning performance at peak processing levels are the most effective ways to prepare for future processing requirements.

Managing Ongoing System Capacity

In our view, capacity planning is just one of the performance management activities that make up the larger field of SPE. This view of the world, however, is not universally held.

In his excellent book on capacity planning, Tim Browning says, "Although performance management is very complex . . . it is only a small part of the capacity planning problem."[9] These differences appear to be largely a matter of how one defines the terminology. Browning is, in fact, comparing capacity planning with the more traditional reactive approaches to performance management that we described in Chapter 4. As evidence of this, he characterizes capacity planning as a *long-term, forward-looking* activity, while he refers to performance management as a *short-term* activity focusing on the *present.*

In fact, Browning's view of the capacity planning function is entirely consistent with our definition of SPE. He lists the following factors as aspects of capacity planning; in our view, all of these factors are the concern of SPE.

▶ **Technical factors**
Hardware and software components
Workloads
Workload trends
Performance modeling
Capacity measures
▶ **Business factors**
Physical planning constraints

---

[9]T. Browning, *Capacity Planning for Computer Systems* (Cambridge, MA: Academic Press, 1995), 15.

Contingency plans
Scheduling constraints and critical workloads
Tuning efforts
▶ **Management factors**
Business units and plans
Service levels
Latent demand
Management policies
Life expectancy of a computing configuration
Formal resource plans
Changing plans

Of course, Browning's view of capacity planning is also the traditional view; it perfectly complements the traditional reactive style of performance management. When performance management is entirely reactive, then all forward-looking activity must, by definition, fall into the realm of capacity planning. But when SPE adopts a proactive stance to performance, what remains to distinguish capacity planning as a separate activity?

To answer, we return to our original discussion of *why a system runs slowly,* at the conclusion of Chapter 3. There we distinguished between two classes of problems: those amenable to *software performance engineering* and those requiring additional *computing capacity.*

We also pointed out that a large gray area exists between these two classes, which can be resolved only by business considerations involving the relative costs of different solutions. Browning echoes this aspect of the planning process. To illustrate the relationship between capacity planning and business planning, he uses a figure similar to Figure 5.9. This figure nicely summarizes the larger business context for capacity planning decisions.

In our view, SPE embraces all aspects of performance management, while capacity planning refers only to the planning and management activities required *to deliver sufficient computing capacity.*

Of course, this definition requires us to define what is *sufficient.* There is little doubt that for both SPE and capacity planning, the goal is to *maintain acceptable performance levels in the face of change.* It is the inevitability of change that necessitates SPE and, of course, capacity planning:

▶ The workload is constantly changing as new applications are written, volumes of work increase, the users' workload mix changes, new users are brought onto the system, or volumes of data increase.
▶ The resources available to process the work also change, as new software features are added, the volumes of competing work change, the hardware configuration changes, or new hardware devices are added.

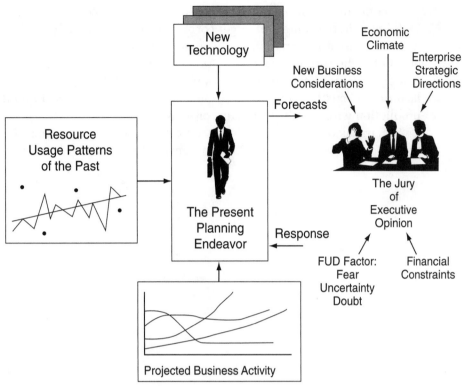

FIGURE 5.9 Capacity planning and business planning.

Each of these changes has a bearing on performance; their effects are related by the general equation, *Performance = Resources/Workload.*

Both SPE and capacity planning address this equation for a particular combination of software, hardware, and workload, and they aim to produce solutions that ensure the desired performance levels. For the capacity planner, the workload is fixed and the resources must be adjusted to match. In the view of SPE, the resources can sometimes be changed, but often they are fixed (or, at best, changing only slowly), so the challenge is to make the workload fit. We return to this subject in Chapter 10, *The Locality Principle,* in our discussion of *degree locality.*

Conclusions

We began our review of SPE activities by focusing on the business factors and objectives that provide the context for all processing requirements. We concluded with a brief review of the role of capacity planning and its relationship to larger business goals.

A common thread here is that software performance engineering is meaningful only in the context of larger corporate goals. Conversely, senior management must treat information systems and computing resources like any other element of the corporate infrastructure. Like a new line of business, new information systems cannot be made ready overnight. Like a production line in a factory, the existing computing resources cannot be expected to double their production with no advance notice or planning.

SPE translates business goals into efficient information systems; the SPE activities are the ways we keep those systems in tune with the business.

CHAPTER 6

Predicting Future Performance

"Never make forecasts; especially about the future."

Samuel Goldwyn

In This Chapter . . .

Performance Prediction Techniques
Introduction to Performance Models
Comparing Analysis and Simulation
Benchmarks and Benchmarking
Benchmarking Complications
Conclusion

Those who look for ways to predict a system's performance divide into two camps—we might call them *designers* and *managers*. Designers want to understand the system better; managers want to know whether to schedule a hardware upgrade or whether a planned application will support the business effectively. Nevertheless, both groups are really interested in the same fundamental questions of system design, even though they might phrase them differently:

▶ What is the system doing, and what will happen if I change parts of it?
▶ When will we hit the next bottleneck (there always is one), and how can we overcome it?

These are the questions that performance analysts and capacity planners set out to answer—a challenging task when the subject is a large production system. There are a variety of techniques that can be useful in predicting software performance:

▶ Published vendor measurements
▶ Rules of thumb
▶ Parametric analysis, simple formulas
▶ Project from an existing workload
▶ Analytic modeling, queuing theory
▶ Macro-level simulation
▶ Detailed simulation
▶ Project from single thread measurements
▶ Benchmarking

Performance Prediction Techniques

Each of the prediction techniques is applicable to different situations and at different stages of the application development life cycle. They range in complexity from the simplest rules of thumb (estimating response time by counting I/Os) right through to the most complex (a time-consuming and detailed benchmark, in which we build an actual version of the software, instrument it, and measure its performance).

As we go down the list, the techniques become more complex. They require that progressively increasing levels of resources be devoted to build the model and exercise it, and that increasingly greater levels of detail characterize the input. In return, they may—depending on the accuracy of that input—yield greater accuracy in the results, as illustrated by Figure 6.1.

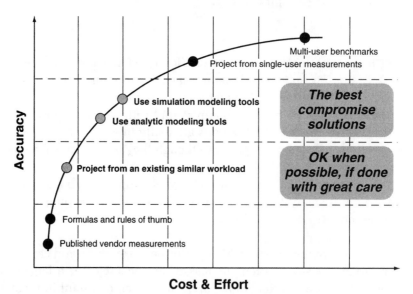

FIGURE **6.1**   Evaluating modeling techniques.

In practice, we pick the most appropriate technique for the time available and the effort we want to expend, factoring into our decision which approach will give us sufficient accuracy and an acceptable degree of confidence in the results. In the sections that follow, we review the pros and cons of the principle techniques.

Published Vendor Measurements

Trying to infer something about the likely performance of an application by looking at published vendor measurements is an inexpensive method, but it also has very low accuracy, as we explain in the section, *Benchmarks and Benchmarking.*

Rules of Thumb

If we are developing a small application quickly, using equipment and configurations that we are familiar with, we often rely on our experience with a particular type of design. In other words, we use rules of thumb, which generally result in relatively good performance if they are applied prudently. But we can't necessarily rely on rules of thumb for more complex applications or for technologies that are unfamiliar to us.

Projecting from Measurements

Essentially, there are two types of performance measurements: *single-thread* and *multithread.*

► A *single-thread measurement* is an application measurement made in a controlled environment, with no competing work. This technique is ideal for capturing an application performance profile. But because the environment is artificial, we cannot use the data to make predictions about performance in a production environment unless we add a lot more data about the rest of the workload mix and then use the *analytic modeling* or *simulation* techniques described in the following paragraphs.

► A *multithread measurement* is really just another term for a *benchmark,* a controlled measurement of a known workload mix. We discuss its limitations later in this chapter.

Analytic Modeling

Analytic modeling is normally done using a body of mathematical methods collectively referred to as *queuing theory.* Actually, this term embraces a variety of different solution techniques, some of which are more precise than others, but all of which involve mathematical analysis of the type of data that is summarized in an application-resource usage matrix. The mathematics first evaluate device utilization levels by accumulating the total impact of all processes on each resource, then compute the resultant delays each process experiences waiting for service. We describe these techniques in more detail in the next section.

Most analytic methods depend on certain assumptions about randomness in the distributions of arrival times of the requests for service and in the distributions of the service times. These assumptions are necessary to make the mathematics work, but they are also realistic—if arrivals were not random but perfectly synchronized, a device could be 100 percent busy but no process would ever have to wait. In real systems, this does not happen.

Simulation Modeling

Simulation involves actually building a software model of each device, a model of the queue for that device, model processes that use the devices, and a model of the clock in the real world. As with analysis, these models must include assumptions about arrival and service time distributions, so that the results represent the kind of randomness that would be evident in a real system.

When the simulation clock starts, simulated processes are generated and arrive in the simulated system, according to their defined arrival frequency. Each simulated process makes its requests for service at the simulated devices, in order, as it was modeled. If a device is busy at the time the request is made, the process must be placed in a wait state in the queue for that device until it can be serviced. The simulator manages the clock all the while, keeping track of simulated time.

To see how busy a device was or how long it took to process a transaction of type *X,* we have to simulate the arrival and processing of a reasonable amount of work, monitor the model while it's running, and then compute some averages. And just as when we monitor a real system, we probably need to let things run for about 10 simulated minutes to be sure that we have simulated an average mix of activity. Otherwise, we can't trust our statistics—because of the randomness of transaction arrivals, a short observation may give us an unrepresentative sample.

Benchmarking

A benchmark is a controlled test to determine exactly how a specific application performs in a given technology environment. Benchmarking differs from routine performance monitoring in two ways:

▶ Monitoring supplies a profile of performance over time for an application already deployed, either in a testing or a production environment.

▶ Benchmarking produces a few controlled measurements designed to compare the performance of two or more implementation choices.

Running a selected application, or workload mix, under controlled conditions and measuring the results is a good way to obtain accurate performance profiles. But to use this approach to make decisions about design alternatives, you would need to build the application in a couple of different ways and measure how each performs under a variety of conditions. This method, while accurate, is usually prohibitively costly because of the development effort required. In practice, only the most performance-critical applications ever justify the time and expense of a benchmark.

Standard benchmarks are normally run by outside organizations—such as industry analysts, magazine publishers, software vendors, and hardware vendors—and the results are published. We discuss this further in the section *Benchmarks and Benchmarking.*

Introduction to Performance Models

To some people, computer performance modeling is a little understood art practiced only by mathematicians and other magicians. If this view closely reflects your own, then the following brief overview of the subject may be helpful.

Our goal in this section is to provide an overview of the performance modeling process, not a complete tutorial. While we may make a believer of you, we cannot convert you instantly into a skilled practitioner.

Therefore, we suggest that readers intending to develop models should already have some relevant skills and experience or should study other, more detailed material first. Ideally, work with someone familiar with performance modeling when you create your first model. Then you can move on to the data-gathering and analysis phases with some confidence that the model is a good representation of your configuration. But make sure that you read the guidelines presented later in this chapter in the section *Using a Performance Model.*

What Is a Performance Model?

You may be familiar with data models like E-R, or object models like OMT, or functional models like data flow diagrams. Whereas these models capture the essence of a data structure or an application's logic, in a performance model the focus is on system resource usage. Of course, if we look closely enough, almost everything in the real system has *some* bearing on resource usage, right down to the particular mix and sequence of COBOL or C++ language statements chosen by the programmer to implement the application logic.

A model, by comparison, is an abstraction of the real system—a simplified representation that hides much of the real-world detail to reveal only those things that are important. Because it is much less detailed than the actual application program, a model is easier to understand and manipulate, and it can be built much more quickly.

A Library for Performance Modelers

Many technical books and papers on performance modeling are written for students of computer science. They focus on the mathematical underpinnings rather than how to apply modeling methods to systems design problems. No book on performance modeling can be entirely free of mathematics, but here are a few of the most approachable sources of information:

1. Ted C. Keller, *CICS Capacity and Performance Management* (New York, NY: McGraw-Hill, 1993).
2. E. D. Lazowska, J. Zahoran, G. S. Graham, and K. C. Sevcik, *Quantitative System Performance: Computer System Analysis Using Queuing Network Models* (Upper Saddle River, NJ: Prentice Hall, 1984).
3. Arnold O. Allen, *Probability, Statistics, and Queueing Theory with Computer Science Applications, 2nd Ed.* (Cambridge, MA: Academic Press, 1990).

If you are not intimidated by mathematical formulas, and have access to a technical library, you may wish to look for the following surveys:

1. *Analytical Queueing Models,* special issue of *IEEE Computer,* 13 (4), April 1980.
2. *Queuing Network Models of Computer System Performance,* special issue of *ACM Computing Surveys,* 10 (3), September 1978.

These two collections of papers are a bit more academic than the books we listed. But despite being almost 20 years old, they still provide good overviews of the theory and application of queuing network models.

Queuing Network Models

A performance model reduces a complex computer system to a set of relationships among a few simple variables:

▶ The number of separate *processes* in a system
▶ The mean service times of *servers*—which comprise *physical devices,* like the processor, disks, or network, and *logical resources* like concurrent threads
▶ The number of times a process uses each server, known as a *visit ratio*

Each modeled process consists of a sequence of requests for service from the modeled servers. Each modeled server has an associated queue where processes must wait for service if the device is busy. One way to describe this is as a *queuing network model* because the processes represent the flow of work among network servers.

Calculated results include system throughput, mean device utilizations, queue lengths, and wait times. The solutions to a queuing network model take into account not only the capacity limitations of the servers, but also the delays introduced into response time by high server utilizations (or "bottlenecks").

It is customary to represent a queuing model using symbols like those shown in Figure 6.2, which illustrates the graphic symbols corresponding to each element of a queuing network and some of the notations used to describe the queuing parameters.

In the literature on computer system modeling, these symbols are combined into networks. Figure 6.3 is a typical example of a queuing network of the type used to model computer systems. It is a version of what is commonly called the *central server model* (of multiprogramming), or simply CSM. The same diagram can be drawn in several ways—for example, three alternative but topologically equivalent versions of the same network are shown to the right of the main figure.

The model shown in Figure 6.3 is annotated for convenience. The interpretation of the model is as follows:

▶ A user, from one of a network of 100 workstations, initiates a request for service (a computer *transaction*), creating a separate process.
▶ Processing for the request consists of alternate requests for CPU and I/O service, until the process completes and a response is returned to the user.
▶ After a delay—examining the output, thinking, sleeping, or whatever—the user submits another request or transaction.
▶ The average transaction requires 19 I/O operations; this is indicated by the branching probabilities of .05 and .95 noted where the flow splits between the workstations and I/O devices, after departure from the CPU server.

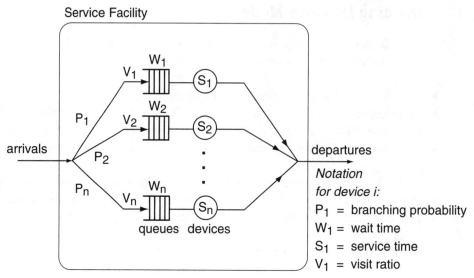

FIGURE 6.2 Elements of a queuing network.

▶ The server CPU is a two-way multiprocessor.
▶ Sixteen I/O devices are modeled, requests being distributed among them with probabilities $p_1, p_2, \ldots, p_{16}$.

Queues and Delays.   Notice that in the model shown in Figure 6.3, no queue is shown at the workstations. This means that the workstation device merely imposes a fixed service time delay on the process, without any queuing over-head. This type of device, which is called a *delay server,* is used to represent any resource that not being investigated by the model. For example:

▶ Since a client workstation is not a shared resource, the total delay introduced at the workstation by application processing and user think time are often modeled in this way.
▶ A delay server can be used to simplify the modeling of disk I/O devices if the model designer expects their utilization to be so low that little or no queuing will occur. Another justification for using a delay server would be the belief that tuning the real I/O subsystem would keep I/O access times stable and thus of little interest to the modeler.

Accuracy, Precision, and Detail

Garbage in, garbage out.
      Earlier, we stated that the reason for performance modeling is to help an-swer some fundamental, if somewhat abstract, questions about the design of a

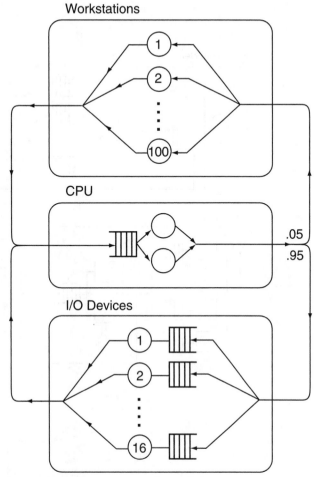

FIGURE 6.3 A typical computer network model.

computer system—questions about its behavior under changing conditions and its ability to handle an increased workload without hitting a bottleneck. To address these concerns, we have to consider other, more concrete questions involving estimates of CPU utilizations, application processing time, device response times, network delays, and so on. For example, we may need to know:

Will the system handle next January's projected volumes for the StockInquiry *application with response times below five seconds—and if not, why not?*

Clearly, we can phrase questions of this nature in a precise way and specify very precise assumptions. But a predictive method can never provide entirely accurate answers to any question, however precise. Any technique we might choose

Equivalent Networks

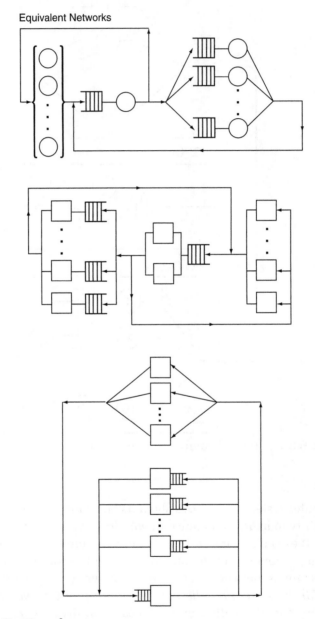

FIGURE **6.3** *Continued.*

to answer the questions is subject to inherent limitations in the accuracy of the input data, the ability of the model to represent the real system, and the modeling technique itself. The following sections review these issues in more detail.

Level of Detail.   Models are never detailed enough to include all the factors that affect performance. For complex systems, the law of diminishing returns applies when adding detail to a model. Applying the **Centering Principle,** which we introduced in Chapter 4, a few key factors usually dominate the performance of a system. Once these are included, adding more factors has progressively less effect on the results; the additional factors complicate the model without substantially improving its accuracy. At some point, it becomes preferable to curtail the quest for greater accuracy in favor of ease of model validation and ease of use. The time needed to build a model and the time it takes to run are important measures of its usefulness.

Scope of the Modeling Effort.   Modeling requires an investment of time, and not every application or resource warrants that investment. Applying the Centering Principle again, most of the benefits of performance modeling are obtained by applying it in a selective way, using the 80/20 rule. We find the 10 percent to 20 percent of critical system components that are likely to cause 80 percent of performance problems, or that are the most significant from a business point of view, and focus our attention on modeling that critical subset. Other components are encapsulated as delay servers or as a background workload—their effects are visible in the model, but their details are not.

Some aspects of the system are deliberately excluded; see the capsule *What Details Are NOT Modeled, and Why?*

The Modeled Workload.   Application *profiles* are notoriously inaccurate—see the capsule in Chapter 5, *Will the Real Application Profile Please Stand Up?* And even with attention to business factors, few organizations can forecast their future *workload volumes* precisely because of business unknowns. The resulting model input is an estimated mix of approximate processing requirements.

Modeling Assumptions.   The mathematical queuing theory methods used to solve queuing network models are now very well established and have proven to be robust and acceptably accurate for a wide range of model configurations. All models, however, introduce assumptions and generalizations that do not exactly match the real system. In queuing network models, assumptions, such as randomly distributed arrivals and service times, infinite user populations, simplified scheduling algorithms, and identical multiserver server threads, are common examples of assumptions. The model results, while accurate for the model itself, are less accurate for the real-world system to which the model is applied.

Conclusions.   Because all predictions are approximations, the goal of modeling is not to produce "the right answer"—an inappropriate concept in this context. Rather, it is to derive an answer that is sufficiently accurate for the business situation. Most modeling or capacity planning situations do not call for the prediction of resource utilizations to the nearest percent, nor for response times to the nearest tenth of a second. Indeed, such accuracy usually implies extensive input at a level of detail rarely, if ever, available.

The appropriate level of detail for a model depends on many variables, including the following:

▶ Our purpose in building a model and the nature of the questions that we want the model to help answer
▶ The degree of variability of the workload profiles to be modeled and the extent to which we need the model to reflect that variability
▶ The quality of the forecasts of future workload growth used as input to the modeling process
▶ The data and tools available for constructing workload profiles
▶ The time available to construct and validate the model, weighed against its expected life span

All this is not to decry the pursuit of accuracy in model building; a misleading tool is worse than none at all. A model should be accurate enough to assist us in answering the questions for which it is designed, and we should clearly understand both its limitations and its margin of error before we base important decisions on its output.

Building the Performance Model

A software performance model represents all five of the fundamental aspects of performance that we introduced in Chapter 3 and illustrated in Figure 3.1. For the system being modeled, the five aspects are combined to create an application-resource usage matrix, and the data in that matrix is analyzed as a network of resources with queues to use those resources. Application processing is represented as a series of demands against these resources, driven by business factors like transactions per second or the number of line items in an order, as illustrated by Figure 6.4.

Figure 6.4 is a conceptual view of a performance model. Separate circles representing the five inputs are not meant to imply that the five variables are independent. In practice, they are interdependent:

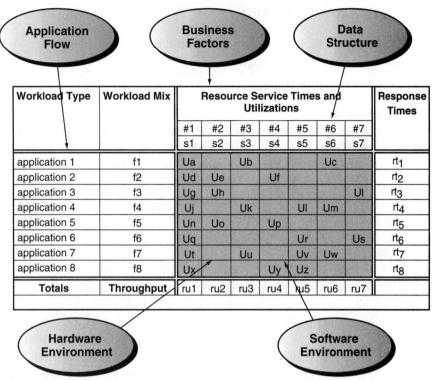

FIGURE **6.4**   Elements of the performance model.

▶ The software environment usually influences the application processing.
▶ The hardware environment can influence the choice of data structures.
▶ The software environment may behave differently depending on the hardware platform (for example, UNIX or Oracle run differently on different hardware).
▶ The application behaves differently based on the choice of software platform.
▶ The database sizes influence DBMS optimizer, which influences application processing.
▶ Sometimes the hardware behaves differently based on the way the software platform drives it (for example, network performance changes based on the choice of Ethernet or token ring).
▶ Everything is driven by the business factors.

The purpose of the performance model is provide a tool exploring these kinds of relationships, to determine which ones are the most significant, and to investigate their combined effect on performance.

Gathering the Input

To build a model, we must understand how the system works. We must answer questions like the following:

▶ Which are the most important application processes from a performance standpoint?
▶ What are their execution frequencies, and how are these tied to business variables like the number of orders per day?
▶ How many CPU instructions will be executed on different processors (client, database server, host, or mainframe)?
▶ How much data is transferred from or to disks attached to each of the processors, in how many I/O operations?
▶ How much data is transferred over a local or wide area network, in what size packets?
▶ How fast are all the devices involved (processors, disks, networks)?
▶ How much competing work is there from other applications or systems?

Many of the answers will, of course, be estimates. But we are building a model, and once it is built we can vary the inputs to see which ones have the most effect on the results. We need hardware device metrics to describe the service characteristics of the hardware environment and software metrics to help us compute what the pattern of request for service will actually look like in the modeled software environment.

For example, to model an SQL workload we must at least estimate how our SQL queries will actually be processed by our target DBMS, which will differ depending on whether it is DB2, Sybase, Oracle, Informix, or whatever. We must estimate database I/O counts and processor usage, split the database I/O and processor load across client and server, and then estimate the network traffic between the two. Typically, we obtain these kinds of metrics from one of three places:

▶ From our previous experience and from measurements of an existing system
▶ From published information supplied by the database vendor
▶ From tools supplied by the modeling tool vendor

Describing the Workload

In the technical literature on performance modeling, this stage is often called *workload characterization*. The first step in describing our workload is simply to identify the resources to be modeled. As we discussed earlier in the section

Accuracy, Precision, and Details, most models need not include any resources except those known to cause delays in processing work. Consequently, most models express relationships between a few key variables like:

▶ Application processing volumes, or transactions per second
▶ CPU utilization, or instructions to be executed
▶ I/O device utilizations (singly or in groups)
▶ Workstation response times, or user think times
▶ Network links

The second step is to describe the work in terms of these resources. At this point, we must determine to what degree our model will represent differences between various types of work. Essentially, we must choose one of three possible levels of detail when designing the model:

▶ Model the "average" workload.
▶ Model work as a group of application areas.
▶ Model workloads at the transaction level.

We illustrate these levels in Figure 6.5 and discuss them in the three sections that follow.

Model the Average Workload.   In this approach, we view all processing as a single homogeneous workload that generates some level of CPU and I/O activity—either per user per minute, or per transaction. We then drive the model by varying the number of users or the transaction arrival rate, as appropriate. This approach lets us investigate CPU and I/O capacity limits, provided that future workload increases can easily be expressed in terms of current volumes. Its advantage is in the relative simplicity of the input data required, and for this reason it may be the ideal model for gross-level capacity planning.

This is probably too much of a simplification if the current workload is really not homogeneous, but in fact consists of many applications, each with different profiles and each growing at different rates. Difficulties arise when we want to translate these various workload projections into model input. Also, with this approach, we cannot investigate any phenomena related to variations within the workload, like differential response times, concurrent thread usage, or I/O balancing.

Model Applications.   The obvious extension of the single workload approach is to break the work up into major application areas and develop a standard profile to represent each. Once again, this can be driven by users or transaction

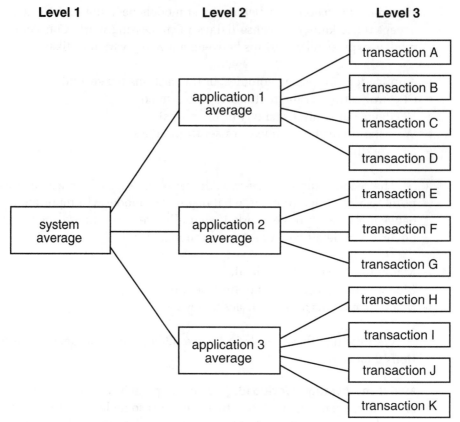

FIGURE 6.5   Levels of detail in model inputs.

rates—this time on a per-application basis. Depending on the number of separate application areas in the model, and on the extent of the real variations within those applications, this approach may permit some investigation of I/O balancing and concurrent thread usage. As a result, we can estimate some differences in response time between applications, though not with any great reliability.

One advantage of modeling at this level is that, although we must now obtain separate input data for each application, this may actually make the model simpler to use. If we choose the application areas properly, making the model reflect business growth that results in workload changes is usually quite easy. Since one goal of modeling is to ensure that the system will continue to support the demands of the business, this is a desirable feature in a model. The model itself can even incorporate links between business factors (as we discussed earlier in the chapter) and workload volumes for various applications.

Model Individual Transactions.   The normal—and most natural—approach is to characterize the workload as individual transaction types. These transaction types, once defined, may be treated differently in different areas of the model. For example, they might be grouped as applications for the purpose of determining their arrival rates, which could continue to be based on users or overall transaction rates per application, as before. But for the purpose of modeling resource usage, they might be assigned to homogeneous workload classes.

Although it incorporates a more detailed workload model than the application-based approach, a transaction-based model can still contain a "front end" that relates workload volumes to business factors. Although it requires more input data, a model constructed at this level of detail is clearly the most useful for investigating system behavior.

The major challenge in constructing such a model is the data analysis required to separate out the workload profiles for each transaction group, a problem that we addressed in Chapter 5 in the section *Uncorrelated Information*. If the available measurement tools do not readily permit this level of analysis, then there is a danger that this level of model, even though it appears to be more precise, may actually furnish less accurate results than a higher-level representation.

Logical Performance Models.   A logical performance model does not take into account the specific hardware and software on which the application runs. Instead, it points out the amount of work the application needs to do—work that will make demands on whatever resources are ultimately involved. As indicated in Figure 6.4, a logical performance model takes into account the business factors, data structures, and processes and uses this information to estimate execution frequencies and the resulting *logical* I/O operations.

We can understand a great deal about an application simply by examining the number of *read* or *write* operations being performed for each type of data. If application designers give some thought to I/O operations as they design an application, then logical performance modeling can provide a more exact way to describe and estimate this information at an early stage. Combining unit costs and execution frequencies like a spreadsheet, a performance model can help application designers understand which specific processes or statements result in large numbers of I/O operations.

Physical Performance Models.   A physical performance model adds performance measures for the specific hardware and software environment. In addition to looking at logical I/O, we can now look at physical I/O operations and

What Details Are NOT Modeled, and Why?

When building a performance model we may deliberately omit details that are important in the real system, typically for one of three reasons: complexity, tuning assumptions, or infrequent occurrence.

Complexity

It may be too difficult to characterize the workload in relation to a particular performance variable. Even though the workload is known to be an area of concern, we may decide to use an alternative method to investigate it.

A good example of this is the impact of database locking. We know that application designers must think about how their application will take locks in the database and whether two applications are likely to contend with each other significantly. All the same, the incidence of severe locking problems is almost always related to particular patterns of use of certain subsets of the data rather than to the total volume of use of a table or database as a whole.

If we were to model two or more applications performing random locking on the data, we would not see the problem in the model. Contention arises because the pattern of locking is not random across the whole database or table; it is related to the data content in some significant way. Therefore, to uncover this problem using a model, the analyst must first think about patterns of locking carefully enough to predict that the nonrandom pattern will exist and may cause problems. At this point, a model does not add much value except perhaps to confirm what the analyst has already realized. Generally, the extra effort of modeling data locking is not worth it, except possibly when the modeler needs to investigate one of those common problem cases—called *hot spots*—in which small shared tables are updated by several applications. We discuss locking and hot spots in more detail in Chapter 12.

Tuning Assumptions

Some performance problems will not occur in practice if the real system is properly tuned, and we generally do not need to waste time modeling a poorly tuned system.

A good example of this is the impact of DBMS cache, or buffer pool, sizes. For example, if we try to run DB2 with very small buffer pools, all kinds of bad things happen to our DB2 database accesses. First, DB2's *sequential prefetch* (read ahead) function is disabled; if the situation is bad enough, blocked asynchronous writes to disk are converted to single synchronous writes. These changes typically have a significant effect on processor and I/O resource use, as well as on application response times. Normally, we do not model them because they really should not occur on a properly tuned DB2 system.

Infrequent Occurrences

Even though the particular performance problem might be quite significant, the event or process that causes the problem happens infrequently, making the problem an intermittent one rather than an ongoing characteristic of the system. Examples of events that can cause all processing to stop for some time are:

▶ Deadlocks among processes
▶ A broadcast storm caused by a faulty device in a network
▶ A server failure at a remote database server
▶ A DBMS recovery log device filling up in a system that does not support immediate automatic switching to a new log device

Situations like these in which "everything stops" are certainly interesting from a performance point of view, but because they are intermittent we have to be very careful about how we treat them in a model. In effect, our real system has two distinct patterns of behavior: the normal pattern and the intermittent problem pattern. If we average them together, the normal dominates and more than likely hides the effects of the problem altogether; if we focus on the problem behavior, we do not get a true picture of how things are the rest of the time.

The approach we usually take is to model the normal pattern and to analyze the problem situation separately to see whether it can be alleviated by tuning. This separate analysis is often done manually since the effects of the problem are obvious (everything stops). The only really interesting question is "For how long will things stop?" The goal of analysis is to design a solution that keeps stoppages as short as possible. Usually, we don't need to model or analyze the impact on the rest of the workload—we don't need a model to show how things perform when they are temporarily stopped.

Guideline 6.1	**Investigate intermittent problem conditions separately**

A real system may have two distinct patterns of behavior—the normal pattern, and an intermittent problem pattern. When modeling, isolate the intermittent condition and model it separately, or investigate it using other methods.

begin to approximate response time. We can evaluate the effects of buffering, processor speed, block size, and concurrent workloads on actual performance.

Solving the Model

For a performance model to be useful, we must evaluate or "solve" it, to obtain the *utilization* of each modeled device, the *queue lengths* for service at each device, and how long each process spends *waiting for service* at each device. From these statistics, we can compute the total response time for each process simply by summing all the device service times and wait times appropriately.

Models encourage "what-if" analysis because they can represent business factors as parameters that are easily changed. Once the model is constructed, we can systematically reevaluate it for different sets of conditions, much like a financial spreadsheet. Varying the business factors can reveal sensitivities:

▶ Which resources and process are particularly sensitive to changes in business factors
▶ Which factors have the most influence on overall performance
▶ Which elements of the data structure, application processing, hardware, or software are critical from a performance point of view

Using a logical model, for example, an application designer and a database administrator might examine the results together and decide that one module could be redesigned for efficiency, while in another area, data tables could be denormalized to reduce database I/O. The model can be modified and rerun to see whether the proposed changes would really result in fewer I/O operations.

Physical performance models provide a more comprehensive view of how the system will perform and so permit more refined "what-if" analysis—trying out different placements of data and processes across the network to evaluate the relative impact of each change on response time.

Using models in this way is called *sensitivity analysis.*

Solution Methods.   There are two principal methods of evaluating any performance model—mathematical analysis and simulation. In the next section, we compare and contrast the two methods. In theory, we can separate the form of the model (that is, the abstract representation of the real-world system under study) from the solution method. And we can solve any given model by mathematical analysis or by simulation.

In practice, however, the design of the model (including the method of characterizing the workload) is heavily influenced by the intended solution technique. There is little value in creating an elegant or detailed general model if there is no easy way to use it to predict performance for specific workloads. For this reason, the form of the model is usually determined by the modeling tool(s) being used. We list some examples of modeling tools here, and we discuss them in more detail in Chapter 18.

Analysis tools: Perhaps the best known example of this type of product is BEST/1 from BGS (www.bgs.com). Dr. Jeffrey Buzen of BGS was one of the pioneers in the development of analytical queuing theory methods to estimate computer system performance.

Other prediction tools that use analytic modeling techniques include:

▶ BEZ*Plus STRATEGIST* from BEZ Systems (www.bez.com)
▶ Digital's *DIGITAL Capacity Planner* (www.digital.com)

Analytic performance models complement traditional analysis and design tools. Some of the information needed to create performance models—like database volumes and application/database interactions—is captured in functional data and process models and can be reused for performance modeling.

Simulation tools: Tools based on simulation are widely used to configure enterprise networks. These tools evaluate enterprise network traffic and help companies to lower overall tariffs by predicting the optimal configuration of network links. Simulators are generally necessary to resolve these types of questions because network architecture and behavior are too complex to analyze mathematically. Examples of network simulation tools are:

▶ Make Systems' *NetMaker XA* (www.makesys.com)
▶ Zitel Corporation's *NetArchitect* and *Capacity Planner* (www.zitel.com)

In Chapter 18, we discuss *SES/Strategizer,* a client/server performance modeling tool that uses simulation from Scientific and Engineering Software, Inc. (www.ses.com).

Comparing Analysis and Simulation

To illustrate the differences between analysis and simulation, imagine that we want to solve a model with the following characteristics:

▶ 10 different processes or transaction types
▶ 1 processor device
▶ 4 disk I/O devices

▶ An arrival rate of 10 transactions per second

▶ Each process makes 10 I/O requests and uses the processor between each

In an analytic model, this means doing some computations for a matrix of dimensions (processes *x* devices)—in our example (10 × 5), or 50 sets of computations. All of this is just number crunching, and it can be done in a few seconds on a workstation.

To obtain the same results, the simulator must generate 10 transaction types, at 10 per second, for (say) 10 minutes. That's 10 × 10 × 10 × 60, or 60,000 transactions. For each transaction, it must simulate 10 I/O and 10 processor requests. That's a total of 20 × 60,000, or 1,200,000 requests to be simulated. Each request involves updating the status of the requesting process, checking the status of the requested device, probably placing the request in a queue for the device, checking all the devices to see which one will complete its service next, updating the process and device statistics for the service time just completed, and updating the simulated clock.

That is a lot of processing. Actual run times depend on the modeled transaction arrival rate, the amount of detail in the model, and the power of the processor running the simulation, but it is not uncommon for a "10-minute" simulation to take anything from 1 to 10 hours to run.

What If . . .

The beauty of a model is that it lets us try out design changes before we spend our valuable resources developing application software. Let's consider the impact of some typical changes we might make in our model:

Double the Arrival Rate.   In the analytic model, the arrival rate of 10 per second is represented somewhere as a variable multiplier in a mathematical formula. If we double it to 20 per second, the same computations are performed using a multiplier of 20 instead of 10, so the time to solve the model analytically does not change.

Doubling the simulated workload, on the other hand, probably more than doubles the simulation run time because not only do we have to simulate twice as many events, we also create more contention for the modeled devices so the simulator spends more time managing the device queues.

Add a Background Workload.   It is not usually realistic to assume that our new application is the only one using the computing resources. Other work normally competes for the processor, disk, and network devices. We take this into account by adding some background work to the model. In an analytic model, we can do this by adding a "background percent busy" factor to each device. This amount is factored into each set of computations as an additive variable, but solving the model does not take any longer.

To add a background workload to a simulator, we have to simulate at least one more process to generate the sum total of all the background activity on each of the devices, so the solution time is extended.

Add a Network Component.   In an analytic model, if we were to add a network component to each transaction as another device, the number of sets of computations would go up from 10×5 to 10×6, or 60 sets, causing a 20 percent increase in the time it takes to solve the model.

If we add a network device to our simulation, then there must be at least two logical I/O requests to this device (an input and output message) per transaction. In our example, this would mean $60,000 \times 2$ or 120,000 more events to simulate. If there are more output messages (for example, to transmit a result table), the event count rises accordingly. To model the network properly, we really need to look at the number of physical packets transmitted, which might easily be four times the number of logical message transmissions. The number of additional events to simulate can be at least 480,000 and probably more than half a million if we model any network overhead activity.

In an analytic model, by comparison, the time needed to solve the model remains the same regardless of how many messages there are per transaction or whether we model logical network I/O (messages) or physical I/O (packets); all we are doing is adjusting the device service time and the number of service requests per process, which are just variables in the formulas.

Model the Network in More Detail.   Even if we decide to model the network in a lot more detail and include 10 new devices within the network model, we still only roughly triple the original solution time of our analytic model, which is measured in seconds. But in the simulator, if the average transaction transmits its messages through 4 of our 10 new devices, we have about 2 million network-related events to be simulated, probably adding hours to the elapsed time.

Recommendations

To sum up:

Analysis: Analytic performance modeling, using queuing theory, is very flexible and complements traditional approaches to performance. It can be used early in the application development life cycle. We do not have to build the actual system, or a version of it, as we would for a benchmark or prototype. This saves tremendously on the resources needed both to build and evaluate a design. In an analytic model:

▶ We can make our model larger and add more devices without its taking forever to evaluate. Analytic models can be quite detailed where detail is appropriate, but the machine cycles needed to evaluate the model do not increase nearly as dramatically as they would if the corresponding model were solved by a simulation method. Desktop or laptop processing power is usually sufficient to evaluate analytic models.

▶ Playing what-if games with the business factors typically makes no difference at all to the solution time because the business variables are just variables in the mathematical formulas being computed. While we might easily run an analytic model 20 times in one afternoon, making 20 runs with a simulator is more likely to take 2 to 4 weeks.

Simulation: In a simulator, as we make our model larger and add more devices, we may need substantially more time to evaluate the results. Playing what-if games with the business factors can also make a substantial difference to the solution time because any increase in modeled processing will result in a corresponding increase in simulated processing.

Considering our discussion, it is reasonable to ask why anyone would want to use a simulator when an analytic solution is available is reasonable. The main reason is that a simulator shows the real world in slow motion.

While the analytical modeling tools can quickly analyze most system behaviors, the mathematics deal in *average* service times and *average* wait times. Simulation modeling tools let us observe actual behavior; if we have unstable conditions, we can see spikes occurring or queues building up and going down again. If we have a concern about extreme variability and spikes, a simulation tool allows us to observe that behavior and plan accordingly; an analytical tool does not.

▶ With a simulation tool, at any time during a simulation run, we can look at an individual device and see exactly what it is doing at that moment—is it busy or is it idle? How long is the queue? We can see where the queues build up. And if an intermittent event occurs that causes a large perturbation in performance, we can actually see the combination of circumstances that caused that event, the effect on the rest of the system, and how long it took for things to return to normal.

For some kinds of systems, especially those that are subject to wide variations in demand, this capability is very useful. But if we do not have that type of requirement, a simulator is overkill.

Three Levels of Modeling.   While it is very useful to have simulation capability somewhere in a development organization, it is quite unnecessary to have it in every project team. We recommend a three-level approach to application modeling, in which each level is a refinement of the level above:

▶ **Logical performance modeling** by analysis in the early stages of development to identify performance-critical components and potential bottlenecks
▶ **Physical modeling** of normal behavior by analysis as the application design is refined, to validate the choice of design options and project performance in the target environment
▶ **Detailed simulation modeling** of transient behavior in complex, performance-critical applications where the cost of modeling is unimportant compared to the potential risk of incurring a performance problem

This scheme should be familiar to performance analysts because it has parallels in the world of performance monitoring. We discuss this scheme in Chapter 5 but generally we use two levels of monitoring for information systems: application-level accounting to track the relative levels of resource demand by application or transaction and resource usage statistics to validate the design of critical applications or DBMS components.

In most cases, these two levels tell us everything we need to know about application and system performance. But sometimes we need to go that one level deeper, to see what is actually going on inside an individual transaction occurrence or inside one component of the DBMS. Then we need a performance trace to give us a blow-by-blow report.

As with monitoring, so with modeling. A simulator is modeling's equivalent of the detailed performance trace. It is expensive to run, and it takes a while to analyze the output. Most of the time we don't use it, but it's nice to have it around for those few situations when we really need it.

Iterate for Success.   To be effective, modeling at the second and third levels must be iterative. No matter what modeling tool(s) we use, they must be augmented with techniques for capturing measurements of the existing system and feeding them back into the model. For arguments supporting this recommendation, see the Chapter 5 capsule *Will the Real Application Profile Please Stand Up?*

Benchmarks and Benchmarking

A benchmark is simply another type of model. We begin with some definitions:

▶ A **benchmark** is a representative set of programs we can use to draw conclusions about the behavior of some larger computer system.

▶ A **custom benchmark** is one that is tailored to our specific needs and interests.

▶ A **standard benchmark** has achieved some degree of recognition within the industry. To be useful, such a benchmark must stipulate both the *programs* that comprise the workload and (ideally, at least) the *rules* for running and measuring them, to ensure that results obtained from separate measurements are still comparable.

▶ The term "benchmark" also refers to the overall process of selecting, running, and measuring a set of benchmark programs and deriving results.

Probably the most comprehensive sources of information about benchmarks for database and transaction processing systems are *The Benchmark Book* by Richard Grace[1] and *The Benchmark Handbook* edited by Jim Gray.[2] For easier reading, choose *The Benchmark Book*.

Deciding What to Measure

We first introduced benchmarks in Chapter 3 (see Guideline 3.5). Benchmarks, as we noted in Chapter 5, are normally used to measure a system's responsiveness at a range of workload levels, and its peak throughput or capacity. We can use a benchmark to measure anything—it just depends on how we vary the test environment, and what measurement data we collect.

Deciding what to measure begins long before we run the benchmark. When we introduced the elements of performance at the beginning of Chapter 3, we pointed out The Law of Measurements: *The result of any measurement will depend upon what is measured, how the measurement is done, and how the results are computed* (Guideline 3.1). Every benchmark program measures something and, by implication, fails to measure some other things. So, before choosing one, we should discover the answer to two key questions:

▶ What exactly does the benchmark measure?
▶ How closely does the benchmark program resemble the normal workload we intend the measured configuration to handle?

For example, the SPEC FP benchmark is designed to measure the speed of mathematical calculations using *floating point* arithmetic, which is common in

---

[1]Richard Grace, *The Benchmark Book* (Upper Saddle River, NJ: Prentice-Hall, 1995).
[2]James Gray, ed., *The Benchmark Handbook* (San Mateo, CA: Morgan Kaufmann, 1993).

engineering and scientific applications, but rarely needed for business information processing. Someone who relied upon SPEC FP benchmark results to select a computer for database management would probably make a poor choice because he or she had not considered the two key questions.

The secret to using a benchmark successfully is to select or construct a benchmark that is representative of our real workload.

Guideline 6.2	**Select a representative benchmark**

Before using a benchmark, answer two questions: "What exactly does the benchmark measure?" and "How closely does the benchmark program resemble the normal workload we intend the measured configuration to handle?" The secret to using a benchmark successfully is to select or construct a benchmark that is representative of the real workload.

Standard Benchmarks

It's a relatively simple matter to develop some programs and label them the "*XYZ standard,*" but defining a complete and watertight set of rules takes a lot more work. As a consequence, the so-called "standard" benchmarks vary widely in the completeness of their rules. Examining the primary sources for such benchmarks will reveal the reasons for this. The principal sources are:

- ▶ Organizations sponsored by a consortium of computer companies
- ▶ Individual computer hardware or software vendors
- ▶ Computer trade publications
- ▶ Universities
- ▶ Commercial benchmarking companies

Is There Safety in Numbers?   Some of the most popular benchmark programs and the most widely published benchmark results come from groups of computer hardware and software vendors acting in consort. RISC workstation manufacturers sponsor the *Standard Performance Evaluation Corporation* (**SPEC**), and DBMS vendors (together with other interested parties) operate the *Transaction Processing Council* (**TPC**).

These consortia create an aura of objectivity despite the fact the benchmarks they sponsor inevitably tend to highlight the group's collective strengths and minimize their weaker points. This is a bit like the tobacco companies forming a "non-profit" research institute to report the "truth" about smoking. For example:

▶ The SPEC INT and SPEC FP benchmarks[3] (the most widely quoted SPEC tests) are calculation intensive (an area where workstations have historically excelled) and perform no disk I/O (an area where a workstation might perform no better than a PC).

▶ The TPC benchmarks[4] emphasize the ability of a database server to process a high rate of transactions, but do not properly account for the load that would also be imposed on the server by all the other components required to actually generate such a high transaction rate in a normal production environment.

As Kayvalia M. Dixit observes in *The Benchmark Handbook,*[5] *"Truth in benchmarking is an oxymoron, because vendors use benchmarks for marketing purposes."*

Single-Supplier Benchmarks.   These market realities make it very difficult for an individual hardware or software company ever to promulgate a standard benchmark, no matter how useful it might actually be. An amusing story contributed by Neal Nelson[6]—a benchmarking specialist—illustrates this:

> Several years ago a major disk drive manufacturer wanted to advance the state of the art in disk drive benchmarking. They made a sincere effort to write a better disk drive benchmark. They wrote a white paper describing their effort. They announced it and offered free copies to interested parties. The benchmark never really caught on and recently I asked a high ranking executive at the company "Whatever happened to that benchmark?" He explained that one of two things happened when the benchmark was used: If the benchmark showed that his company's product was faster, people dismissed the results because the benchmark had been written by the winning company and was therefore presumed to be biased. If the benchmark showed some other disk to be faster then the benchmark

---

[3]Grace, *The Benchmark Book,* Chapter 2, p. 11, and Chapter 10, p. 249; and Gray, *The Benchmark Handbook,* Chapter 9, p. 489.

[4]Grace, *The Benchmark Book,* Chapter 4, p. 61; and Gray, *The Benchmark Handbook,* Chapters 1–3, p. 21–267.

[5]Kaivalya M. Dixit, "Overview of the SPEC Benchmarks," in *The Benchmark Handbook,* Chapter 9, p. 490.

[6]Neal Nelson & Associates, 35 East Wacker Drive, Chicago, IL 60601. Telephone (312) 332-3242.

was presumed to be accurate and the other product was selected. The disk drive manufacturer decided that they did not want to promote any more standard benchmarks.

Those who live by the sword will die by the sword!

Publish or Perish.   In recent years, magazines publishers have become a prolific source of benchmarks. The large magazine chains have equipped and staffed benchmarking laboratories and have created suites of benchmarks that are frequently quite impressive. *The Benchmark Book* includes chapters on the Ziff-Davis Networking and Personal Computer benchmarks.[7]

A potential drawback of these benchmarks is that they are controlled by the publication's editorial staff. If a publisher's major thrust is personal computers, the benchmarks tend to focus on personal computers. The selection of machines for testing and the timing and extent of any tests are governed by the editorial calendar.

On the other hand, if your area of interest matches the editorial focus, and your project's time frame can be adjusted to the publisher's editorial calendar (or you are willing to run the tests yourself), then these benchmarks are usually inexpensive to obtain and run, and fairly complete and unbiased.

A Bit Too Close to Reality?   One might imagine that researchers at universities would be interested in developing standard tests to evaluate the performance of leading-edge technologies, but few such tests have emerged. This is probably because researchers are usually investigating very narrow specialized topics, which would tend to require a custom benchmark that would not be of general interest.

The *Wisconsin benchmark* which measures relational DBMS performance, is a notable exception. It was developed by Dina Bitton, David DeWitt, and Carolyn Turbyfill at the University of Wisconsin from 1981 onwards, and quickly became the de facto standard, because at the time it filled a void. DeWitt writes, "*We never expected this benchmark to become as popular as it did. In retrospect, the reasons for this popularity were only partially due to its technical quality.*"[8]

The Wisconsin benchmark's success was an accidental quirk of timing, its role as a standard has since been assumed by the *TPC benchmarks* we mentioned

---

[7]Ziff-Davis "Networking" and "Personal Computer Benchmarks," in *The Benchmark Book*, Chapter 3, p. 29, and Chapter 7, p. 155.
[8]David J. DeWitt, "The Wisconsin Benchmark: Past, Present, and Future" in *The Benchmark Handbook*, Chapter 4, p. 269.

earlier. But it has not died altogether, its current incarnation is being used to measure parallel database servers.

Getting Help from Vendors

When a sale is on the line, a hardware or software vendor may be willing to help you benchmark their product. Unfortunately, vendors tend to approach benchmarking in the same manner that the automobile manufacturers do the Grand Prix racing circuit:

▶ Hardware vendors want to "prove" that their machine is best. Every computer model and configuration has specific strength and weakness. Every benchmark has an individual workload profile that matches up differently against the strengths and weaknesses of different machines. Just as the RISC workstation vendors endorse the SPEC suite, all hardware vendors will tend to favor and endorse those benchmarks that highlight their strengths and overlook their weaknesses.

When Wizards Go to War, No One Wins

Tom Sawyer is a respected authority on benchmarking whose work with database vendors in the 1980s culminated in the formation of the TPC. He warns that if more than one vendor is vying for your business, an all-out tuning war can result:

> Let us assume vendor A wins the benchmark. Vendor B then says: "Well, we didn't realize vendor A was going to use one-star wizards, whereas we used our branch office folks. We would like to re-run our benchmark with the additional tuning and insight equivalent to that used by vendor A." Vendor A will in turn want to rerun with two-star wizards, claiming that was what Vendor B used, etc. This process can escalate past the four-star wizard ranking, with lots of time lost.[9]

It may be interesting to watch all this wizardry in action, but don't expect it to be particularly educational or useful, because the protagonists usually resort to all kinds of software stratagems that do not work in your real system. To forestall this *war of wizards,* Sawyer recommends telling all the vendors in advance that the benchmark will be "a single trial; no excuses; no reruns."

Sound advice from a battle-scarred veteran of the benchmark wars!

---

[9]Tom Sawyer, "Doing Your Own Benchmark" in *The Benchmark Handbook,* Chapter 11, p. 561.

▶ Software vendors use benchmarks to "prove" that their software is the fastest. They tend to favor benchmarks that are complex and that will respond to extensive tuning to obtain the fastest possible results.

Getting this kind of help from a vendor is a double-edged sword. Even if you define a workload yourself and take it to a vendor test center for execution, you risk being oversold. Remember the old legal saying that "*a person who chooses to be his own attorney has a fool for a client!*"

Since winning a benchmark means closing a sale, vendors employ experienced professional technicians to tune their system before the test. These tuning wizards can nudge and cajole every last ounce of performance from a given machine with a given workload. They know that cached disk I/O runs 10 to 100 times faster than physical disk I/O. They have tools to examine the execution profile of your programs and reveal the best configuration options for your (usually simple) workload.

The result may look impressive, but what happens after the tuning wizards are gone and you have to manage the system yourself? It is reasonable to expect that vendor sales efforts will communicate all of a product's significant strengths, but it is up to you to uncover the weaknesses. So you will still need to run more benchmark tests to reveal the whole story.

Remember that vendor benchmarks are *always* part of the *sales* process. The best test is always to install their software or hardware in your own environment, use it with your own workloads, and develop your own understanding of its capacity. Just get a money-back guarantee first.

Independent Benchmarking Organizations.   The best antidote to vendor influence is the independent benchmarking organization. Some of these companies, like the National Software Testing Labs, work primarily with vendors. Others are more customer oriented. Their goal is to give customers the tools to see clearly through the haze of vendor mis-statements and exaggerated claims. Two leading companies are:

▶ Neal Nelson & Associates, whose standard *Business Benchmark* simulates a typical I/O intensive multi-user business environment. Also, customers can use the *Remote Terminal Emulator* to create and run custom benchmarks using their own programs.
▶ AIM Technology[10] whose battery of benchmark *Suites* are used by UNIX system vendors, system integrators, and MIS technicians. Using a technique AIM

---

[10]AIM Technology, 4699 Old Ironsides Dr, St 150, Santa Clara, CA 95954. Telephone (800) 848-8649 or online at www.aim.com.

calls *load mix modeling,* benchmark users can customize the *Suites* to mimic the characteristics of a user workload.

For a detailed description of the various benchmark services available from these two companies, refer to Chapters 5 and 6 of *The Benchmark Book.*

Benchmarking Complications

Benchmarking sounds relatively straightforward: run some programs and measure the result. But that simple formula hides a maze of complications. To conduct a proper test of a distributed system we must:

▶ Assemble a working distributed environment to serve as a test bed
▶ Obtain or create distributed applications programs that will run on the test system(s)
▶ Load meaningful and representative test data
▶ Either connect and configure a large number of client machines with operators who will perform well-defined tasks with reasonable repeatability, or (more typically) obtain and program a client/server *driver* program
▶ Monitor the system and gather measurement data
▶ Analyze the data, summarize it, and report the results
▶ Vary the workload and/or the environment and repeat the measurement

Complications arise in four major areas: the benchmark *workload,* the benchmarked *environment,* the benchmarking *process,* and the *results.* In the short sections that follow, we discuss some key issues that we must address within these four areas.

The Benchmark Workload

Perhaps the most perplexing aspect of benchmarking is ensuring that the measured workload truly represents the real world (or at least some aspect of it), because it is so hard to know what the "real world" actually looks like. Application profiles are notoriously elusive—see the capsule *Will the Real Application Profile Please Stand Up?* in Chapter 5.

Are There Any Unknown Variables?   Another challenge is to recognize when the benchmark does not take into account significant performance factors that will affect the relationship between a real workload and its environment. If we do not really understand what the key performance variables are, we are likely to misinterpret the results.

For example, as we discuss in detail in Chapter 14, virtually all modern computers use "caches." A cache is a local storage area that is smaller and faster than the "normal" area. An instruction cache is a small area of static RAM that is very fast and close to the CPU, with access times that may be 10 times faster than the system's main memory. For a calculation-intensive program, the same benchmark on the same machine could report results that differed by a factor of 10, depending on whether the program is compiled in such a way that all of its instructions fit entirely in the instruction cache. Caching, and its effectiveness, are important characteristics to measure, but, unless we really know what's going on, is our benchmark measuring the speed of the computer, or the effectiveness of the compiler?

Guideline 6.3	**Loosley's Law of unlikely events**

The probability of an unlikely event occurring during a benchmark measurement is at least as high as its probability in the real system, and typically higher. When some parts of the workload mix have low probabilities of occurring, we may have to run the benchmark for longer than we might expect to account for workload variations.

Are Unlikely Events Overrepresented?   We discussed the extreme case of this problem earlier, in the section *Infrequent Occurrences*. Many relatively infrequent primitives (like creating and deleting files or database tables, building database indexes, or taking database checkpoints) are important enough to measure, but we must take care not to overrepresent them in the mix, or they will tend to dominate the results. But this creates another complication.

At run time, to eliminate the possibility that systematic interactions among the various programs might bias the results in some way, benchmark input is normally generated at random by a program called a *driver* or a *remote terminal emulator*. This creates message traffic that simulates the presence of a large number of active users working at separate workstations or "terminals."

While we rely on randomness to ensure that all *likely* combinations of work actually occur during the course of the benchmark run, it can also lead to the occurrence of some *unlikely* combinations events. Years ago, when designing and running benchmarks of IBM database software (IMS/VS and DB2), I discovered that Murphy's Law applies equally well to benchmarks as it does to real systems. When we have deliberately assigned low probabilities to some parts of the workload mix, we may have to run the benchmark for longer than we might expect to account for workload variations.

The Benchmarked Environment

Earlier we emphasized the importance of clearly defined rules for standard benchmarks. Rules make a benchmark a known and repeatable quantity, which lets us follow the scientific method: *Change the variables of interest one at a time and observe the result.* Even when a benchmark's input is generated at random by a driver program or remote terminal emulator, it should be possible to make *identical* measurement runs, by controlling all the start conditions and using the same *seed* for the random generator.

Making a complex client/server benchmark repeatable involves a lot of work, however, and may not even be possible. Unless we are benchmarking a data warehouse, any business benchmark must update databases. Before the next run, all those databases (and their associated indexes) must be reloaded or restored, to recreate their original states. The starting conditions of every other component must also be controlled.

In practice, achieving exact repeatability is usually not worth the effort. We probably do want to restore the databases to some realistic starting point (as opposed to using an unrealistic set of perfectly organized databases). But we may prefer to rely on randomness to take care of fluctuations elsewhere, making more than one run and averaging the results if necessary.

The Benchmarking Process

Creating a benchmark whose workload we can really *control* is not easy. For example:

▶ How will the programs that control the benchmark ensure that the various activities of interest really do occur at our desired frequencies?
▶ If we are simulating hundreds of users manipulating very large amounts of data, how will we ensure that the activity is spread across an entire database in the proportions we planned?
▶ How will we control the relative proportions of various kinds of database request?
▶ How will we control the sizes of result sets generated by database queries within the workload?
▶ What mechanism(s) will we use to vary any of these workload distributions, when we need to adjust the workload mix?

A poor benchmark suite consists of programs that always do the same thing. A good benchmark has been designed so that all the important workload variables are parameterized. By adjusting an input parameter somewhere, we can adjust the workload mix. This makes the benchmark customizable.

The Results

People crave simplicity; they want a single number that will tell them the truth about computer performance. If one computer scores 10 and another scores 15, the second must be 50 percent faster. Alas! Real life is not this simple. A benchmark that summarizes everything into a single performance score is either very simple itself, or hiding a lot of valuable information.

Can the Benchmark Be Tuned to Improve the Results?   Earlier in this chapter, we discussed the need to curtail the activities of tuning *wizards* while benchmarking. If the results are to be realistic, we should give the benchmark environment a level of attention and tuning comparable to that available in the normal production environment, and no more.

Some benchmarks resist tuning. This may be frustrating to some, but the results may be more useful for predicting performance in the real world. For example, a database application that selects data at random from a very large database cannot be tuned by extra caching. Such a benchmark would measure the efficiency of random data retrievals, regardless of the tuning effort.

Can the Results Be Invalidated by Trickery?   When a sale is on the line, benchmarking trickery knows no bounds. Some years ago the *dhrystone* benchmark was popular. Small, standard, and easy to run, it seemed to contain a meaningful mix of calculation activities. Then some computer equipment manufacturers modified their compilers to scan for the *dhrystone* source code and plug in hand optimized assembler language. These compiler changes had no effect on any real application programs that would ever be run on the machine, but boosted *dhrystone* scores considerably.

Even four-star tuning wizards could not match this! As word of this chicanery leaked out, use of the *dhrystone* benchmark inevitably declined.

In summary: Whenever you look at benchmark results, always make sure you know exactly what the benchmark measured. We repeat our earlier advice; always remember the Law of Measurements (Guideline 3.1): *The result of any measurement will depend upon what is measured, how the measurement is done, and how the results are computed.*

Using a Performance Model

In conclusion, we present some general guidelines on using models. They apply to any modeling tool or method chosen. They are not particularly original;

you can probably find something similar in most modeling textbooks. Nevertheless, we feel that they are important enough to be repeated here.

First Validate Your Model.   Before you set out to use a tool, make sure that it works properly. When selecting any prediction tool or technique, you should always consider (as a factor in assessing its likely accuracy) how well it applies to the situation to be studied. This means understanding the range of questions for which it was designed and the environments in which it has been validated.

Because of the combinations of parameters involved, it is rarely possible to validate a capacity planning model fully. Usually, the best we can hope to do is to take a large number of "spot checks," to satisfy ourselves that the model represents reality within some defined area or range of values of the model's input parameters. The more diverse the validation points, the better the model—so try to get validation data from a variety of workloads on your present system.

Guideline 6.4	**Validate performance models**

Before relying on a model to predict *future* performance, first make some "spot checks" to confirm that it reflects the performance of *current* workloads reasonably well.

Don't Try to Stretch Your Model Beyond Its Natural Limits.   Once validated, a model can be used with confidence within the area of validation, for the kinds of questions it was designed to answer. It can also be used to project system behavior at points outside that area. Were this not so, there would be little reason for building such a model in the first place. You should exercise care, however, in interpreting the results of such projections in any modeled environment where one or more of the resources modeled is approaching its saturation point. Unless the critical resource is the CPU, you must usually consider whether there will actually be a bottleneck in the real system or whether it can be removed by tuning.

Also, be aware that your model can handle only those questions whose answers depend entirely (or, at least, nearly so) on the resources being modeled. A simple model can answer a simple question like "Will the projected work-

Guideline 6.5	**Recognize a model's limits**

A model's usefulness is limited to the effects and behavior of the resources modeled. Be especially careful whenever a modeled resource other than the CPU is approaching its saturation point.

load need a faster processor?", but you will need a lot more detail in the model if you want to use it to balance the load for your I/O subsystem.

Use the "What-if" Approach to Improve Your Model.   You can make the greatest contribution to the accuracy of your predictions by methodical use of your model and its results. A principal benefit of system models is the opportunity they provide to forget about the problems of analyzing data and to concentrate on investigating the dynamics of the system under study. Analytic models, although not particularly complex, are no exception to this.

For example, when you are not sure of the values or relative importance of some input parameters, you can compute the results for a range of possible values and determine the sensitivity of the model to variations in those parameters.

More than likely, you will discover that the model is really sensitive to only a subset of the input parameters; you can then present your results in terms of that subset. This will also help you to decide how accurate your input data needs to be to obtain some desired level of accuracy in your results. Finally, you can determine what additional measurement data needs to be obtained from your existing system, to ensure the desired accuracy in the model projections. When used in this way, the model is sure to increase your understanding of the system.

Guideline 6.6	**Use a model for sensitivity analysis**

When you are not sure of the value or relative importance of some modeled variables, compute the results for a range of possible values and determine the sensitivity of the model to variations in those parameters. Doing this identifies the most significant factors affecting performance.

Don't Let Averages Mask Significant Performance Variations.   Because all models simplify the real world, significant variations in performance may be overlooked. Even if the modeled workload re-creates the variations, their presence will be masked if the model's results are presented only as averages.

For example, the performance of a modern computer is highly dependent on its use of memory for caches. Tasks that execute entirely from cache (either a CPU cache or disk cache) will run up to 100 times faster than tasks that fetch instructions or data from main memory or disks. In practice, an occasional sequential scan of a large database table may flush out the contents of a system's disk cache or a DBMS cache. During this period (which may last several minutes) other tasks that require only moderate disk services but share the cache may run 50 times slower than normal.

No tool can predict when or how often a user might issue the query that forces a sequential scan. Analytic modeling typically misses this type of problem, unless we have designed the model specifically to investigate it. (See Guideline 6.1, "*Investigate intermittent problem conditions separately.*") But simulation or benchmarking can reveal these kinds of performance variations—provided we look beyond simple averages and pay careful attention to the detailed results.

Once we know that such a problem exists, any type of model can estimate the throughput of a system in either domain.

Guideline 6.7	Don't let averages mask significant performance variations

When using a simulation model or a benchmark, always pay careful attention to the detailed results. Significant variations in performance may be overlooked in the results are presented only as averages.

Don't Get Carried Away—The Model Is No Smarter Than You Are.   If you want to use any tool properly, first find out how it works. A perennial risk of prediction tools is that they may be used by someone with insufficient input data and only a partial understanding of the relationship of the tool to the system being modeled. We have all met the manager who believes that a design problem that his staff cannot even formulate properly can be readily solved once they have access to a sufficiently comprehensive model.

Actually, however much care has gone into the construction of your model, it will still obey that most fundamental law of data processing: Garbage in, garbage out. Of course, a large pile of neatly formatted garbage can be very beguiling—you can easily be mesmerized by the beauty and precision of the model's output. Don't forget about the simplications made in the model to achieve that (apparent) precision.

Guideline 6.8	Don't let a model replace common sense

However much care has gone into the construction of your model, it will still obey that most fundamental law of data processing: *Garbage in, garbage out.* Modeling must supplement thoughtful analysis, not replace it.

Conclusion

In this chapter, we have discussed various ways to predict future performance. But no matter which approach we adopt, the outcome will be a failure unless we first understand the present. If you don't know anything about your application's CPU or I/O requirements per transaction, having an analytic or simulation model will not help greatly.

Even benchmarking must be approached with extreme care or its results can be misleading. There was a time when computers were relatively simple devices. They would have a card reader, a printer, a CPU and a disk. One could double the speed of the card reader and know that the input portion of a job would go twice as fast. Those days are long gone. Today, a single computer system could have twenty different components or subsystems that could be the primary bottleneck, depending on the workload. A given benchmark may actually measure only one of those components.

Using a standard benchmark involves trade-offs and limitations. For example, selecting a magazine benchmark is almost certainly faster, easier, and cheaper than developing a custom test. But it is very unlikely that the programs and database activity will match our intended workload. Also, these freely available benchmarks have usually been widely used, and all their functions fully debugged—maybe even optimized—long ago. Most real applications and software packages, in contrast, have inefficiencies and performance bugs—and Murphy's Law dictates that a major bug will appear in the functions that are most critical to our application. We still need controlled load testing to uncover these problems before the system is placed in service.

To run a model is to conduct an experiment; its results are worthless if the conditions of the experiment do not reflect reality. In today's world, to obtain some level of comfort about the future, we must:

▶ Understand our applications and how they interact with the system.

▶ Understand our chosen modeling tools or benchmarks, which components they model or measure (and which they do not), and how they relate to the real world that we need to predict.

▶ Understand which parts of the target environment we *cannot* control, and look for ways to evaluate the worst case scenarios for those components.

▶ Even for those components we *can* control, we should take care not to model or benchmark a system that is tuned for a single application, if such tuning goes beyond the levels we can reasonably expect to exist in the normal "unbiased" production environment. (Be especially careful of this whenever outside consultants or vendors are involved.) If we don't take precautions to limit excessive tuning, we will end up trying to factor its effects out the results, which is like trying to figure out the performance of a standard model Ford by adjusting the results of the *Monaco Grand Prix*.

To sum up, no matter which technique we use, we should never treat a model as a black box that just churns out answers. Rather, we must use the model to help us learn more about the system, continually modifying it to reflect the changes and growth in our knowledge, and the evolution of the systems and applications of interest. Provided we adopt this kind of systematic approach, almost any modeling technique will help us understand *some* aspect of performance better.

Principles

CHAPTER 7

SPE Design Principles and Techniques

"Order and simplicity are the first steps toward the mastery of a subject—the actual enemy is the unknown."

Thomas Mann

In This Chapter . . .

Software Engineering Principles
Software Design Principles
Software Design Techniques
Localization: The Path from Logical Design to Construction
The SPE Design Principles

How should we design good software? Even though many books offer a variety of answers to this question, most ignore performance issues altogether. In some, the importance of performance is mentioned briefly, but it's left to the reader to define what performance really means. In books devoted to performance, on the other hand, performance is presented as the overriding design goal, while other aspects of software engineering are virtually ignored.

As advocates of Software Performance Engineering (SPE), we propose a more holistic view of software development, in which meeting performance objectives is one of the cornerstones of software quality. As we said in Chapter 4, the goal of achieving good performance cannot be separated from the rest of software engineering; that is, *"SPE is simply software engineering with performance in mind."*

In Chapters 5 and 6 we showed how the management goals and practices of SPE are inextricably woven together with those of the broader software engineering process. We now turn to the technical principles and practices of SPE and their relationship to those of software engineering.

203

A Library for Software Designers

If you have ever browsed in the software engineering section of your local computer bookstore, you know that the subject of software design is a rich and well-represented one. Ed Yourdon's *The Programmers Bookshelf* is an excellent bibliography. An annotated version of this list, originally comprising 87 books on all aspects of software design and the development process, was first published in Yourdon's book, *Decline and Fall of the American Programmer,* itself a very readable survey of modern software engineering trends. His recent sequel, *The Resurrection and Rise of the American Programmer,* includes an updated version.

Ed Yourdon maintains an updated version of this bibliography (along with a lot of other useful references for developers) on his Web page at http://www.yourdon.com/.

My own list is a much shorter one. No matter whether you believe that information technology is advancing through a series of technical revolutions or through a gradual process of evolution, these books can give you a well-rounded view of what software design is all about.

First understand how software engineering has evolved as a discipline. For a comprehensive overview, I use *Software Engineering: A Practitioner's Approach,* by Roger Pressman. It would be very difficult for any single textbook to do justice to the entire software engineering life cycle, from management to maintenance, but this book comes closest. A thoroughly reliable reference work that is regularly updated (a completely revised fourth edition appeared in 1997, with much new material on distributed systems and object-oriented methods), its main strength is the breadth of its coverage. And, at almost 800 pages, its coverage is still detailed enough to be useful. But this is a general work on software engineering; do not expect to find extended discussions of client/server architectures, the design of database applications, or software performance engineering.

For lighter reading about today's trends and tomorrow's possibilities, I recommend Ed Yourdon's books and Bruce Tognazzini's *Tog on Software Design.* Yourdon is largely preoccupied with the development process, while Tog's viewpoint takes in the future of the entire computer industry in a world of distributed computing. Provocative and insightful, Tog offers very easy reading while still managing to say a lot about what makes for good software.

Finally, focus on the details of software construction. The ultimate encyclopedia for the software developer is *Code Complete,* by Steve McConnell. Subtitled *A Practical Handbook of Software Construction,* this 850-page book is exactly that. Its stated goal is to narrow the gap between the knowledge of "industry gurus and professors" (Yourdon and Pressman, for example) and common commercial practice, and "to help you write better programs in less time with fewer headaches." It starts out emphasizing the importance of the "prerequisites to construction," including problem definition, requirements analysis, and architectural design. It then settles in to its central subject matter: the detailed design, construction, and testing of software.

After 25 years working on software performance and reading computer books I know that, unless performance is the stated focus of the book, most authors make only passing references to performance, efficiency, or optimization as development goals. Steve McConnell is the exception. He tries hard to give the reader a realistic assessment of the role of performance as an aspect of software quality. Obviously a software engineer himself, he begins his discussion of tuning with the insightful admission that "Programmers like you and me tend to look at the world through code-colored glasses. We assume that the better we make the code, the more our clients and customers will like our software." His discussions of requirements and architecture acknowledge the importance of performance specifications; he points the interested reader to Connie Smith's classic on *software performance engineering* and devotes two long chapters (60 pages) to code-tuning strategies and techniques.

Every developer should own a copy of McConnell's book. Its style and content are thoroughly practical. It even has a short section on "Religious Issues" advising managers how to handle quality goals in sensitive areas that are reflections of a programmer's personal style and tips on "Managing Your Manager" for the software developer saddled with a technically incompetent boss; it concludes with a recommendation to read Dale Carnegie's *How to Win Friends and Influence People*.

Software Design Bibliography: Past, Present, and Future

Booch, Grady. *Object Solutions* (Reading, MA: Addison Wesley, 1996).

Carnegie, Dale. *How to Win Friends and Influence People* (New York, NY: Simon & Schuster, 1981).

Johnson, Jay, Skoglund, Rod, and Wisniewski, Joe. *Program Smarter, Not Harder* (New York, NY: McGraw-Hill, 1995).

McConnell, Steve. *Code Complete* (Redmond, WA: Microsoft Press, 1993).

Pressman, Roger. *Software Engineering: A Practitioner's Approach* (New York, NY: McGraw-Hill, 1992).

Tognazzini, Bruce. *Tog on Software Design* (Reading, MA: Addison Wesley, 1996).

Yourdon, Ed. *Decline and Fall of the American Programmer* (Englewood Cliffs, NJ: Yourdon Press, 1992).

Software Engineering Principles

In our view, SPE is nothing more or less than *good* software engineering. And it's a truism to state that achieving *acceptable* performance must *always* be one goal of good software engineering: If the performance is not acceptable, how can the engineering be judged to be "good" in any sense? Performance may not be the only goal, of course, but it is always one goal among others. And following sound software engineering practices will help, not hinder, the goals of acceptable performance.

In keeping with this view, in this chapter *we present the SPE design principles as natural extensions of the basic principles of good software engineering.*

Software engineering principles, laid down over the years by leading computer scientists,[1] have focused mainly on the logical aspects of software design for which correct behavior, ease of use, code reusability, and ease of maintenance are typical goals. The SPE principles, in contrast, deal with physical consequences of design decisions, where performance is the key indicator of quality.

In Figure 7.1, we identify the key software engineering principles and some relationships among them. In the discussion that follows, we point out some performance-related implications of these design principles.

The key principles divide nicely into three layers of three principles each. We begin with the first layer. The foundation underlying all other principles is a commitment to *formal* or *structured* methods. Three related principles—**Formality, Completeness,** and **Simplicity**—emerge here, of which the last is particularly relevant to performance.

> **Guideline 7.1**
>
> **Software engineering foundation: Formality**
> Apply rigorous or systematic methods throughout the development process.

> **Guideline 7.2**
>
> **Software engineering foundation: Completeness**
> Decompose the problem in such a way that nothing is left out. This may seem obvious, but only systematic methods can ensure it.

---

[1]Over the last 25 years, many industry thinkers such as Dahl, Dijkstra, Jackson, Myers, Ross, Wasserman, and Wirth have proposed similar sets of software engineering principles. In their book *Structured Techniques: The Basis for CASE* (Englewood Cliffs, NJ: Prentice-Hall, 1988), James Martin and Carma McClure argue that sound development practice for information systems must be built on the solid foundation laid by these principles. Roger Pressman's discussion of software design fundamentals reiterates this argument, based on many of the same principles.

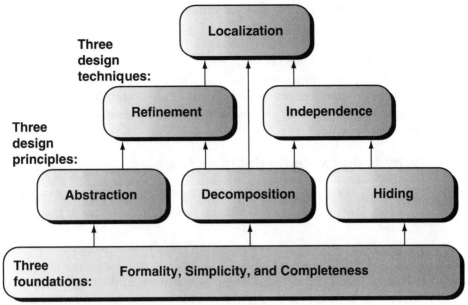

FIGURE 7.1   Key principles of software engineering.

Guideline 7.3	**Software engineering foundation: Simplicity**
	Maintain conceptual integrity and eliminate unnecessary features.

Keep It Clean and Simple

It does not take a great deal of thought to see why *Formality* and *Completeness* are important engineering principles. On the other hand, it is perhaps less obvious why the Simplicity Principle is worthy of note, especially in a book devoted to discussions of physical design and performance. There are good reasons why a simple software solution is usually better, not only logically but also physically:

▶ Logically, a simple design is more likely to exhibit "conceptual integrity"— that is, to be based throughout on a consistent design philosophy and architecture will surely make the design easier to understand and maintain.

▶ Physically, when the designer eliminates unnecessary features, the result will almost certainly perform better.

In software, however, simplicity rarely occurs naturally. Indeed, the opposite is true—simplicity must be carefully cultivated and protected during the development process. Unless you make simplicity your explicit goal, large software systems always tend to become more complex as they are developed.

Why Is Software So Complex?

Knowledge of what users really want often is the single most important factor in the failure or success of a software project. It's also one of the most neglected factors.

Johnson, Skoglund, and Wisniewski

The real world is a complicated place, and we build software to support and serve people as they work in that world. Furthermore, very few potential software users understand the complexities of software design, and few software engineers are truly familiar with the user's world. It's not surprising that everyone involved in the development process tends to act in ways that cause our software to mirror the complexity of the user's world. Consider:

▶ **Users are in the driver's seat.** One of the touted benefits of distributed computing is the emancipation of users, freed at last from the tyranny and oppression of unresponsive data-processing departments. Today, as never before, there is strong pressure to involve the end user in the software design and development process. And most potential users, when consulted, come up with a wish-list of "minor changes" and "small improvements" that would be "nice to have."

▶ **Software designers are creative people.** When confronted with a complex problem domain and a long list of user "requirements" whose relative importance they are not qualified to judge, designers have a natural inclination to dream up features and options that will meet every conceivable need of every potential user.

▶ **Programmers are paid to write code.** They solve problems by writing more code—they are prone to respond to complexity and uncertainty by coding lots of nifty features to handle every possible situation. And it's always easier to add features and options than it is to remove them. Only the most disciplined of programmers are willing to throw away working code.

▶ **Managers are rarely good software architects.** In fact, that's usually why they are managers. They have chosen the management career path in preference to the technical one. There is nothing inherently wrong with that—by the same token, good engineers rarely enjoy managing. Problems arise, however, when those whose task it is to manage large software engineering efforts are not good managers. Unfortunately, this is all too often the case. The rapid pace of change in our industry makes it hard for managers who are no longer actively doing development work to keep pace with the latest technology. Poor management and lack of a consistent architectural vision generally lead to poorly designed and overly complex software.

Even though the first design may be clean and simple, added complexities still tend to creep in as time goes by. In his landmark essay on software engineering practice, *The Mythical Man Month,* Fred Brooks writes about the dangers of "The Second System Effect." He notes that "an architect's first work is apt to be spare and clean" because, aware of his uncertainty, he works "carefully and with great restraint." However, many potential refinements are noted and filed away mentally for future use. So there is a tendency for the second version to include "frill after frill and embellishment after embellishment" as the designer starts to feel more confident of his understanding of the problem domain.[2]

This phenomenon, variously labeled as "feature creep" or "creeping featurism," is well known in software development. How often have you heard a developer say, "We can easily add that"? (Maybe you even were that developer yourself!) Our recommendation is that the next time you find yourself in one of these conversations, try to temper the developer's natural enthusiasm and creativity with a pause for second thoughts like these:

"*. . . , but what will it do to our performance?*"
"*. . . , but is it really needed?*"
"*. . . , is there some other feature I can eliminate to make up for adding this?*"

Jeff Tash, speaking about the benefits of object reuse, likes to say that "the fastest line of code to develop is the line of code you don't have to write."[3]

---

[2]Fred Brooks, *The Mythical Man Month* (Reading, MA: Addison-Wesley, 1975 and 1995).
[3]Jeff Tash, President, Database Decisions, a division of Hewitt Associates. LLC. Telephone (617) 891-3600 (*dbd@tiac.com*).

Where performance is concerned, we could certainly add: "And the best performing line of code is the line of code you leave out." We will return to this topic in more detail in Chapter 8, in our discussion of the Workload Principle.

> **Guideline 7.4**   **Software diet:**
> **The ultimate performance enhancer**
>
> Software, like its creators, has a natural tendency to put on weight. For the best performance, keep your applications on a strict diet. The best performing line of code is the line of code you leave out.

Be Simple, Not Simple-Minded

One note of caution is in order. By all means keep the design simple, but where performance is concerned, do not confuse the admirable design goal of simplicity with the inferior engineering practice of simple-mindedness. Nothing about the Simplicity Principle guarantees that the simplest *implementation* will perform the best. Indeed, the opposite is true. Generally it takes a clever and typically more complex solution to improve on the performance of the simplest algorithm. For example:

▶ A bubble sort is an easy algorithm to code, but it performs terribly if you need to sort anything more than a small number of elements.

▶ It takes a lot more design and coding effort to retain copies of software components in a dynamically maintained memory cache than it does to re-read them from disk every time they are used. But the application will run faster if you eliminate the disk I/O time.

▶ When your application involves reading or writing data and interacting with the user at the same time, creating multiple processor tasks that can run in parallel can speed up performance from the user's perspective. It will always be more complex to create a solution that uses parallel processing than one that is implemented as a simple linear sequence of tasks.

▶ Distributing fragments of your database to different locations is more complex than keeping all the data in a single, centralized database. Maintaining the data consistently, propagating updates from one location to another, providing for remote access—all these issues add complexity. The result, however, can be better performance for those at remote locations who must manipulate portions of the database.

On another level, distributed computing itself is a far more complex solution for the enterprise than centralized mainframe computing ever was. The benefit for the enterprise is the improved performance of the information-processing function. New applications are possible. Data that never existed before, or was available only through periodic batch reports, can now be called up online whenever it's needed.

To sum up then, make the design simple but the implementation smart. The SPE design principles that we introduce later in this chapter provide the guidelines needed to help us build smart, well-performing systems.

Guideline 7.5

Design for simplicity, implement for speed

Keep the design simple but the implementation smart. Generally, it takes a clever and typically more complex solution to improve on the performance of the simplest algorithm.

Guideline 7.6

Software design principle: Abstraction

Abstraction is the guiding principle of design work. Represent problems in a simplified general form to eliminate irrelevant details. Incidentally, this principle is the basis for all types of modeling.

Guideline 7.7

Software design principle: Decomposition

Make large problems tractable by breaking them into smaller ones. This is a fundamental strategy of analysis and problem solving that dates back to Aristotle. It is the reason for the horizontal dimension of the Zachman Framework (which we'll discuss later in this chapter).

Guideline 7.8

Software design principle: Hiding

Isolate each component by letting a component see only that information which is essential to it. Hiding (also called **encapsulation**) simplifies the design by allowing the internal design of a component to be changed without affecting other components.

Software Design Principles

Next comes a layer comprising the three fundamental principles of analysis that we apply during the process of software design: **Abstraction, Decomposition,** and **Hiding.**

Abstraction and Decomposition

By analogy a map illustrates the value of abstraction and decomposition. Employing the abstraction principle, maps are useful because they eliminate most of the details of the real world, presenting an abstract representation of the small subset of information needed for navigation.

In 1989, Doug Stumberger, a friend taking a break from software engineering, spent a month driving across the United States from Boston to Santa Cruz, California. First, he looked at a map of the United States to see which route best suited his purpose. Next, he consulted regional and state maps to refine the route. Finally, he referred to local maps of those places he visited along the way. His strategy was to move from the broad picture to the details by repeatedly decomposing the problem into smaller parts, but to get down to greater levels of detail only when required. Unfortunately for Doug, he arrived in Santa Cruz days before the 1989 earthquake (which, in software engineering terms, might be analogous to massive last-minute changes to handle new and unforeseen government regulations), and so he had to change his plans.

Decomposition pervades human thought. Given a mass of information, we intuitively search for an organizing framework that will allow us to arrange it into more manageable chunks or classes. It's hardly surprising that humans were thinking about the most natural way to assign things to groups 2200 years before information processing was done by computers.[4]

Without using decomposition techniques, humans could not develop complex information systems. Our limited human brains simply cannot comprehend really large problems without decomposing them into smaller ones, a fact that underlies most software engineering methods. Decomposition is also essential if work is to be parceled out among teams of human developers or processed by parallel processors. Over the course of the 35 years or so that peo-

---

[4]In her excellent book Building *Enterprise Information Architectures* (Upper Saddle River, NJ: Prentice-Hall, 1996), Melissa Cook points out that in the fourth century B.C., the Greek philosophers Plato and Aristotle studied classification theory. Plato focused on the search for the *eiodos* or essence of things; Aristotle's interests centered around logical division, or decomposition.

ple have been writing software, schemes for problem decomposition have been continually refined. Even the term **data processing,** the historical name for information systems, itself implies a decomposition—all computing tasks could be decomposed into data and process components, the data being static and the process dynamic.

The Pros and Cons of Hiding

In the construction of software, hiding is a key technique. Callable modules are designed to hide the implementation details behind a defined interface or API. The physical details of data storage are hidden behind an access-method interface or a data-manipulation language like SQL. Client/server design guidelines often extend this idea, suggesting that each shared resource be managed by a server. For example, Paul Renaud, in *Introduction to Client/Server Systems,* writes:

> Any data, peripherals (e.g., printers), or services (e.g., communications) that are shared among several users should be managed by a server. The server should provide a logical abstraction of the shared resource to its clients and hide the details of how the resource is managed, its current state, etc.
>
> A good starting point is to imagine a logical server for each shared resource in the system. Each database, peripheral, and shared service should be viewed as having its own server.[5]

Even though hiding is obviously a useful and important technique of logical design, it can have adverse physical consequences. These arise not so much from the use of hiding per se, a technique that is neutral with respect to performance. The trouble comes from the fact that a mechanism hidden behind an interface becomes invisible to another developer writing client code to use that interface, allowing unwary developers to forget about the physical consequences of their particular usage. Out of sight, out of mind.

Guideline 7.9	**Too much hiding is bad for performance**

If during development you are in too much of a hurry to ask what's hidden behind an API, you will usually have to spend time later finding out why it's causing performance problems.

---

[5]Paul Renaud, *Introduction to Client/Server Systems* (New York: John Wiley & Sons, 1993), 310.

In the worst cases, an unsuspecting developer can create a serious mismatch between the design of the requester software and the operation of the mechanisms hidden behind the server's API. (Note that here we use the terms *requester* and *server* in their generic senses; we are not referring to components of particular products or even to components of a particular technical architecture.) Avoiding these kinds of mismatch is one of the central themes of SPE. It is one that takes on even more significance in the enterprise client/server environment, where systems must be constructed from a variety of components produced independently by different people.

We will revisit this topic in more detail in Chapter 10, when we discuss the Locality Principle and, in particular, the significance of achieving *effectual locality.*

Software Design Techniques

At the top come the final three principles, each of which evokes a fundamental design technique or procedure of software engineering: **Refinement, Independence,** and **Localization.**

> **Guideline 7.10**   **Software design technique: Refinement**
>
> Create the ultimate solution through a systematic process of decomposition and **elaboration**, recursively developing new levels of detail as needed. This key software design and development technique, also called **stepwise refinement,** was originally identified by Nicklaus Wirth in 1971, and follows naturally from the decomposition and abstraction principles. It is the basis for the existence of the successive phases found in every model of the software development life cycle.

> **Guideline 7.11**   **Software design technique: Independence**
>
> Create components that are logically independent of one another, permitting one to be modified independent of the others. While database designers speak of **logical independence,** software designers prefer the term **functional independence.** Deriving from the combination of the decomposition and hiding principles, this principle underlies the techniques of **software layering, logical database design,** and of course, **object-oriented design.**

> **Guideline 7.12**   **Software design technique: Localization**
>
> At the apex of the pyramid is the localization principle: Group logically related items together. Applying this principle creates a wide range of well-designed software elements including modules, objects, tables, messages, windows, and even frames (for devotees of artificial intelligence (AI)).

Decomposition and Software Quality: From Zachman to Pirsig

In the field of software engineering, a great deal of attention has been devoted to devising schemes for performing further decompositions within the domains of data and process. While few people ever questioned the basic data/process conceptual model, in reality it is an overly simplistic one—the complex software applications that run our businesses must actually deal with several other fundamental concepts.

The Zachman Framework

In 1987, John Zachman introduced his *Framework for Information Systems Architecture*.[6] The Zachman Framework (Figure 7.2) is now widely recognized as a simple but comprehensive formalism for organizing ideas about how we develop information systems. Rows in the framework correspond to the various stages of the application development process (planning, analysis, schematic design, technical design, construction, and deployment). Columns correspond to the distinct components of a business application (data, rules, process, location, time, and user role).

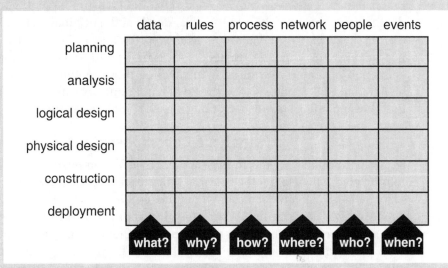

FIGURE 7.2   The Zachman Framework.

---

[6]John Zachman, Framework for Information Systems Architecture, *IBM Systems Journal* 26(3) (1987).

As a method of organizing ideas, the framework can hardly be called original: Partition the problem domain using a two-dimensional grid. We learned to do that in grade school. Indeed, the beauty of the framework is its utter simplicity. But the secret to its usefulness lies in deciding where to draw the dividing lines. With a flash of insight worthy of Plato himself, Zachman observed that if we wish to introduce more rigor into the process of information systems development, then certain partitions of that domain are truly *essential*. That is, they are both natural and vital:

▶ *Natural* because they separate things that are truly different in essence, not simply different representations of the same thing
▶ *Vital* because a failure to recognize these inherent differences must lead to architectures, development processes, and tools that are fundamentally flawed

Although he has modestly denied that he "invented anything" (see, for example, the interview published in *Database Newsletter,* Vol. 17, No. 5, 1989),[7] Zachman deserves full credit for this observation. It is characteristic of ideas that the most revolutionary and surprising ones often appear to be the simplest and most obvious—*once they have been stated.* So the fact that the Zachman Framework now seems so natural is testimony not to its lack of depth, but to the opposite—to the great depth of the original vision. By introducing the framework, Zachman has moved the discussion of software engineering away from its narrow focus on methods and tools to a broader consideration of the architectures within which those methods and tools must operate. Like all good teachers, the Zachman Framework has not provided all the answers; rather, it shows us how to ask the right questions.

Analysis Decomposes

Applying the ideas of the framework involves **decomposing** an application into its component parts (or columns), then refining the design of each part systematically. When developing complex applications, this is an extremely useful analytical discipline. Ultimately, the application will not be correct—or perform well—unless all its parts work together correctly and efficiently.

A recurring theme in life is that "the whole is greater than the sum of the parts"—relationships, the way things are connected, often are more signifi-

---

[7] *Database Newsletter* 17(5) (1989).

cant and carry far more information than the things they relate. For example, think of the atoms in a molecular structure, the cells in a human brain, or the chips in a computer. It's the relationships that bring the otherwise unrelated components to life.

This observation also applies, we believe, to the components created during the design and development of complex information systems, and thus to the cells of the Zachman Framework. Our analysis dissects the problem domain and the design of the solution into Aristotelian subdivisions (components, classes, modules, entities, attributes, screens, windows, or whatever). Like the pieces of a giant jigsaw puzzle, until they are all brought back together in just the right way, an appearance of disharmony and chaos prevails.

Synthesis, Objects, and Quality

After analysis must come synthesis. The goal of good software engineering must be to synthesize—to harmonize the pieces of the information systems puzzle. One of the great attractions of object-oriented methodologies is that *objects* provide a single, unifying representation that is infinitely scalable from the smallest component to the largest system. In theory, objects do not require us to decompose the problem into weaker components; each object can be a tiny system or machine, complete within itself. We simply plug the machines together to build larger ones. In practice, however, we cannot escape the need for analysis, classification, and subdivision—they are at the root of all good object methodologies, too.

Whatever approach we take to software engineering, we will still need techniques for synthesis and performance engineering. Applying the technique of grouping, we can craft useful components and assemble those components into systems. Guided also by performance engineering principles (and, in particular, the goal of effectual locality or *closeness of purpose*), we can deliver systems whose function and performance exactly match their users' needs.

In other words, systems that exhibit the marks of *quality*—for, as Robert Pirsig said, in his classic *Zen and the Art of Motorcycle Maintenance*, "*Quality . . . emerges as a* relationship *between man and his experience*."[8] Quality in software components is not inherent in the components themselves. It emerges as a relationship between those components and their environment.

---

[8]Robert Pirsig, *Zen and the Art of Motorcycle Maintenance* (London, UK: Bodley Head Ltd, 1974), 378.

These last three principles are closely related:

▶ First, the entire software development process must apply the technique of **stepwise refinement,** beginning with an *external* specification of function (what to do) at a high level of abstraction and proceeding through successive iterations to more and more levels of *internal* detail (how to do it). This is the basis for the division of the Zachman Framework into separate rows, representing stages or phases of the development process.

▶ Next, we need a goal for our refinement process: It is to achieve **logical independence.** A good design is one in which components exhibit independence—that is, independence is *what* we should aim for.

▶ Finally, the software design technique of localization suggests *how* to achieve independence.

Two very important subsidiary concepts, **cohesion** and **coupling,** refer to the strength or weakness of the logical relationships and the degree of independence achieved by a particular choice of grouping.

▶ **Cohesion** is normally used in software design to describe the functional "strength" of a software *module,* in that the more help a module needs from its colleagues, the weaker it is. For more details, see Pressman's discussion. He describes a cohesion spectrum ranging from *Coincidental* at the weakest end ("scatter-brained" modules) to Functional at the strongest end ("single-minded modules").[9] Perhaps the best way to remember this is to think of a strongly cohesive module as one that "does the job, the whole job, and nothing but the job." Even though this explanation applies to modules, the concept of cohesion can obviously be generalized to apply in a similar way to other components like objects, data tables, and windows.

▶ **Coupling** is essentially the inverse of cohesion. It refers to the degree of interconnection or interdependence among the modules or data elements of a design. Again, Pressman describes a coupling spectrum for software modules ranging from no direct coupling at the low end through data coupling, control coupling, and external coupling, to common coupling and content coupling at the high end.[10] To embark on a full discussion of these ideas would be a digression—it is sufficient to understand that as the coupling between two modules moves up the spectrum, the modules become more entangled and less independent. Because the components of an information system must work together to provide the complete solution, some degree of coupling among them is essen-

---

[9]Pressman, *Software Engineering,* 358.
[10]Pressman, *Software Engineering,* 359.

tial. A good software design, though, is one in which the degree of coupling is minimized and the types of coupling confined to the low end of the spectrum.

To sum up then, *cohesion* and *coupling* are subsidiary concepts that measure the degree of *localization* in a software design. Independent modules or components will exhibit strong (i.e., a high level of) cohesion and weak (i.e., a low level of) coupling. Both are important:

▶ A modular design with weak cohesion and low coupling is hard to imagine. It is a collection of barely related, poorly structured components.
▶ A design with strong cohesion and high coupling, on the other hand, is too entangled. Such a design will resist change and be hard to distribute without introducing performance problems.

Localization: The Path from Logical Design to Construction

This brings us to a key point in our analysis. You may be wondering how the preceding discussion of software engineering principles is related to our earlier discussions of SPE. Localization—the apex of the pyramid of software engineering principles—is the connection.

Although we could advance purely logical arguments for the importance of localization and the cohesion and coupling concepts, when we turn our attention to the question of *how* to implement a particular logical design, their significance becomes abundantly clear. For the remainder of this chapter, and the next seven chapters in this part of the book, we focus in detail on the six core design principles of SPE. But those principles do not exist in a vacuum, isolated from the rest of software engineering practice.

Consider Figure 7.3. It shows the relationship of the SPE design principles to the software engineering principles and techniques we described in this chapter.

▶ The physical design principles of SPE are all related in some way to the software engineering technique of localization.
▶ The logical (SE) and physical (SPE) principles between them form a single continuum of related principles for constructing high-quality software.

The key connection is the physical design technique of *grouping*. We define grouping as *any situation in which connections are established between separate computing components (hardware or software, data or process) for the purpose of performing a task*. Based on this general definition, it is clear that grouping is a physical design technique that we use in every area of software design. For example, Table 7.1 lists some common areas in which we apply

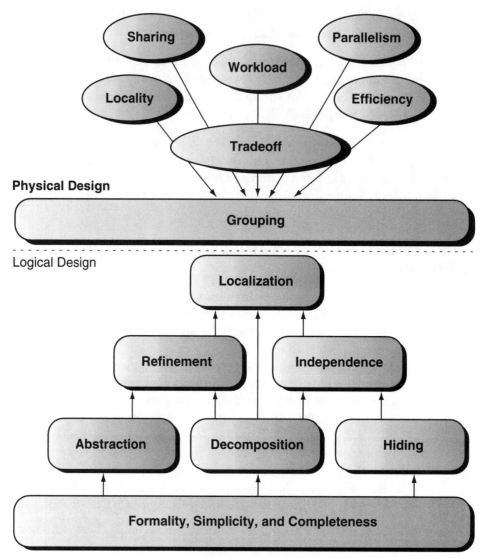

FIGURE 7.3   Six SPE design principles.

grouping techniques, showing in each case the design domain concerned, the class(es) of components grouped, and the aggregate object created as a result of the grouping action.

The ultimate performance of any complex system will depend on the grouping choices and decisions made during the design of that system. This is why

Table 7.1   **Typical Grouping Activities in Physical Design**

Design Domain	Components Grouped	Aggregate Object(s) Created
Program design	Related functions	Applications, processes, routines, or modules
Object-oriented analysis, design, or programming	Related data items and processes or methods	Objects
Database design	Related columns	Records, files, tables, or views
Database application design	Sets of related SQL statements	Stored procedures, database access routines, or database transactions
User interface (UI) design	Related data fields	User dialogs, windows, menus, screens, or reports
Data communications software	Information for transmission	Messages that are transmitted in blocks or packets
Secondary data storage (disk I/O)	Store data	Records, blocks, or pages
Processor memory management	Transient program data	Blocks, pages, buffers, or caches

the software design technique of localization is so important. It is the existence (or absence) of *logical relationships* among a set of components that motivates the *physical action of grouping* (or separating) those components in some way.

While physical design actions cannot *remove* logical dependencies between components, they can certainly *introduce* new ones, so that previously independent elements are now related physically. Ultimately, the performance of the whole system will depend largely on these decisions about the grouping or separating of its hardware and software components.

Figure 7.3 highlights the central importance of grouping and the Localization Principle in good software engineering. We return to the subject of grouping in more detail when we discuss the Trade-off Principle in Chapter 14.

Many key physical design issues hinge around how we apply the technique of grouping, which is used in both logical and physical design. *Independence* and *localization* (and the subsidiary concepts *cohesion* and *coupling*) are crucial to good software design because they have such a strong influence at the intersection of logical and physical design.

Adding Performance to Software Engineering

"The logical designer is a reluctant physical designer."

Paul Winsberg

We have now stepped into the middle ground connecting logical design and physical (or technical) design, and we are about to shift our attention away from the logical view of software engineering principles to the performance-related view. This will lead shortly to a detailed exploration of the six software performance engineering (SPE) design principles illustrated Figure 7.3.

However, before we do shift our focus, we must reemphasize a point we made earlier in Chapters 4 and 5, during our discussions of performance management and the software development process. That is, the order of our presentation of *ideas* does not in any way imply support for an equivalent development *methodology*.

We do not intend by our presentation in this chapter to equate the boundary between logical design and technical design with a switch in focus from logical correctness to performance.

Although it's true that the **Sharing, Parallelism,** and **Trade-off** Principles will be most useful at the technical design and construction stages of development, we should have already started thinking about performance long before the technical design stage. As we noted when we first introduced the design principles in Chapter 4, for optimal software performance we must also keep performance in mind during planning, analysis, and logical design, and start applying the performance principles from analysis onward.

To some, this may seem surprising. Ideally, the counterargument goes, the logical design of a system should be independent of its physical design, allowing the implementation platform to be varied without changing the logical design. Following that reasoning, a natural assumption might be that performance issues do not need to come up until we reach the physical (or technical) design stage.

In the real world, this ideal is simply not achievable. Indeed, it is not practical for logical design to be concerned only with correctness, ignoring issues of technical feasibility. It is usually difficult or impossible to create an acceptable product by tuning the physical design if you start with a bad logical design. This applies equally well to any construction process, whether we're talking about software or cathedrals, submarines or hot air balloons.

Paul Winsberg, when teaching logical database design, always says "the logical designer is a reluctant physical designer," meaning that many logical design decisions cannot be evaluated without reference to the physical consequences.[11] Although conceptual issues should predominate during the analysis and logical design phases, physical issues cannot be ignored.

Guideline 7.14	**Winsberg's Law of Logical Design**

The logical designer must be a reluctant physical designer. Although conceptual issues should dominate our thinking during the analysis and logical design phases, physical implementation issues cannot be ignored. To do so is to risk creating a design that cannot be tuned for performance.

Trade-offs Among Software Engineering Goals

We have noted previously that to achieve acceptable performance, we must make trade-offs. The first such trade-off involves the relative importance of performance and other software engineering goals. Steve McConnell recognizes this key point in his discussion of code-tuning strategies: "Performance is only one aspect of overall software quality," he writes, "and it's probably not the most influential aspect."[12]

Unfortunately, McConnell follows with an argument that does not support his initial statement. "Finely tuned code is only one aspect of overall performance . . .", he argues, "Program architecture, detailed design, and data structure and algorithm selection usually have more influence on a program's size and execution speed than the efficiency of its code does."

The problem with McConnell's reasoning here is that he seems to be trying to equate "performance" with "code efficiency" and then use that as a basis for arguing that performance is not the most influential aspect of quality: His last sentence undermines his own argument. In enterprise information systems, as his last sentence acknowledges, performance depends on much more than just

---

[11]Paul Winsberg (pwinsberg@dbaint.com).
[12]McConnell, *Code Complete,* 694.

the efficiency of a single program's code. Table 1.1 in Chapter 1 listed 40 variables that were likely to influence performance.

We certainly encourage the pursuit of efficiency at all levels of design and implementation, and we devote much of Chapters 8 and 9 to ways of achieving it. We suggest, however, forgetting about the ill-defined notion of performance as somehow meaning "blazing speed" and recall instead the discussion of "identifying business priorities and performance objectives" in Chapter 5. In our view, the only definition of "performance" that makes sense in the real world of software engineering is "acceptable performance in the eyes of the user."

When we define it this way, then it's plain that performance is *always* important. Granted, it's not the only design criterion to which we need to pay attention: Cost, desired function, usability, and maintainability are important goals, too. That's why we have to make the first kind of performance trade-offs. Because no enterprise has the luxury of unlimited budgets, time, and development resources, compromises will always be made, and performance goals must be evaluated against all other criteria.

Who Does Design, Anyway?

In the real world of software development, "design" is an elusive quality. In his book, *The Practical Guide to Structured Systems Design,* Meilir Page-Jones points out a basic problem with the way most companies approach software design—that very, very few people in our industry are designated as "designers." "I'm sure you've met users, analysts, programmers, and even programmer/analysts, but have you ever met anyone with the job title 'designer'?", he asks.[13] We could add architects, data analysts, data administrators, DBAs, and software engineers to that list and still have no better luck finding anyone who we were sure was a designer.

You might think that we all know what design is and what a designer does, so it doesn't matter who does it or what his or her job title is. But the point is that if the design task is assigned to an analyst or a programmer, then it tends to be confused with either analysis or programming.

Page-Jones writes: "If design becomes the domain of the analyst, then the user finds himself treated to a confusing pageant of flowcharts, file layouts, and so on. If design falls into the programmer's jurisdiction, then the overall plan of the system somehow 'just emerges' from the code—if it emerges at all."[14]

This was originally written in the late 1970s. Today, we might prefer to substitute CASE tools, object models, and E/R diagrams as the tools of choice for

---

[13]Meilir Page-Jones, *The Practical Guide to Structured Systems Design* (Englewood Cliffs, NJ: Yourdon Press/Prentice-Hall, 1988), 22.

[14]Page-Jones, *Practical Guide,* 22.

the modern analyst, but the point remains true—design is neither analysis nor programming.

Every project requires attention to design; otherwise, the result will be poorly structured software with poor performance. The design phase occurs when the basic structure of the system is set and the core components identified. In the design phase, a software architecture emerges that will be extended and refined until the production system is completed.

In our experience, when design is done by analysts, either the design or the analysis suffers. Analysts who are not good engineers may assume that it's acceptable to implement a physical version of their logical solution—this leads to poor performance. On the other hand, some so-called programmer/analysts are not analysts at all. They can't avoid thinking about physical optimizations during analysis, so they pollute their logical models with all kinds of implementation artifacts, saying, "I know we will need one of these later." They may create a system that performs well, but it will usually be inflexible and difficult to extend or modify later.

Our advice is to separate analysis from design/construction and then to make design a programmer's responsibility. But be sure to select the programmer carefully. Good programmers—the kind who would qualify for the job title of software architect on a large project—don't just start coding. They don't get bogged down in analysis, either. They spend a lot of time staring out the window and scribbling on scraps of paper before they write a line of code. This is because they are actually doing design, thinking about the problem and searching for the core patterns that will produce an efficient and extensible solution.

Guideline 7.15	**Design is neither analysis nor programming**

Design is neither analysis nor programming
Design is a different activity from either analysis or programming, and it should be conducted separately. Failing to recognize this will usually lead to a system with poor structure and poor performance.

The SPE Design Principles

We now commence our detailed review of the six design principles listed in Table 7.2. We devote a separate chapter to each of the principles listed in the table, beginning with the *Workload Principle.* (Actually, we had so much to say about the *Sharing Principle* that it became two chapters, but you can think of them as one logical chapter.) Each chapter explains the principle, giving examples of how it applies to systems design issues in general and, in particular, to the design of enterprise client/server systems.

The Origins of the SPE Design Principles

Connie U. Smith, the author of *Performance Engineering of Software Systems,* (Addison Wesley, 1990), deserves the credit for first identifying a set of software performance engineering principles—the rules we should follow to engineer performance into our software.[15]

Smith's book describes the following seven principles:

▶ *Fixing-Point Principle.* Establishes connections for responsiveness at the earliest feasible time, such that retaining the connection is cost-effective.

▶ **Locality-Design Principle.** Creates actions, functions, and results that are "close" to physical computer resources.

▶ **Processing versus Frequency Trade-off Principle.** Minimizes the processing times frequency product.

▶ **Shared Resource Principle.** Shares resources when possible. When exclusive access is required, minimizes the sum of the holding time and the scheduling time.

▶ **Parallel Processing Principle.** Executes processing in parallel (only) when the processing speedup offsets communication overhead and resource contention delays.

▶ **Centering Principle.** Identifies the dominant workload functions and minimizes their processing.

▶ **Instrumenting Principle.** Instruments systems as you build them to enable measurement and analysis of workload scenarios, resource requirements, and performance goal achievement.

Over the last few years, several other authors and speakers have adopted Smith's principles as a starting point when presenting ideas about performance management.[16] A good example is Ted Keller's *CICS Capacity Planning and Performance Management,* which includes a 35-page chapter on "SPE Application Design Guidelines" applying Smith's principles to CICS systems.[17] Another author, Dennis Shasha, refers to four design principles in his book *Database Tuning—A Principled Approach.*[18] Although he calls his

---

[15]Smith, *Performance Engineering,* 38.

[16]For an introduction to Smith's SPE design principles, see (Chris Loosley, "Client/Server Forum"), *Database Programming & Design,* March 1995.

[17]Ted Keller, *CICS Capacity Planning and Performance Management* (New York, NY: McGraw Hill, 1993).

[18]Dennis E. Shasha, *Database Tuning: A Principled Approach* (Upper Saddle River, NJ: Prentice-Hall, 1992).

principles by different names, they do correspond fairly closely to four of the principles in Smith's list. Shasha's four principles are:

▶ *Startup costs are high, running costs are low* (the motivation for Smith's Fixing-Point Principle).

▶ *Partitioning breaks bottlenecks* (the motivation for Smith's Parallel Processing Principle).

▶ *Render onto server what is due onto server* (equivalent to a subset of Smith's Locality-Design Principle).

▶ *Think globally, fix locally* (corresponds to aspects of Smith's Centering Principle).

In our own analysis of SPE, we have wrestled with the question of how best to separate the various SPE *activities,* described earlier—which cover the entire development process from planning to production—from the *design principles* to be applied during the system design phases. At one time, we had created several new principles to address issues like these:

▶ Understanding the key business factors
▶ Setting objectives
▶ Having a way to make predictions
▶ Doing performance monitoring

However, because the design and management processes involve such fundamentally different concepts, we eventually concluded that it is clearer to retain the nomenclature of "principles" for the rules of good design and not introduce additional principles related only to the development process. Therefore, we have dropped Smith's Centering and Instrumentation Principles because we feel that they relate more to the conduct of SPE activities. However, we have added a sixth design principle—the Trade-off Principle—that addresses a crucial design issue and is often the key to resolving apparent conflicts among the other design principles.

Combining all these sources, we obtain the following six SPE design principles:

Workload	*Minimize the total processing load.*
Efficiency	*Maximize the ratio of useful work to overhead.*
Locality	*Group-related components based on their usage.*
Sharing	*Share resources without creating bottlenecks.*
Parallelism	*Use parallelism when the gains outweigh the overhead.*
Trade-off	*Reduce delays by substituting faster resources.*

Table 7.2   **The Six SPE Design Principles**

Name	Statement of Principle	Chapter
Workload	Minimize the total processing load	8
Efficiency	Maximize the ratio of useful work to overhead	9
Locality	Group-related components based on their usage	10
Sharing	Share resources without creating bottlenecks	11, 12
Parallelism	Use parallelism when the gains outweigh the overhead	13
Trade-off	Reduce delays by substituting faster resources	14

Like the SPE activities described in Chapter 4, 5, and 6, the design principles are not organized into a methodology. In practice, we may repeat several development stages iteratively, especially if we are using a prototyping or evolutionary methodology to develop parts of the application. Although one principle may be particularly applicable at one stage of one project, in general most of the principles can *and should* be applied across more than one stage to achieve optimal performance.

CHAPTER 8

The Workload Principle

"You can do anything with software, except make pasta and coffee. But just because something can be done it doesn't necessarily mean that it should be done."

Valdo Androsciani

In This Chapter . . .

Minimizing Unit Costs
Trading Off Unit Cost and Execution Frequency
Applying the Workload Principle
Conclusion: Make the Machine a Partner

We now begin our systematic review of the six *SPE Design Principles* that we introduced in Chapter 7.

The first design principle, the Workload Principle, is so natural that we tend to forget about it. Another name for it might be "the bottom-line principle" because it reminds us that two factors contribute to total processing cost, namely unit cost and frequency of execution. The Workload Principle states a logical consequence of this: To minimize the total processing load on the system, we must minimize not either one of these factors, but the product of the two.

Guideline 8.1	**The Workload Principle: Minimize the total processing load**

To minimize total processing load for a workload composed of a number of separate components, minimize the sum across all workload components of **execution frequency** times **cost per execution**.

On the surface, this rule may seem so simple as to be an obvious checklist item for the software designer. It is worth some attention, however, because the formula for total cost brings some important points to light:

▶ Unit cost, or cost per execution, is the starting point of all cost.
▶ We should be alert to trade-off possibilities between unit cost and execution frequency.
▶ In practice, execution frequency tends to dominate the calculation of total workload.
▶ We should use total workload costs to prioritize our design and tuning efforts.
▶ Knowing the workload quantitatively is key to applying the workload principle.

We discuss these points in turn in the sections that follow.

Minimizing Unit Costs

Miss Morgan, my elementary teacher in Wales, devoted her life to giving her charges a well-rounded education. Not content with the daily routine of reading, writing, and arithmetic, she drilled us regularly on the traditional English proverbs. I must have been particularly receptive to these nuggets of encapsulated wisdom because, more than 40 years later, I can still recall many of the sayings I first learned from Miss Morgan.

One of these was *Look after the pence, and the pounds will look after themselves.* (Pounds, shillings, and pence were the currency units in Britain at that time; shillings were later eliminated.) This proverb is surprisingly relevant to computer performance: It reminds us that unit cost, or cost per execution, is the starting point of all cost. Look after module costs, and application costs will look after themselves. Look after application costs, and system capacity will look after itself. Drive down the unit cost of any process or component, and the total processing cost will go down proportionately. Minimize the unit cost, and we minimize the total cost.

Guideline 8.2	**Maximize performance by minimizing unit cost**

Unit cost, or cost per execution, is the starting point of all cost. Optimal performance begins with minimal unit cost.

In Chapter 7, we introduced the *Simplicity* Principle—see *"Keep it Clean and Simple."* Following that fundamental principle of good software engineering will also pay performance dividends, one of those happy situations in which the objectives of logical and physical design coincide. We can aim for simplicity at two distinct levels:

► **First, simplify the applications.** We can reduce the unit costs by eliminating excess code from our applications as a whole. We discuss this in the next section *Weeding Out Unnecessary Features.*

► **Second, simplify the code.** Various optimization techniques can reduce the unit costs of those parts of the application that remain. We discuss this a bit later, in the section *Tuning for Simplicity and Efficiency.*

Weeding Out Unnecessary Features

Most books on software engineering approach this topic from a project management point of view, focusing on the impact of shifting requirements on the development schedule. For example, Johnson, Skoglund, and Wisniewski advise that *"new wants and wishes must be constantly evaluated under the closest scrutiny."*[1] Based on their discussion, here are ten important questions to ask when choosing whether to implement any new feature:

1. Do the end users really require it (is it a need, a want, or a wish)? To find out, ask "What would happen if we left this feature out?"
2. What impact will it have on future versions or releases of the system?
3. How difficult will it be to implement?
4. Will it make it easier or harder to implement other requirements or the rest of the system?
5. Can we implement the requirement effectively by reusing something we have already built?
6. Is this function already available in a well-designed, off-the-shelf component?
7. What effect would it have on the current design or implementation?
8. How will it affect development system resources and performance during development?
9. How will it affect the users' system resources and performance once it's in production?
10. What will be the schedule impact?

Steve McConnell advises *"Make sure everyone knows the cost of requirements changes."* He offers some amusing insights on the psychology of feature creep and how to handle it:

> Clients get excited when they think of a new feature. In their excitement, their blood thins and runs to their medulla oblongata and they

---

[1] Jay Johnson, Rod Skoglund, and Joe Wisniewski, *Program Smarter, Not Harder* (New York, NY: McGraw Hill, 1995), 53.

become giddy, forgetting all those meetings you had to discuss requirements, the signing ceremony, and the completed requirements document. The easiest way to handle such feature-intoxicated people is to say, "Gee, that sounds like a great idea. I'll work up a revised schedule and cost estimate so that you can decide whether you want to do it now or later." The words "schedule" and "cost" are more sobering than coffee and a cold shower, and many "must haves" quickly turn into "nice to haves."[2]

Narrowing our focus to the performance aspects of the decision, we recall our discussion of the SPE activities in Part II of the book. Guideline 5.3, *"Objectives define performance,"* points out that *"Unless we have an objective, we can never have a performance problem."* Guideline 4.9, *"The Centering Principle,"* reminds us to focus on minimizing the processing costs of the dominant workload components. Following this line of reasoning, we can take the questions we noted in our earlier discussion of service-level agreements in Chapter 5, together with those in the list above, and refine them to create a new list of five performance questions we should always ask before adding any requirement to the list:

1. **What** are the business purpose of this feature and the business benefit of adding it?
2. **When** will the business events occur that cause this feature to be used?
3. **How often** will those business events occur, and what would be the consequences of not adding this feature to support them?
4. **Which** additional computing resources (processor, disk, memory, network) will be needed to support this feature?
5. **How much** computing resources will this feature consume each time it is used?

The time to ask these questions is when we understand how the computer will handle a particular business situation. When the processing appears to be particularly complicated, pause for a sanity check. Ask the final question:

6. **But would we really want the computer to do that?**
   Often, even if code could be written to take care of a certain complex business situation, there must still be a human in the loop, making decisions, somewhere. In that case, we should let the machine and the human each do what they do best. Computers are great at handling lots of routine "pa-

---

[2]Steve McConnell, *Code Complete* (Redmond, WA: Microsoft Press, 1993), 31.

per shuffling" and "number crunching" rapidly and without error. Humans are good at making judgments and decomposing large complex problems into several smaller, simpler ones. If we recognize that business always depends on the combination of these two skills, then we will build smaller, better, more efficient systems.

Guideline 8.3	**Improve performance by eliminating feature creep**

Systematically weeding out unnecessary features is one of the most effective ways to improve the performance of any system. As an added bonus, the code will be available sooner, have fewer bugs, and be easier to maintain.

Tuning for Simplicity and Efficiency

Having pared down our application to its most essential features, we must work on optimizing what remains. Although the effect of a particular tuning action will vary depending on the hardware and software environment, some general principles apply widely. Addressing code tuning, Dowd's *High Performance Computing*[3] includes chapters on:

▶ Eliminating clutter
▶ Loop optimizations
▶ Memory reference optimizations

Later, we explain some of the applications of each of these techniques. In *Code Complete,* McConnell covers a lot of the same ground in his chapter *Code Tuning Techniques.* Both are useful references, provided you keep in mind the fundamental differences between *high-performance computing* and enterprise client/server systems.

As we explained in the Introduction, high-performance computing deals with the design of hardware and software to perform massive computations rapidly. It focuses on techniques for optimizing the performance of very large programs to produce answers in the shortest possible time. In contrast, our primary interest in client/server computing is in organizing massive amounts of business information in a distributed enterprise so that large numbers of relatively small programs can obtain access to that information in a timely fashion. We originally summarized these differences in the *Introduction,* Table I.1, but we repeat them here as Table 8.1 for convenience.

---

[3]Kevin Dowd, *High Performance Computing* (Sebastapol, CA: O'Reilly & Associates, 1993).

Table 8.1   **Perspectives of Two Computing Genres**

	High-Performance Computing	Enterprise Information Processing
Workload type	Massive computations	Massive amounts of data
Purpose	Answers to problems	Access to information
Program duration	Long running programs	Short transactions
User population	Small, relatively homogeneous	Large, relatively diverse
Response objective	Minimize program run times	Meet business transaction goals

Of course, the statements in the table are generalizations, and—as with any generalization—there are exceptions. For example, certain kinds of *data mining* applications (see Chapter 21) may involve long-running programs and massive amounts of computation. Also, when we focus on the single issue of reducing unit costs, the fact that we can identify general principles signals the presence of some common middle ground. All the same, the table highlights the existence of two distinct computing *genres* with different performance perspectives.

Thanks to these differences, the tuning techniques of high-performance computing are only partially relevant to our subject. Where code tuning is concerned, we must begin by recognizing the important distinguishing characteristics of the enterprise client/server environment. These are:

► Foreign code
► Expensive primitives
► I/O bound applications
► Remote resources
► Dependence on server tuning
► Exception handling

Each of these characteristics has implications for performance tuning that we discuss in the sections that follow.

Foreign Code.   Typically, the vast majority of the code in any enterprise client/server application is *foreign* code. By this we don't mean that it was coded in C++ by converted COBOL programmers in Korea (although these days, anything is possible). We mean that most of the instructions executed by the application were not written by the programmer who coded the core application logic. It is code that got added from the class library, by the compiler, or by the application generator. Or it is part of the operating system, the presentation manager, the DBMS, the transaction manager, or some other middleware component.

Because of the high percentage of foreign code, the benefits of tuning the core application logic alone are likely to be quite small. The real gains come from reducing the use of system functions or altering the way the application uses those functions.

Guideline 8.4	Focus on the foreign code

In any client/server application, only a small fraction of time is spent processing core application logic. Most significant performance gains will come from altering the way the application uses system functions.

There is another side to this issue. When we develop enterprise client/server systems, we have no choice but to build on top of general-purpose systems software functions supplied by software vendors. This places a premium on performance tuning by the vendor:

► Unless the software vendor supplies performance specifications with the software, the only way we can assess its performance characteristics is by conducting controlled measurements or benchmarks.
► Unless the vendor supplies performance usage guidelines, the only way to find out if the software will suit our requirements is by asking other users or by demanding a trial before buying.
► Unless the vendor supplies tuning knobs, there is probably no way to adjust the software's behavior to match a specific workload.

Guideline 8.5	Unit costs and performance claims by software vendors

Assess the performance characteristics of all general-purpose software *before* depending on it to perform acceptably in any application or system. Be especially careful with any technology that isn't offered with performance specifications, performance guidelines, and performance tuning options.

If a software vendor makes no claims about performance or gives vague answers to precise questions, expect its software to perform poorly. Vendors whose software is designed with performance in mind will *always* use that information when marketing their product.

Expensive Primitives.   Sessions, processes, threads, transactions, messages, RPCs, I/O operations, SQL requests, and so on—these are the fundamental building blocks of information processing systems. In *Transaction Processing:*

Concepts and Techniques, Gray and Reuter point out that these software primitives are *expensive* operations. Not only are they expensive, but some are orders of magnitude *more expensive* than others.[4]

Figure 8.1 is based on a chart originally published by Gray and Reuter in *Transaction Processing Concepts.* On the top, it shows the approximate instruction costs of major operating system, transaction processing, and database operations. On the bottom, these costs are converted to microseconds on a 10-MIPS processor (1 second = 1000 milliseconds). The figure also shows, for comparison purposes, the typical service times of disks, LANs, and WANs.

Clearly, applying the Centering Principle (recall Chapter 5), we can expect to get the maximum performance gains if we focus our tuning efforts on cutting back an application's use of the most expensive primitive operations.

> **Guideline 8.6   Focus on expensive primitives**
>
> The basic primitives of transaction processing systems are *expensive* operations, and some are orders of magnitude *more expensive* than others. For the maximum performance gains, we must focus our tuning efforts on cutting back use of the most expensive primitive operations.

I/O Bound Applications.   Enterprise client/server applications tend to be I/O bound. That is, their speed is mostly limited by the speed of their data input and output operations, not that of the processor. Therefore, as we discussed in Chapter 3 when we introduced the various system resources and the subject of bottlenecks, tuning the code alone may make minimal difference to application responsiveness, although it will help overall throughput.

Figure 8.1 shows that I/O operations are orders of magnitude *slower* than processor operations. Figure 8.1 illustrates the fact that I/O operations also *consume* large numbers of instructions. As a result, any tuning that reduces

> **Guideline 8.7   Focus on I/O operations**
>
> Enterprise client/server applications tend to be I/O bound. I/O operations are orders of magnitude *slower* than processor operations and *consume* large numbers of instructions. Tuning that reduces I/O, especially on a shared server, will improve both application response times and overall throughput.

---

[4]Jim Gray and Andreas Reuter, *Transaction Processing: Concepts and Techniques* (San Mateo, CA: Morgan Kaufmann, 1993), 79.

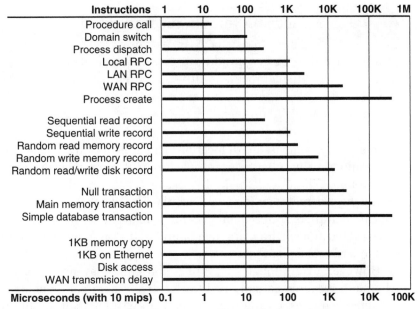

FIGURE 8.1   Comparative performance of typical operations.

I/O, especially on a shared server, will improve both the individual application response time and the overall throughput of the system.

Because I/O operations of all kinds are so expensive, *data compression* may be a viable tuning technique. Compression reduces the quantity of data to be moved and, therefore, the time and instructions required to store and retrieve data from disk or across a network. Provided that there is sufficient data movement to justify the cost of the compression and decompression processes, data compression techniques can lower the unit cost of an application. We discuss data compression in more detail in Chapter 11, *The Sharing Principle.*

Guideline 8.8	**Consider using data compression to reduce unit costs**

Data compression uses processing resources but reduces the quantity of data and, therefore, the time and instructions required to store and retrieve data from disk or across a network.

Remote Resources.   Because we are developing for a distributed environment, our development tools and middleware products may isolate the pro-

> **Guideline 8.9 Focus on remote resources**
>
> Tuning must focus primarily on access to remote resources. There are orders of magnitude differences between the typical instruction cost of dispatching a process locally, on a LAN server, and on a WAN server. Similar ratios apply to data transfer times from local memory, from a LAN server, or from a WAN server.

grammer from some issues of location. This is especially true when we develop applications using client/server development tools that support *application partitioning*. These tools make life easier for the application programmer by letting the program refer to resources (like files, databases, or procedures) using logical identifiers. Subsequent resource placement decisions determine the physical locations, which are then bound to the program through the operation of standard system components.

However, even though the application code may not need to distinguish whether a resource actually resides locally, system components must handle the reference at execution time. And there will be a substantial performance penalty every time those system components receive references to remote resources. Figure 8.1 illustrates the dramatic difference between the typical instruction cost of dispatching a local process (a few hundred), a LAN RPC (a few thousand), and a WAN RPC (tens of thousands). It also shows the orders of magnitude differences in the time required to read data from local memory, a LAN server, or a WAN server. Therefore, to be effective, tuning must take the actual resource locations into account.

Dependence on Server Tuning.   In a client/server environment, the client workstation is dedicated to the needs of its single user and typically has spare processing capacity. The server's resources, meanwhile, are shared by all of its clients. Any client workstation running a poorly tuned application can affect the performance of the whole system. Therefore, there is significantly more opportunity to improve performance by tuning the parts of an application that will run on a shared server.

> **Guideline 8.10 Focus on the server component of an application**
>
> Workstation resources are dedicated to the client application components, but all applications must share server resources. Therefore, tuning the parts of an application that will run on a shared server offers significantly better prospects for improving performance.

Guideline 8.11	Monitor performance as the client population grows

If performance is about the same regardless of the number of users, tune the client side of the application. If performance degrades as more users are added, tune the server side. (Note: This guideline assumes that other variables like database sizes remain approximately constant.)

Exception Handling.   The typical information processing application is like a professional golfer playing the local club course. Although in theory there are hundreds of possible variations, most balls actually fly straight down the middle of the fairway. The application logic follows a well-trodden path from tee to green, needing only the driver, 7-iron, and putter to complete its work. Most of the modules, like the other clubs, stay in the bag. They are there only to deal with exception conditions, ready for the rare occasions when the ball lands in a bunker or behind a tree.

In Chapter 4, we introduced the Centering Principle: *Think globally, focus locally.* It reminds us to identify the dominant workload functions and minimize their processing. When tuning, applying this rule reminds us to focus our efforts on the application's mainline path. If we don't apply the centering principle, we can waste a lot of effort refining the design of components that are rarely used and not performance critical.

Guideline 8.12	Focus on the mainline path

Most application code is rarely used, it exists only to deal with exception conditions. If we do not apply the Centering Principle, we can waste a lot of effort tuning components that are not performance critical.

Eliminating Clutter

In *High Performance Computing,* Dowd defines clutter as *anything that contributes to the run time without contributing to the answer.*[5] He goes on to discuss the overhead costs of subroutine calls, indirect memory references, tests within loops, wordy tests, type conversions, and variables preserved unnecessarily. Three of these items have particular relevance for enterprise client/server systems: subroutine calls, type conversions, and data preserved unnecessarily.

---

[5]Dowd, *High Performance Computing,* 165.

Subroutine Calls.   A few local subroutine calls are harmless enough. *Taligent's Guide to Designing Programs* discusses the trade-off between putting code in a subroutine and moving it inline.[6] It points out that putting a routine inline may increase program size because of the duplication involved. If, as a result, some code gets paged out to disk, performance may well decrease. It estimates that: *One extra trip to the disk costs around 2000 subroutine calls (the faster the processor, the more it costs).* By the same token, remote procedure calls are a lot more expensive than local subroutines, as we noted earlier in the section *Remote Resources.*

With object-oriented development, a common cause of excessive overhead is the use of object inheritance. In most object-oriented environments, inheritance is not free; it has an associated performance cost. It takes time for the software to allocate the necessary memory and create an instance of a derived object class, before that instance can be used. Each time we construct or destruct an object, the object we inherit from must be constructed or destructed.

Unfortunately, developers inexperienced with object orientation often approach inheritance as a sign of membership in the OO fraternity. They have a tendency to overgeneralize, creating class inheritance hierarchies that are seven levels or more deep. Since most of an application's work is handled by instances of objects at the lowest level of the hierarchy, such deep hierarchies generate a lot of overhead processing.

The problem of inheritance overhead is compounded when applications share a class library that resides on a remote server. Then, to support inheritance the software must not only perform additional processing, it must also fetch all the "parent" object structures from the remote server whenever a new instance is created. We discuss this further in Chapter 9, *The Efficiency Principle.*

To minimize module-calling overhead, flatten module or inheritance hierarchies by merging called modules into the calling module or subclasses into the superclass.

Guideline 8.13	**Flatten module hierarchies to reduce overhead**

Modularization carries a performance penalty. Making calls to subroutines or inheriting from a superclass involves additional processing that can be eliminated by merging called modules into the calling module or subclasses into the superclass.

---

[6]*Taligent's Guide to Designing Programs* (Reading, MA: Addison-Wesley, 1994), 64.

Type Conversions. Any time an operation must manipulate two variables of differing types, one (or both) will be usually be converted under the covers. And in a distributed environment, any time data is passed between software components, there is a good chance that some form of data type conversion will take place. The following scenario is entirely possible:

▶ A data item called *busy* is stored by a server DBMS as an integer.
▶ The DBMS converts *busy* to a floating-point number so that it can be passed to a DBMS stored procedure that was designed to manipulate *busy data* of any precision.
▶ The stored procedure creates a *busy table,* comprising a set of busy values with a common decimal precision, to be passed to an application server.
▶ The application server creates an EBCDIC character version of the *busy table* that can be displayed or used as needed by any one of several client applications.
▶ Client/server middleware converts the *busy table* from EBCDIC characters to a *busy data stream* in an encoded form that can be transmitted over the network.
▶ Client software converts the *busy data stream* to an ASCII formatted *busy table* that can be displayed locally in the client environment.
▶ Client application code reads the numeric part of the *busy table* and calls a standard conversion routine that creates a numeric array, producing a set of floating-point *busy data.*
▶ The client application stores this *busy data* in a local table, in a column named *busy* that is defined as integer data type.
▶ The client database software converts the floating-point *busy data* to integers and stores them in the *busy* column.

In this example, some of these conversions are probably necessary and some may be useful. But most are simply wasted overhead. And, of course, any standard routines that perform conversions must do so with the maximum possible precision, probably more than required by the applications most of the time. In practice, most data type conversions are the result of poor design, poor communication, or a failure to create enterprise-wide standards for data representation.

> **Guideline 8.14 Minimize data type conversion overheads**
> Creating and following corporate standards for data representation can minimize the overheads of unnecessary data type conversion as data flows among the components of an enterprise client/server environment.

Data Preserved Unnecessarily.   If we want to make our code run at blazing speed, we could look at how our code assigns and preserves variables across modules and subroutine calls and save a few instructions and some computer memory by scrubbing our code until every wasted byte is eliminated. In the distributed world, as we pointed out earlier, most programs are I/O bound and the real performance gains come from reducing our use of I/O and remote resources.

In a distributed application, the equivalent place to look for savings is excess data being sent or retrieved from a server. This is a very common type of clutter in database and other intensive applications; it comes in four principal flavors.

The first is database requests that retrieve more *columns* than the program really needs. A common example of this is asking for an entire row from a relational database, instead of just the columns needed. In many other DBMSs, especially those that predate relational, the fundamental unit of data for the DBMS was the record or row. Apart from the record's key or unique identifier, it was not until a data record arrived in the program that anyone much cared about what was inside. Perhaps because of this record-oriented mentality, programmers sometimes code the SQL command SELECT * without realizing just how much more it will cost to process. In a relational DBMS, once a row is located, most of the subsequent processing deals with individual columns. The more columns an application asks for, the more it costs the DBMS to extract them and hand them back. Of course, network and memory allocation costs are also roughly proportional to the amount of data retrieved.

Next, programs retrieve more *rows* than the user needs. Examples of this are application specific, but one common pattern is retrieving too much detail. In many applications, the user needs to focus on a small subset of the data at first. Then, in some cases—but not all—the user needs to look at the next level of detail. Any time the application combines this two-stage usage scenario into a single database retrieval operation, a lot of data is sent to the user's workstation but never used. In these situations, we should weigh the cost of a little more application logic against the obvious performance savings. Another application pattern that creates excess data transmission is doing screening in the application that could have been accomplished by sending additional selection criteria to the DBMS. This pattern may be most common in programs written by developers experienced in working with file systems or nonrelational DBMSs, which provided fewer options for screening in the data manipulation language.

Our third category of clutter is performing data-intensive aggregation on the client that could have been done by the server. Any application program that joins data from separate tables or databases "manually," when the work could have been done by the DBMS, incurs a lot of unnecessary overhead transferring data to the program. The same is true of applications that compute statistics like averages, minimum or maximum values, subtotals, and totals when these could have been computed by the DBMS. And for relational databases, there is another whole class of more complex queries that actually can be done using SQL, but for which the SQL technique may not be apparent to an inexperienced programmer. For the programmer who wants to learn more about advanced SQL we recommend Joe Celco's *SQL for Smarties.*[7]

Finally, the client components of poorly designed applications may repeatedly retrieve (or be sent) *the same data.* Web-enabled applications using the *publish/subscribe* (or "push") style of messaging—see Chapter 15 for more details—are especially prone to this problem. Imagine the load that could be generated by a corporate information server sending regular updates of a volatile document database to a very large network of employees, or an even larger network of customers. Exemplifying this problem, many companies discouraged or banned the first release of the popular Web application *PointCast Network* because it used too many workstation cycles and generated too much internet traffic.[8] Even a large, intelligent, client-side cache does not solve this problem, because the data is ever changing. As well as caching data on the client, the publish/subscribe software must be smart enough to send only the changed portions.

Reducing these four types of clutter will normally improve both client processing and network data transmission times.

Guideline 8.15	Minimize the data returned to the application program

Many programs read more data than the application really needs. To reduce application costs, eliminate excess rows and columns from database requests, and make full use of built-in DBMS facilities, and when sending (or retrieving) updates to large data items, transmit only the changed portions.

Optimizing Loops

In *High Performance Computing,* Dowd points out that every program of any significance contains loops somewhere; otherwise, it is a very short

---

[7]Joseph Celco, *SQL for Smarties* (San Mateo, CA: Morgan Kaufmann, 1995).
[8]*PCWEEK,* 14(22), June 2, 1997.

running program.[9] Loop optimization involves removing unnecessary work from loops, removing expensive operations from loops, and interchanging nested loops to improve performance. Once again, we can apply these techniques to enterprise client/server systems.

Earlier in this chapter, we noted that many of the system functions and primitive operations of the distributed environment are *very expensive.* We must be especially careful to keep these operations out of loops. Some examples of things that will cause performance problems in loops include:

- ▶ System calls
- ▶ Calls to user-interface functions
- ▶ SQL or other DBMS calls
- ▶ Disk or network input/output operations
- ▶ Traces and logging

Since such a large fraction of a client/server application's time is spent processing *foreign* code, if we really want to reduce unit costs, we must look for loops outside our own application logic.

One obvious place to look is in the database server. A DBMS loops when joining data from separate tables. If several tables are joined frequently, we may be able to reduce the cost of the join by creating a denormalized table that contains some or all of the data of interest. Of course, this technique works only when we can also arrange to keep the new table updated properly. We discuss this subject in more detail in Chapter 19 *Using DBMS Technology,* and Chapter 20, *Using Data Replication.*

Guideline 8.16	**Lower the unit costs of loops**

By their nature, loops are a good place to look for cost savings. Aim to eliminate expensive system primitives from application program loops, and look for areas to reduce looping in system components. Consider database denormalization to lower the cost of frequently executed database joins.

Optimizing Memory Reference Patterns

Because processors are so much faster than any kind of computer memory, the way the processor interacts with memory can have a significant effect on

---

[9]Dowd, *High Performance Computing,* 187.

processor performance. High-performance computing techniques emphasize the importance of minimizing the cost of transferring *program instructions* and *variables* between the processor and random-access memory locations. In information processing, analogous techniques can help applications optimize their use of disk storage and I/O buffers by improving their locality of reference.

This is an area where we must be careful how we apply some of the specific techniques and guidelines of high-performance computing. For example, to minimize the overhead associated with processing nested loops, the high-performance guideline suggests moving the most active loop to the inner position. The number of loop initializations will be one for each iteration of the outer loop, and one for each iteration of the inner loop. To illustrate, we apply this logic to a nested loop join of two tables, *Tminor* having 10 rows and *Tmajor* 10,000 rows. With *Tminor* as the outer table, the overhead would be proportional to $10 + (10 \times 10,000)$, or 100,010. With *Tmajor* outside, the corresponding figure would be $10,000 + (10,000 \times 10)$, or 110,000. This suggests that *Tminor* should be the outer table when joining.

But this does not account for the impact on the database buffer pool or cache. When *Tminor* is in the inner position, all 10 rows will be brought into the cache, and—because they will be continually referenced for each of the 10,000 rows of *Tmajor*—they will remain in the cache while the code reads through *Tmajor*. When *Tmajor* is in the inner position, it will also be brought into the cache the first time its rows are read, but because of its size, by the time the last rows are being read, the first rows may have been flushed out again to make space available for other concurrent applications. Having *Tminor* in the inner position creates better *locality of reference* in the cache. We discuss locality issues in more detail in Chapter 10, and caching in Chapter 14.

Although there may be some additional processing overhead to manage the looping process, putting the *Tminor* in the inner position will minimize the I/O needed to bring the two tables into memory and keep them there. As we noted earlier, I/O savings usually dwarf any extra processing costs. It will also minimize the number of cache pages used, which helps concurrency, because the cache is a shared resource.

Guideline **8.17**	**Improving locality of reference improves performance**

Improving the locality of reference of computer memory and cache or buffers keeps more data available for immediate processing and reduces the overhead costs of input/output operations.

In relational DBMSs, decisions about such matters as the order of table access in a join are made by the DBMS *optimizer* component, largely outside of the programmer's control. But sometimes there are ways to influence an optimizer's decision by the way in which an SQL statement is coded. Generally, we advise proceeding with extreme caution in this area. However, when tests show that an optimizer's own choice of access path for a multitable loop join produces poor performance, influencing the optimizer to place the smaller tables in the inner positions is usually worth a try.

Also, any time an application program must join tables manually, if those tables are of very different sizes, placing the smaller tables in the inner loop positions will optimize performance. Manual joins are sometimes needed when a program reads data from more than one server.

Guideline 8.18	**In a nested loop join, place smaller tables in the inner positions**

When tests show that an optimizer's own choice of access path for a multitable loop join produces poor performance, influencing the optimizer to place the smaller tables in the inner positions may improve performance.

Trading Off Unit Cost and Execution Frequency

The Workload Principle takes on an added significance when the two factors, *execution frequency* and *cost per execution,* are not independent variables.

In practice, the software design process frequently throws up situations in which the two factors are interrelated. Often the relationship is such that we can lower one at the cost of raising the other, and it's not clear which pair of possible values will be better. That is why Connie Smith named her corresponding principle the *Processing versus Frequency Trade-off Principle.*

At issue here is the scope or complexity of a software *unit of work* and the number of times that unit of work is requested. A unit of work in this context is any software element whose size and scope are subject to design, but which, once created, is processed as a whole. Examples include routines, modules, transactions, windows, messages, tables, and objects. The trade-off involves balancing the computing resources needed to process the unit of work against the frequency of use necessary for users to complete their business tasks.

To find the optimal grouping of more granular software elements into units of work, we must play a balancing game. Larger units of work may benefit from economies of scale, offering the possibility of increasing the efficiency of the overall system by reducing the average cost per software element processed. At the same time, a larger unit of work is more likely to include some wasted processing for certain classes of users. Dividing the work into smaller units lets us build finely tailored systems that do just the right amount of processing for each user and no more—but we lose the economies of scale.

For example, Table 8.2 shows five different design choices for a buffer management component that will load display objects into memory for a hypothetical project management application with a graphical user interface. The software designer has the option of loading all the display objects at initialization time (V_1) or loading objects incrementally according to various other strategies (V_2–V_5).

Keep in mind these notes on memory allocation:

1. The example assumes that fixed memory buffers are set aside to store only one group of display objects. The first group of objects is overwritten when the user moves on to a second group and may have to be reloaded later.
2. Obviously, the cost to load a group decreases with its size, but smaller groupings require more frequent calls to refresh the buffers as the user navigates through the application.
3. The table does not show the memory requirements, which will be highest for design V_1 and will decrease progressively for designs V_2 through V_5.
4. In a real system, this simple design could be improved by using some form of object caching, as we discuss later in Chapter 14.

Table 8.2   **Five Hypothetical Strategies for Loading Display Objects**

Component Version	Implementation Strategy for Loading Display Objects	Refresh Calls per Transaction	I/Os per Call	I/Os per Transaction
V_1	Load all objects at initialization	1	1500	1500
V_2	Load objects for each application functional area, when first used	1.5	600	900
V_3	Load objects for each application function, when first used	5	180	900
V_4	Load objects for each logical group of windows, when first used	10	60	600
V_5	Load objects for each window, when used	60	20	1200

For each design, the table shows an estimate of how many times the component will be called on average and how many disk I/Os it will incur on average. In the example, we see that the lowest total cost will be obtained by design choice V_4, in which the application loads all the display objects for a logical group of windows whenever any window in that group is first used. When we perform this kind of analysis, we are applying the Workload Principle.

In Chapter 7, we introduced the idea that *grouping* related software elements is a fundamental technique of software design. Our example illustrates two points:

▶ When considering the performance consequences of any grouping decision, it is important to apply the Workload Principle. Changing the grouping of elements generally changes the bottom-line costs.

▶ The grouping with the best performance is not necessarily the most obvious choice from a logical design perspective. In the example, simpler alternatives (like V_1 and V_5) do not perform as well as V_4.

| Guideline 8.19 | **Logical and physical grouping** |

We should always pay careful attention to the effect our logical grouping decisions will have later on the physical bottom line of total workload processing costs. We may be able to reduce total processing costs by grouping components differently. The best logical grouping will not necessarily be the best physical grouping.

Execution Frequencies Tend to Dominate Total Costs

The formula for total workload is **execution frequency** times **cost per execution**. This is simple and symmetric. In practical terms, however, the two variables do not carry the same weight, as illustrated by an example. Table 8.3 lists the various unit costs for a hypothetical workload comprising seven applications, the most expensive at the top. Table 8.4 lists the corresponding application execution frequencies, the most frequent at the top.

The interested reader may wish to pause for a moment to consider a hypothetical situation in which reports for the combined workload indicated a capacity problem. If you were considering tuning this workload, would your inclination be to start by looking at the workload totals, at the most expensive applications (Table 8.3), or at the most frequently executed applications (Table 8.4)? Why?

Table 8.3   Sample Workload Ordered by I/O Costs

ID	Application Name	I/Os per Transaction
A	Product sales summary	5000
B	Wholesale order processing	200
D	Telephone order handling	30
C	Customer support inquiry	20
G	Telephone special offers	10
E	Retail point of sale recording	5
F	Call center IVR recording	1

Obviously, to answer that question systematically, we would need to compute the information shown in Table 8.5, which summarizes all seven applications and the combined workload for the group. It also shows the I/O rate of each as a percentage of the total. This time, the table is ordered by the hourly I/O rates per application.

Reviewing Table 8.5, we notice the following:

▶ The characteristics of the combined workload are quite different from those of any individual application. Looking at summary reports for the entire workload would be unlikely to help us identify areas for potential performance improvement.

▶ Transactions A and B show that *low execution volumes can neutralize high unit costs.* Although summary reports and processing of large orders are individually expensive, they happen infrequently enough that their total cost is a relatively small percentage of the total.

Table 8.4   Sample Workload Ordered by Frequency

ID	Application Name	Frequency
F	Call center IVR recording	10 per second
E	Retail point of sale recording	1 per second
G	Telephone special offers	30 per minute
D	Telephone order handling	25 per minute
C	Customer support inquiry	10 per minute
B	Wholesale order processing	30 per hour
A	Product sales summary	1 per hour

Table 8.5   **Sample Workload Ordered by Total Costs**

Application	Transaction Rate	Rate/Hour	I/Os per Trans	I/Os per Hour	% of Total
D	25 per minute	1500	30	45,000	32.1%
F	10 per second	36,000	1	36,000	25.7%
E	1 per second	3600	5	18,000	12.9%
G	30 per minute	1800	10	18,000	12.9%
C	10 per minute	600	20	12,000	8.6%
B	1 per minute	30	200	6000	4.3%
A	1 per hour	1	5000	5000	3.6%
Combined	~12 per second	43,531	3.21	140,000	100%

▶ Transactions E and F show that high execution volumes are less likely to be neutralized by low unit cost. Applications that log every user interaction will consume a lot of resources, no matter how careful we are about their unit costs. In this case, E and F together make up almost 40 percent of the workload.

▶ Transactions C, D, and G show that we cannot ignore an application just because it is not the most frequent or individually the most expensive to run. In this case, C consumes more I/O resources than A and B combined, G consumes the same resources as E, and D is the largest workload of all.

Two guidelines summarize the general conclusions we can draw from this discussion:

Focus on High-Volume Applications.   When designing or tuning a collection of programs, it usually pays to look at those with the highest execution frequencies first. This is because for any class of interactive business applications under study, execution frequencies generally exhibit a wider range of values than unit costs. So the most frequently executed programs are likely to represent a sizable percentage of the workload.

Also, while it's probably not cost effective to spend much time working at saving a couple of database I/Os in a routine that's used once a day, it would definitely be worthwhile if the routine were called once per second. If a high workload cost is driven primarily by a high execution frequency, we should always search carefully for unit cost savings because the unit cost of any process becomes more significant the more frequently that process is executed. Even small savings can be important if the process is called often enough.

Once again, recall the Centering Principle from Chapter 4; the Workload Principle helps us focus our attention on the subset of the workload where tuning efforts are most likely to pay dividends.

> ## Guideline 8.20   Focus on high volume applications
>
> If a high workload cost is driven by a high execution frequency, we should always search carefully for unit cost savings because the unit cost of any process becomes more significant the more frequently that process is executed.

Focus on the Bottom Line.   All the same, we must always pay attention to the bottom line. Example application D illustrates exactly what the workload principle is all about. Because big numbers tend to capture our attention, the combination of a program with moderate unit cost being executed at a frequency well below the maximum rate may well escape unnoticed, even though it actually makes up the largest workload on the whole system.

In the course of developing any major system, programmers may write thousands of lines of code and produce hundreds of modules to handle a wide range of business conditions. Applying the Workload Principle helps us focus our attention on the subset that will have the greatest impact on total resource usage; again, recall the Centering Principle from Chapter 4. They may not be the most important from a business viewpoint, or even the most performance-critical, but tuning that subset may have the biggest impact on system parameters like device utilization levels, throughput, and other measures of total capacity.

> ## Guideline 8.21   Focus on the bottom line
>
> The Workload Principle is fundamental to the entire process of performance engineering. Any time the total workload cost is high, there are almost certainly reasons and opportunities for tuning, whether the reason is high frequency, high unit cost, or some combination of the two.

Know the Workload Quantitatively.   To apply the Workload Principle, we must first understand the workload quantitatively. We must look beyond *what* the application is supposed to do, to discover *who* will use it, *why, when, how,* and *how often.* And we must know something about the relative importance of the different application processes or business transactions involved.

What's more, we need this information early on. If we are going to analyze performance trade-offs and apply the Workload Principle during the design phases, then we must have already obtained the necessary usage estimates and priorities during the earlier analysis phase.

These aspects of the workload principle reinforce our earlier discussion of business factors in Chapter 5. Regardless of what kind of development methodology we use, somehow we must capture from the intended users the "functional specifications" for a new software system—the knowledge of how the new system must process information to support the business. And as we seek out and record this knowledge, as software designers we should never be content simply to understand the processing (or "functional") needs alone; we must also obtain what we might call the *quantitative specification*. That is, we must learn how different parts of the processing will relate to business factors like the number of customers needing certain types of service and the expected frequencies of those business activities.

> **Guideline 8.22   Functional specifications must include performance metrics**
>
> Unless we capture usage estimates or performance metrics during the analysis phase, we cannot expect to apply the Workload Principle to make informed design decisions later in the development process.

Applying the Workload Principle

Compared to the other devices in our enterprise environment, communication networks are slow and prone to error. They frequently are the source of performance bottlenecks. The key to improving network performance is for applications to *ship less data* between locations.

Applying the Locality Principle will help us avoid the need for some data transmissions altogether by locating related processes and data together; we discuss this in Chapter 10, in Guideline 10.4. When data and process are already separated and neither can be moved, we need to look carefully at how applications interact with data at remote locations. In this situation, the Workload Principle reminds us to minimize total network loads by minimizing the product of *remote data requests* times *requesting processes*.

Minimizing LAN Activity

First, minimizing LAN activity means designing the LAN-based components of applications to minimize the number of LAN transmissions between client workstation and workgroup server.

In terms of the various two-tier client/server architectures we introduced in Chapter 2, this goal favors the *distributed logic* model over either the *remote presentation* or *remote data access* models. As illustrated in Figure 8.3, net-

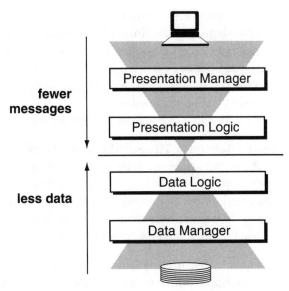

FIGURE 8.3   Volume of interactions between layers.

work traffic is almost certainly minimized when we partition an application within the business logic layer. This is because:

▶ Data selection and summarization activity in the data logic component ensures that not all the data passing between the data management and data logic components needs to flow back to the client.
▶ Much of the information flowing between the presentation logic and presentation manager components relates to screen formatting and application control and flow, which are of no concern to the data logic component.

Guideline 8.23	**Minimize remote data requests using a distributed logic architecture**

Compared to either the *remote presentation* or *remote data access* client/ server architectures, partitioning an application within the business logic layer will minimize network traffic.

Using Stored Procedures

When using client/server DBMS technology (which we discuss in more detail in Chapter 19). DBMS stored procedures are a simple example of the distributed logic architecture. Figure 8.4 illustrates how we can reduce network traffic by using remote stored procedures instead of multiple separate remote SQL requests. The ideal candidate for packaging into a stored procedure is a group of SQL statements that operates on more than one table. For example, several SQL statements making consistent updates to related tables can be grouped together and then invoked as a single procedure.

However, we note some drawbacks of stored procedures.

Longer Perceived Response Times.   Because the entire procedure is a single unit of work, the client application receives no information at all until the entire procedure completes. Therefore, the application has no opportunity to interact with the user before the procedure completes. Although this may or may not extend the *effective response time* of the application as defined in Chapter 3, it may increase the *perceived response time* beyond that which is acceptable.

No Second Chance.   Because the stored procedure is a single unit of work, the application has no opportunity to let the user to change his or her mind about

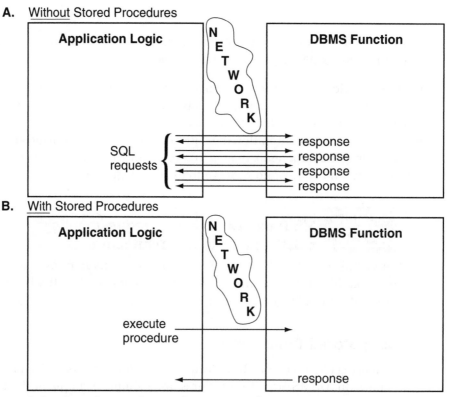

FIGURE 8.4   Stored procedure reduces network activity.

the requested action, based on early feedback from the first interaction with the database.

For many applications, an uninterruptible procedure may be a good thing. As in the example of consistent updates to related tables that we gave earlier, we want the DBMS to *ensure* that the entire procedure completes or fails as a single *atomic,* or indivisible, *transaction.* Securing this property for a group of related updates is one of the benefits we obtain from DBMS-controlled procedures. We will return to the subject of transactions in more detail in Part IV of the book and in Chapter 22, *Transaction Managers and Transaction Monitors.*

But suppose a procedure has a form like these:

▶ *For every X in the database, perform operations a, b, c, ...*
▶ *Locate Y and perform a, b, c, . . . against every related X.*

The user may actually be surprised by the result of the initial scan for occurrences of *X.* Maybe, upon seeing that there are 1000 instances of *X,* or alternatively none at all, the user may question the correctness of the transaction and opt to do some more research first. Therefore, applications that use stored procedures should be designed to give user feedback describing all of the actions taken by the procedure.

Ideally, the intended scope of the action should be discovered and presented to the user for confirmation *before* invoking the update actions. However, to provide this type of feedback and confirmation, an application may need to incur extra database interactions, reading the database once to report on its intentions and then a second time to carry them out. This additional activity creates a safer application but reduces the overall gains obtained by using a stored procedure.

The Workload Principle must be applied to the entire application, with and without the stored procedure.

Guideline 8.24	**Use stored database procedures**

Replacing a group of SQL requests by a DBMS stored procedure will reduce traffic on the network, but it may increase perceived response times. Also, some additional database activity may be required to confirm changes.

Minimizing WAN Activity

In the three-tier environment, we can reduce WAN traffic and improve client response times for frequently used enterprise data by distributing copies or fragments of the shared tables out to the workgroup server level. This is one of the principles behind systematic data replication technology (which we discuss in Chapter 20). For frequently used data, systematic replication can minimize the volume of WAN data transmissions between the enterprise and workgroup servers in support of LAN-based applications.

> **Guideline 8.25   Replicate frequently used enterprise data**
>
> In the three-tier environment, we can reduce WAN traffic and improve client response times for frequently used enterprise data by distributing copies or fragments of the shared tables out to the workgroup server level.

However, when considering data replication, we must not forget that the process of replicating data from an enterprise server to one or more workgroup servers will consume additional WAN resources. So the Workload Principle must be applied to the combination of the information processing workload *and* the replication activity. If data is referenced only lightly, it may be considerably more costly to replicate it than to forward occasional remote requests to the enterprise server.

Complicating matters, the decision can rarely be reduced to simple computations of overall cost. Other objectives and concerns must be taken into account, too. These include the response time objectives of the data retrieval applications and the availability of enterprise data in a suitable format for client processing.

Sometimes the replication activity is part of a scheme to create department-level *data warehouses* or *data marts* (which we discuss in Chapter 21). In that case, the organization may be willing to incur additional WAN costs to create the warehouse or data mart because of the benefits to the business of having the right data available in the right format at the right location.

> **Guideline 8.26   Weigh replication savings and costs**
>
> Although replicating frequently used enterprise data can reduce WAN traffic by applications, the replication process itself consumes additional WAN resources. The Workload Principle must be applied to the combination of the information processing workload *and* the replication activity.

Conclusion: Make the Machine a Partner

During my career in the Performance Department of IBM's Santa Teresa Laboratory, I was fortunate enough to work with Valdo Androsciani, author of the first-ever software performance monitor at IBM in the late 1960s, and a first-rate software engineer. "Software is wonderful stuff!" Valdo used to say. "You can do *anything* with software, except make pasta and coffee." (Valdo, as you may have guessed, is Italian). "But . . .," he would continue, ". . . just because something *can* be done doesn't necessarily mean that it *should* be done."

This is an important insight to bring to the design process. Sometimes designers create overly complex computer systems because they incorrectly assume that the system should be made to take care of every possible problem automatically. The result is an overengineered system that is not flexible enough to adapt to evolving business needs, yet performs poorly into the bargain. The most useful computer systems are the ones that don't try to take over the whole job. So design systems that:

▶ Let the machine do what it does best—rapid, routine, repetitive drudgery.
▶ Free the user to think, judge, and make decisions.
▶ Simplify the processing by keeping the human in the loop.

If we recognize from the outset that the computer is simply a useful business tool, but one that can never entirely displace the role of human knowledge and judgment, then we are freed to create simpler, more flexible, and better-performing systems.

CHAPTER 9

The Efficiency Principle

"First design software that works, then optimize your design."

Greg Faust

In This Chapter . . .

Computing is like cooking. Before we can cook anything, we have to shop for the ingredients and assemble all the pots, pans, bowls, and mixing tools we'll need to do the work. Afterward, we must clean up and put everything away. It's the same with computing. Whenever we want to compute anything, we must first incur a setup cost to organize the work—collecting the data to be processed and creating the processing environment—before we can actually do the work. Afterward, there's usually a corresponding tear-down cost.

Although it's unavoidable, the preparation and cleanup work is really just overhead. Doubling the preparation will not add to the amount of useful work accomplished. To maximize efficiency, we aim to reduce these overhead costs to a minimum. One way to do that is to capitalize on the fact that software is inherently repetitive. It is a very rare program that runs only once, performing a single action on a single object; most programs do the same things over and over again. Sometimes we perform multiple operations on a single object or set of objects. Other situations require the same sequence of actions to be performed on every object.

Whenever we have to do the same thing many times over, we can usually eliminate most of the repeated overheads. Cooking pancakes for six people does not take six times as long as cooking for one, even though we have to cook six times as many pancakes, because we only need to prepare and clean up once. Similarly, to maximize computing efficiency, we aim to go through the setup processes once and then retain the working environment for as long as possible to avoid incurring the same setup costs again.

The Efficiency Principle: Some Examples

Software is a malleable medium. As Fred Brooks wrote in *The Mythical Man Month*, "The programmer, like the poet, works only slightly removed from pure thought-stuff."[1] There are many different ways to accomplish any result, some more efficient than others. This is the subject of our second SPE design principle, the *Efficiency Principle*. This principle (which might also be called the *overhead* principle) states that *the most efficient design is the one that maximizes the ratio of useful work to overhead.*

Eliminating repeated setup costs is probably the most effective way to reduce overhead. Dennis Shasha (in *Database Tuning: A Principled Approach*) captures this idea succinctly in his statement: *"Startup costs are high, running costs are low."*[2] In a broader sense, however, the Efficiency Principle applies to anything we do to increase the ratio of useful work to overhead.

Guideline 9.1	**The Efficiency Principle**
	The most efficient design is the one that maximizes the ratio of useful work to overhead.

In fact, the Efficiency Principle lies behind many familiar techniques for improving performance, such as indexing, blocking, and caching. Table 9.1 lists many computing situations in which we apply the Efficiency Principle.

► The first two columns in the table identify a category of processing and a particular example of work to be performed in that category.

---

[1]Fred Brooks, *The Mythical Man Month* (Reading, MA: Addison-Wesley, 1975 and 1995), 7.
[2]Dennis E. Shasha, *Database Tuning: A Principled Approach* (Upper Saddle River, NJ: Prentice-Hall, 1992), 2.

Table 9.1 **Applying the Efficiency Principle**

Category	Work to Be Performed	Overhead Processing	Efficiency Techniques
User interface	Enter data for processing by an application	Selecting objects and related actions	Use fixed format data entry dialogs, forms
Processing	Execute machine instructions	Compiling high-level language instructions	Use compiled executable modules
	Execute a program procedure	Making a remote procedure call	Use a local procedure
	Execute SQL database manipulation statement	Optimizing (selecting the optimal database access path)	Use static (bound) SQL packages
	Inherit properties of a superclass object	Locating the object superclass and its properties	Use static (compiled) inheritance
	Execute object-oriented methods or procedures	Interobject messaging, method invocations	Use larger object granularity, inline methods
	Use data in computations	Coverting stored data types to match	Design stored data to use matching data types

Data retrieval	Read desired data from the database	Searching for and locate the data in the database	Use indexes, hashing, pointers
	Locate a data item based on multiple search criteria	Dynamically combining data from multiple indexes	Build a static multicolumn index
	Use stored reference data in an application	Reading from a reference table stored on disk	Load reference data into a cache in memory
	Use a remotely located reference table	Fetching table contents from remote location	Store a copy of the table locally
	Use data stored in tables in an object-oriented program	Dynamically converting from relational tables into objects	Store data in an ODBMS
Data manipulation	Process related data in an application	Joining related data tables	Denormalize tables
	Use summary data in an application	Computing data summaries, averages, totals	Precompute summary tables
	Process data sequentially	Sorting data into sequence	Order or cluster the database
	Process data in a remote database	Shipping data manipulation statements to the database	Use remote stored database procedures
Data transmission	Transmit data over a network link	Handling data transmission and receipt activity	Ship data in larger blocks
	Process multiple rows from a remote database	Network transmission overhead per row	Fetch data in blocks, not one row at a time

▶ The third column shows a corresponding class of overhead processing.

▶ The final column shows a technique we might use to increases the ratio of useful work to overhead in each case.

Fixing Point: Early versus Late Grouping

In Chapter 7, we defined the physical technique of *grouping* very generally, to cover any situation in which connections are established between separate computing elements or components (hardware or software, data or process) for the purpose of performing a task. When discussing the relationship of SPE to software design, we highlighted the importance of grouping techniques in both logical and physical software design. Performance depends particularly on two aspects of grouping:

▶ *Which* objects are grouped together
▶ *When* the grouping is done

In Chapter 10, *The Locality Principle,* we discuss the question of how best to select which particular object instances should be grouped. Here we consider the timing of the grouping action. In *Performance Engineering of Software Systems,* Connie Smith uses the term *Fixing* to mean much the same as our *grouping* notion—the action of creating a relationship between two or more computing elements to produce a desired result. The *Fixing Point* is the moment at which the relationship is established.[3]

Smith's *Fixing-Point Principle* states, "*For responsiveness, establish connections at the earliest feasible point in time, such that retaining the connection is cost-effective.*" This principle falls in line with our comments about the repetitiveness of many software tasks and the opportunities for reducing the overheads of setup processing. Relatively static grouping schemes in which the grouping of elements persists for a longer period are likely to reduce overhead costs by comparison with more dynamic alternatives.

Guideline 9.2	**Fixing relationships increases efficiency**

When a set of computing elements (hardware or software, data or process) is used together more than once, a design involving static grouping of those elements will reduce overhead costs by comparison with more dynamic alternatives.

---

[3]Connie U. Smith, *Performance Engineering of Software Systems* (Reading, MA: Addison-Wesley, 1990), 40.

Grouping: A Classification Scheme

In Table 9.2, we list many examples of component groups. We have divided the examples into four classes, using two criteria:

▶ Whether the grouping action creates an aggregate object from components drawn from a single class of object instances (*similar components*) or connects components of different types (*dissimilar components*).
▶ Whether the grouping action takes place early or late, with respect to the time when the aggregate is actually required to exist for processing purposes.

In attempting to name these four classes, we run into the usual confusion of overlapping and imprecise computing terminology. We have selected four

Table 9.2   Examples of Component Groups: Four Classes

Fixing Point	Groups of Similar Components	Groups of Dissimilar Components
Early	**AGGREGATE**	**BIND**
	Software modules	Objects
	Fields in data records	Database stored procedures
	Columns in table rows	Static (compiled) DBMS access
	Denormalized tables	modules
	Data warehouse summaries,	Compiled programs
	aggregates	Distributed database schema
	Fixed menus and user dialogs	OLAP/multidimensional software
	Database physical pages or blocks	Special-purpose hardware
	Database physical clustering	*Database machines*

Fixing Point	Groups of Similar Components	Groups of Dissimilar Components
Late	**COLLECT**	**ASSOCIATE**
	Disk I/O blocking	Interpreted languages
	Communications message blocking	Distributed objects
	In memory cache or buffer pool	Dynamic inheritance
	Dynamic query result tables	DBMS dynamic access path selection
	Dynamic database views	Multidatabase gateways
	Dynamic sorting of results data	OO/Relational mapping middleware
	General-purpose GUIs	General-purpose hardware

verbs whose meanings seem to come the closest to the four types of grouping we have in mind:

▶ **Aggregate.**   To group similar objects into a static aggregate object, prior to execution time.

▶ **Collect.**   To gather similar objects together dynamically during program execution.

▶ **Bind.**   To create a static relationship between dissimilar components, prior to program execution.

▶ **Associate.**   To create a temporary relationship between dissimilar components, during program execution.

In the next four sections of the chapter, we consider how the Efficiency Principle applies to selected examples of all four types of grouping activity.

Aggregating Similar Components

An aggregate is a *static* object structure created by grouping *similar* objects prior to execution time. In this section, we review two areas of software design—user interface design and database design—where we can often increase efficiency by creating aggregate structures that support repetitive usage patterns.

User Interfaces

There has been a great deal of focus in recent years on the advantages of graphical user interfaces (*GUIs*) and object-oriented user interfaces (*OOUIs*) that allow a user to point and click on any object or perform any function in any desired sequence. Chiefly, these advantages center on the added flexibility they afford users to carry out their work in the most convenient way. When an application involves performing a series of repetitive tasks—constantly dealing with the same type of data and performing the same business functions—the user interface should consist of fixed windows, menus, and dialog boxes and should require the minimum of navigation.

When all a user wants to do is perform a fixed set of actions with a specific set of objects, any additional navigation or object selection is just unnecessary overhead. Because users spend a great deal of time working with the application interface, the Centering Principle (which we discussed in Chapter 4) suggests that if we want to tune the application, then improving the UI is a good place to start. In fact, just by streamlining the interface, we can significantly improve the *perceived response time* of the application without tuning any other part of the application code.

> **Guideline 9.3** **Create fixed interfaces for repetitive tasks**
> When an application involves a series of repetitive tasks, the user interface should consist of fixed windows, menus, and dialog boxes and require a minimum of navigation. Streamlining the interface alone can significantly improve the perceived response time of such an application.

Database Design and Denormalization

Logical database design emphasizes the benefits of normalization. A database in which each fact is stored once, and once only, uses storage efficiently and minimizes the chance of applications storing inconsistent data. Normalized database designs are also flexible designs, making the data available in a form convenient for processing by future applications, whatever they may be. These are very important goals.

But, there is a trade-off. Normalization involves separating each distinct entity or object class into a separate table, producing designs with many smaller tables that applications must interconnect (or *join,* in relational database terminology) to retrieve all the related data they need to process. From an application's point of view, joining separate tables to locate the data of interest is just overhead processing that must be done before the useful processing can begin.

If an application needs to repeatedly process related data from multiple separate tables, we may be able to improve its performance by creating a single denormalized table that brings the data of interest together permanently. By joining the separate tables once statically, we eliminate the overhead of performing a join dynamically each and every time the application is run.

Denormalization is an example of a *biasing* technique. Rather than adopt a data storage structure (like that for a normalized relational model), which is neutral with respect to data usage, we choose instead to bias the storage structure in favor of one particular usage pattern. Naturally, the application with this pattern obtains better performance as a result. Depending on the degree of denormalization involved, biasing the storage structure may eliminate the need for many I/Os that would otherwise be required to assemble an object from a collection of normalized tables.

Of course, we should not lightly abandon the advantages of a normalized database design. Generally speaking, we should denormalize only when it's strictly necessary to meet application performance goals. Even then, we have to balance the performance benefits against the consequences for other retrieval and update applications.

Other retrieval applications, with different usage patterns, will not obtain the same benefits. Their target data is now stored in a less compact form because a lot of extraneous data has been interspersed. A DBMS stores and reads data in database pages or blocks, typically 2K or 4K at a time. In a normalized structure, each page contains one type of data only, allowing many rows of that type to be read with a single I/O. To read the same data from a denormalized structure, a program may well be forced to do more I/O to skip over unwanted data. So the performance drops.

One solution is to retain the existing base tables and the existing applications, creating a new denormalized table to support retrieval by only some applications. In this case, we also have to design and implement the programs to maintain that new table by extracting or replicating data. This is the approach usually taken when designing database for decision-support systems (*DSS*) or executive information systems (*EIS*) or when developing a data warehouse (which we discuss next). Often, some delay in propagating updates from the base tables is acceptable for these types of databases. This allows for considerable flexibility in how the updates are handled, as we discuss in Chapter 20, *Using Data Replication.*

If we decide instead to denormalize the base tables, then we must modify the existing update applications accordingly. This might be the appropriate choice if the application retrieving the data needs to see updates immediately. In this case, though, another concern must be handled—denormalizing creates the possibility that our update applications will introduce inconsistencies into the database. In a denormalized database, facts previously recorded in only one object or row are now present in multiple rows. Therefore, the applications must sometimes update data in multiple locations instead of updating the single location required by a normalized design.

Denormalization is a good example of the Efficiency Principle at work (do the join once statically to avoid doing it many times over dynamically), but it does involve making several trade-offs. We should never consider denormalizing until we can answer these three questions:

1. *What will be the effect of denormalization on the performance of other applications?*
2. *How will denormalization affect our ability to meet performance objectives for all applications?*
3. *How will we update the data in the new denormalized table?*

Guideline 9.4	Consider denormalization—and its side effects—carefully

If an operational application must join normalized tables repeatedly, consider creating a denormalized table to eliminate the repeated overhead of the join dynamically. Evaluate these three issues carefully:

What will be the effect of denormalization on the performance of other applications? A denormalized design is biased toward the usage of a particular application and—by implication—away from others.

How will denormalization affect our ability to meet performance objectives for all applications? Denormalize only if other methods of improving performance are not sufficient to meet the objectives.

How will we update the data in the new denormalized table? Before denormalizing, ensure that *all* other applications can be reworked to handle updates correctly without introducing inconsistent data into the database.

Data Warehouses

All databases contain information, but an "informational" database is the term used to describe the counterpart to traditional operational databases. Operational databases contain the raw data used in day-to-day business operations like inventory, order processing, or distribution. The data in informational databases is organized to support executive decision making within a particular segment of the business, like marketing or product line management.

Operational data are the basic facts of the business, organized to support business operations. Informational databases contain subsets of the same data, but enhanced and organized to support the user who needs to see not just the facts, but also the following:

▶ Summaries of the facts (for example, product sales by category by region)
▶ Relationships among the facts (for example, comparing product sales with pricing levels and promotional discounts, by category, by region)
▶ Trends within the facts (for example, product sales by category by month)

The primary motivation for creating informational databases is to put the data into a form more suitable for informational processing. One of the clear benefits we obtain by assembling data into informational databases (or *data marts,* or *data warehouses*) is also increased *efficiency* because we assemble information once and then make it available to a lot of users. Regardless of the particular technology or techniques that we use, when we create an informational database we eliminate the overhead costs of having individual users repeatedly searching for that information in multiple back-end operational databases.

Obviously, the better we are at designing the warehouse—making sure it contains exactly the right combination of data and summaries the users want—the greater these efficiency benefits. Once again, we see how a clear understanding of the user's needs can pay performance dividends.

> **Guideline 9.5** **Denormalize data for informational applications**
> For informational applications, create separate denormalized databases (data marts or data warehouses) organized to support DSS and EIS requirements.

Collecting Similar Components

In this section, we discuss some situations in which we can improve performance by collecting similar objects together dynamically during program execution.

Buffering and Caching

Buffering or caching is a widely used technique for increasing efficiency. When we retain copies of frequently used data or program code in memory, we avoid the overhead of loading it again, either from a local disk or from a remote server. For example:

▶ All DBMSs use this technique to speed up repetitive access to data, particularly for relatively static components of an application that are managed by the DBMS, like stored database procedures, triggers, or previously compiled dynamic SQL statements.

▶ Many Web browsers have a local disk cache that retains copies of recently retrieved HTML and other Web page content. The next time we visit the same Web site, the browser reads from the local cache; if we want to see the latest Web site content we must explicitly tell the browser to refresh our view by reading again from the remote server.

▶ Data warehouses and data marts store precomputed summary data, providing, in effect, a cache of summary data for applications to use. By retrieving this summary data using a relatively inexpensive local disk or network I/O, we eliminate the overhead costs of the complex database queries that would be otherwise needed to compute summary statistics.

We can apply this concept when we build systems. Caching is easiest to implement for static data like reference tables or user profiles. Even for data that is updated, a write-back cache can be created, shipping the updates back to revise the master copy on the server and retaining the updated copy in the local cache at the client. Client/server DBMSs implement this type of caching.

Because caching involves trading local memory for I/O, we discuss it in more detail in Chapter 14, *The Trade-off Principle.*

> ## Guideline 9.6 Cache static or slowly changing data
>
> Whenever the same data must be transferred repeatedly, create a dynamic cache to retain a copy of the data closer to the application that needs it. Caching can be used to eliminate the overhead of retrieving data using disk I/O, network I/O, or even complex database searches.

Blocking and Data Transmission

In a client/server environment, the process of retrieving data from a server database to the client application provides various possibilities for eliminating overhead.

RDBMS Block Fetch. When retrieving large result sets, some fixed overheads are associated with each message sent and received across the network, regardless of its size. These overheads occur in three places:

▶ *Processing* overheads on the *server*
▶ *Data transmission* overheads on the *network*
▶ *Processing* overheads on the *client*

Because these overheads are roughly proportional to the number of messages that pass between the server and the client workstation, sending a result set in larger blocks, rather than one row at a time, reduces the overhead for that result set. Recognizing this, many client/server relational DBMSs allow the DBA to set a tuning parameter that determines the block size to be used when transferring groups of query result rows (the *result set* or *result table*) from the DBMS server to the client requester. This technique is called **block (or blocked) fetch,** or equivalent names like *cursor record blocking.*

If the client application is going to use the entire result set to populate a local object like a table or a spreadsheet, shipping all the data from the server in a small number of large blocks is obviously the ideal technique for optimal client response time and overall system efficiency. A DBMS can actually use the block fetch technique even if the application is written to use an SQL cursor manipulation protocol to process the result set (subject to some trade-offs that we will discuss in a moment). When using cursors, the results of an SQL

SELECT are retrieved and processed by the program one row at a time, through a series of SQL FETCH commands. This works as follows:

▶ The DBMS server first receives and processes the initial SQL SELECT statement that defines the result set.
▶ Because the application is defined as using cursor SQL, the DBMS can anticipate that a succession of SQL FETCH commands will soon follow.
▶ The DBMS server sends the first block of result rows to the client component.
▶ The DBMS client software receives and holds the block of result rows, handing one row to the application in response to each FETCH request received.
▶ Either asynchronously in the background or synchronously when the contents of the first block have all been read by the application, the DBMS client component passes another FETCH request to the server, bringing across the next block of the result set.

Even if the block fetch technique is supported by the DBMS, not all applications using cursor SQL can take advantage of it. If an application also updates or deletes the individual rows retrieved by the FETCH operation, then locking issues come into play. If a program (A) intends to update a row, then once that row is passed to the client, the DBMS must ensure that the same row is not also changed on the server by another concurrent program (B) because B's changes may be lost when A returns an updated row to the server.

Suppose an application uses the SQL processing pattern shown in the following example. (We base SQL examples on SQL-92 syntax; specific products may offer slightly different versions.)

```
DECLARE <cursor> CURSOR FOR
    SELECT <data>
    FROM <table>
    WHERE <selection criteria>
    FOR UPDATE OF <data items>
BEGIN <processing loop for each row>
    FETCH <cursor>
    INTO <program variables>
    . . .
    <process the row>
    . . .
    UPDATE <table>
    SET <update details>
    WHERE CURRENT OF <cursor>
END <processing loop>
```

In this case, the DBMS may decide not to use the block fetch technique, choosing instead to delay retrieval of each row from the database until the corresponding FETCH is actually issued by the program. Delaying retrieval is one way the DBMS can ensure that current data is being retrieved, without locking every row in every block of data passed to the client.

In practice, the DBMS's decision as to whether to use block fetch will depend on three key aspects of the data manipulation request:

► The degree of isolation specified for the application, and the granularity of object locking (for example, row, page, or table locking) used by the DBMS to achieve the requested level of isolation between applications
► Whether the cursor is declared as being FOR READ ONLY (which automatically disallows any UPDATE or DELETE operations using the same cursor)
► The nature of the SELECT statement, and the access path selected by the DBMS to produce the result set

In particular, block fetch can always be used if an intermediate result set must be computed before selecting the first row to be returned to the application (to sort data to satisfy an ORDER BY or GROUP BY clause, for example), because such cursors are never updateable (in other words, they are always "read-only").

This is a complex issue requiring a detailed understanding of DBMS access paths and locking techniques. Of course, a DBMS must implement a conservative policy to prevent update conflicts because it must handle all possible applications. In practice, many tables are never subject to concurrent updates because of application design choices as to which programs or users may update the data. Unless the application design actually requires the DBMS to prevent concurrent updates to the selected data once the initial SELECT has been issued, we recommend that developers code separate UPDATE or DELETE statements instead of using the WHERE CURRENT OF syntax. This approach will allow block fetching of rows whenever possible. The trade-off will be some extra processing on the server to locate the rows to be updated or deleted.

Guideline 9.7	Avoid cursor SQL UPDATE and DELETE operations on large result tables

Except to permit concurrent updating of data in a single table, avoid using a cursor for large updates. To do so may cause the rows to be transferred one at a time from the DBMS server to the client. Substituting a separate SQL UPDATE or DELETE statement may permit block fetching of rows to the client. The trade-off will be some extra processing on the server to locate the rows to be updated or deleted.

ODBMS Block Fetch.   The block fetching concept is not confined to relational databases. Although the behavior is different, some Object DBMS (ODBMS) vendors offer a similar facility in their products. For example, Figure 9.1 illustrates the behavior of the *ObjectStore* ODBMS from Object Design Inc. In *ObjectStore,* a page fault occurs on the client machine if a required page of data is not in the client's extended working storage. The server software is designed with the assumption that applications will have a *locality of reference* in their use of the stored data. In other words, if an application wants to read an object from one page, then there's a good chance that shortly thereafter it will also need to read some related object instances from the adjacent pages. Rather than retrieving a single *page* from the server machine, it retrieves a data *segment* —a group of adjacent pages—the size of which is determined in advance by an ObjectStore parameter called a *fetch policy.*

The Block Fetch Trade-off.   When using block fetch, one design consideration is the delay that occurs before the application is handed the first row of the result set by the DBMS. Choosing a block size may mean making a trade-off between perceived response time and the overall efficiency of the application:

▶ If the user needs to see and process the data one row at a time, even though blocking the results will reduce the cost of handling the entire result set, the perceived response time for the application will be slower when larger block sizes are employed.
▶ When the application displays multiple rows of the result set together, a compromise might be to make the block size large enough to handle the data needed to fill the first display screen.

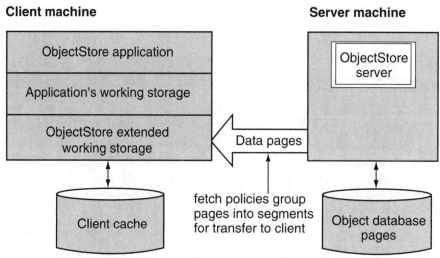

FIGURE 9.1   *ObjectStore* ODBMS fetch policies.

Ultimately, the right decision in these cases depends on the performance goals for the application and the relative importance of response time and overall throughput. We discuss the subject of design trade-offs in more detail in Chapter 14, *The Trade-off Principle.*

> **Guideline 9.8**
>
> **Fetch data in blocks, not one row at a time.**
>
> Because some fixed overheads are associated with each message sent and received across the network, regardless of its size, many client/server DBMSs use a technique called blocked fetch or block fetch to minimize the overhead of sending large result sets from the server to the client. Sending a result set in larger blocks, rather than one row at a time, reduces the overhead.

Finally, if we are building a system that will need to make frequent large data transfers, we should take a different approach altogether. Instead of the synchronous client/server design, in which an information server receives requests and responds to each request on demand, we should set up an asynchronous server. When clients submit requests for data, they are placed in a queue for later processing. This allows the server to achieve optimal efficiency by handling all requests in a controlled and orderly manner without unscheduled interruptions from other client requesters. The requested data is then returned to the client using a file transfer protocol that is more efficient than that used by a DBMS, possibly even using a compressed file format for network efficiency. We discuss this approach in more detail in Chapter 16, *Architecture for High Performance.*

Binding Dissimilar Components

We define *binding* to be the action of creating a static relationship between dissimilar components prior to program execution. In this section we discuss some situations in which we can improve performance by binding.

Compilation Techniques

The most obvious example of binding is anything we call *compilation.* We bind a logical processing requirement expressed in a general-purpose, high-level language to a particular target processor by compiling the program into executable machine instructions that will run on that processor.

Unless we write our source code directly in machine language, or in a low-level assembler language that maps directly to machine language instructions, whatever logic we write must eventually be converted into machine language instructions that can be executed. In essence, there are four distinct ways for software products to handle the conversion process: *static compilation, dynamic compilation, interpretation,* and *Just-In-Time Compilation.*

Static Compilation.   Static compilers convert the entire source module into machine language once and store a permanent copy of the executable version for repeated use later.

For any module that will be used repeatedly, this technique will clearly give the best performance at execution time because it maximizes the ratio of useful work (program execution) to overhead (compilation). Furthermore, compilers are probably our profession's most mature technology. Compiler writers today build on 25 years' experience with code tuning and optimization. The best compilers not only convert the source code into machine instructions, they also perform all kinds of tricks with the machine code to make it run as fast as possible on the target processor. For the modern multiprocessor computer, this type of machine-aided optimization is essential and usually produces much better machine code than most humans can. For more on this subject, see Kevin Dowd's *High Performance Computing.*[4]

Dynamic Compilation.   Dynamic compilers convert the entire source module into machine language at execution time, possibly retaining the compiled version temporarily in a cache for subsequent use, but *not* retaining a permanent copy of the compiled code.

Dynamic SQL is a case in point. The user composes a processing request in a high-level language (SQL), and the system takes care of converting that request into executable instructions (a database *access path*) and acting on it. For unplanned and infrequently executed processing, like *ad hoc* SQL queries submitted to a DBMS, this approach makes sense. The performance cost of compilation is a reasonable price to pay for the power and flexibility of direct database manipulation by any user. For repeated work, like stored queries that produce standard reports (sometimes called *"canned queries"*), dynamic compilation imposes an excessive and unnecessary level of overhead. We discuss this issue further in a later section, *SQL Gateways and Access Path Selection.*

In a move designed to combine the technique of dynamic compilation of client SQL requests with the efficiency of static or compiled SQL procedures, relational DBMS servers like Oracle and IBM DB2 Universal Database now cache the compiled versions of SQL statements, procedures, or packages on the server. The compiled code can then be reused if an identical request is received.

Interpretation.   An *interpreter* is a program that proceeds instruction by instruction through the source code at execution time, reading the source code, and acting on it.

---

[4]Kevin Dowd, *High Performance Computing* (Sabastapol, CA: O'Reilly & Associates, 1993).

For program logic, perhaps the most common alternative to static binding is dynamic interpretation of the high-level language at execution time. One benefit of interpretation is that it lets developers create a single version of the program logic that will run in multiple environments. Historically, it has been widely used by application generators and object-oriented languages like Smalltalk; more recently it has been used for portable Internet languages like Java and HTML. It is also the basis for the object-oriented property of *dynamic inheritance,* a technique we discuss later in this chapter.

Although interpretation does have some advantages, performance is certainly not one of them. Estimates of the relative speed of compiled to interpreted code range all over the map, from as little as a factor of 5 to 50–100 times faster. Obviously, any quoted number must be specific to a particular product and a particular processing context, but there seems to be a consensus that a compiled program typically runs 15–20 times faster than its equivalent in interpreted pseudo-code.

Also, interpretation consumes more of a server's scarce resources, making any environment that uses it less scalable. It uses extra processor cycles, and needs additional memory over and above the source code, and any data areas, to store the interpreter or *run-time* component. Finally, because the source code is used as the basis for the program logic, there is little or no opportunity for the kind of code optimization tricks a clever compiler can use.

Do not jump to the conclusion that compiling previously interpreted code will cut a 20-second *response time* down to one second. Recall (from Chapter 3) that an application's response time depends on a lot more than just processing speed. For most business applications, disk I/O and network delays—not CPU time—predominate.

Just-In-Time Compilation.   Systems using a Just-In-Time (JIT) compiler proceed through the source code instruction by instruction at execution time, converting the source code into machine code and then immediately executing the result, ideally retaining the converted instructions in case they are reused (in a program loop, for example). This might be called a hybrid approach; it has been popularized recently by software vendors in the Internet/Web arena who are seeking to speed up the execution of *Java* applets or methods.

At execution time, a Java Virtual Machine using this technique takes the *bytecodes* previously produced by a Java compiler and passes them to the JIT compiler, which compiles them into the native code for the machine it's running on. Executing the native code is faster than interpreting the original bytecodes, and these performance gains increase the more often the compiled Java methods are called. Therefore the benefits will be more noticeable for more complex, longer running, applications.

**Guideline
9.9** **Compilers and interpreters**

For optimal performance at execution time, any module that will be used repeatedly should be compiled into machine language once and a permanent copy of the executable code used thereafter.

For unplanned and infrequently executed processing, dynamic compilation at execution time makes sense. For repeated work, like stored queries that produce standard reports (sometimes called "*canned queries*"), dynamic compilation imposes an excessive and unnecessary level of overhead. For optimal performance, eliminate dynamic SQL from production applications, or ensure that the compiled version is cached on the server.

Interpreted code does not perform well. To boost performance, use a Just-In-Time (JIT) compiler if one is available. A program that calls the same function or method repeatedly will obtain the greatest improvement from a JIT compiler.

Stored Database Procedures

Another example of binding is the technique of collecting a set of SQL statements into a database procedure or package and storing that procedure at a remote location with the server DBMS whose data they manipulate. This technique maximizes the ratio of useful work (executing the data manipulation statement) to overhead (shipping the SQL requests from the client application to the server DBMS).

The processing overhead will be further reduced if the stored procedure can be compiled (or "*bound*") and the resulting database *access path* or *plan* stored with the DBMS for repeated use. We discuss the issue of *dynamic* versus *static* SQL in more detail in a later section.

**Guideline
9.10** **Stored database procedures**

Minimize repeated network overhead by storing SQL in remote procedures or packages stored with the server DBMS whose data they manipulate. Minimize processing overheads by compiling the procedure once and storing the compiled *access path* or *plan* with the DBMS.

Object DBMSs

In a normalized relational database, multiple different attributes that pertain to a single customer are stored in multiple different tables (for example, the address, information about their various accounts, and so on). When we use object technology, however, we often collect the data for a particular application into a single object. In an object-oriented database, then, the information comprising a single application object may be stored together in an instance of a stored object rather than scattered among several stored tables.[5] As a result, there is a natural tendency for object-oriented databases to be denormalized. In this respect, objects are an example of the Efficiency Principle. This is why objects perform well when used by the application they were designed for and why ODBMS technology is ideally suited for a high-performance application server.

As we noted earlier in the chapter, denormalization is a *biasing* technique. An object class in an ODBMS may be *reusable,* but it will not necessarily give *repeatable performance* when reused. Suppose a new application (B) reuses an object class (Oa) that was previously created for use by application (A). If application B needs to refer only to a subset of the information in Oa, it will not obtain the performance benefits of denormalization originally seen by application A. To reach the subset of data of interest, application B will have to read and skip all the information it doesn't need. A denormalized design is biased toward the usage of a particular application and—by implication—away from others.

This rule applies regardless of the logical data structure or technology because it applies to *physical structures,* not to *logical design.* A database may be called an ODBMS, an RDBMS, a network DBMS (like IDMS), or a hierarchical DBMS (like IMS DB), but as long as databases store and retrieve data from disks, we are still making the same kinds of decisions about *matching* the stored pattern to the usage pattern. We discuss this subject in more depth in Chapter 10, *The Locality Principle.*

Guideline 9.11	ODBMS technology is ideally suited for a high-performance application server

In an object-oriented database the information comprising a single application object may be stored together in an instance of a stored object rather than scattered among several stored tables. This is why objects perform well when used by the application they were designed for and why ODBMS technology is ideally suited for a high-performance application server.

Associating Dissimilar Components

We define *associating* to mean creating a temporary relationship between dissimilar components, dynamically, during program execution.

---

[5]C. J. Date, Why the "Object Model" Is Not a Data Model, *InfoDB* 10 (4). Date argues that object databases are inevitably application specific, and that object DBMSs actually support only a storage model, not a true data model.

At the beginning of the chapter, we quoted Smith's *Fixing-Point Principle*— "For responsiveness, establish connections at the earliest feasible point in time, such that retaining the connection is cost-effective." Another name for fixing is *binding,* the act of making a connection. And *fixing for efficiency is in direct conflict with dynamic association techniques.* For efficiency, we emphasize the advantages of early fixing or early binding; creating dynamic associations, on the other hand, is what programmers call *late binding.* Software engineers, however, like late binding for reasons that have nothing to do with performance—late binding removes many reasons for recompilation and so simplifies program maintenance.

In this section we discuss two important uses of dynamic association techniques: SQL gateways and access path selection, plus dynamic object inheritance.

SQL Gateways and Access Path Selection

Before it can actually execute an SQL data manipulation request, a DBMS must first *optimize* it. A relational DBMS *optimizer* analyzes an SQL statement, then examines a variety of statistical information from its catalog about the sizes of the target tables and any available indexes. For complex queries involving several tables, the optimizer typically evaluates many candidate access paths before it finally selects the one it considers likely to be the most efficient. Although this access path selection process is essential, it is also clearly an overhead that we incur because we are using a high-level data manipulation language. For optimal performance, we should aim to minimize this overhead cost.

To support this goal, DBMSs provide two ways to handle SQL requests:

▶ **Dynamic SQL.** This refers to the style of processing in which a DBMS receives an SQL statement at program execution time, evaluates various possible ways of processing that SQL request against the data, selects an *access path,* and then performs that access path. Dynamic SQL statements are recompiled with each request, unless (a) a cache is provided on the server to retain the access path information and (b) the statement is reused frequently enough for the access path to remain in the cache.

▶ **Static SQL.** This refers to SQL that is compiled in advance of its execution by the DBMS and whose access path details are stored in a DBMS catalog or directory for later use. At program execution time, the access path information is retrieved, executed, and typically kept in a cache where it is available for reuse subsequently.

Dynamic SQL is intended to be used by end-user query applications, which allow the user to determine the nature of database requests at execution time. These types of applications have no choice but to ship SQL statements to the DBMS and let the DBMS decide what to do with the SQL statements when they get there. Static SQL, on the other hand, is designed for applications that submit the same SQL requests repeatedly.

Because production SQL applications always process the same SQL, applying the Efficiency Principle guides us to *eliminate dynamic SQL from production applications.*

Gateways to Heterogeneous Databases.   A heterogeneous database gateway ships SQL requests to multiple back-end databases and supports join operations across databases. But it must also understand performance.

Suppose, for example, we want to combine data from Sybase and DB2 databases. If the gateway understands SQL syntax and knows where the various tables are located, then it can recognize that one part of the SQL statement needs to go to DB2 and that another part needs to go to Sybase. It can also retrieve the information and join it on the gateway processor, then pass the results back.

If it doesn't know anything about performance, though, it may not process the data in the most efficient way. To be effective, the gateway must be able to figure out the most efficient way to process the SQL statement—much as the optimizer for a single relational DBMS does—taking into account such factors as:

▶ The likely sizes of all intermediate result sets
▶ The likely delays involved in shipping intermediate result sets between locations
▶ The relative speeds of the processors at the various locations

This technique is called **global optimization.** For example, if a query needs to join two rows from a DB2 database at one location with a million rows from a Sybase database at another, it would not be smart to bring the million rows to the gateway processor. A gateway using global optimization would recognize that it will be much more efficient to fetch the two rows from DB2 and send them to the Sybase DBMS, perform the join there, and bring only the result (a few rows) back.

IBM's DataJoiner is probably the best example of this type of remote data access gateway. It incorporates an optimizer that understands the characteristics of the various relational database optimizers. For more about this product, see the capsule "If you can't beat 'em, join 'em" in Chapter 19, *Using DBMS Technology.*

> **Guideline 9.12**   **Remote data access gateways and dynamic SQL**
> Beware of application generators and other tools that access remote data via SQL gateways because the SQL will be recompiled with each request, unless (a) a cache is provided on the server and (b) the statement is reused frequently enough to remain in the cache. For optimal performance, look for a remote data access gateway like the IBM DataJoiner that compiles the SQL and optimizes the access path to the distributed data.

Dynamic Inheritance

Object inheritance is a programming mechanism that allows the properties (attributes and associated methods) of one object to be propagated to other objects, through the definition of a *class hierarchy* or *inheritance hierarchy.* In a hierarchy, an object can inherit (and override) the properties of any of its ancestor objects. Meilir Page-Jones points out that, in one sense, inheritance is similar to lexical inclusion in a block-structured programming language.[6] For example, code inside an inner **begin . . . end** block can see the variables defined in any of the outer blocks within which it is nested and redeclare (override) them. However, the features of an inner block are private and invisible to the code in outer blocks.

Of course, this is a limited analogy only. In most other senses, objects are more like separate programs or modules—they can be separately defined, stored, and executed. When an object participates in an inheritance hierarchy, its inherited properties are defined externally, in another object, while its private properties are defined internally. The object-oriented development environment must provide a way to merge the two, either before the object is used (through some kind of compilation process) or dynamically at execution time. These two approaches are called *static* and *dynamic inheritance.*

Static inheritance is really just an object-oriented *compile and link* or *build* process; the logic from many separate source modules is combined into a single executable. To illustrate how dynamic inheritance works, consider the example shown in Figure 9.2.[7]

The arrows on the left side of the figure describe the following sequence of development activities:

---

[6]Meilir Page-Jones, *What Every Programmer Should Know about Object-Oriented Design* (London, UK: Dorset House, 1995).

[7]The figure and associated discussion expands on a simple three-level inheritance example by Emily Kay published in *Datamation* 41 (5), March 15, 1995. One can easily imagine the many further variations that may exist in a real business situation.

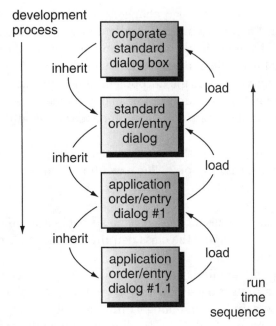

FIGURE 9.2   Dynamic inheritance.

▶ First, we develop a *corporate standard dialog box*—a window containing some standard layout information and the corporate logo.

▶ Next, we develop a *standard order-entry dialog* for use in all order-entry applications. It inherits from the corporate standard dialog but adds some fields and layout details required in all order-entry situations.

▶ Next, we create *application order-entry dialog #1* for use by a particular application. It inherits the standard order-entry window but adds some specific fields required for this particular application.

▶ Finally, we create a window for the special case when we have a back order. This window is just like the previous order-entry window but also needs to display some additional information about the status of the order. This is *application order-entry dialog #1.1,* which inherits from *dialog #1.*

For the application developer, this scenario has two very attractive features: *reuse* of previously developed code and layout definitions and (almost) automatic *maintenance.* The reuse aspect is obvious; this is how the maintenance side works:

Because of inheritance, if someone decides to change the company logo in the corporate standard dialog box, then nobody else has to change any code. As soon as the corporate logo changes, all other windows inherit the new logo from their "parent" window. Thanks to dynamic inheritance, the change gets propagated automatically when it happens. The next time a user runs an application that uses one of these lower-level windows, he or she will automatically get the new version of the corporate logo on the screen. From a development point of view, this amounts to free maintenance—a very attractive benefit since most programmers hate doing maintenance and would far rather be working on neat new stuff.

But, as we noted earlier, there is no such thing as a free lunch: Dynamic inheritance is a case in point. The execution time behavior of the back-order application is indicated by the arrows on the right side of Figure 9.2:

▶ First, the user comes along and requests back-order dialog #1.1, whereupon the software managing the class definitions loads into memory everything associated with #1.1.

▶ Next, the software finds that, because of dynamic inheritance, some of the class definitions it needs are actually defined in dialog #1, so it also needs to load the definition of dialog #1 into memory.

▶ It does so, only to find that it then needs to load the standard order-entry dialog.

▶ After loading that, it finds that the corporate standard dialog box is now also required.

▶ It loads that and can now finally complete the display and pass control back to the user.

Clearly, this process requires several disk I/Os to load all the necessary definitions. Of course, we always have to load a program into memory before we can execute it, but if the program has been previously compiled and linked together into a single executable module, then we can usually load it quickly with a short burst of sequential I/O operations. In this case, we have to load the necessary components piecemeal, which will obviously end up using more I/O operations and taking longer.

But that's not the whole story. In a client/server environment, the presentation interface is running on a client workstation on a LAN, but the object class definitions—being shared by all client workstations—reside in a library on a shared disk on a network server. Every one of those I/O operations to fetch definitions is not a local I/O; it is a remote I/O, going back and forth across the network to the server. You may recall (from Chapter 3) that remote disk I/Os are a couple of orders of magnitude more expensive than local I/Os.

Note that this is not a problem created by the design or implementation of a particular software *product.* Using any object-oriented application development tool or language (like *Smalltalk*) that supports the *technique* of dynamic inheritance, developers can produce situations like the one we just described. With dynamic inheritance, a lot of things have to happen under the covers between the time the user clicks on an object and the instant that the system can display that object on the screen. The result is the characteristically sluggish feel of this type of application, which some users have dubbed "point, click, and wait."

Combining Inheritance and Performance. There are three ways to get around the performance overhead of dynamic inheritance:

1. **Use static inheritance instead.** The first way is the obvious one—don't use it. Use inheritance during the development process, to obtain the benefits of object reuse, but then compile the resulting objects to create a single static executable module. For example, *Delphi* from Borland works this way. The compilation process copies in all inherited class definitions, eliminating all the overhead of run-time interpretation. Borland's marketing has always stressed the performance of *Delphi* applications, and independent assessments of the product support Borland's claim that compiled Delphi programs run much faster than those built using other development tools that require a run-time interpreter.

2. **Minimize the depth of the inheritance tree.** This approach is a compromise, but limiting inheritance hierarchies to a few levels will eliminate the worst excesses of dynamic inheritance. With this approach, inheritance hierarchies tend to grow horizontally, rather than vertically. We might decide to copy properties from one object to another, in effect making multiple versions of an object at the same horizontal level, rather than going another level deep. Of course, when we do this, we lose the benefits of dynamic inheritance if any of the copied properties change. We will probably get better performance, but we will have to keep track of the copying, and we will have additional maintenance work to do when things change.

3. **Cache objects when they are first used.** If the software environment that supports dynamic inheritance also manages a cache, the first time a user retrieves information, it is stored in the cache, typically in memory on the client workstation. It may take awhile to track back through the hierarchy and load all the ancestor objects into the cache the first time an object is referenced, but if the user requests the same information over and over again, it will stay in the cache on the workstation—thereby eliminating the performance hit incurred with the initial request.

   Depending on the size of the cache, however, and the way it is managed, the user may experience a performance hit again if he or she uses another application and then returns to the initial task. In this case, it may be necessary to download the referenced information from the server once again—repeating the hierarchical search and reloading all of the ancestor objects back into the cache.

> **Guideline 9.13   Dynamic inheritance**
>
> Application development tools that employ dynamic inheritance may perform poorly because of repeated requests from client to server to retrieve inherited components. To eliminate the overheads of dynamic inheritance, select a tool that creates compiled executable modules. When using dynamic inheritance, reduce its overheads by flattening inheritance hierarchies.

Other Techniques for Improving Efficiency

In this section, we briefly review some further techniques for eliminating overheads and processing work more efficiently.

Replicated Reference Tables

Client software on the user workstation may repeatedly use certain reference tables. Examples might be to validate input or to look up and substitute coded identifiers for the business names entered by users. Even though these are common tables, shared by all users, if they are available only on the server, much unnecessary network overhead will result. For optimal performance, a copy should be resident locally to minimize repeated network access to the database server.

These tables will inevitably change from time to time, so we must plan to use replication techniques (which we discuss in more detail in Chapter 20) to maintain the local copies. Such tables can be refreshed daily at workstation initialization or periodically when changes occur.

> **Guideline 9.14   Replicated tables**
>
> Download essential tables (for example, those used to validate input) to the client workstation periodically to minimize repeated network access to the database server.

Indexing

Without some kind of indexing mechanism, any request for data from a database involves a scan through the entire database to find the instances of the rows whose fields or columns satisfy our particular search criteria. Once it locates those instances, the DBMS, in effect, creates a list of the items that correspond with the search condition.

This is exactly what we do when we build an index. In the *Order* table, for example, if we build an index on *CustomerNumber,* the index records every instance of every distinct *CustomerNumber.* The next time we need to find all the orders for a given customer, we can go straight to the index. Scanning the table and building the index once eliminates the overhead of scanning the table and recreating the list of customers every time.

We discuss indexes in more detail in Chapter 14, *The Trade-off Principle,* and Chapter 19, *Using DBMS Technology.*

> **Guideline 9.15 Indexing**
>
> Create indexes to minimize the disk I/O needed to locate frequently used data. For rapid access to data that is used repeatedly, building an index is more efficient than searching the database each time.

Batch versus Online Transactions

At the beginning of this chapter, we pointed out that *software is inherently repetitive.* This is especially true for the class of software that we are primarily concerned with in the enterprise client/server arena—business information processing. There are many business situations in which we must process a large number of identical transactions or perform the same sequence of actions on a large number of objects.

Although this type of processing can be handled interactively, treating each set of actions against a single object as a separate transaction, that is not the most efficient way. Unless business reasons require continuous incremental updates to the databases, it is much more efficient to accumulate a file or table of high-volume business transactions when they are generated and process them later in batches.

Obviously, for some business applications (like airline reservations and stock trading) the databases must be kept continuously up to date. But for every such application, there are several others where periodic updates are quite acceptable, provided the data in the database is kept internally consistent. For these applications, batch processing is most efficient.

> **Guideline 9.16 Use batch processing for efficiency**
>
> Unless business reasons require continuous incremental updates to the databases, it is much more efficient to accumulate a file or table of high-volume business transactions when they are generated and process them later in batches.

Batch processing is definitely not the same as a large number of randomly generated online transactions performed consecutively, and it should never be designed to work that way (unless the designer cares nothing for performance and is simply looking for a "quick and dirty" solution). When a large batch of input must be processed against a database, a sort/merge technique is almost always optimal. The application first sorts the input so that the intended updates are in the same sequence as the target database. It then reads the sorted input and the target database sequentially, in parallel, applying all the updates.

The sort/merge technique eliminates the many separate database searches that would otherwise be required to handle the updates in their original, random order, replacing them by a sort of the input and two sequential scans.

> ### Guideline 9.17   Batch processing requires a different approach
>
> Processing a million updates in batch is not like a million online transactions, back to back. A sort/merge technique should be used to minimize the overhead of repeatedly searching the target database for the location of the updates.

Data Replication

Whenever we need to copy data and maintain those copies as the source data changes, many distinct performance issues arise in both the source and target systems. We devote Chapter 20 to the performance of data replication technology. In the context of this chapter, however, if updates must be replicated asynchronously, the most efficient techniques are those involving batching. In particular, it is always more efficient to use high-performance database load utilities than to process changes one at a time, for example using SQL.

> ### Guideline 9.18   Use high-performance utilities for data replication
>
> When replicating data, it is always more efficient to use high-performance database load utilities than to process changes one at a time.

Checkpointing

Any time we must repeat work, that is overhead, much of which can be avoided by the technique of *checkpointing*. A checkpoint is a relatively recent point of consistency that is recorded in persistent memory to allow for rapid restart in the case of an error. For really large batch jobs involving millions of updates, the application should create periodic checkpoints that allow processing to be restarted relatively quickly. If we design such an application without taking the possibility of intermittent failures into account, then any error can mean having to repeat all processing from the beginning. This is especially frustrating when—in accordance with Murphy's Law of Program Errors—the failure occurs in the last phase of a four-hour process.

Checkpointing large data transfers is always advisable because a device somewhere in the network may fail or lose data during the transfer. This is particularly true of transfers over a WAN and is also good practice for heavily loaded LANs. When a session between a client and server must be restarted from the beginning of a large data transfer, we waste the resources of the client, the server, the network, and the human user.

Adding checkpointing logic to an application can sometimes be difficult because the server must keep track of data that it has sent to a client in previous sessions. The investment in development time, however, is usually quickly repaid in reduced operational costs and improved user productivity.

> **Guideline 9.19 Checkpoint large data transfers**
> Any time we must repeat work, that is overhead. Although it takes more development effort to write the code to take checkpoints, making long batch jobs restartable after a failure will save time and computing resources in the long run. This is particularly important for long data transfers over relatively slow networks.

Activity Tracing and Logging

Systems software often contains options to switch on a variety of activity logs or traces. There are four principal reasons for tracing:

1. **Serviceability or debugging.** Systems software is often shipped with internal traces turned on, usually to allow the software vendor to diagnose the causes of problem conditions. Application developers create their own traces to aid with debugging and then forget to remove them in the production code.

2. **Auditing.** This may be needed from time to time, but only a few applications with stringent audit requirements need a continuous audit trace over and above the normal records kept by the application itself.

3. **Accounting or resource chargeback.** Some tracing may be essential—for example, to support chargeback in a time-sharing environment. Even this requirement might be better addressed by a simpler method involving less overhead or by assigning a smaller, dedicated processor.

4. **Performance monitoring.** As we discussed in Chapter 5, it is useful for software to allow various levels of performance monitoring. Routine performance

statistics can be collected fairly cheaply; for example, many DBMSs record statistics in the database catalog. Usually, the only reason for continuous, detailed tracing is performance problem solving; typically, short periods of tracing are sufficient.

In Chapter 8, when discussing Table 8.5 we stated, *"Applications that log every user interaction will consume a lot of resources no matter how careful we are about their unit costs."* Similarly, no matter how careful developers are to control the cost of tracing, detailed traces are an expensive overhead. A well-designed trace, when turned off, should consume fewer than 10 instructions at each trace point in the code, that being the cost of testing whether the trace point is actually active. Running production workload volumes with these kinds of traces turned on continuously is a sure way to consume additional resources. First there will be the CPU cycles to collect the trace data and format a trace record, then there will usually be more processing and an I/O operation to write out the trace record to a disk or tape.

In general, try to avoid tracing continuously for any reason. Look for ways to gather data by occasional tracing and other, less expensive statistics-gathering techniques.

Guideline 9.20	**Switch of unnecessary tracing and logging**

Check all software carefully to make sure that all unwanted traces are switched off. In general, try to avoid tracing continuously. Look for ways to gather data by occasional tracing and other, less expensive statistics-gathering techniques.

Conclusion

Fred Brooks[8] observed that software is fun to work with because it is *". . . such a tractable medium."* Being so malleable, software offers numerous opportunities for optimization, at all stages of development life cycle. In this chapter, we have highlighted some of the most significant and common of these, but every project will present its own new and different possibilities. If we are following the path of SPE (*"software engineering with performance in mind"*) then we will be alert for these opportunities, and our software will be that much the better as a result.

We began this chapter with *Greg Faust's golden rule* of good software engineering: *"First design software that works, then optimize your design."*[9] Notice

---

[8]Brooks, *The Mythical Man Month*, 7.
[9]Greg Faust, Microsoft Corp., Redmond, WA.

how far this is from the alternative of: *"If the software works, ship it!"* This Machiavellian management maxim is sometimes adopted by those who—beaten down by deadlines and technical complications—may not be finding software development to be quite as much fun as Brooks suggested.

In response, we cannot offer any magic that will eliminate the need for careful attention to the concerns of efficiency. We can only reiterate Connie Smith's remark that: *"You can always tune it later, but the results are never as good."* So don't wait until you are almost done before you start thinking about optimization; apply Greg Faust's rule at every stage of the software life cycle, at both the micro level (modules, objects, or components) and the macro level (subsystems, systems, and business processes). But do so wisely—avoid wasted effort by applying Guideline 4.9, *"The Centering Principle,"* and in particular, Guideline 8.12, *"Focus on the Mainline Path."*

Guideline 9.21	Faust's golden rule of good software engineering

First design software that works, then optimize your design.
  Apply Faust's rule at every stage of the software life cycle, at both the micro level (modules, objects, or components) and the macro level (subsystems, systems, and business processes).

We note two caveats:

▶ First, since this is a chapter about efficiency, we have stressed the reduced overheads of larger groups and earlier grouping. But grouping does have other consequences too; in practice we must also weigh the counterarguments for the flexibility afforded by smaller groups and later grouping.

▶ Second, many grouping actions involving shared components—like data structures, computer memory, or processing resources—are *biasing* techniques. That is, they bias the design in favor of a particular application or usage pattern. Therefore, there can exist (in theory, at least) another workload with another usage pattern whose performance will be affected adversely by the same design choice. When tuning for efficiency we generally focus on the positive side, but it is always important to look out for any potential negative side-effects for other workloads. Once again remember *The Centering Principle.*

As the saying goes, there is no such thing as a free lunch. In the world of systems, once we step beyond the domain of the Workload Principle and code tuning that we covered in the Chapter 8, there is no such thing as free performance gain. We return to these concerns in Chapter 14, *The Trade-off Principle.*

The Locality Principle

"It is not the facts but the relation of things that results in the universal harmony that is the sole objective reality."

Robert Pirsig

In This Chapter . . .

Locality: Matching Components to Usage
The Four Types of Locality
Holistic Design and Software Tuning
Case Study: The Consolidated Software Corporate Shared Calendar System
Conclusion

The third design principle, Locality, addresses the performance benefits we can obtain by creating software and systems that match closely their intended usage.

Notice the two key ideas underlying this principle. The first, of course, is that of *closeness*—when explaining the different ways of applying the principle we find ourselves repeatedly drawn into using synonyms for locality like *grouping, proximity,* and *matching.* The second idea is that of matching a particular *usage pattern.* Of the many design choices available for grouping elements of the software and hardware solution, we will get the best performance when any resource or server (such as a routine, file, database, processor, memory, network, or storage device) is configured to match the *demands* placed on it by the workload.

Stated this way, the ideas behind the Locality Principle may seem obvious; our goal in this chapter is to suggest some systematic ways in which we can harness this transparently simple idea to create better-performing software designs.

Locality: Matching Components to Usage

Connie Smith states the Locality Principle as "Create actions, functions, and results that are 'close' to physical computer resources."[1] Dennis Shasha's whimsical database design principle, "Render onto server what is due onto server," embodies the same thought.[2]

We take Smith's original definition as a starting point, but we do not wholly endorse it. In our view, it states the principle backward, in a way that seems to reflect the mindset of a performance analyst working in a static and inflexible mainframe or centralized computing environment. In contrast, one of the fundamental tenets of distributed computing is its flexibility in the face of changing demands. When designing a new *distributed system* then, rather than regarding the physical computer resources as fixed and tuning the workload to fit, we would surely prefer, if possible, to organize the physical resources to match the logical processing demands.

In practice, the real world of enterprise computing will probably present us with situations somewhere in between these two extremes. Typically (as we discussed in Chapter 5), we have to balance application goals with enterprise constraints and client needs with server capacity, leaving us only partial flexibility to specify the computing environment.

Therefore, since the method of matching the system to the workload can include both *designing the application* and *tuning the environment,* we prefer to state the Locality Principle in a neutral way as "Group components based on

---

| Guideline 10.1 | Locality Principle: Group components based on their usage |

We will get the best performance when any resource or server (such as a routine, file, database, processor, memory, network, or storage device) is configured to match the demands placed on it by the application workload. To apply the locality principle, we must do the following:

▶ Design components and applications to match the demands of the business.

▶ Design a computing environment to match the logical processing needs.

▶ Design and time applications to match the processing resources available.

---

[1]Connie U. Smith, *Performance Engineering of Software Systems* (Reading, MA: Addison-Wesley, 1990), 44.
[2]Dennis E. Shasha, *Database Tuning: A Principled Approach* (Upper Saddle River, NJ: Prentice-Hall, 1992), 5.

their usage." This definition makes no distinction between software and hardware components, and it contains no assumptions about how and when the grouping is to be accomplished when applying the principle.

Know the User

Applying the Locality Principle highlights how vitally important it is for the software designer to *know the user.* If, during an earlier requirements or analysis phase, we have identified the business factors and objectives (see Chapter 5), we can approach the task of software engineering:

▶ Knowing *why* the business needs this application
▶ Knowing *how* each particular function will be used
▶ Knowing *when* and *how often* a user will actually invoke those functions

Flowing from that knowledge should come a design in which the application software closely matches the user's needs and makes use of system software components (middleware, DBMS, operating systems, and so on) in a harmonious fashion.

> **Guideline 10.2** **Know the user**
> The software designer who knows why, how, and when an application will be used can create software that closely matches the user's needs and uses system software components harmoniously.

The Four Types of Locality

There are four types of locality—*spatial, temporal, degree,* and *effectual.* Each one emphasizes a different aspect of design, and each plays an important role in the performance of a distributed system.

▶ **Spatial locality** refers to *closeness in distance.*
▶ **Temporal locality** deals with *closeness in time.*
▶ **Degree locality** addresses *closeness in capacity.*
▶ **Effectual locality** is about *closeness of purpose.*

Figure 10.1 illustrates the four types of locality and the relationships among them, showing that they form a hierarchy.

Starting at the lowest level, *spatial locality* again emphasizes the fundamental performance techniques of *grouping* and *fixing,* collecting together elements that will be used together (recall Chapter 9 and the Efficiency Principle).

No matter what the context, it takes time to cross distance. Computers are machines operating at finite speeds, often much slower than we would like, and the closer we bring things together, the faster we can move between them.

While spatial locality is often the technique we use to make things go faster, there are limits to its applicability. Try as we might, we can't compress the entire universe of enterprise client/server applications into a single PC. *Temporal locality* brings us to the goal itself—to bring related things closer in time. It refers to the performance benefits of completing a group of related actions at the same time or sequentially without delay.

Degree locality complements spatial and temporal locality, each of which is concerned primarily with the response time, or *application* perspective on performance. Degree locality, in contrast, addresses capacity, a key issue in *systems* design. To ensure degree locality, we must match the data storage, transmission, and processing demands imposed by the business workload with the capacities of the hardware and software resources that make up the system.

Effectual locality refers to the overall mindset that is needed when grouping components onto systems. We must create components and interfaces that will work well together. Another term for effectual locality might be *synergy*. This synergy must be based on how the components themselves work and on how the workload patterns of our particular applications stress those components. In many respects, effectual locality is the glue that holds the first three types of locality together; without it, all our design efforts in the other areas may still not produce the expected performance benefits.

Even without any of the elaboration that follows in the remainder of this chapter, we can immediately see from this introduction that there are substantial differences in the way these four concepts will influence our design decisions. But there is a common thread. All four types of locality are concerned

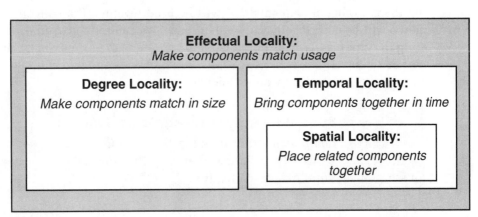

FIGURE 10.1   Relationships among the four types of locality.

with *relationships*—how to respond to *logical relationships* and how and when to create *physical relationships.* In fact, the four types of locality help us decide on the most effective way to *relate* our various software and hardware components in response to (that is, in *relation* to) the demands imposed by the users' workload.

Spatial Locality

Spatial locality refers to *closeness in distance.* It has much in common with the software engineering concept of *cohesion* that we introduced in Chapter 7. In programming, it is sometimes called the *principle of proximity,* which in *Code Complete,* Steve McConnell states as "Keep related actions together."[3] McConnell's guideline works, provided that we adopt the right interpretation of the word "related." In a large system, components may be connected by many overlapping relationships, but for spatial locality, *usage pattern* is the one that matters. In other words, *components that play together should stay together.*

This guideline applies equally to many different grouping of components; for example:

▶ Related columns in database rows
▶ Related rows in database tables
▶ Related tables in physical database structures
▶ Related attributes in objects
▶ Code fragments in software modules
▶ GUI components in a window

In fact, it can be applied to any collection of elements that need to be used together. The Efficiency Principle (Chapter 9) highlighted the issues surrounding the grouping of elements that will be used together. If a collection of elements will be used together more than once, we can reduce overheads by creating the group as early as possible (*static grouping* or *early fixing*). The upper half of Table 9.1 lists many situations in which we use the technique of early grouping to improve software efficiency.

> **Guideline 10.3**   **Spatial locality: *Closeness in distance***
>
> *Components that play together should stay together.* If a collection of elements will be used together more than once, then we can reduce overhead by grouping them statically.

---

[3]Steve McConnell, *Code Complete* (Redmond, WA: Microsoft Press, 1993), 181.

There is another side to grouping, namely *separation.* Recall our earlier discussion of *coupling* and *cohesion* in Chapter 7. When we do a good job of grouping related components together, the consequence is that *unrelated components are separated.*

In a large distributed system, the separation can be just as important as the grouping. Components that are not well separated are *entangled.* They will resist distribution, causing performance problems when we try to distribute them. A component in a distributed system will operate most efficiently when it does not have to know anything about what is going on in some other part of the system.

Guideline 10.4 is based on one of the conclusions reached by M. Satyanarayanan during the design of the *Andrew* and *Coda* Distributed File Systems at Transarc Corporation and Carnegie Mellon University.[4]

Guideline 10.4	**Minimize the need for system-wide knowledge**

In a large distributed system, it is difficult to be aware, at all times, of the entire state of the system. It is also difficult to update distributed or replicated data structures in a consistent manner. Designs that rarely require global information to be monitored or atomically updated are more scalable.

Applying the Spatial Locality Principle

As we noted earlier, in computers, *closer* usually means *faster.* So spatial locality has always been crucial to performance no matter what the computing environment. But it takes on an even greater significance in a client/server environment precisely because the whole idea of distributed systems is to separate things. Distribution is the enemy of spatial locality! Distribution takes designs that used to perform perfectly well on a mainframe and ruins them by introducing separation. Distribution allows new application architectures with abundant potential for new separation problems. *Distribution promotes spatial locality to even greater prominence than before.*

Here are some broad guidelines for improving performance by achieving good spatial locality in an enterprise client/server computing environment. We discuss each briefly in the sections that follow and return to them again later in the book.

► Minimize data transfers between clients and server.
► Perform all-user interface logic on the client workstation.

---

[4]M. Satyanarayanan, "Distributed File Systems," in *Distributed Systems,* edited by S. Mullender (Reading, MA: Addison-Wesley, 1993), 353–383.

▶ Aim to group related data at a single location.

▶ Avoid the remote presentation architecture.

▶ Limit use of the remote data access architecture.

▶ Use distributed logic architectures and middleware.

▶ Use stored database procedures.

▶ Consider replicating widely used data.

▶ Consider merging data in a data warehouse.

▶ Consider using object database technology.

Minimize Data Transfers Between Clients and Server.   This recommendation is not so much an example of spatial locality as a consequence of it. Communication networks are probably the slowest and most error-prone of all the devices in our systems. As a result, they have the poorest performance characteristics. They are also a shared device, which introduces further potential for delays. Chapters 3 and 11 address these issues in more depth. Here we simply note that our goal should always be to minimize data transfers over the network. If we create good spatial locality between data and processes, we will contribute to optimal performance by minimizing the need to transfer data before it can be processed. Techniques for achieving this goal are the subject of Part IV of this book.

Guideline 10.5	Minimize data transfers between clients and server

Communication networks are probably the slowest and most error-prone of all the devices in our systems. As a result, they have the poorest performance characteristics. Creating good spatial locality between data and processes will contribute optimal performance by minimizing the need to transfer data before it can be processed.

Perform All User Interface Logic on the Client Workstation.   Practically speaking, this guideline means the same things as *Avoid the remote presentation architecture,* which we discuss a bit later. But we list it here to make sure the point is not overlooked. Unless you are designing for a very high-speed LAN environment, separating user interface logic from the presentation manager is a sure way to load up the network and slow down the user.

Aim to Group Related Data at a Single Location.   For distributed information systems, probably the single most influential factor in the performance of any application is the location of its data.

When planning for distributed data, put spatial locality as high on your list of objectives as political realities and other design criteria allow. The first goal of any data distribution scheme must be to identify those subsets of data that are most likely to be used together in applications. Ideally, these should be stored at the same location. If this is not done and logically related data becomes separated physically, then no amount of juggling with the processing will avoid the performance penalty of moving some of the data between locations.

In general, once we decide to distribute *any* data, we can never eliminate *all* data movement by applications. No matter what distribution scheme we select, there will always be some applications that do not have perfect locality of reference. As usual, the decision will involve compromises and trade-offs among applications, a subject we examine in more detail in Chapter 14.

To ensure optimal locality in our distributed system designs, we need to consider all of the following factors:

▶ The need to move data closer to the user for responsiveness
▶ The frequency of user access to the data
▶ Database size and projected growth rates
▶ The capacity of server disks
▶ The server disk speed at peak utilization levels

The last three items also relate to *degree locality,* which we discuss later in this chapter. Data distribution and guidelines for using DBMS technology in a distributed environment are covered in Chapter 19.

Guideline 10.6	Aim to group related data at a single location

The first goal of any data distribution scheme must be to identify those subsets of data that are most likely to be used together in applications. Ideally, these should be stored at the same location. If logically related data becomes separated physically, then no amount of juggling with the processing will avoid the performance penalty of moving data between locations.

Avoid the Remote Presentation Architecture.   Recall (from Chapter 2) that in the *remote presentation* client/server architecture, only the presentation manager layer resides on the client workstation; all other architectural layers (presentation logic, data logic, and data manager) run on the server. Obviously, this architecture, with a network link separating the closely related *presentation manager* and *presentation logic* layers, gets a very poor rating for spatial locality.

To achieve good spatial locality, aim to perform all user interface logic on the client workstation. Positioning the user interface logic close to the user interface itself will minimize the need for the application to go back and forth across a network while organizing information for display.

Limit Use of the Remote Data Access Architecture.   In the remote data access architecture, the presentation manager, presentation logic, and data logic layers all reside on the client workstation, and only the data manager resides on the server. Again, a network link separates two closely related components, this time the *data logic* and *data manager* layers. This is not as bad as the remote presentation architecture because the volume of data manipulation requests (SQL, for a relational DBMS) to the data manager is typically much lower than that of user interface calls to the presentation manager. But it still gets a low score for spatial locality because processes that manipulate the database are separated from the data itself. For good spatial locality, we need to get the two closer together.

Despite its inherent performance limitations, remote data access gateway technology is widely used and can give quite acceptable performance for some applications. We discuss this subject in Chapter 9, in the section *SQL Gateways and Access Path Selection,* and in Chapter 19, in the section *Design for the Existing Application Environment.*

Use the Distributed Logic Architecture.   In the *distributed logic* architecture, the network link is placed between the presentation and data logic components, with the presentation manager and presentation logic residing on the workstation and the data logic and data manager residing on the client. In comparison with the remote presentation and remote data access models, it is clear that this arrangement minimizes network traffic and maximizes spatial locality on both the client and the server. We discuss distributed logic architectures and middleware extensively in Part IV of the book.

Guideline 10.7	Use distributed logic architectures and middleware

Both the *distributed presentation* and the *remote data access* client/server architectures suffer from poor spatial locality. For optimal performance, use the *distributed logic* architecture.

Use Stored Database Procedures.   DBMS-supported *stored procedures* are one of the simplest implementations of the distributed logic client/server model. Although their function is limited in scope and not suited to all applications, stored procedures containing a collection of data processing statements are located with the database(s) they manipulate. In that respect, they score high on spatial locality. Stored procedures eliminate the need to ship processing requests across the network and may, if the procedures are precompiled, also eliminate the overhead of repeated compilation of those requests. We discuss this subject in more detail in Chapter 8, in the section *Using Stored Procedures* and in Guideline 8.24: *Use stored database procedures.*

Consider Replicating Widely Used Data.   Consider replication schemes to distribute copies of operational data closer to its users. We discuss replication in more detail in Chapter 20.

Consider Merging Data in a Data Warehouse.   Consider systematic warehousing schemes to reorganize and distribute appropriate subsets of data closer to its users. We discuss data warehousing in more detail in Chapter 21.

Consider Using Object Database Technology.   A computer *object* (in the object-oriented sense) is a representation of some real-world object, implemented as a collection of related attributes of different types that, in some context, belong together. Usually that context is an application or set of applications that need to process that object. Therefore, objects have inherent spatial locality—using object technology is a sure way to create physical data structures in which all the elements needed for processing are stored together. Because of this, object databases are ideally suited to the role of dedicated application servers, as we noted previously in Guideline 9.11. From the viewpoint of a single application, or a set of related applications, an object database can provide a physical data model with a high level of spatial locality.

Guideline 10.8	**Consider using object database technology**

Objects have inherent spatial locality—using object technology is a sure way to create physical data structures in which all the elements needed for processing are stored together.

Data Partitioning and Distribution

In the area of database design, the technique of *data partitioning* is another good example of the Spatial Locality Principle. Sometimes, even though a database as a whole is shared by many users, in practice each user refers to a distinct subset of the information, with only an occasional need to look at the entire database. This is typical of databases containing customer information when customers are segmented by geographical areas, regions, or buying patterns. In these situations, we can partition the database using the particular segmentation pattern. Partitioning can improve performance in two ways:

▶ Rather than storing the entire database on a central single server, several smaller databases are created. If these are then placed on separate servers, each server has a lower level of use.
▶ Often, when we partition a large database, the geographical structure of the enterprise lets us move a partition closer to the physical location of its users.

In this case, we can improve performance by giving users local (LAN-based) access to the data instead of remote (WAN-based) access. This is a key goal of any data distribution scheme, which we discuss next.

The occasional need to process the entire database can be handled by distributed processing or by periodically propagating summaries from the partitions into a central summary database. We discuss data partitioning in more detail in Chapter 13, *The Parallelism Principle*.

> **Guideline 10.9   Partition large shared databases**
>
> Partitioning large shared databases and distributing the partitions can improve performance by eliminating inessential sharing of a key resource and by reducing the distance between the resource and its users.

Data Distribution Guidelines Based on Spatial Locality

Because of the crucial importance of spatial locality, we suggest that organizations establish a corporate design guideline for the way in which distributed applications interact with their data. The guideline might be something like this:

> *Unless performance objectives or response time estimates indicate otherwise, online applications should be designed to perform 85 percent of all processing against local data.*

Creating such a guideline will certainly not guarantee *acceptable* performance; that is not its purpose. Acceptability is subject to specific objectives that must be set for each application (recall the discussion of performance objectives in Chapter 5). A corporate goal of this type can be a catalyst; its purpose may be more political than technical. If observed, it will introduce the importance of spatial locality into every discussion of application architecture or data distribution. Creating and pursuing such a goal can do the following:

▶ Encourage an organization to settle on a corporate strategy for enterprise data management and provide a concrete objective for data distribution decisions (see Chapter 19).
▶ Drive decisions about data architectures, including the use of data replication and data warehousing technologies (see Chapters 20 and 21, respectively).
▶ Create a framework for thinking about different application-processing models and influence application architecture choices (see Part IV of the book).
▶ Provide numeric criteria for evaluating vertical application packages from software vendors.

We note two caveats:

▶ In spite of the emphasis on spatial locality, we should not forget that some transactions do not require fast response times. Some users really don't mind waiting while their software laboriously assembles a report by searching and retrieving data from several remote databases. Perhaps the application is producing summaries that were not previously available or is replacing a periodic batch report. In these situations, the users may be delighted just to have up-to-date information available online at relatively short notice, and they may be quite willing to schedule their other work to accommodate the long-running transaction required to produce it.

▶ This guideline is intended to influence our thinking about the design of *interactive* applications. It should not apply to batch reporting, batch update applications, mass data extracts, table loads, or other utility programs that process entire databases. Nor should anyone be allowed to count such programs against the corporate target. Running a weekly report against an 8.5 million row table does not justify making 1.5 million new remote data access requests in an online customer profile application that supports the help desk.

Finally, we should be ready to relax the goal based on analysis of specific application needs and the expected performance of specific applications. Over time, we can revise the goal based on evolving technology and our experience in using it. After all, devices keep getting faster. So it's possible that in 5 or 10 years we will find satisfaction at lower levels of locality.

Guideline 10.10	**Set an overall data locality guideline**
	Establish a corporate design guideline, like this one:

Unless performance objectives or response time estimates indicate otherwise, online applications should be designed to perform 85 percent of all processing against local data.

If observed, this type of guideline will introduce the importance of spatial locality into every discussion of application architecture or data distribution.

Temporal Locality

Temporal locality refers to *closeness in time*. Whenever we have grouped related elements together (achieving spatial locality) then, for that group, temporal locality usually follows automatically. But in practice, it is not *always* possible to use spatial locality to optimize performance. Consider the following:

▶ Components can be grouped in only one way. Static grouping is exactly that: static, unchanging, *fixed.* Once we've chosen an optimal grouping scheme, other potentially useful groupings are then excluded.

▶ Group size limitations or other physical implementation constraints may require a particular grouping.

▶ Logical design criteria (or other objectives unrelated to performance) may dictate a certain grouping of components.

So what happens when usage calls for a different grouping? In those situations, the Temporal Locality Principle guides us to look for techniques other than physical proximity to ensure that related actions are performed in a group or in immediate succession.

This guideline often goes hand in hand with the Efficiency Principle (Chapter 9) because by doing a group of related things at the same time we tend to minimize any associated overhead costs.

Guideline **10.11**	**Don't squander scarce spatial locality**

Any collection of system components can be grouped in only one way—we must choose carefully. Once we've chosen an optimal grouping scheme, other potentially useful groupings are excluded.

Guideline **10.12**	**Temporal Locality: *Closeness in Time***

After we have grouped related elements in one way, we may still need a different group of those same components to work together efficiently. In this situation, we need to look for techniques other than physical proximity to ensure that related actions are performed in a group or in immediate succession.

Applying the Temporal Locality Principle

We now discuss two areas of client/server design where the *Temporal Locality Principle* is particularly applicable: user interface design and remote database gateways.

User Interface Design.   User interface design for an imaginary application provides a good example of spatial and temporal locality. Figures 10.2 and 10.3 illustrate two design proposals for the user interface for a hypothetical bank teller application, possibly even an advanced version of an automated teller machine. The boxes represent distinct UI *views* provided by the application.

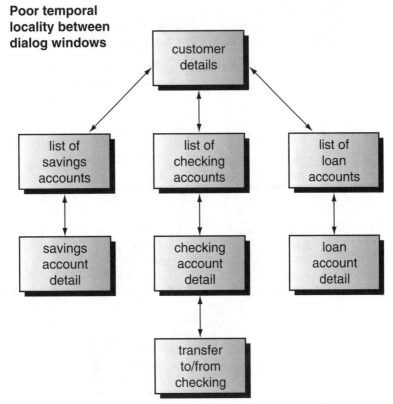

Poor temporal locality between dialog windows

FIGURE 10.2   Initial UI dialog design.

We will call them *windows;* you may think of them as screens, dialog boxes, menus, panels, displays, or views depending on your mental model of the implementation technology. The lines connecting the boxes represent user-navigable relationships among the windows.

Assume that, in any given window, the application designer has included all the information relevant to that particular application function. Then we might conclude that the application has good spatial locality—items that are used together have been grouped together. And, since both designs provide access to the same account information using the same set of windows for the various application functions, their spatial locality is identical.

The initial UI dialog design (Figure 10.2) is an example of very poor temporal locality. Reminiscent of the typical ATM, it offers the user a hierarchy of potential actions with no means of navigating between related account functions such as viewing checking and savings account details. A user of this interface would be forced to perform the functions associated with each account type individually, before moving on to work with the next account type, and so on.

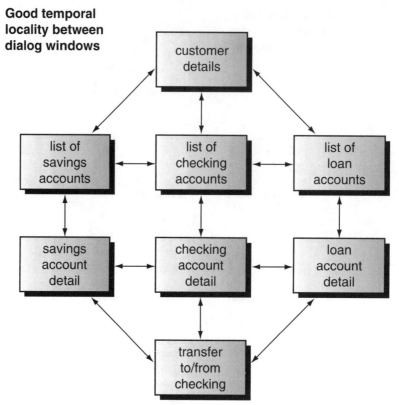

FIGURE **10.3**   Revised UI dialog design.

While the initial dialog design might be acceptable for some transactions, it would be very frustrating for others because *the sets of related actions the user needs to perform are not available together.* There is no easy way to compare savings and checking balances, moving from one to the other, and then to transfer funds from savings to checking.

This problem is solved in the revised design (Figure 10.3). An example of good temporal locality, it permits efficient navigation among the various account types and functions. Although it would take a little longer to develop the lateral navigation paths and the associated user interface elements to invoke them, the result would be well worth the effort in terms of the overall quality of the application.

We emphasize that this *is* a performance issue. When the interface does not support the natural flow of business actions, users cannot possibly perform their jobs efficiently. This makes the whole system inefficient. Conversely, we can make significant improvements in the user's perception of system performance simply by adhering to the Locality Principle in user interface design, without even touching the rest of the application code.

> ### Guideline 10.13 Create UI paths to support usage scenarios
>
> In user interface design, the Locality Principle reminds us to make sure that the related actions the user needs to perform are available together. Improving UI efficiency alone can make significant improvements in a user's perception of performance.

Federated Databases.   A class of application with poor temporal locality is the federated or multidatabase application that assembles its data at execution time from databases at separate locations. We discuss this type of remote data access technology in more detail in Chapter 9, in the section *SQL Gateways and Access Path Selection.*

If a frequently used application needs to process data from multiple databases, we may want to consider an alternative architecture. Because this type of application typically reads from multiple databases but updates, at most, one, we can create a data server at the departmental or workgroup level that supplies only the subset of information the application needs. The data server can be refreshed periodically or, if necessary, updated by replicating data from the source databases, as we discuss in Chapter 20. For the data server, an object DBMS is a good candidate.

This approach eliminates the processing overhead and response time delays of collecting and joining data at execution time. It has much better temporal locality than the federated database solution, and it will give better performance for the retrieval applications.

> ### Guideline 10.14 Federated databases
>
> Federated or multidatabase applications that assemble their data at execution time from database at separate locations have poor temporal locality. For performance-critical applications, create data servers at the departmental or workgroup level that supply only the subset of information the application needs. This will eliminate the processing overhead and response time delays of collecting and joining data at execution time.

Degree Locality

Degree locality refers to *closeness in capacity*. As we noted earlier, to ensure degree locality, we must match the data storage, transmission, and processing demands imposed by the business workload with the capacities of the hardware and software resources that make up the system.

Clearly, this guideline applies to the sizing of *physical or hardware resources*—processor speed, memory, disk space, communications channel bandwidth, and so on—to match the users' workload. Perhaps less obvious, but equally important in practice, are those situations where software components impose limits on *logical resources* like locks, threads, regions, address spaces, or buffers. These logical resources can be show-stoppers if they are not available in sufficient quantity to match the workload.

We discuss logical resource limits again later in this chapter, in the section *Tuning and Side Effects.*

Degree locality is a central principle of effective client/server design because most enterprise-distributed computing systems embrace a wide range of processor speeds, processor memory sizes, disk speeds and capacities, and network bandwidths. We cannot simply develop software that has a fixed requirement for processing, files, tables, buffer pools, cache, or message handling and expect it to run anywhere and everywhere without problems.

Among the theoretical advantages claimed for distributed systems are their flexibility and scalability in the face of varying workload demands. These are indeed desirable properties, but, like most good things in life, they do not come free. If we want to obtain the benefits of scalability, then we must design with scalability in mind. Client/server systems that run smoothly are those assembled from software components that have been *carefully scaled to fit on their respective processors.*

Guideline 10.15	**Degree locality:** *Closeness in capacity*

For optimal system performance, we must match up the data storage, transmission, and processing demands imposed by the business workload with the capacities of the hardware and software resources that make up the system.

Applying the Degree Locality Principle

The principle of degree locality reinforces the importance of *identifying the sensitivity of the application design to key business factors, predicting performance on the target platform,* and *managing ongoing system capacity*—three SPE activities we introduced earlier, in Part II of the book. To ensure that a design matches software needs with hardware capacities, *we must have already analyzed the projected demand.* Knowing expected workload volumes and their relationship to key business factors is the only way we can be confident we have sized the client, network, and server components correctly.

Finally, because distributed systems are inherently more modular than centralized ones, sometimes we actually do have the luxury of designing the distributed computing environment itself, as opposed to merely creating an application that must be made to run in an already existing environment. In these situations, the inverse statement of the locality principle is the most important one to remember: *"(Re)organize the physical computing resources to match the logical processing needs."*

Guideline 10.16	**Know the capacity requirements**

Knowing expected workload volumes and their relationship to key business factors is the only way we can be confident we have sized the client, network, and server components correctly.

Degree Locality and Peaks in Demand

When projecting expected workloads, we must be careful not to fall into the trap of designing a system to handle the average workload. It will be the peaks in demand that challenge our ability to meet the performance objectives. In our discussion of *The Centering Principle* in Chapter 5, we observed that—even if we can handle today's peaks successfully—volumes grow continually in most systems. (Guideline 5.22 notes a useful rule of thumb: *Today's peak is tomorrow's average.*) It is only by tracking the peaks and planning for performance at peak processing levels that we can create a truly scalable system architecture.

Guideline 10.17	**Plan for system scalability**

When designing a new distributed system, identify its peak processing requirements, and project *all* workload volumes well beyond their current levels. With these artificially high requirements in mind, select a system architecture that will let you match future workload growth with gradual increases in the capacity of the physical computing resources.

Effectual Locality

Effectual locality refers to *closeness in purpose.* When we build enterprise information systems, achieving effectual locality means making sure that separate components work together smoothly to satisfy the user's needs. This can mean many things—dedicating physical resources to match the nature of the workload, building or selecting software components that mesh together, or picking software that suits the user's workload.

To explain effectual locality, Connie Smith uses the obvious example of special-purpose hardware.[5] That is, if your purpose is to support data-mining

---

[5]Smith, *Performance Engineering*, 46.

Locality: A Logical or Physical Issue?

In the world of IT, we all have different backgrounds and experiences. It is common for people who have to think about processing resources and capacity to have worked primarily in the "systems" side of the organization. People with a systems perspective tend to focus on processing the maximum amount of work using existing resources, managing conflicts for computing resources, and minimizing the need for new hardware purchases. An important goal for systems people is to keep everything working smoothly because bottlenecks in shared resources can affect many areas of the business.

Physical Biases

Degree locality is a key issue in systems design because it deals with ideas of capacity. People with a systems perspective may be tempted to see the concept of degree locality as an argument for skipping *logical* design activities like data or process modeling and jumping straight into physical design.

This probably occurs because they have a strong bias toward viewing the computing environment as a resource with a fixed capacity and the new applications as potential sources of excessive demand. So they tend to be very impatient with logical designs that they "know will never fly" and want to start right away to build with the performance limitations of the existing environment in mind.

Logical Alternatives

Let us offer a slightly different perspective. In our view, the Locality Principle actually supports the need for logical design for two reasons:

▶ First, having a very clear understanding of the logical processing requirements is always the starting point for good physical design.
▶ Second, mapping a logical design to the available physical resources may reveal areas where we must make adjustments. At this point we can analyze more than one possible solution and make an informed choice. If we

applications, then a parallel processing database machine with hardware (and probably software too) that is optimized for processing complex queries against massive databases is ideally suited for the task. While this is a good example, it is somewhat limited in its scope. It does not illustrate the real significance of the effectual locality principle, which applies to a much wider and more general range of design decisions than the use of special-purpose hardware. In a

do have to compromise the best logical design for reasons of performance, we will have made a conscious decision to do so. This is much better than the alternative, which often amounts to making unplanned compromises simply by following rules of thumb about performance that may not really apply.

On the other hand, the Locality Principle also reminds us that if we care about performance, then we cannot simply implement our logical designs without regard for the physical consequences. Spatial and temporal locality emphasize the impact on *application performance* of various design choices. Degree locality adds to that a concern for *system performance* based on workload volumes and capacity.

None of this is an argument for abandoning logical design altogether. Analysis and logical design provide the security of:

▶ A firm foundation of business facts and requirements
▶ A complete plan for mapping those facts and requirements into a technical solution

Without these, software construction is like paying a contractor to build a house without blueprints. We may get a house that can withstand an earthquake, we may get a house we can afford, or we may get a house that meets our needs as owners and occupants. But if we want to be sure of meeting all three goals, we should hire an architect to design the house before we begin building.

Guideline 10.18 Locality: A logical or physical issue?

If we care about performance, then we cannot simply implement our logical designs without regard for the physical consequences, both for applications and for the system as a whole. We will be better placed to make physical design choices if we start from a clear understanding of the logical requirements and a clear plan for translating them into software.

complex distributed system, after all, the hardware is just one layer of the total solution, and most systems are built using general-purpose hardware. Yet the goal of effectual locality is one of the strongest motivations for distributed computing itself, which aims to replace or supplement the proprietary mainframe with an open and scalable network of smaller processors that can be more responsive to the needs of users.

In our view, the effectual locality principle applies in *all* areas of distributed system design. It is the principle that shows us how to ensure that all the separate parts or layers of the system *fit together* effectively. When we introduced the fundamental software engineering principles (formality, simplicity, completeness), we pointed out how creating a design with *conceptual integrity* was an important aspect of simplicity. The SPE design principle of effectual locality addresses the way we actually achieve that logical software engineering goal of conceptual integrity.

To get the best performance, we must design the software functions and organize and distribute the workload across the available computing resources in such a way as to match the following as closely as possible:

▶ The behavior patterns and information processing needs of the user
▶ The behavior and processing demands of the software
▶ The availability, responsiveness, and capacity of the hardware resources

> **Guideline 10.19** **Effectual locality:** *Closeness in purpose*
>
> For optimal performance, design software functions and distribute the workload across available computing resources so as to match:
>
> ▶ The behavior patterns and information processing needs of the user
> ▶ The behavior and processing demands of the software
> ▶ The availability, responsiveness, and capacity of the hardware resources

Mixing Workloads.   If effectual locality suggests matching workloads with processing resources, how are we to reconcile an immediate need to process large decision-support queries with an ongoing transaction workload that demands high throughput and short response times? The more resources consumed by queries, the fewer remain to process transactions, and the larger the impact of the query workload on transaction throughput.

On the other hand, if we try to maintain overall throughput by artificially restricting the resources allocated to queries, queries take much longer. This alone can cause political problems unless expectations have been set properly. There is a potential side effect, however, that is even more damaging. If the DBMS holds any database locks for a long-running query, subsets of the transaction workload may have to wait until the query completes, causing erratic transaction response times.

The usual resolution of this dilemma is to *avoid mixing short transactions with long-running queries* in the first place. We refer to this as *Inmon's rule* because the well-known speaker and author Bill Inmon spent many years during the 1980s evangelizing this concept, making the rounds of the database user groups, talking about the importance of separating operational from informational processing. In many respects, the current trend toward separate database machines and separate processors for data warehousing is a logical application of the effectual locality principle and of Inmon's Rule, in particular.

> **Guideline 10.20** **Inmon's Rule**
> *Don't mix short transactions with long-running queries.*
> When we have high-performance operational workloads, we should keep them on a separate processor, separate from *ad hoc* or unknown queries, which may have massive processing requirements.

Of course, Inmon's rule is not just for transactions and queries. It can be applied to any mix of workloads that have different performance characteristics. We should consider:

▶ Setting aside dedicated software (DBMS) and hardware (processor, disks) for query workloads. These are usually called *operational data stores* and *data warehouses,* and we discuss them in Chapter 20, *Using Data Replication,* and Chapter 21, *Using Data Warehouses and Mining.*

▶ Using parallel processors for massive queries. We discuss this further in Chapter 13, *The Parallelism Principle.*

▶ Splitting off work onto a dedicated server whenever a single application (or a group of related applications) has a high volume of processing and critical performance objectives.

> **Guideline 10.21** **Dedicated application servers**
> Consider splitting off work onto a dedicated server whenever a single application has a high volume of processing and critical performance objectives.

Effectual Locality and the Two-Tier Architecture

Dennis Shasha's database design principle said, "Render onto server what is due onto server." Another way of saying this is that we should *put things where they belong.* When we design two-tier client/server systems, some things *belong* on the server; others *belong* on the client. Consider the following:

▶ Those parts of an application that require only the immediate user's context belong on the client workstation; those that depend on volatile, shared information belong on the server. The difficult design decisions involve parts of applications that support a single user but use shared information. We address this subject in more detail in Part IV of this book.

▶ For usability and responsiveness, we need immediate validation of user input on the client. For data integrity, we need verification of data-related business rules on the database server. Sometimes this may mean running the same checks twice; however, the motivations are different. On the client, the purpose of input validation is to help an individual user; on the server it's there to protect a community resource (the shared database) from corruption by any user.

▶ Computationally intensive parts of the application belong on the client. They include processing all kinds of media, *text, graphics, sound, voice,* and *video,* unless the result of the processing will be used by multiple clients. And all kinds of computation, whether it's *compilation, calculation, ciphering,* or even *contemplation* (or whatever it is that expert systems do under the covers while they are looking for patterns in data)—all these activities belong on the client. (Note that this statement applies to typical *business* workloads, in an environment in which a server must support an ever-growing population of clients. It may not apply to computationally intense *scientific* workloads that could overwhelm the processing capabilities of a client workstation.)

▶ Following the dictates of spatial locality, some application functions have no natural home. Like shadows, they follow their data wherever it goes. These include query optimization, data compression and decompression, encryption and decryption, sorting, searching, and statistical analysis. For shared data, these functions belong on the database server.

> **Guideline 10.22** **Natural client processing**
> When we design two-tier client/server systems, all functions that support a single user belong on the client. The initial design goal should be to offload all single-user computation, except for that related to processing shared data, to the client workstation.

> **Guideline 10.23** **Natural server processing**
> When we design two-tier client/server systems, all shared functions belong on the server. These include all processing of shared data on behalf of all clients, until that data is reduced to suitable form to hand over to the client workstation or store in the database, as appropriate.

Effectual Locality and the Three-Tier Architecture

Moving up from two-tier systems to three-tier or enterprise client/server systems, we again see that effectual locality leads to a natural architecture, as illustrated in Figure 10.4. We have named the three levels of the architecture based on their respective relationships to business data: *Consumption, Context,* and *Content.* We discuss each level briefly.

Data Consumption.   As before, the purpose of the client or workstation layer is primarily to support *data consumption* by a single user. This layer is usually the ultimate *consumer* of corporate data (and sometimes the producer, too). This level handles most data preparation and presentation and some data collection. Located at this level are small amounts of dedicated user data, user processing context information, GUI or object-oriented user interfaces, menus, forms, and dialog boxes, as well as validity checking—in fact, everything needed to make the user's life as painless as possible. The consumer is king!

Application Context.   Located in the middle—at the departmental level—we find the *application context.* Data used by applications at the department or workgroup level is usually organized and stored in the most effective way for the purpose of that department. That is, it has effectual locality. Objects, and object DBMSs, because they are constructed with a particular application in mind, fit naturally at this level of the architecture. Finally, because of the emphasis on applications, transaction management and data integrity rules are issues that must be managed in this layer. Both are concerned with the correctness and consistency of data in the context of application processing.

Enterprise Data Content.   We call this layer the *enterprise data content* layer because a lot of the organization's core business data may originate here, being generated by enterprise-wide operational systems. Here the focus is not on a single application. Instead, data at this level has an enterprise context. Ideally, it would be normalized. In practice, data found here is either in prerelational or relational form, organized according to the needs of an operational system and the corresponding DBMS. Cleaned and reorganized data stores like enterprise-level data warehouses and operational data stores also belong at this level; these do exist in some organizations.

> **Guideline 10.24   Natural three-tier architectures**
>
> When we design three-tier client/server systems, applying the ideas of effectual locality produces a natural division of data and functions across the three tiers. Briefly, the three architectural layers focus on data consumption, application context, and enterprise data content, respectively.

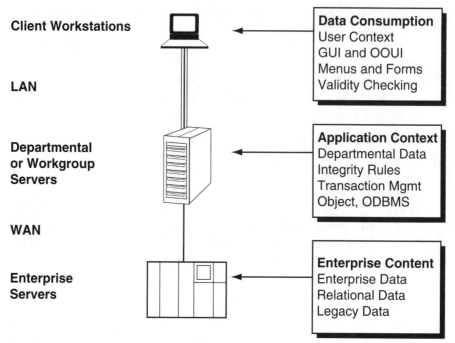

FIGURE 10.4   Locality and the three-tier architecture.

Bottom-Up Design and Systems Software

One of the perennial debates among software engineering methodologists concerns the relative merits of top-down decomposition (also called stepwise refinement) and bottom-up composition as strategies for creating a modular design. This subject is covered in most books on software engineering or structured design, and we do not propose to review the details here. The most balanced discussions (for example, McConnell's *Code Complete*)[6] concede that design should be a heuristic process in which the two strategies are complementary.

One aspect of this discussion deserves mention, however, because it relates in an important way to the locality principle, particularly effectual locality. It concerns the question of how shared modules or common subroutines should be developed. In the top-down approach, common functions arise almost by accident. For example, a designer, working down one functional decomposition path, sees that a function now required is similar to one previously identified. The existing function is reworked, generalizing it to create a common subroutine serving both purposes. This approach is not entirely satisfactory; shared

---

[6]McConnell, *Code Complete*, 145–7.

modules created in this way tend to be hybrids that are not well designed for either context.

In bottom-up design, common functions arise in the earliest stages when the designer is thinking about the characteristics (and limitations) of the underlying technology and the general requirements of the software solution. Common low-level functions are designed to offer new and useful services constructed from the elementary building blocks of the underlying technology. These, in turn, will be used by higher-level functions later in the design process. At this stage, the specification of the common functions is quite independent of any particular context in which they might be used.

Bottom-up design is generally felt to be the preferable technique for designing common modules. However, in their book on *Software Engineering*, Doug Bell, Ian Morrey, and John Pugh provide an important insight about this strategy. It is that "*bottom-up design requires an act of faith on the part of the designer, that suitable features have been devised. There is no guarantee that the features that are implemented will turn out to be useful.*"[7]

We would add the further note of caution, "Even if the function implemented is useful, there is no guarantee that its performance will be acceptable." This is where the Effectual Locality Principle comes into play. It states that paying attention to a component's purpose is an essential step in software performance engineering. Therefore, we should be extremely cautious about including any common function or routine that was not explicitly designed for the purpose for which our system intends to use it. Remember the Business Factors Principle and our admonition earlier in this chapter to "*know the user*"!

Applying this thinking to the development of enterprise client/server systems, we see that all software development includes bottom-up design. Every developer must make use of general-purpose systems software functions that have been created and supplied by others, without any knowledge of a specific application. Everyone must build on top of the functions supplied by operating systems, database management systems, transaction monitors, and other middleware. Concern about whether a module is suitably designed for our intended purpose must extend beyond just the application modules we develop ourselves, to include all general-purpose, low-level functions the application uses.

---

[7]Doug Bell, Ian Morrey, and John Pugh, *Software Engineering* (Upper Saddle River, NJ: Prentice-Hall, 1992), 71.

| Guideline 10.25 | **Effectual locality and general-purpose software** Assess the behavior and performance characteristics of all general-purpose software *before* depending on it to perform harmoniously and acceptably in any application or system. |

Holistic Design and Software Tuning

Effectual locality is all about holistic design; it continually reminds us that *the whole is greater than the sum of the parts.* When systems are assembled from independent but cooperating layers or components, it is not enough to design each part well.

For optimal performance, the entire set of components must operate harmoniously and efficiently when subjected to the processing demands of the user. It is not possible to achieve that degree of harmony unless the design of each component, and of the overall system, is driven by a clear vision of the system's overall purpose. In other words, the design must observe the principle of effectual locality.

> **Guideline 10.26** **Effectual locality and layered systems**
>
> For optimal performance, an entire set of components or layers must operate harmoniously and efficiently when subjected to the processing demands of the user. It is not possible to achieve that degree of harmony unless the design of each component or layer, and of the overall system, is driven by a clear vision of the system's overall purpose.

Software Tuning Knobs

Sometimes the designers of systems software products allow us to defer the analysis of grouping possibilities until after implementation by supplying tuning parameters ("knobs") that let us adjust the degree of grouping in some key area of the product's operation.

For example, many DBMSs have a tuning parameter to control the block size used for "blocked fetch"—the action of transferring groups of query result rows from the DBMS server to the client requester. A DBMS administrator is expected to consider the effect of different block sizes, perhaps by applying the Workload Principle to select a block size that will minimize the cost of transferring the result rows to the client for a "typical" database query.

In practice, however, the total processing cost for different block sizes is a difficult thing for a DBA to estimate in advance, and to complicate matters further, total processing cost may not be the only performance-related issue. Increasing the data transfer block size has several effects:

▶ It *reduces* the number of separate data transfer operations needed to transfer large result sets.
▶ It *delays* the client's opportunity to process the first row of a large result set until all the rows in the first block have been extracted from the database server and shipped across the network to the client application.

► It *increases* the possibility of wasted processing on both the client and the database server if a user discards most of the results after examining the first few rows.

To weigh the significance of these different effects, we must consider them in the context of our system and our user population. Without the context of our own performance goals, we have no way to determine the relative importance of the different performance variables. In other words, we must appeal to the effectual locality principle to help us make the best design choice *for our purposes.* Typically, this involves making trade-offs among workloads, which we discuss further in Chapter 14, *The Trade-off Principle.*

Guideline 10.27   **Effectual locality and tuning**

In a complex environment, tuning changes affect more than one application. To weigh the significance of these different effects, we must understand their relative importance for our particular system and our user population. To tune effectively, we must understand clearly the purpose of each application and the purpose of the tuning change.

Tuning and Side Effects

In Chapter 3, we noted that computer systems are composed of many logically and physically related components. Before tuning such a system, we must understand these relationships. Otherwise, a change designed to help one component might hinder another, producing a net drop in performance. Ideally, we should understand how each component works and how those components use the system resources—the processors, memory, disks, and network.

Next, we would ideally like to be able to measure separately the performance of each system component. Then we could easily see the effect on the entire system of a change in any one component. In practice, as we discussed in Chapter 6, the available monitoring tools produce only a few snapshots of a system's more visible corners. Typically, we can monitor an overall performance parameter of interest (like response time, processor utilization, or transaction rate), together with some details of a subset of the system components.

In this situation, we must assume that the remaining components are not affected by our tuning changes or regard them jointly as a "black box" whose inner workings we do not need to understand, provided that the overall result of our tuning efforts moves the performance parameter in the right direction. If a shortage of time or tools limits us to measuring only a subset of the system, then this approach may be the only one possible.

In the long run, though, tuning based on limited information can itself produce problems. Complex systems are often susceptible to sudden "de-tuning" or performance degradation as a result of a relatively small change.

Generally, this degradation is not caused by having overcommitted the physical computing resources. As physical resources become increasingly overloaded, the result is usually experienced as a gradual overall slowdown, causing a general malaise affecting performance for all users. Sudden drops typically occur because a shared logical resource created by a programmer (like buffers or threads) has reached a certain critical point. Even if that critical point can be predicted (although usually it cannot), if that parameter is not being monitored, we may be confronted by unexpected performance problems in spite of previous tuning work.

> **Guideline 10.28** **When tuning, beware of side effects**
> Tuning a single component of a system is dangerous without a clear understanding of the bigger picture. Tuning often has side effects; fixing one thing may make others worse.

Logical Resources: An Old Example.   Years ago, part of my job was to tune IMS systems. (IMS is a comprehensive mainframe transaction management software product from IBM.) In one highly tuned IMS installation where real memory was constrained, adding some new applications that involved more database processing than previously used resulted in a sudden, dramatic loss of performance. There were a number of reasons for this:

▶ Although there was enough memory to load application programs, the system did not have enough memory to store the corresponding database descriptors in the memory pool (called a *PSB pool*) reserved for this purpose.
▶ As a result, the level of multiprogramming dropped, reducing the overall throughput and causing incoming messages to back up in the transaction input queues.
▶ This caused the message queues to grow too large to be stored entirely in memory, requiring the queue manager to begin unloading messages from the queues to disk to make space available for new messages.
▶ This introduced even more delays because while the queue manager was busily managing the queues, it was not handling any user input or output.

All of this took place in spite of previous tuning in which memory allocations had been "tuned" to free up the maximum amount of memory for programs. It is clear, of course, that this exercise had been carried too far—but there was no way of knowing until the users began to complain.

Modern Equivalents.   Although IMS developers long ago eliminated this particular bottleneck, every complex software system has its own PSB pool (as users of Windows know only too well). Corey, Abbey, and Dechichio call them *show-stoppers*. Their book, *Tuning Oracle*, devotes a chapter to the topic, pointing out examples of operating system limits and DBMS limits that, if reached or exceeded, can bring the system to its knees.[8]

Because every software product is unique, there is no single guideline that covers all the potential hazards. But look out! If a software product has *installation variables* or *setup options* or *initialization parameters*, never simply accept the default values. Be very careful whenever you set aside space for anything, or allocate the maximum number of concurrent instances of files, threads, users, open tables, log buffers, or any other widget of which you may need more than one.

▶ Think about the current workload.
▶ Think about planned growth.
▶ Think about the peak periods of the day or month.

Read the product manuals, and unless there is a good reason to put a cap on a logical resource (for example, to control the number of concurrent tasks to match the power of the processor), allocate enough logical widgets for the worst processing mix your system could be expected to handle, and add a few more for safety.

In summary, if we want the security of a well-tuned system, there is no substitute for a complete picture of how the system works and what work it's doing. This has been confirmed many times over by practical experience and painful surprises.

Guideline 10.29	**Allocate enough logical resources**

If a software product has *installation variables* or *setup options* or *initialization parameters,* never simply accept the default values. Be very careful whenever you set aside space or allocate a maximum number of any logical resource. Plan for the worst processing mix your system could be expected to handle, and add a margin for safety.

---

[8]Michael Corey, Michael Abbey, and Dan Dechichio, *Tuning Oracle* (Berkeley, CA: Oracle Press, 1995), 139.

Case Study: The Consolidated Software Corporate Shared Calendar System

The Consulting Services division of Consolidated Software (CS/cs), a large firm of software consultants, is headquartered in Santa Cruz, California. It has branch offices in the major cities and employees everywhere, many working from their homes. In the past, branch offices were relatively autonomous, each managing its own projects, often using its own pet project management and tracking tools. With the growth of tele-commuting, there is an ever-increasing tendency for employees to be assigned to several projects based on their special skills, so that many of the company's projects now involve employees from more than one branch.

This change has complicated the process of project tracking and time reporting. A recent audit concluded that CS/cs had lost a lot of potential revenue on larger, fixed-price projects because the project leaders had no easy way to keep track of the real costs, and no one had the time to figure out how to match up the project data from all the different branch office tracking systems.

Under the leadership of development manager, Chuck "Cubie" Brown, the company is currently developing a new corporate client/server application to handle all project tracking and time management and to coordinate individual, project, departmental, and corporate calendars and schedules.

The Corporate Shared Calendar System (CS/cs3) has three main functions:

▶ It allows employees to maintain their own calendars, schedule meetings with other employees, and stay abreast of meetings and events scheduled by others at the departmental and corporate level.

▶ It has a project management component that allows groups of employees to create and maintain schedules for shared projects, to assign tasks, and to report on the status of their assigned tasks and of all the projects in which they are involved.

▶ It supplies a company-wide internal e-mail service that is integrated with the calendar scheduling and task reporting functions.

A Problem for Joe Tuna

In CS/cs3, all project history details were maintained on a DB2 system running on a single dedicated project server machine in Santa Cruz. Now that the system was live, all the branch offices were busy migrating their existing project data into the DB2 database, and more and more employees were starting to use the new project tracking component. But they were not impressed.

The corporate architecture group at CS/cs had recommended using DB2 because they felt it could handle the large databases and high transaction volumes expected. But as use of new system grew, its performance went downhill fast. Cubie Brown had to install a help line to deal with employees from all over the country who were calling to complain about periods of extreme sluggishness. The help line didn't help. Some project managers even threatened to go back to using their old branch office systems if Cubie didn't fix the problem soon.

Cubie called in Joe Tuna, the performance analyst on the CS/cs3 project. Joe was busy with his pet programming project—*TuneIT,* a little utility that would suggest tuning changes to the index structures by analyzing SQL access paths. *"It would be really useful for the next big DB2 project,"* Cubie agreed, *"but there may not be another one unless we figure out how to make this one run faster. The history application is obviously screwed up, and right now I've got the whole company on my back. I need you to drop everything else and find out why."*

Resisting the urge to answer by telling Cubie about the difference between reactive and proactive performance engineering, Joe nodded "OK." Heading for his office, he tried to refresh his memory of the project history application. He had reviewed and approved the original SQL design. He knew that whenever an employee requested a project history report, the client application submitted an SQL request to DB2 on the project server, retrieving just his or her own project's data. Managers could see all the projects they or their employees were working on. The application generated a default SQL query with a standard WHERE clause specifying the projects to be reported on and the level of detail in the report. And just last week, while he was working on some ideas for his *TuneIT* code, Joe had been doing a routine check of indexing standards; he was pretty sure that the project ID and employee ID columns in the history table were indexed properly.

Back at his desk, Joe started browsing through the data he had been collecting to test the *TuneIT* code. He remembered that users could customize the WHERE clause with other selection criteria if they wanted to. "I'll bet this is some dumb query from one of the new projects," he thought to himself. "If I had my *TuneIT* routine working, I could find it right away." He had statistics from the DBMS catalog and performance traces showing SQL usage patterns on all the major databases at various times of the day.

After a while, he noticed something odd.

Large numbers of active SQL requests for data were being aborted by the client application. After some work to match up the aborts with the corresponding SQL calls earlier in the trace, he could see that this problem did not seem to be related to the project ID; it was happening on several projects. Further analysis showed that in almost all the cases where these aborts occurred, the SQL requests were made to the history database.

The big trace file didn't actually list the SQL text, but in another file Joe had assembled just the SQL calls and the corresponding access paths from the trace. He printed the file and worked through it, marking the aborted SQL calls. He was pleased to find a pattern. In most cases, the application was requesting all the history records for one or more projects, sorted by date, in descending date sequence.

At first he thought there was a bug in the history client application code and spent some time working with Missy Take in the QA group trying to reproduce the problem on her test system, but without success. Finally, he started up a very limited DBMS trace of the history database, routed the output to his workstation, and sat at his desk waiting for the SQL abort command from a client to appear.

Before long his persistence was rewarded; he quickly traced the user ID. It was Will Hackaway in Madison, Wisconsin, the chief programmer on the MOO project. Will had a large project developing object-oriented applications for the milk marketing board. Joe called Will and told him he was trying to debug a performance problem in the project history application.

"Glad to know you guys are working on the problem, response times have been really bad sometimes," said Will. But to Joe's surprise, Will had not experienced a failure of any kind. Puzzled, Joe turned on a detailed trace and asked Will to repeat his last interaction with the system.

Nothing happened.

"What did you just do?" Joe asked.

"I displayed a list of all the employees on my project and sent them an e-mail message about a possible design bug I had uncovered."

"Weren't you looking at the project history database?" Joe asked.

"Not now. I was earlier, when I was thinking about the bug. I was looking to see if anyone else had reported it. Can't you see me in your trace?"

"Maybe. . . ," said Joe, ". . . anyway, why don't you do it again—look at the project history again, I mean. Just as you did last time."

"OK—here goes. . . ."

Joe waited. He saw the trace of the SQL request, followed by the FETCH request for the results. But that was it—still no abort command. He waited.

"What's happening? Are you tracing me?"

"Yes, but I don't see anything. Are you paging through the results?"

"No, . . . but I will if you want me to."

"What did you do last time?"

"Well, normally I just look at the first couple of screens, to see what's happened on the project recently. The history report shows the most recent project activities first and continues all the way back in date sequence. I check it regularly, so the things I'm looking for are generally near the top."

"What did you do next?"

"*That's it. I was studying my code for a while—maybe 10 minutes or so. If I wanted to, I could respond directly to the person responsible for any line item in the history report by just clicking on that line in the report. Then the system gives me a list of project management actions I can take at that time. In this case, though, I wanted to fire off a message to everyone on the project, so I had to go into e-mail. I pulled up the address list for the project team and sent the e-mail, as I showed you before. Because I'm the project manager and the message is for the whole team, it gets recorded in the project history database too.*"

"Oh, really! I didn't realize that e-mail got recorded too."

"*Yes! There's a constant stream of project-related stuff in e-mail. Plans, project notes, spec modifications, design changes, new versions of design documents, meeting notifications, status reports, updates to the current baseline code. The bigger the project, the more e-mail. The project history database is like a central bulletin board for the whole project. In the first release, recording wasn't optional, so the history database even ended up tracking all kinds of important project events like notification of free food in the kitchen. Now we can turn off recording for those types of messages. It's not so interesting, but I guess it saves a lot of wasted space in the database.*"

"OK, do it again now."

This time Joe saw the abort request come across. He asked Will to repeat the sequence of actions, and the same thing happened. He thanked Will for his time and promised to do what he could to fix the performance as soon as possible. Then he went to look for Dee Coda, the programmer who had designed and written most of the client side of the CS/cs3 application.

Taking a diagram (see Figure 10.5) from her desk, she showed Joe how the code worked:

"*After it issues the SQL query and gets the OK back from the database, the history display routine issues the FETCH command to the database and waits for the first block of data to arrive in the client buffer. Then it formats the first page of data, sticks it in the history display window to give the user something to look at, but continues to issue more fetches to get more blocks of data. When the buffer is full, control goes back to the user interface, which lets the user page down through the data in the buffer and select any line item for action. If the user tries to page down past the end of the buffer, or print a report, the client software saves the current buffer to a temporary spool file on disk and goes back to the server database to get more blocks of data and fill another buffer, and so on. . . .*"

It made sense, but Joe was still puzzled. He showed Dee Coda the printout of the trace he had run earlier. "Why don't we see more FETCH requests?" he asked.

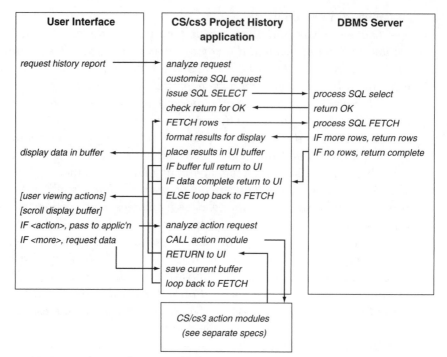

FIGURE 10.5   CS/cs application diagram.

"Well, Joe," she said, ". . . you should be proud of us! We tuned it. After looking at some of the current project systems, we figured that most projects would eventually include large numbers of tasks and checkpoints. So our first design decision was to use a large buffer in the client application and a large block size to transfer the results of the SQL queries from the project server back to the workstation.

"Then we matched up our default buffer size in the client with the size of the DB2 message buffer for block fetch on the database server. Actually, a user can change the buffer size on the client if he or she wants, but most of them don't bother to find out about how the code works—they just run with the defaults. And since the projects were all pretty big, we set the default buffer size at 32K. The history rows are variable length, and most of the status entries are quite short, but we figured on an average of about 100 characters. So the buffer can hold about 320 rows on most projects, which is 15 or 16 screens of the report."

"Sounds like more than enough for most users," said Joe, recalling his conversation with Will Hackaway.

"Well, since there were going to be a lot of users sharing the history data-base, we knew you would want us to make sure our database requests were as efficient as possible. We try to get in and get out fast with all the data we need. Most of the time we get enough data in the first block, and we never have to go back into the database for more.

Joe smiled. "OK, that's good. So when do you issue this SQL abort?" he asked, pointing to the trace.

"Abort? I never do that—my code never fails!" She paused. *"Actually, I think that must be done by CSam—that's our common SQL access module. Moe from the corporate systems group wrote it. It handles everything to do with connecting to server databases and shipping off the actual SQL requests. I just call CSam with a SELECT parameter when I want to search the history data-base. I get some data back from the SELECT and then I say FETCH if I want to get more."* She paused, thinking. *"Oh yes! I also call CSam with a TERMINATE parameter when the user clicks on the CANCEL or EXIT buttons. That's all I ever do in my code."*

"Thanks, Dee," Joe said, picking up his notes and heading for the coffee machine. He could already see that it might take more than one change to the history tracking system to fix the problems, but at least he was starting to see what some of the problems might be.

Back at his desk Joe drank his coffee and stared out of the window. It was late afternoon, and the low sun sparkled on the bay. Volume on the tracking system would be peaking soon, as people logged in their day's activities. If performance was poor already, he knew better than to risk making things even worse by running more traces right now. He took out the trace printout again and started to make notes. Then he dug out an old copy of the CSam spec and skimmed through it, marking one page with a yellow tag. It read:

"CSam should always be called from an application's CANCEL and EXIT routines, to enable proper termination of any open database transaction. CSam will ensure that no client has more than one open database transaction with a given database server. An attempt to initiate a second SQL transaction with any database server during an open transaction with that server will trigger CSam to terminate the current transaction before submitting the new request."

"Another piece of the puzzle," he said to himself triumphantly, borrowing one of Cubie Brown's favorite expressions. He still had some loose ends to tie up, but he was pleased with his progress. He began jotting down some notes and questions.

Notes on the Project History Tracking System.   Joe's notes listed these questions:

1. Big projects generate a lot of history records—like a bulletin board. Need capacity planning?
2. People use the project management system constantly. Percentage recording versus reviewing status?
3. Project managers use the system several times a day. How often? Mostly reviewing?
4. Free-form SQL query facility not used—requires SQL skills. Any user training?
5. Standard history report is a quick way to check on all recent project activity. Cost?
6. Users rarely page forward to view older line items. How many pages needed on average?
7. Users can spend unlimited time viewing information in a history report. Typical viewing time?
8. Eventually, user either responds to a report line item or exits from the application. Percentages?
9. See CSam spec, section 4.2, on transaction termination. Why issue Abort?
10. Moe Wok (C/Sam)—DB2 systems experience?

A whimsical idea struck him. "Maybe I should create a project now and use the project history system to track myself. What would Cubie say if I told him I couldn't make progress because the tracking system was slowing me down?!" He chuckled to himself.

Debugging Questions

What might be causing the response time problems in the CS/cs3 history tracking application? To test your debugging skills, you may wish to pause at this point to consider the evidence. Questions to consider are these:

1. Is the problem in DB2, in the application code, or in C/Sam?
2. Where would you look, and what information would you look for to confirm your hypothesis?
3. What solutions would you suggest?

Back to Joe Tuna's Office

After some more investigation, Joe drew some conclusions about the design of the History Tracking system. He decided to write a short memo, summarizing his observations about the design parameters and their impact on performance.

FETCH Block Size versus Client Application Logic: Performance Issues

As a result of the recent performance problems in the project history application, I have reviewed the design of the application and the database. Here are some observations:

Client Application Externals

▶ Most users are not trained in SQL and are not using the free-form query facility. I suggest we provide SQL training and consider adding some standard templates to the application to address common user reporting requirements.

▶ The application offers users the opportunity to display a history report for a single project or for all projects the user is assigned to. There is no facility to limit reporting to recent events only. As a result, it appears that some users may be requesting history reports as a way to report on recent entries in the project history database for their project(s). This results in unnecessary database processing.

▶ I suggest we do some more analysis to better determine user requirements for reporting. It may be possible to provide an option for employees to report on some recent subset of the project data that would address the real purpose behind many requests for history reports.

Client Application Internals

▶ The history reporting application always uses a database FETCH block size of 32K to control the number of rows retrieved before the first screen is displayed.

▶ The application uses its internal buffer size to control the fraction of the result set to be retrieved before pausing to wait for a user action. Currently, this also defaults to 32K, but it could be increased.

▶ If there are more result rows to fetch, then the application keeps its SQL cursor open in the DB2 table(s) from which the data is being fetched while the user examines the first set of results.

▶ In the history database, data is stored by date within project code. For SQL queries that retrieve data on more than one project, DB2 sorts the data into time sequence across all projects and stores the results in a temporary table prior to retrieval by the user.

▶ For multiproject queries, an unfinished transaction causes the user's cursor to remain open in the temporary table. Because temporary tables are not shared, this does not interfere with any other users.

▶ For single-project queries, the optimizer figures out how to get the data in the right sequence directly from the base table, so no temporary table is created by DB2. For these queries, when the cursor is held open some pages are locked in the history base table, which can lock out other users who need to update the history database for the same project. This is a likely cause of the erratic response times many users have experienced.

Server-side Solution

The current server message buffer size setting for database FETCH requests is large, but we could increase it even further. This would:

1. *Reduce* the number of data transfers needed to transfer large result sets.
2. *Delay* the client's opportunity to process the first row of a large result set until all the rows in the block have been extracted from the database server and shipped across the network to the client application.
3. *Increase* the possibility of wasted processing on both the client and the database server whenever a user discards most of the results after examining the first few rows.

Advantage: Using a larger buffer on the server would probably solve the current problem.

Disadvantage: Selecting an even larger block size creates other problems that will only get worse as the projects grow. Doing so means taking a position on the relative importance of these different performance variables for our database server and our user population. Also, there is the question of how large it should be. We would need more research to come up with a proposal. Finally, making this change on the server reduces the possibility of tuning the client-side settings for any project because the client's buffer must be large enough to accept whatever the server sends.

Client-side Solutions

There are three ways to solve the client-side problem:

1. Increase the size of the client buffer to make it large enough to retrieve all history report rows before the report is formatted and displayed. Based on the current client-side logic, this technique would permit the client to retrieve all its data and immediately close the DB2 cursor before

user viewing of the report begins. As a result, once the report is initially displayed, paging through the report would not require any further access to DB2, and other users would be free to access and update the tables used in the query.

Advantage: This solution is easy to implement, provided there are no client buffer size limitations due to the capacity of the client platform.

Disadvantage: Retrieving all the rows before displaying the first screen will mean that sometimes it will take much longer for the user to see a response. On balance, though, this design will probably lead to less erratic response times.

2. Another possibility would be to add a "maximum rows" parameter to the client application, to limit the rows retrieved. The default for this could be set to be less than one buffer full of data, but the user could override it if he or she really wanted to see more data. The client would then terminate the query on reaching the defined row count, which would release any locks being held in DB2.

Advantage: The additional application logic is conceptually simple. The result is flexible, with user control. It allows for differences among users and projects.

Disadvantages: This solution is more work than the first; in particular, it involves some new UI. Also, someone would have to educate the users. What if a user overrides the default one day and doesn't bother to set it back down again? Then we're back to the same problem as now. To prevent this, we could force a low default and not retain any overrides beyond the current application session. Then maybe we'd have some people complaining about having to reset the parameter every time. Therefore, I suggest we collect more information about typical user viewing requirements before we consider this solution.

3. A more elegant design would be to continue the present approach of retrieving just one block of rows before the first screen is displayed. Give control back to the user, but if there are still more rows to retrieve, then also create a separate FETCH task that runs in the background. The FETCH task will continue issuing more FETCH commands for the remaining data, updating the buffers and moving data out to the temporary spool file as necessary. Typically, all this would complete while the user is still viewing the first set of results, so by the time the user needs more

data, it would all be on the workstation. The users could print reports, do more analysis, or do whatever they wanted, all without going back into DB2.

Advantage: This design combines quick response for the user with minimal time holding cursor position in the base tables.

Disadvantage: This approach requires much more complex programming. Because this is a "system" approach, requiring multiple concurrent database connections, we could ask Moe Wok in the Corporate Systems group to research it and make a proposal.

Conclusion

In many areas of software component design, the grouping decision can have a significant effect on performance, as we discussed in Chapter 7 under the software design technique of *Localization.* Frequently, the right grouping choice will be the one that best achieves effectual locality between one software component and another, between the software and the typical usage pattern, or between the software and the hardware components.

On the other hand, without attention to effectual locality, even a collection of well-designed components can produce poor performance (as *"Joe Tuna"* discovered in the *CS/cs3 Case Study*).

> **Guideline 10.30** **Grouping and effectual locality**
> The grouping choice that produces the best performance will usually be the one that best achievesx effectual locality between one software component and another, between the software and the typical usage pattern, or between the software and the hardware components.

The Sharing Principle

"Any noise annoys an oyster, but a noisy noise annoys an oyster most."

Job Loosley

In This Chapter . . .

Use Shared Resources Carefully
Grouping and Sharing
Shared Resources
Shared Servers
Shared Databases
Shared Networks
Conclusions

Up to this point, our investigation of the first three SPE design principles (*Workload, Efficiency,* and *Locality*) has mostly concentrated on how to improve the performance of individual applications or their components. But as we turn to the *Sharing Principle,* our attention shifts away from the individual or application perspective and toward the community or systems perspective.

An *application-resource usage matrix*—a design concept we introduced in Chapter 3—can describe a system as a collection of application workloads, system resources, and their relationships. Figures 3.5 and 3.6 illustrated such a matrix in detail; Figure 11.1 is a reminder of its general form. Each row describes an application, or a group of applications having similar processing characteristics. Each column represents a *physical resource* like a processor, a disk device, or network link, or a *logical resource* like an object, a table, or a database.

The information recorded in the matrix describes how the set of applications (the rows) uses the set of resources (the columns). Each cell at the intersection of a row and column records the use of a particular resource by a particular application. In the illustration, these usage statistics are shown as

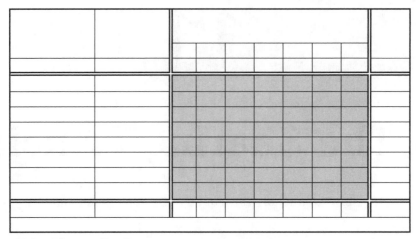

FIGURE 11.1   The application-resource usage matrix.

$U_a \ldots U_z$. Notice, incidentally, that many cells are empty—not every resource is used by every application.

The information in the matrix is the key to performance. Previous chapters on the Workload Principle (Chapter 8) and the Efficiency Principle (Chapter 9) have concentrated on the rows of the matrix—on the applications. The Locality Principle (Chapter 10) dealt with the goal of matching the resources to the applications. We now turn our attention to the columns of the matrix, the resources, and, in particular, to those resources that are shared by many applications.

Use Shared Resources Carefully

The Sharing Principle is short and simple: *Share resources without creating bottlenecks.* Connie Smith shortens it even further with her version: *Share resources when possible.* She then adds the useful guideline: *When exclusive access is required, minimize the sum of the holding time and the scheduling time.*[1] This simple rule is the key to understanding the performance of shared resources.

First let's review some terms that we first introduced in Chapter 3, in the section *Estimating Waiting Times for Resources.* When any computing resource is shared among many processes, the average time each process spends using (or being served by) the resource is known as its average *holding time* or *processing time.* The busier a shared resource becomes, the longer the average

---

[1]Connie U. Smith, *Performance Engineering of Software Systems* (Reading, MA: Addison-Wesley, 1990), 52.

time that processes must spend waiting to be served. This *wait time* or *waiting time* may also be referred to as the *queuing time,* or the *scheduling time.* The sum of wait time and holding time is the *service time* of the resource.

Now consider the application-resource usage matrix. If it includes every computing resource in its columns, then everything an application does to complete its work—apart from sitting idle while a user decides on the next input—is represented in the matrix. For completeness, even the user's response time can be represented as a column, a resource, in the matrix. In fact, the human user is by far the slowest I/O device of all. So achieving high performance often involves keeping user interactions to a minimum.

For any application or row of the matrix, there are no other components of response time except those represented by the nonempty cells in that row. And the only interactions between a process and a resource are *using the resources* and *waiting for the resource.* Therefore, all response time comprises these two components: using and waiting.

To sum up then, Smith's guideline draws attention to two important facts:

▶ Any time we share limited resources, it is inevitable that processes will sometimes have to wait because other processes are using a required resource.
▶ What's important for performance is the total service time—the time we spend using the resource plus the time we spend waiting for it.

About 25 years ago, I read a paper on the second law of debugging: *If you can't see the bug, you are looking in the wrong place.* I have long since forgotten what the first law was, but I have always found the second law invaluable. Its usefulness extends far beyond program debugging, to many of life's more puzzling pursuits, from hunting for lost car keys to diagnosing performance problems.

To make a significant improvement in performance, we must tackle the right problem. In particular, redesigning an application to reduce the time spent using a shared resource will not help much if the real problem lies in the time spent waiting for that resource.

The Two Dimensions of Response Time: An Example

Suppose we were to investigate two applications, *DataMiner* and *DataReporter,* with the goal of improving their performance. We discover that each has the same response time—22 seconds. We also obtain the information shown in Table 11.1:

▶ In the *DataMiner* application, we have a couple of seconds of I/O time (mostly waiting time, because 200 milliseconds is a very long time for a disk I/O) and

Table 11.1   **Sample Application Workloads**

	DataMiner		
	Processing Demand	**Device Performance**	**Response Time**
Disk	10 I/Os	200ms per I/O	2 seconds
CPU	1 billion instructions	50 MIPS CPU, dedicated	20 seconds
		Total response time	**22 seconds**

	DataReporter		
	Processing Demand	**Device Performance**	**Response Time**
Disk	1000 I/Os	20ms per I/O	20 seconds
CPU	1 million instructions	50 MIPS CPU, 99% busy	2 seconds
		Total response time	**22 seconds**

about 20 seconds to process 1 billion instructions on a dedicated 50 MIPS processor.

▶ In the *DataReporter* application, we process 1000 I/O events in 20 seconds—about 20 milliseconds each. We then take another 2 seconds to process 1 million instructions because a 50-MIPS processor that is 99 percent utilized performs like a half MIPS processor. We explain this reasoning in more detail later in the section *Estimating the Response Time of a Shared Resource.*

Now consider how we might tune either of these applications. From the eight statistics available (frequencies and response times, for CPU and disk I/O, for two applications), we can deduce quite a lot about these applications and how to approach tuning them.

DataMiner.   When tuning *DataMiner,* our attention would be drawn to the processing demand of 1 billion instructions. Clearly the problem here is CPU utilization. We would ask, "Why are we using all of these instructions? What are we doing?" One billion instructions is a very large processing load, and we should focus our tuning efforts on finding the reasons for it, with the aim of reducing the demand.

The I/O times for *DataMiner,* although individually slow, are not a major contribution to overall response time. They do, however, certainly indicate severe contention for the I/O device in question, which is almost certainly causing problems for other applications. Even though our present focus is on *Data-Miner,* we cannot turn a blind eye to this statistic. Seeing it should trigger further research. Devices do not become severely overloaded when no one is using them, so some other work is affected.

DataReporter.   Turning to *DataReporter,* most of the response time appears to come from disk utilization. To speed up the reporting process, our first thought would be to investigate its database access pattern, to see whether we could redesign it to use a more efficient access path involving fewer I/Os. At 20ms per I/O, the disks themselves are operating reasonably efficiently for random access, although speeding up a sequential scan may be possible. Evidently, *DataReporter* uses different data from *DataMiner,* or we would be seeing the same 200ms I/O times and a very different total response time for *DataReporter.*

On the processor side, contention for the CPU does not appears to be affecting the *DataReporter* application because it is very efficient, at 1000 instructions per I/O. However, since the processor handling *DataReporter* is so busy, it is quite possible that some of the 20ms being reported as I/O time is actually being caused by CPU contention because it may include some time that elapses while the *DataReporter* program waits to be redispatched by the CPU following an I/O. This phenomenon is quite common for I/O time measurements recorded by software monitors, depending on how (and where in the operating system) the beginning and end of the I/O event is actually measured.

We could test this hypothesis by running *DataReporter* during an off-peak period and comparing I/O times. If CPU contention is indeed the problem, we could improve *DataReporter* performance by scheduling it to run at a less busy time. Alternatively, being more proactive, we may want to ask, "Who else is using the processor, what are they doing, and why?" In this case, the culprit may well turn out to be *DataMiner!*

Conclusions.   The first observation is that most of the actions we might take to tune *DataMiner* would have no effect on *DataReporter,* and vice versa. The corollary to the second law of debugging is found in the story of the drunkard who was searching for his lost wallet underneath the lamp post because the light was better there. When troubleshooting, we have a tendency to pay attention to the most visible symptoms. To be effective, though, we must also be sure they are the true cause of the problem.

Second, all devices are not created equal. Because the CPU is a much faster device than disks and because it is shared by all processes, a workload needing 20 seconds of processor time is not comparable to one needing 20 seconds of disk I/O time. In the situation we've described, *DataMiner* is an example of the kind of programs colloquially referred to as "pigs"—they hog all the processing resources and cannot share the computer gracefully with any other work, except possibly work that is I/O bound, like *DataReporter.* And the best way to keep pigs under control—to prevent them from making the shared environment uninhabitable for everyone else—is to put them in a separate pen. In this instance, if we had enough *DataMiner* work, we would probably consider allocating a powerful dedicated processor for it.

Guideline 11.1	**The laws of tuning**

1. All elapsed time in computing is composed of the sum of time spent waiting for computing resources and time spent using computing resources.
2. To tune an application effectively, we must first know where it is spending its time.
3. Tune utilization problems directly; tune contention problems indirectly.
4. A contention problem in one application is a utilization problem in another.

Summary: A Framework for Removing Bottlenecks

Let's review a theoretical performance debugging process using the application-resource usage matrix as a framework. To investigate a specific application:

▶ Looking at a row of the matrix, we can see if the total response time is acceptable.
▶ Looking at the cells in that row, an excessively large value in a particular cell may tell us that an application spends too much time using a particular resource. Therefore, we can focus on reducing the utilization of that resource by the application.
▶ If there are no *utilization* problems within the application, the problem must arise from resource *contention*—the application spends too much time waiting for some resource. Examining the resource utilization totals, we can see which of the resources used by the application are overloaded.
▶ Examining the column(s) for the overloaded resource(s) shows which other applications are causing the contention. We can then focus on those applications to reduce their use of the critical shared resource(s).

To reduce the holding time of shared resources, we can:

▶ Reduce the number of times we make a request
▶ Reduce the size of the request
▶ Speed up the processing of the request
▶ Route some requests elsewhere

In Chapter 8, *The Workload Principle,* and Chapter 9, *The Efficiency Principle,* we provided many examples of the first two techniques. We also discussed trade-offs between the frequency and size of requests, an important issue for shared resources and one that we revisit in the next section, *Grouping and Sharing.*

Processing speed can usually be improved by replacing the critical resource with a faster one. We can also increase the *effective speed* of a resource—its power to perform useful work—by reducing its utilization level, a topic we address in the section *Shared Resources* later in this chapter. Later, in the section *Shared Servers* we also discuss techniques of workload partitioning, a subject that we take up in more detail in Chapter 13, *The Parallelism Principle.*

Grouping and Sharing

Earlier chapters (especially Chapters 7, 8, and 9) have stressed the importance of grouping as a software design technique and its influence on performance. Usually, a larger unit of work is created by grouping smaller elements together. When evaluating possible grouping options, we should take into account the way the final unit of work will interact with shared resources. Grouping elements into small units of work tends to optimize individual process response times, whereas grouping into large units of work tends to optimize overall system resource usage.

> **Guideline 11.2 Shared resources and the size of units of work**
> In design situations involving shared resources, grouping elements into smaller units of work tends to optimize individual process response times, whereas grouping into larger units of work tends to optimize overall system resource usage.

Actually, the reason why large units of work cause response time problems is not their size *per se,* but the increased service time variability they introduce into the overall workload. Conversely, when the average unit of work is smaller, service times typically vary less, and response times are lower.

To explain why widely varying service times cause response-time problems, we could appeal to the mathematical methods of *queuing theory,* introduced earlier in Chapter 6 in the section *Queuing Network Models.* However, in our experience, most software engineers find intuitive reasoning more persuasive than pages of mathematical symbols, so we use that approach.

Randomness and Queuing

Consider any system involving demands for a shared resource. From our day-to-day experiences, we know that delays are inherent in shared systems like banks, supermarkets, and highways. Furthermore, in these systems, once the utilization level rises above a certain point, queues start to develop. We encounter queues for bank tellers, checkout lines in the supermarket, traffic jams on the highway. And the higher the utilization, the longer the queues.

Although it may not be obvious, unless the shared resource is permanently overloaded with work, these queues are entirely due to variations in the level of demand for service. As a counterexample, imagine a highway that is full of perfectly synchronized traffic, the nose of one vehicle immediately following behind the tail of another. In theory, if everyone drove at the same speed, we could achieve the maximum possible highway throughput—100 percent utilization of the highway with no delays. In practice, a completely full highway is a parking lot.

This is because in the real world, driving styles vary, vehicle performance varies, and people's daily schedules vary. In statistical terms, we would say that the car-driving population exhibits randomness in its pattern of demand for highway space. It's this randomness that prevents us from ever achieving 100 percent utilization of any shared system.

First, the pattern of *arrivals* in the system varies—cars enter the highway randomly. Random arrivals create peaks and troughs in demand, leading to queues. This is why traffic engineers install monitoring lights on busy highways to smooth the flow of cars entering the highway. The smoother the flow of arrivals, the fewer queues develop.

Guideline 11.3	**The arrival distribution law**

The delay introduced by a shared resource will increase with the variability in the arrival distribution of requests for service.

Second, the pattern of *service times* also varies—some vehicles move more slowly than others. Unless the highway system is completely overloaded, individual commute times are shortest when everyone drives their cars on their own chosen route directly from their home to work. On the other hand, if a large group of people drive to the bus depot, wait there for the bus, and travel to work together on the bus, they use the highway more efficiently, but they will probably spend more time to get to work.

In practice, commuters can even use both cars and buses according to their different needs and still reap some benefits of an overall reduction in highway traffic—provided everyone drives in the same lanes at the same speed. But problems can arise when the two classes must share the same resource—in this case, the highway—and one class has a tendency to lock up the resource for extended periods. If a few buses take up all the lanes and also travel more slowly than the cars, then large numbers of cars will get backed up behind the buses, greatly reducing highway efficiency.

In shared systems, long-running things tend to slow everything else down. Little things get stuck in line behind the big things and have to wait—much like waiting in line at the bank teller. If the little old lady ahead of you in line is depositing her life savings out of a shopping bag, you're going to have to wait a long time—even if you're next in line. That's why most banks use a single queue/multiserver solution—so that one long-running task doesn't slow down the whole process.

The same is true with computer systems. Indeed, the mathematical bases for most of the *queuing theory* methods used to predict computer systems behavior include assumptions about randomness in the distribution of arrival times of service requests at the devices and in the distribution of service times for those requests. These assumptions are necessary to make the mathematics work, but they are also realistic. Like our earlier example of traffic on the highway, if requests for service by computer devices were not random but perfectly synchronized, with completely uniform service times, a device could be 100 percent busy, but no process would ever have to wait. In real systems, this does not happen.

To reduce the queuing delays associated with variable demands for service, software designers often break up large units of work into smaller chunks to improve overall response time. A good example of this is the ATM network transmission protocol, which breaks up all kinds of information (data, voice, image, video), no matter how large the real messages, into small 53-byte packets for network transmission. Using this technique, messages of vastly different sizes can be intermixed yet still flow smoothly without tiny 100-byte data messages being forced to wait in a queue somewhere while the network is tied up transmitting megabytes of live video images.

This discussion highlights some obvious parallels between the behaviors of computer systems and transportation networks, a topic we return to in more detail later in this chapter when we discuss communications networks. It also explains the technical reasoning behind Inmon's rule, *Don't mix short transactions with long-running queries,* introduced in Chapter 10. We now generalize Inmon's rule to obtain the more widely applicable *service distribution law.*

Guideline 11.4   The service distribution law

Don't try to mix small and large units of work if they must share the same resources. The delay introduced by a shared resource will increase with the variability in the unit of work size.

Shared Resources

When a shared system resource such as a processor, a disk, or a network link is busy handling work for one client application, it is unavailable to process other requests from other clients. Those requests must wait in a queue for service. The higher the percentage of time that a resource is occupied, the longer each queued request must wait for its turn. In fact, the service time of a shared resource grows exponentially as its utilization level increases. This fact is captured in a pair of simple formulas that can be used to estimate the *expected response time* and *expected waiting time* at a shared resource.

[Note: Technically, the term *expected* is used in its statistical sense here, namely the mean, or average, of a statistical distribution. In this case, it refers to the distributions of response times and waiting times that are derived mathematically by making assumptions about the distributions of arrival times and service times. However, in the context of estimating response times, the more usual interpretation is also correct.]

Estimating the Response Time of a Shared Resource

Guideline 11.5 describes a pair of simple formulas that anyone can use to estimate the response time for a request for service from a shared resource when we know (or can estimate) how busy that resource will be. One formula gives the *expected response time,* which includes both the time spent waiting for the resource and the time actually using it (that is, receiving the requested service). The second gives the *expected wait time.* These formulas are well known among performance analysts and capacity planners, but they may not be familiar to other developers, even though they are quite easy to understand. In the following paragraphs, we explain the formulas using an example and discuss some of the assumptions and limitations of their derivation.

A Response Time Example.   This formula is easy to explain by intuitive reasoning:

If a resource is busy, it is not 100 percent available to perform work. In general, if it is X percent busy, then it is $100 - X$ percent available. For example, if it is busy 10 percent of the time, then it is available only during the other 90 percent. In other words, if its utilization is $U,$ its availability is $1 - U.$ To an arriving process-seeking service, it looks like a slower resource, operating at a fraction of its full power. Instead of operating at its full power (1), providing S units of service in a time of $S/1,$ or $S,$ it operates at reduced power $(1 - U),$ and so takes $S/(1 - U)$ units of time to provide the same amount of service.

Guideline 11.5	Response time and waiting time formulas

Increasing average holding time of a shared resource tends to increase scheduling time exponentially. For any shared resource having utilization U and service time S, estimates of the response time R and the scheduling time or waiting time W are given by the formulas $R = S/(1 - U)$ and $W = S \times U/(1 - U)$, where:

▶ U, the resource utilization, is a value between 0 (free) and 1 (100 percent busy). For example, for a resource that is 35 percent utilized, $U = .35$.
▶ S, the service time, is the service time for a particular interaction between a requesting process and the resource, excluding all waiting time.
▶ R, the expected response time, is an estimate of the total delay imposed on the requesting process by the resource at utilization level U.
▶ W is an estimate of the expected waiting time for the same process, that is, $R = S + W$.

Here's a concrete example:

Suppose we need to process 100 million instructions, which would normally take 2 seconds on a 50 MIPS processor. Suppose the 50 MIPS processor is 90 percent busy. Then a process needing CPU cycles, instead of seeing a 50 MIPS processor, sees what appears to be a 5 MIPS processor because the other 45 MIPS are already taken. Because the processor appears to operate at one-tenth of the power, the process will take 10 times as long to complete.

Using the response time formula, we would have written:

$$R = 2/(1 - 0.9)$$
$$= 2/(0.1)$$
$$= 20$$

That is, the expected response time for our process is 20 seconds—again, 10 times as long as the 2 seconds that we might have expected on a 50 MIPS processor working at full power. Voila! Or, as all aspiring mathematicians are taught to write, Q.E.D.

Here's another example. Suppose the average data access time for a disk device is 10ms and the disk is 40 percent busy. Then an estimate of the response time is 10ms/0.6, or 16.67ms. Alternatively, an estimate of the waiting time is 10 ms $\times$ 0.4/0.6, or 6.67ms, again producing a total response time of 16.67ms for the device (6.67ms waiting plus 10ms processing).

Service Multipliers.   Another way of using the response time formula is to compute a *service multiplier* $[1/(1 - U)]$, the factor by which response time is extended at various resource utilization levels U. The service multiplier is also referred to as an *expansion factor;* for example, see Renaud.[2] Table 11.2 lists the service multipliers for various utilization levels.

The left column of the table, labeled *Class of Device,* is not meant to be read as a precise classification scheme. Except at the extremes, the classifications are meant to indicate typical ranges (note the gray areas between them). But these ranges do provide some useful insights into the effects of utilization level on shared resources.

▶ When devices are lightly loaded, the service multiplier has only a mild effect—the waiting-time component of response time is only a fraction of the service time.
▶ At more typical levels, once device utilization passes 0.5 (50 percent busy), the service multiplier passes 2. Waiting times now exceed service times.
▶ As the utilization climbs past the 70 percent level, the service multiplier is 3.33 and rising quickly. At 75 percent, a request that needs 1 second of service will take 4 seconds; at 80 percent, 5 seconds. Typically, we would like our

---

[2]Paul Renaud, *Introduction to Client/Server Systems* (New York, NY: John Wiley & Sons, 1993), 284.

Table 11.2   Service Multipliers for Open Systems

Class of Device	Resource Utilization	Service Multiplier
Client	0.00	1
Lightly loaded server	0.10	1.11
	0.20	1.25
	0.25	1.33
	0.33	1.50
	0.40	1.67
Typical server	0.50	2
	0.67	3
	0.70	3.33
	0.75	4
Busy server	0.80	5
	0.90	10
	0.95	20
Congested server	0.99	100
	0.999	1000
Unavailable	1.0	infinity

monitoring activities to detect the rise in response times caused by utilizations in this range before a resource becomes a bottleneck.

▶ At 90 percent utilization, it takes 10 seconds to complete a 1-second request. When resources are this busy, the effects will certainly be felt somewhere in the workload, for two reasons. First, applications using the busy device(s) will experience noticeably longer response times. Second, relatively small fluctuations in the load will cause quite large swings in the service multiplier, resulting in erratic response times for the applications affected.

▶ As resource utilizations approach 100 percent ($U = 1$), waiting times increase rapidly because the divisor ($1 - U$) in the formula approaches 0. The system is entering a critical state.

▶ When a device is 100 percent busy, the service multiplier is infinite; in effect, the device is unavailable.

At least, that's what the response time formula predicts, thereby raising some interesting questions. Although we may like to joke about infinite response time in some systems we deal with, we know it never really happens. There are reasons for this, which we discuss next.

Guideline 11.6	Design monitoring to detect high shared resource utilization levels

When resource utilizations climb past the 70 percent level, the service multiplier is rising quickly. Typically, we can observe the effect of this by monitoring response times. Design monitoring activities to detect utilizations in this range before a resource becomes a bottleneck.

Open and Closed Systems

The response time formula we have described is based on a set of statistical assumptions called an *open single-server system,* in which work is generated at a fixed rate by an unlimited population of users. Computing environments that come closest to satisfying the open system conditions might be an online system serving thousands of users, such as a very busy Web server or a national airline reservation system.

In reality, most computer systems are not open systems—they are *closed systems.* That is, a limited number of users generate a limited number of processes that compete for all the resources. When some resources are busy because processes are already tied up waiting for service, the arrival rate of new requests for service does not continue at the same level as previously; it slows down.

Most real systems also have other natural governors built in, especially when human users are involved. When devices bottleneck and service slows, users lose patience. Work waiting for service evaporates as users decide to do some other work for a while until service levels improve again. Not surprisingly, as work evaporates, utilization levels drop and service picks up again.

To take some of these moderating conditions into account, we need more complex mathematical formulas. These exist, but are beyond the scope of this book. However, we can show some results. The three center columns of Table 11.3, which is based on a discussion of these issues by Ted Keller,[3] show the service multipliers obtained by modifying the open system assumptions to produce a closed system, as follows:

▶ The number of users is fixed at 10, 30, or 90, respectively
▶ The average time between those users' requests for service is adjusted to produce various resource utilization levels ranging from 10 to 95 percent

The right-hand column of Table 11.3 shows the corresponding service multipliers obtained using the open system assumptions of Table 11.2, for comparison purposes.

_____

[3]Ted Keller, *CICS Capacity Planning and Performance Management* (New York, NY: McGraw Hill, 1993), 118.

Table 11.3 **Service Multipliers for Closed Systems**

Average Resource Utilization	Closed Queuing Numbers of Users			Open Queuing
	10	30	90	
.10	1.1	1.1	1.1	1.11
.25	1.3	1.3	1.3	1.33
.33	1.4	1.5	1.5	1.50
.50	1.7	1.9	2.0	2
.67	2.2	2.6	2.9	3
.75	2.6	3.2	3.6	4
.80	2.8	3.7	4.4	5
.90	3.6	5.2	6.9	10
.95	4.3	6.8	9.8	20

Comparing the open and closed system results, we can see immediately that the open system assumptions are actually quite conservative. This means that the response time formula is usually a safe method of obtaining a rough estimate for the service time of any shared resource. It errs on the side of overestimation, especially as resource utilization levels rise above 70 percent—the region where device wait times begin to have a significant effect on application response times. But, as the saying goes, it is better to be safe than sorry!

Shared Servers

In client/server systems, we should design applications to minimize the holding time of the slowest shared resources, such as server disks or the wide area network. The slower resources are the most critical because they are the most likely to become bottlenecks.

Another way to speed up processing is to divide and conquer, providing more parallel servers; we discuss this further in Chapter 13, *The Parallelism Principle*. In a client/server environment, one way to reduce the load on a shared server is to move work elsewhere. In previous chapters we have already suggested many possibilities, including the following:

▶ Create additional workgroup servers to handle long-running batch applications separately from response-critical transaction work
▶ Create data marts or a data warehouse to separate data analysis workloads from operational database applications
▶ Offload data mining applications to a more powerful dedicated processor

In addition to separating work of different classes, we can minimize the load on shared servers by properly *partitioning* individual applications among processors. The shared server needs to handle only that processing that is truly multiuser in nature and requires the multiuser context provided by the server environment. Processing that can be done separately for each user or client can be moved to the client workstation. We recommended this first in Chapter 10, where our discussion of *Effectual Locality* concluded that there were some *natural ways to partition* client and server function. The Sharing Principle now reinforces our previous conclusion.

Queuing theory, as expressed in the response time formula for shared resources, makes a persuasive argument for redistributing work in a client/server environment. Although the devices at the client workstation may be less powerful than those at the server, devices at the server are shared by all clients. Client devices, on the other hand, are dedicated to a single user and so process requests at full power, undiluted by contending demands. Any work arriving at

> **Guideline 11.7**
>
> ## Clients have spare capacity for small tasks
>
> Processing that relates only to a single user's application should be pushed onto the client workstation to conserve scarce server resources. By minimizing server resource consumption per client, we improve overall scalability.
>
> On the other hand, moving a really large function from a local client platform to a dedicated remote server will improve quickness of response if the function can be performed asynchronously.

a client device encounters zero utilization—in the response time formula, the divisor $(1 - U)$ is 1. As Table 11.2 shows, the service multiplier is 1.

When we redistribute work, we can take advantage of this. Consider the following example:

▶ Suppose a 1 MIPS server supporting a large network of clients is handling requests at a rate of 16 per second and requests take an average of 60,000 instructions to process. Then the total processing is 16 × 60,000, or 960,000, instructions per second. The server will be 96 percent utilized. Processing 60,000 instructions takes only .06 second, but at 96 percent utilization (U = .96), the service multiplier $1/(1 - U)$ = 25. The expected response time for each request will actually be (25 × .06), or 1.5 seconds.

▶ If an average of just 10,000 instructions per request (one-sixth of the work) could be offloaded to the client workstations, the average service time for the remaining 50,000 instructions would drop to .05, and server utilization would drop from 96 to 80 percent, for which the service multiplier is 5 (see Table 11.2). The expected server response time would be 5 × .05, or 0.25, second.

▶ Offloading just one-sixth of the load to the client would drop the server response time to one-sixth (coincidentally) of its former time, from 1.5 seconds down to .25. Even after adding back some time to process the extra 10,000 instructions on the client workstation, overall application response time would surely drop.

This example illustrates the benefits of any tuning action that reduces the load on a shared resource, once that resource starts to become a bottleneck. Of course, as we discussed in the previous chapter under *Tuning and Side Effects,* we must ensure that the process of removing a bottleneck in one resource does not create a new bottleneck in another. In this case, the resource most likely to be affected by any redesign involving partitioning is the communications network. We must take care that repartitioning an application does not introduce a lot more message traffic between its components.

> ### Guideline 11.8 Lighten the load on a shared server
>
> Although the devices at the client workstation may be less powerful than those at the server, devices at the server are shared by all clients, whereas client devices are fully available. Provided that repartitioning in application does not introduce any significant additional communications overhead, systematically removing even relatively small amounts of work from a shared server can produce surprising improvements in overall application response times.

Shared Databases

Databases allow data to be shared by many users. A DBMS maintains the integrity of the data while supporting lots of users who need to read and write concurrently from the same database. To prevent concurrent programs from accessing inconsistent data, DBMSs use locking mechanisms to isolate the programs from one another. Database locking, because it reduces concurrent access, is an important design issue. In fact, it's so important that we have given it its own chapter. See Chapter 12, *Database Locking*.

Shared Networks

Any shared resource is a potential source of application response time delays. When we consider the shared devices in an enterprise client/server environment, the communications network is probably the first device that comes to mind. Busy networks, because they are usually the slowest and most error-prone of all the shared devices in a distributed system, can contribute significantly to application response times.

Enterprise networks are complex computing infrastructures incorporating many smaller local area, campus, and wide area networks. Continually evolving and expanding, they link hundreds, even thousands, of communications devices whose performance capabilities vary widely. Many writers have compared the role played by a communications network with a transportation infrastructure consisting of city streets and traffic lights, local highways, intercity tollways or autobahns, trains, airlines, and so on.[4] It is an apt analogy and a useful one as far as performance is concerned. There are many parallels between the behaviors of traffic in the two types of networks, as we noted earlier in this chapter.

---

[4]Martin Nemzow, *Enterprise Network Performance Optimization* (New York, NY: McGraw Hill, 1995), 12.

Many factors influence actual network performance. As might be expected, these follow the pattern of performance factors first introduced in Chapter 3, in Figure 3.1. For convenience, we provide a network version as Figure 11.2. Briefly, the factors are:

► **Application workloads.** For network performance, the relationship between the business drivers and all aspects of network traffic.

► **Application design.** When, where, and how much the application uses the network.

► **Application media.** What is being transmitted, for example, data, voice, graphics, video.

► **Network software.** The network protocols used.

► **Transmission media.** The physical path used, for example, twisted pair, coaxial cable, optical fiber cable, wireless.

► **Network devices and topology.** The architectural layout of, and interconnections among, all the physical devices that compose the network.

Network performance optimization is a sufficiently broad subject that it qualifies as a separate discipline from SPE. An enterprise network will not deliver acceptable performance unless it is designed and cared for by specialists

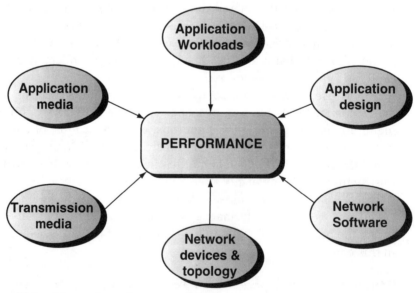

FIGURE 11.2 Network performance factors.

in network design and performance optimization. In the sections that follow, we review some aspects of network performance without going into much detail. We list some recommended reading in the capsule *A Library for Network Designers.*

Application Bottlenecks and the Throughput Chain

To determine the overall performance of a complex network of interconnected components, we must know where the bottlenecks are. Recall our discussion of the *Fundamental System Resources* in Chapter 3—every system has a bottleneck device, the first device to saturate as the workload increases. From this fact we deduced the first rule of system tuning: *Find the biggest bottleneck and eliminate it* (Guideline 3.6).

In his book, *Introduction to Client/Server Systems,* Paul Renaud describes the concept of the *throughput chain.*[5] Similar to the concept of the critical path in project management, the throughput chain identifies all the devices involved in one application's interaction with a client/server computing environment.

Noting that it is hard to spot bottlenecks in a large client/server system because of the number of components involved, Renaud concludes that we can *use the throughput chain to spot bottlenecks.* Once we have identified the components in throughput chains, we can quickly zoom in on likely bottlenecks because a chain is only as strong as its weakest link!

He explains the concept using the following example, illustrated in Figure 11.3:

- ▶ A client CPU can process 500 transactions per second.
- ▶ Network interface cards can handle 2400 packets per second.
- ▶ The LAN can carry 1200 packets per second before saturating.
- ▶ LAN/WAN routers can forward 7000 packets per second.
- ▶ The WAN can handle 650 packets per second.
- ▶ The server's CPU can handle 120 transactions per second.
- ▶ The server's only disk can perform 30 I/Os per second.

Renaud claims that this type of analysis *quickly tells (us) what maximum throughput can be.* Reviewing the example, Renaud concludes (in effect) that we can ignore the first six items because the system's throughput is obviously limited by the server's disk, which can perform only as many transactions as 30 I/Os per second permits.

---

[5]Renaud, *Introduction,* 282.

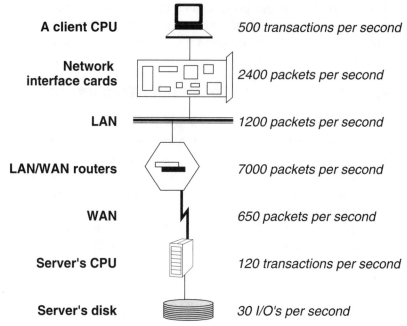

FIGURE 11.3   The throughput chain.

In one sense, this is an important point because it highlights the fact that, in Renaud's interpretation of this example at least, *the bottleneck is not in the network; it's in the application.* Without this insight, we might waste a lot of time tuning the network for greater throughput without making much of an impression on application response time. If we want to get more work through, then we must eliminate the disk bottleneck—either by installing a faster disk or by spreading the data across several disks.

Guideline 11.9	**Application behavior determines throughput**

Even though we may think that the network limits application throughput, in reality it is an application's use of resources that limits its throughput. To find the bottleneck, we must consider all the resources the application uses.

Sufficient Information?

Unfortunately, the throughput chain *described in the example* does not actually prove that the server's disk is the bottleneck. It merely suggests a likely problem because 30 is such a low value relative to the other numbers. In fact, in drawing his conclusion, Renaud is obliged to add this qualifying statement: *assuming that a transaction requires only one disk I/O.*

In that it identifies the set of devices an application uses, the throughput chain is closely related to a single row of the application-resource usage matrix introduced earlier in this chapter (see Figure 11.1). But the lesson of the application-resource usage matrix is that we cannot determine bottlenecks by focusing on only one application or on only one subset of the resources. We must look at both the *application demands* and the *resource capacities* to find the bottleneck. In Renaud's example the following factors are apparent:

▶ The client CPU is definitely not the bottleneck because the server CPU will bottleneck first. Incidentally, unless the client workstation is submitting previously *batched* transactions to multiple servers, then the client CPU is significantly overpowered for the application.

▶ Assuming that there is a 1:1 relationship between the various types of packets mentioned as they flow through the network, then it seems unlikely that the network interface cards or the LAN/WAN routers could be bottlenecks because either the LAN or the WAN will bottleneck first.

▶ Even with the assumption of one disk I/O per transaction, only the server CPU is eliminated because the server disk will bottleneck before the CPU.

Without knowing all the details of the application-resource usage matrix, it is impossible to say whether the LAN, WAN, or server disk will bottleneck first, because we have no information about the number of LAN or WAN packets per transaction.

> ### Guideline 11.10   Throughput chains
>
> Identifying throughput chains can be a useful way to focus attention on likely bottlenecks in a large networked environment. Bottlenecks are created by a mismatch between *application demands* and *resource capacities*. We cannot identify bottlenecks with certainty unless we know the *application-resource usage matrix*.

Network Delays

Communication networks introduce another dimension into application design. Of course, there is the obvious contribution to response time associated with shipping data between components. The network itself, though, because it is a shared resource, can be also be a source of seemingly random delays, unexpected application errors, unexplained data loss, or even periods of total failure.

A Library for Network Designers

In addition to the general books on client/server computing that we refer to elsewhere, there are many books on data communications and networking. Here are a few that focus on performance related topics:

▶ Frank Derfler, *PC Magazine Guide to Connectivity,* Emeryville, CA: Ziff-Davis Press, 3rd ed., 1995
▶ Gilbert Held, *Internetworking LANs and WANs: Concepts, Techniques and Methods,* New York, NY: John Wiley & Sons, 1993
▶ Gilbert Held, *LAN Performance: Issues and Answers,* New York, NY: John Wiley & Sons, 1997
▶ Martin Nemzow, *Enterprise Network Performance Optimization,* New York, NY: McGraw-Hill, 1995
▶ Martin Nemzow, *LAN Performance Optimization,* New York, NY: Windcrest/McGraw-Hill, 1993
▶ Kornel Terplan, *Effective Management of Local Area Networks: Functions, Instruments, and People,* New York, NY: McGraw-Hill, 2nd ed., 1996
▶ Harrell J. Van Norman, *LAN/WAN Optimization Techniques,* Boston, MA: Artech House, 1992
▶ Craig and Colleta Witherspoon, *Optimizing Client/Server Networks,* Foster City, CA: IDG Books, 1996

Parts of every book will eventually be made obsolete by the constant advance of network technology. Those we list here are, however, still in print at the time of writing, and contain useful guidance on enterprise network design and network management issues that will remain current, even as networking protocols and products evolve.

Bandwidth.   In its simplest terms, using our transportation analogy, bandwidth is like the traffic capacity of the highway. Network bandwidth is a measurement of the rate at which data flows between two points in a network. It is a function of the transmission medium (the highway itself) and protocol used (the speed limit). Unfortunately, no network ever transmits application data at its full rated speed.

If we did not know anything about networks, we might assume that we could compute network transmission time for an application simply by dividing the number of bytes of application data by the rated bandwidth. It is usually true that data, when transmitted, moves at the rated speed. But the *effective* bandwidth drops because there are times when no data is transmitted at all and a lot of the data actually being transmitted is overhead, not useful application data.

Indeed, there are many built-in inhibitors to network performance, each one of which takes another bite out of the rated bandwidth. We describe the most significant ones in the following sections.

Protocol Limitations.   Transmission protocols control the actual rate at which data is transmitted between connected devices on the network. Because of limitations on packet sizes and on when packets can be sent, no pair of devices ever communicates at the rated bandwidth for the network, and the network as a whole does not achieve its rated capability.

Protocol Conversion and Encapsulation.   When networks that developed separately are interconnected, different network protocols must be reconciled. Not only do LAN and WAN protocols differ, but each type of network can use several different protocols. An enterprise network may have to support data being transmitted using TCP/IP, SNA, IPX/SPX, DSLW, and NetBIOS, for example. Bridges and routers must either convert packets from one protocol to another or encapsulate packets using one protocol as data inside another. Translation takes time, and encapsulation dilutes the data stream by adding another layer of overhead.

Device Latency.   *Latency* is the technical term for *delay*. No matter what we do to boost application throughput, transmitting data introduces delays. We can build a wider highway and raise the speed limit, but computer networks have an absolute speed limit: the speed of light. It takes time (about 0.25 second) to send data via a satellite link, 100ms to send data across the United States. Even more significant, any large enterprise network has many segments, linked by hubs, bridges, routers, gateways, and switches. And every device has latency, usually more than the transmission time. So a certain minimum time is required to send messages in multiple hops to remote locations. This phenomenon produces a lower bound on network service time.

Guideline 11.11	**Bell's rule of networking**

Money can buy bandwidth, but latency is forever.[6]

Tom Bell

No matter what the bandwidth of a network, it takes time to send data around the world via satellite links or over multiple hops in a large enterprise network. Every device in a network path contributes to the minimum time required to send messages.

---

[6]Thomas E. Bell, "Performance of Distributed Systems" (paper presented at the ICCM Capacity Management Forum 7, San Francisco, October 1993).

Congested Servers.   If one device in a network (for example, a hub, a router, or a server) is really overloaded, every now and then it will miss packets that it is intended to service. Provided the overloading is not too severe, network hardware and software typically resolve this problem transparently to the applications. However, recovering from errors is certainly not free. The lost packets generate unproductive error message traffic (see the next section), and portions of messages then have to be resent.

Error Handling.   Like accidents on the highway, device failures in a network cause serious slowdowns. Links fail, causing traffic to be rerouted, increasing congestion elsewhere. Faulty devices can drop data packets or saturate the network with gibberish. Among the most common causes of errors are:

Network Busy, Net Work Zero

Here is an amusing example, from the front page of *The Wall Street Journal* on January 10, 1997, describing how a single network error can overwhelm an entire network.[7] In this example, 36 people out of 100,000 responded to a faulty message. In a computer network, an analogous broadcast message could have reached a far higher percentage of devices connected to the network. To ignore this type of network problem is to invite occasional periods of erratic application performance.

The text of the article follows.

Run for Your Lives! Beepers Go Berserk, Refuse to Be Silenced

Hundreds of Messages Harass the Hopelessly In-Touch

Thousands of relentlessly in-touch wireless warriors got their comeuppance yesterday: A technical problem on the SkyTel paging network led to a nationwide bout of beeper madness, as a digital deluge of erroneous call-me-back messages swept over more than 100,000 unwitting pager customers.

The high-tech snafu sent thousands of customers reaching for the pagers on their waistbands and in their pocketbooks, clogged digital memories with reams of bogus missives and, on the West Coast at 5 A.M., roused legions of sleeping beeper addicts who couldn't bear to simply turn the pesky gadgets off.

---

[7]David D. Kirkpatrick and Jared Sandberg, "Run for Your Lives! Beepers Go Berserk, Refuse to Be Silenced," *The Wall Street Journal* (January 10, 1997), 1.

- ▶ Timing errors caused by wrongly configured network devices
- ▶ Errors caused by network layouts that exceed the maximum permitted distances
- ▶ Noise introduced by damaged and poorly fitting physical connections and other wiring flaws
- ▶ Excessive traffic generated by inappropriate use of device monitoring protocols

Paradoxically, because network components are designed to recover from errors, the more errors that occur, the more error-recovery traffic is generated. So the more systematic an error condition, the greater is the fraction of network bandwidth devoted to the overheads of error handling, and the lower is its effective capacity. This, in turn, causes application delays, which result in users, perhaps familiar with much shorter response times, canceling work. Of course,

None of these hapless recipients knew who had reached out into the ether to touch them. Yet thousands obligingly tried to return the call. It got worse: SkyTel customers' beepers can display text messages, such as news headlines, and also numbers that can represent identification codes or the phone numbers of whoever is trying to reach them. So three dozen especially diligent customers assumed they had been beeped by another SkyTel customer who had left such an identification code on their beepers.

Wireless Jam

They dialed up the SkyTel network, entered that code to leave a message for the mystery caller and then entered in their own phone numbers so the stranger could call them back. Unbeknownst to them, the SkyTel system then efficiently zapped those real phone numbers out to the same 100,000 pager customers. Ever eager, thousands of them then returned calls to the diligent three dozen, tying up phone lines and jamming voice-mail queues.

The result was an embarrassing communications chasm in the Wireless Age, a 26-minute snarl that underscored how heavily we have come to rely on this high-tech wizardry and how fragile is the underpinning of staying in touch "anywhere, anytime." It raised a disturbing prospect: Maybe we're all too much in touch.

Technoid Response

SkyTel quickly offered up a fittingly technoid, furrowed-brow explanation for the mess: "One frequency of our one-way nationwide network experienced an anomaly in the database that caused customers to be paged erroneously," said a spokesman.

the cancellations generate more traffic, as do the resubmissions of work that follow promptly thereafter. On the surface, the network may appear to be operating normally. In reality, its effective capacity is almost zero. This condition is sometimes called a *network panic*.

Data Compression

In the past, the main justification for data compression was to save disk space. This was an important issue for users of PCs and workstations whose hard disks and diskettes kept filling up. On larger servers and particularly on mainframes, storage space was less of an issue, and when it did become an issue it was just as likely to be dealt with by archiving as by compression.

Historically, apart from its use to speed up expensive data transmissions over public telephone networks, compression has not been widely used to save time. When processors were slower and processing resources were scarce, the amount of processing required to compress and decompress data was itself a significant concern.

Today, the way in which we use data compression has changed. Every year, storage costs decrease while processor speeds increase. To balance the scale, the volume of data to be managed by our applications keeps rising. As a result, in many organizations the reduced storage cost of compressed data still can more than pay for the additional processing needed to compress data.

But from a performance viewpoint there is an even more significant trend. Table 3.4 in Chapter 3 highlights the vast differences in the speeds of various computing devices. As we all know, technology advances relentlessly and computers keep getting bigger and faster. But historically, the speed of storage devices, and networks—particularly WANs—has not kept pace with the increases in data capacities and processing speeds.

In the world of enterprise distributed computing, in which we often need to move large volumes of data across relatively slow WAN links, data compression is becoming increasingly attractive, not so much for its cost-saving aspects, but as a way to boost performance.

Compression touches on several of the performance principles. Because it involves the ratio of an overhead cost (the compression/decompression activity) to the cost of the useful work (storing, retrieving, or transmitting data), the usefulness of compression involves the Efficiency Principle. Data compression is also a good example of a resource trade-off, discussed later in Chapter 14. We expend additional processor cycles to compress and decompress data and, in return, reduce the I/O overhead of storing, retrieving, and transmitting the data.

When considering the value of data compression, some issues to consider are:

- ▶ Resource speed
- ▶ Resource utilization
- ▶ Unit of work size
- ▶ Compression technique
- ▶ Type of data

Resource Speed.   The slower the medium, the greater the performance benefits of applying fast processor cycles to compress data. In the past, compressing for disk storage was rarely a good idea, while compressing for network transmission often was. Today, thanks to increased data volumes and faster processors, performance can often be improved by compressing data for disk storage. In the same vein, compressing data for network transmission is almost always a winner, especially if data is being transferred across a relatively slow WAN. With the growth of the Internet and the widespread use of Web browsers, we have all become much more familiar with compression as a technique to cut down on data transmission times.

> **Guideline 11.12 Compression and resource speed**
> The slower a device, the greater the probability that compressing its data will improve application performance.

Resource Utilization.   Guideline 11.8, *"Lighten the load on a shared server,"* noted that when a shared resource is used heavily, lowering its utilization level even a small amount can reduce delays significantly because of the impact on the service multiplier for the resource at high utilization levels. In a high-speed network, the time it takes to compress data may not be justified when compared to the saving in data transmission time alone. If that network is heavily loaded, compressing long messages to one-third or one-fourth of their length can significantly reduce contention, which may produce a noticeable reduction in waiting times.

> **Guideline 11.13 Compression and resource utilization**
> The higher the device's utilization, the greater the probability that compressing its data will improve application performance.

Unit of Work Size.   As we discussed in our coverage of the Efficiency Principle, any time we need to do anything in computing, there is always an initialization cost. For small blocks of data, the overhead of applying compression techniques may not be worth the savings in space or transmission time. But for large blocks, compression will always save network bandwidth and usually reduce application response times.

Guideline 11.14   **Compression and data volumes**
The larger the volume of data to be moved or stored, the greater the probability that compressing it will improve application performance.

Compression Technique.   In data compression, there are horses for courses. *Lossless* methods like run-length encoding (RLE) are not the most efficient, but they preserve every bit of the original data, as is essential with most binary, numeric, and text data.

The alternative, *lossy* methods, can be applied to graphics, continuous voice, and full-motion video images, where a trade-off can be made between performance and the quality of the data delivered. One well-known example is the JPEG technique. JPEG is widely used for transmitting graphic images over the Internet and is recognized and converted automatically by Web browsers. Incidentally, JPEG stands for Joint Photographers Expert Group. And for the next trivia question, . . .

Guideline 11.15   **Use lossy compression whenever possible**
Use *lossy* compression methods for greater compression of graphics, voice, and video data whenever you can trade network performance for some loss of quality in the data delivered.

Type of Data.   Some types of data are more easily compressible than others:

▶ Text usually compresses slightly more efficiently than numeric data, with both typically compressing in the region of 50 percent.
▶ Executable programs may compress to only 80 or 90 percent of their size.
▶ Graphics may compress to 75 to 85 percent of their size.
▶ CCITT Group IV facsimile compression can compress scanned text images to as little as 5 percent, but it performs poorly on digitized pictures.

Pick the best technique for your data and stick to it; don't try to "double compress."

> ### Guideline 11.16   Don't try to overcompress
> Trying to compress already compressed data is usually (a) a waste of processing resources, (b) a waste of time, and (c) ineffective. Pick the best technique for your data and stick to it; don't try to "double compress."

Design for the Normal Daily Environment

Estimating the impact of network conditions on a new application is always difficult. Because the communications network is a shared resource, any increase in utilization generated by one client effectively reduces the network bandwidth available to other clients. If we know something about current network conditions, we may be able to estimate a service multiplier for the network by applying the shared resource law.

However, simply estimating average utilizations usually is not enough. The production environment always involves larger databases, more users, and transient peaks in demand. Peaks in the data transfer rates increase the likelihood of bottlenecks, lost packets, and wasted bandwidth devoted to error recovery. Production environments also mean that other work competes for shared devices. Parts of the enterprise network may be overloaded at certain times of day because of factors completely outside our application.

In Chapter 5 we advocated using *production data* for testing. We also advocated generating *production transaction rates*. These recommendations address the need to test an application at production *utilization levels*. We must also consider production *contention levels*. In the case of the network resource, because it's almost impossible to simulate typical network conditions in any other way, testing client/server applications in the environment where they're going to be used is essential. That way, any performance problems can be uncovered and addressed before the application is placed into production. There are plenty of war stories about applications that worked fine during weekend testing but slowed to a crawl as soon as the remote printers on the network were started up.

> ### Guideline 11.17   Test for network contention
> It is almost impossible to simulate typical network conditions during development. Plan to test client/server applications in the environment where they're going to be used so that any performance problems can be addressed before placing them into production.

Conclusions

In an enterprise client/server environment, there will inevitably be:

▶ Fluctuations in the distribution of work to be done, as business volumes rise and fall
▶ Fluctuations in the availability of network and processing resources

Even if we have designed our systems to accommodate peak processing volumes, servers or some part of a large network are normally out of action some of the time. Therefore, if we design applications that require all resources to be available before we can complete any useful work, we reduce the availability of the whole system to the level of its most error-prone component.

For optimal performance, we should design applications to accommodate unexpected peaks in the workload, server outages, and resource unavailability. This means application and system design must:

▶ Emphasize concurrent operation in preference to workload serialization
▶ Prefer asynchronous to synchronous connections between clients and servers
▶ Place requests for service in queues and continue processing, rather than waiting for a response
▶ Create opportunities for parallel processing of workload components
▶ Distribute work to additional servers to accommodate peak volumes
▶ Provide redundant servers to take over critical workload components during peaks and outages

We return to these ideas in more detail in Part IV of the book.

If there is a single conclusion to be drawn from our long discussion of the Sharing Principle, it is this: *Design applications that don't wait.*

Guideline **11.18**	**Bell's law of waiting**

All CPUs wait at the same speed.[8]

Tom Bell

For optimal performance, design applications that don't wait.

---

[8]Bell, *Performance of Distributed Systems.*

Database Locking

"The use of riches is better than their possession."

—Fernando de Rojas, *La Celestina,* Act II

In This Chapter . . .

DBMS Locking Strategies
Hot Spots in Shared Data
Locking Summary

A primary reason for using a DBMS is to allow data to be shared by many users. Sharing involves maintaining the integrity of the data while supporting concurrent users who need to read and write from the same database. To prevent concurrent programs from accessing inconsistent data, DBMSs use locking mechanisms to achieve isolation between applications. When all applications that need to update a data item must first obtain an exclusive lock, the updates are serialized. This approach eliminates the possibility of two applications concurrently updating the same data item, which could produce incorrect results.

Even with only one updating process, locking is still essential to ensure the integrity of shared data. A program cannot safely read a page of data while another process is simultaneously reorganizing the page to insert a new row. To solve this problem, most DBMSs[1] get a shared lock while reading and an exclusive lock while updating. The shared locks are held only for the duration of the data access, but they are essential to avoid corrupting the data structures.

---

[1]Oracle, which uses a nonblocking read technique, is a notable exception. By maintaining a *system change number,* and noting when a data page changes, Oracle can ensure that a transaction already in progress always sees consistent data. If a data page is updated during a transaction, Oracle reads its log records and reconstructs the earlier version. For a more detailed discussion of this technique, see C. M. Saracco and C. J. Bontempo, "Getting a Lock on Integrity and Security," *Database Programming & Design* (August 1996), 36.

Locking, therefore, is inevitable. The performance cost of locking is that it reduces the level of data availability and so increases response times.

DBMS Locking Strategies

One important difference between database locks and other computing resources is that we do not directly *control* the actual locking strategy used by the DBMS in any particular processing situation. Rather, it is selected by the DBMS itself, based on several parameters:

▶ The lock size(s) specified for the table(s) involved (row, page, table, and so on)
▶ The isolation level specified for the program (dirty read, cursor stability, repeatable read)
▶ The type of processing involved (SELECT, UPDATE, and so on)
▶ The number of items expected to be locked for the particular request
▶ The access path chosen by the DBMS optimizer to satisfy the processing request (table space scan, index scan, index lookup, and so on)

Because we have only an indirect influence on what actually happens, it is particularly important for application and database designers to understand how *their particular DBMS* implements locking and what design options are available. This is a particularly complex aspect of DBMS design, rich in functional details and design possibilities. (In other words, *it's fiendishly complicated!*)

However, although locking implementations and options do differ from DBMS to DBMS, the above list highlights several common themes, which we now discuss.[2]

Lock Modes

We have already pointed out that a DBMS gets a *shared* (S) lock while reading and an *exclusive* (X) lock while updating. These are known as lock modes. Shared locks are compatible with other shared locks—that is, two processes can simultaneously hold shared locks on the same data item. But a shared lock is incompatible with exclusive locks. A third commonly used lock mode is *update* (U), which is compatible with other *shared* locks but not with another *update*. DBMSs also use a variety of *intent* locks: *intent shared* (IS), *intent exclusive* (IX),

---

[2]For a more complete discussion of program isolation and locking, see Part IV of *Transaction Processing: Concepts and Techniques*. Whereas Gray and Reuter address the subject from the point of view of a DBMS implementor, we focus more on how to use the options provided by most DBMSs.

and *shared intent exclusive* (SIX). An intent lock is acquired on a table or tablespace, prior to requesting more finely grained locks on a row or a page.

Table 12.1 is a compatibility matrix that summarizes the way in which these various lock modes interact. Each cell of the table shows whether a lock is granted when the lock is requested in the mode shown in the row and when another process already holds a lock in the mode shown in the column. Notice that update locks are asymmetric; they are like a reservation for an upcoming update. An update lock is granted when shared locks are held, but once granted, it prevents other shared locks from being acquired. Upon completing the update, the DBMS usually downgrades the update lock to a shared lock to allow other updating processes to proceed.

Also notice that exclusive locks are just that: They exclude every other type of lock, and every other type of lock prevents an exclusive lock from being obtained. This explains why it is so easy to get contention between readers and writers, especially with small tables. When monitoring delays caused by lock contention, always look for exclusive locks—either locking large objects (tables, tablespaces, databases) or being held for a long time. Or worse still, exclusive locks can exhibit both conditions, effectively making part of the database unavailable to any other processing. In the sections that follow, we note some situations that may cause exclusive locks to be held for extended periods.

For a more detailed explanation of the way these different types of locks are used, see Gray and Reuter.[3] For a shorter discussion, see "Getting a Lock on Integrity and Security" by C. M. Saracco and C. J. Bontempo.[4]

---

[3]Jim Gray and Andreas Reuter, *Transaction Processing: Concepts and Techniques* (San Mateo, CA: Morgan Kaufmann, 1993).
[4]C. M. Saracco and C. J. Bontempo, "Getting a Lock on Integrity and Security," *Database Programming & Design* (August 1996), 36.

Table 12.1 **Typical Lock Compatibility Matrix**

Lock Mode Requested	Lock Mode Already Granted						
	None	IS	IX	S	SIX	U	X
IS	yes	yes	yes	yes	yes	no	no
IX	yes	yes	yes	no	no	no	no
S	yes	yes	no	yes	no	no	no
SIX	yes	yes	no	no	no	no	no
U	yes	no	no	yes	no	no	no
X	yes	no	no	no	no	no	no

Lock Size or Granularity

Relational DBMSs support four common levels of *lock size* or *locking granularity,* as illustrated by Figure 12.1.

▶ *Row locks* protect against concurrent manipulation of a single row or index entry.

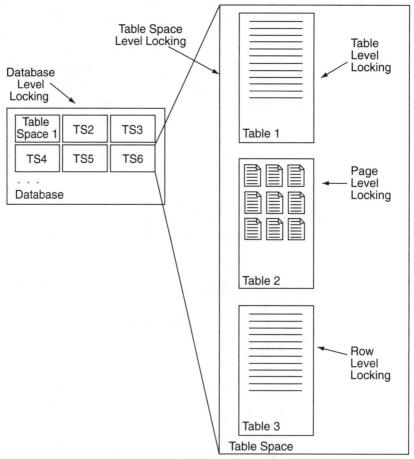

FIGURE 12.1 Database locking granularity.

► *Page locks* protect all rows in a database or index page, usually 2K or 4K, depending on the DBMS and the operating system environment.

► *Table locks* prevent concurrent access to an entire table.

► *Database locks* prevent concurrent data manipulation activities or changes to the structure of any table in the database (usually a named collection of tables).

Although row-, page-, and table-level locking are common, not every DBMS supports all four levels. In some products, row-level locking is not available; others do not use database locks. Yet other lock variations used by some DBMSs include *index subpage locks* (on a logical subset of an index page), *extent locks* (on a physical collection of data or index pages), and *tablespace locks* (on a physical file containing one or more tables). Tablespace locks are also illustrated in Figure 12.1.

Whether to use row-level, page-level, or table-level locking is usually defined as the property of a table when it is created. This property controls the size—and, to some extent, the timing—of the locks that the DBMS will acquire and release when programs need to manipulate data in that table.

Because they minimize the amount of data locked, *row* locks maximize concurrent access to different data items in a table and generally offer the best performance. Locking a 4K data page can easily tie up more than 100 rows; locking an index page can be even more restrictive because index entries are much smaller than whole rows. Ultimately, choosing the best lock size involves applying the Degree Locality Principle, as discussed in Chapter 10. For online transactions that need to process only a few rows, *row* locks are best. But if an application will systematically update a large number of rows, then page locks, or even a table lock, may be the fastest and most efficient way to handle that application and get it out of the way of others.

A DBMS may make this type of decision internally, raising the user-specified lock level to a higher level because of the type of processing to be done. This technique is called *lock promotion* when implemented statically or *lock escalation* when it is done dynamically during program execution. We discuss lock escalation in more detail in a later section.

Most DBMSs also allow an application program to escalate the locking level manually; for example, by issuing an explicit SQL statement like *LOCK TABLE*. This option should be used with care because there is usually no way to release the table lock until the application completes. For the mass update application, however, it is appropriate and more efficient than waiting for the DBMS to escalate the lock dynamically.

Finally, for read-only data, specify the largest lock size possible, usually TABLE or TABLESPACE (which may contain several tables). If no application will ever update the data, all readers can safely acquire a single large shared lock and process merrily away without giving another thought to locking. This is obviously the most efficient locking strategy for any data that is refreshed periodically but not updated online, as is usually the case in a data warehouse.

Guideline **12.2**	**Optimize table lock sizes to match the processing**

- ▶ For online transactions that need to process only a few rows, *row* locks are best.
- ▶ If an application will systematically update a large number of rows, then page locks, or even a table lock, may be the fastest and most efficient way to handle that application and get it out of the way of others.
- ▶ Programs intending to issue mass updates against a table with row level locking should first lock the table explicitly. This is more efficient than waiting for the DBMS to escalate from row locking to table locking dynamically.
- ▶ For read-only data that is never updated online, as in a data warehouse, use the largest lock size available to minimize locking activity.

Deadlocks

Deadlocks can occur when two (or more) programs issue locks in the process of reading and updating the same data. Like two petulant children, one has the bat and needs only the ball, and the other has the ball and wants to get hold of the bat. Each wants what the other has, and nothing useful gets done until someone—in this case the DBMS deadlock detection mechanism—intervenes and makes one side let go of its treasure.

Ideally, deadlocks should be broken promptly because not only are the deadlocked programs halted, but as long as the deadlocked programs hold database locks they will further inhibit concurrency for other applications. But not all deadlocks are recognized as such at the time the request is made, either because more than two programs are involved or because the DBMS activates its detection mechanism only periodically. To perform deadlock detection for every lock request would be prohibitively expensive; it is more efficient to perform it at regular intervals. In this case, the DBMS usually provides an installation parameter to control the *deadlock detection interval.*

If deadlocks are truly related to the content of the data, then one potential side effect of using many smaller row locks is an increased possibility of deadlocks between applications. Conversely, if applications obtain table locks,

Guideline 12.3 — Tune server deadlock detection intervals for the rate of deadlocks observed

Monitor the frequency of deadlocks on a database server, and set the detection interval accordingly. Ideally, deadlock detection should occur at least 10 times as often as deadlocks, to ensure that all deadlocks are resolved relatively promptly.

Because deadlock detection is an expensive overhead, if there are very few deadlocks, raising the detection interval will improve overall throughput. Select an interval close to the maximum acceptable response time for occasional error conditions.

If deadlocks occur often, lowering the interval will improve overall throughput and response times. Select an interval in the range of 15 seconds to 1 minute.

there is little risk of deadlocks (except possibly among badly designed applications that update multiple tables), but little concurrency either. Some DBMSs use a slightly less heavy-handed approach to deadlock avoidance; they obtain all the locks required by a program before beginning any processing, but this, of course, also inhibits concurrency.

The best way to avoid true data-related deadlocks is to fix the problem at its source. Investigate all deadlocks until a pattern emerges, then review how the applications involved process the shared tables. Usually there is a way to eliminate the deadlock by redesigning the application logic.

However, in our experience, it is much more common for deadlocks to be an artificial consequence of a particular combination of lock size and physical database design. The stalled applications (locked in the so-called *deadly embrace*) are not really waiting to process the same *data;* they just happen to be working with the same data or index *pages.* In this situation, dropping the lock size to *row* may well make many deadlocks disappear. If this does not work, then we probably need to revise the physical database design, to spread the pattern of database lock requests more evenly across the stored tables or indexes involved in the deadlocks.

Finally, there is one important thing to remember about tuning applications to avoid deadlocks. Deadlocks may be very bad for performance, but all lock waits are bad for performance, and at least two programs must be waiting to create a deadlock. So if we tune our applications to minimize waiting, deadlocks will automatically be minimized, too. To quote Miss Morgan's monetary analogy again: *Look after the pence, and the pounds will look after themselves.*

> **Guideline 12.4** **Avoid deadlocks**
>
> Investigate the cause of all deadlocks until a pattern emerges. If deadlocks are truly related to the content of the data, then using *row*-level locks can increase the possibility of deadlocks. If the deadlocks occur because applications just happen to be working with the same data or index *pages,* then consider locking at the *row* level. If this does not work, revise the physical database design to spread the lock requests more evenly across the tables or indexes involved.

Distributed Deadlocks. In some situations, a single process can update distributed databases, using a two-phase commit process to synchronize the updates at the separate sites. However, as our earlier discussion of locks and deadlocks indicates, the more delays involved in any process, the greater the potential for contention and deadlocks with other processes. Because of the inherent communication delays involved in all distributed processing, the probability of contention and deadlocks in a distributed database application increases substantially in proportion to the number of sites involved.

This is not due to any deficiency of the two-phase protocol. Two-phase commit is a perfectly sound logical solution to the problem of synchronizing resource managers. It simply does not work well in practice with independent distributed systems because when any one of the participants is delayed for any reason, that delay gets propagated into the other participating DBMSs because of the need to synchronize databases.

This is why the more popular approach to data distribution is to use replication schemes to copy data and propagate updates. Although not without its own complications, as we discuss in more detail in Chapter 20, *Using Data Replication,* this approach does avoid many of the unpredictable locking delays inherent in attempting to maintain data consistency dynamically across multiple sites.

> **Guideline 12.5** **Avoid distributed two-phase commit**
>
> Use schemes to copy data and replicate updates to avoid the delays inherent in attempting to maintain data consistency dynamically across multiple sites.

Lock Escalation

Other important considerations in the selection of lock size are the cost of acquiring all the locks a program needs and the memory or disk storage required to record the details of those locks. The number of bytes needed to record each outstanding lock varies among DBMSs in the range of 50–250 bytes, but suppose, for example, it takes 200 bytes per lock. Then a program defined with repeatable read isolation level and row-level locking that scans database rows could tie up as much as a megabyte of memory for every 5000 rows scanned. Even at 50 bytes per lock, scanning a million-row table would tie up 50 megabytes of memory. If the application has many users, recording its lock activity could make a significant dent in the shared memory resource.

Because of this aspect of locking, most DBMSs automatically override the requested lock level, raising it to a higher level when doing so will significantly reduce the number of lock requests. When this decision is made statically, before the application is run, this is called *lock promotion.* For example, at application bind time, DB2 automatically promotes the locking level of programs having the *repeatable read* isolation level to *tablespace* if their processing calls for a table scan; otherwise, every row in the table would have to be locked individually.

Many DBMSs also incorporate a *dynamic lock escalation* facility to further manage the trade-off between memory use and concurrency at execution time. When a single process has acquired an excessive number of locks, the DBMS raises its lock level dynamically to *table* from *row* or *page,* lessening its impact on the system's shared memory resource. Lock escalation also lowers the response time of an application requesting many locks because getting a single table lock is much quicker than getting a few thousand row or page locks.

SQL Server, for example, escalates from a page lock to a table lock when a process obtains too many page locks against a single table. The default *lock escalation threshold* is 200, but it can be modified using the *sp_configure* stored procedure. This holds for both the Microsoft and Sybase products.[5,6] DB2 and CA-OpenIngres operate similarly.

On the other hand, Informix and Oracle do not support lock escalation. In fact, Oracle claims that this design decision maximizes concurrency and allows "contention free queries."[7] Although it may make marketing sense, this claim is technically misleading—if memory is plentiful, users of SQL Server and DB2 can obtain similar behavior to Oracle's by establishing high lock escalation thresholds. Doing so effectively switches off lock escalation, except in

----

[5]Jim Panttaja, Mary Panttaja, and Bruce Prendergast, *The Microsoft SQL Server Survival Guide* (New York, NY: Wiley, 1996), 37.
[6]Shaibal Roy and Marc Sugiyama, *Sybase Performance Tuning* (Upper Saddle River, NJ: Prentice Hall, 1996), 180.
[7]See the Oracle 7.3 data sheet at *www.oracle.com*

the case of "run-away" applications that request very large numbers of locks. Oracle users, however, do not have the safety net of lock escalation to rescue them from a bad combination of processing and locking level.

> **Guideline 12.6**
>
> ## Lock escalation
>
> The purpose of lock escalation is to act as a safety net to trap "run-away" processes that are acquiring a very large number of row or page locks on a table. Set the escalation threshold so that all normal transaction processing against a table will not be affected, but excessive locking activity will be escalated as promptly as possible because all locking activity by a run-away's process is overhead.

Global Lock Limits.   Although they do not support lock escalation, initialization parameters in both Oracle (*DML_LOCKS*) and Informix (*LOCKS*) do enforce global limits on the numbers of various kinds of locks that can be held by all users concurrently. DBMSs usually implement this type of global limit for reasons related to memory allocation. For simplicity, DBMSs set aside a fixed area of memory to record information about all concurrent locks and do not have code to deal with overflow situations. Instead, they depend on an administrator to guess at a suitable limiting value and let applications fail if they are unlucky enough to attempt to exceed the limit.

Global lock limits, however, cannot be used as a substitute for lock escalation. When the limit is reached, the next program to request a lock will fail. Even though a run-away program may be acquiring an excessive number of locks, another concurrent program may be the one that hits the limit.

The default value of the Oracle DML_LOCKS setting is four times the number of concurrent users. Gurry and Corrigan recommend raising the multiplier to eight;[8] Corey recommends a multiplier of 10,[9] but even these values may be too low for workloads with a relatively small number of update intensive applications. As a general rule in all situations of this type, we recommend setting high global limits to avoid unexpected program failures, then investigating any situations in which the limit is hit.

> **Guideline 12.7**
>
> ## Beware of global lock limits
>
> Set high global limits to avoid unexpected program failures, and investigate any situations in which the limit is hit.

---

[8]Mark Gurry and Peter Corrigan, *Oracle Performance Tuning* (Sebastopol, CA: O'Reilly & Associates, 2nd ed.), p. 363.

[9]Michael Corey, Michael Abbey, and Dan Dechichio, *Tuning Oracle* (Berkeley, CA: Oracle Press, 1995), 161.

> **Guideline 12.8** **Monitor locking levels**
>
> Monitor lock usage by programs and overall locking levels in the system, to see if global lock limits are approached or exceeded.

Program Isolation Levels

In most single-user systems, there is no need to lock data and isolate programs from each other. For database servers, though, DBMS vendors provide program isolation features to support database integrity in the face of concurrent database processing by multiple clients.

As a further refinement, server DBMSs allow various *isolation levels* to be specified for an application program. These control the *degree* of data integrity enforcement in database applications. Listed from the weakest to the strongest, these are roughly as follows:

▶ **Dirty Read.**   Locks are ignored. Applications may read data that has been updated but not yet committed to the database (*dirty data*), and that may never be committed if, for some reason, the updating application fails before it completes.

▶ **Committed Read.**   Applications may not read dirty data and will be prevented from overwriting another application's dirty data.

▶ **Cursor Stability.**   A row read by one application will not be changed by another application while it is being used. With page-level locking, a page will remain locked until the application moves on to the next page.

▶ **Repeatable Read.**   This causes all data items read to be locked until the application reaches a commit point, so that any data item, if re-read, will contain the same value as previously. This level is also called *serializable* because it creates the same results (in the programs and in the database) as if the programs had been run serially, rather than concurrently.

From a performance viewpoint, the stronger the isolation level, the greater the potential for lock contention and response time delays. Therefore, we should design applications to use the weakest level that is consistent with the correct working of the application. For example:

▶ If the data in a table is not updated during normal online processing, as is usually the case with a data warehouse, for example, all programs should use dirty read for efficiency. Even for data subject to concurrent updates, programs that simply report on data can often tolerate the *dirty-read* level, unless consistency among reported data items is essential. Statistical reporting, which usually does not need exact answers, can also use this level.

▶ Programs that both read and write data but do not depend on nor maintain consistency between the data items read and those written may be able to use the *committed-read* level.

▶ Selecting *cursor stability* provides the greatest concurrency without loss of data consistency for most applications that access a given row only once. But, for example, a query that computes a total may not return a correct value, even though each row is read only once—another program may have been in the process of making a set of related changes while the sum was being computed, and the cursor stability isolation level does not prevent some of those changes from being included in the sum.

▶ Applications that read the same row several times must use the *repeatable read* or *serializable* option to guarantee data consistency. For optimal performance, use repeatable read sparingly because it locks every data item an application touches and restricts concurrent access to tables by other work. Unfortunately, sometimes the only way to create the appearance of serialized operations by a set of programs that are manipulating the same table(s) is actually to serialize much of their processing.

Guideline 12.9	**For optimal performance, weaken isolation levels**

For optimal performance, always specify the weakest isolation level consistent with application correctness and data integrity. Use dirty read for read-only data and for all programs that can tolerate small inconsistencies in the source data that might be introduced by concurrent updates. If possible, avoid using the *repeatable read* or *serializable* level because it causes the most locks to be held for the greatest duration and prevents a lot of concurrent processing.

This is a highly complex and technical area of DBMS design; our discussion is necessarily incomplete. Complicating matters, it turns out that the implementations of these various isolation levels by DBMS vendors vary widely. For example, most DBMSs do not distinguish between *committed read* and *cursor stability,* nor between *repeatable read* and *serializable.* Furthermore, the DBMS implementations differ from those defined in the SQL standard.[10]

---

[10]For some varied and rather sketchy details of particular DBMS implementations of isolation levels, see the footnotes in Chapter 19. For a short discussion of isolation levels and the SQL standard, see C. J. Date and H. Darwen, *A Guide to the SQL Standard,* 4th ed. (Reading, MA: Addison-Wesley, 1997), 60–62. For a thorough treatment of program isolation concepts, see Gray and Reuter's 70-page chapter in *Transaction Processing: Concepts and Techniques,* 375–445.

Lock Duration

In Chapter 11, we noted Connie Smith's statement of the Sharing Principle, *"When exclusive access is required, minimize the sum of the holding time and the scheduling time."* The technical term for the time an application spends holding locks is *lock duration,* and it depends primarily on application logic. There are two areas in which application design can help minimize lock duration:

Choosing DBMS lock duration options. Although the DBMS may provide the option of acquiring locks at program initialization time, the greatest concurrency is usually obtained by selecting the DBMS options that delay lock acquisition until each data item is processed and releasing all locks as soon as possible thereafter—either immediately after processing the data item or at the next commit point, depending on the locking strategy being implemented.

Designing the application's data manipulation logic. When coding programs that manipulate shared data, minimize the duration of any update portion of the application. We should:

▶ Complete as much processing as possible before any data manipulation request that obtains update or exclusive locks. For example, do not declare a cursor with the FOR UPDATE OF . . . clause unless the update in question is scheduled to happen promptly thereafter. If the program may not actually update the data, or if a delay is possible before the update occurs, read the data with a share lock and defer getting a lock for the update request until an update is sure to happen.
▶ Minimize the total amount of processing done after locks are acquired.
▶ Release locks as soon as possible, by issuing a COMMIT or terminating the program promptly. Therefore, we should be careful not to create programs that combine database update activity with subsequent data browsing.

Guideline 12.10   Minimize lock durations

To minimize lock contention, minimize the time an application spends holding locks. Defer lock acquisition until the latest possible time, minimize processing while holding locks, and commit or terminate the program promptly.

Hot Spots in Shared Data

Although locking is essential for maintaining data integrity, excessive contention can occur when too many concurrent applications need to lock the same data item or the same small set of data items. Database designers call this type of locking bottleneck a *hot spot.* Because several applications are reading and writing to the same portion of a database, it is quite common for deadlocks (discussed earlier) to be caused by hot spots. A hot spot can arise for one of three reasons:

Natural hot spots exist in the business data. It is very rare for activity to be evenly distributed across all areas of the business—recall the Centering Principle introduced in Chapter 4. Sometimes, thanks to a highly skewed distribution of work, a large percentage of database updates apply to a small fraction of the business data.

▶ Suppose, for example, a software vendor records and maintains status information about all customer service hot-line calls and any follow-up activity, in a table ordered by date and time. If the company responds to its callers promptly, most database activity will center on the most recent data in the table.

▶ Another example might be a mail order company whose product line includes a small number of very popular items. If telephone order processing maintains stock levels dynamically, many order takers will be reading and updating the same rows in the stock table.

Automating these types of business applications tends to create database hot spots naturally, unless we are careful to design the databases and the associated processing to eliminate them.

The application's design creates artificial hot spots. When applications are designed to maintain the current value of a derived statistic like a sequence number, a total, or an average, instant hot spots are created in databases because every instance of a program must read and update the same data item.

Locking protocols against physical data structures create artificial hot spots. Even though applications are not manipulating the same data, they may well be reading and writing to the same physical data or index pages, which will cause contention if page-level locking is being used. Common examples of this type of problem occur when all the rows in a table fit on a small number of pages or when data is inserted sequentially on the last page of a table based on a time or a sequence number.

In the following sections we discuss some possible solutions to these common problems.

Timestamped Data

When data is stored and processed in time sequence, hot spots commonly occur on the last page of a table or an index. This is usually an artificial hot spot caused by the physical data structure. Often, row-level locking will eliminate this type of hot spot because it is the data or index pages, not the data records themselves, that are in demand. If row-level locking is not possible, storing the data in a different sequence eliminates the hot spot in the data but makes it a bit more expensive to retrieve data in time sequence. If the timestamp column is indexed, however, there may still be a hot spot on the last page of the index. However, even in data that is updated, the timestamps themselves are rarely updated. The problem may be less severe in an index than in the corresponding table, as long as page locking can be avoided in the index.

To reorder timestamped data that has no other column of unique values available as a suitable ordering key, create a new column containing the reversed timestamp and use it as the ordering key. For example, the successive timestamps 18.37.52.469, 18.37.52.470, and 18.37.52.471 would become 964257381, 074257381, 174257381, respectively. As the example shows, this technique randomizes the sequence of the stored data relative to the true timestamps but still leaves the true timestamp in the table and available to applications as needed. When the reversed timestamp key is stored elsewhere as a cross-reference or foreign key, other processes will be able to access the data via the index on the reversed timestamps, reducing the use of the index on the true timestamp.

The whole subject of temporal data is a complex one, and many issues come into play when selecting the best way to store temporal data in a relational database, of which performance is just one. For this reason, *time-series* is one of the extended data types likely to be better supported by an object-relational or "universal" DBMS. For a short review of the subject, see Mike Stonebraker's book, *Object-Relational DBMSs.*[11]

Guideline 12.11 Timestamped data

Avoid application and database designs in which data is inserted and stored in timestamp sequence. Use a different column as an ordering key. If no other suitable column is available, consider using a reversed form of the timestamp for the ordering key and for foreign keys in related tables.

Allocating Sequence Numbers

Storing data sequentially based on artificially assigned sequence numbers poses all the same problems as those discussed previously in the section,

---

[11]Mike Stonebraker, *Object-Relational DBMSs: The Next Great Wave* (San Mateo, CA: Morgan Kaufmann, 1996), 45.

Timestamped Data. However, there is an additional risk of a hot spot if, in the process of allocating the sequence number, every application reads and writes to a single *CurrentHighSeqNo* record in a database.

Often, sequence numbers can be replaced in the application design by ascending values like timestamps. This should be done whenever possible. If sequence numbers are essential, one way to avoid database locking problems is to use an optimistic allocation scheme involving a unique index. For this technique, create a DBMS index that enforces uniqueness of the sequence number column in the table of interest. Have each application read the previous highest sequence number (S)—usually, the DBMS's MAX function will use the index to get this value quickly without scanning the table—and then attempt to insert its new entry using the next highest sequence number (S + 1). Because the unique index prevents duplicates, if the insert fails it means that some other application has taken the sequence number S + 1, so the application must re-read the table to obtain the new maximum value.

This technique will work provided that all applications can obtain access to the shared data in about the same amount of time. *It will not work in a high-volume environment with a wide range of data access times.* Slower applications, probably those running at remote locations, will be preempted by faster ones. They will rarely be able to read and update the database before another application "steals" their intended sequence number. Remote users will grow frustrated waiting for their transactions to complete and will begin calling the support line to complain about highly erratic response times.

In this situation, to minimize contention, a single process should read the current maximum sequence number, immediately add 1, and insert the new entry. The entire process must run as rapidly as possible while holding a database lock on the current maximum sequence number. The easiest way to achieve this goal is to create a stored database procedure that performs all three actions. In this case, the maximum throughput of the system for applications needing to maintain the sequence number will be determined by the elapsed time to dispatch and execute the stored procedure. Since the process runs in its entirety on the database server machine, no network I/O will be included in the elapsed time. Also, at high volumes, no disk I/O time should be involved either because the database and index page(s) containing the highest sequence numbers will be continually in use, causing them to remain loaded in memory in the DBMS cache or buffer pool.

If the application can tolerate gaps in the sequence numbers, then a simple *Sequence Number Server* can be created. This process reads the current highest sequence number once at initialization, caches it internally, and thereafter hands out the next highest number to any requester. Invoked by an RPC, this is even faster than using a database procedure. It does not matter if some sequence numbers handed out never make it into the database. For this to work, *every application must use the same technique;* otherwise, duplicate sequence numbers can occur. Even with a unique index to catch duplicates, having two different techniques to request a new sequence number is sure to cause collisions and delays as application volumes rise.

> ### Guideline 12.12   Allocating sequence numbers
>
> To avoid a hot spot when allocating unique sequence number, do not use a database table to maintain the current highest sequence number.
>
> ▶ At low volumes, use an optimistic allocation scheme in which every process reads the current maximum value from a unique index and simply adds 1, repeating the process in case of collisions.
> ▶ At high volumes, create a stored database procedure that reads the current highest value, adds 1, and stores the result.
> ▶ For maximum throughput, create a special-purpose Sequence Number Server, accessed via a remote procedure call.

Summary Statistics

For occasional use, summary statistics like averages or totals should be recomputed when needed because the overhead of maintaining them continuously probably does not justify the savings. If suitable indexes are available, a DBMS can compute many summary statistics (like COUNT, MIN, MAX, SUM, and AVERAGE) directly from an index. This is almost always a lot faster than reading every row in the table because many fewer pages must be read, and—for busy tables—the indexes are often already in memory in a DBMS cache. We discuss caching in more detail in Chapter 14, *The Trade-off Principle,* and Chapter 19, *Using DBMS Technology.*

When an application needs averages or totals to be available continually, and needs these same statistics to reflect recent database activity, we risk creating hot spots if the design causes every user to update the same statistics in the database.

One approach is to maintain periodic batch totals and to record recent transaction history using a batch of database inserts, not updates. Periodically, the most recent batch of inserts is totaled and the batch totals inserted as a new row in a table of batch totals. Using this technique, the processing required to compute a current (or nearly current) total or average value is more complex, but it requires reading of only previously inserted data, thus eliminating the contention that occurs when every application locks and updates a single data item. To maintain the highest level of summary statistics, we could design a rapid read-and-update process that reads the batch totals and inserts a new set of overall summary statistics, as we suggested for sequence numbers, making sure to eliminate all I/O delays at high processing volumes to minimize contention.

If desired, a series of summary levels like *hourly, daily, weekly,* and *monthly* statistics can be maintained in this way. This summarization process is illustrated in Figure 12.2.

When data is extracted into read-only databases, as is the case with a data warehouse, a variety of summaries, averages, and totals can also be precomputed and stored. For applications that need summary data, the most efficient solution is one involving periodic light summarization, followed by further summarization as time goes by. Applications then have a variety of levels of detail available to address most reporting needs. We discuss this subject further in Chapter 21, *Using Data Warehousing.*

Guideline 12.13	**Summary statistics**

When averages or totals need to reflect recent activity, maintaining those statistics in the database can create hot spots. Instead, use the combination of a transaction log and periodic summaries. Record recent transition history using database inserts, not updates. Periodically, total the most recent batch of inserts and insert the batch totals as a new row in a table of batch totals. Periodically compute overall statistics from the batch totals, again using a database insert to record the result. Hourly, daily, weekly, and monthly summary statistics can be maintained in this way.

Small Tables and Indexes

Small tables and indexes that are updated are a classic source of hot spots in database systems. Often, small shared tables contain various types of application control data rather than true business data. In addition to the obvious example of database servers for shared business data, in a distributed computing environment we often create shared servers for administrative data. For example, managing user identification and authentication from a single security server allows applications running on separate processors to share security services.

Such shared servers may minimize operational costs, but we must always beware of creating bottlenecks. If a relatively small number of shared data elements are updated by many users, we must take care to avoid creating artificial hot spots by the way we use locking mechanisms. In small tables, whatever

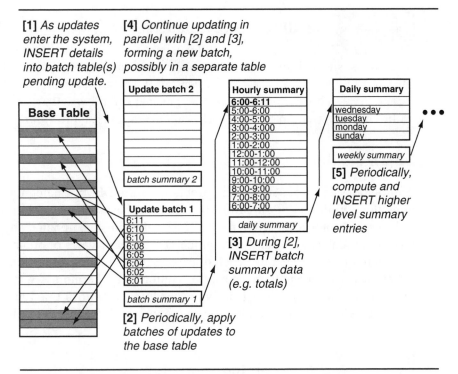

[1] *As updates enter the system, INSERT details into batch table(s) pending update.*

[4] *Continue updating in parallel with [2] and [3], forming a new batch, possibly in a separate table*

[5] *Periodically, compute and INSERT higher level summary entries*

[3] *During [2], INSERT batch summary data (e.g. totals)*

[2] *Periodically, apply batches of updates to the base table*

FIGURE 12.2   Maintaining summary data without hot spots.

data they contain, concurrency will be severely affected if any application is allowed to lock any more than the row or rows it needs to process.

Therefore, row-level locking is essential for small tables. In a DBMS that does not offer row-level locking as a design option, or in any situation in which the table may be subject to page-level locking, then we should spread out the data artificially so that it occupies more pages. To spread out the rows, we can insert extra free space in the table, insert dummy rows, or pad each row with a large unused column.

Indexes on small tables are usually not useful since the DBMS can scan the entire table with one or two disk I/Os. In fact, since the DBMS may not even use the index, we should consider dropping small indexes. Any time there is sufficient activity against a table that a small index becomes a source of lock contention, we must ask ourselves whether the benefits of having the index outweigh the overhead of maintaining it and the additional locking delays it introduces. Given the volume of activity, if the index were dropped, then the entire table would probably reside comfortably in the DBMS cache anyway.

> ### Guideline 12.14   Small tables and indexes
>
> Small tables and indexes are a classic source of hot spots in database systems. Use row-level locking, or spread out the data artificially so that it occupies more pages. To spread out the rows, we can insert extra free space in the table, insert dummy rows, or pad each row with a large unused column. If small indexes incur lock contention, consider dropping them.

DBMS Catalog

Another classic source of locking problems is the DBMS catalog itself. It contains the definitions of all DBMS objects—databases, tables, columns, views, indexes, SQL procedures, and so on. The catalog must be updated any time any one of these objects is modified, which can lock out users of other objects. In fact, in our experience, unrestricted use of SQL DDL (data definition language) always causes some amount of catalog contention. Therefore, we strongly recommend introducing administrative procedures to control this type of definitional activity in a production environment, scheduling it during low impact hours.

> ### Guideline 12.15   DBMS catalog contention
>
> Unrestricted use of SQL DDL (data definition language) always causes some amount of catalog contention. In a production environment, create administrative procedures to control this type of definitional activity, scheduling it during low impact hours.

Locking Summary

To sum up our review of database locking, we return to the four ways of reducing contention for a shared resource, namely: reduce the *number,* and *size* of requests, *speed up* processing, and *divert* some requests elsewhere. To minimize the performance impact of database locking, we must design applications and databases with these four factors in mind:

▶ Select the weakest *isolation level* consistent with application correctness. This will help minimize the frequency, size, and duration of lock requests.
▶ Unless all applications will read a large percentage of rows in a table, select the smallest *lock size* for tables. This will help minimize the size of requests and the incidence of lock contention.

▶ In applications that intend to perform mass updates, issue the LOCK TABLE command to escalate the lock size explicitly. Try to schedule these applications away from peak processing times.

▶ Design application logic to delay requesting locks until the last possible time, to minimize the amount of processing done after locks are requested, and to release locks as promptly as possible. This will minimize the time spent holding locks.

▶ Design applications, tables, and their associated lock-related parameters to spread lock requests evenly across tables and indexes. This will minimize the incidence of hot spots and deadlocks in the database.

This completes our two chapters on the Sharing Principle. In the next chapter we look at another way to make systems more responsive—*divide and conquer* techniques that employ the **Parallelism Principle.**

The Parallelism Principle

"Many hands make light work."

Anonymous

In this Chapter . . .

Workload Growth and Parallelism
Parallel Processing Possibilities
Who Needs a Parallel Processor?
Parallel Database Processing
Conclusions about the Parallelism Hierarchy

In Chapters 11 and 12 we discussed the performance of shared resources and how to minimize the delays caused by bottlenecks. When there is excessive demand for a single shared resource, one way to break the logjam is to divide and conquer. Dennis Shasha's database design principle, *"Partitioning breaks bottlenecks,"* concisely expresses this motivation for processing work in parallel.[1]

The idea behind parallelism is simple: Take several items of work and process them at the same time. Naturally, this approach is faster than processing the same work serially. But while it may be an obvious and attractive design technique, processing in parallel does introduce new problems of its own. Not all workloads can be easily subdivided, and not all software is designed to work in parallel. Processing related pieces of work in parallel typically introduces additional synchronization overheads and, in many situations, produces

---

[1]Dennis E. Shasha, *Database Tuning: A Principled Approach* (Upper Saddle River, NJ: Prentice-Hall, 1992), 3.

new kinds of contention among the parallel streams. Connie Smith's version of the Parallelism Principle recognizes these complications: "*Execute processing in parallel (only) when the processing speedup offsets communication overhead and resource contention delays.*"[2]

To sum up, Smith's and Shasha's two views nicely highlight the dilemma facing every designer when considering parallelism.

Guideline 13.1	The Parallelism Principle: Exploit parallel processing

Processing related pieces of work in parallel typically introduce additional synchronization overheads and often introduce contention among the parallel streams. Use parallelism to overcome bottlenecks, provided the processing speedup offsets the additional costs introduced.

Workload Growth and Parallelism

Contention for a shared resource, like the network or a small table, or excessive amounts of database processing on a relatively slow server will cause performance problems even in small departmental systems. But, if everything about the application remains small, we can usually find a way to remove the bottlenecks and tune the application code or the database structure to reduce excessive processing to a manageable level.

When we scale up from a departmental client/server systems to enterprise-wide distributed computing, however, a whole new set of challenges arises. To stay competitive, a large modern enterprise needs a comprehensive information system. In Chapter 5, we pointed out that the sheer scale of enterprise information processing can introduce performance problems. We showed how, as information systems grow, performance issues arise along six distinct dimensions. These were originally presented in Table 5.1; we're repeating it here as Table 13.1 for convenience. Parallel processing techniques are particularly relevant to four of the dimensions in the table—*large databases, large objects, high transaction rates,* and *complex data analysis.* And to the extent that these four phenomena are a consequence of growth along the other two dimensions—large networks connecting large populations of computer users generally lead to large workloads—we could reasonably argue that techniques involving parallelism apply to every one of these six dimensions.

---

[2]Connie U. Smith, *Performance Engineering of Software Systems* (Reading, MA: Addison-Wesley, 1990), 55.

Table 13.1   **The Six Dimensions of Growth**

Growth Area	Characteristics
Databases	Transactions, queries, and reports must work with progressively larger and more complex operational and decision support databases.
Stored objects	Originally, databases stored relatively short alphanumeric business records; increasingly, they must store graphics, voice, and video information, too.
User populations	Progressively more users need online access to business information.
Transaction rates	Very high transaction processing rates can occur, especially at peak business periods when responsiveness is critical to the profitability of the business.
Data analysis	Traditional transaction processing recorded relatively simple business events. Now online systems must support progressively more complex data analysis.
Networks	Linking departmental-level local area networks with corporate wide area networks creates ever more complex enterprise networks.

Scalability and Speedup

We can evaluate the benefits of parallelism using two important concepts: **scalability** and **speedup.** Although these terms are most often used in technical literature to describe the characteristics of different multiprocessor *machines* (which we discuss later in this chapter), they apply equally well to entire information processing *systems.* In essence, *scalability* refers to capacity or *throughput* increases, while *speedup* refers to reductions in *response time.* We now discuss these two concepts in more detail and review the related issues of *load balancing* and *Amdahl's law.*

Scalability.   *Scalability* refers to the capacity of the system to perform more total work in the same elapsed time. A system or machine would have *linear* or *perfect scalability* if increasing its compute power by some percentage had the effect of increasing its capacity to process work by the identical percentage. For example, an OLTP system processing 25 transactions per second would, assuming linear scalability, handle 50 per second if we doubled the number of processors.

Speedup.   *Speedup* refers to the capacity of the system to perform a particular task in a shorter time. A system or processor would have *linear speedup* if increasing its compute power by some percentage had the effect of reducing the elapsed time for a task by the inverse percentage.

In other words, with linear speedup, twice as much hardware would perform the same task in half the elapsed time. If 2 processors can complete a task in 10 minutes, 4 should do it in 5 minutes, and 8 should take 2.5 minutes.

> **Guideline 13.2**   **Scalability and speedup**
> *Scalability* refers to the capacity of the system to perform more total work in the same elapsed time when its processing power is increased.
> *Speedup* refers to the capacity of the system to perform a particular task in a shorter time when its processing power is increased. In a system with *linear* scalability and speedup, any increase in processing power generates a proportional improvement in throughput or response time.

Overheads and Load Balancing

Whenever we process work in parallel, two factors threaten to limit our ability to exploit the full potential of our parallel resources: **parallelism overheads** and **load balancing.**

Parallelism Overheads.   When we split work into parallel streams, a variety of overheads appear that are not present when the same work is processed serially. Good examples are:

▶ The cost of splitting work into parallel streams
▶ Operating system processing for task or context switching
▶ Processor and I/O delays for memory swapping
▶ A reduction in the efficiency of hardware or software caching
▶ Contention for data shared by the parallel streams
▶ Delays for synchronization among the parallel streams
▶ Additional processing for synchronization

The impact of these types of overhead almost always gets worse as the number of parallel streams increases, which limits scalability.

> **Guideline 13.3**   **Overheads in parallel systems**
> Whenever we split work into parallel streams, a variety of synchronization and contention overheads appear that are not present when the same work is processed serially. These overheads almost always get worse as the number of parallel streams increases, which limits scalability.

Load Balancing.   Assuming that we have a workload we can subdivide without introducing excessive overheads, the next challenge is getting the separate components balanced. For maximum scalability, if we have four processors, we should be *using* four processors. If we have 20 disks, our data should be spread over 20 disks, and we need to be *using* all 20 equally. Unless we can balance the load on our parallel resources, one will become a bottleneck while others have spare capacity.

In this chapter, we discuss many different possibilities for employing parallelism. These range in scope from splitting up entire workloads down to parallel processing of program instruction streams. Regardless of the particulars of the scheme, *successful load balancing is essential for scalability.*

As Figure 13.1 illustrates, this fact has implications for all five performance factors: workload volumes, application processing, database content, hardware, and systems software. For example:

▶ Does the workload mix vary? How do the resulting processes distribute across the resources? If, for example, we optimize a relatively static resource, like the distribution of stored data, for one workload mix, what happens when the mix changes? How does the parallel scheme handle dynamic workload fluctuations?

▶ Is the application a single massive process or a large collection of small processes? If the former, how and where can we actually subdivide it? If the latter, to what degree can we run them in parallel? In the world of parallel database processing, these two concerns are called *intraquery* and *interquery* parallelism.

▶ Can we partition the database in such a way that data requests are evenly spread across disks and across processors if disks are not shared?

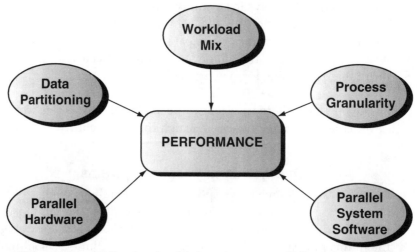

FIGURE 13.1   Factors affecting load balancing in parallel systems.

▶ Does the system software exploit parallelism in the hardware with data and process partitioning schemes? Can the software do dynamic load balancing as workloads change? What degree of user intervention is needed to obtain effective parallelism?

▶ To what degree does the hardware support parallelism? Do all devices operate at equal power? Does the hardware have inherent bottlenecks in some components that inhibit load balancing?

To obtain linear scalability we would need a system that had no overheads from parallel processing and a workload that could keep all devices equally busy. This explains why linear scalability is an ideal and never the practical reality.

> **Guideline 13.4** **Load balancing in parallel systems**
> Unless we can balance the load on parallel resources, one will become a bottleneck while others will have spare capacity. Regardless of the particulars of any parallel-processing scheme, successful load balancing is essential for scalability.

Speedup: Amdahl's Law

In 1967, Gene Amdahl, who later became famous as the founder of the mainframe computer company that bears his name, observed that there is a limit to the amount that we can speed up any task if we optimize only one part of it. This principle has become known in the industry as Amdahl's Law. It provides an upper bound on the maximum speedup that can be obtained from parallel processing.

For example, suppose a data-mining application runs for an hour but spends only six minutes of that time processing and the rest reading the database. In this case, substituting an infinitely fast parallel processor will not reduce the execution time below 54 minutes, and it may not even achieve that if some of the database I/O originally overlapped with the processing. Since an infinitely fast machine would produce a 10 percent speedup at most, wheeling in a machine that was only four times as fast would probably not make a noticeable dent in our response times *for this application.*

We should save our faster machine for applications like the *DataMiner* program we discussed in Chapter 11 (see Table 11.1), which is processing more than 90 percent of the time (20 seconds out of a total elapsed time of 22 seconds). If we could cut its processing time to 5 seconds, our maximum overall reduction would be 15/22 or 68 percent.

To sum up Amdahl's Law: *For any application, the maximum speedup we can obtain by optimizing any component of a program or system depends on the percentage of time the application spends using that component.*

Applying Amdahl's Law

Although Amdahl was originally referring to the potential benefits obtainable from parallel computers, notice that the law as stated is actually completely general—it can be applied to a wide variety of tuning situations and to any technique for achieving speedup. It applies equally well to any sequential activity that comprises distinct subtasks or components, including:

▶ Manual workflows
▶ Tasks that combine manual and automated components
▶ Entire information systems
▶ Software applications
▶ Software processes

In fact, Amdahl's Law provides the technical basis for applying the Centering Principle to tuning, as we discussed in Chapters 4 and 5. It tells us that to obtain the greatest potential for performance improvement we must focus on:

▶ The most frequently executed components (the *mainline* path through the application)
▶ The slowest devices
▶ The busiest devices
▶ The part of the application where we spend the most time

This is an important insight for the design of high-performance client/server information systems. As we pointed out in our introduction to enterprise client/server in Chapter 2, system performance problems are often rooted in excessive (and relatively slow) communication among distributed components rather than within the components themselves. Amdahl's Law explains why scaling up the performance of the individual components does little to relieve such problems.

Guideline 13.5   Amdahl's Law

There is a fundamental limit as to how much you can speed up something if you optimize only one portion of it. For any application, the maximum speedup we can obtain by optimizing any component of a program or system depends on the percentage of time the application spends using that component. Conversely, optimizing the largest component of any application offers the greatest potential for performance improvement.

Parallel Processing Possibilities

We can apply the Parallelism Principle at many different levels. Starting with the information processing requirements for the entire enterprise, a workload can be subdivided into components (see Figure 13.2) at progressively lower levels of detail, as follows:

Level-1. Enterprise information processing requirements normally comprise several workload classes.

Level-2. A single workload class comprises many business workflows or transactions classes.

Level-3. A single business workflow or transaction class may generate many software application or transaction instances.

Level-4. A single software application may comprise several software processes or tasks.

Level-5. A single software process may contain several data manipulation requests or "queries."

Level-6. A single data manipulation request or "query" may access several data structures (tables and indexes).

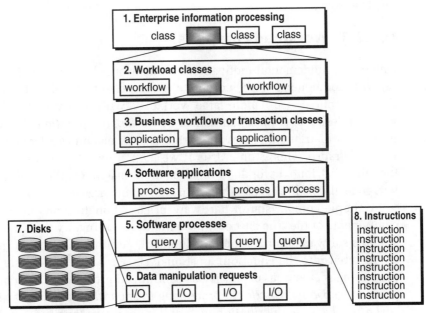

FIGURE 13.2   Workload components.

Level-7. A single large data structure (table or index) may reside on many disks.
Level-8. A single program contains many CPU instructions.

Applying parallel processing techniques at any one of these eight levels can increase throughput and reduce response times. Therefore, to simplify our discussion of the concepts and design choices available, we now introduce some terminology to define these eight distinct levels of parallelism. They are:

Level-1. Workload parallelism
Level-2. Workflow parallelism
Level-3. Program parallelism
Level-4. Process parallelism
Level-5. Data manipulation (DML) parallelism
Level-6. Intraquery parallelism
Level-7. I/O device parallelism
Level-8. CPU parallelism

We discuss each of the eight levels briefly in the next eight sections and summarize the levels in Table 13.2. In addition to the level number and name, Table 13.2 identifies the class of work being subdivided and the elements being processed in parallel. It also shows the motivation for each level, the principal mechanisms involved in implementing it, and some of the design issues we must resolve.

Level-1: Workload Parallelism

One of the fundamental motivations for distributed computing in general is to *separate* components of the corporate workload to be handled by different processing resources. To handle large workloads with relatively small processors, we must design to exploit parallelism by *workload separation*. A common justification for distributed processing is that smaller machines offer better price/performance ratios. This is often true if we look at only the hardware costs. Even though a distributed workload requires more machines, the total machine cost will generally be lower than that of an equivalent large central server.

A simple comparison of hardware prices, though, omits many significant components of the true cost of information processing. By the time the costs of systems software, application development, administration, and maintenance are factored into the equation, most analysts agree that large-scale distributed processing is at least as expensive as centralized processing. The consensus appears to be: *Do not distribute processing to separate machines on the basis of cost alone because distribution may cost more in the long run.*

Table 13-2 **Eight Levels of Parallelism**

Level	Parallelism Type	Applies to . . .	Process in Parallel	Design Motivations	Mechanisms Involved	Design Issues
1	Workload	An enterprise workload	Workload classes	Business workload exceeds the power of a single processor Different workload classes don't mix well Workload is growing rapidly Workload volumes fluctuate a lot	Distributed processing Dedicated servers Distributed data Data partitioning Replicated tables	Would a larger processor be more effective? How will we route work to the server? What will be the response times of remote requests? Is data partitioning feasible? Is data replication feasible? How will we propagate updates to replicated tables?
2	Workflow	A workload class	Business workflows or transaction classes	Performance-critical business process involves serialized stages Performance-critical business process can be simplified	Business process re-engineering Workflow design	Does the business process subdivide into logical stages? Is the entire process atomic? What happens if any stage fails?

Table 13-2 **Eight Levels of Parallelism (*Cont'd*)**

Level	Parallelism Type	Applies to . . .	Process in Parallel	Design Motivations	Mechanisms Involved	Design Issues
3	Program	A business workflow or transaction class	Software application program or transaction instances	A large transaction processing workload Growth and fluctuations in transaction arrival rates A large client population	Transaction monitor Message queuing middleware	How many server tasks per active client workstation? How much server memory per concurrent client connection? Does middleware queue and schedule server requests? Does middleware do load balancing across multiple servers?
4	Process	A software application program	Software processes or tasks	A large program requiring a fast response	Manual parallel programming techniques	What is the overhead of dispatching multiple subtasks or threads? Do response time gains justify the additional coding complexity?
5	DML	A software process	DML requests	Slow response time caused by extensive database processing in multiple DML requests	Parallel DBMS DBMS optimizer operating on a database procedure	Does a set of database requests contain no sequential interdependencies? How does the DBMS optimizer know that two DML requests are logically independent?

6	Intraquery	A DML request	Data structures (indexes and tables)	Response time delays caused by complex processing of one or more massive data structures by a single DML request	Parallel DBMS DBMS optimizer operating on a single database request (typically an SQL statement)	Can the data of interest be spread across multiple disks? Can the processing be spread across multiple processors? Does the DBMS actually exploit these possibilities for parallelism? Do response time gains justify the additional database design and maintenance effort?
7	I/O Device	A single table or data structure	Disks	Applications that search very large databases Response time delays caused by the disk I/O component of database processing	RAID technology Parallel DBMS	Which data partitioning scheme will best suit the application processing pattern, and promote parallel I/O operation? How well does the DBMS support data partitioning and parallel I/O?
8	Instruction	A program	Instructions	Response time delays caused by massive amounts of computation Processor capacity limits exceeded by large workloads	Parallel processing algorithms Parallelizing compiler	Are special programming skills required to allow parallel processing to occur? Can the workload be parallelized more easily at a higher level in the hierarchy?

Once we accept this conclusion, we are forced to focus more carefully on the other costs and benefits of distribution, either of which may include performance:

▶ Distribution introduces delays when related components are separated—recall Guideline 10.3 and our discussion of the *Spatial Locality Principle* in Chapter 10.

▶ On the other hand, separating workloads that do not mix well can improve performance by reducing the contention for shared resources. For example, for optimal performance we should separate an online production transaction-processing workload from a decision-support workload, as in a data warehousing environment. Inmon's rule, which we introduced in Chapter 10 (see Guideline 10.20), provides one of the motivations for this type of separation, namely: *Don't mix short transactions with long-running queries.*

The goal of client/server design is to get the benefits of separation while avoiding the costs. Therefore, we must always stay alert for opportunities to replace large central servers with several smaller ones by subdividing the workload.

When we look for parallelism at Level-1, we must consider these key design issues:

▶ **Feasibility.** Is installing a larger central processor actually a feasible solution, and if so, would that approach be more effective? Either the sheer volume of processing requirements or an incompatible workload mix may rule out a single-processor solution.

▶ **Network delays.** If we create a dedicated server for a particular class of processing, how do we route work to the server? What will be the impact on response times for users whose location is remote from the dedicated processor?

▶ **Data partitioning.** If distinct classes of work share common data but are assigned to separate processors, is some form of data partitioning feasible? For example, a customer database is a shared resource, but perhaps it does not have to reside on a single central server. An alternative may be to split the data by sales region and store each region at a separate regional database server. If this type of partitioning is indeed feasible, then several smaller servers can give us both *better throughput* and *higher availability* than the equivalent large centralized server. We discuss data partitioning in more detail later in this chapter.

▶ **Data replication.** If data partitioning is not possible, is data replication feasible? If so, how will we propagate updates among the replicated portions? We discuss technologies for systematic data replication in detail in Chapter 20.

Guideline 13.6   Coupling inhibits parallelism

Parallel processing is best suited to classes of work with nothing in common. The greater the degree of logical coupling among workload classes, the more complications arise when attempting to process those classes in parallel.

Level-2: Workflow Parallelism

Because this level deals with the way a business workload is subdivided into business transactions, introducing some types of parallelism here may not directly affect the performance of the computerized portions of the information system. However, it will usually have an indirect effect, because performing business tasks in parallel increases the potential for parallel processing at the next level.

In some cases, however, there is a direct relationship because subdividing the business process into separate steps often allows the automated portions to be implemented differently.

Workflow Parallelism and Perceived Response Time.   Perhaps the most compelling reason for employing workflow parallelism is to reduce perceived response times. Response times will be longest when:

▶ All work is done sequentially.
▶ The user waits for all processing to complete.

There is no reason to design an application to work this way if the business transaction can be subdivided into phases. Then:

▶ Some phases, or parts of phases, can often be processed in parallel.
▶ Some phases may not require the user to wait. The system can either guarantee an action once the user has supplied some input, or supply a response later.

These techniques all lower perceived response times. We discuss these subjects in more detail in Part IV of the book.

Guideline 13.7   Workflow parallelism can lower perceived response times

If we can subdivide an application into a series of separate phases, some phases can often be processed in parallel while other phases may not require the user to wait. We can exploit these possibilities to lower perceived response times.

When we discussed *effectual locality* in Chapter 10, we emphasized the importance of *matching* business processing needs, software behavior, and hardware resources. Our brief discussion of workflow parallelism confirms just how important the manual business process is:

- ▶ It contributes to the overall response time for a business task.
- ▶ It influences the pattern of demand for processing resources.
- ▶ It has a big influence on the response time the user experiences.

Later, when we examine client/server middleware technologies (in Chapter 15) and consider the optimal architectures for performance (in Chapter 16), we will once again see the significance of the business workflow as the starting point for all distributed design. In Chapter 17, we consider some design issues associated with this level of parallelism, such as the atomicity of tasks, interdependencies among tasks, and task completion rules.

Level-3: Program Parallelism

We call this level program parallelism. In the database world, the terms *parallel transactions* and *interquery parallelism*[3] are common. On a uniprocessor machine, the only true parallelism that exists is among the various hardware devices—a CPU and many disks are all working in parallel on different tasks. On a multiprocessor, the right operating system software can drive even more parallel processes, keeping multiple CPUs and even more disks busy. To exploit the full power of the multiprocessor, the operating system and other layers of middleware must cooperate to keep all the CPUs equally busy. If one of four CPUs is 99 percent busy, but the other three are at 33 percent, we are operating the machine at half its potential.

Program parallelism is particularly relevant to any shared server in a client/server environment. Typically, the number of concurrent requests for service at any time depends on the overall behavior of the client population, which, in turn, depends on the peaks and troughs in the business workload. Some key design considerations in this environment are server capacity, handling peak volumes, and load balancing.

- ▶ **Server capacity.** For a particular combination of processor and workload, what is the optimal level of concurrency?

---

[3]In our view, the term *interquery parallelism* ought really to refer only to Level 5. In a DBMS-centric context, however, Levels 4 and 5 are usually not distinguished at all, and "interquery parallelism" usually refers to Level 3. Our recommendation: Always double check to make sure you understand what the term means to its user.

Multiprogramming and Multiprocessors

Ever since the first commercial operating systems appeared in the 1960s, large shared mainframe machines have created the illusion of parallel processing. Even on uniprocessors—machines with a single CPU—multiple programs appear to be running in parallel. In reality, this is *concurrency,* not *parallelism.* At any point in time, the CPU is executing only one process, and every other process is waiting for its turn.

For commercial data processing, which typically involves quite a lot of I/O, this arrangement works fine most of the time. Like a highly skilled juggler, the processor touches each task momentarily, just long enough to throw it into its next I/O operation. Processing instructions is very fast compared with disk I/O, so a single CPU can support a large number of tasks and keep up the impression that each one has its own processor. This software juggling act was originally called **multiprogramming.** In recent years, the terms **multitasking** and **multithreading** have been more in vogue.

The terms *multiprogramming* and *multitasking* are more or less equivalent. They refer to the operating system mechanisms to support parallel processing of separate dispatchable units. *Multithreading,* in contrast, refers to mechanisms (usually outside the operating system's control) to create parallel execution streams *within* a single operating system dispatchable unit. Because they are not managed using system calls, threads have lower overheads than separate tasks or processes; they are often referred to as *lightweight threads* for this reason.

But whatever we call it, and whatever it costs, it differs from **multiprocessing,** which refers to applying the power of more than one processor or CPU to a single task. This can only happen on a **multiprocessor**—a machine with multiple CPUs.

Guideline 13.8	**Multiprogramming and multiprocessors**

Multiprogramming and multiprocessors

Multiprogramming is a software technique for running programs concurrently using a single CPU. Multiprocessing involves applying more than one CPU to a single task. It requires a multiprocessor—a machine with multiple CPUs.

The CPU power and memory capacity of a server determine its ability to handle concurrent tasks. In an enterprise client/server system, as the number of client workstations grows, the rate of requests hitting the server rises, too. Every concurrent request demands its own allocation of memory for the server application code to run in, some CPU time to process instructions, and I/O resources.

If we keep driving up the rate of requests, eventually even the biggest server with the most efficient software will run out of capacity somewhere.

▶ **Handling peak workload volumes.** Must servers be configured with sufficient spare capacity to handle peak processing volumes, or can the systems software smooth out peaks in the arrival rate of requests?

▶ **Load balancing.** If the server is a multiprocessor, can the middleware keep all the processors equally busy?

The Role of Middleware

Because *middleware* is the software mechanism by which clients and servers communicate, all the design issues we have noted can be summarized in one question: *How does the middleware (which, of course, works with the associated server operating system environment) handle multiple concurrent client requests for service?* If the middleware works in such a way that an independent operating system process or task is created for every separate client request, then the overhead of process management on the server can become excessive. On the other hand, if all requests must wait for a single server application process, then the server will become a bottleneck as the client workload rises.

We briefly consider the three principal middleware technologies for interprocess communication. In order of complexity, they are: *remote procedure calls, message-oriented middleware,* and *transaction monitors.* Here, we focus only on issues of parallelism. In Chapter 15, *Middleware and Performance,* we describe all these technologies in greater detail, and in Chapter 22 we address the performance of transaction managers and transaction monitors.

Remote Procedure Calls.   Because a remote procedure call (RPC) is a synchronous request for service, each concurrent RPC request is typically handled by starting a separate server task for each request. As a result, with RPC-based middleware, the degree of server parallelism is typically determined by the demands and schedule of its clients, and the clients must wait for the server to respond.

Programmers can create more sophisticated arrangements by building additional function using the basic RPC mechanisms as a building block—for more detail refer to the section *Remote Procedure Calls* in Chapter 15. Most organizations, however, would prefer to purchase the additional function in standard middleware components.

Message-Oriented Middleware (MOM).   With message-oriented middleware, each program has its own associated queue, and two programs communicate with each other by leaving a *message* on the message queue of the other.

Because a program can place messages on multiple queues, a calling program can activate many called programs that run on different nodes and all of which run in parallel. In the case of a temporary peak in requests, the queue acts as a buffer between clients and servers—requests can build up on the queue without the server's being overwhelmed. In a parallel-processing environment, there can be multiple servers for the same queue. Since each server pulls messages off a queue at its own optimal rate, load balancing across multiple parallel servers occurs naturally, without a great deal of special programming effort being required.

Transaction Monitors. Transaction monitors (TMs) are even more sophisticated than message queues. A TM can take advantage of multiple processors by responding dynamically to demand from client application modules. As demand increases, the transaction manager can "spawn" more instances of a server application module to achieve dynamic workload balancing. Later, when demand falls, the transaction manager reduces the number of server instances to a predefined limit.

When the server runs on an SMP multiprocessor (which we'll discuss later in this chapter), to maximize the use of the hardware, each instance of a server application can run on a different CPU. To ensure optimal parallel execution of business transactions, the transaction manager can then use a load-balancing algorithm to distribute requests across all instances of server application modules.

Guideline 13.9	**Prefer transaction monitors, or MOM, to RPC**

RPC is an adequate communication mechanism for small-scale environments in which a small client population creates a relatively stable level of demand for dedicated servers. It does not scale well to large client populations generating highly variable levels of demand. Under these conditions, transaction monitors or message-oriented middleware can smooth out peaks in the distribution of requests and prevent a server from being overloaded.

Levels-4/5: Process and Data Manipulation Parallelism

On a server, parallel processing can be applied to requests from multiple clients, as we discussed at Level-3, or to an individual client's request. On a client, parallel processing can allow the user to interact with application code while other activity (like sending or receiving data) continues in the background. Obviously, the first requirement for such parallelism is a multitasking operating system like OS/2, Windows NT, UNIX, or MVS. Perhaps less obviously, a multiprocessor is not essential—as we discussed earlier in the capsule *Multiprogramming and Multiprocessors*.

In practice, Levels-4 and -5 are often not distinguished at all. Both address the opportunities for breaking a single task into multiple subtasks and processing them in parallel. To aid in the discussion of this area, consider the example of a process that uses a DBMS, shown in Figure 13.3.

Figure 13.3 illustrates a single process P, which consists of sequences of program instructions interspersed between file I/Os and calls for service to a DBMS. The DBMS requests, in turn, are serviced by further instruction sequences and I/Os.

Levels-4 and -5 represent two ways of introducing parallelism into process P:

▶ At Level-4, *overtly,* through manual parallel programming techniques
▶ At Level-5, *covertly,* by using a DBMS optimizer.

We distinguish them as separate levels because, even though neither technique is common, they could in fact be used separately or in combination. (Note that we are purposely deferring discussion of a third possible technique—using a parallelizing compiler—until Level-8.)

Manual Parallel Programming.   Using **parallel programming** techniques, we can create lightweight threads by manually subdividing (*forking*) P into smaller processes that can be run in parallel, then synchronizing (*joining*) the results later.

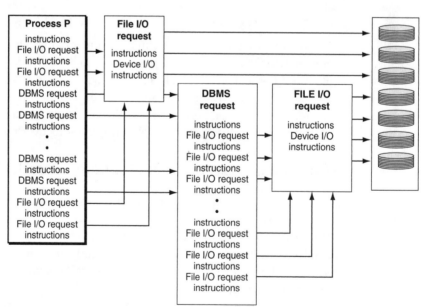

FIGURE 13.3   Components of a DBMS process.

Developing multithreaded servers with lightweight threads can reduce the need for some processes to wait and eliminate the overheads of using multiple system managed tasks. The trade-off, though, is more complex application logic. The parent process must play the role of a dispatcher. It must keep track of the server processes and perform some kind of load balancing among them. And what does the dispatcher do with requests that come in when all server processes are busy?

These solutions are also exposed to more potential error conditions because an errant server thread can bring down others—or the entire server. We do not recommend this approach unless you are using middleware that provides good support for high-performance multithreading or have developers with experience developing, testing, and maintaining systems software.

Parallel Tasks from a DBMS Optimizer.   A **DBMS optimizer** typically supports intra-query parallelism, which is the next level in our scheme. To generate DML parallelism, however, an optimizer would need to examine a group of database requests (DML statements) and determine automatically that two or more of them could be processed in parallel. Although this is theoretically possible for a set of unrelated queries, most relational DBMS optimizers today work only on single SQL queries. The interface between a program and a DBMS is inherently sequential, since it follows the program's flow. To parallelize a set of queries from a single process, the queries would have to be submitted as a group, as in a stored procedure. The optimizer would also need to recognize (or be told) that there were no dependencies among the queries. If any query includes a program variable (as is normally the case for SQL embedded in application logic), then it is impossible to determine its independence without also compiling and tracing the application logic, which pretty much rules out processing that query in parallel with others.

Some exceptions do exist, however. NCR's *Teradata* RDBMS—a parallel processing database engine—supports a "multi-statement request," in which a batch of independent SQL statements can be submitted as a group to be optimized for parallel execution. The product also has a "multiload" utility that can process multiple database transactions in parallel against a single file of input—another example of DML parallelism. Finally, a kind of reverse parallelism: Because the Teradata query optimizer is aware of parallelism, it can actually *combine* independent parallel database scans of the same data into a single task, reducing overhead costs (an application of The Efficiency Principle), a feature called "synchronized scans." For more information on Teradata, see NCR's Web site at www.ncr.com.

Nevertheless, we conclude that most enterprise client/server applications not already split into parallel streams higher in the hierarchy are not likely to benefit greatly from parallelism at Levels-4 or -5. They are much more likely to benefit from parallelism at Levels-6 or -7.

Level-6: Intraquery Parallelism

Because of the power of the declarative query language SQL, a single data manipulation request or "query" often requires the DBMS to process several tables and/or indexes. Therefore, considerable scope exists for DBMS optimizers to speed up the processing of individual data manipulation requests through parallel processing. We discuss this subject in detail in the later sections *Parallel Database Processing* and *Parallelism and Warehouse Database Design.*

The RAID Advisory Board (RAB) Online

To find out more about how RAID devices exploit I/O parallelism, visit the *RAID Advisory Board's Storage System Information Center,* at www. raid-advisory.com. This Web site has a lot of useful material explaining and comparing the various RAID technologies, and information about RAID products and vendors.

Although they can enhance performance, the main idea of RAID devices is to use additional disks (the "R" in RAID stands for "redundant") to provide a more reliable storage medium. Reflecting this, the RAB now advocates the alternative term *Extended Data Availability and Protection* (EDAP).

Level-7: I/O Device Parallelism

Most business workloads are I/O bound—in other words, the time spent waiting for I/O operations either to begin or to complete is a major element of most application response times. Therefore, whenever we can process multiple I/O streams in parallel, we will usually lower the response time of some application. We obtain the most dramatic reductions when we can take a single I/O bound process (like a large database scan) and split it into several smaller parallel processes. The two principal methods of accomplishing this are:

▶ Using disk devices that employ RAID technology. For more details, see the capsule *The RAID Advisory Board (RAB) Online* and the section on *Disk striping and RAID* in Chapter 3.
▶ Using a Parallel DBMS. We defer discussion of this technology until the later section *Parallel Database Processing.*

To achieve the maximum benefit from any scheme involving parallel disk I/O, we must first decide how best to distribute our data across the disks, given the likely processing requirements. Here in this common thread, as always, the Locality Principle is a hard taskmaster. It rewards us with better performance when we remember its advice to "*Group components based on their usage,*" but also punishes us with long delays if we forget.

Level-8: CPU Parallelism

Finally, if we have not found any larger units of work to split into parallel processing streams, we can work on the program instruction stream itself. Referring again to Figure 13.3, one way to speed up program P is to compile it using a **parallelizing compiler,** to exploit any opportunities for parallelism within the program instruction sequences.

Using a Parallelizing Compiler.   In the Introduction, we listed the principle differences between *high-performance computing* and *enterprise information processing* and summarized these differences in Table I.1.

With respect to the potential benefits of applying parallelism, the most significant difference is that workloads of the former type are dominated by processing, whereas those of the latter type are dominated by I/O activity. Or to put it another way, high-performance computing is compute bound, and enterprise information processing is I/O bound. This explains why the techniques of high-performance computing have only limited application in the world of enterprise client/server.

Parallelizing compilers are particularly useful for those compute-bound *high-performance computing* applications. However, since *business information systems* usually have a high ratio of I/O time to processing time, a paralleling compiler may not produce much speedup—recall our earlier discussion of Amdahl's Law.

The one class of information processing that may benefit from massively parallel processing is data mining. Some data mining applications may perform complex statistical analysis on relatively small amounts of data. But the most computationally intensive types of statistical analysis used during data mining still involve a significant amount of I/O to read database tables. As a result, their performance needs are far more likely to have already been addressed by *Query Parallelism* at Level-6, or *I/O Parallelism* at Level-7. We discuss data mining in more detail in Chapter 21.

Finally, to exploit CPU parallelism, we need multiple processors to process the parallel instruction streams. Since parallel processing is our next major topic, we now suspend our review of the parallelism hierarchy, deferring our conclusions until the end of the chapter.

Who Needs a Parallel Processor?

"If you build it, he will come."

W. P. Kinsella

Business applications and computing technology are like the proverbial chicken and egg—it is sometimes difficult to tell which one came first. Business needs drive technological innovation and refinement, which, in turn, create opportunities for new kinds of business applications, and so on. This cycle is particularly apparent in the realm of parallel processing. Although more than 90 percent of the machines sold today are single processors, the demand for more computing power is leading to increased use of multiprocessor machines and associated parallel-processing architectures.

In the next section, we review briefly some of the technological motivations for parallel processors, noting also some of the most common applications.

Technological Motivations

Computers that can perform parallel processing using more than one CPU are commonly referred to as multiprocessors (*MPs*)—distinguishing them from uniprocessors, machines with a single CPU. Over the last 25 years, multiprocessor machines have been developed to address a variety of technical challenges, chiefly:

To overcome capacity limits. When a machine already uses the fastest CPU available, the only way to increase throughput is to add more processors. Historically, the largest mainframe machines have had multiprocessor architectures to overcome the inherent capacity limits of uniprocessors. These machines are used for a wide range of commercial data processing applications. In many cases, large machines are used to consolidate workloads that could actually be run on several smaller ones, so there is little real need for parallelism in the workload itself.

To increase speed. In a shared server environment, as we discussed in Chapter 11, increasing the overall processing capacity can improve response times by reducing the time processes must wait for their turn on the CPU. Sophisticated hardware and operating systems software can achieve even greater response time reductions by applying the power of more than one CPU to a single task. For scientific computing involving a lot of number crunching, the only way to speed up the process is to apply more processors to the task. In a commercial data warehouse environment, data-mining applications often involve computationally intensive statistical analysis and also need I/O parallelism to read large database tables.

To increase reliability and availability. In a multiprocessor, if one CPU fails, another is still available for critical processing. For applications that need to run continuously—like banking, defense, and space exploration—redundant hardware has long been used to provide better availability. Tandem Computers, as its name implies, is probably the company best known for selling hardware with parallel components to provide fault tolerance. These machines range from small computers with as few as two CPUs to massively parallel processors.

Parallelism, Price, and Performance

Hardware vendors also incorporate multiprocessing technology in the more powerful models of midrange machines (now generally referred to as *servers* of various kinds) and large workstations. This is not because building, or buying a faster CPU is impossible, but because doubling the number of CPUs is a lot less expensive than doubling their speed.

Anyone buying a computer naturally wants to get the most *bang for the buck.* Therefore, the *price/performance ratio* of a machine is an important metric. "Unhappily, . . . ," Harold Lorin points out in his comprehensive review of the Information Technology, *Doing IT Right,* ". . . it is difficult to determine the (true) price of a computer, . . . and impossible to determine its performance, since the behavior of a program . . . is affected by so many factors of hardware, software, and use. The concept is firm, but the metrics are a little shaky."[4]

Since the advent of the microprocessor, hardware manufacturers have sought to maximize price/performance ratios by building machines that combine the power of large arrays of relatively inexpensive Intel or RISC chips in massively parallel architectures. Beginning with Teradata and its DBC/1012, almost all large computer manufacturers have followed this path.

Lorin points out that the terms used to describe various classes of computer have only fuzzy definitions and summarizes the economics of computer hardware using a table similar to Table 13.3.[5] Although a thorough investigation of price/performance ratios is beyond the scope of this book, Table 13.3 does highlight the enormous range of computing possibilities available for constructing the enterprise client/server systems. The issue facing us is this: *Can we actually use this hardware effectively to process our workload?*

---

[4]Harold Lorin, *Doing IT Right* (Upper Saddle River, NJ: Prentice-Hall, 1996), 51.
[5]Table 13.3 is based on Table 3.2 in *Doing IT Right,* 55.

Table 13.3   **Weighing Application, Price, and Performance**

Class of Computer	Principal Uses	Attributes	Price Range ($)
Supercomputer	Scientific/engineering	High FLOPS	2.5–25M
Highly parallel	Scientific/engineering/ database	500-64K processors	100K–7M
Mainframe	General purpose/commercial	Old technology	700K–25M
Mini-super	Scientific/engineering	Symmetric MP	100K–1.5M
Enterprise server	General purpose/commercial	Symmetric MP	200K–2M
Departmental server	General purpose/commercial	Symmetric MP	50K–500K
Group server	General purpose/commercial	Microprocessor	7K–25K
Supermini	General purpose/commercial	Symmetric MP	200K–3M
Workstation	Scientific/engineering	Microprocessor/ SMP	5K–50K
Personal	General purpose	Microprocessor	1K–5K

Multiprocessor Architectures

All computers are assemblies of CPUs, memory, and disks. The key differences among multiprocessor architectures are how these resources are interconnected and which resources are shared. We can classify a multiprocessor architecture informally as one of three groups:

▶ Shared memory or shared everything
▶ Shared nothing
▶ Shared disks

Figure 13.4 shows simplified views of all three architectures. The difference between them lies in the placement of the interconnect linking the resources together.

▶ With **shared memory,** the CPUs are all connected to the shared memory by the interconnect, with the memory being linked to all disks. Therefore, the interconnect to the shared resource (memory) carries requests for that shared resource or for data residing in that shared resource.
▶ With **shared nothing,** the interconnect links the processors only. Each processor has its own complement of memory and disks. It is a slight misnomer to call this architecture *shared nothing* because the interconnect itself is a shared resource.

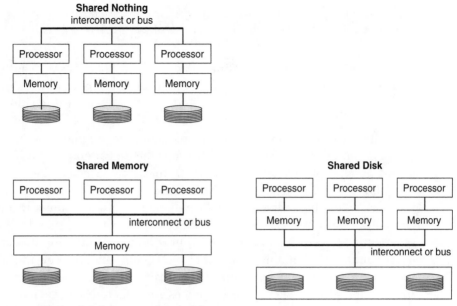

FIGURE 13.4   Multiprocessor architectures.

▶ **Shared disk** places the interconnect between the memory and the disks. Each processor has its own memory, but all the memories use the interconnect to satisfy the data access requests from all disks. All data stored on all disks is available to all processors via the memory.

The shared disk architectures can be combined with the others to achieve **hybrid** or **cluster** designs. For example, multiple shared memory (SMP) nodes can be linked together (clustered) with a common interconnect to have access to a shared disk resource, as illustrated in Figure 13.4.

We now discuss these various architectures in more detail. Before we begin, however, we must emphasize that no architecture is "the best" in an absolute sense. To quote Dan Graham, "If asked 'Which type of building is better, a house, a store, or an office?' the correct answer would be 'Each is better for a different purpose.' So it is with computer architectures."[6]

The Locality Principle applies here—the best architecture for any enterprise is the one that best matches the workload. As part of our

---

[6]Dan Graham, "SMP vs. Multi-Purpose Parallel Computers," *InfoDB* 10(3–4). This article was published in two parts; the reference cited appears in the first part, on page 20.

A Brief History of Parallel Processing

"The machine can be brought into play so as to give several results at the same time, which will greatly abridge the whole amount of processes."

(Luigi F. Menabrea, 1842)

With these words, General Menabrea recorded his support for Charles Babbage's proposed *Analytical Engine,* perhaps the first attempt to build an automated parallel processor. Even in 1840, the benefits of parallel processing were obvious to Babbage; if a machine could process several tasks in parallel, the work would be done faster. His Analytical Engine was literally a parallel computing machine—an assembly of cogs and gears—that could carry out several indexing arithmetic and multiplication operations simultaneously.

Too much friction and insufficient funds combined to prevent Babbage's mechanical vision from becoming a practical reality. But once the era of *electronic* computing began, parallel-processing machines have made steady progress toward the mainstream:

▶ The very first computer, the ENIAC, was built in 1949. It used vacuum tube technology to perform 5000 additions per second on 11 parallel accumulator stacks.
▶ By 1966, Dan Slotnick had built the ILLIAC IV, which successfully combined the power of 64 processors.
▶ In 1983, Teradata brought out its special-purpose Parallel Database Machine, the DBC/1012.

review, we comment on the types of workloads best suited to the various architectures.

Buyer Beware . . . We begin with a caution: This is an area where it is dangerous for prospective computer buyers to believe too strongly in general rules of thumb. Regardless of multiprocessor architecture, the key question is *"Can the particular software that we intend to use actually exploit the full potential of the parallel processors, for our particular workload?"*

The only way to answer this question is to run the workload and measure it. In the complex interaction of hardware, software, processing, and data, it is easy to overlook some critical bottleneck that reduces the effective power of a multiprocessor to the speed of its slowest component.

The best hardware in the world will run only as fast as the software drives it, and the software behavior depends on the application and its data. This is espe-

▶ In 1985, Denelcor released its $7 million baby, the Heterogeneous Element Processor. It did not sell well.

▶ By 1986, however, more than a dozen companies (including Bolt Beranek & Newman, Cray Research, DEC, IBM, Intel, Alliant, Encore, and Thinking Machines) were selling parallel processors.

▶ In 1994, MasPar released the MP-2, a massive parallel-processing system that can be configured to have up to 16,384 RISC processors combined into a single Processor Array. It was aimed at the decision-support marketplace. It did not sell well enough to keep the company in business; in 1995, MasPar changed its name to NeoVista, and switched its focus to parallel database software for decision support.

▶ Today, almost every computer manufacturer sells parallel-processor machines. There are many different types, ranging from a shared memory configuration with 2 to 64 processors, to massive parallel-processor machines having hundreds, or even thousands, of processors.

In the near future, even larger configurations will become standard. They will be assembled from multiprocessor chips (for example, the Intel P6), each of which will contain four-way processors.

References

Theme section "Multiprocessing," *Byte Magazine,* Volume 10, Number 5 (May 1985), 169–252.

In-depth section "Parallel Processing," *Byte Magazine,* Volume 13, Number 12 (November 1988), 272–320.

cially true for multiprocessors, which need multiple tasks to process. Just because a particular software product *runs* on a certain parallel processor, it does not necessarily follow that the software fully *exploits* the power of the hardware. If a DBMS does most of its work under a single task, or if an application

---

Guideline 13.10   **Can your software exploit parallel hardware?**

In the complex interaction of hardware, software, processing, and data, it is easy to overlook some critical bottleneck that reduces the effective power of a multiprocessor to the speed of its slowest component.

The key question is "*Can the particular software that we intend to use actually exploit the full potential of the parallel processors, for our particular workload?*" The only way to answer this question is to run the workload and measure it.

involves many points at which separate tasks must synchronize, or if all the application's data resides on a single disk, then a lot of processors can be sitting idle waiting for one to complete.

We discuss software parallelism in more detail later in this chapter.

Multiprocessor Scalability and Speedup

Earlier in this chapter we introduced the general concepts of *scalability* and *speedup.* Here, we consider how those concepts apply to multiprocessor machines. Recall that *scalability* refers to the capacity or *throughput* increases that we can obtain by adding more CPUs; *speedup* refers to reductions we can achieve in *response time.* Ideally, by adding more processors, we can maintain performance as workloads increase or, alternatively, improve the performance of current workloads.

The perfect multiprocessor would exhibit *linear* scalability and speedup—doubling throughput, or halving response times, when the number of CPUs is doubled. Although a benchmark might exhibit linear **scalability** for an artificial workload, in practice, we can never achieve linear scalability for realistic information processing workloads. No matter how efficient the multiprocessor architecture, scalability is always less than perfect because of:

▶ The overheads inherent in splitting work into parallel streams
▶ Delays due to contention for shared resources
▶ The need for periodic synchronization among the parallel streams

For real workloads, these overheads and delays always grow worse as more CPUs are added to a multiprocessor configuration, although the actual measure of scalability depends heavily on the workload and type of processor.

Linear **speedup** is a desirable attribute as databases grow in size. For example, in a data warehousing environment, a query that takes an hour to complete on a uniprocessor would run in less than 4 minutes if we could substitute a 16-way machine and get linear speedup.

Obviously, as with scalability, the degree of speedup we can achieve in practice is less than this. How much depends on the hardware, the software, and again—most important—the nature of the workload:

▶ For CPU-intensive workloads, being able to perform parallel processing is the most important.
▶ For I/O bound work, doing parallel I/O is essential.

Finally, for some types of work—like data-mining operations in a warehouse environment, which typically involve some fairly intensive processing against a lot of data—we need an environment that supports both parallel CPU and parallel I/O well.

SMP: Shared Memory

Also called *shared everything,* these machines are a simple extension of the common single-processor computer architecture and have been around for a long time. Instead of a single CPU, they have multiple CPUs (typically between 2 and 32), all of which share the same memory and the same set of disks, as shown in Figure 13.5. These machines are sometimes called *symmetric multiprocessors* (SMP) or *tightly coupled multiprocessors* (TCMP).

Because SMP machines have a single shared memory, they are particularly suitable for workloads that need to share a lot of information, like online transaction processing against shared databases. Single copies of code, control information, message buffers, and DBMS cache(s) can reside in the shared memory where they can easily be shared among many concurrent processes. A single operating system manages all processes, handling I/O interrupts and scheduling CPUs to process work. The shared memory makes scheduling simple because every CPU has access to the same data.

But this strength is also a weakness. In the SMP architecture, the bottleneck is the *interconnect,* or *bus,* that connects the memory to the CPUs. Every byte processed by every CPU must be read across this bus and be written back when modified. As the number of CPUs grows, contention for the bus grows, too. So adding more CPUs does not support a corresponding increase in the number of concurrent active processes. The greater the number of CPUs already installed, the less the effect of adding more—for more details, see the capsule *Estimating SMP Scalability.* This is exactly what we would expect, based on our discussion of *service multipliers* for shared resources in Chapter 11, *The Sharing Principle.*

Traditionally, multiprocessor mainframes did not scale well beyond 4 to 8 processors. Advances in interconnect technology have increased this range to 8 to 16 today, and even larger numbers are available from the hardware vendors, but experience is limited.

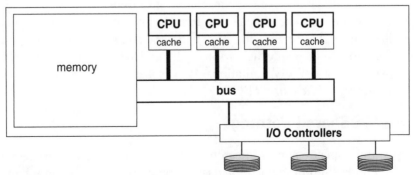

FIGURE 13.5   Shared memory architecture.

Estimating SMP Scalability

"Too many cooks spoil the broth."

Anonymous

Dan Graham[7] quotes a formula—derived from IBM measurements of TPC-C workloads on various UNIX systems—for estimating the scale-up of SMP machines.[8] It is:

Effective UNIX CPUs $= N \times X \times K^{N-1}$

where $X = 0.89$
$K = 0.97$
$N =$ number of processors installed

In this formula, if N processors are used, their maximum power is reduced by two factors:

The first factor (X) is a measure of the sophistication of the operating system and represents loss of efficiency due to the extra overheads of multiprocessing. Operating systems software always lags behind hardware developments, and it takes time for vendors to tune their software to exploit new hardware capabilities. For a truly mature, well-built OS that has been running on SMP systems for many years (like MVS or UNISYS OS1100), X is probably closer to 1.0, or should be. UNIX systems are still maturing, and NT will probably lag behind UNIX.

[7]Graham, "SMP vs. Multi-Purpose," Part 1, 23.
[8]According to Graham, the formula that we cite in this capsule is based on IBM's measurements of TPC-C workloads on UNIX systems from Sun, HP, DEC, Compaq, IBM's RS/6000, and a few others. There were some typographical errors in the original published version of this formula, but the version reproduced here is correct.

We strongly advise anyone planning to depend on a "pure" SMP machine with more than eight processors first to run benchmarks using their own workloads (see Chapter 6). This advice may be somewhat academic since hardware vendors are busy adding various bells and whistles to their SMP machines to overcome scalability limitations. We discuss this trend a bit later, in the section *Clusters, Hybrids, and MPPC.*

MPP: Shared Nothing

At the opposite end of the architecture spectrum from SMP, each CPU or *node* in a shared-nothing machine has its own allocation of memory and disks. Orig-

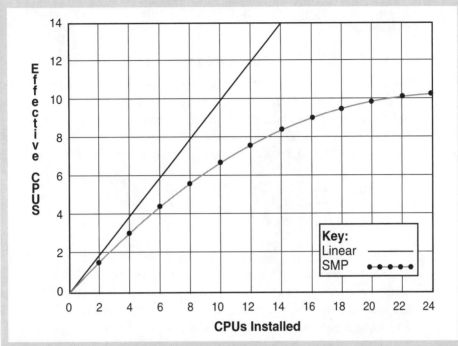

FIGURE 13.6   Typical SMP scalability curve.

The second factor (K^{N-1}) represents the progressively increasing overheads of such activities as lock management and processor scheduling.

Figure 13.6 shows the drop-off in performance predicted by the SMP scalability formula, compared to the straight line of perfect linear scalability. For example, a 10-way UNIX machine can process the equivalent of 7 separate CPUs, but adding another 10 CPUs boosts the multiplier only from 7 to about

inally, each node had a single processor, as shown in Figure 13.4; newer machines have SMP nodes, as shown in Figure 13.7. This greatly reduces contention for the interconnect compared to SMP. Because of this, proponents claim that this architecture scales linearly to hundreds or thousands of processors.

With the right workload, this may theoretically be true. But the perfect workload for achieving scalability on an MPP would have its processing and data requirements spread evenly across all the nodes, and each CPU would need to process only the data resident on disks located at that node. Of course, such a workload does not need an MPP; it could be run equally well on lots of

10. Although "your mileage may vary," this scalability curve is typical of SMP behavior.

The 32-Processor Limit

If we accept that SMPs exhibit scale-up characteristics like those described in Graham's formula, then a little mathematical reasoning shows why a 32-way SMP machine is the largest we should ever expect to see. Consider how the formula behaves when we increase the value of N to $N + 1$. The relative improvement in effective processing power will be given by the ratio:

$$((N + 1) \times X \times K^N) \div (N \times X \times K^{N-1})$$
or $$((N + 1)/N) \times K$$
or $$((N + 1)/N) \times 0.97$$

When $N = 32$, this multiplier is 1.0003; when $N = 33$, it is 0.999.

In other words, at 32 processors, adding one more produces a negligible benefit and, after that, further increases actually drive the effective power of the machine down. According to Graham, "there are many rumors of SMPs scaling to 32-ways successfully, but no publicly available proof."[9]

Guideline 13.11   **The SMP scalability curve**
Do not assume that a machine with a pure SMP architecture will scale linearly above an 8-way processor. Use the typical SMP scalability curve (see Figure 13.6) as a guide, but plan also to run benchmarks with real workloads, and discuss performance experiences with other users.

---

[9]Graham, "SMP vs. Multi-Purpose," Part 1, 23.

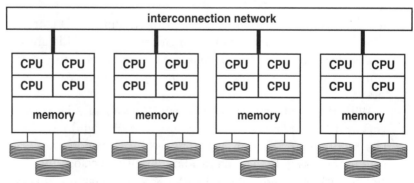

FIGURE 13.7   Shared-nothing architecture with SMP nodes.

separate processors. It would be a lot simpler to address the performance requirements of such a workload with parallelism at Level-1 or Level-3 in our parallelism hierarchy, rather than trying to solve the problem with a parallel processor at Level-8.

The real challenge for an MPP is the workload that *cannot* be split apart earlier in the hierarchy because it is either a single large process or a collection of processes that manipulate common data. Unless we can break up that large process into smaller chunks and route them to separate CPUs, our MPP machine will run no faster than a single CPU. And unless we can spread the data that processes need across all the nodes, some subset of the disks and CPUs will be busy while others are idle.

Limits to MPP Scalability.   Even if we do a good job of load balancing for both data and processing, studies show that mixing OLTP and decision-support workloads can significantly impede scalability. To get optimal performance for a decision-support workload with a lot of parallel read I/O, the software and hardware must cooperate to maintain a continuous data "pipeline" from disk to memory to processor cache to CPU. Any update activity disrupts this flow from disk to CPU. The different workloads do not even have to be processing the same *data*—simply running processes that read and write to the same *disks* concurrently interferes with optimal parallelism.

Perhaps the biggest challenge to using a pure MPP machine effectively is finding the ideal workload.

Shared Disk

An intermediate form of parallel processor architecture is obtained by sharing only the disks. This allows large databases to be shared by several processors, each with their own separate memory components. This architecture eliminates the SMP *interconnect* bottleneck that we described earlier, but the connection between the shared disks and the separate processor memories can be a bottleneck. High-speed bus technology and RAID disk controllers are needed to minimize the contention here.

Another problem arises when data from a single disk is shared by several processors. To minimize disk I/O delays, each processor has its own cache memory. This works well when all programs are reading data, but if any program updates a data item, then the caches can no longer operate independently because their contents may overlap. A lot of locking and synchronization messages are needed to prevent conflicting updates by two or more processors. As update activity increases, these synchronization overheads become the bottleneck.

A shared disk system works well for a read-only workload like that of a data warehouse or data mart. The ideal update workload is one that partitions itself naturally across the processors, and requires only a relatively low level of data sharing. Less predictable update workloads will not scale well without special purpose components like those used in the IBM Parallel Sysplex. These high-end machines include sophisticated *global lock management* and *cache coherency* mechanisms implemented by a high-speed hardware *coupling facility*, to speed up the exchange of synchronization messages among the processors and minimize processing delays.

> **Guideline 13.12   Shared Disk Systems**
>
> A shared disk system works well for a read-only workload like that of a data warehouse. The ideal update workload partitions itself naturally across the processors and requires only a relatively low level of data sharing. Less predictable update workloads will not scale well without high-speed hardware mechanisms for *global lock management* and *cache coherency.*

Clusters, Hybrids, and MPPC

The three hardware architectures we have described constitute the basic building blocks of modern parallel processors. However, hardware designers are continually tinkering and inventing new ways to connect the basic components together. Among the evolutionary developments are:

▶ **Shared-Everything.** This is a version of SMP that uses more sophisticated memory to CPU interconnections called *cross-bar switching*—essentially an interconnect grid that provides many paths between each CPU (and its associated instruction cache) and each bank of memory. Cross-bar switching avoids bus contention, provided that two CPU's do not need access to the same memory bank simultaneously. This works well if there are not too many hotspots in the data.

▶ **NUMA,** or **non-uniform memory architecture.** This is another version of SMP in which the memory component is partitioned, and the partitions are each connected to a group of CPUs on a bus, and to each other by a slower link. As a result, every CPU can access all the memory, but some memory is "local" and other memory is "remote." The partitions become, in effect, the memory cache for their local CPUs—data in remote memory must be moved to local memory before a CPU can process it. To get the most out of a NUMA machine, it must have a smart operating system that understands the significance of maintaining affinity between a CPU and its local memory partition. If the systems software can arrange the processing so that each CPU works predominantly with data in its local memory partition, everything runs smoothly. Hardware vendors promoting this architecture may suggest that it will somehow (magically?) let standard uniprocessor software scale up naturally without hitting the SMP interconnect bottleneck. In fact, it requires a cooperating workload and some sophisticated scheduling algorithms.

We recommend Gregory Pfister's book, *In Search of Clusters*.[10] Pfister defines a **cluster** as "*a type of parallel or distributed system that consists of a collection of interconnected whole computers, and is utilized as a single unified computing resource.*"[11] Because engineers can invent many ways to interconnect computers, this definition is a good one. It captures the basic ideas without being pedantic about the method. One popular arrangement is the *SMP cluster*, a collection of SMP machines linked in a larger shared-nothing configuration like the one shown earlier in Figure 13.7.

This is a broad and complex field that is continually evolving as the manufacturers look for a competitive edge in price or performance. Graham[12] concludes that the outcome of this evolution will be a hybrid blend of *MPP* and *cluster* architectures that he calls *Multi-Purpose Parallel Computing* (**MPPC**).

Multiprocessor Conclusions

To sum up, parallel processing can be done on machines with SMP, MPP, or various hybrid architectures. A wide range of parallel machines is available today, and we are bombarded with marketing arguments as to why one particular hardware vendor's architecture is better than another's. Many of these arguments are very technical, often unintelligible, and prove very little.

Regardless of the hardware architecture, the objective is to increase processing power by adding more processors. But depending on both the workload and how the processors and other devices are interconnected, other hardware constraints, for example, the memory or I/O bus, can prevent the full exploitation of the additional processors. If some other component is the bottleneck, we obtain no benefit from adding more processors—in fact, we may even make the bottleneck worse.

One solution is to remove the constraint by giving each processor its own memory and/or its own disk subsystem. This solution, however, complicates system software development. For example, database software must coordinate the contents of in-memory data caches across the different processors if each

---

[10]Gregory F. Pfister, *In Search of Clusters* (Upper Saddle River, NJ: Prentice Hall, 1995).
[11]Pfister, *In Search of Clusters*, 72.
[12]Graham, *SMP vs. Multi-Purpose Parallel Computers*, Part 1, 27.

processor has its own dedicated memory. Removing hardware constraints may simply move the problem to the software unless the software has been specially written to overcome these problems.

We now turn our attention to software issues.

Parallel Database Processing

No matter what the hardware architectures may be—SMP, MPP, shared disk, clusters, and so on—the key questions are these:

▶ Is there a good fit between the DBMS and the underlying hardware architecture?
▶ Does the hardware in any way restrict the scalability of the DBMS?

If we focus too closely on the interesting computer technology of parallel processors, we are in danger of losing sight of the real goals, which always should be:

▶ Does the combination of hardware and software meet our business goals?
▶ Can we develop and run our application(s) on this system in the time available, for the price we are willing to pay?
▶ In other words, is this interesting technology really *usable?*

For parallelism to be maximally usable, we would just write a program or a database query and then let the software take over, exploiting parallelism as and when appropriate. Unfortunately, this ideal vision of full and efficient automation without any human design assistance is rarely achieved by any computing technology. So the real issue is not *whether* we must contribute some design skills, but *how much must we do* to exploit or control parallelism, and *how much is done automatically* by compilers, database optimizers, other middleware, and operating systems.

Figure 13.8 shows the various architectural layers needed to bring parallel processing to bear on our applications. As the figure shows, the DBMS software layer plays a crucial role in making hardware parallelism available to our information processing applications. Without it, as our earlier discussion of Levels-4 and-5 in the parallelism hierarchy pointed out, we would have to resort to laborious hand-coding of parallel programs to exploit parallel hardware.

DBMS Support for Parallelism

To bring about parallel database processing, a DBMS must support a variety of functions, including:

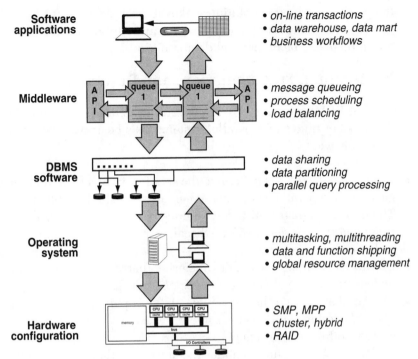

FIGURE 13.8   Parallelism and architectural layers.

▶ Spreading the data across enough disks to allow it to be processed by parallel I/O streams

▶ Breaking apart database queries and then processing some parts in parallel

▶ Bringing together a data manipulation task and the rows to be manipulated, either by moving the data to the processor running the task (I/O shipping, or data shipping), or by dispatching the task on the processor where the data resides (function shipping); for all but the most trivial amounts of data, function shipping is more efficient

▶ Managing locking and cache consistency issues as required to synchronize the activity of cooperating parallel subtasks within a larger data manipulation process

▶ Performing database utilities (like loading, indexing, and reorganizing data) in parallel for separate data subsets or partitions

▶ Reporting on its own parallel access path generation and parallel processing to enable performance monitoring and tuning

We should not assume that every parallel DBMS product does an equally good job in all these areas. Parallel database is still a maturing technology, and the pace of hardware evolution makes it hard for the software to keep up. But the one area that every parallel DBMS must support is data partitioning. Without it, there can be no parallel database processing.

Partitioning, Fragmentation, and De-clustering

Parallel DBMS systems provide several schemes for partitioning data across the disks or nodes of a parallel system. Let's begin with some parallel DBMS terminology:

▶ A *partition* (or *table partition*) is the set of rows of a table that reside on a single node of a parallel processor. It can also be called a table *fragment.*
▶ The process of distributing rows among partitions can be called *partitioning, fragmentation,* or *de-clustering* (because the rows are no longer clustered together on a single node).
▶ DBMSs can support partial de-clustering (partitioning across some *subset* of nodes) and full de-clustering (across *all* nodes).
▶ The number of nodes across which a table is partitioned is termed the *degree of de-clustering,* which is the same thing as the number of partitions in a shared-nothing environment.
▶ Tables may be assigned to nodes in such a way that they are *fully overlapped* (share the same nodes), *partially overlapped* (share some nodes), or *nonoverlapped* (have no common nodes).

We illustrate the four major schemes in Figure 13.9 and review them in the paragraphs that follow. They are:

▶ **Schema partitioning.** One table on one disk; another table on another disk, and so on.

▶ **Range partitioning.** Sequenced ranges are placed on different disks; for example, A–E, F–I, J–N, O–Z.

▶ **Hash partitioning.** A hashing algorithm used to determine on which disk to place the row.

▶ **Round-robin.** First row on first disk, second row on second disk, third row on third disk, and so forth.

Schema Partitioning.   Schema Partitioning (see Figure 13.9) is the simplest scheme—we simply allocate each table to a separate disk (or set of disks). This simplifies administration and may work for certain workloads consisting of a large number of small diverse transactions or queries.

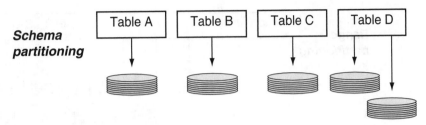

FIGURE **13.9**   Schema partitioning.

Hash Partitioning.   Hash partitioning (see Figure 13.10) is often associated with shared-nothing architectures and is a random placement of rows, based on a hashing function. Because of this, the data does not become disorganized. Often a DBMS stores data in some logical keyed (*clustering*) sequence, based on the contents of a column or columns. Later, as we insert more and more data into the database, the keys become progressively more disorganized because there is not enough space on the pages where the new rows belong, so they are placed elsewhere by the DBMS. To recover the required ordering of rows, we must run a reorganization utility, which consumes time and processing resources and makes the data unavailable for normal processing.

A strong argument made in favor of hash partitioning is that we don't have to reorganize the data. This is particularly important when dealing with very large data volumes in the terabyte range. We also do not need to have the spare disk capacity in which to carry out the sorting involved in reorganization, and, of course, the database administrator's work is simplified—leaving more time for other performance tuning, perhaps.

In a data warehouse or other decision-support environment with read-only data, this benefit evaporates because we never need to reorganize data that is not updated.

Range Partitioning.   Range partitioning (see Figure 13.11) can cause data skewing because of the uneven value distributions common in all business

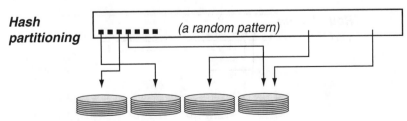

FIGURE **13.10**   Hash partitioning.

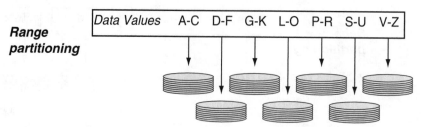

FIGURE 13.11   Range partitioning.

data and execution skewing when many queries need to process data from the same ranges. Essentially, this is another manifestation of the database hot-spot problems that we discussed in Chapter 12. To overcome these problems, we must spread the hot spots across multiple nodes. To make this possible, we must define a larger number of smaller ranges, giving ourselves more flexibility in assigning ranges to nodes.

Expression Partitioning.   Some DBMS products permit a general logical expression to be used as the basis for partitioning. If using a simple value range produces unevenly sized partitions, or uneven usage patterns against the partitions, we might be able to find a more complex expression that corrects this skewing. So expression partitioning offers a mechanism for fine-tuning but requires the ability to repartition data on line and in parallel.

Before choosing a sophisticated partitioning scheme such as expression-based partitioning, a database administrator should monitor data usage patterns *at the SQL statement level.* Tools like Hewlett-Packard's IW Advisor, IBI's Smartsite, and Mercury's Interactive SQL Sniffer can help in this area.

Round-Robin Partitioning.   Round-robin partitioning (see Figure 13.12) is typically used with SMP shared disk architectures because all disks are shared by all processors. MPP systems offer no benefit here, since on shared-nothing systems, the DBMS doesn't know which node contains the data.

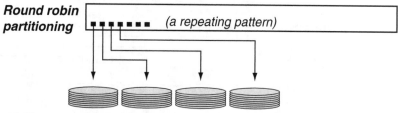

FIGURE 13.12   Round-robin partitioning.

Database Design Is More Complex

In a multiprocessing system, database design can have a significant effect on application performance. Typically, it involves using all the options described in the previous paragraphs, and more. Not all the partitioning schemes we described are available for all DBMSs, but there are many other database design options in addition to these. And the more options we have, the more likely we are to make a mistake. When we have no choice, we have no decision to make, but when we have choices, trying to pick the correct one is a problem. An example may illustrate the kinds of decisions involved.

One reason for using fully overlapped tables is that they are related and frequently joined. If that join operation is crucial to application performance, in a shared-nothing environment we might decide to partition both tables using the identical range or expression partitioning scheme based on the contents of the join columns in either table. That approach would cause matching rows from the two tables to be assigned to the same node. This partitioning scheme would, in turn, permit partitions of the two tables to be joined at each node without moving any data among nodes—a key design goal for shared-nothing systems.

This simple example illustrates the additional complexity of database design in the shared-nothing environment, as compared to an environment with shared disks in which every processor has access to all disks.

Other Data Partitioning Issues

Note that, as usual, we have focused mainly on the performance related aspects of data partitioning. However, partitioning also raises a variety of other concerns for the DBA, including:

▶ **Administration.** Data partitioning support is important for both parallel query *performance* and administration. Partition *independence* is needed to allow administration operations to be done on individual partitions (for example, for data loading, backup, and recovery). These features become more critical as data volumes grow. Recovering a terabyte of data in a warehousing environment is not practical.

▶ **Design assistance.** Some products offer *multiple partitioning schemes.* This complicates physical database design, so any assistance in this area from design tools is a plus, especially for an MPP system where correct partitioning plays a large role in achieving optimal performance and scalability.

▶ **Repartitioning.** Incorrect partitioning in a shared-nothing configuration can seriously degrade performance. So it is important for administrators to have the

Parallelism and Warehouse Database Design

One key issue in database design for a data warehouse concerns the use of star schema designs instead of the normalized designs typically used in operational databases.

Star Schema versus Normalized Design

A star schema consists of one or more large fact tables and several small *dimension* (or *reference*) tables. The fact tables contain the information of interest to the business, and the dimension tables enable us to view the data across different dimensions (for example, time, product, or market). The key of a fact table is normally a combination of keys of the dimension tables. Compared with normalized tables, a start schema design has the following characteristics:

- ▶ Significant denormalization
- ▶ More update anomalies
- ▶ Fewer joins
- ▶ Fewer tables
- ▶ More tolerance of access path changes
- ▶ Faster join processing when using large table/small table join strategies
- ▶ Large indexes

When compared with a star schema design, normalization produces

- ▶ More tables
- ▶ One fact in one place
- ▶ Efficient update processing

ability to *repartition* the data, either to get better performance in an existing configuration or to take advantage of incremental additions to the hardware. If this can be done online, so much the better. Shared disk environments, including single SMP and SMP clusters, are likely to be more forgiving since all processors see all disks.

▶ **Referential integrity.** Some DBMS products may not enforce system-maintained referential integrity for partitioned data. While this imposes additional responsibility on update applications in an operational environment, it is irrelevant in a data warehouse where the database is read-only.

► More table joins
► Rapid access to data via indexes on key columns

Therefore, a star schema design appears to provide some performance advantages in a data warehousing system. Let's look at the use of such a design on SMP and MPP shared-nothing systems.

Star Schema and SMP Systems.   On an SMP system, we can use the shared-memory component of the hardware along with the DBMS buffer cache as a *window* on the large fact table, allowing efficient joins to take place in memory. Furthermore, since all the columns associated with different dimensions are indexed separately, the impact of access path (i.e., dimension) changes is not a major issue. With some DBMS products, join operations are performed by first creating an intermediate result set that is the cartesian product of the small dimension tables, then joining this result set and the fact table. Provided that the cartesian product does not grow too large to be contained in the cache, this access path minimizes I/O, because it requires only a single scan of the large fact table.

Star Schema and MPP Systems.   On MPP shared-nothing systems, scanning of the fact tables is very fast. A large fact table is typically partitioned across multiple nodes of the MPP based on hashing index. Partitioning may present problems on MPP systems if the user query employs an index that is not the index used to partition the data. In this situation, the DBMS may be forced to redistribute rows in the large table across nodes because it has no other way to get the required data to the correct nodes. Hence, some of the benefit of using multiple indexes on the key of the fact table is lost. In this situation, the use of a star schema design may not be beneficial on an MPP system. Row redistribution, however, is likely to be more efficient in SMP node MPP systems since some of the work can be done in memory.

Conclusions About the Parallelism Hierarchy

At the beginning of the chapter, we introduced the parallelism hierarchy with its eight levels of potential parallelism. By reviewing this hierarchy systematically, we've reached a few conclusions about how to use parallelism effectively:

► Introduce parallelism where it occurs naturally in the hierarchy.
► For optimal performance, introduce parallelism as early as possible in the hierarchy. Introducing parallelism later can be thought of as a belated attempt to

improve the performance by parallelizing a piece of work that was not split apart earlier either through lack of forethought or because it could not be split.

► Higher in the hierarchy, we can use *overt* workload management and application design techniques to create parallel processing streams because we are dealing with large workload components that are under our control.

► The lower we go in the hierarchy, the more automated (or covert) the parallelism mechanisms must become because we are dealing with interactions that are closer to the hardware device level.

► Workload parallelism is easier to implement than software parallelism, which is easier to implement than device parallelism.

No matter which level of parallelism is implemented, eliminate synchronization between parallel streams whenever possible. Remember: *Synchronization kills parallelism.*

The Trade-off Principle

"It depends . . ."

Akira Shibamiya

In This Chapter . . .

Management Trade-offs Revisited
Technical Trade-offs for Optimal Performance
Grouping and Performance
Caching and Buffering
Indexing Trade-offs
Data Compression
Applying the SPE Design Principles

What makes design challenging—but interesting, or even fun, depending on your point of view—is that it always involves balancing conflicting goals. The operations of large human endeavors are contrived from the collective imaginations and intellects of all the people of the enterprise; developing software systems to support them properly is no simple task. It is typically a long and complex process during which the designer is confronted with many choices and decisions. *You cannot simply follow a single rule or apply a single principle and be done.*

Earlier (in Chapter 5) we saw that establishing performance objectives always involves balancing the goal of *acceptable performance* with other design criteria like *correct function, high reliability, data integrity, portability, reusability, ease of maintenance,* and so on. Whenever we aim for multiple goals, issues of priority, of balance, and of compromise arise. In this chapter, we turn to the technical aspects of trade-off and compromise. The sixth and final design principle points out that—once a particular set of quantitative performance goals is established—making trade-offs among workloads and computing resources is one of the key techniques we must use to achieve those goals.

Management Trade-offs Revisited

Earlier, when discussing software performance engineering, we dealt with the subject of trade-offs from the management point of view. The following is a brief summary.

Simplicity Comes First

We begin by restating a very important point. No matter what we might conclude about the need for balance and compromise, making trade-offs should never extend to compromising the fundamental aims and practices of good software engineering, as we discussed in Chapter 7. Functional simplicity and code efficiency should continue to be our goals at every stage of design and development.

The most effective way to improve performance is to reduce the workload by eliminating features of marginal value and removing inefficient code from our applications. For specific recommendations, see *Minimizing Unit Costs* in Chapter 8, *The Workload Principle.*

Trade-offs Among Software Engineering Goals

Performance is simply one of many software engineering goals, requiring managers to make trade-offs when setting objectives. Also, there is no absolute definition of *good performance.* Good performance for any computer system or application can be defined only for a particular hardware and software environment and in the context of requirements and expectations.

Akira Shibamiya, an IBM performance specialist who surely knows more about DB2 performance than anyone else, when asked about the performance implications of any hypothetical DB2 design choice, invariably begins his answer with the qualifier, "It depends. . . ." After pausing for a moment to reflect on all the conditions and assumptions that could influence the answer, he then continues, not with an answer, but with another question as to the assumed environment and performance goals.

In Chapter 5, we discussed the need for users, application designers, and systems staff to establish performance objectives jointly, through a service-level management process that promotes compromise in pursuit of larger organizational goals. Ideally, this process involves drawing up service-level agreements that will provide a formal basis for ongoing performance management and capacity planning efforts.

> ### Guideline 14.1   Akira's standard performance answer
>
> To any hypothetical question about performance, begin your answer with "It depends. . . ." Pause for a moment to reflect on all the conditions and assumptions that could influence your answer. Then continue, in the style of Socrates, not with an answer, but with questions as to the assumed environment and performance goals. After responding to several of these, your questioners will see for themselves the obvious answer to their original question.
>
> You will soon gain a reputation as a wise and patient performance teacher.

Trade-off Individual, Community, and Enterprise Goals

Achieving good performance means different things to different people in the organization. Users have an *application perspective* on performance; *response time* is their priority. People with a *systems perspective* on performance are concerned about overall *throughput* and *capacity* needed to support the entire population of users.

Because our existing hardware resources and budgets usually impose limits on capacity, management must balance the particular performance needs of individual applications with those of the whole community of users. This always involves making trade-offs; we addressed the management aspects of this issue in Chapter 5.

A given set of computing resources can always be arranged to give increased responsiveness for one particular application if we are willing to sacrifice overall capacity by removing all potentially competing work. Alternatively, we can generally achieve high throughput at the expense of response time. For most organizations, neither of these extremes is politically acceptable. The issue that we must address as we design our systems is how to strike a balance between maximizing the overall system's capacity to process work and increasing the responsiveness for particular subsets of the workload.

Enterprise goals, like delivery dates for new application functions, are also a factor. A simple implementation will be available sooner, but it may not perform well. Poor performance may cost us business or drive up other costs. On the other hand, if we wait for the more complex solution with better performance, we may lose so much business that the application is no longer profitable. Factors like *reliability, data integrity, portability, reusability,* and *ease of maintenance* also have associated costs that vie with performance for development dollars.

Technical Trade-offs for Optimal Performance

The Trade-off Principle deals with the more technical aspects of trade-offs. In the previous six chapters we explained how applying five fundamental SPE design principles can help to optimize the use of scarce computing resources in the pursuit of application or system-level performance goals. But in most design situations, more than one of those principles applies. That fact will be clear by now from the many examples we have offered in the last six chapters.

If we set out to apply the SPE design principles to a particular design problem, we usually find that the principles tend to pull us in different directions. While this may be disconcerting at first, it cannot be avoided because each principle emphasizes a different aspect of performance. So to make decisions and move forward, we must strike a balance.

The remainder of this chapter focuses on the role that technical trade-offs play in the practice of good design—trade-offs among the computing resources, among workloads that share those resources, and even among the SPE design principles themselves.

Making Trade-offs Among Computing Resources

Performance optimization has two phases: *absolute* and *relative* tuning. Once we have made our applications as efficient as possible through *absolute* tuning of our design and code, all further performance gains will be *relative* ones. We must make trade-offs, improving one application or resource at the expense of another. The ability to recognize and implement resource trade-offs successfully is the hallmark of the good software engineer.

In Chapter 3, we introduced and described the principal computing resources. We also explained the role that hardware and software resources play in determining application performance and the significance of *resource bottlenecks*. In Chapter 4 we introduced the Centering Principle, noting that every system develops bottlenecks as the workload grows and that the fundamental rule of all performance tuning is to *eliminate the biggest bottleneck.*

At the most basic level of analysis, there are only two ways to remove a resource bottleneck:

▶ Increase the power of the resource to process the demand
▶ Reduce the demand

Assume for the moment that we cannot increase the power of the resource and that we have already reduced the inherent demands of the workload to a minimum by tuning for efficiency, eliminating unnecessary work, and so on (see *Minimizing Unit Costs* in Chapter 8). The only way left to remove a bottleneck is to alter the software design, reducing the demand for one resource by making increased use of another.

Designing for performance always involves looking for ways to make effective trade-offs among the available computing resources: chiefly processor cycles versus space in memory versus disk I/O versus network bandwidth. For example:

▶ Distributing or replicating fragments of a database from an enterprise DBMS server to middle-tier workgroup servers uses more disk space on the workgroup machines. In exchange, client workstations can retrieve the data locally through an efficient LAN connection, reducing the traffic on a bottlenecked WAN or the processing load on a bottlenecked mainframe.

▶ Storing an SQL procedure on a LAN-based DBMS server requires some server disk space and probably some disk I/O time to load the procedure when it is invoked. But, in return, we avoid sending that set of SQL requests repeatedly from the client to the DBMS every time the application is run. This reduces the bottleneck on the shared LAN resource and lowers our overall transaction response time by eliminating the round trips across the LAN needed to submit each SQL statement individually.

▶ Storing a file of common derived statistics like sales totals or monthly averages on the client or on a network server lets a client application replace the sizable processing and I/O cost of evaluating a complex database query by a simple disk or network I/O to read the precomputed data values.

> **Guideline 14.2   Make trade-offs among computing resources**
> The software engineer who understands performance strives to eliminate bottlenecks by creating a design that makes the best possible use of *all* the available computing resources. Exchanging resources with spare capacity for a bottlenecked resource will usually improve both overall throughput and response times.

Types of Resource Trade-offs

In theory, there are as many possibilities for resource trade-offs as there are distinct combinations of computing resources. But some make more sense than others. Typically we look for ways to:

▶ Substitute faster devices for slower ones
▶ Divert work from heavily loaded devices

▶ Substitute memory and processor cycles for disk I/O

▶ Substitute local resources for network I/O and remote resources

▶ Make the processor the bottleneck

▶ Substitute memory for processor cycles

We consider each of these trade-off strategies in the following paragraphs.

Substitute Faster Devices for Slower Ones.   In Chapter 3, we introduced the major classes of computing devices and pointed out the wide variation in their speeds. (For convenience, we repeat the summary here as Table 14.1; refer to Table 3.3 for explanatory notes). The table shows the *typical* hierarchy of computing resources found in an enterprise client/server environment, organized by relative speed with the fastest at the top. To improve an application's performance, we must look for design changes that will make its resource usage pattern migrate upward in the hierarchy.

Divert Work from Heavily Loaded Devices.   In any situation involving performance bottlenecks, the Sharing Principle is particularly relevant. It provides a quantitative basis for resource trade-off decisions that will improve performance. Remember that when making resource trade-offs for performance, we are always aiming to *reduce delays by substituting a faster resource* for the one that is the bottleneck. But also recall that for shared resources we must always pay attention to the sum of waiting time plus service time. In Chapter 11, we recommended: *Lighten the load on a shared server* (Guideline 11.8). The fastest resource is not simply the one with the fastest rated service time—we must also take into account the likely waiting time due to resource contention.

For example, it would not be a good idea to move data from a relatively idle disk (*A*) with a 25ms access time to another (*B*) that has a 10ms access time but

Table 14.1   **The Hierarchy of Computing Resources**

Device Type	Typical Service Time	Relative to 1 second
High Speed Processor Buffer	10 nanoseconds	1 second
Random Access Memory	60 nanoseconds	~6 seconds
Expanded Memory	25 microseconds	~1 hour
Solid State Disk Storage	1 millisecond	~1 day
Cached Disk Storage	10 milliseconds	~120 days
Magnetic Disk Storage	25 milliseconds	~4 weeks–25 days
Disk via MAN/High Speed LAN Server	27 milliseconds	~1 month
Disk via Typical LAN Server	35–50 milliseconds	~6–8 weeks
Disk via Typical WAN Server	1–2 seconds	~3–6 years
Mountable Disk/Tape Storage	3–15 seconds	~10–50 years

is 90 percent busy. In fact, we could probably improve overall performance by moving some data in the opposite direction. Using the simple rule of

$$R = S/(1-U)$$

for estimating the response time of shared devices that we introduced in Chapter 11, we can see that the actual response time of disk B is probably closer to 100ms than to its rated access time of 10ms.

Substitute Memory and Processor Cycles for Disk I/O.   Database caching or buffering reduces the cost of re-reading frequently reused portions of a database by retaining them in memory, improving responsiveness by trading off memory for processor resources and disk I/O. Of course, the costs of searching for data in a cache are all wasted overhead when the data isn't actually there. This situation is termed a *cache miss.* The relatively small overhead of cache misses must be weighed against the larger savings we get whenever there is a *cache hit.* Typically, no matter how large the cache, cache hits consume fewer processor cycles and a lot less time than would the corresponding disk I/O.

The previous paragraph, however, does highlight an important facet of cache design: The benefits of any cache depend on the ratio of cache hits to cache misses. We examine this issue in more detail later in this chapter, in the section *Caching and Buffering.*

Substitute Local Resources for Network I/O and Remote Resources.   Usually a client process can retrieve data from a disk on the client workstation faster than it can from a shared disk on a network server. One exception to this rule is when we have much faster disks on a lightly loaded server machine on a high-speed LAN. In that case, it can be faster for clients to retrieve data from a server disk. In most client/server environments, though, the added delays due to LAN transmission time and contention for server resources outweigh any benefits obtained from faster disks on the server.

Whenever we relocate or copy data or processes for performance reasons, our motivation is to exchange additional storage and processing resources at the target location for network I/O. No extensive calculations are required to tell us that colocating process and data will produce faster response times than either transferring data to the site of the process or shipping a process to the data location. This trade-off is one of the fundamental strategies of client/ server design. For more details, see the Locality Principle (Chapter 10) and Part IV of the book.

Make the Processor the Bottleneck.   Many tuning actions involve making trade-offs among several resources. In almost all cases, the design that offers the best performance will be the one that adds processor cycles while reducing the use of some other resource(s). The reason for this is simple: The processor is the fastest hardware resource (see Guideline 5.21). Unless the processor is already overloaded with competing work, substituting more processing for some other, slower resource *always* improves performance.

Data compression is the perfect illustration of this rule. Compressing and decompressing data takes processor cycles but pays dividends by reducing the number of I/Os needed to store, retrieve, and transmit the compressed result. That's why PKZIP is so popular.

Substitute Memory for Processor Cycles.   And what if the processor *is* overloaded? Then the only thing faster than processing is *no* processing. Often we can eliminate repeated processing by retaining derived or computed information in memory or by retaining information about the state of an ongoing process until it is needed again, rather than discarding that information and having to recompute it later.

Servers that must handle requests from many clients use this technique when they retain in memory a pool of operating system processes or threads that are always available and ready to process the next request from any client. Doing this eliminates the overhead costs of having the operating system repeatedly initiate and terminate server processes. We discussed this common technique earlier (in Chapter 9) in connection with the Efficiency Principle and the concept of the *fixing point*.

In all such cases, we improve overall throughput by freeing up processor resources for other work, and we improve response time because it is usually much faster to re-read a stored copy of anything from memory than it is to recreate it from scratch.

Guideline 14.3	**Reduce delays by substituting faster resources**

When making trade-offs among the available computing resources, reduce response times by substituting faster resources for any resource that is a bottleneck. Strategies for improving performance include substituting disk storage for network I/O, processor cycles for disk I/O, and memory for processor cycles.

Prioritize and Trade Off Among Workloads That Share Resources

When all other trade-off possibilities are exhausted, we must assign priorities to groups or classes of work that share computing resources and trade off performance among them. Of course, *deciding which workload gets priority is a management issue,* the resolution of which requires defined *Performance Objectives* as we discussed in Chapter 5. At least, it should be a management issue, but this is an area in which systems people often take the law into their own hands as long as no one complains. But here we are concerned with the technical questions of how, once priorities are assigned, we can actually use that decision to adjust the performance landscape.

Making these kinds of trade-offs is an extremely common activity in all kinds of system-level tuning work. Indeed, in shops where application developers do not operate within a strong framework of service-level management, juggling workload priorities is probably the prevailing method of system-level tuning. This is because there are not many ways to make absolute performance improvements in any application without touching the code.

▶ **Adding Indexes.**   A database table is a shared logical resource. Improving the responsiveness of interactive query applications against a shared table by adding several indexes will almost certainly slow down any update operations against the same table because the indexes now have to be updated, too. (The net effect of adding an index involves several other considerations that we discuss elsewhere; here we just want to illustrate the aspect of a trade-off among classes of work.)

▶ **Denormalization.**   Denormalizing is an optional strategy in physical database design (see Chapter 19). Suppose we take a set of three related tables, joining them to create a single physical table. This will improve the performance of applications that actually need all the joined data but slow down other applications that need only a subset of the data. (As with indexes, there are other consequences too.)

▶ **Workload Scheduling.**   Because we are working with a fixed pool of resources, any time we adjust operating system task scheduling (or dispatching) priorities we are choosing to improve the performance of one class of work at the expense of another. For example, to improve the performance of online transactions, we could relegate all batch reporting to a single logical task or address space with a low operating system scheduling priority.

Response Time versus Throughput.   Tension always exists between throughput and response-time goals. Increasing overall throughput is likely to drive down average transaction response times because competition for resources drives up device utilization levels, extending device wait times. Conversely, by allocating disproportionate resources to a specific application, we can lower its response time, but we do so at the expense of overall throughput.

Shared database systems often present this dilemma, particularly when we try to mix long-running queries with high-volume transaction workloads. We reviewed this issue earlier under the Locality Principle. For a short summary, remember Inmon's Rule: *Don't mix short transactions with long-running queries.* For a longer discussion see Chapters 10 and 19.

Grouping and Performance

When we explained (in Chapter 7) how the six SPE design principles were related to the fundamental software engineering principles, we introduced the subject of **grouping.** Grouping is a physical design technique that we use in every area of software design. As we pointed out in more detail in Chapter 7, in Table 7.1:

▶ We group related functions into processes, routines, or modules.
▶ We group related data items and methods into objects.
▶ We group related columns into records, files, tables, or views.
▶ We group sets of related SQL statements into stored procedures.
▶ We group related data fields into dialogs, windows, screens, or reports.
▶ We group data for transmission into messages, blocks, or packets.
▶ We group stored data into database blocks or pages.

Since most of these design situations offer more than one way to group the low-level components, it is interesting to consider whether the design principles of software performance engineering can help us select an optimal grouping for performance.

In Chapter 7, we looked at grouping and software engineering goals from the logical design viewpoint only, in which the primary motivation for grouping small components into larger units is to create a simpler and more logically cohesive design. But the logical measures of cohesion and coupling are not the only criteria by which to judge a grouping decision.

Grouping and the SPE Design Principles

In Chapter 9, we saw that the Efficiency Principle was directly related to the question of when objects were grouped. Both the timing and the group size decision affect the efficiency of a design. Relatively static grouping schemes in which the grouping of elements persists for a longer period are likely to reduce overhead costs by comparison with more dynamic alternatives.

Similarly, the motivation for using larger groups is also to obtain some economy of scale, typically by reducing the average amount of processing or storage required per element grouped.

Reducing overhead is certainly an important goal, especially if our greatest concerns are in the areas of system throughput and capacity. But there is generally a price to pay in return for reducing overheads. Larger, more static groups are less flexible in a number of ways. In fact, the grouping decision can potentially involve *all five SPE design principles* and, therefore, can involve making trade-offs among them. Many examples in the following sections illustrate this.

Guideline 14.4	Grouping—the two critical decisions for performance

Grouping software elements together is a fundamental technique of physical design. Typically, two aspects of any grouping decision have significant performance implications:

▶ *Fixing point* (the timing of the grouping operation)
▶ *Group size*

The Significance of Group Size

Each potential choice of group size can have a different impact on performance. Smaller groups tend to produce more responsive solutions, while larger groups favor throughput and overall efficiency. Often there are other consequences too because of interplay among the SPE design principles. Here are some examples:

▶ **Program design.** Depending on the relationship between modules and separately executable processes, small modules start up faster and need less memory, but they are likely to consume more resources in process management overhead. Large modules do the opposite.

▶ **Database design.** If the physical database design is highly normalized (typically comprising many small tables or records), programs take longer to read the data, but updates are faster. While larger denormalized tables improve performance for those applications that need the larger group of data, other applications may run more slowly because of the time wasted retrieving unwanted data.

▶ **Database application design.** A large SQL stored procedure can replace a series of separate SQL requests from the client software to the database server. This reduces network traffic and should speed up response time for client applications that need the full set of database processing. On the other hand, running a lot of large stored procedures at once can clog up the database server and make it less responsive to smaller SQL requests.

▶ **UI design.** Displaying a standard window or dialog showing everything about a customer reduces requests for additional details and speeds up the agent's work. But the system may be doing a lot of unnecessary processing to retrieve and display all that customer data if, for most transactions, the agent needs only the customer's name, phone number, and account number.

▶ **Data communications.** Every packet of every block of every message adds its share of overhead, slowing down the effective data transmission rate. On the other hand, the transmission protocols may be able to handle a workload mix composed of smaller blocks more effectively than one that includes some very large blocks.

▶ **I/O subsystem.** For small data requests, small I/O block sizes are ideal; large block sizes waste I/O time, channel capacity, and processor memory. For large requests, small block sizes waste time and processor resources.

The Group Size Trade-off: A Summary

The many dimensions of the group size decision are summarized in Table 14.2 and discussed in more detail in the sections that follow. To simplify things, we

Table 14.2   **Group Size and the SPE Design Principles**

	Workload	Efficiency	Locality	Sharing	Parallelism
Large group advantages	Can match a large workload	Increased efficiency and throughput	May increase spatial locality		
Large group disadvantages	More chance of wasted work	Less responsive	May reduce functional cohesion	May increase contention	May inhibit parallelism
Small group advantages	Can match a small workload	More responsive	May increase cohesion	More flexibility, better for sharing	More opportunities for parallelism
Small group disadvantages	May not minimize costs	May reduce throughput	May increase coupling	Minor increase in deadlocks	

have reduced the spectrum of grouping possibilities to the two extremes: *large groups* and *small groups*. The table lists some of the advantages and disadvantages of each with respect to each of the five design principles. While responsiveness is not strictly a concern of the Efficiency Principle, it is frequently a casualty of increased throughput so we show it in that column. Note that the primary concern of first three principles is the performance of individual applications; the last two address community or system performance issues.

> **Guideline 14.5** **The SPE design principles and grouping**
> All software design principles can have a bearing on grouping decisions. But the principles don't all pull in the same direction where the grouping decision is concerned. Therefore, we must anticipate the effect of any proposed grouping on all applications affected by the decision, taking into account their various performance objectives.

Caching and Buffering

John von Neumann, who first defined the architecture of the modern computer, wrote in 1946: "*Ideally one would desire an indefinitely large memory capacity such that any particular word would be immediately available . . . We are . . . forced to recognize the possibility of constructing a hierarchy of memories, each of which has greater capacity than the preceding but which is less quickly accessible.*"[1]

> *Preliminary Discussion of the Logical Design of an Electronic Computing Instrument,* 1946

Because of the vast differences in the speeds of devices used in a computer system, caching is one of the most widely used techniques to improve software and hardware performance. Much of the technical literature focuses on processor design, where caching is used to speed up data transfers from slower to faster memory components or from RAM to the CPU. Reviewing the architecture of modern computer systems, Gray and Reuter explain the role of caching in the context of a **memory hierarchy** of:

► High-speed electronic cache memory (or *processor registers*)
► Slower-speed random-access memory (or *main memory*)

---

[1]A. W. Burks, H. G. Goldstine, and J. von Neumann, "Preliminary Discussion of the Logical Design of an Electronic Computing Instrument," *Datamation* 8:36–41 (October 1962). A reprint of the design notes of John von Neumann and his team in 1946, written during the period when the architecture of the modern computer was first defined.

► Nonvolatile electronic or magnetic online external storage (or *fixed disks*)
► Near-line archive storage (mountable disk or tape *cartridges* managed by *robots*)
► Off line storage (*tapes*)[2]

As we show in Table 14.1, distributed computing adds yet more memory layers to this list—the various storage devices located at other nodes in the network.

How Caching Works.   A cache works by applying the Trade-off Principle to speed up access to any storage device (the **cached device**). Actually, the cached device continues to operate at the same speed, but the caching mechanism makes it seem faster. It does this by retaining copies of frequently used data items—the cache—in a smaller but much faster device and then searching the cache first for any requested data element. Because the cache is usually invisible to the requesting process, it gives the appearance of a reduced access time for the underlying device.

Caches are typically implemented in memory, giving very fast access times, although other fast devices like solid-state disks can be used to improve the access times of slower devices. In general, using Gray and Reuter's hierarchic memory model, *small, fast, expensive memories at the top act as caches for the larger, slower, cheaper memories used at the lower levels of the hierarchy.* When implemented by systems software, a cache may be called a **buffer pool,** a **buffer cache,** or simply **buffers.** Similarly, the caching mechanism or technique is sometimes called **look-aside buffering.**

Finding an element in the cache is referred to as a **cache hit;** the inverse is a **cache miss.** The success of a cache is measured by its **hit ratio** or **hit rate,** the fraction of all cache requests that are satisfied from the cache.

The likelihood of finding any requested data element in a cache depends on three factors:

► The reference pattern for the cached data
► The relative sizes of the cache and the underlying cached data
► The cache management mechanism

Most data has an uneven reference pattern. Following the 80/20 rule (recall the Centering Principle), a small subset typically receives the bulk of all requests. As a result, cache hit rates of 80 percent and above are quite common,

---

[2]Jim Gray and Andreas Reuter, *Transaction Processing: Concepts and Techniques* (San Mateo, CA: Morgan Kaufmann, 1993), 54.

provided the cache is large enough relative to the size of the underlying data. In some applications, highly skewed reference patterns permit hit rates of 90, 95, or even 99 percent.

Caches can be **static** or **dynamic.** Whereas the content of a static cache never changes during normal operation, a dynamic cache is continually updated to reflect the workload. Both types are useful. Which type is most appropriate for any given situation depends on how frequently the data is updated and how soon those updates need to be reflected in the cache.

For example, a DBMS-managed data replication scheme is basically just a static preplanned caching mechanism. It works well in certain situations, such as maintaining remote copies of code lookup or translation tables that change only occasionally—recall Guideline 9.6, *Cache static or slowly changing data.*

Many design situations, however, require dynamic caching for performance. The volatility of commonly accessed data, and the unpredictable and ever-shifting nature of workloads, makes it very difficult for us to design and implement static caches that retain their usefulness over the course of time.

In a dynamic cache, a cache management mechanism keep tracks of the contents, marking elements as they are reused. When a cache miss occurs, the new data element read from the cached device is stored in the cache for possible future reuse. A replacement algorithm like **least recently used (LRU)** selects the least popular element(s) currently stored there to be overwritten. Tom Cushing, a consultant and teacher who is well known for his performance expertise, offers this easy way to remember how dynamic caching works: *If you don't use it, you lose it.*[3]

Guideline 14.6	**Cushing's law of caching**

In a dynamic cache with LRU replacement: *If you don't use it, you lose it.*

Cushing's caching corollaries: Cushing's Law reminds us of the relationship between the overall frequency and variability of cache references, the size of the cache, and the expected interval between references to any cached data item. For a fixed-size dynamic cache with an LRU replacement algorithm:

1. For a particular workload, items in a cache have an average *half-life* time. Once the interval between references to a data item exceeds this time, it is more likely than not that the cached copy will be flushed out and must be reloaded on the next reference.
2. Increasing the cache size increases the half-life time of its contents.

---

[3]Thomas Cushing, Advanced Computer Services, Inc.; telephone (203) 457-0600 or online at *tcushing@cshore.com.*

Levels of Caching

Because caching is such a common technique in software design, general-purpose software components in every layer of a system are likely to have caches built in. Quite often there is even a parameter to adjust the cache size. Figure 14.1 illustrates some of the typical locations of caches in an enterprise client/ server system:

▶ Software components designed for client/server operation use client-side caching to cut down on repeated server requests.
▶ Every self-respecting DBMS uses adjustable caches or buffer pools (and usually several of them) to minimize disk I/O requests.
▶ Underneath the DBMS, the operating system and its access methods or device drivers offer more levels of caching.
▶ Below that, there are hardware caches before we finally get down to the actual device.

All these layers are trying to reduce the need for network or disk I/O. The slower the device, the more layers of caching we're likely to find above it.

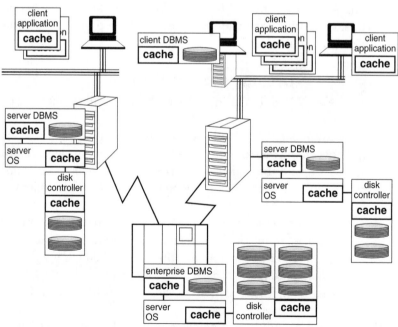

FIGURE 14.1   Caching is an enterprise client/server environment.

Estimating Effective Access Time for Cached Data

While the idea behind caching is fairly simple, there appears to be some confusion among authors about how to evaluate the benefits numerically:

▶ Derfler and Schireson, writing about disk caching in *PC Magazine* in 1993, claim that "*The difference in performance achieved by doubling the available cache, for example, could be as high as 20 or 30 to 1.*"[4]

▶ Nemzow, citing Derfler and Schireson, claims a 2,596 percent improvement for an example in which hit rates increase from 30 to 69 percent.[5]

▶ Gray and Reuter, on the other hand, argue that unless the hit ratio is close to 100 percent, effective access time is *much closer* to that of the slower device than to that of the cache.[6]

Who is right? As you may have guessed, *it depends* on your assumptions.

Two Examples

Derfler and Schireson give the following examples: "Suppose your server takes 20 milliseconds (ms) to process a request if it involves a disk access and 0.1ms if it does not. Say that 60 percent of the requests can be filled with data available in RAM: a 60 percent hit rate. Then your server can process 100 requests in 806ms. If by increasing the amount of cache, 99 percent of requests could be found in cache, 100 requests could be processed in 29.9ms: a 2,596 percent performance improvement." They go on to argue that "Even a more modest improvement—from an 85 percent hit rate to 98 percent—would improve performance by about 600 percent."[7]

In our view, these examples are misleading. In the first place, to claim *a 2,596 percent performance improvement* is itself a questionable use of statistics. We would prefer to say simply that access times were cut from 806ms to 29.9ms—a 96.3 percent reduction. More importantly, both examples produce startling "percentage improvements" only because they employ a final hit rate close to 100 percent. Here's how it works.

A Simple Approximation

A quick and easy way to estimate effective access time is to assume that cache hits have a zero access time. Relatively speaking, this is not an unrea-

---

[4]Frank J. Derfler and Max Schireson, "Maximizing the Performance of Your Server," *PC Magazine* 12(18) (October 26, 1993).
[5]Martin Nemzow, *Computer Performance Optimization* (New York, NY: McGraw Hill, 1994), 56.
[6]Gray and Reuter, *Transaction Processing*, 55.
[7]Derfler and Schireson, "Maximizing the Performance."

sonable simplification when the cache is a couple of orders of magnitude faster than the cached device (and why use caching in the first place unless the cache is substantially faster?).

If hits cost nothing, then the only access times we need to consider are those caused by cache misses. So, *to estimate average access time, simply multiply the fraction of cache misses by the device access time.*

To illustrate this approximation, we apply it to the first example. When the hit rate is 60 percent, the miss rate is 40 percent, so the average access time is roughly 40 percent of 20ms, or 8ms. For 100 requests, that's 800ms. Notice that in the example, the hits do not actually happen in zero time, so the total time (806ms) is a little bit higher, but the difference is insignificant. (Mathematically speaking, by ignoring the cost of hits, the approximation produces a lower bound for effective access time.)

Guideline 14.7	**Estimate effective access time for a cached device**

To estimate the effective access time of any cached device, simply multiply the fraction of cache misses by the device access time.

The approximation shows why the earlier examples give such good results. Improving from *any* miss rate higher than 10 percent to a miss rate of 1 or 2 percent is going to look good because the calculated "percentage improvement" depends on the ratio of the effective access times, which is the same as *the ratio of the miss rates*. Using the logic of the examples, a 1 percent miss rate is "500 percent faster" than a 5 percent miss rate, and so on. Clearly, the miss rate ratios are not nearly as dramatic when the hit rates are lower. Apparently this fact was overlooked by Nemzow, who modified Derfler and Schireson's example so that hit rates increase from 30 to 69 percent instead of from 60 to 99 percent, but who then claimed the same 2,596 percent improvement.[8] Unfortunately, even going from no cache at all to a cache with a 69 percent hit rate will produce only an improvement of about 100/31, or just over 322 percent (to use the percentage calculation), so Nemzow's result is obviously incorrect.

---

[8]Nemzow, *Computer Performance.*

So it's not unusual for data to pass through four or five caches on its path from disk to application program, and even more in a distributed environ-ment.

With so many caches, how should we select the cache sizes at the different levels? In a discussion of computer architectures, Gray and Reuter approach this question from a cost viewpoint. They first give an obvious guideline: *Frequently*

How Much Faster?

Finally, how are we to interpret Gray and Reuter's position? Even a hit rate of 67 percent produces an average access time that is approximately one-third that of the slower device. On a linear scale, this is certainly not *closer* to that of the slower device than to that of the cache.

But because they are writing about orders of magnitude differences in speed between the layers of a memory hierarchy, Gray and Reuter are thinking in terms of a logarithmic scale.[9] On a linear scale, 13ms is much closer to 0.1ms than it is to 39ms. If you are concerned about orders of magnitude, 13ms is 130 times slower than 0.1ms, and only 3 times faster than 39ms.

This appears to be a classic example of the glass being viewed as half empty or half full, depending on the viewer. The computer architect sees the glass half empty; to the application developer it is half full. Gray and Reuter are thinking about what they call *the perfect memory,* which is as fast as the cache itself (an impossibility, of course, but a design ideal nevertheless). They focus on how much slower the effective speed is compared to the cache. And, of course, *we cannot achieve an effective access time close to that of the cache itself unless the hit rate is close to 100 percent.*

The application developer is less concerned about achieving blazing speed; he or she is more interested in practical techniques to trim application response times. To the application developer, despite Gray and Reuter's pessimism about low hit rates, a cache with a hit rate of 67 percent that cuts average access times by a factor of 3 may be just what's needed to meet the performance objectives.

---

[9]Gray and Reuter, *Transaction Processing,* 54–55.

Guideline 14.8 **Estimating improvements in effective access time**

To estimate the relative change in effective access times produced by a change in cache size, compute the ratio of the cache miss rates before and after the change. For example, improving the hit rate from 70 to 80 percent produces about a 3:2 drop in access times (a one-third drop); improving from 80 to 90 percent roughly halves access times.

accessed data should be in main memory, while it is cheaper to store infrequently accessed data on disk. Acknowledging the vagueness of this guideline, they go on to define *frequently* as once every five minutes or less, supporting this with an argument based on relative costs per byte of computer memory and disk storage. For more discussion of the *Five-Minute Rule,* see section 2.2.1.3 of Gray and Reuter.

> ### Guideline 14.9 The Five-Minute Rule of cache size
>
> As a starting point for cache design, recall Gray and Reuter's rule of thumb: Keep a data item in electronic memory if its accessed at least once every five minutes; otherwise, keep it in magnetic memory.

The *Five-Minute Rule* is a useful rule of thumb during systems design. Restated in terms of Cushing's second corollary, it asserts that we should have enough electronic memory set aside for caching to achieve a cache half-life of five minutes. However, it does not take into account the particular performance requirements of different applications. So it does not help us with the design decisions and trade-offs involved in allocating limited computing resources to caches for specific applications.

Since most software caches (regardless of which component supplies the cache) draw on the same pool of shared processor memory, how should we divide our fixed pool of real processor memory? And how should we spend our hardware budget, if we can choose between primary and secondary processor caches and disk cache?

To tackle this trade-off we review the Efficiency and Locality principles. There are several reasons why the cache that is closest to the application is the most suited to the application's purpose and will give the best return on our investment in cache size.

Caching and Efficiency

Because caching is a technique for getting the same amount of real work done with less overhead, we first pointed out its benefits in Chapter 9, *The Efficiency Principle.* Applying the Efficiency Principle to environments with multiple *levels* of caching, it is clear that *looking for data in all the wrong caches* is also an unwanted overhead—one that is minimized if the software can find the data in the first cache in which it looks. In practice, this is likely to be either one that we build ourselves inside an application component or one provided by systems software like a DBMS or a transaction monitor.

If we have the choice, a dedicated application cache is the most efficient by far because data cached inside the application is available for processing immediately at a very low cost. In contrast, suppose another local software component reads the data from its cache and returns it to the application. In that case, we do avoid any I/O delay, but the application still incurs significant processing overheads. Issuing a database or system request and having another component pass back the result take processor cycles. And if this interaction involves an operating system-managed process switch or task switch, even more overhead accrues.

Also, having several levels of cache creates a **skimming** effect. The first cache to receive an application's requests "skims off the cream" of frequently requested data items, passing only the cache misses through to the next level. So the second cache handles only those data items that are less likely to be needed again by the first. The third cache handles only the cache misses from the second cache, and so on recursively. Clearly, this phenomenon reduces the effectiveness of lower-level caches and usually means that lower-level caches need to be significantly larger to achieve the same hit rate as their neighbors above them.

Guideline 14.10	**Don't look for data in all the wrong caches**

Allocate memory locally to minimize caching overheads; the closest cache to an application provides the maximum benefit at the lowest cost. Adding memory to a DBMS cache or buffer pool will be more effective than adding the same amount to an operating system or hardware disk cache.

Because of the skimming effect, it is very hard to achieve high hit rates in lower level caches. Despite this, the lower-level caches are not completely redundant. Sometimes application software is designed to cache one type of request but not others. For example, a DBMS may provide extensive caching for databases but not for certain kinds of application descriptors or other system-level data that is stored in files associated with (but not in) the database. Granted, this may be a design flaw in the DBMS, but we have to learn to live with flawed software. In a case like this, a disk-level hardware cache can come to our rescue, providing a performance boost that compensates for the absence of higher-level caching.

Guideline 14.11	**Let lower-level caches mask missing software**

When tuning individual applications, focus any available resources on improving the hit rates of the highest-level caches. Apply resources for lower-level caches only when these are shared by applications that have no higher-level caching available or when some of an application's I/O requests are issued by software components that bypass the higher-level caches.

Caching and Locality

Next consider the Locality Principle and the notion of effectual locality, or closeness of purpose. As Figure 14.1 illustrates, hardware and software components in an enterprise client/server environment are arranged into giant tree structures. Each instance of user interface logic inhabits a separate leaf of the tree; the data in the enterprise databases is stored on devices buried at the base of the trunk. Caches close to the leaves serve only the needs of a small group of users, perhaps only a single application; a cache close the ground (the storage device) serves *all* users of the device.

Assuming that the stored data is shared by several applications, as we move away from a leaf toward the ground, the flow of data requests increases. Also, the pattern of data references becomes flatter, as the combined interests of multiple applications average out. So the farther a cache is away from an application, the less it can serve the particular needs of that application, and the more it must reflect the needs of all its users.

Also, if an application controls how its cache is used, it can be smarter about which data is likely to be needed again. As a result, dedicated application caches typically contain more useful data in less cache space, achieving higher hit rates than general-purpose caches placed farther away.

Guideline 14.12	Create a dedicated cache to maximize application performance

For performance-critical applications, creating a small dedicated cache inside the application is likely to be more effective than adding a larger amount of memory to DBMS buffers or any other general-purpose cache. Depending on the application, a cache may be useful on the client workstation, in an application server component, or both.

Read–Ahead Logic.   In an even more telling use of effectual locality, systems software sometimes incorporates special logic designed to actively exploit the existence of a cache, employing **read-ahead logic** and **anticipatory buffering**. Knowing the application, systems software can retrieve more data than is needed to satisfy an application's current request, anticipating its future requests for related data.

This is efficient; it's cheaper to read and transfer a few large blocks of data than many smaller ones. More importantly, this technique can employ the Parallelism Principle, scheduling read-ahead operations in the background to fetch the next blocks of data into the cache at the same time as the current blocks are being processed by the application.

Analogous to the **pipelining** mechanisms used in CPUs to fetch computer instructions for processing, this technique is common in DBMS software. A DBMS can use read-ahead logic whenever it knows that an application either is processing a physical cluster of related data items or is reading through many data items sequentially. Provided the application continues to read data in the anticipated pattern, all its data requests will be satisfied from the cache, minimizing response-time delays for disk I/O.

Caching and Real Memory

If caching is so useful, why not simply create huge memory caches everywhere and cut out all the disk I/O? Obviously, we cannot do this with hardware caches because the hardware cache device itself dictates the size of the cache. But software is more flexible; so what happens if a cache (or the combination of several caches) uses more virtual memory than the real memory available on the computer? Unfortunately, far from eliminating all I/O, this will actually generate I/O.

Every virtual page we use must be assigned to a real page of computer memory. And once we start to fill up all the computer's real pages with our cache, the operating system will step in and start paging out some of our cache pages to free up space. This means real I/Os to a real file on a real paging disk somewhere. And if we ever try to read one of those cache pages again, the operating system's demand paging logic will perform another I/O on our behalf to bring that page back in. For more details, see the capsule *Squeezing a Quart into a Pint Pot* in Chapter 3.

Therefore, it's important not to over-allocate memory to caches or buffer pools. Real memory pages are needed for the operating system, for middleware and subsystems like a DBMS, and for every concurrent application process. Although some system software components like DBMSs place limits on the number of buffers that can be allocated, these do not apply to caches developed in application code. But there is no free lunch! If caches eat up too much real memory, the only result will be excessive paging or swapping activity somewhere in the system—and no performance gains.

> **Guideline 14.13 Avoid over-caching in memory**
> When allocating memory for caching, restraint is essential. If the space allocated to caches exceeds the real memory pages available, the operating system overhead of shuffling cached pages in and out of memory can cancel out the intended benefits of the cache. Aim for a balance point that maximizes I/O savings from caching without introducing too much additional paging I/O.

> **Guideline 14.14 To discover optimal cache sizes, monitor total I/O rates**
> To find the optimal cache sizes to minimize local I/O, monitor total I/O rates (including paging I/O, of course) before and after increasing cache allocations. Cache sizes can be increased as long as total I/O rates continue to drop.

Caching and Remote I/O

There is one situation in which even over-allocating memory to cache can still produce an overall performance improvement: when we use a local cache to eliminate I/O to a remote device. Remote data requests are orders of magnitude more expensive than local ones (see Guideline 3.11). So the resource and response time costs of re-reading data from a remote database can easily outweigh any additional paging overhead generated by storing data in a local cache.

To speed up remote data access, creating a local cache on disk is a good strategy. If you have been "surfing the Net" with your Web browser lately, you will be familiar with the following software behaviors:

▶ The browser creates a local cache on your workstation's hard disk of everything you read.

▶ The next time you select a previously read object, the browser retrieves it directly from the local cache, with noticeably faster response time.

▶ To keep track of what's in the cache, the browser also maintains an index of the contents so that it does not have to search the entire cache every time you click on an object.

▶ The cache has a specified maximum size. When it fills up, the least recently referenced objects are over-written.

▶ To obtain a new copy of any cached object, you must specifically request it by selecting the *reload* option.

▶ Also, you can flush the entire cache periodically, if you wish.

Because of the percentage of static data in Web pages and the probability of repeated visits to some pages, these techniques work particularly well for Web browsers. However, they are all examples of relatively simple methods that application developers can also adopt to speed up remote data access for any application that has some probability of re-reading data items.

Guideline 14.15 Trade local I/O for remote I/O

Since remote data requests are much more expensive than local ones, local caching is particularly effective if local applications must read data from remote devices. Even if a local in-memory cache causes an increase in paging I/O, it may still yield a net reduction in application response times. Alternatively, consider creating a cache on a local disk.

Guideline 14.16 Create an index to eliminate cache searches

To avoid having to search through the entire cache, create an index of the cache contents and always look there first. For a disk-based cache, cache the index itself in memory to eliminate expensive system calls or disk I/Os to read a disk directory. Even for an in-memory cache, using an index minimizes access to the cache pages, which, in turn, minimizes paging overheads.

Guideline 14.17 When caching to reduce remote I/O, monitor response times

When using a local cache to eliminate I/O to a remote device, to find the optimal cache size, monitor response times. Cache sizes can be increased as long as average response times continue to drop, even though some additional local paging may occur.

Guideline 14.18 Add computer memory to maximize cache benefits

On a server, as workload volumes and client populations rise, increased competition for computer memory from concurrent processes will reduce the effectiveness of in-memory caches. Monitor paging rates to detect this trend. If paging rises significantly, consider adding more real memory to return paging rates to their previous levels.

Updated Data and Write-Back Caches

This introduction to caching techniques has focused on the benefits of caching data that is read repeatedly. In an environment with shared data, as long as applications only *read* the cached data, every client workstation can have a separate cache, and those caches can contain copies of the same data. But if any application *updates* a shared data item that was read from its cache, then to maintain the integrity of the shared data, the following must occur:

▶ The cache must be updated to reflect the change.
▶ The data source on the underlying cached device must be updated.
▶ All other caches must be notified that their current copy is no longer valid.

If the cache includes mechanisms to handle this added complexity, it is called a **write-back cache** or a **write-through cache.** Because this introduces additional complications related to the design of update transactions, we return to this subject in Part IV of the book, and in Chapter 19, *Using DBMS Technology.*

Indexing Trade-offs

Earlier we cited the decision to add an index as a (relatively simple) example of a trade-off between update and retrieval workloads. In practice, the decision to add an index in such situations is a complex one, involving several design principles. First, an index is an example of the Efficiency Principle (see Chapter 9), at least in so far as the retrieval workload is concerned. If we have a large enough cache and the table is used often enough, then a well-tuned DBMS will actually retain a copy of the entire index in the cache where it can be read without a single disk I/O interruption—another example of the Efficiency Principle.

Next, in a mixed query and update environment, if we need to optimize for the total cost of processing or for the capacity or throughput of the system as a whole, then we must apply the Workload Principle. Only after we consider the relative frequencies of queries and update transactions, and the effect of any index on their processing, can we estimate whether the net effect of adding that index would be a positive or negative one.

Third, indexing involves the Trade-off Principle because several resources are involved. Indexing a large database table takes up extra disk space to store the index, some extra disk I/O and processor cycles to read it, plus additional I/O and processor cycles to update it whenever the indexed data changes. In return, it eliminates most of the disk I/O time (and the associated processor cycles to handle the I/O) that would be consumed if we had to rediscover the location of data items every time they were needed.

Finally, the Sharing Principle (Chapter 11) applies. In some DBMSs, some programs acquire locks on index pages. In these cases, because indexes are more compact than the corresponding data tables, adding indexes can actually increase the likelihood of contention between queries and updates.

In Chapter 19, *Using DBMS Technology,* we discuss several other issues involved in the design of database indexes.

Data Compression

Data compression is a pure example of a resource trade-off although the usefulness of compression also involves the Efficiency Principle. We expend additional processor cycles to compress and decompress data and, in return, reduce the I/O overhead of storing, retrieving, and transmitting the data. Because data compression is so useful as a way to reduce the load on shared devices, we discussed data compression issues in Chapter 11, *The Sharing Principle.*

Applying the SPE Design Principles

In Part III of the book, we have discussed the SPE Design Principles and ways to apply them. We have not tried to organize these principles into a prescriptive sequential methodology for performance engineering. In any design situation there is always interplay between the principles and therefore room for the designer to make judgments and trade-offs in the course of applying them. The principles actually deal with the different perspectives we pointed out when we first discussed performance in Chapters 3 and 4.

To return to an analogy we introduced earlier (see *Caching and Locality*), we can imagine these various perspectives on the enterprise as different views of a single tree, in which the **community** is the trunk and the branches are successively smaller groupings of applications, until eventually we reach the **individual applications** or **components** at the leaves. Then:

▶ The *Workload, Efficiency,* and *Locality* principles apply mainly to the smaller branches and leaves.
▶ The *Sharing* and *Parallelism* principles focus more on the larger branches and the trunk.

Table 14.2 highlighted some consequences of these systematic differences of perspective among the first five principles. In this context, to take an **organizational** perspective mean to apply the Tradeoff Principle to resolve any apparent conflicts among the other principles. Guideline 14.19 summarizes the various kinds of trade-offs we have discussed.

In any design situation, exactly how we should apply the principles and which trade-off we might be willing to make among them will depend largely on which part of the spectrum most concerns us. For example, we can often reduce response times for individual applications by using *caching* (a resource trade-off). However, the same tradeoff may or may not be effective as a way to lower overall disk usage—it all depends on the application mix.

In theory, if two principles (*Efficiency* and *Sharing,* for example) appear to be in conflict and all else is equal, we advise adopting the simplest solution. In practice, such a situation is a rarity. In our experience, if we have done our homework properly, we generally know the relative priorities and performance goals of various workload classes and have a good feel for the overall conceptual integrity of the design. Once everything is known and understood, design decisions usually make themselves because overriding reasons always tip the scales in one direction or another.

In our view, the design principles should never be applied as if they were precise prescriptions for design actions. Rather, they should be viewed as a set of techniques for reasoning about design decisions—tools that can lead us to new insights about the consequences of those decisions.

In the next part of the book, we apply the principles in just that way, to help us reason about the design of distributed transaction systems.

> **Guideline 14.19** **Summary of SPE trade-offs**
>
> Achieving acceptable performance means making trade-offs. Here is a summary of the different SPE trade-off areas discussed in Chapters 5, 7, and 14.
>
> ▶ Never compromise the fundamental software engineering goal of simplicity (Chapter 7).
> ▶ If necessary, make trade-offs among software engineering goals (Chapter 5).
> ▶ Always look for effective trade-offs among available computing resources (Chapter 14).
> ▶ Prioritize and trade off among workloads that share resources (Chapter 14).
> ▶ Balance individual/application needs and community/system needs (Chapter 5) and make trade-offs among the SPE design principles themselves (Chapter 14).

Applications

Middleware and Performance

"The medium is the message."

Marshall McLuhan

In This Chapter . . .

Communicating Processes
Middleware Manages Communication
Processing Transactions
Distributed Object Technology
Distributed Transaction Monitors: *TP-Heavy*
The RPC versus Messaging Debate

When our applications must operate in a distributed computing environment, many issues arise that do not exist when all data is stored and processed by a single central computer.

The technology that implements client/server communication will be some form of *middleware.* But to make it clear that we do not intend to descend into a purely technical discussion of client/server middleware and its features and functions, we repeat a key guideline (*10.2 Know the user*) from our earlier discussion of the Locality Principle: *The software designer who knows why, how, and when an application will be used can create software that closely matches the user's needs and uses system software components harmoniously.*

This guideline is crucial to the design of effective distributed systems. In this chapter, we argue that because it is so much harder to build distributed applications, unless applications are designed to work in very close harmony with the way the business operates, they are likely to fail altogether or to be the source of continuing performance problems as the business grows.

We have looked at enterprise client/server computing at a fairly high level (in Chapter 2), introduced some performance-related concepts and activities (in Chapters 3 through 6), and spelled out a set of SPE design principles (in Chapters 7 through 14). In the next three chapters, we consider in more detail the enabling technologies, the architecture, and the design of enterprise client/server systems.

Our goal in these chapters is to use the SPE design principles to answer the question: *How should we use the technologies of distributed computing to build high-performance systems in the enterprise client/server environment?*

Communicating Processes

When an application involves two (or more) processes running on different computers, those processes must communicate. Figure 15.1 illustrates the high-level components involved in this communication. As the figure shows, the communication actually takes place at more than one level:

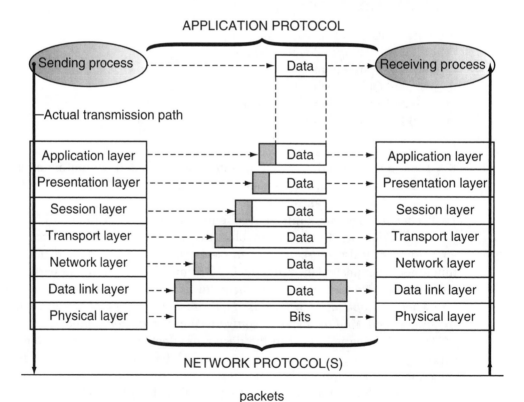

FIGURE 15.1   Communicating application processes.

▶ Network software and hardware make the communications work at the lower levels.

▶ Application architecture and design determine content and purpose of the communication taking place at the uppermost layer.

▶ Middleware determines the way distributed application components use the network software and hardware to communicate.

After introducing these three levels, we will return to a discussion of the various types of middleware available and draw some conclusions about performance.

Network Communications

Any discussion of network communications usually includes an illustration like Figure 15.2. This is the OSI Reference Model, which is intended to show how the various layers of networking software should fit together. We do not need to review the OSI Reference Model in detail. We include it here for two reasons. First, it provides a graphical illustration of the relationship between middleware protocols (like RPC) and various popular networking protocols

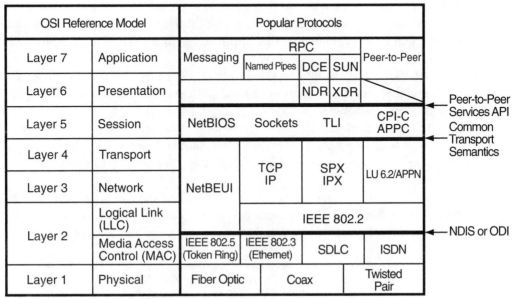

FIGURE **15.2** The OSI Reference Model with examples.

The Travel Agent

Imagine designing an online system to replace a travel agent. To book a single business itinerary, a travel agent must interact with many independent "systems" or "agents," including:

▶ The client, in person or by telephone
▶ An airline reservation system for the flights
▶ Hotel reservation systems, some automated, some handled via the telephone
▶ Rental car companies
▶ Restaurants
▶ Ticket agencies

All the interactions are part of a single business transaction, but different rules govern them. For example, the instructions to the travel agent might be:

▶ Book a round trip air ticket, two nights in a hotel, and a rental car.
▶ If there are no convenient flights, delay the entire itinerary by one week.

like TCP/IP, LU6.2, Ethernet, and ISDN.[1] Second, it emphasizes that the discussion of messaging protocols in this chapter will be at the level of the application program interface (OSI layer 7), and not of the lower-level network communication protocols used to implement the messaging (OSI layers 2 through 5). Network communications at these lower layers use a variety of *formats and protocols,* or *FAPs,* implemented using many different kinds of messages, data packets, and acknowledgments that applications never see. For example:

▶ Although two processes may be communicating synchronously at the application level, the underlying communication path may be engaged in full-duplex, asynchronous exchanges.
▶ Although there may be no response to a request at the application level, many lower-level acknowledgments usually will be sent and received by the communications software; some acknowledgments may even be seen by the middleware.

Our discussion in the next section is not about the messages sent and received under the covers by network communications software. It concerns the application-level protocols by which components send and receive messages to

---

[1]Figure 15.2 is based on the discussion in *The Essential Client/Server Survival Guide,* 2nd Ed., by Robert Orfali, Dan Harkey, and Jeri Edwards (New York, NY: John Wiley & Sons, 1996), which gives a brief overview of this subject. For a more detailed discussion, see R. J. Cypser's *Communications for Cooperating Systems* (Reading, MA: Addison-Wesley, 1991, 1992).

> ▶ Some hotels are more convenient than others; try them in order of preference.
>
> ▶ A hotel reservation is important, but it would be OK to be on a waiting list for a preferred hotel, rooms are available elsewhere as a backup.
>
> ▶ Book a restaurant, one near the hotel, for dinner on the first evening.
>
> ▶ If it turns out that no hotel rooms are available, then the whole trip must be rescheduled.
>
> ▶ The rental car is desirable, but not essential, since a limousine service is an alternative. If there are no rental cars, reserve one on a waiting list, and book a limo service.
>
> ▶ If a rental car becomes available, cancel the limo booking.
>
> A real travel agent takes into account even more complications than this—such as customer budgets, cabin class, special fares, special meals, airline preferences, seating preferences, and so on—but these are sufficient to illustrate some of the issues that arise when designing distributed applications.

other components, orchestrated by the application programmer who wrote the code. Following that, we discuss middleware, whose purpose is to hide all the details of the low-level network protocols from the application programmer.

Application-Level Protocols

A crucial step in designing distributed applications is deciding how the parts should communicate. To communicate, two programs must follow an agreed style or protocol. Suppose program A sends a message to program B and waits for a single response. Things do not work well if B sends zero or five responses or decides to send a message to program C instead of a response to A.

In the simplest client/server model, all communication is direct and synchronous. This, however, is not the only way for processes to cooperate. Several different styles of communication are possible, based on various combinations of attributes, which we discuss in the following sections:

▶ Synchronous/blocked or asynchronous/unblocked
▶ Connection-oriented or connectionless
▶ Conversational or pseudo-conversational
▶ Direct or queued
▶ Client/server and cooperative roles
▶ Partner availability and connection
▶ Number of partners

To illustrate some of the issues involved, we will use what is perhaps the classic example application of a business transaction in a distributed computing environment—the travel agent (see the accompanying capsule).

Synchronous/Blocked or Asynchronous/Unblocked.   Figure 15.3 illustrates two communication styles. When communication is **synchronous,** the initiating process sends a message (typically called a *request*) and waits for a *response* before it can continue processing. This is also referred to as **blocked** communication because the initiating process is blocked from proceeding until it gets the response. If communication is **asynchronous,** the initiating process is **unblocked**—it can continue processing after sending the request, possibly sending further messages to the same target process or to others in the meantime.

Procedure calls provide the most simple and commonly used example of a synchronous or blocked protocol. For processes running on separate machines, the same behavior is obtained by using basic *remote procedure call (RPC)* middleware to communicate. RPC processes can be unblocked if they use multiple threads to send and receive. Asynchronous or unblocked message sequences require middleware that supports a *point-to-point (P2P)* messaging model.

The travel agent typically has a synchronous communication with the airline reservation system and a concurrent asynchronous communication with the client sitting at her desk.

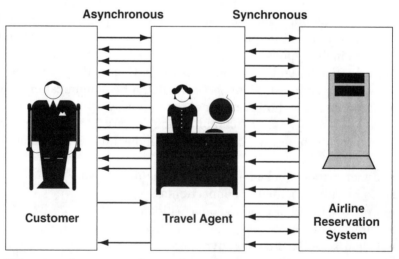

FIGURE 15.3   Synchronous and asynchronous communication.

Connection-Oriented or Connectionless.   A **connection-oriented** application protocol (shown in Figure 15.4) is one in which the two parties first *connect,* exchange messages, and then *disconnect.* The exchange of messages is often synchronous, but it can be asynchronous—for example, a client sending a request to a DBMS could receive multiple messages containing data in response. In a **connectionless** protocol, the initiator does not enter into a connection with the target process. The recipient of a message simply acts on it—and if appropriate, responds—but retains no further relationship with the requester.

The travel agent typically has a connection-oriented communication with a telephone caller, but a series of connectionless interactions with the reservation system while retrieving information about airline schedules and prices.

Note that application-level behavior does not imply anything about whether the low-level protocols are connection-oriented (that is, reliable *datastream* communications with static routing and message acknowledgments) or connectionless (that is, broadcast *datagrams* with dynamic routing and no acknowledgments). Most middleware implementations use connection-oriented protocols for their reliability, but some also support faster (but less reliable) connectionless versions.

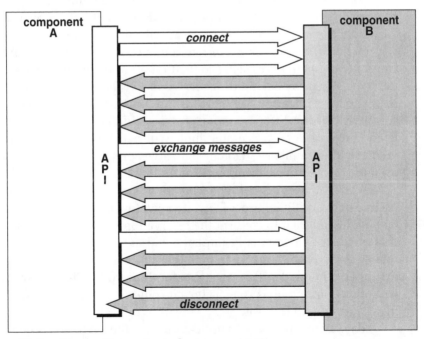

FIGURE **15.4**   Connection-oriented communication.

Conversational or Pseudo-Conversational.   A connection-oriented exchange of messages between two communicating processes is also called a **conversation.** The exchange is usually synchronous. But blocking inhibits parallel processing, so unblocked communication is supported as long as the API allows partners to send and receive data continuously.

In true conversational processing, such as the travel agent talking to the client on the telephone, the two processes remain active throughout an exchange of messages. In the synchronous case, each one waits while the other takes its turn processing, then continues where it left off when the next message arrives.

When a server handles a very large population of requesters (that is, clients), implementing true conversational processing leads to a very large number of concurrent server processes. Typically, most of these processes are actually idle, waiting for the next client message, because the client side of the application is interacting with the user and so runs for a lot longer than the server side. This ties up a lot of server memory. Managing so many concurrent processes is expensive because of the operating system overheads involved in continually scanning long lists of active processes. Most operating systems were designed for batch and time-sharing environments where a relatively high overhead per active process is not a significant problem.

About 25 years ago, the developers of large, mainframe-based transaction processing systems like CICS and IMS/TM invented a clever way to mimic conversations using connectionless protocols. Upon completion of a request/response pair, the server process terminates, instead of remaining active and waiting. But first it saves some context information, either by passing it back to the requester or by saving it on the server. When any message arrives, a new server process is started. It first reads the context information and then acts accordingly. With a little bit more programming effort, developers have simulated conversational processing, but with better performance because of the much smaller number of concurrent server processes required. This is called **pseudo-conversational** communication.

The travel agent's airline reservation system is almost certainly using pseudo-conversational processing. It may allow the agent first to look for a seat on a flight and then to confirm the reservation later if the seat is available, but these two steps are actually implemented as two separate nonconversational interactions. There is no guarantee that the seats available at the time of the first interaction will still be available for the second. This is why a travel agent will often book a seat as soon as the customer shows an interest in a particular flight, just to hold the seat.

Today, many Web-based applications use the same technique to create the illusion of conversational processing for the user. Nondisplayed HTML fields in Web pages are used to store context information, which gets sent to and fro between client and server with each "conversational" interaction.

Direct or Queued.   As we see in Figure 15.5, two styles of communication are possible.

In **direct** communication, middleware accepts the message from the initiating process and passes it directly to the target process. Synchronous processing can be combined with either direct or queued communication, but asynchronous processing typically implies some form of queued communication because it is difficult to design a process that is running but can also accept messages at any time from another process.

With a **queued** protocol, the initiating process (or *queue manager* middleware) places the message in a queue; the target process retrieves the message later at its convenience. A response, if required, flows back via a similar route. Message queuing applications are unblocked when the queue manager receives the message. This precedes the message's receipt by its target process, so using queues is essentially an unblocked style of communication.

The travel agent might need a direct connection to the process that books the airplane seat, but a queued connection to a hotel reservation system with an unpredictable response time ranging from seconds to more than an hour.

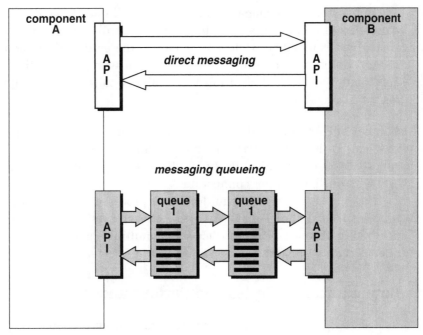

FIGURE **15.5**   Direct and queued communication.

Client/Server and Cooperative Roles.   Object and traditional application designs tend to be client/server, cooperative, or a hybrid of the two:

▶ In **client/server** (or *requester/server*), one process plays the role of the requester and the other responds.
▶ In **peer-to-peer** (or *cooperative*), either process can initiate a request; responses are not necessarily paired with requests.

The conversational style allows processes to reverse cooperative roles, while message queuing makes client/server roles reversible. The use of an RPC implies that the caller is a client and, therefore, is not inherently reversible.

Partner Availability and Connection.   Some communication styles require the processes to be available and connected; for others, this requirement is unnecessary, impractical, or undesirable. For example, the travel agent needs the airline reservation system to be available, but the procedure for making a hotel reservation can begin with a phone call to the hotel's reservation desk, regardless of whether its system is available at the time.

Conversations and RPCs generally require partner connection and availability. There are exceptions to this—RPCs using UDP/IP (User Datagram Protocol/Internet Protocol) messages are connectionless. When processes send messages to a queue, the queue management software will relay the message to its destination or hold it until the receiving partner is available for connection.

Partner availability is closely related to the earlier discussion of blocked versus unblocked communication. An event-driven server with multiple partners cannot be blocked, as it must be available to respond to requests regardless of message status.

Number of Partners.   Like the travel agent, some processes will need to communicate with multiple partners during a transaction, either simultaneously or serially. Most communication styles allow parallel requests to partners, generally with one partner per connection.

With queue management middleware, processes connect to a queue manager rather than directly to their partners. A connection to a single queue manager can give the application access to multiple queues, and each of those queues can, in turn, be read by one or more partners.

Communication Styles and Performance

Before comparing the various types of middleware available to implement communication, we point out that the way components communicate can have

A Parable of Communications

Imagine that you work in the customer service department of your regional telephone company, *American DingBell*. When customers call, you and your coworkers solve their problems. Surveys show that most customers hate interactive voice response (IVR) systems, so *DingBell* gives them direct access to a service representative. Whenever a phone rings, company policy insists that you interrupt whatever you're doing and answer it because customers don't like to wait.

You can keep abreast of the calls until, in a stunning stock market coup, *DingBell* acquires its much bigger rival, *DongBell*. During the transition, the customer billing system gets scrambled. Droves of irate *DongBell* customers call to complain. Banks of telephones ring incessantly. As soon as you pick up one phone, another rings, then another. You juggle phones frantically, inefficiently, while the callers wait, their frustrations mounting. Profits at *Ding-DongBell* drop sharply as customers switch to AT&T.

Finally, management realizes that putting callers in a queue may serve a useful purpose after all. They bring in an IVR system, which routes most callers to the *DongBell Billing* office. They hire queue jockeys to entertain the waiting callers with soothing alternative jazz. Life in customer service assumes a more orderly pace. You remark that *"All's well DingDongBell."* A passing marketing executive overhears you, and a new advertising slogan is born. Customers switch back from AT&T. Profits soar. *The end*.

The moral of this story is: *Direct access is disruptive; queuing smoothes things out.*

a significant effect on an application's performance. The capsule, *A Parable of Communications,* may be enlightening.

Any server has a limited capacity to process concurrent requests. Each concurrent request consumes some amount of the server's memory and CPU resource. If we try to drive the server to a higher level of concurrency than its memory and CPU capacity permit, instead of getting more work done, we actually get less done because the overheads of memory swapping and task or context switching take up more of the processor's resources.

If a very large population of client workstations keeps submitting requests at a rate higher than the server can handle, the system gets overloaded. Requests get backed up, and performance spirals downward at an ever-increasing rate until the users get frustrated and take a coffee break or stop working and start playing *Hunt the Wumpus* on their workstations. When some people stop using the system, performance improves for the remainder.

We discussed this phenomenon briefly in Chapter 11, in the section, *Open and Closed Systems*. If a server in an open system must respond synchronously to any client's request, then, because the number of clients is very large (in theory, unlimited), the server can be overloaded by a high rate of client requests. When server utilization nears its limit, peaks in the workload can cause very long delays in service.

Guideline 15.1	**Synchronous calls disrupt service**

If a server in an open system must respond synchronously to any client's request, when the number of clients is very large, the server can be overloaded by peaks in the rate of client requests.

Defining Middleware

Middleware is often referred to as the slash (/) in client/server. This is probably the simplest way to explain it because, according to Orfali, Harkey, and Edwards: *"Middleware is a vague term that covers all the distributed software needed to support interactions between clients and servers."*[2]

Unfortunately, although this definition matches common usage within the industry, it is too broad to be particularly useful as a framework for discussion.

Where Is the Middle in Middleware?

The problem is that the location of the middle depends on who you are. The OSI Reference Model is helpful as a starting point because everyone can agree that, as Figure 15.2 shows, layer 7 in the OSI Reference Model contains basic middleware services. Beyond that, viewpoints differ:

► From the viewpoint of a network specialist using the OSI Reference Model as a framework, everything above level 7 must be an application, by definition. This includes databases, operating systems, and every other piece of software that is not involved in the details of network communications.

► From the viewpoint of the application developer, middleware is the software that sits between distributed components and lets them communicate. The application itself, by definition, is not middleware, but everything below it is. More sophisticated IPC services are built on top of the services provided by the OSI Reference Model's layer 7, but those services are still middleware, not part of the application.

---

[2]Robert Orfali, Dan Harkey, and Jeri Edwards, *The Essential Client/Server Survival Guide* (New York, NY: John Wiley & Sons, 1996), 16.

If clients operate independently, the only way to prevent a server from becoming overloaded is to restrict the number of clients using the server—in other words, to create a closed system. We can do this by putting a queue in front of the server, buffering it from the peaks and troughs in the arrival of new requests for service.

> ### Guideline 15.2 Queuing calls minimizes wait times
>
> Using a queue to decouple requesters from a server smoothes out peaks and allows the server to process requests at its optimal pace. By eliminating the overhead of interruptions, queues maximize server performance and so minimize the time a requester must wait for service.

The way to reconcile these two views is to assume that each side knows where the middle begins. So we conclude that a reasonable working definition of middleware is: *The layers of software that let application components interact with network software.*

Notice that this definition deliberately excludes vendor-supplied application-related software like DBMSs, workflow managers, or e-mail software. It also excludes the software in communication *stacks* that implement network protocols like TCP/IP. In our view, to classify either of these as "middleware" contributes nothing to our understanding of how systems are assembled and is just as unhelpful as the network-oriented view of the world that regards everything above OSI layer 7 as an "application." Incidentally, this discussion also underscores why it is so difficult for application developers and network specialists to communicate; it may provide an alternative definition for middleware: *Middleware is the reason why network specialists and application programmers cannot communicate directly.*

> ### Guideline 15.3 The middleware muddle
>
> Middleware defies precise definition, so here are some working definitions. Middleware is. . . :
>
> ► . . . the slash (/) in client/server
> ► . . . a vague term that covers all the distributed software needed to support interactions between clients and servers
> ► . . . the layers of software that let application components interact with network software
> ► . . . the reason why network specialists and application programmers cannot communicate directly

Middleware Manages Communication

Any time we have distributed components, whether they are data or process components, there must be middleware to allow them to communicate. Middleware can supply a variety of services that support client-to-server communication, such as:

▶ **Directory services,** to assist in routing client requests to the location of their intended servers.
▶ **Security services,** to prevent unauthorized clients from connecting to a server.
▶ **Message construction,** or *marshaling*—packing the parameters of the client request into a message to send to the server—and then *unmarshaling* (unpacking) them at the receiving end.
▶ **Character set translation,** to support interoperation between client and server platform that use different character formats. (In OSI terms, this function belongs at layer 6, the presentation layer, but middleware product functions do not always follow the OSI Reference Model, especially at the upper layers.)

The basic function of middleware, however, is to enable interprocess communication by providing an application programming interface (API) that isolates the application programmer from the details of the low-level network communication formats and protocols (FAPs).

> **Guideline 15.4**   **Middleware**
> Middleware is software that enables interprocess communication. It provides an application programming interface (API) that isolates the application code from the underlying network communication formats and protocols (FAPs).

Three Classes of Middleware

Middleware can distribute an application at a variety of levels. In Chapter 2, we introduced three models for two-tier client/server communication. These were originally shown in Figure 2.4, which we now extend by adding boxes to represent the necessary middleware layers. The result is Figure 15.6, which shows the class of middleware required to implement each of the three communication models.

Since there is little agreement on an organizing framework for middleware, for simplicity, we have chosen to name the three major classes according to the three kinds of logic (*presentation, application,* and *data*) found in an enterprise information-processing application. (For reference, we originally discussed

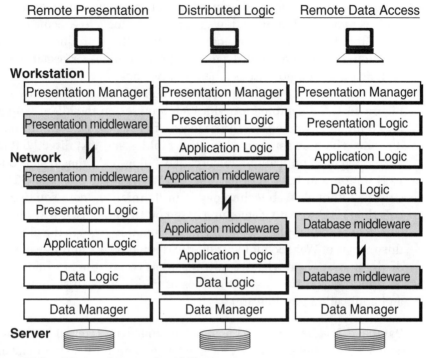

FIGURE 15.6 Three classes of middleware.

these in Chapter 2 and summarized them in Table 2.1). So our middleware classes are:

► Presentation middleware
► Application middleware (which is also called *distributed logic middleware*)
► Database middleware

For more details of middleware products in each class we recommend *The Essential Client/Server Survival Guide,* by Orfali, Harkey, and Edwards.[3]

We now review each of these classes of middleware. Because application middleware is the most important for building enterprise client/server applications (later we explain why), we deal briefly with the other two classes first. We then look at application middleware in more detail.

Distributed Presentation Middleware. Presentation logic can be split between what you see at one location and how you see it at another by using

---

[3]Orfali, Harkey, and Edwards, *The Essential Client/Server.*

screen-scrapers or terminal emulation software. Remote presentation software such as Motif/X Windows allows presentation logic to execute at a location remote from business function logic. Although these products do serve a useful function, they do not play a significant role in high-performance client/server systems, so we do not discuss them in this book.

More interesting is the growth of Web-enabled applications. As shown in Figure 16.1, the combination of a Web browser on the client workstation, the HTTP protocol, and a Web server together act as distributed presentation middleware. The browser displays static graphics and text directly. It can also invoke "helper" applications (also called "plug-ins") that reside on the client workstation and handle other object types embedded in the HTML message stream. Although Web technology is in its infancy, more sophisticated protocols than HTTP are now emerging based on DCOM or CORBA. These can move components or "applets" containing presentation logic to the client. Over time, this merger of Web technology and distributed object middleware will blur the distinction between what we now regard as two distinct technologies (the Web and objects) and two distinct classes of middleware (distributed presentation and application middleware).

Database Middleware.   Almost all of the departmental or two-tier client/server applications currently in existence were built using database middleware. This style of application is also known as a *fat client* because most of the application logic resides on the workstation. Only the DBMS is on the server.

Fat client applications issue SQL requests to a relational DBMS such as DB2, Informix, Oracle, SQL Server, or Sybase. These SQL requests are handled by proprietary *database middleware* supplied by the DBMS vendor. The middleware ships the SQL requests over the network to the DBMS and later returns data in the other direction to the application. For an example of this, see Figure 3.2 and the section *A Response Time Example* in Chapter 3.

The other most common examples of database middleware are database gateways, typically supporting an ODBC API, that provide remote database access.

Application Middleware

In the following sections we discuss five types of application middleware, giving examples of products of each type. In approximate order of relative complexity, they are:

▶ Point-to-point, or direct messaging middleware (P2P).
▶ Remote procedure call (RPC).

▶ Message queuing middleware (MQM). The combination of direct messaging (P2P) and queued messaging (MQ) is called Message-Oriented Middleware, or MOM.

▶ Object request broker (ORB).

▶ Distributed transaction monitor (DTM).

Application middleware differs from database and presentation middleware in a very significant way. Database or presentation middleware supports communication between a user-written application component on one side and a software vendor-supplied component on the other. In that situation, the user has very little design flexibility because the software vendor (or an industry standard like SQL) has already defined most of the rules—the formats and protocols—for the communication.

Application middleware, in contrast, is much more like a general-purpose programming language. Its purpose is to let two user-written components communicate in any way that suits the application designer and developer. The choice of the desired *communication style* is the key application design decision.

Application Middleware APIs.   Of the many styles of communication used by processes, the three most popular are conversations, remote procedure calls, and object messages. These styles are implemented as interface standards such as CPI-C, the OSF/DCE RPC, and CORBA, respectively. Message queuing introduces an additional style and uses its own API, such as IBM's Message Queuing Interface (MQI).

All the communication possibilities offered by a particular middleware product can be used in any way that makes sense to the developer. But obviously, each product has its own limits; we can't invoke an object method with an RPC or coordinate distributed two-phase commits with message queuing middleware (or maybe we can, but it would be an unnatural act that would take a lot of ingenuity to make it work). The desired style usually implies a particular API, and after that, it is difficult to rewrite an application to use a different API.

Application Middleware Interoperates.   Application middleware not only connects distributed processes but also can interconnect different types of middleware. In the first example in Figure 15.7, one application is issuing RPC calls, which are transmitted by underlying P2P software such as PeerLogic's PIPES. In the next example, MQ software such as IBM's MQSeries is using RPC services to transmit a queued message. The last example shows how an MQ queue manager sends a message with underlying P2P software, for example, MQSeries using PIPES as a transmission medium.

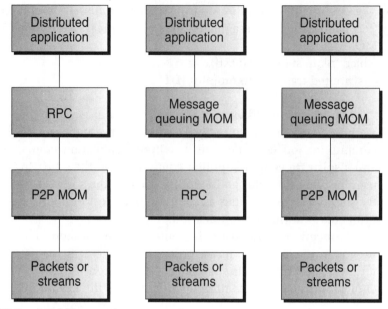

FIGURE 15.7   Middleware interoperation.

This kind of interfacing is possible because the different types have many similarities. Although products are not necessarily implemented in this way, it may be helpful to think of the various types of application middleware as successively more powerful layers of software, each of which incorporates and builds on the functions offered by the layer(s) below, as shown in Figure 15.8. Some object request brokers (ORBs) are actually built using RPC communications but provide a much higher level of function. Distributed transaction monitors interoperate with all the other classes of middleware to support the concept of distributed transactions—that is, transactions that involve interrelated updates to a collection of distributed resources. There is also considerable convergence—both MQ and ORB middleware increasingly are acquiring features formerly found only in distributed transaction monitors (DTMs).

Point-to-Point Messaging (P2P)

P2P middleware relays a message between two or more partners that are connected and available. In other words, P2P middleware supports *direct communication,* as shown in the upper part of Figure 15.5. Communication can be either synchronous or asynchronous. Synchronous communication is blocked and conversational, while asynchronous communication is unblocked.

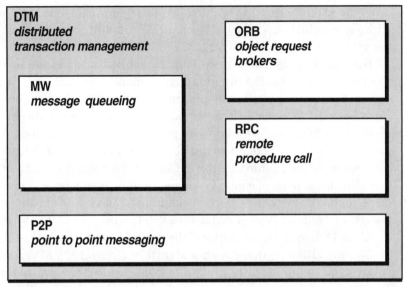

FIGURE **15.8**   Five types of application middleware.

Note that P2P is not identical to *peer-to-peer* communication. Although it supports a peer-to-peer model for communicating processes, P2P technology places no restriction on the logical roles of the processes within an application. It can be used to build a wide variety of distributed applications, in which components may perform the roles of clients, servers, or cooperating peers, as needed.

Obviously, many more sophisticated protocols can be built using P2P as a building block. The most popular example of P2P middleware is PeerLogic's PIPES. But like programming in a low-level language, building applications using P2P alone is complex.

Remote Procedure Calls (RPC)

A remote procedure call, or RPC, is a mechanism that lets a program call a procedure located on a remote computer in the same fashion as a local one within the same program. One of the purported advantages of RPCs is that programmers are used to coding procedure calls, so they don't need to learn anything particularly new.

Actually, coding an RPC is different because a remote procedure does not share the calling program's dispatchable unit. As a result, the parameter-passing options are restricted, and the two procedures cannot share any resources other than the parameter list passed with the call. To mask these differences (and allow procedures to move between local and remote status without recoding the caller), a "local RPC" function gives local procedure calls the syntax and semantics of an RPC!

But appearances can be deceiving. No matter how similar an RPC may look to a procedure call to the programmer, it actually invokes a new process on the server. Figure 15.9 shows an outline of what actually happens and reveals some key performance differences between a local procedure call and an RPC.

First, an RPC involves a lot more processing. Calling the client stub is a local procedure call, but to complete the RPC many more exchanges have to take place between modules. In *Introduction to Client/Server Systems,* Renaud lists 24 steps including three pairs of context switches on the client (either side of the *send, receive,* and *acknowledge response* operations), plus a pair of context switches for the server process. Typical estimates of RPC cost are "10,000 to 15,000 instructions" and "several hundred times" the cost of a local procedure call.[4]

Second, although these are not shown in Figure 15.9, RPC software also involves requests to *security* servers to control the access to remote programs. These requests, although important, do add to the cost of an RPC. Some implementations use *dynamic binding* of the client to the server, meaning that the client RPC runtime software must first query a directory or *naming* service on the network to determine the address of the server for this particular type of service. This also adds to response time.

Third, RPC technology is synchronous. For communication to occur successfully, both the local and remote programs must be bound to the RPC, and both components must remain available.

Synchronous communication between client and server works well for small LAN-based workloads. It is not as good when we want to scale up to larger systems that must support hundreds or thousands of clients, for the reasons we discussed earlier (see Guideline 15.1, *Synchronous calls disrupt service*). To recap, the problems are these:

▶ The server is driven by the demands of the requester, and the requester must wait for the server to respond.
▶ The number of concurrent requests for service depends only on the overall behavior of the client population.
▶ Peaks in the arrival distribution of requests can overwhelm the server.

This is not the ideal arrangement for achieving high performance—things run a lot more smoothly when separate components are each allowed to work at their own optimal pace.

---

[4]Paul Renaud, *Introduction to Client/Server Systems* (New York, NY: John Wiley & Sons, 1993), 186.

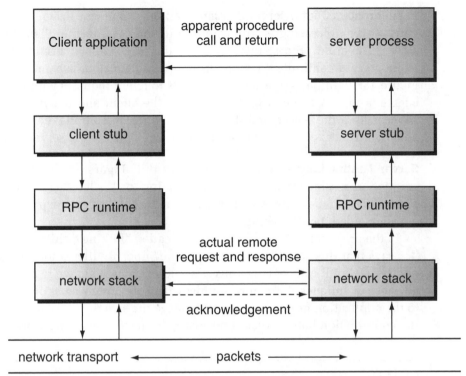

FIGURE **15.9**   RPC implementation.

Guideline 15.5   **Synchronous RPCs do not scale well**

For a LAN-based server, RPCs are fine. But when we need to support hundreds or thousands of clients, basic RPCs are not an appropriate, scalable solution.

Extending RPC

Of course, the RPC mechanism is just software, and, as my colleague Valdo Andosciani often said, "You can do anything with software. . . ." Software can always be extended with more software. Using the simple synchronous RPC as a building block, programmers can create asynchronous client/server communication mechanisms with multithreading and load balancing on the server. Here are some examples based on John Bloomer's discussion of these techniques in his book, *Power Programming with RPC*.[5]

[5]John Bloomer, *Power Programming with RPC* (Sebastapol, CA: O'Reilly and Associates, 1992), Chapter 9, 235–282.

Asynchronous Client/Server Communication.   One way to achieve asynchronous server processing is to create a child process on the client to call the server. The child process then waits for the response synchronously, but the main process continues. A second, more sophisticated, scheme is shown in Figure 15.10. Initially, the server responds to client requests with an acknowledgment only. A daemon process runs on the client and receives the real responses from the server, and the client's main process polls the daemon periodically to check whether the results have arrived from the server yet.

Server Multitasking.   Building on top of this, Figure 15.11 illustrates how parallel-processing mechanisms incorporating load balancing can be built on top of RPC middleware. A master task can accept a client request and start a new dependent task to handle it.

In the programmer's vernacular, this is called "forking a child task." Our editor says that this sounds really nasty—and probably illegal too. Actually, it's not illegal, but it can be dangerous if we don't know what we're doing because all these techniques do require sophisticated programming skills. In addition to the application function, we must manage the scheduling of child tasks and the coordination between tasks necessary to make everything work. We must

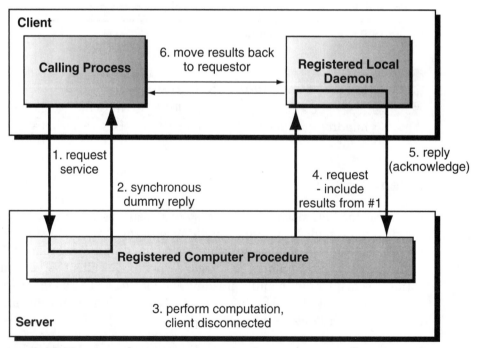

FIGURE 15.10   Asynchronous communications using two client processes.

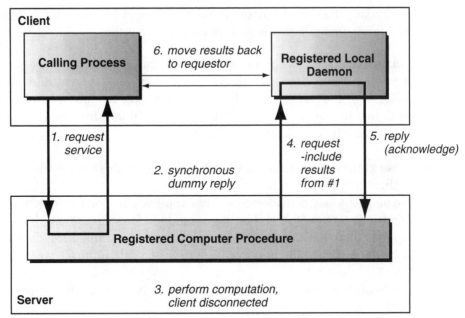

FIGURE 15.11   Server multitasking with RPCs.

also consider the appropriate degree of parallelism for the machine that is running the server process.

Among the performance-related issues that we would need to consider are:

▶ What happens if the processor is replaced by a bigger one? Ideally, the level of multithreading should adjust automatically; otherwise, the faster server may not be used fully.
▶ What other work is running on the same server? If many applications share the same server, middleware really ought to be concerned with the degree of parallelism across *all* applications, not just within a single application.

There are issues in other areas too, including what to do when either a client or a child subtask fails.

Server Multithreading.   A multitasking solution incurs a lot of operating system overhead to start tasks and switch among them. To avoid the overhead of creating new processes at run time, we can create a pool of server processes at server initialization time. Then the parent server process acts as a dispatcher, receiving requests from clients and issuing a second local RPC to one of the child processes. Another alternative is to code a multithreaded server, using lightweight threads instead of operating-system-managed processes. As we concluded when we discussed multithreading in Chapter 13 *(see Manual Parallel Programming)*, this is even more tricky to write.

Conclusions.   At this point, it seems only fair to Valdo, who we quoted at the beginning of this discussion of RPC-based extensions, to remind you of the second half of his advice: "But just because it *can* be done doesn't necessarily mean that it *should* be done." With this thought in mind, the inescapable conclusions are that, in this case, Valdo is right:

▶ These kinds of system-oriented concerns lie outside the domain of the typical application programmer.
▶ Anyone seriously considering writing application code to create significant extensions on top of RPC should instead look for standard middleware that supplies those extensions. Using more powerful, standard middleware will make the extended features available for use by all applications.

This is the type of function the next two types of middleware—MOM and DTM—provide.

Message-Oriented Middleware (MOM)

Max Dolgicer of the International Systems Group defines MOM as: "A layer of software which supports multiple communication protocols, programming languages, and execution platforms. It resides between business applications and the network infrastructure."[6]

Message-oriented middleware (MOM) is a relatively new distributed computing technology. MOM is commercial messaging middleware that supports application-to-application communication using a high-level messaging API. It allows one application to send a message to another application, at any location, and for any purpose. Messages may contain data, control information, or both.

The messaging model may be direct (P2P) or queued (MQ), as shown earlier in Figure 15.6. Since we have already discussed P2P messaging, we now focus on message queuing, which is by far the most important class of MOM. The most well-established MQ product is IBM's *MQSeries*.

Message Queuing

MQ middleware supports both asynchronous and synchronous dialogs. An application using MQ writes to a queue rather than directly to a process (see Figure 15.5). In a dialog between two programs, each program has its own associ-

---

[6]Max Dolgicer, International Systems Group, Inc. (mdolgicer@isg-inc.com).

ated queue, and they communicate with each other by leaving a *message* on the message queue of the other. The queue manager middleware takes care of moving messages between the queues.

Because each process reads from and writes to a queue, rather than connecting directly to its partner, the processes can run independently, at different speeds and times, with or without a logical connection. The remote program does not even have to be available.

Unlike an RPC-based solution, participating programs do not have to be precompiled or bound to each other. As a result, new components can be added to a system dynamically.

Like most middleware, MQ software compensates for environmental differences. The MQ middleware supports the same high-level API on every platform it runs on, thereby reducing development costs and allowing applications running in different environments to communicate easily. MOM can be used to provide location transparency, tier separation, scalability, independence, and support for event-driven applications. MQ middleware can be used to integrate new applications with legacy systems.

The Queue Manager. The queue manager stores and manages queues. It must support operations that will create queues, destroy them, and change their attributes, such as their size or who is permitted to use them. The queue manager must be able to start and stop a queue. It is often in control of flexible routing of messages to remote queues. The queue manager must be able to provide information about the state of elements in the queue.

The resemblance of a queue manager to a database manager is striking. In fact, it has led many to suggest that the queue be placed in a database. This strategy would make use of the sophisticated transaction mechanisms of the DBMS to ensure durability and consistency of the queue. Some vendors do use this approach (for example, New Era of Networks, or NEON), but using the DBMS can incur significant locking overhead due to the numerous write operations required to implement it (recall our earlier discussion of locking and *hot spots* in Chapter 12).

Performance Benefits of MQ Middleware. Compared to synchronous methods, MQ middleware has several advantages:

▶ Because it allows programs to operate asynchronously, each communicating program can proceed at its own optimal pace. The requesting program can *leave* a message on a queue and get on with other things.

▶ If appropriate, a program can leave messages on the queues of many servers' programs, and they can all carry out the request when they are active and ready to do so. Hence, a calling program can activate many called programs that run on different nodes, all of which run in parallel.

▶ In the case of a temporary peak, a queue of requests can build up without the server being overwhelmed. The server can pull the messages off the queue at its own optimal rate. There can even be multiple servers for the same queue, if necessary.

Later in this chapter, we discuss transaction management with MQ middleware.

Other Messaging Facilities

Note that MQ is not the same as special-purpose *e-mail* or *workflow* software. MOM is basic software componentry that can be used to build systems. As such, it should not be confused with electronic mail or automated workflow products, which are software products that include messaging capabilities to support a particular business application.

MOM technology is also distinct from Electronic Data Interchange (EDI), a widely used standard for transferring information between companies. EDI standards define how messages are to be formatted, transmitted, and handled so that information can be exchanged between discrepant systems. Because the U.S. government mandated its use by 1997, EDI is becoming widely used for electronic commerce. Documents and business forms formatted according to EDI standards can be transmitted using MOM technology or other client/server middleware.

Guideline 15.6	**MOM smoothes server operations**

MOM allows communicating programs to operate asynchronously, so that each can proceed at its own optimal pace. During a temporary peak, a queue of service requests can build up without the server's being overwhelmed. A server can pull the messages off the queue at its own optimal rate. There can even be multiple servers for the same queue, if necessary.

Guideline 15.7	**Message queuing can speed up client response**

When unblocked communications are used in a message queuing environment, client response time is not affected by server processing delays. The transmitting (client) program is freed from waiting as soon as the messaging queuing system receives the message.

The Publish/Subscribe Messaging Model. The publish/subscribe model is a totally asynchronous messaging model in which the sender of information (that is, the publisher) does not need to have any knowledge at all about the

MOM and EDI Online

The Message-Oriented Middleware Association (MOMA) site at www.moma -inc.org/ provides a list of MOMA member companies, their URLs, and the messaging products they provide.

The Data Interchange Standards Associations (DISA) site at www.disa .org/provides a wealth of information about EDI. David Robert Lambert's site at pages.prodigy.com/edibooks/ lists books on EDI and has other useful links.

message recipient (that is, the subscriber), other than his or her address. The subscriber is anonymous.

This model allows almost complete independence of the participating processes. Subscribers establish *profiles,* which filter the published information based upon its content at the time of publication. Publishers then simply broadcast messages to "anonymous" subscribers, based upon their profiles.

Because the publisher does not have to modify its processes as new subscribers are registered, the publish/subscribe model is highly scalable and can be used in a wide variety of contexts. New Era of Networks' *NEONet* (www. neonsoft.com) and Active Sofware's *ActiveWeb* (www.activesw.com) are examples of message middleware products that implement a publish/subscribe model. Data warehousing products such as *deliveryAGENT* by VIT and *Tapestry* by D2K use the publish/subscribe model to let warehouse users control the information they receive, its format, and its delivery schedule.

Processing Transactions

In our review of the classes of application middleware shown in Figure 15.9, we now move beyond simple messaging to more complex requirements, one of the most important of which is support for *transactions.* To appreciate what this involves, we must first understand how computers handle business transactions.

To illustrate interprocess communication styles, we have been using an example of a business transaction—making a set of reservations for a business itinerary. As the travel agent completes each reservation, a record is created somewhere. This is part of what makes it a *transaction*—unlike a simple inquiry, every transaction involves a change in the state of some recorded information.

Life is a series of recorded transactions. An item is posted to a bank account, a name is added to a list, a hotel reservation is created, an order is placed, priced, fulfilled, shipped, invoiced. In every case, information is recorded. If the enterprise is using a computer, an information system must update a file or database somewhere.

Indeed, it is crucial that the information *is* recorded and is recorded *correctly.* In many situations today, the computer has the only record of the transaction. You may recall the philosophical question about the tree falling in the forest: *If no one is there to hear it fall, does it make any sound?* The operation of many business systems today poses a similar question: *If there is no computer record, did the transaction actually occur?* Often the answer is no:

▶ If the ticket agency loses your concert reservation, then you do not have a reservation and there will be little good in complaining after all the tickets are sold.

▶ If the bank loses the record of your cash deposit, you did not make one, and your account will not be credited. Unless you spot the error, the transaction never occurred.

Of course, there is usually a manual process for correcting errors—if you take your dated and stamped deposit slip back to the bank, they do have a way to credit you the cash. But in a very real sense, the assets recorded in a bank's information systems are the only assets the bank owns.

To sum up, the success of a business transaction depends on the computer system correctly *recording* the transaction. That means that business systems must have what are collectively referred to as "the ACID properties."

Transactions: The ACID Test

In a computer system, a transaction is a collection of processing steps that has four properties:

▶ Transactions are **atomic.** Any changes to the state of the persistent information maintained by the system (for example, the data in files or databases) are made completely or not at all.

▶ Transactions are **consistent.** The database is maintained in a consistent state.

▶ Transactions are **isolated.** Even though other transactions may be processing concurrently, any changes happen as if the transaction were serialized with all other transactions.

▶ Transactions are **durable.** Any changes, once made, are permanent and are not affected by subsequent failures.

Commercial transaction processing (which we discuss in more detail in Chapter 22, *Transaction Managers and Transaction Monitors*) is about observing these "ACID properties" to ensure that each business transaction is processed once and once only, accurately and appropriately.

The Challenge of Distributed Transactions

Now consider what happens as we distribute the processing. Let's begin with some assumptions about distributed systems:

▶ A distributed transaction system can involve two or more workstations, running under DOS, Windows, UNIX, or MacOS, two or more mainframes, or any combination in between, from PCs to minis to servers to hosts.
▶ Those systems have components that sometimes act as peers, clients, and servers, with roles changing according to circumstances.
▶ Those components may well have been developed at different times by different developers.
▶ A business transaction initiated in this environment should either complete or fail in a dependable manner, as appropriate, to satisfy the business situation.

Now take the travel agent example—the travel agent is the coordinator of a *distributed transaction,* a transaction that itself is composed of several smaller transactions involving distributed resources (in this case, the various service providers).

Suppose we want to automate the travel agent's service. You may be tempted to argue that this is not feasible with centralized or distributed processing because of the amount of human judgment needed to do the job. We would tend to agree but ask you to set that issue aside for the moment:

▶ Assume that, based on our long experience as business travelers, we have already created an expert system that captures the travel agent's knowledge and decision-making processes. (Incidentally, we did all the design while our plane was waiting in line for takeoff at DFW airport.)
▶ Assume, too, that all the service providers (airlines, hotels, rental cars, restaurants) have online reservation systems, but their response times are extremely variable. Some, like the airlines' systems, have short response times and are reliable. Many are Web-based and have a tendency to fail altogether at peak periods, losing all trace of the requests currently being processed.

The challenge is to design a system that will handle the travel agent's transaction correctly under all possible conditions. Most importantly, after any failure, we should not be left with any partial itineraries, any itineraries in which we are double-booked, or any itineraries in which we fly to New York only to find that there are no hotel rooms available because of a major international conference on *Distributed Transaction Processing.*

Misplaced Optimism

Naive client/server developers operate under the optimistic assumption that all transactions will complete and that, if they do not, rollback and/or recovery will "just happen." If an application fails, then "the system" (or someone with systems responsibility) will restore things correctly from backups. Such optimism may seem fine when an application is working well, but it is unacceptable in most business situations.

Some degree of faith in the systems software was justified in the past on small departmental systems. Support for transaction processing was embedded in operating systems like OS/400, VMS, or MPE/ix. Users had terminals that handled only presentation logic, and the operating system had complete control over the transaction. UNIX, for example, does not possess similar transaction integrity facilities. The DBMS vendors (Oracle, IBM, Sybase, Informix, et al.) have had to build extensive support for transactions into their databases to provide degrees of transaction integrity under UNIX.

RPCs and Transactions.   Earlier we discussed RPC middleware. The *basic* RPC mechanisms do not support transaction semantics. Some *implementations* of RPC, however, do support *transactional RPCs.* For example, BEA's TUXEDO has a function called TxRPC that implements the X/Open standard of the same name for transactional RPCs. It is based on the standard DCE RPC but extended to support transactions. In the language of distributed transactions, the program called by a TxRPC becomes *infected* by the caller's transaction. But for this to work, the programs must already be running in an environment managed by a distributed transaction manager like TUXEDO, which means we are not simply using a basic RPC mechanism to communicate between processes. We discuss transaction managers (and X/Open) a bit later; here we are considering the properties of basic RPCs only.

Microsoft's Distributed Transaction Coordinator.   Microsoft is evolving a Distributed Transaction Coordinator (DTC), code named *Viper,* for its Windows platforms. The first stage appears in SQL Server 6.5 and supports distributed SQL Server transactions (see *Relational Database Transaction Processing: TP-Lite,* a bit later). Ultimately, Microsoft could extend *Viper* to support enterprise-wide transactions on heterogeneous platforms. Microsoft's major technological thrust in this area, embodied in its Component Object Model (COM) and its distributed counterpart (DCOM), is to let developers assemble applications from software components that have been separately developed by different vendors at different times.[7]

Microsoft's goal of support for heterogeneous transactions is not available in today's client/server environment. In the meantime, any developer optimism stems not from technological knowledge but from ignorance of the issues. In an enterprise client/server environment, any such optimism is misplaced. Today, once we move application logic off the central processor to intelligent workstations or distributed servers, applications will not guarantee transaction integrity unless we take the necessary development steps to ensure it.

> ### Guideline 15.8 Don't assume that everything will work properly
>
> In an enterprise client/server environment, optimism is misplaced. Many different kinds of failures can and will occur. Unless these are planned for, systems may well process business transactions incorrectly.

Relational Database Transaction Processing: TP-Lite

Client/server database servers support certain kinds of transaction processing by incorporating a limited form of transaction support in the DBMS. Single remote SQL requests can be processed, with each request being treated as a transaction, as illustrated on the left side of Figure 15.12. Or requests can be packaged into database procedures, and the entire procedure then treated as a transaction.

This approach is called *TP-Lite,* to distinguish it from full-scale transaction monitor products that we'll discuss later. Using a DBMS that can manage its own transactions is an attractive way to solve the problems of transaction processing, but it works only for simple transactions. There is a long list of actions that a program might take that are not treated as part of the commit scope of the typical TP-Lite transaction. For example, if a stored procedure invokes a second procedure, they are treated as two separate transactions. The first can fail while the second succeeds, violating atomicity. TP-Lite also is not designed to cope with transaction requirements like those shown on the right side of Figure 15.12, in which a single transaction involves multiple SQL requests and procedures at multiple sites.

---

[7]If and when Microsoft's DTC capability becomes a reality, it may well be supplied as part of a DCOM-compliant Object Request Broker. Charles Brett, "Microsoft Steps Up to Transactions," *InfoDB* 10(5) (February 1997).

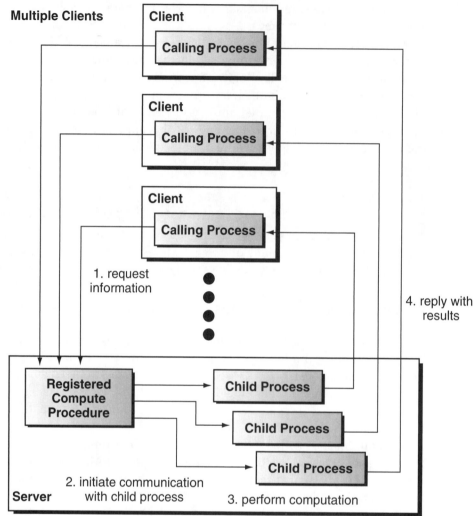

FIGURE 15.12   TP-Lite versus TP-Heavy.

TP-Lite cannot deal with the following:

▶ Distributed or federated databases that link data in multiple DBMSs, at multiple sites
▶ Applications using multiple, different relational DBMS products or multiple data manager types (relational, hierarchic, flat file, and so on)
▶ Multiple applications with different presentation managers (3270, GUI) accessing same database

Distributed Databases. The transactional support within DBMS products keeps improving, and some DBMSs have ways to handle homogeneous distributed transactions—transactions that touch multiple copies of the product at different locations.

In multiplatform distributed database systems, also known as *federated databases,* support for transactions is sparse and largely untested. The official standard, ISO Remote Data Access (RDA), is as good as dead because the SQL database vendors are not implementing it. Only Microsoft and IBM appear to be developing products that consider the problems of using federated databases and envision coordinating and recovering updates dependably.

For example, Microsoft's SQL Server 6.5 provides (for Windows 95 and NT developers) the ability for client programs to initiate transactions across multiple SQL Server databases, irrespective of whether they are local or geographically dispersed.

Microsoft's declared intention is to extend the current DTC component of SQL Server 6.5 to support heterogeneous systems. It remains to be seen how other DBMS vendors will interface with DTC and how quickly this will happen. Also, although DTC is currently part of the SQL Server DBMS, the heterogeneous version of the future will probably be closer to a transaction monitor, which we discuss in the next section.

IBM's solution has been around longer. The Distributed Relational Database Architecture (DRDA) is IBM's protocol for exchanging SQL among its DB2 family of relational DBMSs and the de facto standard for interconnecting heterogeneous SQL database systems. A few years ago, many people in the database community expected that widespread adoption of DRDA would lighten the application developers' load by supporting distributed multidatabase transactions. DRDA has made some progress in this direction—the standard has been licensed by many database and gateway vendors, some of whom have incorporated DRDA support into their products.[8] But despite some successes, DRDA is not in widespread use (compared, for example, to other middleware standards, like CORBA, that we discuss later).

The Real Problem with Distributed Databases. Heterogeneous distributed SQL applications are not widely used because they suffer from two inherent problems: heterogeneity and distribution.

---

[8]On their Web site at *www.software.ibm.com,* IBM lists companies that have announced support for DRDA in their products. At the time of writing, these include Attachmate Corp., File Tek. Inc, GrandView DB/DC Systems, Informix Software Inc., Object Technology International, Oracle Corp., Rocket Software Inc., StarQuest Software Inc., Sybase/MDI, Wall Data Inc., and XDB Systems Inc.

The X/Open Transaction Model

The open systems consortium X/Open—now part of *The Open Group*[9]— has defined a *Distributed Transaction Processing Reference Model.* The 1994 version specifies four essential components of a distributed transaction (see Figure 15.13):

▶ *Application program,* which defines transaction actions and boundaries between transactions
▶ *Resource managers,* including databases and file access that provide access to shared resources
▶ *Transaction manager,* responsible for identifying individual transactions and controlling transaction completion and recovery from failure
▶ *Communication manager,* responsible for managing communications processes

X/Open also specifies operations that must be observed by both transaction managers and resource managers if they are going to participate in the distributed transaction environment. Examples include:

▶ **xa_start.** Informs a resource manager that a transaction will be started by a specific application

▶ **xa_commit.** commits work for a specific transaction

---

[9]The Open Group—an industry consortium dedicated to the advancement of multivendor information systems—was formed in 1996 by the merger of the two leading open systems consortia, X/Open and The Open Software Foundation (OSF). The Open Group's Web site is at *opengroup.org;* for X/Open, see *xoweb.xopen.org.*

▶ **Heterogeneity.** In 1995, David Stodder commented that "DRDA works great if everybody complies with the server's SQL syntax and semantics. But in a heterogeneous world, IS organizations might have to wait a long time for that compliance."[10] This observation sums up the problem of interoperation at the level of the SQL API—every DBMS vendor implements a different set of SQL extensions, to distinguish itself from its competition. To use DRDA successfully, an application must either stick to the lowest common SQL denominator or use only the SQL dialect that the server will accept—in which case, DRDA allows interconnection but not interoperability.

---

[10]David Stodder, *Database Programming & Design* (October 1995).

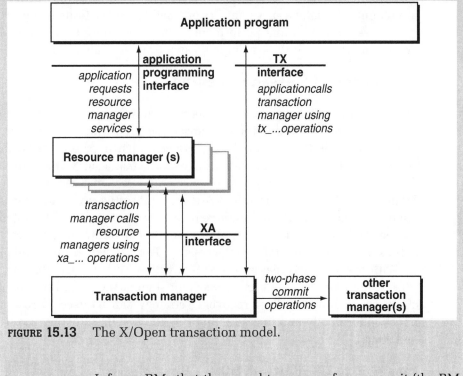

FIGURE 15.13 The X/Open transaction model.

▶ **xa_prepare.** Informs RMs that they need to prepare for a commit (the RM places the work in a "hardened" state in preparation for the commit)

▶ **xa_rollback.** Rolls back work for a specific transaction

Each transaction monitor will define a set of verbs and variables to implement the standard. These coordinate with the values the RM expects.

▶ **Distribution.** The second problem with DRDA is that it binds the separate DBMSs together through its use of the two-phase commit protocol. As we noted in Chapter 12 on database locking, two-phase commit is a perfectly sound logical solution to the problem of committing the actions of multiple resource managers, but it simply does not work well in practice.

The problem is not with the protocol itself, although the four rounds of communication required between the participants do introduce some additional delays. The main problems are caused by repeatedly imposing synchronization points on supposedly independent systems.

The result is that when any one of the participants is delayed for any reason (but typically related to locking), the delay gets propagated into the other participating DBMSs. Almost inevitably, as workload volumes grow across the interconnected database systems, coordinating transactions using distributed two-phase commit limits performance more and more by making all useful processing stop until the participants synchronize their databases.

Transactional Message Queuing

MQ software is designed to move messages and may not have all the features needed to support the distributed transaction-processing requirements we described earlier in the chapter. It can, however, participate in transactions, depending on its ability to function as a resource manager. X/Open, for instance, defines *queues* as XA-compliant resource managers that can be managed by a TP monitor. Queues managed by XA-compliant software can also participate in a syncpoint across multiple resource managers (for example, file systems, database systems, and other queues). For more details on X/Open and XA-compliant resource managers, refer to the capsule *The X/Open Transaction Model.*

With transactional message queuing, if there is a failure, the entire enterprise cannot be recovered to a consistent state at the same time (that is, synchronously). But a "rolling recovery" strategy can be used to recover failed nodes individually and to gradually bring the system into a uniformly consistent state.

From ACID to TRI-ACID with MOM.   We now describe how message-queuing middleware can use secure queues to move messages between components.

In the example shown in Figure 15.14, Application A sends a message to Application B. This is treated as three transactions:

▶ **TX1.** Application A puts a message onto Queue 1 indicating a destination of Queue 2.

▶ **TX2.** The queue manager moves the message from Queue 1 to Queue 2.

▶ **TX3.** Application 2 gets the message from Queue 2.

Because each of these stages is a separate secured transaction, it is recoverable in the case of a failure. Therefore, once Queue 1 accepts the message from Application A, TX1 is complete, and Application A can terminate or move on to other processing because the queue manager is guaranteed to perform TX2. Application A does not need to know anything about how and when Application B will get the message, or even anything about the existence of Application B. Conversely, Application B can be ignorant of Application A.

Because it implements the ACID properties in three separate steps, this approach is sometimes called a *Tri-ACID* implementation of messaging.

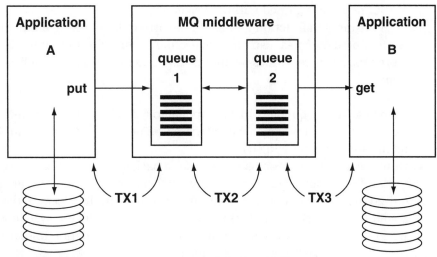

FIGURE 15.14   Tri-ACID messaging with MQ middleware.

Methods of enforcing transaction integrity based on this technique are key to the process of distributed application design. We use them whenever we design a multiphase distributed application. For example, to complete a full requester/server interaction, as many as five separate transactions may be required:

▶ The client writes a request to its own output queue.
▶ The queue manager moves the request from the client's output queue to the server's input queue.
▶ The server dequeues the request, performs the required service, and places the response on its output queue.
▶ The queue manager moves the result from the server output queue to the client input queue.
▶ The client dequeues the response from its input queue.

The Performance Implications of Using MQ Middleware

Transactional messaging offers three major performance advantages:

1. Clients do not wait for servers—they may initiate transactions even when servers are not available by placing a transaction on a queue.
2. Servers do not wait for clients—they may provide output to transactional requests even when the client is not available.
3. Having all servers take requests from a single "first-come, first-served" queue helps in load balancing.

But nothing is gained without price.

A business transaction that could be carried out in a single unit of work if it were implemented as a single synchronous computer transaction may require more processing resources when it is implemented as a message-based application:

▶ Each change to a queue is like an update to a database that demands the same transactional guarantees that a database update would demand and, therefore, incurs similar processing costs.

▶ However, all of this processing is done in background. A client does not have to wait for the subsequent transactions to complete. Participants are not required to hold resources and wait during conversations. Because the shared resources, the servers, are taking requests from a queue, the system will scale well to fluctuations in transaction load. The main limitation to scaling is the server capacity to process transactions.

Of course, there is no magic here—transactional messaging is not immune to performance degradation. Background transaction service rates are still subject to resource bottlenecks, even if these may not be apparent to the client. If one machine cannot service its requests at the same rate as other servers, eventually it will impact the overall throughput of the system. Reasons for a bottleneck might be:

▶ A server running on a slower machine
▶ A long-running process dominating the server's resources
▶ Resource locking on the server
▶ Scheduling priorities that determine how the server processes requests on the queues

When long queues build up for a slow server, a faster machine must be substituted, or some work must be shifted to other, more efficient servers. The advantage of an asynchronous MQ-based application design is that neither the existence of the server bottleneck nor the tuning actions need affect the client application.

The Design Implications of Using MQ Middleware

In Chapter 2, when we discussed enterprise client/server systems, we pointed out that the conceptual architecture of a three-tier system involved an *application logic* layer that decomposes *global transactions* into *local transactions* and directs each local transaction to the correct node.

A MOM application works this way. It decomposes a complex *global* transaction involving update activities at several nodes in a distributed system into several smaller *local* transactions. System software can still be used to guarantee the integrity of the local transactions, and the MQ software guarantees all message deliveries between the local transactions. But if any local transaction fails, no system software will back out all the previous local transactions within the global transaction. Therefore, the application must make sure that the global transaction follows the *ACID* properties.

This complicates application design because we must design compensating transactions to take care of a variety of recovery scenarios. However, the design work involved in dividing a global transaction into local transactions and identifying compensating transactions is no more difficult than designing a complete manual system to handle the same transaction, provided that we approach application design in the right way from the start.

We return to this subject in our discussion of *decoupled processes* in Chapter 16, *Architecture for High Performance.*

Distributed Object Technology

Up to now, our discussion of application middleware has focused on how distributed *programs* can communicate; we now explain how to make the right connections among *distributed objects.* This field is so broad that we cannot hope to summarize it in a few paragraphs. It is also the latest "hot" technology. Practically every week in the trade press someone writes about this year being (finally) "the year of distributed objects." Only a recluse, or someone recently returned from an extended *walkabout* in the Australian outback, can be altogether ignorant of the subject. So to keep things short, we will simply give some definitions, briefly list some performance concerns, and suggest some recommended reading.

Distributed Object Definitions

First, to really understand *distributed* objects you must know what an *object* is. Mercifully, there are already enough good tutorials on object orientation available that we don't need to write another one. We'll just recite the mantra "encapsulation, polymorphism, inheritance" once, and move on. When objects are distributed, we need middleware to connect them. Just as RPC middleware or an MQ manager acts as a message broker for *programs,* an **object request broker (ORB)** is middleware that enables communication among *objects* in a distributed environment.

The **Object Management Group (OMG)** is a consortium of object technology vendors founded in 1989,[11] and charged with specifying a set of common interfaces to permit interoperation between different vendors' object oriented software. The OMG has created the **Common Object Request Broker Architecture (CORBA),** which, as its name suggests, specifies a standard *architecture* (not an implementation) for *object request brokers.* Any ORB that adheres to this specification is said to be *CORBA-compliant.* Using CORBA-compliant ORBs, objects can invoke each other's services transparently, independent of OO languages, tools, platforms, and locations.

Some Performance Concerns

We illustrated the conceptual relationship among the various classes of middleware in Figure 15.8. Like RPCs, communicating objects depend on synchronous connections. The key difference is that ORBs must handle *inter-object* messaging, and can therefore be subjected to a great deal more traffic when fine-grained objects interact. Now recall Figure 15.8. ORBs provide a layer of function over and above basic RPCs; some are actually built on top of an RPC service. This extra function, of course, adds an extra layer of overhead. So if an application is constructed using fine-grained objects, and those objects are then distributed, the accumulated overheads and network delays contributed by inter-object messaging activity through an ORB can be a significant drag on performance.

This is a definite area for concern. Although we might expect ORB performance to improve over time, the idea of a "lightweight ORB" is almost an oxymoron (see the next paragraph). The obvious solution—combining object calls to create larger grained objects—obviously undermines the goals of reuse and ease of maintenance that make objects attractive for software engineering.

Guideline 15.9	**Distributing objects can create performance problems**

Object request brokers add a layer of overhead to basic RPC services. If an application is constructed using fine-grained objects, and those objects are then distributed, the accumulated overheads and network delays contributed by inter-object messaging activity through an ORB can be a significant drag on performance.

---

[11]According to the Object Management Group's Web site at *www.omg.org,* OMG membership numbers over 700 companies at the time of writing (June 1997).

Compared to P2P, RPC, and MOM, ORBs are a complex and ambitious technology. They are also less mature, and largely unproven as a basis for enterprise client/server applications. Object enthusiasts like to say that "everything is an object," and the corresponding mission statement for ORBs must be "object brokers support everything." ORBs are becoming the Swiss army knife of the middleware world. Their capabilities are expanding to provide every possible middleware service: internet access, database gateways, transaction management, and so on. Unfortunately, generality has a price; in our experience, general-purpose software always performs poorly. Recall Guideline 7.2, *Software diet: The ultimate performance enhancer,* and Guideline 10.19, *Effectual Locality: Closeness in purpose.*

From this short discussion, we infer that any conclusions we may reach about the suitability of RPCs as a basis for computing within the distributed enterprise will apply with even greater force to distributed objects. As with RPC-based techniques, distributed objects are not unusable, but they do need to be used with care. If we need to establish SPE standards and procedures to ensure reasonable performance from RPC-based applications, we can be sure that even more stringent measures will be required to make distributed objects perform acceptably.

> **Guideline 15.10   Manage the application of distributed object technology**
>
> Any design criteria and SPE standards and procedures developed for communicating programs should be applied with even greater force when implementing applications using distributed objects.

Recommended Reading

Here are some useful references:

▶ *Business Engineering with Object Technology,* by David Taylor[12] provides a readable and insightful introduction to the uses of object technology
▶ The OMG's Web site at *www.omg.org* supplies details of the OMG and CORBA, including full CORBA specifications
▶ T.J. Hart's article, *"Questioning CORBA,"*[13] published in DBMS magazine in March 1997, is a short critique of CORBA

---

[12]David A. Taylor, *Business Engineering with Object Technology* (New York, NY: John Wiley & Sons, 1994).
[13]T. J. Hart, "Questioning CORBA," *DBMS* (March 1997), 52–53.

▶ Douglas C. Schmidt (*schmidt@cs.wustl.edu*) maintains a comprehensive set of CORBA-related bookmarks at *www.cs.wustl.edu/≈schmidt/* including a section describing research on high-performance CORBA.

▶ *The Essential Distributed Objects Survival Guide* by Robert Orfali, Dan Harkey, and Jeri Edwards[14] is a comprehensive and readable reference work on *distributed objects* technology

Distributed Transaction Monitors: *TP-Heavy*

Transaction monitors like IBM's CICS and IMS-TM and NCR's TOP END were originally developed to support host-based *online transaction processing* (OLTP), which has traditionally been the most robust transaction-processing environment available. These products support the ACID requirements through facilities like transaction logging, rollback, and recover.

The newer Distributed Transaction Monitors (DTMs) like *Encina* from Transarc (now wholly owned by IBM), BEA's *TUXEDO,* and the distributed versions of CICS and TOP END, have evolved from foundations laid down by the host-based products but now support transaction processing across multiple systems. DTMs manage transactions explicitly from inception to completion, providing the highest level of transaction-processing reliability.

Compared with DBMS TP-Lite facilities, DTMs are called *TP-Heavy.* This name was not acquired without reason. Among the strengths of transaction monitors are well-rounded administration and security facilities, flexible data communications options, and support for DBMS and non-DBMS resources (that is, messages, files, and queues). Unlike the original proprietary OLTP products we mentioned earlier, DTMs permit interoperability with development tools and other system software through their support for industry-standard interfaces to resource managers, security services, and naming services.

Finally, because transaction processing is a style of application processing that has been in use for almost 30 years, people with OLTP development skills are readily available in traditional IT shops. We discuss transaction monitors in more detail in Chapter 22, *Transaction Managers and Transaction Monitors.*

Transaction Monitor Performance

DTMs have several interrelated features that are useful for ensuring good performance when handling large transaction workloads.

---

[14]Robert Orfali, Dan Harkey, and Jeri Edwards, *The Essential Distributed Objects Survival Guide* (New York, NY: John Wiley & Sons, 1996).

Offline Transaction Processing: A New Technology?

In a geographically dispersed enterprise, it is not always possible for all clients to remain connected to the enterprise network at all times. Remote workgroup servers and members of the "new migrant cybernetic worker class"[15] need to continue working, even though they may be disconnected from the network for extended periods, and only connect when they need to send or receive data.

When we want to extend transaction-oriented applications to disconnected clients, we often find that we need a layer of function on an application server that acts as a surrogate for clients that are not present. One approach is to assemble the necessary services using messaging middleware and custom written code. An alternative is the new class of **Off-line Transaction Processing (OFTP)** middleware.

OFTP middleware is actually a hybrid of workflow, transaction management, messaging, data access, rules management, and data replication facilities. But rather than just supplying the basic building blocks, OFTP middleware offers an integrated set of services designed specifically to support components that are available only intermittently. Using OFTP, those components can participate in long-lived transactions of the kind that are common within enterprise-wide business applications.

Caprera, from Tactica Corp.,[16] is perhaps the most sophisticated example of this emerging technology. For more details, see *www.tactica.com.*

---

[15]Jim Johnson and Molly Baunach, "OFTP: Off-Line Transaction Processing for the New On-Line World," *Application Development Trends* (April 1997), 33–37.

[16]Tactica Corp., Portland, OR 97223. Telephone (800) 831-6161 or online at *www.tactica.com.*

► **Scalability.** Compared to the TP-Lite approach, a transaction monitor can typically provide better performance and scalability when a large number of workstations (greater than 50 to 100) have to be supported and/or when supporting high transaction loads. This is because DTM software typically uses:

- ► Queued input to buffer the server against peaks
- ► Priority scheduling for high-priority messages
- ► Server threads to minimize the overheads of server multitasking
- ► Load balancing to keep all server processes equally busy

All of these features can be used in combination to create server environments that maintain the desired performance characteristics in the face of workload peaks. This is particularly important in any large distributed system where the client activity is subject to large and unpredictable fluctuations. These fluctuations often occur in systems that are connected directly to the customer, such as servers for Internet-based applications. In these situations, there is no pool of customer contact workers (service representatives or salespersons, for example) to buffer the impact of customer demand on the enterprise systems.

▶ **Transaction queuing and priority scheduling.** DTMs have queuing, routing, and messaging built in, which typically may use or bypass the transactional controls. As part of the queuing process, we can assign priorities to classes of messages so that high-priority applications jump to the head of the queue for server resources.

▶ **Load balancing.** If properly configured, a TM can respond gracefully to peaks in the distribution of work. As demand increases, the transaction manager can "spawn" more instances of a server application module to achieve dynamic workload balancing. Later, when demand falls, the transaction manager reduces the number of server instances down to a predefined limit.

   As we discussed in Chapter 13, *The Parallelism Principle,* when the server runs on an SMP multiprocessor, each instance of a server application can run on a different CPU so as to maximize the use of the hardware. Using a load-balancing algorithm, a TM can distribute requests across all instances of server application modules, thereby maximizing the opportunity for parallel execution of business transactions.

▶ **Threads.** As we also discussed in Chapter 13, threads are less expensive to manage than full-fledged operating system processes. They can be implemented by the TM itself or by the operating system. In either case, there will be a performance gain compared to starting a separate task for each concurrent transaction.

DTM Limitations

All the same, DTMs are not the panacea they might seem to be. First, because they are so powerful, they are also more complex to use:

▶ Interfacing with a transaction monitor makes application development more complex; the support for DTMs in application tools is limited compared to that for developing *TP-Lite* applications using a relational database. The TP-Lite approach is simpler and more portable, and it provides faster application development, ideal for low-volume applications. For more discussion of development tools, see Chapter 18.

▶ Making two different OLTP managers work together is all but impossible (who manages the managers?).

The next problem with today's DTP products is that they provide only limited support for managing the workstation portions of distributed transactions. Even IBM's CICS—now available on such diverse non-IBM *server* platforms as HP's *HP/UX,* Digital's *UNIX,* Siemens Nixdorf's *SINIX,* and Microsoft's *Windows NT*—does not support *client* workstations well.

These are legitimate concerns but not necessarily show-stoppers. If we need industrial-strength middleware, we could pick a DTM product and find ways to work with it, selecting other products to match if necessary.

Another issue is of far greater significance. Suppose, perhaps through the expanded reach of IBM's CICS and Encina or of Microsoft's DTC product, the limitations of platform support were removed and every client and server platform had transaction management software available. Even so, giving each component in a heterogeneous distributed system the capability to participate in a single global transaction still does not solve the inherent problems of coordinating the components. We discuss this in the next chapter.

The RPC versus Messaging Debate

In this chapter, we have surveyed the field of client/server middleware. Broadly speaking, as we illustrated in Figure 15.8, the various classes of application middleware are based on either synchronous RPCs (and, more recently, ORBs), or asynchronous messaging techniques.

Whenever there are several ways of doing the same thing, people want to know which is the "best." When choosing middleware, people tend either to insist that "objects are the only viable technology" or to take sides in the "RPC versus messaging debate" which is really a debate about synchronous and asynchronous communication styles. The key issues in this debate are:

1. RPC advocates believe that the synchronous, blocking transaction provides the best control of data integrity. They assert that asynchronous access of databases cannot ensure that updates are always applied in the correct order and at the correct time. The information database may be out of date, leading to incorrect results.
2. Messaging advocates believe that synchronous, blocking transactions are inconsistent with event-driven programming required in complex environments. Event-driven processes do not want to wait passively for other processes to complete their work; event-driven processes need to retain control so that they can act on new messages from other processes.

3. RPC advocates assert that the RPC is faster than the store-and-forward processing employed by message-based middleware.
4. Messaging advocates assert that message-based systems can achieve much better peak load performance because all requests are placed in a queue and the servers simply take new tasks from the queue.

One of the results of the debate has been to stimulate both camps to add new capabilities to their own approach. As a result, there is some convergence in the two approaches. Some RPCs are acquiring asynchronous support, and messaging approaches support persistent sessions between queues. ORBs, in true object-oriented fashion, are likely to inherit characteristics from all other middleware classes.

In our view, both synchronous and asynchronous styles are essential because they reflect different processing needs. Indeed, in the next two chapters we show how to create high-performance client/server architectures and application designs by using a combination of these technologies.

Architecture
for High Performance

"Form ever follows function."

Louis Henry Sullivan

In This Chapter . . .

A Reference Model for Client/Server Architecture
The Real Problem with Distributed Transactions
Abandoning the Single Synchronous Transaction Paradigm
Architectural Patterns
Application Design Patterns

In this chapter, we explain how to apply the performance principles to determine an architecture for high performance—an overall framework for designing and building enterprise client/server applications.

Perhaps you are thinking that architecture is boring and much too theoretical to have any real effect on how the system actually works. We disagree. In our opinion, choosing the right architecture is the key to developing a successful distributed system. Architecture constrains our design and product choices, and so it determines how a system is constructed and how it works.

In Chapter 15, we introduced the middleware technologies that enable client/server communication. In this chapter, by following several connected lines of reasoning, we draw some surprising conclusions about how to build systems using those technologies. These conclusions, which we have hinted at in earlier discussions, are now spelled out clearly for the first time.

We say that the conclusions are surprising not because they differ from everything we have discussed in previous chapters, but because they may cause you to think twice about trying to build high-performance applications using *synchronous* technologies like remote procedure calls, database gateways, distributed databases, distributed transaction monitors, and distributed objects.

Our conclusion is that, while all these technologies do have roles to play, the most important technologies are the ones that link components *asynchronously,* letting us design applications as *multitransaction workflows* using *decoupled processes.* To discover the definitions of those terms, and to find out why we reach these conclusions, you'll have to read this chapter.

A Reference Model for Client/Server Architecture

In this chapter, we focus on systems and application architectures and on design foundations, continuing on to more detailed design issues in Chapter 17.

For an overview of the subject, we introduce the client/server computing roadmap (Figure 16.1) as a reference model. This framework, produced by DataBase Associates, illustrates how various kinds of middleware can be used to unify Web-based applications and existing enterprise client/server applications.

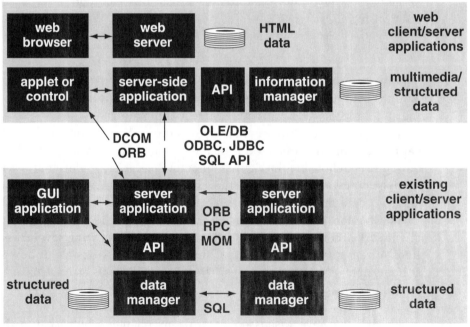

FIGURE **16.1**   A client/server computing roadmap.

The Client/Server Computing Roadmap Online

If you want to locate the key client/server products and vendor information online, the client/server computing roadmap is a good place to start. Find it at DataBase Associates International's InfoIT site, at *www.infoit.com.*

The Real Problem with Distributed Transactions

In the last chapter, we expressed the concern that many of today's middleware technologies are not ideally suited to building high-performance client/server systems for the distributed enterprise. Some of these technologies are quite popular in the trade press; distributed transaction monitors and distributed objects are even seen by many as "the future direction of enterprise computing." However, in our view, for the distributed applications of the future to perform acceptably, these enabling technologies must first be transformed to incorporate asynchronous operations.

The real problem is not in the products; it is in the concept of distributed transaction management on which the products are founded. The concept of a single integrated focus for transaction management from initiation to completion, with recovery and management of databases as part of its competence, is sound and well proven in the world of host-centered computing. But it is not nearly as well suited to applications in the distributed world. In fact, distributed transaction monitors really work well only when the business transaction is not too complex and the behavior of the participating computer systems is not too diverse.

What exactly do we mean by *diverse* in the context of a distributed computing environment? Using the travel agent system introduced at the beginning of Chapter 15 as an example in each case, here are four areas where diversity is a potential cause of problems:

▶ **Variable capacity.** Components operate at different speeds. For example, the airline reservation portion of the itinerary can probably be accomplished quickly thanks to the airline's high-speed reservation system. Smaller reservation systems could be limited by the capacity of their server to process concurrent requests.

▶ **Variable contention.** Components operate in different processing environments, so that some may be subject to delays due to sharing resources (for example, CPU, network links, disks) with other work. The car rental system could be overloaded with requests and subject to long delays.

▶ **Variable availability.** It is hard to ensure that independently controlled components are all available simultaneously. For example, a restaurant's reservation system may be temporarily unavailable. Some may not operate at all at certain times of day.

▶ **Variable demand.** The division of the global transaction among the components may be uneven by its nature. One component may be asked to perform a task that takes minutes or even hours to complete, while another portion can be accomplished in seconds. For example, it may take the travel agent system a long time to search for available rooms in all the possible hotel systems.

Of course, this is just another instance of the problem of synchronization that we saw in Chapter 15 on the *distributed database* approach to coordinating updates to separate databases.

The travel agent example makes it quite plain that, even though we are handling what is logically *a single business transaction,* it does not always make sense to coordinate all the actions of the separate distributed systems involved in that business transaction within the scope of *a single global computer transaction.* The nice thing about the travel agent example is that it is so obviously unsuited to being implemented as a single synchronous transaction that it forces us to look for an alternative approach.

Abandoning the Single Synchronous Transaction Paradigm

The real problem, in our view, is that the concept of a heterogeneous distributed database with synchronized updates is a vision of utopia that swims against the tide of computing technology. The tight controls over application processing that are possible on a mainframe are incompatible with many aspects of the move to widespread distributed processing.

From everything we have discussed up to this point, in Chapter 15 and earlier in the book, we conclude that *decoupled processes and multitransaction workflows are the optimal starting point for the design of high-performance enterprise client/server systems:*

▶ **Decoupled processes.** Decoupling occurs when we can separate the different parts of a distributed system so that no one process ever needs to stop processing to wait for the other(s). The driving force behind this recommendation is Bell's law of waiting: *All CPUs wait at the same speed* (Guideline 11.17).

▶ **Multitransaction workflows.** Often, we can split up the business transaction into a series of separate computer transactions. We call the result a *multitrans-*

action workflow. The motivation for this recommendation is the Locality Principle, *Group components based on their usage* (Guideline 10.1), and the Parallelism Principle, *Workflow parallelism can lower perceived response times* (Guideline 13.7).

In the following sections, we summarize the many arguments that lead to this recommendation. They relate to:

▶ The limited ability of systems software to enforce transaction integrity
▶ The conflict between independent distributed systems and controlled transactions
▶ The analogy of designing applications to exploit massively parallel processors
▶ Our collective experience of designing manual systems
▶ The recommendations of established software design principles
▶ The desire to build systems from separately developed components

Figure 16.2 illustrates these points.

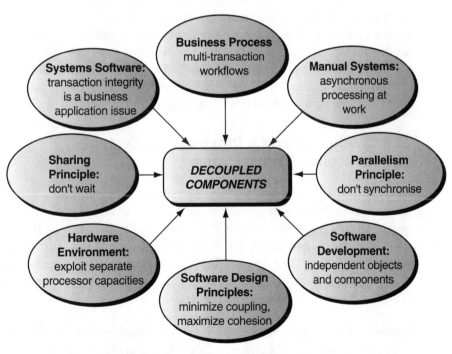

FIGURE 16.2 Arguments for decoupled processes.

The Limited Safety Net of Systems Software

First, let's take another look at the ACID properties and the level of support we can reasonably expect to get from systems software like a DBMS or a transaction monitor.

It is important to understand that observing the ACID properties means a lot more than just using a DBMS or a transaction monitor, or both. In fact, the successful, dependable, and robust applications of the past—which still support today's businesses—were built using *a combination* of systems software, application code, and business processes that enforced these properties.

DBMSs use locking techniques (which we discussed in detail in Chapter 12) to achieve *isolation* and have logging, backout, and recovery facilities to enforce *atomicity* and *durability*. When any data is updated by a program, the application programmer is responsible for many aspects of *consistency*. Although system software can maintain the structural integrity of stored data, and even enforce some kinds of predefined consistency rules among data items, no system software can ever know whether every change to stored data is actually correct and consistent with all business rules.

The best we can achieve, even within a tightly controlled mainframe environment, is to create a well-behaved application program, wrap it within a cocoon of protective systems software and systematic backup and recovery processing, and hope that the business process is not compromised by mistakes or deliberate tampering and fraud. But we still cannot rely on systems software to manage transactions correctly in the face of errors in the business process or the application code. Ultimately, correctness and consistency are the responsibility of the business process and the application programs that implement it.

The Conflict Between Independent Systems and Controlled Transactions

In a distributed environment, the protective cocoon afforded by system software is full of holes, and—in the majority of enterprises—those holes cannot be sealed without imposing severe limitations and restrictions on the flexibility of the shared information systems. Even attempting to make independent distributed operating systems behave like a tightly controlled centralized environment would undermine the very reasons why we chose to move to distributed systems in the beginning:

▶ Enforcing the integrity of distributed transactions within a single unit of work requires control, coordination, and synchronization among the component processes.

▶ Exploiting distributed computing resources effectively requires independence of the components.

This is a fundamental conflict that can be resolved only by changing our processing paradigm.

The Analogy of Parallel Processors

When we considered parallel processing technology in Chapter 13, we saw that to make a multiprocessor machine perform well, we must do everything possible to encourage parallel processing; otherwise, the entire network of computers runs only as fast as the slowest (or even slower, thanks to the added communication delays). *Synchronization inhibits parallel processing.* Or, to state it the other way, to enable parallelism, we must support *asynchronous* processing of application components.

The other lesson from massively parallel processors is that when a process and its data are separated, one or the other has to move. The best design is the one requiring the least amount of data movement, because while the moving is going on, the processor is probably not doing much useful work. The conclusion is that unless the amount of data involved is very small, it's usually faster to invoke the process where the data resides (function shipping) than to move the data (data shipping).

Applying this logic to distributed DBMSs makes it clear that if we want to achieve high performance, we should look for ways to update the separate databases without synchronizing the updates and to distribute the processing across the platforms where those databases reside, not ship data between systems.

The Experience of Designing Manual Systems

Designing a computer system based on multitransaction workflows is not a particularly revolutionary proposal. Indeed, if we had somehow been able to skip the first 40 years of the computer age and start automating our business systems using today's technology, we would probably not have thought it the least bit unusual because all manual systems work this way.

But like our computers, our reasoning can be so logical that it lacks real thought. Occasionally, we need to balance our linear thinking with a small dose of simple wit like that ascribed to the Irish farmer who, when asked by strangers for directions to a distant town, began his answer by saying "Well, I wouldn't start from here!"

Starting from the Wrong Place.   Most of our troubles stem from the fact that, when trying to reach the destination of distributed systems, we keep starting from the wrong place, namely the application designs and systems software of centralized computing:

▶ Design discussions dwell on how best to "partition" applications for the distributed environment. Manual systems, however, are already partitioned naturally—the supposedly monolithic application that is being "partitioned" would not exist in the first place if it had not been conceived as "the right solution" by a designer with a centralized computing mindset.

▶ The reason we have been devoting so much attention to making *distributed* databases and *distributed* transaction managers work is because they are extensions of the core mechanisms of *centralized* information processing— shared databases and transaction monitors. Rather than trying to force these centralized mechanisms to work in the distributed environment, we should design new mechanisms that are more appropriate.

Starting from the Right Place.   In fact, we should start from the design of manual business systems. All large-scale human systems are inherently distributed and asynchronous in nature. Even the participants in close-knit team efforts operate asynchronously. We find chorus lines, cheerleaders, marching bands, and synchronized swimmers so interesting because they are such an aberration. So, before the advent of the centralized mainframe, the idea of recording an entire business transaction with a single synchronized set of human actions did not arise because it is so absurdly impossible.

Traditionally, the business process is divided into its natural components (or phases), according to the roles of the various human processors (or workers). Work flows through the phases, and information is recorded as necessary along the way. If anything goes wrong along the way, the appropriate set of compensating actions must be taken to undo whatever partial progress has been made. And the whole operation is designed to ensure that no irrevocable actions are taken too early in the process—usually meaning before the money is in the bank. Companies that mail out the diamonds before cashing the checks soon learn how to design a more effective multiphase business process.

When we do a good job of distributed systems design, it becomes an integral part of business process design. Rather than bending the business process to meet the needs of a centralized computer, we must blend the power of distributed computers into the business process.

Software Design Principles

In Chapter 7, we discussed software design principles. In the area of localization, we emphasized that a good software design is one that minimizes the degree of coupling among cooperating components and maximizes the degree of cohesion within components.

We will achieve this goal by designing a staged business process that minimizes the need for coordination across locations and then by creating components that closely match the separate stages of that business process. In Chapter 17, we discuss some implications of this conclusion.

Building Systems from Separately Developed Components

Traditionally, when software was developed for centralized systems, there was a single point of control. Components of a system were all designed, built, and deployed by a single group or team of developers with shared knowledge and objectives.

In a distributed environment, developers trying to build an entire application with Windows clients, a UNIX server, a CICS transaction monitor, and an Oracle DBMS must understand all the platform environments and the communications among them. Usually the result is a monolithic design that is difficult to test, maintain, or change. Few individuals have the breadth of skills to deliver it.

A decoupled approach changes this. Components that encapsulate a single business subtask can be developed separately. To deploy them, they need only to communicate successfully with messaging middleware. After that, the middleware takes over, reliably delivering messages to other components. With this approach, it is easier for different groups to build parts of systems at different times. It is also easier to integrate new components with existing legacy applications. For an example, see the capsule *Decoupled Development.*

In Chapter 15, we discussed *transactional message queuing,* pointing out that it is an essential aspect of distributed application design. To guarantee the integrity of a business transaction that is implemented using decoupled components, we must design with three objectives in mind:

▶ Decoupled processes that obey the ACID properties
▶ Guaranteed message delivery between the processes
▶ Compensating processes to handle any situations in which a process cannot complete

We discuss these design issues, and others, in more detail in the next chapter.

Guideline 16.1	**Decoupling is the key to high performance in distributed systems**

Decoupled processes and multitransaction workflows are the optimal starting points for the design of high-performance enterprise client/server systems.

Decoupled Development

Decoupling occurs when we separate the different parts of an application (transactional or not) across one or more systems (or "nodes"). In Figure 16.3, node 1 has Application A, which communicates with Application B (on node 2) and Application C (on node 1) This is a simple but representative example of a distributed application.

Our example has five components when decoupling is considered:

▶ **Application A**
▶ **Queue1,** which is a queue manager on node 1 that communicates to other similar queues via an agreed mechanism (whether via messaging, RPC, or conversational middleware does not matter)

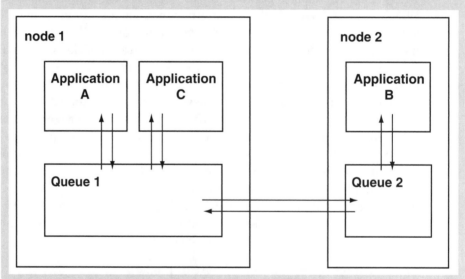

FIGURE 16.3   Decoupled components.

Architectural Patterns

In Chapter 2, we introduced the concepts of client/server computing and described the evolution to enterprise client/server systems and three-tier architectures. In Chapter 10 on the Locality Principle, we concluded (*Guideline 10.24*) that there exists "a natural division of data and functions across the three tiers" of an enterprise client/server architecture and that these "three ar-

▶ **Queue2,** which is a queue manager on node 2 (also communicating with other queues—including Queue1)
▶ **Application B**
▶ **Application C**

Assume the following:

▶ The queue managers (Queue1 and Queue2) can communicate reliably with each other.
▶ Application A's development tool (and thereby each completed application) can write to (and read from) Queue1.
▶ Application B's development tool (and thereby each completed application) can pick up information from Queue2 (as well as write back to Queue2 for any returns/responses).

Given these assumptions, we can write Application A once we have agreed on the application-level communication protocol between Applications A and B and between Applications A and C. After that, all three applications can be developed separately and in parallel, with each developer using different skills and little knowledge of each others' environments.

Applications A, B, and C could also be replaced by new components because components can be swapped in or out as long as the operating environment and the supporting queuing mechanisms do not change. This capability is particularly important because it lets an enterprise evolve gradually from legacy applications to newer ways of working.

Guideline 16.2	**Decoupled components let us tie unlike systems together**

The decoupled approach to linking components offers a simple way to connect dissimilar systems within a distributed environment, without the performance and development costs of forcing them to interact synchronously.

chitectural layers focus on data consumption, application context, and enterprise data content, respectively."

But, as Orfali, Harkey and Edwards point out, *three-tier is an overloaded word in the client/server literature.*[1] And our discussions of "three-tier architectures"

---

[1] Robert Orfali, Dan Harkey, and Jeri Edwards, *The Essential Client/Server Survival Guide,* 2nd Ed. (New York, NY: John Wiley & Sons, 1996), 19.

have not really made it clear that there are two distinct definitions of "three-tier" involved:

▶ The *logical layering* of function into presentation logic, application logic, and database logic
▶ The *physical distribution* of function across client workstations, departmental servers, and enterprise servers

Although there is a natural affinity between the two concepts, they are not identical. We now consider the relationship between these two concepts.

Logical and Physical Architectures

Logically, systems need components to play three fundamentally different **roles.** To aid in memory, we refer to these roles as *consumers, context,* and *content.*

Consumers are application-related components that interact with users and handle the *presentation, preparation,* and *collection* of information.

Context refers to application *processing* logic that accepts information requests from consumers, decomposes them, and directs them to the correct content layer. It understands the application *processing context,* so it can handle any "business rules" that are not properly part of either the presentation or data logic layers. *Correct processing,* enforcement of data *integrity rules,* and *transactions* are all concepts that are understood in this layer.

Content refers to corporate information and the management services that organize and manage it. In the past, this was simply *data* and *databases;* now it extends to include other media and other resource managers, too.

Now consider the physical architecture. Theoretically, an optimal arrangement of these components is illustrated by Figure 16.4, which is based on Bernard Boar's synthesis of ideal business, data, and processing architectures.[2]

Theoretical Three-Tier Architecture Benefits.   In what sense is this optimal? To answer that, we must consider the requirements for an enterprise information architecture. For a large organization, moving to an enterprise client/ server system represents a major shift from monolithic systems with fixed distribution to dynamic, heterogeneous, pervasively networked environments. The next generation of systems will be an order of magnitude more dynamic—always running, always changing—with thousands of machines in huge networks.

---

[2]Bernard Boar, *Implementing Client/Server Computing* (New York, NY: McGraw Hill, 1993), 57.

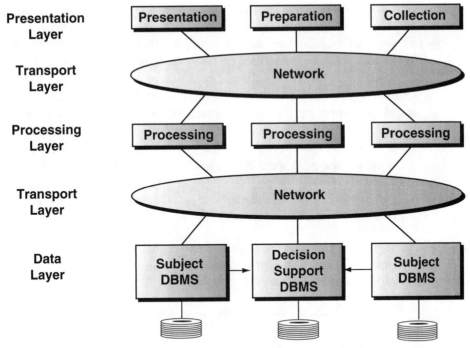

FIGURE 16.4   Optimal architecture for enterprise client/server.

In such an environment, content components (service providers like DBMSs) and service consumers (GUIs, for example) must be continually added and removed.

The key to doing this is the middle tier, the hub of the three-tier architecture. In the first place, this central layer acts in a connecting role to let individual clients access multiple content servers, and (of course) servers support multiple clients. A separate central tier can also:

▶ Provide a set of *services* that can be dynamically invoked by both the consumer and content layers
▶ Allow new services to be added without major reconfiguration
▶ Allow services to be removed dynamically without affecting any participant not using those services
▶ Allow one service provider to be replaced by another

These are all vital characteristics in a distributed computing environment. Unfortunately, however, they cannot be obtained quite as easily as Figure 16.3 implies because of some physical limitations of client/server technology.

A Practical Three-Tier Architecture.   Very soon (if not today), using distributed object technology, it will be possible to implement systems using exactly the physical architecture shown in Figure 16.4. But we don't recommend it. Figure 16.4 is a nice theoretical picture that does not map well to the real three-tier world of client workstations, departmental servers, and enterprise servers.

If we were to implement applications using this physical architecture, they would perform very poorly. A consumer's request for data must be passed across two transport layers to reach the content layer, and in the real world, one of those transport layers is probably a relatively slow wide area network.

So the mapping between the logical and physical layers cannot be nearly as clean and simple as Figure 16.4 suggests. In practice, an optimal architecture for high performance will embody a set of relationships between the logical and physical layers like those we show in Figure 16.5:

▶ The vertical axis shows the *logical roles*—consumers, context, and content.
▶ The horizontal axis shows the *physical tiers*—workstations, departmental servers, and enterprise servers.

To simplify the discussion of this area, we will drop the term *layer* except to refer the generic concept of *layering*—the subdivision of a system into a hierarchy of interconnected components.

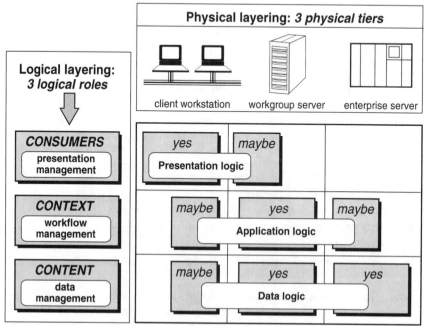

FIGURE 16.5   Logical and physical layering in practice.

The positions of the three horizontal boxes in the table show how presentation, application, and data components must be assigned to the three physical tiers.

The figure shows that there is indeed a natural affinity between *logical roles* and *physical tiers,* as we pointed out in *Guideline 10.24.* To build systems that work effectively in a heterogeneous distributed environment, however, we must employ an application architecture in which:

▶ Presentation management is centered on the client workstation, but some aspects are handled by the workgroup server. Actually, this is not essential in traditional client/server environments and is probably best avoided there. But in Web-based environments, the Web server does have a role to play in presentation management.

▶ Application logic and workflow management are centered on the workgroup server, but some aspects are handled by the client workstation and some by the enterprise server.

▶ Data management is spread across all three tiers, although the majority of the responsibility is shared between the workgroup and enterprise servers.

Communication Paths.   Applications that are implemented using this architecture must incorporate several different types of interprocess communication. Using the numeric identifiers shown in Figure 16.6, a variety of possible communication paths are possible.

We can organize the various communication paths into five major classes, as follows:

1. Within role and tier (*1-1, 2-2,* etc.).
2. Within tier, between roles (*1-2, 2-3, 4-5, 5-6, 8-9*).
3. Within role, between (adjacent) tiers (*1-4, 2-5, 5-8, 3-6, 6-9*).
4. Between roles on adjacent tiers (see the note that follows) (*1-5, 4-8, 5-9*).
5. Between remote tiers (see the note that follows) (*1-8, 3-9*).

Note: An application design in which communication skips either a logical or a physical layer is not recommended because it compromises the software engineering benefits of layering and hiding that we discussed in Chapter 7. But it does happen in practice:

▶ A logical example (*4-6*) is a simple two-tier Web browser application in which presentation components interface directly to data management on the local server.

▶ A physical example (*3-9*) would be a data replication component on a mobile computer uploading data directly to the enterprise server.

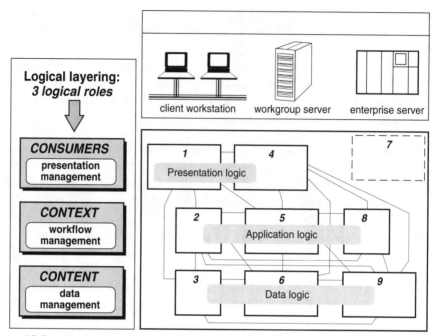

FIGURE 16.6   Communication paths in a distributed application.

Performance Implications.   To obtain optimal performance we should apply three rules:

1. Minimize the number of communications across tiers, especially across those connected by a WAN.
2. Limit synchronous communications to the faster communication paths within a single tier or between tiers connected by a high-speed network.
3. For slower communication paths, use asynchronous communication coupled with other design techniques that eliminate processing and communication delays from the user's perceived response time.

This conclusion has some consequences for our choice of application communication styles or protocols. We discuss this next.

Distributed Application Patterns

We began the previous chapter by describing a variety of different *communication styles* that are available for the components of a distributed application. We are now going to organize those styles into a smaller number of standard patterns. These patterns are the building blocks from which we can construct larger systems.

In recent years, patterns in software architecture and design have been receiving attention from a number of authors. The goal of those who form the "patterns community" is to document and disseminate information about standard ways of solving software problems. We do not have space in this book to discuss this idea in detail, but we do recommend *A System of Patterns* as a good starting point.[3]

In the following paragraphs, we list a small number of standard communication patterns that can be used to create distributed systems. Our patterns are not defined rigorously—to document any pattern properly requires a complete specification of its purpose and behavior. However, *A System of Patterns* does describe some related patterns: the *Broker* architectural pattern and the *Forwarder-Receiver, Client-Dispatcher-Server,* and *Publisher-Subscriber* design patterns, the last three of which are lower-level building blocks than those on our list.

From our earlier review of process communication styles in Chapter 15, we identity the collection of standard patterns shown in Table 16.1:

▶ The first column of the table lists communication patterns that might be used for data retrieval applications or by components that do not participate in a software transaction.

▶ The second column lists patterns that can be used within transactional applications.

---

[3]Frank Buschmann, Regine Meunier, Hans Rohnert, Peter Sommerland, and Michael Stal, *A System of Patterns* (New York, NY: John Wiley & Sons, 1996).

Table 16.1   Synchronous and Asynchronous Patterns

	No Software Transaction Involved	**Within a Software Transaction**	**Using an External Broker Service**
Synchronous	Request reply Conversations	Local transaction Global transaction	Object request broker Web request broker
Asynchronous	Request reply Publisher/subscriber	Store, forward, and forget Multitransaction workflow	Message broker Groupware

▶ The third column lists patterns that can be used when components use an independent software component to manage the communication.

▶ The first row lists synchronous patterns, the second asynchronous.

Notes on Table 16.1.   The table is not intended to list all primitives available for interprocess communication (for example, basic P2P messaging does not appear); it lists only those patterns that we regard as the most useful for creating distributed applications.

The table is an attempt to generalize away from particular middleware categories. So, for example, RPC is not listed because it is an example of *synchronous request-reply*. DBMS and DTM products support several of the patterns, so they do not appear either.

Conclusions.   We began our coverage of enterprise client/server in Chapter 2 where we introduced the basic concepts of client/server technology and architecture. In Chapter 15, we extended our discussion of client/server architecture with a detailed evaluation of middleware technologies. In this chapter, we have argued that to achieve the promised flexibility and scalability of distributed systems, we must adopt a new approach to the design of information processing applications. Table 16.1 lays out the fundamental design patterns of high-performance client/server computing. Combining these patterns with the conclusions of an earlier section (see *Performance Implications*) produces an architecture for high performance.

Application Design Patterns

Before moving on to consider detailed design issues in the next chapter, we spell out some application design foundations—the core design guidelines and patterns that can be used to create distributed applications. These can be thought of as the building blocks from which we can assemble enterprise client/server systems. They are based on our conclusions about architecture and on the SPE design principles we presented in Chapters 7 through 14.

Core Design Guidelines

As we review these key design patterns and summarize imperatives for good performance, we recall relevant guidelines that we introduced in our discussion of the SPE design principles. Throughout this section, the guidelines appear indented and in italics, with the associated guideline number appearing in boldface.

Don't Skimp on Logical Design.   Good logical design is important—we cannot overturn the carefully established and sound principles of software engineering. Good logical design goes hand in hand with good physical design.

7.14 *Winsberg's Law of Logical Design.*   The logical designer must be a reluctant physical designer. Although conceptual issues should dominate our thinking during the analysis and logical design phases, physical implementation issues cannot be ignored. To do so is to risk creating a design that cannot be tuned for performance.

Design for High Cohesion.   A high degree of *cohesion* exists naturally within the stages of a well-designed business process. Translating this into the design of the supporting information systems can help to promote local data access and minimize the need for distributed processing.

10.3 *Spatial locality: Closeness in distance.   Components that play together should stay together.* If a collection of elements will be used together more than once, then we can reduce overheads by grouping them statically.

When designing individual components, achieving high cohesion requires grouping services by function, complexity, and frequency of execution. When we do this, we simplify the task of performance tuning. Related functions are grouped together and so can be invoked with fewer messages; it is easier to separate short-running simple functions from longer-running complex ones and to optimize the performance of the most frequently used components.

7.13 *Grouping is a key decision in logical and physical design.*   Many key physical design issues hinge around how we apply the technique of **grouping,** which is used in both logical and physical design. *Independence* and *localization* (and the subsidiary concepts *cohesion* and *coupling*) are crucial to good software design, in part because they have such a strong influence at the intersection of logical and physical design.

Segregate Distinct Workload Types.   Like oil and water, certain classes of work just don't mix. By separating business transaction processing from information analysis for decision support, and by assigning each to separate servers, we can improve the performance of both.

10.20 *Inmon's Rule: Don't mix short transactions with long-running queries.*   When we have high-performance operational workloads, we should keep them on a separate processor, separate from *ad hoc* or unknown queries, which may have massive processing requirements.

When things are grouped properly, it's easy to separate the groups and give each the right treatment.

> **9.5** *Denormalize data for informational applications.*   For informational applications, create separate denormalized databases (data marts or data warehouses) organized to support DSS and EIS requirements.

Process Local Data.   Of all the performance principles we have discussed, *locality* is the one that has the greatest impact on the performance of distributed processing. Whenever we must process remotely located data, either the time to communicate with the remote server is perceived directly as delay at the client interface or else we must create a more complex design using caching and/or asynchronous data manipulation to mask the remote processing delay. Having the right data located close to the client simplifies application design enormously.

> **10.10** *Set an overall data locality guideline.*   Establish a corporate design guideline like this one: *Unless performance objectives or response time estimates indicate otherwise, online applications should be designed to perform 85 percent of all processing against local data.* If followed, this type of guideline will introduce the importance of spatial locality into every discussion of application architecture or data distribution.

Don't Clog Up the Server.   The most effective designs are those that make optimal use of all available resources to process the work. Client workstations are the ideal place for client-related processing; servers should be reserved for work that needs access to shared information.

> **11.7** *Clients have spare capacity for small tasks.*   Processing that relates only to a single user's application should be pushed onto the client workstation to conserve scarce server resources. By minimizing server resource consumption per client, we improve overall scalability. On the other hand, moving a really large function from a local client platform to a dedicated remote server will improve quickness of response if the function can be performed asynchronously.

Design for Low Coupling.   Messages between processes are the main source of slow performance. This can be true for complex applications running in a single processor environment and it is certainly the case when the communicating processes are distributed. Usually, the problem does not lie in the volume of information to be exchanged, but rather in the processing overheads and response time delays associated with each message. Low coupling between components minimizes the number of messages.

Guideline 16.3	**Douglas's Rule of distributed application performance**

For a distributed application, response time problems are far more likely to be caused by the number of messages it requires than by the size of those messages.

No amount of fancy new technology can overcome the limitations of space and distance.

> **10.6** *Aim to group related data at a single location.* The first goal of any data distribution scheme must be to identify those subsets of data that are most likely to be used together in applications. Ideally, these should be stored at the same location. If logically related data becomes separated physically, then no amount of juggling with the processing will avoid the performance penalty of moving data between locations.

Create Decoupled Components. Typically, there is a low level of coupling among the stages of a well-designed business process. If we translate this into the design of the supporting information systems, we arrive at application designs that use the following techniques as building blocks:

▶ Decoupled software components
▶ Carefully controlled parallel processing
▶ A workflow style of interprocess communication
▶ Function shipping rather than data shipping
▶ Asynchronous scheduling of workload components
▶ Batching of asynchronous workload components

Assembling systems from decoupled components is the key to exploiting the full power of a distributed processing environment. Decoupling occurs when we can separate the two parts of a single process so that neither one needs to stop processing to wait for the other.

The opposite of decoupled components is *entangled components*—a system with many interconnections among the components. This kind of design is the result of doing a poor job of grouping. Entangled components perform poorly as workloads change and grow.

> **10.5** *Minimize the need for system-wide knowledge.* In a large distributed system it is difficult to be aware, at all times, of the entire state of the system. It is also difficult to update distributed or replicated data structures in a consistent manner. Designs that rarely re-

quire global information to be monitored or atomically updated are more scalable.

Carefully Control Parallel Processing.   To improve performance and scalability, we must create and exploit opportunities for parallel processing. One way is through replicated services, especially file or data services. Another is by breaking apart application processes into parallel processing streams. Decoupling components enables parallel processing. However, we must always use parallelism carefully because it involves a trade-off, as embodied in the Parallelism Principle.

> **13.1** *The Parallelism Principle: Exploit parallel processing.*   Processing related pieces of work in parallel typically introduces additional synchronization overheads and often introduces contention among the parallel streams. Use parallelism to overcome bottlenecks, provided the processing speedup offsets the additional costs introduced.

Subdivide Complex Applications into Multitransaction Workflows.   All but the simplest of business processes are conducted in stages. A business transaction is carried out by a network of separate but related business activities, connected by a flow of information. When these activities are implemented as a network of separate but related computer transactions, we call the result a multitransaction workflow.

We strongly recommend implementing complex applications as multitransaction workflows. They are natural, since their structure is derived directly from the business process they support. They are also very good for performance and scalability because they enable asynchronous and parallel processing by separate computers. Finally, multitransaction workflow designs typically improve perceived response times because they handle the user's computer interactions using smaller, more responsive components.

Use Function Shipping Rather Than Data Shipping.   When a process and its data are separated, something has to move. Unless the amount of data involved is very small, it's usually much more efficient to invoke the processing where the data resides (function shipping) than to move the data. As a practical rule, the best design is usually the one that moves the least amount of data.

Schedule Workload Components Asynchronously.   When components operate asynchronously, each one can be designed to operate in the most efficient way possible for its own workload. Components linked by synchronous connections, on the other hand, tend to operate at the speed of the slowest part of the whole system.

Asynchronous connections do not mean slow connections. In a well-designed high-performance system using asynchronous links, work can flow rapidly. In fact, occasional peaks in the workload usually cause much less disruption than they would in the equivalent system with synchronous links.

> **15.1** *Synchronous calls disrupt service.*   If a server in an open system must respond synchronously to any client's request, then when the number of clients is very large, the server can be overloaded by peaks in the rate of client requests.

Batch Asynchronous Operations Whenever Possible.   Grouping operations into larger batches usually improves efficiency and, hence, overall system throughput and scalability, but—when processes are connected synchronously—these gains usually come at the cost of individual process response times. Separating a portion of the total processing into an asynchronous batched component can improve *both* perceived application response times *and* overall system efficiency. For high performance and scalability, we should design systems to exploit the increased efficiency of deferred batch processing whenever business constraints permit it.

> **11.2** *Shared resources and the size of units of work.*   In design situations involving shared resources, grouping elements into smaller units of work tends to optimize individual process response times, whereas grouping into larger units of work tends to optimize overall system resource usage.

> **9.16** *Use batch processing for efficiency.*   Unless business reasons require continuous incremental updates to the databases, it is much more efficient to accumulate a file or table of high-volume business transactions when they are generated and process them later in batches.

Use Caching Techniques to Minimize the Need for Access to Remote Data.
Caching is an essential technique of distributed design. No large distributed information system will perform well without extensive use of caching at many different levels. Hardware, operating systems, middleware, and applications can all make effective use of caching techniques. And since the key to successful caching is to know the usage pattern, caching by applications can be the most effective of all. Referring to Figure 16.5 and the associated discussions about architecture, effective caching can move vital data from cell 9 to cell 6, or from cell 6 to cell 3, and in so doing convert remote processing into local processing.

14.15 *Trade local I/O for remote I/O.*   Since remote data requests are much more expensive than local ones, local caching is particularly effective if local applications must read data from remote devices. Even if a local in-memory cache causes an increase in paging I/O, it may still yield a net reduction in application response times. Alternatively, consider creating a cache on a local disk.

Minimize Exclusive Use of Shared Resources.   Requiring exclusive use is *not* sharing. Applications that share resources perform well. An application that demands exclusive access lowers performance for others; two such applications can kill performance for everyone, themselves included. This is embodied in the Sharing Principle: *Share resources without creating bottlenecks.* In practical terms, this means creating designs that minimize the time any component needs to spend holding exclusive control of any shared resource.

12.1 *Exclusive use inhibits sharing.*   Any use reduces sharing, but exclusive use reduces sharing the most.

The Final View

Manual systems always permit asynchronous operation of their separate components because no other mode of operation is possible. Only computers make synchronous changes even possible. To a degree, centralized computing could deliver synchronous changes to related databases because the same computer managed all the system resources. Peaks in the workload could cause contention and delays, but provided the machine kept running, a congested machine acted as its own governor.

Processor technology does not allow the centralized computing model to scale up without limits. When the workload surpasses the capabilities of the largest centralized processor, the only way to keep growing is to divide and conquer—to create a network of computers. Networked computers demand a different approach to application design. Pursuing the vision of enterprise-wide synchronization of information through networked computers can cause delays and inefficiencies when any part of the whole system operates below par. This is the Achilles' heel of interdependent systems—the whole is no stronger than its weakest part.

Therefore, the rigid concept of synchronous transactions must be replaced by a wider range of possible application designs:

▶ The older, synchronous methods are still appropriate for changes that are within the scope of a single processor, or even for occasional communication between components separated by a very carefully controlled, high-speed LAN

▶ These must be combined with asynchronous designs in which the user must accept that unconfirmed changes will be reflected in the enterprise database(s) at a later time.

Ironically, these changes bring us almost full circle back to the days of manual systems. In a manual system, it is normal for changes to be recorded quickly in one location, but for those changes to take a few days to percolate through the system. The only difference is that distributed computing has shortened the time frames enormously. But drawing the analogy to the way manual systems work is an observation that will help us to design new, faster distributed systems.

Design for high performance is the subject of our next chapter.

Design for High Performance

"A good scientist is a person with original ideas. A good engineer is a person who makes a design that works with as few original ideas as possible. There are no prima donnas in engineering."

Freeman Dyson

In This Chapter . . .

Real-Time Systems Design
Designing a Distributed Application
Guidelines for Data Distribution
How to Group Process and Data
Designing the Application Flow
Control, Transactions, and Rules
The Response Time Reference Model
Rules of Thumb for Estimating Response Times
Conclusions and Management Guidelines

Architecture and design principles give us a guiding framework, but they allow for many different designs. We must choose a particular design to match the user's requirements. In this chapter, we examine that design decision in more detail, recalling many of the guidelines that we laid out in the previous chapters on SPE design principles. Throughout this chapter, the guidelines appear indented and in italics, with the associated guideline number appearing in boldface.

Earlier in the book, we explained that the goal of achieving good performance cannot be separated from the rest of software engineering. In Chapter 4, we defined software performance engineering (SPE) as *"software engineering with performance in mind."*

We now refine that idea further. If we have performance in mind during the design phase, our design philosophy will be *"Design applications that don't wait."* We first proposed this important guideline (Guideline 11.18) in the context of Bell's Law of Waiting: *All CPU's wait at the same speed.* Bell's Law embodies an important insight—applications that wait obviously make poor use of computing resources—but that is not the whole story. There is another angle to this guideline that is equally important: *Applications should not make the user wait.*

Real-Time Systems Design

A good business information system is designed to be a real-time system for the business process. Real-time systems must always run as fast (or faster) than the external process they support. Similarly, a business process should not be expected to wait for a computer process that is supposed to support it. For example:

▶ Users read, use, and update corporate information. Computers supply shared information by reading and updating databases. A responsive computer system should keep several copies of the most useful information in different locations, so that there is a copy handy whenever a user needs one.

▶ Some high-performance applications require high-speed access to remote data. In that case, every component on the path from client to remote server should be especially designed and monitored to make sure that it supports this particular application. When a client workstation waits for a process running on another node in the network to complete, not only is the workstation being used inefficiently, but the user is also wasting valuable time.

▶ For most business purposes, information supplied to users does not always have to be current. Some information can be a few seconds, minutes, or hours out of date. Other information can be dated summaries. Users just need to know how current the information is and should be given information appropriate for the business task. They should not have to wait for information that is more current than they need.

▶ The computer system must keep all the information consistent. Users don't care how, when, or where that happens. They should not be expected to have anything to do with that process, and certainly not have to wait for it to be done.

As software engineers and designers we don't always distinguish the user's role from that of the computer. Often, our mental viewpoint is that of the computer system itself, especially when we have to focus on issues of efficiency and scalability.

But during the application design process we must also step outside our normal roles as software engineers to imagine ourselves in the shoes of the user for whom we are designing the perfect application. As the user, we are the masters, in control. The computer system should be a willing servant, doing our bidding—but unobtrusively, in the background, without ever expecting us to wait for things we don't care about. We should design all systems to work this way.

10.1 *Locality Principle: Group components based on their usage.* We will get the best performance when any resource or server (such as a routine, file, database, processor, memory, network, or storage device) is configured to match the demands placed on it by the application workload. To apply the locality principle, we must:

▶ Design components and applications to match the demands of the business

▶ Design a computing environment to match the logical processing needs

▶ Design and tune applications to match the processing resources available

Designing a Distributed Application

When designing a distributed application, we must make a series of decisions at seven distinct levels, which we can summarize as:

1. The business process
   ▶ What are the successive stages or tasks of the business process?
   ▶ What are the performance requirements for those tasks?
   ▶ We discuss some related issues in the next section, *Understanding What the Business Process Needs.*
2. The information to support the process
   ▶ What data must be read, displayed, captured, or updated during the business process?
   ▶ For data that is read, how current must it be?
   ▶ For data that is captured or updated, how quickly must the changes be made available to other applications?
3. The location of that information
   ▶ What are the source and/or target locations of that data?
   ▶ See the related section a bit later, *Guidelines for Data Distribution.*
4. How to connect the process with the data
   ▶ Where should data processing occur? Should we fetch the data to the process or ship the process to the data?

▶ Should this connection be made dynamically (at execution time) or statically at an earlier time?

▶ See the later section, *How to Group Process and Data.*

5. The logical application flow

▶ What is the logical flow of the application that implements or supports the business process?

▶ How will the application components interact with their user(s) and with each other?

▶ See the later section, *Designing the Application Flow.*

6. Task completion rules

▶ For each stage within the business process, what happens if we cannot complete the task?

▶ What are all the things that can go wrong, and how will the application design handle them?

▶ See the later section, *Control, Transactions, and Rules.*

7. The software mechanisms needed to make it happen

▶ What type of system software and middleware should we use?

▶ What kinds of messages must be sent and received among the application components?

▶ See the later section, *How Is Control Enforced?*

In the sections that follow, we discuss each of these seven areas in turn, repeating the guidelines that focus on the actual design process and emphasize the performance consequences of the various design decisions.

Understanding What the Business Process Needs

Good design depends on knowledge of the processing requirements:

▶ We cannot produce a reasonable design for performance unless we know the business. Application performance always depends on usage patterns. When we design distributed systems, usage should control the design.

▶ Although "good performance" is usually part of the informal requirements, performance requirements must be made explicit.

▶ The distributed business process will determine the choices available for improving the performance of an application.

▶ The business transaction provides the basis for all constraints on data integrity and consistency, which, in turn, influence our ability to improve performance by relaxing synchronous integrity enforcement.

▶ Business transactions and their performance requirements are the starting point for design. We cannot design optimal systems by assembling separate solutions to low-level functional requirements.

As we pointed out in Part II of the book in our discussions of SPE, good design also requires a realistic assessment of the system's capabilities. We conclude this chapter with some techniques for projecting the likely performance characteristics of different types of distributed applications.

> **10.2** *Know the user.* The software designer who knows why, how, and when an application will be used can create software that closely matches the user's needs and uses system software components harmoniously.

> **10.16** *Know the capacity requirements.* Knowing expected workload volumes and their relationship to key business factors is the only way we can be confident we have sized the client, network, and server components correctly.

Design Involves Management Trade-offs. Performance is never the *only* goal; it is simply one among many important goals. Performance is neither free nor an automatic by-product of pursuing some other goal. Achieving acceptable performance requires development skills, time, and money—all of which are in limited supply. Management must weigh performance goals against the competing claims for those scarce resources.

> **5.5** *Objectives must balance individual, community, and enterprise goals.* An ideal world of instantaneous, simultaneous read and update access to all corporate data by all users is not technologically feasible. When setting objectives, we must strike a balance among:

> ▶ The need for responsiveness in particular subsets of the workload
> ▶ The need to maximize overall throughput given the resources available
> ▶ The cost of implementing computing solutions to business problems
> ▶ The time to deliver those solutions

Design Involves Technical Trade-offs. Performance design is a process of making trade-offs, the goal of which is always to get the work done in the most efficient way that meets the users' objectives for responsiveness.

> **14.2** *Make trade-offs among computing resources.* The software engineer who understands performance strives to eliminate bottlenecks by creating a design that makes the best possible use of *all* the available computing resources. Exchanging resources with spare capacity for a bottlenecked resource will usually improve both overall throughput and response times.

> **14.3** *Reduce delays by substituting faster resources.* When making trade-offs among the available computing resources, reduce response

times by substituting faster resources for any resource that is a bottleneck. Strategies for improving performance include substituting disk storage for network I/O, processor cycles for disk I/O, and memory for processor cycles.

Facts Are Our Friends.   When designing systems, facts beat prejudices, superstitions, and hunches every time. Performance in distributed systems is often seen as a function of network efficiency. But performance can also be limited by the processors at a particular node, by the speed of storage devices, or by contention for shared data resources. In fact, actual performance is always the combination of an application's processing, its environment, and its usage. There is no substitute for understanding all three.

> **3.13** *The application-resource usage matrix.*   An application-resource usage matrix describes how a set of applications uses a set of computer resources. Knowing this information is the key to understanding the performance of those applications and how to tune either the applications or the resources.
> Given application frequencies, the matrix can yield useful insights into likely causes of performance problems in the areas of resource capacity or application response time.

Guidelines for Data Distribution

From our previous discussions of architecture, recall that the logic behind data distribution in the enterprise client/server environment is for business process workflows to determine the processing and for the location of processing to (ideally) determine data placement. Having said that, we must deal with various complications and constraints.

The Basic Guidelines

Most data placement decisions involve balancing the following four issues:

1. *The Locality Principle:* Logically related tables will probably be used together.
   ▶ Make sure you understand the logical database design.
   ▶ Avoid separating logically related data (recall Guideline 10.6).
2. *Ownership:* The department that owns and updates the data often determines where the master copy of certain data resides. As a result, important tables may need to be replicated elsewhere.
3. *Environmental constraints:* When considering where to place data in the enterprise, environmental constraints other than performance may be the most important. For example:
   ▶ What are the data security and availability requirements? In a corporate network, some nodes may be more secure or reliable than others.

▶ Capacity limitations may inhibit data relocation. How large is the database or database fragment being considered for distribution? Compare projections of table growth with the disk capacities of servers. (Recall Guidelines 10.15, 10.16, and 10.17.)

4. *Usage patterns and sharing:* Understand how the data is actually used.

   ▶ Are some tables shared by multiple locations? Which locations use the data most? If possible, for shared data, compile a usage matrix of tables by user location.

   ▶ Evaluate the effect of moving shared tables to a shared enterprise server, considering the performance penalty of WAN access.

   ▶ Prefer LAN access to WAN access. Consider distribution schemes like splitting rows, columns, and fragments across locations, to keep remote data access to a minimum.

Resolving Conflicts Among the Guidelines

Notice that this set of guidelines can lead to fundamental conflicts that must be resolved. These are illustrated by Figure 17.1.

Recall that the sixth performance principle (which we discussed in Chapter 14) is the Trade-off Principle. The need for trade-offs arises because it is difficult to create a single design that will address the performance needs of individuals, applications, and the system as a whole, when:

▶ Individual users in different locations need rapid access to shared data.

▶ Various applications use the same data in different ways.

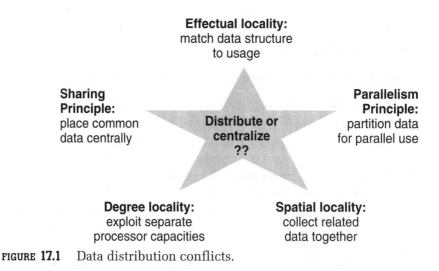

Effectual locality:
match data structure
to usage

Sharing Principle:
place common
data centrally

Distribute or centralize ??

Parallelism Principle:
partition data
for parallel use

Degree locality:
exploit separate
processor capacities

Spatial locality:
collect related
data together

FIGURE **17.1**   Data distribution conflicts.

▶ The entire enterprise needs to maximize its use of scarce computing resources

   To resolve these kind of conflicts, we can:

▶ Review the performance objectives of applications that need access to data
  shared across locations, to determine whether depending on remote access to
  shared data will be fast enough.
▶ When deciding which applications need faster access to data, weigh application performance objectives, business priories, and processing frequencies.
▶ Consider replicating shared tables at local servers to improve response times.
  Especially good candidates for replication are slowly changing code tables
  and other reference tables that can be updated periodically. For other tables,
  consider the volatility of the information and the level of currency required by
  the business application.

Multiphase Updating of Replicated Data

If possible, avoid any design that requires multisite updates within a single
transaction. Prefer a multiphase asynchronous approach to updating, like the
one shown in Figure 17.2.

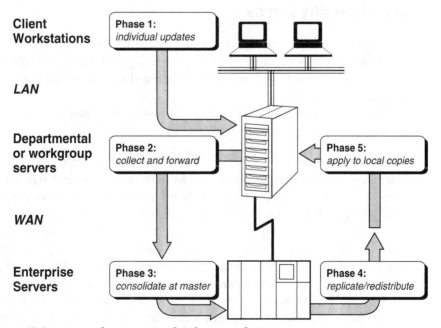

FIGURE **17.2**   Asynchronous multiphase updating.

Phase 1: Update.   Updates are first recorded in a copy of the database at a local node. The local database copy acts as a more current cache of a master version stored centrally. If possible, the local version is a fragment of the master, containing only the subset needed for typical local operations. If data can be perfectly partitioned—for example, when each region stores and uses only regional data—then there is no need for phases 4 and 5 of this process. However, not all shared data can be partitioned in this way.

Phase 2: Collect.   Copies of the local updates are then forwarded asynchronously to a master copy of the data at a central location. There are a variety of ways to do this—as individual update messages, as a batch, or using DBMS replication software.

Phase 3: Consolidate.   Updates are posted to the master version of the data, possibly in batches, depending on the appropriate balance of data currency and update efficiency.

Phase 4: Redistribute.   Updates are later propagated asynchronously to the dependent copies at the local nodes.

Phase 5: Apply.   Updates are applied to the data fragment at the local node.

Data Integrity Issues

For more discussion of this style of processing, see Chapter 20, *Using Data Replication.* However, note that this processing *style* does not require a replication *product*—it can be implemented using distributed application logic and application middleware.

When data is distributed and/or replicated, we must evaluate several data integrity issues.

Multisite Consistency.   If related tables are located at separate sites, how will multisite updates be accomplished? In particular, how and when will any intertable integrity rules be enforced? Even though such relationships may exist, processing will be simplified and perform better if business requirements allow intersite consistency to be relaxed for short periods during the updating process. For example, even though the central master copy of data may be maintained in a consistent state, the local copies may be temporarily inconsistent because of the delays in an asynchronous updating process.

The style of processing we have described might be called *bidirectional replication.* Whether it is actually possible for *the same data element* to be updated simultaneously at more than one location depends on the application. In many cases, although updates flow in both directions, the nature of the business process is such that these updates are to different data elements. Often this occurs because although all nodes in the network may see all the data, update authority is partitioned among the nodes. An example of this would be customers assigned to a particular sales office or products assigned to a particular factory. When the business uses these kinds of partitioning schemes, the information processing flow can be simplified because we do not need to create elaborate procedures to resolve potential update conflicts that cannot actually occur in practice. For more about this subject, refer to Chapter 20.

Batching and Data Integrity.   When planning to handle updates to replicated data synchronously using a batch process, estimate how long the update process will take as application and data volumes grow. Here are some issues to consider:

▶ Replication has its own costs. What will be the impact of replication on network traffic? How long will it take to refresh large replicated tables? Recall Guideline 8.26.
▶ Large updates should be done using high-speed batch utilities, never as a long series of individual update transactions. Recall Guideline 9.17.
▶ Can we make the data temporarily unavailable during the update "window" without disrupting normal business operations?
▶ Will it be better to partition the data and perform the update in smaller batches, one partition at a time?
▶ Will the design selected still maintain the right balance between data currency, batch size, update frequency, and data availability as volumes grow?

We discuss replication performance issues further in Chapter 20, *Using Data Replication.*

> **8.26** *Weigh replication savings and costs.*   Although replicating frequently used enterprise data can reduce WAN traffic by applications, the replication process itself consumes additional WAN resources. The Workload Principle must be applied to the combination of the information processing workload *and* the replication activity.

> **9.17** *Batch processing requires a different approach.*   Processing a million updates in batch is not like a million online transactions, back to back. A sort/merge technique should be used to minimize the overhead of repeatedly searching the target database for the location of the updates.

How to Group Process and Data

When designing applications for performance, evaluate the choices of data access techniques using the following order of preference:

1. Store data at the local server, using a replication scheme if necessary. Data replication is basically just a static, preplanned caching mechanism.
2. Use an intelligent dynamic caching scheme to retain a local copy of frequently used data that resides at a remote location.
3. Invoke the required processing at the remote location where the data resides (function shipping).
4. Use a multiphase design that will retrieve the minimum amount of data necessary before unblocking the client process. Use additional asynchronous tasks to return any further data required.
5. Use remote data access middleware to fetch all the data required to the client.

If you have been keeping the SPE design principles in mind, you will see immediately that this list is derived by applying the Efficiency Principle. For more detailed discussions, refer to Chapter 9 and, in particular, Guideline 9.2: *Fixing relationships increases efficiency.*

> **9.2** *Fixing relationships increases efficiency.*   When a set of computing elements (hardware or software, data or process) is used together more than once, a design involving static grouping of those elements will reduce overhead costs by comparison with more dynamic alternatives.

Designing the Application Flow

How should the application be partitioned into components? This is the key decision of logical design because once it is made, it is difficult to redesign the application, and it may even be difficult to tune its performance.

> **2.1** *Logical layering mistakes cannot be easily resolved at the physical level.*   The logical design for a distributed software application should ensure maximum cohesion within layers and minimum coupling between the layers, while the physical design should maximize the performance of each layer and each link between layers. Effective physical design depends on having a sound logical design to optimize.

Often a large business process subdivides itself naturally into several smaller and logically separable stages. But what about those business stages?

Can they be subdivided further into small processing tasks that can be processed rapidly, possibly even in parallel, in a distributed computing environment?

Task Atomicity

Obviously, a crucial issue is the atomicity characteristics of a task. In practice, with a little thought, even seemingly atomic tasks can often be subdivided into subtasks, especially if we have a way to make the intermediate results secure.

Once again, the analogy with manual processes is helpful. Suppose you want to total up 10,000 checks you just received in the mail. Rather than doing the whole process in one step, you would do it in batches, recording subtotals. This approach allows several people to work on the job in parallel and also guarantees that the process can be restarted from an intermediate result after a failure.

Here are three examples of how computing processes can be subdivided to improve perceived response times:

▶ When retrieving a set of related information, the user typically does not need all the information at once. The retrieval process can therefore be thought of as two (or more) stages, in which the most essential subset of the information is retrieved quickly, with the balance coming later in a second batch. The 80/20 rule can be applied to most data retrieval situations to identify the critical subset of data. We can even design the database to optimize the retrieval of this subset.

▶ Fetching the second batch of data can be made optional and triggered by a user action. Alternatively, it can always be fetched in parallel with the first, but by a second, longer-running, parallel task. Or—in a further subdivision—the second batch might first be extracted into a temporary holding area on the server and later brought to the client only if and when it is requested.

▶ When updating a set of related data, rather than having the client application wait for all the updates to complete successfully, the update request can be simply logged quickly in a (secure) queue of updates. If the queue is implemented as a DBMS table, the DBMS's recovery facilities protect it from accidental loss. Or secure MQ middleware can be used to guarantee delivery of the request to another queue in another location. Later, a separate process can read the queue and make the real updates. This separates the update request, which is fast, from the update process, which may be a lot slower, depending on the network and server environments. The update may be delayed because the server is busy or because of contention between the updating process and other database work.

In the third of these examples, by allowing some delay between stages, we are able to subdivide one update process into three (or four) stages: <*decide* on updates>, <*record* decision>, possibly <*transfer* the update request to another location>, and <*update* database>. If either of the first two fails, we must start again. After that, the update is guaranteed to happen.

Notice how much this differs from the TP-Lite approach of using DBMS-managed stored procedures on the databases' server. With that technique, all the successive phases of the update happen as a single synchronous transaction controlled by the client.

Designing Multiphase Applications

Distributed applications consist of processes and messages. To design a multiphase application, we must understand and clearly define and document each process, each message, and the message paths.

Process Attributes.   Processes are defined by business functions, and business functions have some very specific requirements that can be classified as attributes. The relationships between processes dictate additional attributes. Issues that must be considered include:

▶ **Repeatable or nonrepeatable.** A repeatable process is simply one where the user (or another process) has no effect on an important resource. An inquiry can be repeated, but the update to a bank balance cannot.

▶ **Updating or nonupdating.** Some processes make permanent changes to data, others read data, yet others simply participate in the application flow.

▶ **Visible or invisible.** If several successive updates are made to a single data element, then provided there are no other side effects, all but the last update is invisible. This is significant when we plan to batch updates or replicate updates at another location.

▶ **Revocable or irrevocable.** When any phase of a multiphase business process cannot complete, the appropriate set of compensating actions are taken to undo whatever partial progress has been made. When we identify an *updating* process, this usually triggers a requirement to design a *compensating process,* which we discuss a bit later. An irrevocable process is one whose effects cannot be backed out.

Obviously, it is important to identify any irrevocable processes because they require very careful handling. Provided the information system is designed with business requirements in mind, this happens fairly naturally. After all, the majority of *business* transactions do include irrevocable actions, so most business processes already take this issue into account. Once again, keeping the computer system's design close to that of the business system can help us to avoid doing things in the wrong order.

▶ **Compliant or noncompliant.** A compliant process always accepts requests; a noncompliant process may reject requests. We may have to treat external systems that are outside our control as noncompliant. In the travel agent example in Chapter 15, the hotel reservation system may be a noncompliant process, while the airline reservation system would be assumed to be compliant.

Message Attributes.   For each message between processes, we must identify whether it is persistent, to a local or remote process, whether a reply is required, and whether it is synchronous or asynchronous.

Performance Attributes

The preceding attributes apply primarily to the logical design of the application. From a performance viewpoint, there are three further issues to consider:

▶ **Responsiveness.** When users need to receive information to support their business activity, the system must supply that information promptly, as defined by the needs of the business process.

▶ **Synchronous or asynchronous.** Users should not have to wait for processing that only the computer system cares about. Identifying asynchronous processes is the first step in creating high-performance systems. Asynchronous processes minimize perceived response times and create opportunities to apply parallel processing and batching techniques. Some synchronous processes cannot be avoided, however; these need careful design to minimize any response time delays.

▶ **Sequential or parallel.** We must determine which tasks must be performed sequentially and which, if any, can take place in parallel. For scalability, the ideal design is one that consists of many small, independent tasks that can potentially be processed in parallel.

Compensating Transactions

Interdependent tasks constrain our processing options. On the other hand, splitting an application into many small stages complicates the analysis of possible task failure scenarios and the design of compensating transactions and recovery processing. In practice, we will probably need to balance performance and complexity concerns.

Next, we consider some further aspects of task *interdependency* and *completion rules*.

Control, Transactions, and Rules

For each stage within each business process, we must decide what happens if we cannot complete a stage. Is the entire business process atomic, or can some parts complete and other fail? The concept of *spheres of control* is helpful here. Conceptually, we can think of completing a business process as the successful invocation of a hierarchy of concentric spheres of control.

Spheres of Control

The concentric rectangles in Figure 17.3 represent the hierarchy of spheres of control for a typical business process. The business process is implemented by a combination of manual actions and software applications. Software applications consist of multiple components, many of which manipulate data stored in a database managed by a DBMS.

Ultimately, our objective is to read and write that data correctly. So, within each sphere of control, mechanisms must exist to ensure that all actions taken (which include, of course, invocations of processes at the next lower level) complete successfully. A failure within each sphere of control must be handled appropriately by the next higher *calling* sphere of control. We must design business and software processes accordingly.

Looking at the spheres of control in this way helps us to understand what different kinds of middleware and standard software componentry can be used for. In Figure 17.4, we have added annotations within each sphere of control, showing the roles of various components of a system.

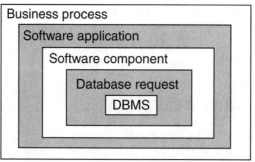

FIGURE 17.3   Spheres of control.

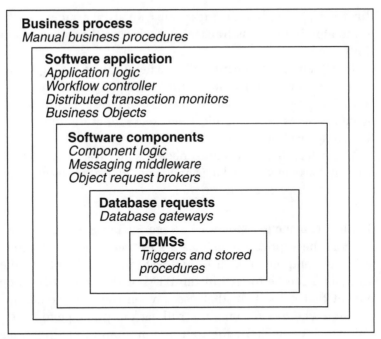

Business process
Manual business procedures

Software application
Application logic
Workflow controller
Distributed transaction monitors
Business Objects

Software components
Component logic
Messaging middleware
Object request brokers

Database requests
Database gateways

DBMSs
Triggers and stored procedures

FIGURE 17.4   Software scope.

Can the DBMS Enforce Business Rules?   Database professionals sometimes argue that (ideally, at least) all integrity rules, since they concern the correctness of data, should be enforced by the DBMS. Figure 17.3, however, makes it clear that responsibility for correct operation of the whole system cannot be isolated within a single low-level component like DBMS-enforced integrity rules. To begin with, two practical limitations make this suggestion unworkable:

▶ To determine correctness, a rule would need a lot of information about user roles and authorities, locations, time, and application context that simply is not stored in a DBMS today.
▶ In a distributed environment, with federated databases, individual DBMSs support variable levels of integrity enforcement. So overall rule enforcement across heterogeneous database servers cannot possibly reside within an individual server; it obviously must occur outside the scope of a single DBMS.

But even if a DBMS stored all the necessary data, it would still not be possible to enforce data integrity entirely within the DBMS. As Figure 17.4

illustrates, individual business rules are always subject to the larger concept of the atomic business transaction, which either succeeds or fails in its entirety.

DBMS-enforced integrity rules, whether they are implemented as methods in an object-oriented DBMS (OODBMS) or as triggers and stored procedures in an RDBMS, cannot possibly be aware of all the conditions that are understood by components of the application executing at the higher levels—they are at the wrong level in the control hierarchy.

Ultimately, the DBMS must obey the application's rules of consistency because it does not know what is and is not logically a transaction. This is the application's responsibility.

Can the Transaction Monitor Enforce Business Rules?   If we choose to implement the application using a distributed transaction monitor (DTM)—the software component with the widest sphere of control—then some of this awareness can be lodged in the DTM or the highest-level application component that calls it. In that case, when the time comes to make the final decision whether to commit or roll back any change to the database, that decision will be made by the transaction monitor (TM), which is the "coordinator" of the whole process, and not by the DBMS, which is just a "participant."

The idea that we can enforce data integrity from inside the DBMS is a fundamentally mistaken one. On the other hand, to enforce integrity using a distributed transaction monitor, we must be willing to tie all the components of the application together into a single, interconnected, synchronous process.

Rules Servers.   In some quarters of the industry, there is considerable interest in the idea of creating separate rules servers that record the definitions of business rules in a single central location. The goal is to eliminate the problems caused by duplicate versions of business rules becoming buried and lost inside code. While this is a good idea in theory, in our view, for a rule server to work, it will have to be an integral component of workflow controller middleware that understands the process flow between components.

To maintain data integrity, software applications must be designed to be aware of the scope of business transactions and to handle them correctly. When business transactions are implemented as multitransaction workflows, integrity is something that is achieved only through the combined efforts of all components. Ultimately, it can be enforced only by the business process at the highest level.

Table 17.1   **Client/Server Application Patterns**

What Is in Control?	Single phase	Multi-phase
Client in Control	▸ Application using heterogeneous database gateways ▸ Client applications using RPC	▸ Groupware applications
Application Server Layer in Control	▸ Server-based application using distributed transaction monitors	▸ Server-based applications using MQ middleware
Broker Software in Control	▸ Applications using DBMS stored procedures ▸ Applications using distributed DBMS	▸ Workflow controller middleware ▸ Publish/subscribe middleware
Distributed Peers, No Single Point of Control	▸ Applications using distributed objects	▸ MQ-based apps, store, forward, and forget ▸ Applications built using agents

How Is Control Enforced?

Table 17.1 looks at a related issue: *Which component of a distributed application controls its logical flow?*. The table shows eight possibilities. The first column lists the options for single-phase applications; the second lists those for multiphase. Within each, there are four options for enforcing the flow of control:

▸ The flow of control is directed by client code.
▸ The flow of control is directed by application server code.
▸ The flow of control is handled by an independent broker component.
▸ No single component is in control. During the business process, the locus of control moves among peer components.

The table lists some possible implementation techniques within each category. Based on the conclusions we drew in Chapters 15 and 16, we have highlighted the lower three boxes in the rightmost column. We believe that these are the approaches most suitable for developing scalable, high-volume distributed applications.

We are certainly not arguing that no other techniques can ever be used successfully. Hardware keeps getting faster, and operating systems, systems software, and middleware products keep improving. Obviously, there is an enormously wide range of potential applications waiting to be built and an equally diverse range of potential computing environments. And success stories will appear in every category.

Our conclusion concerns *the probability of success* using various techniques and relates, in particular, to the six dimensions of growth that we introduced in Chapter 13 (see Table 13.1). In our view, as we move up this scale of complexity, successful high-performance applications are most likely to be built using products and techniques that follow the approaches we have highlighted in the lower-right corner of Table 17.1.

Case Studies: How Is MQ Being Used?

In this section, we'll look at two design implementations of a bank loan system.[1] We will also explore the experiences of a major international bank in using the product for migration and coexistence with a legacy system, as well as the development of the replacement system. These studies will give us a glimpse of MQSeries application design and performance as well as a taste of what users like and don't like about the product.

Bank Loans.   The requirements for this application seem fairly straightforward. A walk-in customer applies for a loan. The bank has advertised fast service and would like to approve the loan within 10 minutes. After approval, the branch confirms the loan and hands over the cash. To finish up, the branch notifies the head office.

There are two alternative approaches to this problem, neither of them perfect. Making the process synchronous and revocable would be best for the

---

[1]This case study was first published in an article by John Kneiling, "Distributing Applications with Message-Oriented Middleware," that appeared in the February 1996 and April 1996 issues of *InfoDB*. It is adapted from IBM's *An Early Look at Application Considerations Involved with MQSeries* (GG24-4469).

bank's financial integrity, but the required availability of all processes might not allow for 10-minute processing. An asynchronous and irrevocable approach would be good for customer service, but there's always the chance that an undeserving customer will walk out the door with the bank's cash. We can also question whether a loan is actually an irrevocable process. This scenario is not quite as straightforward as it seems; it requires some very careful discussion with the users who define business requirements and assess the risks of either approach.

The Synchronous Approach

In the synchronous message flow (see Figure 17.5):

▶ The branch interviews a customer, then sends a message over queue *MsgRequestLoanClearance* to process *RequestLoan,* also at the branch. (It is noteworthy here that *InterviewCustomer* is a human process, and that the computer's primary logic is simply sending a message. MQ designs often cross the man-machine boundary.)

▶ *RequestLoan,* in turn, sends message *MsgHQLoanRequest* to the head office, which approves (or disapproves) the loan, returning the reply (*MsgHQLoanOK*) to process *HandMoney* at the branch.

▶ This process then sends *MsgLoanClearanceOK* to *InterviewCustomer.* The human participant in *InterviewCustomer* then notifies the customer of the result and, if approved, the bank hands over the money.

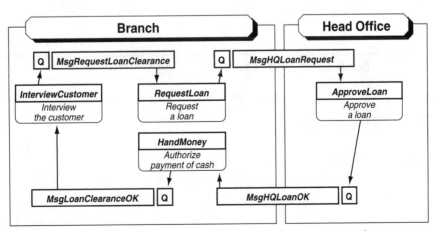

FIGURE 17.5   Bank loan applications: The synchronous approach.

Tables 17.2, 17.3, and 17.4 briefly describe the process relationships, process attributes, and message attributes for this flow. Process *InterviewCustomer,* for instance has a downstream process of *RequestLoan.*

In the synchronous solution, all processes must be revocable before *ApproveLoan.* The head office takes responsibility for approving the loan.

Table 17.2   **Bank Loan Application: Process Relationships**

Upstream Process	*InterviewCustomer*	*RequestLoan*	*ApproveLoan*	*HandMoney*
Downstream Process	*RequestLoan*	*ApproveLoan*	*HandMoney*	*InterviewCustomer*
Message Name	*(MsgRequestLoan Clearance)*	*MsgHQLoan Request*	*MsgHQLoanOK*	*(MsgLoan ClearanceOK)*

Table 17.3   **Bank Loan Application: Process Attributes**

	InterviewCustomer	**RequestLoan**	**ApproveLoan**	**HandMoney**
Repeatable	Y	N	N	N
Updatable	N	Y	Y	Y
Visible	N	Y	Y	Y
Revocable	Y	Y	N	N
Compliant	N	N	N	Y

Table 17.4   **Bank Loan Application: Message Attributes**

Message	Reply	Persistent	Synch	Remote	Comments
MsgRequestLoanClearance	Y	Y	Y	Y	May be manual dialog
MsgHQLoanRequest	Y	Y	Y	Y	
MsgHQLoanOK	Y	Y	Y	Y	
MsgLoanClearanceOK	N	Y	Y	N	Concludes when cash is handed over

The Asynchronous Approach

In the asynchronous approach (see Figure 17.6), *InterviewCustomer* issues a request (message queue MsgRequestLoan) to the loan approval process (at the branch this time, not the head office). If the loan is approved, *ApproveLoan* passes control to *HandMoney* (with or without using a message), which uses message *MsgLoanClearanceOK* to ask *InterviewCustomer* to disburse the loan. *ApproveLoan* also issues a message over queue *MsgHQLoanInform* to inform the head office about the loan so that it can be properly recorded.

Using this approach, *ApproveLoan* may be irrevocable, and the local branch office takes responsibility for the loan.

Core Banking System: MQI Applications

Our next study involves a system that needed to perform high-volume IMS/DB and CICS-DB2 replication between cities with a delay of less than one second for its legacy system. (See Chapter 20 for a discussion of replication) The system also needed to exchange messages with the new system (UNIX- and NT-based), with message integrity and short delays. Messages also needed to be exchanged within the new system itself.

The first problem was that the bank has three major banking centers in cities A, B, and C. Some of the business is in City A, which centralizes all of the IMS database customer records. These records must be current and presented as a single database image. The large number of accesses to the database requires high performance.

The solution (in effect since February 1995) was to use MQSeries to replicate all three regional databases to a central database in City A. The replicated database appears local to applications in City A. This local access produces high availability and is transparent to legacy applications. Sending applications are insulated from target system availability problems, as MQSeries will queue for hours or days if necessary. The performance impact has had negligible effect on updating applications, and reading applications still have local access to data.

The Send and Receive components of the solution architecture update the source database with IMS DL/I, which activates an IMS capture exit. The exit passes the updated segments to an Apply program with the MQPut command, which uses MQGet to retrieve them, then updates the remote database with the appropriate database call.

The transport component consists largely of MQSeries, which moves messages as soon as possible. In this application, queue and log buffers were large (measured in the thousands). Transport happens in real time if MQM Transmission Channel and MQM are active and enabled. If they are not, transport is

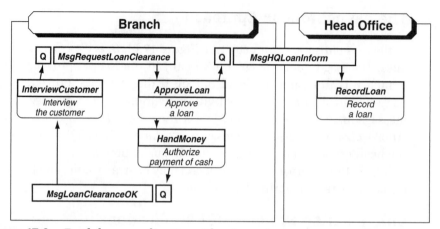

FIGURE 17.6   Bank loan application: The Asynchronous approach.

delayed until they are started. Good performance was attributed to the logger, which is reliable and offers high performance, providing warm-start support without loss of duplicate records, even after system crashes.

The system supports between 1 and 2 million messages per day between three systems in three cities, and over half a million messages within one system. On peak days, the system handles 10 million messages overall. The queue datasets are 4 gigabytes, and approximately 6 million segments are transmitted daily. The system has been able to absorb high volume when the link or target system is down.

System throughput is very encouraging, handling more than 700 messages per second within one MVS and one MQM on an untuned system. Between cities, the rate is 240 messages/second per 1 megabit/second network link. The application exploits 70 percent of the nominal bandwidth of the network for data transfer, with a delivery delay between source and target database updates of less than 1 second when the link is not overloaded. IMS BMP/batch performance depends on the time interval between the application's two commits.

MQSeries series was chosen for this problem because of its high integrity and performance and its support of major MVS environments. More important, however, the entire banking system is currently being replaced with an architecture of MVS, UNIX, and Windows NT. The new system will be highly distributed, with interfaces to as-yet unknown external and internal applications. MQI will be used for communication within the new system, migration from the legacy system, and interfaces to external applications. What's missing are performance-monitoring tools that can identify problems with alerts when transmission queues aren't delivered and when the number of queue messages increases.

The Response Time Reference Model

In this section we look at the components of response time for a distributed application. To do this, we present and review a response time reference model. The model comprises 20 stages, representing the 20 principal elements of transaction response time, as shown in Figure 17.7.

We will review the model in three stages:

► First, we introduce the model.
► Next, we look at the major components—client, local server, remote server, and networks.
► Finally, we consider each of the 20 stages.

During our review, we continue our practice of repeating important performance guidelines from earlier chapters, where they apply.

About the Model

The model represents the typical flow of a transaction in an enterprise client/server environment. A *request* is initiated at the workstation and is

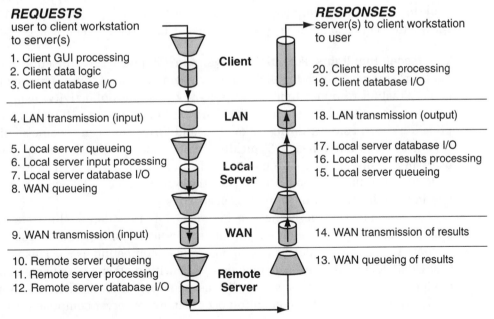

FIGURE 17.7   The response time reference model.

processed by both a local and a remote server and the connecting networks, and *results* are passed back from the servers to the originating client. Although not shown in Figure 17.7, the model is intended to cover applications that use zero, one, or many servers, either locally via a LAN or remotely via a WAN. Also, although we use the terms "request" and "results," the model can represent either query or update processing, since the only difference is the amount of data being passed in either direction.

Response Time of Synchronous Processing.   The purpose of the reference model is to remind us of *all* the different things that *could contribute to application response time* in an enterprise client/server environment. Because it comprises 20 distinct elements, the model may appear to be overly complex. In practice, of course, not every application will have components corresponding to every one of the 20 elements.

Note that any asynchronous parallel or deferred processing of parts of an application would not be included in the model because it does not contribute to response time. The purpose of the model is to help us understand the components of response time that lie on the application's synchronous processing path.

Model Variations.   As it appears in Figure 17.7, the model illustrates the traditional three-tier client/server configuration. The same ideas apply equally well to applications implemented using Web technology. As Figure 17.8 shows, the sequence of the stages simply needs to be rearranged.

The Model Highlights Potential Delays.   In Chapter 11 we discussed the Sharing Principle, which highlights a basic characteristic of computer systems, namely that all response time comprises only two types of activity: *using* resources and *waiting* for resources. The contributions to response time by an application's *use* of slower devices like disks and WAN links can become significant if usage is fairly heavy. Typically, when resources are shared by many users in an enterprise environment, applications will spend even more time *waiting* to use those same devices. And the waiting time will increase exponentially as the number of competing users rises.

The placement of the funnels in Figure 17.7 is intended to illustrate this phenomenon—all the funnels except the first indicate components whose sole purpose is to represent delays in response due to competing users. This is not to say that device contention cannot also occur within other components of the model, such as waiting for a server disk as a component of database I/O time. Typically, some amount of contention occurs in every server component—it is just not represented by a separate component in the reference model.

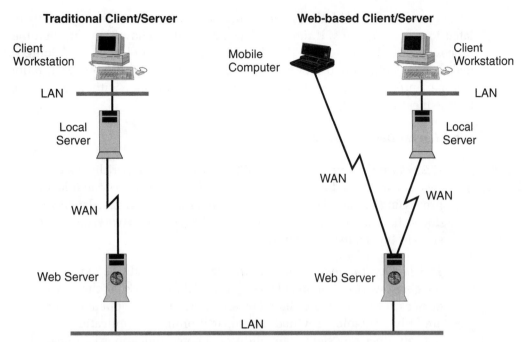

FIGURE 17.8   Two reference model variations.

8.7 *Focus on I/O operations.*   Enterprise client/server applications tend to be I/O bound. I/O operations are orders of magnitude slower than processor operations, and consume large numbers of instructions. Tuning that reduces I/O, especially on a shared server, will improve both application response times and overall throughput.

Major Components of the Model

Here we note a few guidelines that relate to the major components of the model—client, local server, remote server, and networks.

Workstation Design Guidelines.   Earlier in the book we stated Guideline 10.22:

10.22 *Natural client processing.*   When we design two-tier client/server systems, all functions that support a single user belong on the client. The initial design goal should be to offload all single-user computation, except for that related to processing shared data, to the client workstation.

Let's revisit this guideline. Even though some processing may be directly related to a user's actions, if the user does not need to know about it, then that processing can be shifted off the client and performed elsewhere if doing so makes the system more responsive. On the other hand, if the client workstation has spare processing capacity and if work can be done there without disrupting the business process, by all means do it on the client.

Local Server Design Guidelines

10.23 *Natural server processing.*   When we design two-tier client/server systems, all shared functions belong on the server. These include all processing of shared data on behalf of all clients, until that data is reduced to a suitable form to hand over to the client workstation or store in the database, as appropriate.

11.8 *Lighten the load on a shared server.*   Although the devices at the client workstation may be less powerful than those at the server, devices at the server are shared by all clients, whereas client devices are fully available. Provided that repartitioning an application does not introduce any significant additional communications overhead, systematically removing even relatively small amounts of work from a shared server can produce surprising improvements in overall application response times.

Enterprise Server Design Guidelines.   Designing for an enterprise server component usually means interfacing with the existing enterprise systems, possibly including DBMSs and transaction monitors. Because enterprise servers are likely to be the busiest, to optimize application response times we must minimize the size and frequency of requests. Guideline 11.8, *Lighten the load on a shared server,* which we repeated in the previous section on local servers, applies here also. For high performance, a distributed application should not include any synchronous requests to an enterprise server.

Network Design Guidelines

10.5 *Minimize data transfers between clients and server.*   Communication networks are probably the slowest and most error-prone of all the devices in our systems. As a result, they have the poorest performance characteristics. Creating good spatial locality between data and processes will contribute to optimal performance by minimizing the need to transfer data before it can be processed.

11.17 *Test for network contention.*   It is almost impossible to simulate typical network conditions during development. Plan to test client/server applications in the environment where they're going to be used so that any performance problems can be addressed before placing them into production.

Detailed Components of the Model

We now briefly review each of the 20 components of the reference model.

Stage 1: Client GUI Processing.   For the user, the first major delay in getting the job done occurs right here in the user interface (UI), even before the transaction really gets started. Presentation managers like Windows are certainly not renowned for their speed, but having the right graphics hardware on the client workstation can help speed up this phase.

GUI design is important here, too. A well-designed UI that helps the user get the input right the first time and minimizes the number of actions he or she must take to get to the starting line can cut seconds off the user's true response time, without even touching the rest of the application code.

Applications built using Web-based clients tend to be slower if components of the UI must be downloaded from the Web server. For applications used repeatedly from the same client workstation, static components of the interface should remain in a client-side cache. If there are any dynamic components, then the additional trips across the network (more than likely a WAN) must be factored into the response time.

> **9.3** *Create fixed interfaces for repetitive tasks.*   When an application involves a series of repetitive tasks, the user interface should consist of fixed windows, menus, and dialog boxes, and require a minimum of navigation. Streamlining the interface alone can significantly improve the perceived response time of such an application.

> **10.13** *Create UI paths to support usage scenarios.*   In user interface design, the Locality Principle reminds us to make sure that related actions the user needs to perform are available together. Improving UI efficiency alone can make significant improvements in a user's perception of performance.

> **3.2** *Perceived response time.*   The perceived response time is the amount of time that a user *perceives* a task to take. It is disproportionately influenced by the longest response times. One rule of thumb is that the perceived value of average response time is the 90th percentile value of the response time distribution.

The time required to submit the initial request also contributes to perceived response time. Streamlining the user interface can make significant improvements in the user's perception of a system's performance.

Stage 2: Client Data Logic.   In this stage, we do relatively simple things like validate the user's input and construct the request that will be shipped to a server. If this step is slow, it is usually because some disk I/O is going on (see stage 3) or, more likely, because some network I/O is going on under the covers to retrieve additional information or code from a network server.

> **9.6** *Cache static or slowly changing data.*   Whenever the same data must be transferred repeatedly, create a dynamic cache to retain a copy of the data closer to the application that needs it. Caching can be used to eliminate the overhead of retrieving data using disk I/O, network I/O, or even complex database searches.

> **9.13** *Dynamic inheritance.*   Application development tools that employ dynamic inheritance may perform poorly because of repeated requests from client to server to retrieve inherited components. To eliminate the overhead of dynamic inheritance, select a tool that creates compiled executable modules. When using dynamic inheritance, reduce its overhead by flattening inheritance hierarchies.

Stage 3: Client Database I/O.   Database I/O on the client at this stage might validate input data against tables that have been cached on the client workstation for convenience or log input data for asynchronous transmission in batches to a server.

> **9.14** *Replicated tables.*   Download essential tables (for example, those used to validate input) to the client workstation periodically to minimize repeated network access to the database server.

> **3.11** *Local versus remote disks.*   It is always important to limit disk I/O activity to optimize application performance. If the disk in question is located on a remote server, then this guideline is even more important because of the significantly longer access times involved.

Theoretically, on a fast LAN, shifting I/O from the client to a faster disk device on a local server could actually shorten overall response times, even after allowing for the added LAN transmission time. In practice, we doubt whether any small gains in response time justify placing the extra load on the server.

Stage 4: LAN Transmission (Input).   LANs are fast, but they can become congested if there are lots of competing users, especially if the users are shipping print files and graphic images around in large numbers. A congested LAN is a problem that needs to be addressed and fixed by network specialists; it really should not be the subject of application design. However, if you know you will have to contend with LAN problems, package your requests to minimize the number of LAN transmissions.

> **9.10** *Stored database procedures.*   Minimize repeated network overhead by storing SQL in remote procedures or packages stored with the server DBMS whose data they manipulate. Minimize processing overheads by compiling the procedure once and storing the compiled *access path* or *plan* with the DBMS.

Stage 5: Local Server Queuing.   If we use a transaction monitor (like CICS) or message-queuing middleware to manage our server resources, then our transaction may wait for a free server process to be available. The alternative is the approach typically used by client/server database middleware, in which a new server process is initiated for every concurrent requester. This eliminates stage 5, but as the number of concurrent clients rises we may more than pay for it in contention during stages 6 and 7.

> **10.15** *Degree Locality: Closeness in Capacity.*   For optimal system performance, we must match up the data storage, transmission, and processing demands imposed by the business workload with the capacities of the hardware and software resources that make up the system.

> **10.21** *Dedicated application servers.*   Consider splitting off work onto a dedicated server whenever a single application has a high volume of processing and critical performance objectives.

Stage 6: Local Server Input Processing.   Here we perform processing for the core application logic, enforcing business rules and so on. As with stage 2, this is typically not a long process. In an environment with multiple back-end servers, this is the step where we might break the users' input into separate requests to multiple remote servers. Potential delays here come from I/O (see stage 7) and from contention with other users for the processor, as noted under stage 5.

> **9.9** *Compilers and interpreters.*   For optimal performance at execution time, any module that will be used repeatedly should be com-

piled into machine language once and a permanent copy of the executable code used thereafter.

For unplanned and infrequently executed processing, dynamic compilation at execution time makes sense. But for repeated work, like stored queries that produce standard reports (sometimes called "*canned queries*"), dynamic compilation imposes an excessive and unnecessary level of overhead. For optimal performance, eliminate dynamic SQL from production applications.

Interpreted code does not perform well. Quoted ratios of the relative speed of compiled to interpreted code apply to a single product and processing context, but there seems to be a consensus that a compiled program typically runs 15–20 times faster than its equivalent in interpreted pseudo-code.

Stage 7: Local Server Database I/O.   How much data from how many tables must actually be read to satisfy the user's request? Are there indexes in all the right places, and can the local server DBMS actually use them? Sometimes a relational DBMS has to do an awful lot of I/O just to find a few rows of data.

> **9.15** *Indexing.*   Create indexes to minimize the disk I/O needed to locate frequently used data. For rapid access to data that is used repeatedly, building an index is more efficient than searching the database each time.

> **9.11** *ODBMS technology is ideally suited for a high-performance application server.* In an object-oriented database, the information comprising a single application object may all be stored together in an instance of a stored object rather than scattered among several stored tables. This is why objects perform well when used by the application they were designed for and why ODBMS technology is ideally suited for a high-performance application server.

Stage 8: WAN Queuing.   The local server may use custom-built software or message-queuing middleware to manage a queue of requests to be shipped to remote servers. Whatever the technique, there may well be some delay in getting our input onto a busy corporate WAN.

Stage 9: WAN Transmission (Input).   There will always be some delay getting our input to the remote server; how long depends on the amount of data being sent, the bandwidth of the link, and the distances involved. Tom Bell, a popular speaker on performance issues, once said that "Money can buy bandwidth, but latency is forever!"[2] In other words, the problem with a WAN is that even if we can buy a big pipe to send our data down, we still cannot make it get there any faster.

> **11.11** *Bell's rule of networking. Money can buy bandwidth, but latency is forever.* No matter what the bandwidth of a network, it takes time to send data around the world via satellite links or over multiple hops in a large enterprise network. Every device in a network path contributes to the minimum time required to send messages.

Stage 10: Remote Server Queuing.   Typically transactions arriving at an enterprise server will be managed by transaction management middleware like IMS/TM, CICS, TUXEDO, or TOP END. One purpose of these systems is to ensure efficient sharing of scarce server resources by managing a queue of requesters (recall stage 5 on the local server). Any time spent waiting in the queue contributes to overall response time. Fortunately, these software environments usually offer plenty of tools for prioritizing different classes of transactions and for monitoring workload behavior, so at least this element of response time should be predictable.

Stage 11: Remote Server Processing.   As with stage 6, this stage is typically very short unless there is a lot of database query processing. In that case, the time for I/O (stage 12) will dominate.

> **9.12** *Remote data access gateways and dynamic SQL.* Beware of application generators and other tools that access remote data via SQL gateways—the SQL will be recompiled with each request unless (a) a cache is provided on the server and (b) the statement is reused frequently enough to remain in the cache. For optimal performance, look for a remote data access gateway like the IBM DataJoiner that compiles the SQL and optimizes the access path to the distributed data.

Stage 12: Remote Server Database I/O.   In most production applications, because we know the nature of database requests in advance, we can generally optimize their performance by building the appropriate indexes in the database. However, if remote data access middleware is being used to ship across SQL requests, not only may the execution time of the queries be unpredictable, but there will also be the overhead of binding (compiling) the SQL prior to execution at the remote server.

---

[2]Thomas E. Bell, Rivendell Consultants, 2921 Via Pacheco, Palos Verdes Estates, CA 90274. Telephone (310) 377-5541.

Stage 13: WAN Queuing of Results.   This stage is the inverse of stage 8, except that for queries the response to a single request may comprise multiple messages. Depending on the nature of the request (for example, if results need to be sorted), it may be necessary to generate the entire set of responses before the first can be sent. This can make quite a difference in response time.

Stage 14: WAN Transmission of Results.   This stage is the inverse of stage 9, but it may involve many more messages.

> **9.7** *Avoid cursor SQL update and delete operations on large result tables.*   Except to permit concurrent updating of data in a single table, avoid using a cursor for large updates. To do so may cause the rows to be transferred one at a time from the DBMS server to the client. Substituting a separate SQL UPDATE or DELETE statement may permit block fetching of rows to the client. The trade-off will be some extra processing on the server to locate the rows to be updated or deleted.

> **11.12** *Compression and resource speed.*   The slower a device, the greater the probability that compressing its data will improve application performance.

> **9.19** *Checkpoint large data transfers.*   Any time we must repeat work, that is overhead. Although it takes more development effort to write the code to take checkpoints, making long batch jobs restartable after a failure will save time and computing resources in the long run. This is particularly important for long data transfers over relatively slow networks.

Stage 15: Local Server Queuing.   This stage is the inverse of stage 5, except that now, in addition to waiting for local server processing resources, we may need to wait for more than one request to different remote servers to complete before processing (stage 16) can proceed.

Stage 16: Local Server Results Processing.   Here, separate sets of results can be coordinated and assembled into the single view the application needs. Once all the results are back, this should not be a slow process.

> **10.14** *Federated databases.*   Federated or multidatabase applications that assemble their data at execution time from databases at separate locations have poor temporal locality. For performance-critical applications, create data servers at the departmental or workgroup level

that supply only the subset of information the application needs. This approach will eliminate the processing overhead and response time delays of collecting and joining data at execution time.

Stage 17: Local Server Database I/O.   Here we store responses in local tables, possibly also joining them to other data that is stored locally. We may log transaction completion status, among other things. For queries with large results sets, we may have to scroll through already stored data to retrieve a subset to be sent to the client.

> **9.18** *Use high-performance utilities for data replication.*   When replicating data, it is always more efficient to use high-performance database load utilities than to process changes one at a time.

Stage 18: LAN Transmission (Output).   The stage is the inverse of stage 4; it is typically short.

> **9.8** *Fetch data in blocks, not one row at a time.*   Because some fixed overheads are associated with each message sent and received across the network, regardless of its size, many client/server DBMSs use a technique called blocked fetch or block fetch to minimize the overheads of sending large result sets from the server to the client. Sending a result set in larger blocks, rather than one row at a time, reduces the overhead.

Stage 19: Client Database I/O.   Here we store results and retrieve formatting instructions and other user-related data stored on the client workstation so that we can know how to present the results to the user.

   If our application still needs to do extensive amounts of disk I/O at this stage—for example, to sort and report on the contents of a large result table—we need to remember that workstation disks are probably the slowest disks in the system. Ideally, if the data originated at the server, then we can sort it there before transmission. Similarly, some complex analysis and reporting tasks should be done at the server.

Stage 20: Client Results Processing.   Finally, we can assemble, format, and display the data graphically, interacting with the presentation management software. With queries, is there any overlap between the storing (stage 19) and displaying (stage 20) processes, or must the user wait until the entire result is stored before seeing the first data item? This can make a significant difference in response time if the result set is large because (in the extreme case) it is the difference between the time to retrieve the first and last rows of the result.

8.15 *Minimize the data returned to the application program.* Many programs read more data than the application really needs. To reduce application costs, eliminate excess rows and columns from database requests and make full use of built-in DBMS facilities.

Rules of Thumb for Estimating Response Times

Before we head down the path of design for the distributed environment, it is best that we discard any unrealistic expectations. In this section, we suggest some likely ranges of response times that can be achieved using various design patterns. Or to view these recommendations another way, we suggest the appropriate design approach given a particular set of performance objectives.

We acknowledge that this is a risky undertaking. Technology is wonderfully malleable, and people can use it in clever and unexpected ways. So any time we conclude that a particular design approach is unlikely to work, we fully expect someone to contact us and let us know that their organization has been using exactly that approach successfully for the last year and a half.

On the other hand, for our advice to be useful, we must take positions on difficult design questions. If all our recommendations are obviously correct—such as *"Don't try to get subsecond response time from an application that retrieves and sorts a million rows from a remote database"*—then our advice is also redundant.

Our goal in this section is not to define the limits of what is technologically feasible because highly tuned, special-purpose systems can achieve much better performance than the average system. Our intent is to suggest what types of designs might be reasonable and which might be risky and to suggest when it might be sensible to consider redesigning an application rather than attempting a design with a low probability of success.

We also recognize that different organizations possess different levels of skill and experience in implementing distributed systems. So, in Tables 17.5 and 17.6, we suggest both a conservative and an optimistic view of what is feasible for the performance of a particular design pattern.

Key. The columns of these two tables contain the following information:

- ▶ Column 1: Row sequence number, for ease of reference to entries in the table.
- ▶ Columns 2, 3, and 4 are a measure of the complexity of the application workload.
- ▶ Column 2: Number of requests (1 or >1) for information from a server.
- ▶ Column 3: Size of the request (small or large), really a measure of processing complexity on the server.
- ▶ Column 4: Location of the server(s)—local, remote, or distributed—(more than one remote)

Table 17.5 **Conservative Assessment of Performance Possibilities**

No.	Workload		Some Workload Types	(A) 1–2 Seconds— Slick System	(B) A Few seconds More—Sluggish System	(C) Minutes or Longer— Time for a Cup of Coffee
					Response Objectives	
1	1 Sm	local	Simple LAN-based transactions	VERY HARD (tuned two-tier c/s)	NORMAL (normal two-tier c/s)	EASY (any two-tier c/s)
2	1 Sm	remote	Simple remote transactions	VERY HARD (too much network delay)	NORMAL (tuned three-tier c/s)	EASY (any three-tier or Web c/s)
3	>1 Sm	local	Complex LAN-based transactions	VERY HARD (highly tuned two-tier c/s)	HARD (tuned two-tier c/s)	EASY (any two-tier c/s)
4	>1 Sm	remote	Complex remote transactions	UNLIKELY (too much network delay)	VERY HARD (too much network delay)	EASY (any three-tier or Web c/s)
5	>1 Sm	distrib	Most applications built using distributed objects	NO (too many remote servers)	UNPREDICTABLE (too much remote servers)	EASY (any three-tier or Web c/s)
6	1 Lg	local	Typical data mart requests	NO WAY (too much processing)	HARD (tuned two-tier c/s)	NORMAL (Normal two-tier c/s)
7	1 Lg	remote	Simple enterprise data warehouse requests	OBVIOUSLY NOT (see previous entries)	VERY HARD (tuned three-tier c/s)	NORMAL (normal three-tier or Web c/s)
8	>1 Lg	local	Complex data mart requests	IMPOSSIBLE (way too much processing)	UNLIKELY (too much processing)	NORMAL (normal two-tier c/s)
9	>1 Lg	remote	Typical enterprise data warehouse requests	DOUBLY IMPOSSIBLE	UNATTAINABLE (way too much processing)	NORMAL (normal three-tier or Web c/s)
10	>1 Lg	distrib	Federated database via multidatabase gateways	ARE YOU CRAZY?!	YOU MUST BE JOKING	POSSIBLE but avoid (multidatabase gateway or application server)

Table 17.6 Optimistic Assessment of Performance Possibilities

No.	Workload			Some Workload Types	Response Objectives		
					(A) 1–2 Seconds—Slick System	(B) A Few Seconds More—Sluggish System	(C) Minutes or Longer—Time for a Cup of Coffee
1	1	Sm	local	Simple LAN-based transactions	HARD (tuned two-tier c/s)	EASY (normal two-tier c/s)	EASY (any two-tier c/s)
2	1	Sm	remote	Simple remote transactions	VERY HARD (too much network delay)	NORMAL (tuned three-tier c/s)	EASY (any three-tier or Web c/s)
3	>1	Sm	local	Complex LAN-based transactions	VERY HARD (highly tuned two-tier c/s)	HARD (tuned two-tier c/s)	EASY (any two-tier c/s)
4	>1	Sm	remote	Complex remote transactions	UNLIKELY (too much network delay)	HARD (too much network delay)	EASY (any three-tier or Web c/s)
5	>1	Sm	distrib	Most applications built using distributed objects	UNLIKELY (too many remote servers)	HARD (too many remote servers)	EASY (any three-tier or Web c/s)
6	1	Lg	local	Typical data mart requests	VERY HARD (too much processing)	HARD (tuned two-tier c/s)	NORMAL (normal two-tier c/s)
7	1	Lg	remote	Simple enterprise data warehouse requests	UNLIKELY (see entries 2A and 6A)	HARD (tuned three-tier c/s)	NORMAL (normal three-tier or Web c/s)
8	>1	Lg	local	Complex data mart requests	IMPOSSIBLE (way too much processing)	UNLIKELY (too much processing)	NORMAL (normal two-tier c/s)
9	>1	Lg	remote	Typical enterprise data warehouse requests	DOUBLY IMPOSSIBLE (see entry 8A)	UNLIKELY (too much processing)	NORMAL (normal three-tier or Web c/s)
10	>1	Lg	distrib	Federated database via multidatabase gateways	ARE YOU CRAZY?!	YOU MUST BE JOKING	POSSIBLE but avoid (multidatabase gateway or application server)

▶ Column 5: A common workload type that could have the characteristics listed in columns 2–4.
▶ Columns 6–8: These represent performance objectives. These three columns are also named A, B, and C, for ease of reference to entries in the table. For example, entry 6A is in row 6, column A.
▶ Column 6: The response time objective is 1–2 seconds (a slick system).
▶ Column 7: The response time objective is 5–15 seconds (a sluggish system).
▶ Column 8: The response time objective is a minute or more (time for coffee).

The performance objectives are deliberately vague, but the three time ranges are ones that a typical user would experience as noticeably different.

Using the Table Estimator.   Using the estimator is easy. Simply decide which row your application's workload falls in, then read the table to find out your chances of achieving the three response time goals. Assuming that you do have a particular goal for the application, look in the column for that goal (A, B, or C), to find your probability of success.

▶ If your goal is going to be HARD to reach, try to tune the application to move it into an easier category.
▶ If your goal is rated a high risk (VERY HARD or UNLIKELY) or IMPOSSIBLE, then redesign it using multitransaction workflow analysis, to move the user response portion(s) into the EASY categories.

Conservative or Optimistic?   The reason for the two versions is to allow for the wide variation in the skills available to organizations building distributed applications. *If* your enterprise has people skilled in current technology *and* has already had success building and managing distributed applications, *and if* the same group of skilled people are working on the current project, *then* use the optimistic estimates. Everyone else should be conservative.

Creating Your Own Estimator.   If our tables do not fit your environment, construct a simple response time estimator of your own. You will need to devise a simple formula with three factors, the general shape of which is this:

$$\text{Response Time Estimate} = \text{SizeFactors} + \text{LANFactors} + \text{WANFactors}$$

For example, suppose you selected the following factors:

▶ Size factors: Small = 1, Medium = 2, Large = 5, Very Large = 10, Massive = any value
▶ LANFactors = 1 per application request crossing the LAN
▶ WANFactors = 3 per request application request crossing the WAN

Then an application that runs one large process (5) at a local server (1) and two small processes (2) at remote servers (6) would score a total of 14. But 14 of what? The aim would be to select factors so that the final total is a response time estimate in seconds. To do that you would have to load a few standard applications with known workloads, run them, measure their response times, and construct your factors accordingly. In your calculations, ignore any part of the application that does not contribute to a user's perceived response times.

Conclusions and Management Guidelines

Designing for high performance in a large distributed system using synchronous techniques is an ambitious undertaking. It requires the same type of engineering skills from application designers and developers that were once demanded of designers of operating systems. Even when those skills are applied, the system will still not produce a high-performance application without continual, careful management of the environment.

Asynchronous application designs are less ambitious and, therefore, more likely to work, provided that designers are willing to become business process reengineers. The key to effective information processing in a the world of enterprise client/server is to design the business system and the information systems at the same time. This requires a multidisciplinary approach, in which the team members understand the needs and constraints of the other side. Although computer systems must serve the business, an "ideal" business process will be the source of performance problems if it demands too much of the information infrastructure.

Technologies

Performance Tools

"A fool with a tool is still a fool."

Anonymous

In This Chapter . . .

Design Tools
Application Development Tools
Performance Management Tools
Conclusions

A s with many things client/server, we have a habit of throwing tools at problems. Performance is no different. While there are many good tools that can optimize client/server performance, there are bad tools that can kill a system. Selecting the wrong tool can be the third rail of client/server. In this chapter, we take a quick walk through the world of client/server performance tools, concentrating on tools that assist architects and developers in designing, developing, and monitoring high-performance client/server systems.

Clearly, selecting the proper tool is no easy task. Application architects and developers need to understand the enabling technology, the industry, and the wide range of available products. We must take the time to understand a world that's complex and changing rapidly. We need to know how to pick the best tool for the job and map our requirements to a tool set.

In this chapter, we cover a variety of tools including design tools, application development tools, simulation tools, testing tools, and monitoring tools. Our aim is to tie together some of the concepts that we've already presented in the book with real products that are available today.

Design Tools

In one sense, the category of "design tools" could include most of the performance management tool categories that we discuss later in this chapter. For instance, design involves prediction, and a tool that helps with *prediction* often does so by exercising a particular choice of *design* in a controlled environment and *measuring* the outcome. But strictly speaking, such a tool is doing *design evaluation* rather than true design because the user still has to do the actual work of designing the application or system. We discuss this aspect of database design in the next chapter.

Given the inherent relationship between logical and physical design discussed in Chapter 7, a well-designed application is likely to be a well-performing application. So for our purposes here, we'll narrow the definition a bit: The goal is to create a modular (or "partitioned") application and, to simplify our discussion, we may refer to those partitions, layers, modules, or objects as *components.* Design tools help us to create and evaluate the design of a system or its components, rather than the behavior of that design. We might say that *design tools focus on the cause of performance, rather than its effects.*

Design Tool Examples

Design tools include CASE (computer-aided software engineering) tools such as:

▶ Cayenne Software's *Terrain*
▶ Rational Software's *Rational Rose*
▶ Logic Work's *ERWin*
▶ *Select* from Select Software
▶ *Cool,* originally developed (as *IEF,* then *Composer*) by Texas Instruments and subsequently acquired by Sterling Software

A detailed discussion of CASE tools is outside the scope of this chapter, but it's helpful to look at the features of a few of them.

Cayenne Software's *Terrain.* The *Terrain* family of tools from Cayenne Software provides a graphical database design environment for more than 20 different RDBMS products. The design tools incorporate expert design rules and interactive guidance, which help users to complete optimized database designs and also enhance their database design skills. Once a database design has been created, *Terrain* supports bidirectional synchronization with the RDBMS, to simplify change management.

Logic Work's *ERWin.* *ERWin* (see Figure 18.1) is a CASE tool dedicated to database design. It provides application architects with the ability to design, refine, and deploy both multidimensional and relational databases. *ERWin* is able to reverse-engineer an existing database and generate DDL for a target database. It can also link to popular application development tools such as Sybase/Powersoft's *PowerBuilder* and Microsoft's *Visual Basic.*

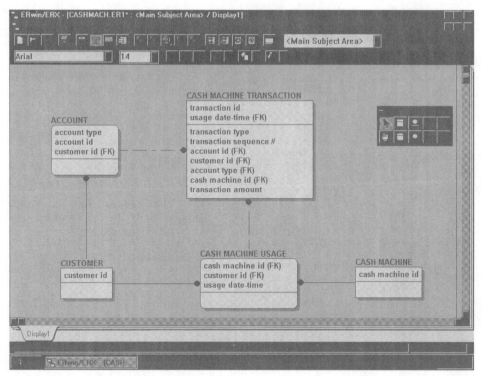

FIGURE 18.1 Logic Work's *ERWin.*

ERWin's database design process is straightforward. Developers simply create the logical database model that serves as a basis for the physical database design. From there, they can generate the SQL definitions (DDL) to create the tables, columns, keys, and stored procedures for the target DBMS.

Rational Software's *Rational Rose.* Where *ERWin* does database design, *Rational Rose* does object-oriented application design. The *Rational Rose* family of products (illustrated in Figure 18.2) originally supported the Booch OOA/OOD methodology, but it is now rapidly shifting to a *Unified Methodology* created jointly by Booch, Rumbaugh, and Jacobsen. This methodology uses a common set of notations known as the *Unified Modeling Language* (UML), which is intended to replace the dozen or so OOA/OOD methods and notations we have today. The UML was largely developed by Rational during 1996, but has been endorsed as a de facto standard by many companies including HP, IBM, MCI SystemHouse, Microsoft, Oracle, and Texas Instruments.

Lately Microsoft and Rational have teamed up to create Microsoft's *Visual Modeler,* which could have the effect of propelling CASE technology into the

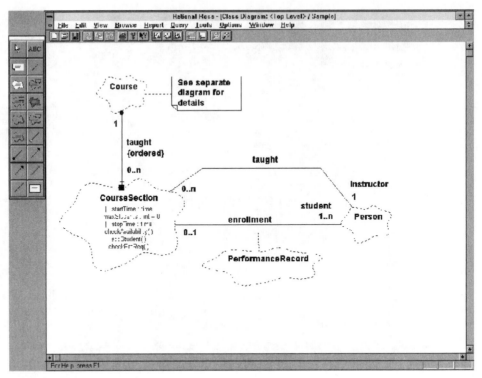

FIGURE 18.2   *Rational Rose.*

popular world of Microsoft development technology. *Rational Rose* is one of the few CASE tools that provides "round-trip engineering." This means that the CASE tool is able to convert existing code into an object model, allowing the application architect to alter the OO design inside of the tool. Once the design is complete, the application architect is able to regenerate the code. *Rational Rose* is able to generate and reverse-engineer code from *Java, Forte, Smalltalk, C++, Ada, PowerBuilder,* and *Visual Basic.* Of course, there are limits to what can be accomplished by any "automatic" reverse engineering tool. Even the most sophisticated algorithms cannot convert your existing spaghetti code into well-structured objects.

Application Development Tools

Applying the arguments and conclusions of Chapters 15, 16, and 17, we should design applications as a collection of *decoupled components.* Synchronous implementations are fine for carefully controlled local (that is, LAN-based) connections, provided that we can tune the environment to produce short response times. However, once the application involves remote (that is, WAN-based) connections, these should be asynchronous.

That means (summarizing our previous conclusions) that distributed components may work if they are not widely distributed and if they are not too fine-grained. But anything more than a small amount of synchronous communication over a fast LAN connection is a recipe for unpredictable performance once we begin to scale up to large volumes of users, data, and transactions.

Taking this concept to application development tools, we need to find tools that provide software architects with the flexibility to create solutions incorporating *both* synchronous *and* asynchronous communication features. We have good news and bad news here. The bad news is that few tools support such flexibility and also provide the kind of quick development cycles required for a rapid application development (RAD) process. The good news is that things are changing quickly—see, for example, Precise Software Solutions' *QBooster* (www.precisesoft.com).

To make better sense of application development tools, it's helpful to separate tools into two categories: open solutions and proprietary solutions.

Open Solutions

Traditionally, an open solution—in this case, a development tool—is one that employs a vendor-independent approach designed to interconnect with any number of products. This requires adherence to a set of standards that is controlled by many organizations. In other words, it is a nonproprietary approach.

In the world of development tools, the open solutions are the numerous, general-purpose programming languages and tools that create programs using these languages, the most popular of which are C++ and Java. Pascal, Ada, and even COBOL are also in the mix.

Today, C++ tools support advanced client/server application development through built-in database connectivity, interactive development environments (*IDEs*), and object-oriented development environments. Examples of C++ development tools include:

► C++ *Builder* from Borland
► *Visual* C++ from Microsoft (see Figure 18.3)

C++.   What makes C++ open is the flexibility of the language. C++ is a standard language. While there are differences in the libraries that come with the tools and differences in the native implementations, the language is basically the same from tool to tool, operating system to operating system. By using C++, we can merge native, application-specific, and third-party libraries into a single development environment. Developers can customize a particular

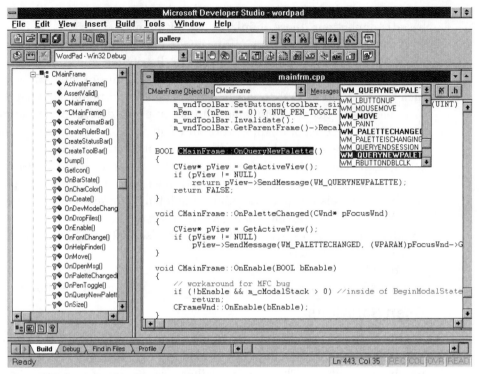

FIGURE 18.3   Microsoft's *Visual C++*.

C++ development tool to meet the requirements of the application. We could, for example, use the native database connection feature of the C++ development tool, use commercial middleware for C++, or create our own custom extensions. Thus, we can specify how we want to handle middleware, database connectivity, and native API interfaces.

Another advantage of C++ is its ability to remove the developers from the complexities of the native procedural APIs. What's more, developers do not have to change the native API calls when moving from platform to platform.

A final advantage of using a C++ approach is that individual modules are likely to perform well. Because C++ generates true native 32- or 16-bit applications using a true compiler, the resulting object code is faster than the interpreted code typically produced by proprietary client/server development tools. On the downside, developers have to suffer through long compile and link cycles, and most C++ development environments don't provide visual development features, which makes them poor RAD tools.

Proprietary Solutions

Proprietary tools include specialized client/server development tools (that is, tools created for the sole purpose of creating client/server applications) that provide developers with an easy-to-use, visual development environment. Examples of proprietary tools include *PowerBuilder* from Powersoft (see Figure 18.4), *Visual Basic* from Microsoft, and *Delphi* from Borland. While these tools do facilitate speedy development, they are not at all flexible. Custom DLLs are necessary to accommodate special requirements like access to a TP Monitor, and in many cases customization is next to impossible.

Most proprietary tools provide some sort of IDE, which allows developers to create databases, build windows, add proprietary 4GL code, and compile and deploy an application using a single interface. Typically, the applications are not submitted to a true compile, but run through an interpreter that does not provide the same level of performance (recall Guideline 9.9, *Compilers and interpreters*). However, to compete with the performance of tools like Delphi (which incorporated Borland's long-established compiler technology in its first

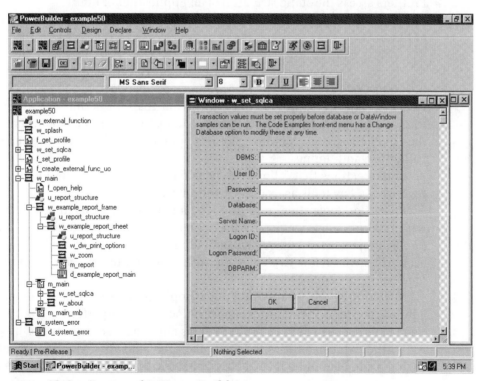

FIGURE 18.4   Powersoft's *PowerBuilder.*

release), the trend is to retrofit these tools with true compilers. Such is the case with tools such as PowerBuilder.

Clearly, the trade-off when moving to proprietary tools is speed of development and flexibility. For instance, even though we can create applications visually and quickly, building applications that are modular in nature is difficult. Many organizations, however, prefer to sacrifice flexibility for shorter development cycles.

Performance Management Tools

As you may recall from our discussion of software performance engineering in Chapter 4, performance management tools fall into four broad categories: catalogs, monitors, profilers, and history tools. We have described these categories in terms of the functions the tools perform. We can also understand the categories in terms of the type of data they collect and report on.

▶ Catalogs collect data on system configurations.
▶ Monitors assess the dynamic behavior of the system.
▶ Profilers assess the static structure of an application or query.
▶ History tools collect summary performance statistics over an extended period of time.

Figure 4.11 relates these categories to the 10 SPE activities that they support. The first two activities, determining workload factors and identifying performance objectives, provide the context and goals for performing all the activities and using all the tools. In practice, most tools support more than one of the 10 SPE activities. Monitors, for example, help with monitoring, analyzing, validating, and tuning.

In the sections that follow, we focus on the most important tool categories, reviewing a few tools as examples within each category.

Prediction tools attempt to provide us with feedback as to how our system will perform before we deploy the actual system. In Chapter 6, we compared the techniques used by analysis and simulation tools, and listed examples of each. Here we review two categories of prediction tools: *simulation tools* and *load-testing tools.*

Monitoring tools, simply put, allow application architects, developers, and administrators to view how system components are performing in real time. Such tools can also help us find problems and diagnose their causes by providing drill-down capabilities to isolate the problem subsystem. We can also use such tools to determine if corrective action really solved a problem. We review two classes of monitoring tools that address client/server system performance:

those for *monitoring distributed networks* and those for *monitoring database servers.* Finally, we note some future possibilities for *monitoring applications.*

Simulation Tools

Although simulation tools can be used to verify both performance and design, their application in the world of client/server is new. So while we've been simulating central processing, network, database, and CPU performance separately for years now, few of us have attempted to simulate systems that tie together all of these components. But, as we noted at the very beginning of the book, the challenge of client/server design is in making the right connections, and—if they are to be useful—simulation tools must step up to this challenge.

By using simulation tools, it's possible to estimate the performance of a client/server system during the design and architecture stage. This is accomplished using performance models, mathematical and graphical representations of the client/server architecture considering all components in the system including processors, memory, network, database, application, and middleware. By using such models, the application architect is able to determine overall client/server system performance before actually obtaining, configuring, and installing the physical components. Or at least that's the idea.

Building models is a difficult proposition for client/server. We have to consider all of the components, including hardware, operating systems, networks, and servers. Once we know what we're working with, we need to define the behavior of each system component—for instance, how much of the CPU or memory resource is required to process a single transaction? We can then use this model to track cost information as well as application and user behaviors.

SES/Strategizer.   *Strategizer* from SES is of the few client/server performance simulation tools available. *SES/Strategizer* is a Windows NT-based simulation tool supporting distributed system performance modeling. *Strategizer* is able to model most system components including clients, servers, networks, routers, applications, and databases. *Strategizer* simulates system performance by allowing us to determine end-to-end response time, network capacity, server capacity, data distribution, and cost. Thus, we can do anything we need to with the model, including performing what-if analysis to identify the optimal system configuration, analyzing the effect of a change in architecture, or finding areas where we can reduce cost without affecting system performance.

The general idea behind *Strategizer* is to let the tool user define a system architecture at a high level by dragging and dropping graphical objects—representing workstations, servers, mainframes, network topologies, users, server processes, database process, and database tables—onto a visual workspace, as we see in Figure 18.5. Application architects simply select and place icons into a model, connect them, and set the model's parameters by adding such information as names, operating system, number of processors, types of processors, RAM allocations, and disk information. We can define these parameters ourselves or select them from a large number of predefined models supplied by SES.

The core of *Strategizer* is an Application Definition Notation (ADN) that provides applications architects with a standard way of representing applications of varying degrees of complexity, thus defining common performance characteristics. ADN allows application architects to turn application logic into system behavior. For example, architects can capture information for message passing and send and receive statements, control logic, and I/O requested using execute statements. It is also possible to use ADN to define workload specification and end-user behaviors.

Strategizer also provides architects with the ability to collect data from system performance data points such as a disk or the network. This ability allows us to consider real data in our model and adjust our model after considering

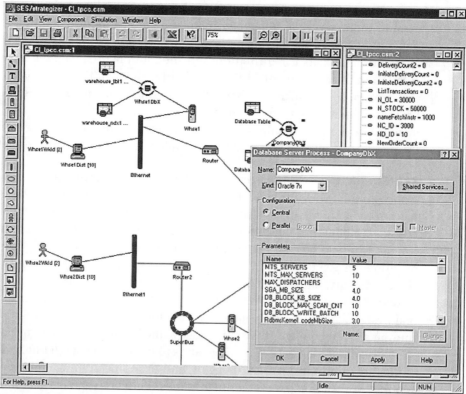

FIGURE 18.5   SES *Strategizer.*

such data. While this does provide some real-time information, *Strategizer* is not a true performance-monitoring tool.

When building a model using *Strategizer*, we need first to define the behaviors of each system component and end user. Thus, we have to understand the user and the components in order to create a useful model. Next, we need to define the processes and services that take place in support of the application (or applications). Finally, we need to define user instances and link them to a component (that is a workstation or server).

Tools such as *Strategizer* take us only so far. We need to be sure to include a solid system monitoring foundation as well. Thus, we need to adjust assumptions with real data from pilot systems and benchmarks. With this methodology, we should be able to catch most performance problems before deploying the client/server system. It's certainly easier to adjust the model and simulate new architectures before spending the big money on the real stuff and real staff.

Controlled Measurement or Benchmarking

Load testing is the process of running a client/server application under an increasing user or processing load to determine how it will behave under high stress. That means abusing the client/server system to determine where it will break. All applications break under some load level. This testing practice determines the application's ability to scale, since scaling is just a matter of handling a larger and larger processing and user load.

In most cases, we want to load test a system by running an application continuously using a large number of varied testing procedures to simulate hundreds, sometimes thousands of users, depending on the requirements of the application. We then increase the load until a problem develops. The types of errors to look for include saturation of the server or the client operating system, memory leaks on the front-end application, concurrency problems, processor and disk performance, or sudden, unexpected system crashes.

The problem with load testing is that it's a pretty expensive venture to load test even a two-tier client/server application, not to mention a more complex multitier client/server application that supports higher loads. The large number of clients required to simulate a high user load means that a large number of PCs must participate in the test. For example, when doing some testing for a Web server, we have to employ more than 100 PCs, all running Web browsers and testing software, to place the appropriate load on the Web server during the test.

We discussed some of the challenges of benchmarking in more detail in Chapter 6, *Predicting Future Performance*.

Load Testing Tools

The friends of the load testers are the testing tools built to automate load-testing procedures. The number of clients running the testing software determines the load we want to place on the system. Better solutions are available to simulate large user loads using a limited number of clients. We capture the user interaction with the application in test scripts, then use the testing software to run multiple instances of the test scripts. This means that we can perform such tricks as simulating a thousand or so users with only 100 or so clients.

The vendors of load-testing tools may suggest that this is really just a matter of recording a typical user session with our application and playing that session back over and over to simulate multiple user interactions. But the load placed on the system will not be realistic unless we can vary the user input. And creating a realistic input *distribution* is crucial. For example:

▶ If we request the same data items from the server repeatedly, those items will probably remain cached on the server, and possibly even on the client, depending on the caching scheme. We will probably underestimate both response times and throughput.

▶ If all clients update the same data items, we will create hot spots and lock contention in the database. We may overestimate response times and underestimate throughput.

▶ If we attempt to insert or delete the same data items repeatedly, we will probably incur database errors instead of normal processing. Response times and throughput estimates will be worthless.

▶ Unless database accesses are spread across the entire database, artificial disk I/O bottlenecks may occur. The application may truly be I/O bound, but we will not be entitled to draw this conclusion from our tests unless we are sure that the test workload is representative of a typical real workload.

Assuming that we have taken care to make the load test a realistic one, then we usually want to monitor as many data points as possible. For instance, by using the native performance management features of our database server, we can watch how the load testing affects cache, buffers, and disk performance. We can do the same thing with the network and client. It's a good idea to keep a log of these performance indicators using performance monitoring tools like those we discuss later.

Mercury Interactive's *LoadRunner*.   Mercury Interactive's *LoadRunner* is an integrated client/server and Web load-testing tool that can perform load testing for most client/server applications and systems. *LoadRunner* allows testers to

Rational Assembles a Load Testing Suite

In the beginning of 1997, Rational Software (previously known mainly for visual modeling tools) created a stir in the load testing marketplace by acquiring, in quick succession, three independent vendors of load testing and function testing products—*Performance Awareness, Pure Atria,* and *SQA.*

Apparently, the eventual goal will be to integrate these overlapping acquisitions into a single comprehensive suite of testing tools, but it's too soon to say how. For the latest news, stay tuned to Rational's Web site at *www .rational.com.*

monitor system behavior and performance during various simulated user and processing loads.

LoadRunner can load test both the client and the server through the client load-testing (end-to-end) component and the server load-testing component. This means that a portion of the testing tool runs on the client, and a portion runs on the server. The goal is to simulate an intense user load, control the load through a synchronization point, and monitor the performance of the systems and applications under test. Client load testing provides accuracy, speed, and repeatability information in a multiuser, automated testing environment that lets us drive the test from a single client. *LoadRunner* can simulate many users across a network, each running an application. Using a single client as the sync point, *LoadRunner* can synchronize all the clients and collect the results for analysis.

On client workstations, *WinRunner* or *Xrunner* agents can act as virtual users running GUI applications. *WinRunner* (which we describe in the following section) supports Windows clients, and *XRunner* supports X Windows. Such an agent can, for example, click the OK button, wait for the results to appear, and record the time the system took to respond. This measures transaction response time as the user would see it on the workstation.

Alternatively, for server load testing we can dispense with workstations altogether and test a server's capacity by simulating the processing load of many clients. The server half of *LoadRunner* lets us simulate live message traffic from multiple clients using a multitasking database and *virtual users.* The advantage is that a single machine can replicate client requests for service at the volumes required to stress the server. We can simulate SQL calls to a server, such as those encountered with two-tier client/server, or messages or transactional RPC requests, such as those that occur with three-tier technology such as TP monitors.

Load-testing tools like *LoadRunner* can never eliminate the need for carefully thought-out testing procedures. But they do give us the ability to simulate multiuser processing loads while an application is still in development.

WinRunner.   *WinRunner* is the client-testing component of Mercury's *LoadRunner*. The best feature of *WinRunner* is RapidTest, a mechanism that creates a full suite of GUI test cases for client/server applications. The idea is to get the testers up and running fast and to avoid the laborious process of creating tests by hand.

RapidTest uses a Wizard to create the test scripts after it learns the application automatically by navigating its way through the menus, menu items, and all available dialog boxes. RapidTest can generate scripts that provide full regression testing for an application, and Script Wizard creates a test script for every window and object that it finds in the client/server application.

Client/server GUI testing tools such as *WinRunner* are particularly important within an iterative development methodology. If repeated testing is relatively quick and easy, developers are more likely to test their applications systematically as they evolve toward the final production version.

Monitoring Distributed Systems

Distributed monitoring tools observe and report on system performance in a networked environment. The simplest such tools may provide some network performance data, but they typically are designed for network management only. For example, from an administrator's workstation, a tool like Ipswitch's *What's Up Gold* can poll and report on the status of a wide range of devices in an enterprise network, using only basic TCP/IP capabilities. Web server support allows its reports to be viewed from any Web browser.

More sophisticated tools use the Simple Network Management Protocol (SNMP). Originally developed as a quick solution to support network device monitoring, SNMP became the dominant protocol for sharing network management information and diagnosing problems. Consequently, tool vendors wanted to extend SNMP beyond its original communications view of the distributed system (*Network Management*) to support the hardware and systems software views—the activities most commonly labeled as *Systems Management.*

In their attempts to broaden their monitoring capabilities, the tool vendors have created an alphabet soup of so-called standards and protocols—CMIP, MIB, MIB II, SNMPv2, RMON, RMON-2—a lot of confusion, and little in the way of true standards. Your best bet is to let the vendors sort out this mess. Meanwhile, don't use any of these acronyms as a way to select a monitoring product—focus on the functions provided.

Software Agents.   To monitor the behavior of software across a large distributed network, we can use software agents. Resident remote agents are like surrogate administrators; they can monitor activity at remote locations and report on predefined problem conditions when they arise. Not only does this free us from the drudgery of repetitive monitoring, it is the only viable approach in a very large distributed environment.

BMC *Patrol.* One of the most sophisticated examples of the agent-based approach is BMC Software's *Patrol,* an enterprise system monitoring product that uses the SNMP protocol to share information. *Patrol* automates control of distributed applications, networks, and even database servers. It uses a series of intelligent agents, management consoles, and *knowledge modules.* These expert modules know how to monitor various operating systems, databases, transaction monitors, and popular vertical application products including Lotus Notes, Oracle Financials, and SAP R/3.

Agents run on each node or "managed server" in the network, and the knowledge models provide the agent with the information on the configuration of each component, allowing a single agent to manage all components and objects associated with a server. The original idea was to use agents to monitor network performance. *Patrol,* however, can use the same mechanisms to monitor application and database server performance as well.

DBMS Monitoring

Database monitoring tools allow us to determine the health of a DBMS and its host processor environment, which combined make up the database server. DBMS monitoring tools need to provide information to an administrator at any given moment, as well as monitor the server over time. These tools must provide both the performance information and the analytical power to make sense of it.

There are many ways in which DBMS performance monitoring tools can determine database server performance. Some tools, such as *Strategizer* (see the earlier description), use detailed simulation models to predict performance and do some monitoring to validate assumptions. These tools are typically the most expensive solutions. Some tools use analytic queuing models that are less expensive. These tools are most useful in the early stages of a project, when the actual operational environment is not available to measure.

Once an application moves into the production environment, the most effective performance monitoring tools leave simulation and assumptions aside. They reside with the DBMS to monitor real-time activity, gather data, and assist the DBA and application architect in figuring out what all the data means. The tools do this using one or more of the following capabilities:

▶ Real-time monitoring
▶ Recent-past monitoring
▶ Historical data analysis

Tools that support all three of these features are known as three-way DBMS monitoring tools. These tools reside on the processor close to the operating system and the database server. They also provide a front-end interface (known as the console) and a statistics-gathering mechanism for tracking behavior. These tools are also able to measure storage space, disk fragmentation, I/O performance, and buffer performance, to name only a few of the data points.

There are two basic forms of data collection: event-driven and sampling. Event-driven data collection requires a data collection process that runs close to the operating system and database server, counting events as they occur. For example, when a delete operation occurs, the counter is incremented. Although effective, event-driven data collection places a burden on the host operating system and the DBMS. Thus we can actually cause performance problems when using event-driven tools—recall Guideline 5.9, *The Uncertainty Principle.* This is especially true on smaller systems where there is not as much excess capacity.

With a sampling approach, however, a tool is able to measure the operating system and DBMS at random times. Sampling, therefore, is more likely to monitor the system without affecting its performance. Also, many operating systems and DBMSs collect some standard statistics continuously, recording them in centrally accessible locations like catalogs or common data tables. Monitoring tools can find out about the recent history of the system by reading these statistics. By using a combination of selective sampling and system-maintained statistics, a tool can estimate the characteristics of a population by analyzing data from just a portion of that population.

Typically, tools let us set the *sampling interval* between checks on the DBMS or other client/server system components, depending on the degree of accuracy with which we want to characterize the DBMS's resource utilization. The higher the number of samples, the more load we put on the system but the more accurate the reading. Obviously, the reliability of any sampled information depends on such things as sample size and the variability of the measure.

The best way to describe this technique is to use a simple example. Taking a set of samples per hour, we can calculate the average value and thus determine what the DBMS is up to. However, by examining the dispersion of the values from the sample as related to the mean value, we can calculate the variation from the sample. This provides us with a real-time depiction of how the database server performed in the past and how it's performing now. Observing a pattern among the samples can even provide us with insights as to how the DBMS will perform in the future.

There are essentially three types of DBMS performance monitoring tools: those that come with the host operating system, those that come with the DBMS, and those that come from a third-party vendor.

Operating System Tools.   Even though they are not built specifically for DBMSs, several tools that come with most (if not all) operating systems allow us to monitor DBMS performance. Although these tools are not particularly sophisticated, they have the advantage of being free and widely documented and discussed in books, manuals, and technical literature. The UNIX 'sar' (system activity reporter) command, for instance, provides information on CPU utilization, memory, and disk activity. It knows nothing about the subsystems of a DBMS, but it's a good quick-and-dirty guide to monitoring and diagnosing DBMS performance and DBMS performance problems. Other operating systems include similar utilities, such as the *Performance Monitor* in Windows NT. For more details about these standard monitoring tools, we recommend:

▶ *System Performance Tuning* by Mike Loukides (Sebastapol, CA: O'Reilly, 1990)
▶ *Optimizing UNIX for Performance* by Amir H. Majidimehr (Upper Saddle River, NJ: Prentice Hall, 1996)
▶ *Optimizing Windows NT* (Microsoft Windows NT Resource Kit, Version 3.51) (Redmond, WA: Microsoft Press, 1996)

Standard DBMS tools.   Most DBMSs incorporate some basic performance monitoring and DBMS administration tools. Although they usually lack the sophistication of the higher-priced third party DBMS monitoring tools, these tools work well, are customized for a specific brand of DBMS, and are always there when we need them. Oracle, for example, builds in *SQL*DBA,* which provides DBMS administration features such as a real-time database monitor for Oracle 7.X. *SQL*DBA* allows us to examine the historical database access log, look at what database locks are present, and even look at the current user load. Informix On-Line provides *DB-Monitor,* a menu-driven utility that provides the DBA with some rudimentary database monitoring features such as usage, backup and recovery, and the ability to adjust system parameters. Informix's *DB-Cockpit* provides real-time and historical database server monitoring information. Informix offers other utilities as well, including a program to report on disk fragmentation and a program to view the contents of a transaction log.

Compuware *EcoTools*.   *EcoTools* is an example of a third-party DBMS monitoring tool. It provides a graphical console that allows us to view the performance of the DBMS. *EcoTools* moves the performance information back to the DBA using graphs, allowing the DBA to determine the performance of the DBMS with a single glance. The information ranges from high-level summary graphs to detailed information pertaining to the performance of particular subsystems. Like BMC's *Patrol* (described earlier), *EcoTools* uses hundreds of intelligent agents that monitor DBMS subsystems, operating systems, and network data points. We can set *EcoTools* to watch for particular warning signs and trigger an alarm, such as when the disk is in danger of filling up or when performance goes below a certain threshold. We can even program *EcoTools* to take some corrective actions automatically (subject to certain inherent limitations that we discuss in later comments on *Monitoring, Tuning, Intelligent Agents*).

Bradmark *DBGeneral*.   *DBGeneral* allows DBAs to monitor Oracle or Sybase database servers. It supports unattended distributed agent technology that continually analyzes the server and alerts the DBA when a problem occurs. *DBGeneral,* which is illustrated in Figure 18.6, comes with a standard set of rules that can be used right out of the box or customized to meet the exact needs of the system. Unlike other monitoring tools, *DBGeneral* does not require a dedicated console. The agents function independently from the console, and any PC connected to the network can function as the console. This product provides a noninvasive monitoring technique, linking directly into the subsystems of either Oracle or Sybase.

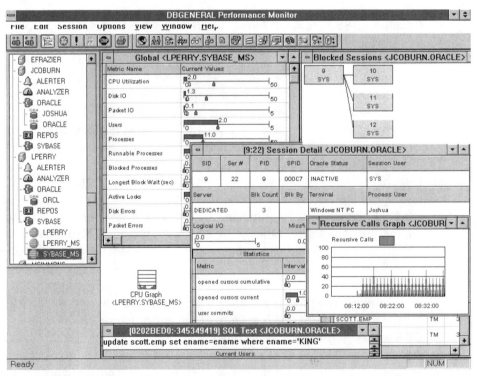

FIGURE 18.6   *DBGeneral.*

Platinum Technology *DBVision*.   Platinum's *DBVision* provides monitoring features for Oracle and Sybase. *DBVision* monitors more than 85 data points of DBMSs and host operating systems. This performance data is represented as strip charts, bar charts, or tables. The DBA can drill down to monitor specific database server subsystems by simply clicking on the graphical display. Since *DBVision* supports continuous monitoring, it is also possible to analyze the data using built-in statistical functions to determine performance trends or to find problems that occurred in the past. Using *DBVision,* a DBA can tract CPU utilization, user connections, database lock information, available space, and other customizable resource usage statistics.

BMC *Patrol*.   *Patrol's* distributed agent-based monitoring architecture (described earlier) supports database monitoring as well as network monitoring. BMC supplies specific *knowledge modules* incorporating expertise about each DBMS. These can monitor all major subsystems and report information back to the DBA at a central location. DBAs can monitor common components using the standard *knowledge modules* or customize *Patrol* to watch other portions of a system.

Monitoring Applications

Earlier we noted the confusion surrounding the role of SNMP. The Desktop Management Task Force (DMTF), an industry consortium of more than 120 workstation vendors, has had better success. Their Desktop Management Interface (DMI) has become the de facto standard protocol for managing networked PCs, Macs, and other workstations. Extensions have connected DMI to SNMP; in 1996, DMI 2.0 added a *Software* Management Interface File (MIF) that makes it possible to manage software at remote workstations.

Using this interface, agents can check for a required hardware and software environment, install and uninstall applications, provide customized support information, and maintain an inventory of installed components. While this type of monitoring is not strictly concerned with performance metrics like device utilization, performance problems can often be traced back to configuration errors.

Exemplifying the trend toward integrating application management with system and network management, Tivoli recently released the Tivoli Manager for Application (TMA), which exploits this MIF interface. A related software developer kit lets developers create the necessary specifications to allow their applications to be managed by TMA. This SDK supplies an important element of an enterprise system management (ESM) solution because even if management tools are available, someone still has to transfer all the necessary management information to the tools.

In Chapter 5, we recommended (Guideline 5.14) creating applications that could monitor their own response times because of the near impossibility of monitoring response times in a distributed environment using external tools. To address this problem, Hewlett-Packard and Tivoli Systems have developed the Applications Response Measurement (ARM) API, a mechanism to permit software to report on end-to-end application response times. Vendors who have signed up to support the ARM API include the traditional leaders in analysis of enterprise performance data like Boole and Babbage, Candle, Compuware, and SAS Institute.

If enough software components support the ARM API, eventually standard reporting tools that also support the API will be able to report on the response time performance of distributed applications. In the meantime, don't assume that you can capture the response time components of a multitier application using standard monitoring tools.

Monitoring, Tuning, Intelligent Agents

Earlier we discussed the trend toward agent-based monitoring tools. There is a limit to what these "intelligent" agents can be expected to do. A utopian vision of enterprise systems management is the self-managed, self-tuning system. Do you suppose that this amazing system would replace faulty network interface cards at remote locations and fix its own bugs (including the occasional small bug in the bug fixing software itself, of course)? Does this remind you of *Star Wars?* A small dose of reality might be helpful here.

In our opinion, the most useful monitoring tools will be the ones that don't try to take over the whole job, especially in the area of system tuning and performance management by rules-driven agents. Automated operations management is one area where rules-based systems have been used successfully because most of the rules fit a simple pattern: "IF *condition* THEN *action*." In contrast, tools that offer rule-based problem diagnosis may look good in demos, but I am not convinced they can achieve significant productivity gains because most problems that require tuning actions are too unpredictable to match a previously encoded rule. It takes human expertise to find them and human ingenuity to fix them.

Conclusions

Selecting tools is a key aspect of performance management. Referring again to Figure 4.11, the service-level management teams should review tools in all four categories to support all 10 SPE activities. The team should try to acquire tools that work together and cover as many activities as feasible. After that, there is no substitute for hands-on experience—we need to test all tools in our own environment. Each type of tool that we have discussed has a role to play in achieving acceptable client/server performance. The individual tools very greatly in features, price, and supported platforms. Marketing literature is fine for initial investigations of function and costs, but the "devil is in the detail."

Using DBMS Technology

"Becoming an expert in data structures is like becoming an expert in sentence structures and grammar. It's not of much value if the thoughts you want to express are all muddled."

William Kent

In This Chapter . . .

Designing Database Systems
Business Factors and Database Design Goals
Database Applications
The Influence of Relational Database Optimizers
The Database Design Process
Database Design Checklists

Earlier in the book, we discussed software performance engineering and the design process in general. Because our subject matter is high-performance *information systems,* throughout the book many of our examples and guidelines deal with ways to design and use databases. In this chapter, our goal is to take a more focused and systematic look at SPE and the design process as they apply to DBMS technology and its use in heterogeneous distributed environments.

This presents an immediate challenge of scope. While it is obviously too important to ignore, database performance is such a broad topic that it's hard to know where to begin. Entire books are devoted to database design alone; others address DBMS tuning. For any particular DBMS, you can buy a small library of helpful textbooks. Obviously, we cannot possibly squeeze into a single chapter a concise summary of everything that can be said about database performance.

Our goal, therefore, is to provide a useful overview of how to get acceptable performance from database technology by discussing techniques and guidelines that apply to every DBMS. Where space limitations preclude a more detailed treatment, we include checklists of important aspects of design and tuning that apply in most DBMS environments.

For detailed tuning recommendations for any particular DBMS you must turn to product manuals supplied by the DBMS vendors and to one (or more) of the many books now available giving DBMS-specific performance guidelines. For example, *Oracle Performance Tuning* by Mark Gurry and Peter Corrigan contains 940 pages of advice, including a handy 70-page appendix of "Hot Tuning Tips" that answers many questions the authors are asked most frequently.[1] Similar books are available for other DBMSs; we include an extensive list of these at the end of the chapter.

Our central focus is on *relational databases,* which store the vast majority of enterprise data today, for both operational and decision support (or *data warehouse*) applications. However, many new operational applications are being developed to use *object databases* and *universal servers* (alias *extended relational databases,* or *object-relational databases*), while data marts use *multidimensional databases.* We include short sections on the performance aspects of these new database technologies.

In addition, five other chapters address the performance aspects of various DBMS-related topics:

▶ Chapter 12 is devoted to the performance implications of *database locking.*
▶ Chapter 13 includes a discussion of some *parallel database processing* issues.
▶ Chapter 18 reviews a variety of *tools* that can help in the deployment of DBMS technology.
▶ Chapter 20 covers the performance aspects of *data replication.*
▶ Chapter 21 discusses many performance issues associated with *data warehouses* and *data marts.*

Designing Database Systems

The title of this section is deliberately vague. As in most areas of our industry, database design terminology is imprecisely defined and widely misused. In books and magazine articles about database technology, terms like *database design* and *DBMS tuning* are used to include almost any of the 10 SPE activities that we described in Chapters 4–6. In this chapter, we try to use distinct terminology for the various activities, as shown in Table 19.1.

---

[1] Mark Gurry and Peter Corrigan, *Oracle Performance Tuning* (Sebastapol, CA: O'Reilly & Associates, 1996).

Table 19.1   **DBMS Technology: Distinct Design Activities**

DBMS-Related Activity	Definition
Performance planning and analysis	Identifying how the users' most critical processing requirements relate to application and database design decisions
Application design	Designing applications that will use the DBMS efficiently, including the best way to code data manipulation statements like SQL
Application partitioning	Distributing the processing components of applications for optimal performance given an existing geographical distribution of data
Application load testing	Testing and verifying the performance of complex SQL code and processing logic
Application profiling	Monitoring and analyzing application behavior to determine how a particular program uses DBMS resources, or how a particular data manipulation request interacts with a particular database or set of databases (for example, by using a DBMS-supplied *explain* facility)
Database design	Selecting among the logical and physical database structures offered by a particular DBMS, to meet application performance goals
Data distribution	Determining the optimal scheme for distributing data among DBMSs situated at various locations in a distributed enterprise
DBMS tuning	Adjusting the many software options provided by a DBMS vendor to customize the behavior of a particular DBMS to best suit a particular mix of databases and application programs
Environment tuning	Adjusting the hardware or software environment within which the DBMS and the applications operate

---

Who Does Database Design?

Table 19.1 reflects some important distinctions among database-related activities. These distinctions are useful for discussing SPE and the design process. But when you actually develop an information system, such divisions are often blurred.

First, not all design tasks can be conveniently confined to a single activity. As we first pointed out in Chapter 3, the performance of database applications depends on many *interrelated* factors in five distinct areas, as illustrated by Figure 19.1, namely:

- ▶ Business factors and design goals
- ▶ How the application uses the data
- ▶ The DBMS software
- ▶ The hardware environment
- ▶ Database structure and content

In this chapter, although we touch on all five areas, we focus mainly on DBMS software and the design of database structures.

The "Designer."   In a book, we may refer to the individual who makes a design or a tuning decision as "the designer." But (as we pointed out in Chapter 7 in *Who Does Design, Anyway?*), very few people in our industry are actually given the title of *designer.* Where databases are concerned, a designer may be called an *application developer,* a *performance analyst,* a *database specialist,* or a *database administrator* (DBA).

Although sometimes a single designer carries out many of the activities in Table 19.1, more often, as Figure 19.1 suggests, the identity of the relevant individual varies according to the context of the design activity being discussed.

In this chapter, we try to use distinct terminology for all the different activities and generic titles like *application designer, database designer, developer,* and *DBA,* depending on the context. In practice, although most enterprises

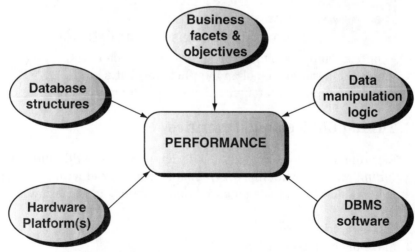

FIGURE 19.1   The five performance factors.

implementing information systems have developers and DBAs, people's titles, roles, and responsibilities vary widely:

▶ Application analysts and software developers certainly have a lot to say about how information flows among the various databases that are spread across the distributed enterprise. They may even design some new databases.

▶ For small databases, it is reasonable to free database users from MIS schedule and resource limitations by giving them reporting tools that can directly manipulate data where it resides. They may even design new "private" databases for themselves or their coworkers.

But, once a collection of information is identified as a corporate asset, to be shared by several applications or queried by users from more than one department, then its ongoing care and management must become a community (or "system") responsibility. And to ensure that very large databases can be used without running into performance problems, then someone with specialized database design and tuning skills must be involved. This person (or team) will be responsible for most of the activities listed in Table 19.1.

These types of design and tuning decisions are usually made by DBAs, not application developers. In fact, in many organizations, developers expect DBAs to make all decisions concerning DBMS design, tuning, and performance. Sometimes this expectation even extends to all decisions concerning the performance of any application that uses the DBMS. This is a bit like expecting a piano tuner to guarantee a flawless performance, regardless of the pianist.

Guideline 19.1 **Don't expect miracles from your database administrator**

Application performance depends on many factors. Expecting a DBA to guarantee the performance of any application that uses the DBMS is like asking the piano tuner to guarantee a flawless performance, regardless of the pianist.

Tuning Choices and Priorities

Regardless of who is doing it, the design process should follow *Nagraj's law of tuning choices* (Guideline 3.14). That is, when faced with a performance problem, we should evaluate potential tuning actions in the following order:

1. Do less work.
2. Make the best use of what you have.
3. Steal from Peter to pay Paul.

4. Water down the requirements.
5. Throw money at the problem.

In this chapter, we focus primarily on the first three options and—like all writers addressing the optimal use of DBMS technology—devote most of our attention to options 2 and 3. This is not because option 1 is less important; on the contrary, it is the best way to improve performance and should always be the starting point, as we originally pointed out in Chapter 3 and explained in more detail in Chapter 8, *The Workload Principle.*

Tuning the Applications.   In the database context, doing less work means changing the application processing, rather than the database structures, the DBMS, or the software or hardware environment. We emphasize that application-processing demands are the starting point for all performance (for example, recall Guideline 11.8, *Application behavior determines throughput*), and application design is usually the most important determinant of DBMS performance.

Having said that, however, we must acknowledge that sometimes tuning applications is not an option. Perhaps no change is possible; perhaps it's too expensive to make the necessary changes; perhaps we don't have the power. For many DBAs, the political situation is like that described by Kevin Loney in the opening words of a chapter on "Managing the Development Process" in the *Oracle DBA Handbook:*

"*Controlling application developers is like herding cats. Since developers can't be controlled, the best way to manage the development process is for DBAs to become an integral part of it.*"[2]

Focusing on DBMS Issues

Whatever the reason, eventually we must move on to other tuning options centered on the DBMS itself. Because each DBMS implementation is unique, offering generic guidance is difficult. Most DBMSs come with a large number of tuning options, the most significant of which are likely to be related to resource allocation in some way.

We discussed aspects of DBMS performance earlier in the book, suggesting guidelines where possible; for example:

▶ Controlling the number of parallel execution threads (recall Guideline 13.3, *Overheads in parallel systems.)*

---

[2]Kevin Loney, *Oracle DBA Handbook* (New York, NY: McGraw Hill, 1994), 109.

Budget for DBMS Performance

We discussed management issues in Part II, but a reminder is in order. Managers who have the power to allocate budget and skill resources should remember that there are no shortcuts to good DBMS performance: *Performance costs money.*

DBMSs are continually evolving. And although the DBMS vendors may claim that the performance of their products improves over time, the benefits are usually available only if you know what you're doing. So, despite all marketing claims to the contrary, don't count on your DBMS vendor to bail you out with some new software magic—getting acceptable performance from new software usually requires an *additional* infusion of skilled resources.

In our view, this is an inescapable management trade-off: Either spend the money to keep your skills up to date or accept lower performance levels.

Guideline 19.2   DBMS performance costs money

Because DBMS software products offer so many design and tuning options, obtaining optimal performance requires database design skills and product-specific expertise. You must either spend the money to keep your skills up to date or accept lower performance levels.

▶ Controlling the size(s) of database cache(s) or buffer pool(s). (Recall Chapter 14 and, in particular, Guideline 14.14, *To discover optimal cache sizes, monitor total I/O rates.*)

▶ Allocating application classes to particular caches or buffer pools (recall Chapter 14).

▶ Allocating memory for recording database locking activity (recall Guidelines 12.7, *Beware of global lock limits,* and 12.8, *Monitor locking levels*).

▶ Allocating memory for sort operations. Many complex database joins necessitate sorting of partial results, and the internal sorting components of database engines are typically a bit less efficient than their standalone cousins, the high-performance *Sort* utilities. In particular, internal sort performance is usually strongly influenced by the amount of cache memory available to the sort, relative to the amount of data to be sorted. (Recall our discussion of *Optimizing Memory Reference Patterns* in Chapter 8, and Guideline 8.17, *Improving locality of reference improves performance.*

▶ Allocating memory buffers and disk device(s) for the recovery log. Recovery logging is essential in a DBMS environment, and so the log can be critical to DBMS throughput. (We did not discuss this issue directly, but it is an example of Guideline 8.12, *Focus on the mainline path.*)

► Controlling the frequency of database checkpoints, which is usually related to the database update rate. Often, a DBMS's default checkpoint interval is set for a relatively low volume system, and needs to be adjusted as volumes rise. Increasing checkpoint frequency shortens recovery time after a failure, but unless it's crucial to minimize down time, extra checkpoints are simply an unnecessary overhead. We discussed checkpointing in Chapter 9 (see Guideline 9.19, *Checkpoint large data transfers*).

► Controlling the granularity and/or frequency of routine monitoring (recall Guideline 9.20, *Switch off unnecessary tracing and logging*).

These areas are likely to be common across all DBMS types. Finally, don't forget Guideline 10.29, *Allocate enough logical resources*. Every DBMS is susceptible to these "show-stoppers"—the Achilles' heel of complex software, especially when it is exposed to substantial growth in processing volumes.

Ainsworth's Ishikawa Diagram.   Writing about client/server database performance (in the context of a Sybase DBMS), Bill Ainsworth identifies the following "six keys to performance":

► **Management capability** to coordinate the organization's paradigm shift to client/server
► **Team capability** to put new tools and techniques into effective use
► **Database structure** (design) and **size** (row count)
► **Access paths** that interact with that structure, such as stored procedures or SQL
► **Physical allocation** of server resources, such as table placement on devices
► **Environment parameters,** such as cache or network configuration variables[3]

Ainsworth elaborates on these six key areas to produce a long checklist of potential performance factors similar to the one we provided in Table 1.1. Using an Ishikawa diagram similar to Figure 19.2, he shows how these factors can be grouped and ranked.

The Ishikawa diagram, also known as fishbone diagram because of its shape, is used to organize ideas about cause and effect. Along each arrow, the contributing factors are recorded as smaller arrows, with the most significant factors placed closest to the arrowhead.

Ainsworth's diagram shows his view of the *typical* importance of various factors *in a Sybase environment*. However, we endorse it as a good starting

---

[3]Bill Ainsworth, "Managing for Performance—A Disciplined Approach," *SQL Forum* (May/June 1994).

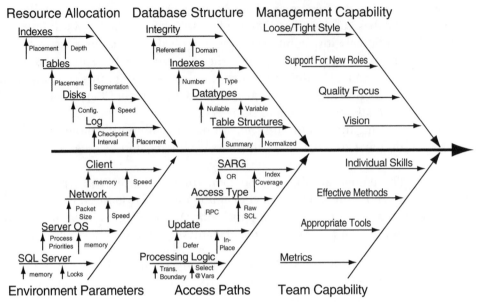

FIGURE 19.2   Ishikawa diagram of database performance.

point for prioritizing design and tuning efforts for *any DBMS environment,* provided that its limited scope is recognized.

1. It is DBMS-centric and does not reflect the full scope of the SPE process that we have been describing in the rest of this book.
2. It does not address application tuning, as we discussed earlier.
3. It assumes a reasonably well-tuned DBMS environment.

The first two caveats require no elaboration, but we need to explain the third. As we noted earlier, the performance of the system as a whole depends on *all* of the design activities and all the individual performance factors. Because they are all interrelated, before we separate one factor and say that it is less important, we must at least know that it is not so badly out of tune that it is the bottleneck for the whole system.

Almost any performance factor can be made into a bottleneck if we try hard enough. For example, according to Figure 19.2, SQL Server memory appears as the least important environment parameter, which is the least important of the six classes of performance factors shown in the diagram. Although this may be true in Ainsworth's experience for typical SQL Server environments, it is easy to imagine a (badly designed) heavily loaded server environment in which throughput is constrained by memory shortages.

In our view, this caveat does not diminish the value of the fishbone diagram in general or the value of Figure 19.2 in particular. We see the diagram as a useful tool and Bill Ainsworth's example as a good summary of the *typical* ranking of various performance factors. It suggests that in most enterprises:

▶ The most significant determinants of DBMS application performance are the skills of the management and developer teams.
▶ Next in importance come the database structures and the ways in which applications access those structures.
▶ In the third tier come the hardware resources and the DBMS software and other environment parameters.

Obviously, every DBMS environment is different. So, rather than debating the correctness of Figure 19.2 with questions like "*Are nullable data types more important than the types of indexes?*" each organization should construct its own version tailored to its own applications, databases, and computing environment.

Know Your Own DBMS.   A DBMS is a large and complex piece of software that offers many possibilities for tuning. Except in the most obvious situations, opinions typically vary as to the most effective design or tuning techniques, even among experts in a particular DBMS. Because of this, we recommend taking the experimental approach of the scientific method:

▶ Attend classes and network with fellow developers.
▶ Obtain more than one reference book on performance tuning for your particular DBMS (we list some at the end of this chapter).
▶ Read and compare their guidance.
▶ Form your own opinion and plan of action.
▶ Verify your decisions by observing the results of your tuning actions.

This last point is crucial. There is no substitute for experience gained from designing and tuning your own applications in your own environment. By adopting systematic approaches to software performance engineering (SPE) like those we proposed in Part II, you can reasonably expect to gain that experience *before* a performance crisis develops.

Business Factors and Database Design Goals

Naturally, performance objectives are a fundamental part of the database design process; if it were not so, a DBA could simply take a normalized entity relationship model produced by a data analyst, implement every entity as a separate DBMS table, and be done. Data distribution or replication would rarely be needed. This is obviously not the case—but neither does the DBA need to go to the opposite extreme of attempting to implement data structures that will absolutely minimize the elapsed execution time of every application.

Design to Meet User Performance Objectives

Let's summarize the ideas first introduced in Chapters 4 and 5:

▶ In principle, for each application, the DBA must work to meet an associated performance objective, such as "We need subsecond response time," "We must be able to process 20,000 per day," or "It must run in less than three hours."
▶ Constraints such as these cannot be deduced from the applications or the databases themselves. They are externally supplied (either formally or informally) through application *requirements* specifications, *service-level agreements,* installation standards, and so on.
▶ Performance goals have a strong bearing on all design decisions. They indicate where optimization efforts are needed and, equally important, when to stop trying to improve the design.

Because databases are frequently shared by multiple applications, the performance objectives for databases may involve a variety of application types:

▶ **Synchronous transaction processing.** Rapid handling of certain commonly executed synchronous *data retrieval* and *update* transactions.

▶ **Asynchronous transaction processing.** Replicating updates promptly at remote locations, within the agreed delay time for asynchronous data propagation.

▶ **Batch processing.** Completing *batch update* programs within the time available (the "batch window").

▶ **Reporting.** Efficient processing and delivery of *standard reports.*

▶ **Synchronous query processing.** Handling a steady flow of *ad hoc queries* without disrupting other work.

To complicate matters, other, potentially conflicting, database design goals include:

▶ **Content.** A database must contain the *right information,* to provide users with the exact data they need to do their jobs.

▶ **Integrity.** The database design must exploit DBMS facilities that support data *integrity, consistency,* and *recovery.* For further discussion of *transactions* and their ACID *properties,* see Chapters 15 and 22.

▶ **Flexibility.** The *logical structure* of the data should be *flexible* enough to support both current and future data processing needs.

▶ **Security.** Sensitive data must be placed in a secure physical location, and access to the data must be controlled. Protecting the data from unauthorized use often places artificial constrainst on design decisions concerning authorized use.

▶ **Capacity.** The physical machine(s) supporting the database must have sufficient capacity to store the data and handle the processing load as the volumes of data and users grow. Recall Table 5.1, *The Six Dimensions of Growth.*

▶ **Management.** The organization, physical placement, and overall design of the data structures must not prohibit timely execution of DBMS utilities such as copying, backup, and reorganization. These data maintenance activities are an essential part of the production schedule.

Therefore, a good database design is almost always a compromise—a balance between many data processing goals, of which performance is just one. To help us find the right balance, performance goal should also include formally or informally expressed business *priorities* that help the designer decide which applications and tables to work on first.

For a more extensive discussion of the trade-off between performance and other goals, refer to the early part of Chapter 5, especially the section, *Identify Business Priorities and Performance Objectives.*

Problem Requirements. Design is a process of optimization, but within the constraints imposed by technology and other business factors such as cost, development resources, or schedules. No matter how thoroughly we plan and manage the design process, potential users will sometimes specify objectives that cannot be satisfied—either within the design constrainsts imposed by our current environment or under any conditions whatsoever. For example, one objective could be *"Process 1 million rows in 1 second."*

Recall Guideline 5.6: *Never accept impossible performance objectives.* A design process employing SPE techniques like those we advocate in Part II should spot problem requirements like these early in the development process.

Database Applications

Database design cannot take place in a vacuum; we must design for one or more applications—that is, for some combination of data and data processing requirements. We need that knowledge when designing both the application processing and the database structures. In fact, *knowing what the applications are actually going to do is probably the single most important piece of information to have* when optimizing data structures for performance.

To do a good job of design in a database environment, the designer needs to know as much as possible about the execution frequencies and behaviors of application programs and SQL procedures, including the actual SQL data manipulation statements:

▶ First, this information includes a subset of what we referred to earlier (see Chapter 3) as the *application-resource usage matrix.*
▶ Next, to support the additional kinds of analysis needed to make decisions about data distribution and application partitioning in a distributed environment, many authors and speakers suggest adding "location" as the third dimension, creating (in effect) an application-resource-location matrix.
▶ Finally, some form of affinity analysis can be used to show how processes use data and which distribution of processes and data might minimize communication overheads and delays.

Although this all makes sense as a conceptual framework for the design decisions of data and process distribution, in practice we rarely have such a "pure" design situation that we can simply perform this type of affinity analysis, find the optimal distribution, and implement the result. Let's look at the practical realities.

Design for the Existing Application Environment

Database design is not a one-time activity; it is a task that continues throughout the lifetime of an application, in response to change. Application requirements evolve; new applications are developed to process old data; processing volumes and priorities change. Many of today's relational and object databases have been migrated from older DBMSs, often requiring extensive redesign. And, as data is migrated to new releases of a DBMS, changing performance characteristics may require further design changes.

Unless we are implementing a brand new distributed system that shares no data with existing systems, the existing application environment almost always restricts our ability to move certain data or process components, or both. Most large organizations have an enormous investment in existing applications and databases. They cannot afford, nor do they wish, to turn their backs on this investment.

Also, there are other design constraints, such as:

▶ Data that cannot be moved for political or environmental reasons like ownership, storage capacity, or security

▶ Differences in frequency, priority, or response objectives among various applications that share common data

These kinds of practical complications typically prevent us from using pure design algorithms based on affinity analysis or any other similar, mechanical technique. Instead, we must usually approach distribution decisions in a more intuitive fashion that involves:

▶ Beginning with the most important applications (see the next section)

▶ Adopting an iterative approach to design like the one we discuss later in this chapter in *The Database Design Process.*

▶ Applying design guidelines and techniques like those we discussed in Chapter 17, *Design for High Performance.*

Checklist: Selecting Applications to Focus On.   Not all database application programs need the same level of attention; the following characteristics indicate a critical application:

▶ High-priority applications

▶ High-volume applications

▶ Applications with short response time requirements

▶ Applications that update small shared tables or tables with small indexes

▶ Applications that support multiple users against common subsets of data

▶ Applications that require the *Repeatable Read* isolation level (for more details, refer to Chapter 12).

Checklist: Data Manipulation Issues

1. Can we convert dynamic SQL to static SQL applications?
2. If dynamic, will the SQL run often enough for the DBMS to cache the access path?
3. Are we designing for the average or for peak-period application volumes?
4. Can we project the SQL access paths, using *explain* or a similar tool?
5. How many rows do we expect to be returned from each table access?
6. Is access through indexes; if not, how will it perform?
7. Does this application access "popular" columns in frequently accessed tables?
8. Is data being sorted; if so, how much data?
9. How will multitable joins perform? (See the capsule *If You Can't Beat 'Em, Join 'Em*)

If You Can't Beat 'Em, Join 'Em

Although Dr. E. F. Codd of IBM invented relational databases almost thirty years ago, in recent years newcomers like Oracle, Informix, Sybase, and Computer Associates have captured large sections of the market that IBM pioneered with its *DB2* technology. Now IBM has found a new way to outflank their competition—by joining them (or joining their tables, to be more precise).

Despite our conclusions about the inherent performance limitations of remote multidatabase gateways, anyone who shares our interest in DBMS technology should take a look at IBM's *DataJoiner*. If your application calls for heterogeneous database access, then *DataJoiner's* global optimization capabilities set a standard against which any other such gateway should be evaluated. It optimizes multidatabase SQL queries against any combination of DB2 (all versions), Oracle, Informix, Sybase, and Microsoft SQL Server. It can also connect to any other database through an ODBC interface, but with a less sophisticated level of optimization.

Not only does the *DataJoiner* understand how to orchestrate the optimizers of the other DBMSs, it can also drive their *explain (showplan)* facilities and produce a unified report explaining how a multidatabase query will be processed. Neat stuff!

Perhaps the key question is: *Can IBM keep this very clever product up to date, as its competitors' optimizers continue to evolve?* The company claims to be committed to doing so, and we hope they can—technology as good as this deserves to succeed. But then, as diehard database techies, perhaps we're a little bit biased. Look for more detailed *DataJoiner* information on IBM's Web site at www.software.ibm.com.

Beware of Remote Data Access.   In Chapter 9, in the section, *SQL Gateways and Access Path Selection,* we discussed the performance limitations of database gateways, especially those that support heterogeneous database access. (To locate the section, look for Guideline 9.12, *Remote data access gateways and dynamic SQL*). To sum up this aspect of database technology:

▶ Many database gateways are based on Microsoft's *Open Database Connectivity* standard (ODBC), or Javasoft's JDBC standard for Java applications. For two-tier client/server applications, these can provide access to a wide variety of database engines through a common API.

▶ If viewed as a fundamental architectural pattern, database gateways in general are not compatible with our conclusions in Part IV about high-performance architecture and design. Typically, their primary goals are ease of development and portability across DBMSs, not high performance and scalability.

▶ Many applications do not demand high-volume, high-performance processing; for them database gateways may be the right solution.

▶ Synchronous, multidatabase gateways are simply not the right architecture for connecting remote workstations to disparate enterprise databases, for all the reasons we described in Part IV.

Don't Overlook Database Maintenance Utilities

DBMS utilities must be run regularly and must meet elapsed time objectives. Furthermore, gains in data retrieval performance are often obtained by complicating the stored data structures—by denormalizing, indexing, adding derived data (like totals), and so on. Such gains are usually achieved at the expense of elapsed execution time for utilities such as *load, recover,* and *reorganize.*

The key performance issues for large batch and database utilities are:

1. The projected workload volumes, namely the number of batched transactions or the table sizes to be processed by database utilities.

2. Whether the input or output data needs to be separately sorted, and if so, the time and resources needed for sorting. Sorting input data into the same key sequence as the target table(s) is a key technique for optimizing batch processing. Recall the section, *Batch versus Online Transactions,* in Chapter 9.

3. The elapsed time or throughput objectives for individual batch or utility processes, or (more often) the overall elapsed time goals for multiphase batch processes that need to be completed within a "batch window." *The Performance of Batch Processing,* in Chapter 3, contains some introductory remarks on this subject.

4. Whether the overall elapsed time can be reduced by parallel processing techniques. As database sizes grow, the DBMS must support the option to partition large tables and work on the partitions in parallel. For more details, see Chapter 13, *The Parallelism Principle.*

5. The time required to load and reorganize large tables and their indexes, and the frequency at which these activities are needed to maintain acceptable performance levels.

6. The frequency of checkpoints and database backups and the time needed to recover databases and resume normal operation after a catastrophic failure. This process is considerably more complicated when databases are distributed or replicated than it is for a database at a single site because of the synchronization involved. Unless the entire process of restarting after a database failure is carefully designed, the performance of distributed applications is likely to be further affected by delays and errors.

7. The time needed to identify, archive, and delete aging data from current production databases. Sometimes we can use a time-based data partitioning

scheme to support and simplify a rolling archival strategy, such as the monthly archiving of data that is more than a year old.

We must take utility processing requirements into account as part of the design process, treating their performance objectives just like those of any other application.

The Influence of Relational Database Optimizers

To understand database design, we must first understand a central issue of relational database performance: the role of the *query optimizer*. When designing for performance, optimizers, despite their name, are not always helpful—in fact, they can actually make life more difficult for the designer.

Benefits of the Relational Database Optimizer

One of the fundamental strengths of a relational DBMS is that it separates the logical (relational) view of the data from its stored (physical) format. The SQL language lets us manipulate the relational view using table names, column names, and data values only, independent of the underlying data structures.

The component that makes this possible is the query optimizer. It maps the SQL query onto the physical data structures and generates an *access path*—a set of data access requests to the DBMS's lower-level internal access methods. This process is called *automatic access path selection;* it is illustrated by Figure 19.3.

A relational DBMS is only as good as the access paths it generates; the query optimizer must live up to its name. Most obviously, it is the mechanism that enables end users to access the database and that simplifies database programming by interpreting high-level SQL requests; equally important is its role in achieving good performance. Databases evolve as data volumes grow, as data structures change, and as DBMSs introduce new physical data structure options.

Thanks to the optimizer, a DBA can tune the stored data structures in response to these changes and *automatically* obtain more efficient access paths for many programs and SQL queries. When applications and data are moved into multiprocessor environments (like those we discussed in Chapter 13, *The Parallelism Principle*), query optimizers can do automatic load balancing across multiple processors.

Limitations of the Relational Database Optimizer

We may be tempted to assume that the performance benefits of query optimization, because they derive from a component of the DBMS itself, can be obtained freely by every relational database user. Unfortunately, this is not the

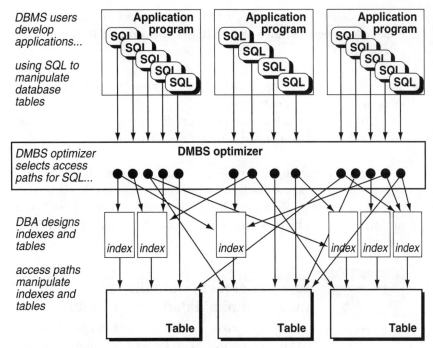

FIGURE 19.3   Automatic access path selection.

case. Furthermore, the quality of a particular DBMS optimizer, although it is an important factor to be weighed when selecting a DBMS product, is not even the key issue. In most DBMSs, the optimizer does an adequate job, even if there is still room for improvement.

A more fundamental issue lies at the core of relational database technology. To understand this, consider the following definition of the three mechanisms that a relational DBMS uses to support efficient processing from "Introduction to Query Processing" in *Query Processing in Database Systems:*

1. A physical design environment that *allows* the physical structure of the database to be adapted to an expected usage pattern
2. A transaction management mechanism that allows multiple access sequences to be executed concurrently but without mutual interference that would lead to inconsistent data
3. A query-processing subsystem that evaluates queries efficiently *within the constraints* created by the two previous mechanisms[4]

---

[4]Jarke, Koch, and Schmidt, "Introduction to Query Processing," in *Query Processing in Database Systems;* S. Reiner, & D. S. Batory, editors; (New York, NY: Springer-Verlag, 1985).

This definition provides a useful framework for thinking about relational database design because it highlights two crucial limitations of the DBMS's mechanisms:

▶ The optimizer works only *within the constraints* created by the database design and transaction subsystem.
▶ The DBMS merely *allows* the physical data structures to be adapted to the workload; it does not actually *adapt* the structures itself.

Often, redesigning the physical structures can allow an optimizer to discover improved access paths that produce substantial gains in processing efficiency for some applications. But before the full benefits of "automatic" query optimization can be realized, *someone must work at optimizing the data structures.*

Guideline 19.3	**Automatic query optimizers need a human database designer**

An "automatic" query optimizer works only within the constraints created by the database design. To obtain the full benefits of query optimization, someone must work at optimizing the data structures.

This is possibly the most significant weakness of relational DBMS technology—a query optimizer is still only as good as the physical data structures it has to work with. Despite the strength of relational optimizers today, they remain passive, reactive mechanisms. Unless a proactive designer creates a suitable index on a table, an optimizer cannot select that index as an access path. And DBMS products offer few facilities to analyze the SQL workloads and suggest changes to the data structures, far fewer to make changes to those structures automatically. Query optimization may be automatic, but database design optimization certainly isn't.

Guideline 19.4	**Query optimizers do not suggest new indexes**

Unless a proactive designer creates a suitable index on a table, an optimizer cannot select that index as an access path. The DBMS products offer few facilities to analyze the SQL workloads and suggest changes to the data structures, far fewer to make changes to those structures automatically.

Cybernetics or Clairvoyance?

"Expert systems have no 'bad days'; they always attend to details."[5]

Expert systems always sound like a good idea—until you actually start to build them. A Microsoft project, code-named AutoPilot, is working on ways to monitor usage and automatically adjust database parameters to improve SQL Server performance.[6] This is a fine goal, but there are many barriers to practical success. For example, adding indexes can slow down existing applications, and dropping a lightly used index may kill the performance of a data request that, although it is run only infrequently, is vital to the business. In our view, unless the DBMS is also supplied with business priorities, the potential for automatic adjustment is limited.

In practice, a human designer, usually the DBA, must figure out the most appropriate set of indexes to satisfy all of the different SQL applications that have to process a table, a task that grows progressively harder as the number of applications grows. Furthermore, it is a paradox that the task of relational database design is made *more complicated* by the presence of the query optimizer!

What the Database Designer Must Understand.   As we noted earlier, database design cannot take place in a vacuum; we must design some combination of data and data-processing requirements. Therefore, *knowing what the applications are actually going to do is probably the single most important piece of information to have when designing a database.*

This means much more than knowing the SQL data manipulation requests—that is just the beginning:

▶ We do not design for some abstract relational DBMS; our designs must work in a particular DBMS environment. We must understand how that DBMS works.
▶ To project the performance of a particular SQL request, we must compare it to the database structures and estimate how the DBMS might actually process it. In particular, this involves understanding when the DBMS can and will use an index and which index is likely to be selected if more than one is available.
▶ Having estimated *how* an SQL request is likely to be processed, the next stage in design is to decide whether the combination of a data structure and processing against it will meet the performance objectives for the application. To do this, we must understand the operation of the low-level DBMS access

---

[5]Paul Harmon, David King, *Expert Systems* (New York, NY: John Wiley & Sons, 1985), 7.
[6]Juan Carlos Perez, "Microsoft Eyes 'AutoPilot' for DBs," *PC Week* (April 20, 1997).

methods (tablespace scan, matching index scan, and so on) sufficiently to estimate the likely cost of processing any particular request.

▶ Because database design takes place in the context of already existing DBMS objects, there are implications to many possible design actions. These can range from the trivial to the catastrophic. Creating an index on a new table is unlikely to ever cause problems. Adding an index to an existing table, though, can disrupt a tuned system if the relational optimizer then decides to select the new index in preference to one that is better suited to existing high-priority applications.

Now look at Figure 19.3 again. The query optimizer, while isolating the programmer and SQL user from messy physical access details, also isolates the database designer from those same details. Without this knowledge, we must evaluate potential data structures by guessing at how and when the DBMS will use them.

Explaining SQL Access Paths.   To reduce this kind of guesswork, relational DBMSs have an optimizer option called **explain** (in Sybase and SQL Server, this is called **showplan**). When an SQL statement is submitted with the *explain* option activated, the optimizer generates a table containing the details of the access path it actually selected. This *explain* table can itself be read using SQL, but because its contents are a trifle obscure and need careful interpretation (*explain* is probably the least aptly named of all DBMS options) they are usually analyzed and reported on by another program.

Although *explain* helps with database design, it is *not* strictly a design tool; it is a design *evaluation* tool. This may seem to be an overly subtle distinction, yet it is an important one. The *explain* output shows only the optimizer's reaction to a particular design option; it does not suggest new design possibilities. Identifying these remains entirely the responsibility of the designer.

Limitations of the Explain Option.   In many application design situations the databases are not yet loaded with production data volumes. So the optimizer's selection algorithms will not have access to the appropriate catalog statistics, and the *explain* output will be of little value.

Most DBMSs try to overcome this limitation by allowing updating of the statistics columns in the DBMS catalog tables. Even if these statistics can be updated by a program prior to running an *explain,* a designer must still decide on the appropriate values to place there to represent a future database. Some statistics, like table cardinality (number of rows), are relatively easy to estimate, but others that involve the number of distinct values in a column or index, or distributions of the most common values, are much harder to predict correctly before the real data is available.

Before running *explain,* the designer must complete all the work of defining a particular data structure and its statistics to the DBMS, so that the relevant information gets recorded in the DBMS catalog tables where the optimizer can read it. This fact alone makes *explain* an unsuitable basis for repeated experiments, particularly on production databases.

Harnessing the Optimizer.   From time to time, researchers and even DBMS vendors have explored the possibility of creating a database design tool that harnesses the power of the *explain* option. The idea is that by repeatedly exercising the explain option for a collection of SQL queries while manipulating the DBMS catalog tables to simulate the existence of indexes, it should be possible to determine an "optimal" set of indexes for that set of SQL queries.

About 10 years ago, IBM released a product of this type, based on a prototype developed by IBM research. The prototype had the unimaginative name of *DBDSGN,* but, with a stroke of imagination worthy of IBM at its best,[7] the product was renamed Relational Design Tool (RDT).[8]

RDT computed the "optimal" design that minimized the total cost of executing all the SQL statements submitted. Unfortunately, this result was based on faulty assumptions:

▶ All the SQL statements were given equal weight in the algorithm. In reality, each would be executed with different frequencies.
▶ The algorithm assumed that minimizing processing costs would produce the optimal solution. In reality, the SQL statements would come from applications with differing priorities and response objectives.

Arguably, given more extensive input describing the workload mix and the performance objectives, a better algorithm could be devised to offset these limitations.

Limits to Design Automation.   Even so, the whole RDT approach still suffers from two significant drawbacks:

▶ Despite their name, *cost-based* optimizers contain cost formulas and pruning algorithms that select a particular access path *relative* to all other candidates,

---

[7]IBM's IMS/VS product once included an option called *Utility Control Facility,* which should surely win some kind of award for unimaginative product names.
[8]The research prototype is reported in S. Finkelstein, M. Schkolnik, and P. Tiberio, "Physical Database Design for Relational Databases," *ACM TODS* 13(1) (March 1988). The product is described in *Relational Design Tool SQL/DS—Program Description and Operations Manual* (IBM document number SH20-6415).

but they do not necessarily produce an *absolute* estimate of execution cost for each access path. If the decision algorithm uses comparisons of the optimizer's own cost estimates (as RDT did), then it cannot take into account additional information that a user could supply to improve that cost estimate once the access path is known.

▶ A fully automated design tool is a "black box" that does not educate its user about database design. Each run produces a single output—*the* solution. The only way to vary the result is to vary the input. If we could be certain that we could always accept the solution without modification, this would not be a problem. But since no one has yet produced such a tool, skepticism is in order.

A Library for Database Designers

Of all the books on data modeling and logical database design, the best starting point is *Designing Quality Databases with IDEF1X Information Models* by Thomas A. Bruce.[9] Unless you work for the government or already use *ERWin* from Logic Works (see Chapter 18), you may not be familiar with the graphical data modeling language IDEF1X. Don't let this deter you—of the many flavors of entity-relationship (E-R) data modeling in use, IDEF1X is really the only standard, and Tom Bruce's book is required reading on IDEF1X and is good on E-R data modeling in general.

In *Data Model Patterns,* David C. Hay describes a collection of standard data models, distilled from 25 years' experience in business data modeling.[10] Of course, each organization is different, and there is no substitute for knowing yours thoroughly. But Hay's book could supply a sound foundation for many business data-modeling projects, and would be especially useful to anyone who has learned the fundamentals of data modeling but wants to see practical examples.

Experienced data modelers interested in the philosophical foundations of their work may enjoy *Data and Reality* by William Kent.[11] Even though his book (subtitled *Basic Assumptions in Data Processing Reconsidered*) dates from the mainframe era, Bill Kent's musings on the meaning of data still make thought-provoking reading for anyone whose mission is either to capture the right information in a database or to draw correct inferences from

---

[9]Thomas A. Bruce, *Designing Quality Databases with IDEFIX Information Models* (New York, NY: Dorset House, 1992).

[10]David C. Hay, *Data Model Patterns* (New York, NY: Dorset House, 1996).

[11]William Kent, *Data and Reality* (Amsterdam, The Netherlands: Elsevier/North Holland, 1978).

The real challenge of design is not to produce the optimal *solution* to a completely specified design problem. Although there are only a few design options for each table, there may be thousands of possible combinations of options in a complete design, and the actual processing needs are continually evolving and changing, never completely specified. The goal of database design, therefore, is to find a design good enough to meet the performance needs of the organization.

Design Tools: Conclusions.   To sum up, relational database design is a difficult task. A relational database designer does not control the way in which the database structures are used—it is the *query optimizer* that selects the access

existing data. At the very least, reading Kent may help explain why reaching agreement on *the right way* to model your business is so hard.

For a concise and practical review of database design issues, we recommend *Relational Database Design: A Practitioner's Guide* by Charles J. Wertz.[12] This well-written book captures the essentials of a big subject in fewer than 300 pages, concluding with a 35-page example of the database design process from a business problem, to data analysis, and all the way through to physical design.

The 600-page *Handbook of Relational Database Design,* by Fleming and von Halle, is a systematic DBMS-independent guide to database design.[13] Organized around 195 database design rules, this book starts with data modeling, then moves on to relational and physical database design. Some of the later tuning examples (using DB2 and Teradata) may be outdated, but most of its advice about database design is timeless.

Finally, for an overview of current database technology, we suggest *Database Management: Principles and Products* by C. J. Bontempo and C. M. Saracco.[14] Unlike the five previous suggestions, each of which aims to prescribe approaches to design, this book is largely descriptive. It contains well-written explanations of current relational, object, and object-relational database technology, and separate chapters describing IBM's *DB2,* Oracle's *Oracle,* Sybase's *SQL Server System 10,* Tandem's *NonStop SQL,* and Computer Associates' *CA-OpenIngres.*

---

[12]Charles J. Wertz, *Relational Database Design: A Practitioner's Guide* (Boca Raton, FL: CRC Press, 1993).
[13]Candace Fleming and Barbara von Halle, *Handbook of Relational Database Design* (Reading, MA: Addison-Wesley, 1989).
[14]C. J. Bontempo and C. M. Saracco, *Database Management: Principles and Products* (Upper Saddle River, NJ: Prentice-Hall, 1995).

path to be used for any DBMS query. And the levers available to the designer have only an *indirect* (and incompletely specified) influence on the optimizer's decisions. A skilled designer may create the potential for good performance, but the optimizer plays a crucial role in determining what actual performance will be.

Doing this well is more an art than a science. It involves the exercise of *heuristics,* or rules of thumb, rather than exhaustive analysis. In our experience, the problem with building a really useful expert system for this type of problem is capturing all the knowledge and expertise of the human designer. In this case, *explain* and prediction tools can help, but they can never replace human intuition and experience.

What the designer really needs is a comprehensive design tool that understands *the current processing environment* and can estimate the effects that *varying the design* may have on existing and projected applications (not single SQL statements). Neither *explain* alone nor derivative tools like RDT address this need. In fact, it is questionable whether any automated tool can be built to handle the entire task because of the level of knowledge it would need to incorporate and the amount of input needed to make decisions.

On the other hand, there is certainly a role for tools with less ambitious objectives, like IBM's *DB2 Estimator,* which estimates the cost of processing individual SQL statements for a given design. There are always opportunities for tools to help with boring mechanical computations. DBMS space and free space calculations, like those performed by Cayenne Software's *Terrain,* for example, are not only boring, they are positively byzantine in their complexity. This is ideal work for a computer to do.

To maximize the value of "expert" database design tools, they must be used *in partnership with human expertise,* not viewed as a replacement for that expertise. This means incorporating them into an iterative design process like the one we describe in the next section.

The Database Design Process

Ideally, relational database design takes place at three distinct levels:

1. An initial *data analysis,* or *conceptual design* phase, during which an abstract *data model* (entities, attributes, and relationships) is identified
2. A *logical design* phase, during which that abstract model is represented as a *relational design* (relational tables, columns, primary keys, and foreign keys) that could be implemented in any relational DBMS
3. A *physical design* phase, when we specify all the *DBMS access structures* (files, partitions, indexes, pointers, and hashing schemes) that determine how those tables are to be stored and accessed

For databases, these correspond to the *analysis, schematic design,* and *technical design* phases of the generic development process we introduced in Part II of the book. Because (in a data context) the term logical design is sometimes used to encompass both of the first two phases and sometimes as a synonym for analysis alone, it minimizes confusion to use the terms *data analysis, relational design,* and *physical design* for these three major phases, and to avoid the use of the term *logical* altogether.

For more about data analysis or data modeling, see the references provided in the capsule *A Library for Database Designers.* Our focus is primarily on the relational and physical design phases, typically the responsibility of a DBA. To bring these two phases into sharper focus, Table 19.2 also distinguishes the *core* design decisions that necessarily precede decisions about *details* and thereby partition the DBA's task into four distinct but related phases.

For convenience of reference only, we have labeled these four phases as A–D. Although this sequence also reflects a logical sequence for tackling the four phases, the actual process is slightly more complex, as we now describe.

Data-Driven versus Process-Driven Design

Any application development process must eventually address the design issues pertinent to all four quadrants of Table 19.2. But a debate sometimes arises as to whether that process should be *data driven* or *process driven.* This debate occurs because in most organizations, data specialists—like data administrators in those larger companies that employ people in that role—are greatly outnumbered by software developers, who focus on processing issues.

In addition, discussions of performance (including ours) tend to highlight the core physical design issues of quadrant C. For a given application-processing demand, as Figure 19.2 indicated earlier, database access structures are the most important *technical* determinant of performance. As a result, there may appear to be a sound basis for the process-driven viewpoint.

On the other hand, a database created by application developers without thought for potential future uses of the same information typically is badly

Table 19.2   **The Four Phases of Database Design**

	Relational (Logical) Design Decisions	Physical Design Decisions
Core decisions	A. Tables and keys	C. Access structures
Details	B. Columns	D. Physical options

designed, inflexible, and hard to integrate into the wider realm of enterprise information processing. Database designers must step outside the narrow requirements of the current application's processing and take the time to think about the inherent logical structure of the information to be stored.

This is not to say that we can ignore performance altogether during relational design. In Chapter 3, Winsberg's law of logical design pointed out that:

> *The logical designer must be a reluctant physical designer. Although conceptual issues should dominate our thinking during the analysis and logical design phases, physical implementation issues cannot be ignored. To do so is to risk creating a design that cannot be tuned for performance.*

Therefore, although this chapter tends to focus on the physical design issues, our suggested design process addresses both relational and physical design and includes both data-driven and process-driven phases. It is an iterative one that can be incorporated into any development methodology.

The Data-Driven Phases.   The first four steps, illustrated by Figure 19.4, are based on analysis of the data requirements only. Stepping through the four phases of Figure 19.4 in order, they are:

1. Organize columns into **normalized tables.**
2. Determine optimum column **data types** and **column ordering.**
3. Define **indexes** for primary and foreign keys only.
4. Select remaining physical design options, like **space** and **free space.**

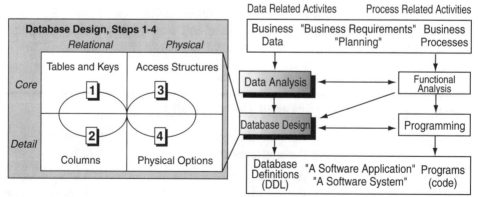

FIGURE 19.4   Database design steps 1–4.

For those readers familiar with the *Zachman Framework (ZF)* for information systems architecture that we introduced in Figure 7.2 of Chapter 7, we can describe this proposal as follows: *First work on rows 2 (analysis), 3 (schematic design), and 4 (technical design), focusing on the data column only.*

The Process-Driven Phases.   Next we must shift our attention to the processing requirements for the data. (In the terminology of the ZF, we now address the relationship of the process column to the data column.) This stage, illustrated by Figure 19.5, involves six further steps:

5. Add new **access structures** (typically **indexes**) to support frequent access requirements.
6. Select remaining **physical options** for any new physical objects created in step 5.
7. If necessary to meet performance objectives, **over-normalize** or **denormalize** tables.
8. Review column **data types** based on the intended processing, and define **data types** and **ordering** for any new tables created in step 7.
9. Define **access structures** for any new tables created in step 7.
10. Select remaining **physical options** for any new physical objects created in steps 7 and 9.

As Figure 19.5 shows, steps 5–10 do not involve new activities, only a new focus. In fact, the entire database design process is continuous and iterative. We have shown only 10 steps, but steps 7–10 may be repeated many more times as we refine the physical design to meet the performance objectives for the applications that will use the database.

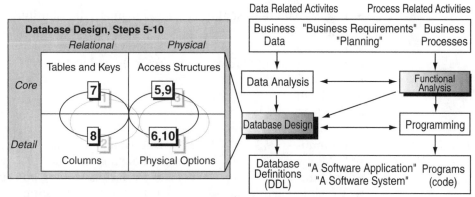

FIGURE 19.5   Database design steps 5–10.

For Ever and Ever . . . In practice, steps 7–10 continue throughout the life of the database, in response to changing requirements. Interestingly, this is illustrated by the shape of the symbol created by following the flow through the design phases—it is the mathematical symbol for infinity.

Database Design Checklists

Table 19.3 shows the principal design concerns within each quadrant. In the following sections we review each quadrant and provide some checklists of typical database design issues and questions. For simplicity, both the table and the bulk of the following discussion use relational database terminology. However, many of the same concerns must be addressed when designing databases for other DBMS types such as object, multidimensional, and object-relational (or *universal*). Despite all claims—particularly by the advocates of object DBMSs—of inherent performance advantages:

▶ All DBMSs, whatever they are called, deal with the same fundamental concerns—allowing a variety of different applications to store and retrieve shared data from persistent storage media (most usually disks).
▶ All DBMSs are subject to the physical law that a particular set of data can be stored in only one sequence on a disk.
▶ No DBMS possesses a magic formula that lets it read or write data from disks faster than any other DBMS.

Table 19.3   **Principal Relational Database Design Tasks**

	Relational Design Decisions	Physical Design Decisions
Core decisions	**A. Tables and keys**	**C. Access structures**
	▶ Normalization	▶ Table partitioning
	▶ Logical data representation	▶ Fragment distribution
	▶ Primary keys	▶ Table indexing
	▶ Foreign keys	▶ Storage structure
	▶ Splitting/joining tables	▶ Table co-location
	▶ Denormalization	
	▶ Replication	
	▶ Summary/derived data	
Details	**B. Columns**	**D. Physical options**
	▶ Data types	▶ Locking options
	▶ Column lengths	▶ Buffering/caching options
	▶ Variable length data	▶ Free space allocation
	▶ Column ordering	▶ Space/storage device allocation

▶ For every DBMS, regardless of vendor or type, database design involves the same set of trade-offs. We can improve performance for a particular database usage only at the expense of other goals such as the ability to query the data easily, the performance of other applications, or the effort and time required to manage and maintain the database.

Therefore, relational DBMSs provide a *lingua franca,* a common set of ideas and associated terminology for any *general* discussion of database design. Unfortunately, when we move from general concepts to *specific* details, we encounter many significant implementation differences even within the class of relational DBMSs. In fact, it is never safe to assume that a design rule of thumb learned for one RDBMS can be applied without change to another.

Where there are *systematic differences* (as opposed to mere quirks of implementation) among the DBMS types, we do note them in the sections that follow.

> Guideline **19.5** **Never assume that different DBMSs work the same way**
>
> Although DBMSs may offer similar features, implementations usually differ. Never assume that a design rule of thumb learned for one DBMS can be applied without change to another.

Core Relational Design

The upper left quadrant of Table 19.3 lists some *core relational design* issues. In our suggested 10-step design process (Figures 19.4 and 19.5) these issues are addressed during step 1 and step 7, as we now discuss.

▶ **Step 1.** The goal of the first phase is to produce an optimal set of tables, columns, and keys that will support both current and future processing requirements. If, as is often the case in practice, this phase is preceded by a *data analysis* or *data modeling* phase (as shown in Figure 19.2), then step 1 of the design process involves translating or "*mapping*" the entities, attributes, and relationships of the data model into relational tables, columns, and keys. If we have already been using data analysis tools like those from Cayenne Software described in Chapter 18, a lot of the work of step 1 can be automated.

Checklist: Typical data modeling issues.   Here are some data modeling issues to consider during this phase, or earlier:

1. Is there a data model?
2. Is it maintained in a modeling tool?

3. Is it current?
4. Is it normalized?
5. Does it identify all relationships among entities?
6. Are there any one-one relationships? Why?
7. Does it identify supertype and subtype entities?
8. Does it identify all data integrity constraints?
9. Does it identify the business factors that determine data volumes?
10. What is the quality and detail of the documentation?

Checklist: Integrity enforcement.   Here are some data integrity issues to consider during this phase, or earlier:

1. What is the primary key?
2. What are the data types of the primary key columns?
3. Is the primary key "artificial"?
4. Are foreign keys which refer to this primary key documented?
5. Do primary and foreign key data types match?
6. For each foreign key, are the update/delete rules documented?
7. How are the update/delete rules implemented?
8. Are there any exposures to uncontrolled updates (i.e., by methods that bypass the rules)?
9. Are any additional types of integrity rules documented and implemented?
10. Do we understand all the performance implications of the integrity enforcement scheme(s)?

▶ **Step 7:** When we revisit this phase at step 7, our relational design actions have physical intentions. For example:

    ▶ Splitting an already normalized table into two tables with a 1:1 relationship ("over-normalization") can reduce I/O for some applications that need only a subset of each row, provided that they scan the table sequentially, while those reading single rows via an index may not be affected at all. On the other hand, applications that insert or delete rows or that read some columns from each of the new tables must now do at least twice the work.

    ▶ Merging previously normalized tables or replicating selected columns in new tables (denormalization) can reduce the I/O costs of separate table accesses for some retrieval applications. Other applications that needed only a subset of the merged data will pay the penalty of additional I/O, and most update processing will be more complicated. For more detail, refer to the discussion leading to Guideline 9.4: *Consider denormalization—and its side-effects—carefully.*

These kinds of changes complicate the database design and, by biasing it in favor of a particular (current) style of processing, make it less likely to support other (future) processing needs. Therefore, we should always be clear about the nature and purpose of the database we are designing, and about the strengths and weaknesses of different DBMS technologies:

▶ It is reasonable to denormalize a database on a *departmental application server,* if that is the *only* way to meet the processing and performance needs of that department's applications.

▶ Pure object DBMSs (like Object Design's *ObjectStore*), which use highly denormalized data storage structures, are ideal for high-performance application servers when there is little or no concern for the performance of new applications of the same data. We explained this earlier; see the discussion leading to Guidelines 9.11 and 10.8.

▶ It is standard practice to denormalize data warehouses and data marts that are designed for retrieval only. (Recall Guideline 9.5.) Multidimensional databases, in particular, are designed for a particular style of processing, and they depend on certain kinds of denormalization (derived data, flattened dimensions) for their performance benefits.

▶ Object/relational or "universal" DBMSs, on the other hand, can be used as general-purpose data servers, and they may or may not store data in denormalized structures. It all depends on how the DBMS is customized to support a particular extended data type.

▶ In contrast, we should make every effort to avoid denormalizing relational databases on *enterprise servers* whose data must be shared by many current and future applications.

This approach is consistent with our earlier discussion of the Locality Principle in Chapter 10 (see *Effectual Locality and the Three-Tier Architecture*) and with our recommendations concerning architecture and design in Chapters 16 and 17.

Checklist: Typical Table Design Issues.   Here are some table design issues to consider during this phase:

1. Does the table represent an entity from the data model?
2. If not, is it normalized?
3. How large is the table (number of rows and row length)?
4. What business factor(s) determine the number of rows?
5. How are subtype entities implemented?
6. Are there any "repeating groups"? If so, what is the performance justification?

7. Is the table denormalized or overnormalized? If so, what is the performance justification?
8. How are one–one relationships implemented?
9. Does the table contain any derived data like totals or averages? How are they maintained?
10. Should there be some (further) denormalization for performance reasons?

Relational Design Details

The lower left quadrant of Table 19.3 lists some *relational design details.* In our suggested 10-step design process (Figures 19.4 and 19.5), these issues are addressed during step 2 and step 8, as we now discuss.

▶ **Step 2.** The second phase deals principally with the data types of all columns. This is usually straightforward, but it involves checking lots of details. Every design decision has a performance consequence, and column data types are no exception. DBMSs vary in their internal operations, but in general:

   ▶ Giving columns of a data domain the same data types in all tables is not only sound practice, it probably improves DBMS and application performance, too (recall Guideline 8.14, *Minimize data type conversion overheads*).
   ▶ When a table includes *nullable* or *variable length* columns, the DBMS must do extra work to retrieve any specific data item from a row. It must recalculate the column offsets separately for every row, whereas for fixed column length, the offsets need only be calculated once for an entire table. This may seem like a small amount of work, but, for a query that manipulates a subset of columns in a very large table, this processing overhead mounts up. On the other hand, if data values (such as long text descriptions) vary greatly, variable-length data types use storage space more efficiently, and so reduce retrieval I/O costs, which is even more significant. The DBMS can compute a lot of column offsets in the time it would take to read one more page of data from disk.
   ▶ Nullable columns (columns that permit *nulls*), because they vary in length, may have side effects similar to variable-length data types, but this should not be made into an argument for using nulls. Missing information (how to represent it in a database and how to handle it in programs) is a complex subject that generates much controversy, even between the leading experts in the database world; we suggest that any minor performance implications be disregarded entirely when deciding whether to use nulls.

Column ordering can also affect the cost of data retrieval and change logging, but in the overall scheme of things, the net effect on performance is probably insignificant for normal applications. (If your application design involves reading and updating very long variable-length rows at rates that stress the DBMS recovery log, then a pause for careful redesign may be called for.)

▶ **Step 8.** Most of these details can be settled during step 2 of the process. But as with core relational design, some questions—particularly those about how best to handle variable-length columns—are related to the way data will be used, and so (logically, at least) they belong in step 8. But don't get too pedantic about it.

Checklist: Column Design Issues.   Here are some column design issues to consider during this phase:

1. Data types are appropriate for domains of allowable values?
2. Variable-length versus fixed-length data types?
3. Nulls or default values?
4. Stored table column order is important?
5. Are any columns "overloaded"? If so, what is the performance justification?

Core Physical Design

The completed relational design is input to the third phase, during which the data structures—the physical files, tablespaces, partitions, and indexes—are designed. The upper right quadrant of Table 19.3 lists some *core physical design* issues. Since it determines the way the data can be accessed by the DBMS, this quadrant has the greatest bearing on eventual application performance and so is generally regarded as the most important. In our suggested 10-step design process (Figures 19.4 and 19.5) these issues are addressed during step 3, step 5, and step 9, as we now discuss.

▶ **Step 3.** The cost of processing data and the appropriate ways to access it depend on how much data there is and on the structure of the data. Normally, primary and foreign keys are identified and indexed at this stage. Other characteristics, such as the number of unique values of a key or column (key or column *cardinality*), the correlation between columns, and the distribution of such values, will also influence the eventual cost of processing. To some degree, these characteristics can also be used during step 3 to refine the basic set of indexes obtained by indexing the key columns. There is little point in making too many physical design decisions until the processing requirements are considered in step 5.

▶ **Steps 5 and 9.** A key decision during this phase is how to index the data. Indexes are a vital mechanism for speeding up access to specific data items in large tables. Indexing, though, is a double-edged sword. Depending on whether the DBMS issues index locks for concurrency and on the isolation levels (or lock levels) specified for the various programs, adding indexes can also introduce the possibility of locking delays because of contention for the pages of indexes being updated. And if contention can occur, then the probability of contention for any given index page is higher than for the corresponding set of data pages because indexes are more compact than the underlying tables (that's why indexes are useful in the first place). We discussed some related matters in Chapter 14, in *Indexing Trade-offs.*

Checklist: Index Design Issues.   Index design is a large subject with many DBMS specific details because the value of any index depends entirely on the chances of the DBMS using it. Here are some issues to consider:

1. Which application justifies creating this index?
2. Is this index required for structural or integrity reasons?
3. Should we index volatile columns; will it create index "hot spots"? (See Chapter 12.)
4. Should we use single-column or multiple-column indexes?
5. Which index should be selected for clustering or sequencing the data?
6. When will indexes be created?
7. When are indexes reorganized? (For some types of index, this is not required.)
8. Will the DBMS optimizer actually use the index?

Bitmap indexes.   Until recently, the predominant form of indexing available in RDBMSs was the B-tree index. With the growth of data warehousing and data mart applications, bitmap indexes have become common, especially in multidimensional databases. For more details of these technologies, see Chapter 21, *Using Data Warehousing.*

The bitmap index consists of strings of bits indicating whether column values match a particular key value. For a particular key value, a bitmap index maps occurrence of the value to the rows in which it occurs.

A B-tree index generally associates a pointer (a *row-identifier,* **ROWID,** or **RID**) to a row with a specific key value. In the case of nonunique values, an individual key is associated with multiple pointers. For example, if student grades were being indexed, a B-tree index of would consist of a grade (A, B, C, D, or F), followed by pointers to all the rows where that grade occurred. Each pointer is normally four bytes long, so if there were 8 million rows in the table, the resulting index (containing a four-byte pointer per row) would require about 32MB, if we ignore the overhead costs of storing the five key values themselves.[15]

---

[15]Yes, we know all about non-leaf pages, and other index overheads too, but this is an illustrative example, so we are ignoring them. Peace!

A bitmap index, on the other hand, consists of a long bitstring for each distinct grade. Each bitstring has one bit for every row in the table. The first bit corresponds to the first row of the table, the second bit to the second row, and so on. As illustrated in Table 19.4, whenever a row contains a particular grade, the corresponding bit is set to a 1 in the bitstring for that grade; otherwise, it is set to a 0.

Because there are 8 million rows, each grade has 8 million bits in its bitmap— that is, 1MB per grade (conveniently). So indexing five grades would take 5MB, compared with the 32MB of pointers that we'd need for a B-tree index.

Obviously, the size advantage of a bitmap index diminishes as its cardinality increases. Suppose that instead of letter grades, the base table contains integer percentage scores. Now the B-tree index *could* come out ahead. It remains unchanged at one pointer per row, or 32MB as before, whereas the bitmap index now needs a 1MB bitstring for each of the 100 distinct key values (or 101, if both 0% and 100% can occur). Uncompressed, the bitmap index now takes up about 100MB, although compression can reduce this significantly at the expense of some additional processor cycles.

Table 19.4   **Bitmaps for Student Grades**

Row	Grade	A Bitmap	B Bitmap	C Bitmap	D Bitmap	F Bitmap
1	A	1	0	0	0	0
2	C	0	0	1	0	0
3	D	0	0	0	1	0
4	A	1	0	0	0	0
5	B	0	1	0	0	0
6	F	0	0	0	0	1
7	C	0	0	1	0	0
8	C	0	0	1	0	0
9	D	0	0	0	1	0
10	C	0	0	1	0	0
11	F	0	0	0	0	1
12	C	0	0	1	0	0
13	C	0	0	1	0	0
14	A	1	0	0	0	0
15	B	0	1	0	0	0
16	•	•	•	•	•	•
17	•	•	•	•	•	•
18	•	•	•	•	•	•

However, any storage benefits are secondary; the primary benefit of the bitmap index is retrieval performance. It improves CPU utilization during searches and counting by allowing direct manipulation of the bitstrings. This works best when the bitstring is relatively dense. If the bitstring is sparse, then the B-tree index is more efficient.

These characteristics make bitmap indexes a good fit for data warehousing applications. When a database is designed as a star-schema like that shown in Figure 21.7, bitmap indexes can be used for the dimensions because—relative to the large central fact table—each dimension table typically contains a very small number of rows. In fact, when designing warehouses using bitmap indexes, there is a big advantage to keeping the dimension tables small. To satisfy queries against the fact table, a DBMS can quickly manipulate the relevant bitmap indexes to identify the subset of all rows that qualify. For an explanation of how this is done, see "Accelerating Indexed Searching."[16]

Guideline 19.6	**Bitmap and B-tree indexes**

Use bitmap indexes to improve access performance to columns having low cardinality. Use B-tree indexes when columns have high cardinality or when they have very irregular data distributions.

Checklist: Identifying Critical Tables.   Not all tables need the same level of design attention; the following characteristics indicate that a table is a candidate for careful review:

1. Large tables
2. Tables that are accessed frequently
3. Small tables that are updated by all (or many) users of an application
4. Tables that are on an application's critical path
5. Tables that are shared by two or more applications
6. Tables that participate in performance-critical joins

Physical Design Details

The lower right quadrant of Table 19.3 lists some *physical design details.* In our suggested 10-step design process (Figures 19.4 and 19.5) these issues are addressed during step 4, step 6, and step 10, as we now discuss.

---

[16]C. J. Bontempo and C. M. Saracco, "Accelerating Indexed Searching," *Database Programming & Design,* 9(7) (July 1996), 37–43.

▶ **Steps 4, 6, and 10.** In the final phase, all the essential details of physical design are completed to create a set of physical database specifications that the DBMS can implement. For relational databases, these include, for example, allocating storage space on physical disks, specifying a percentage of space to be left available as embedded free space to accommodate inserted rows, and choosing lock sizes (row, page, table, and so on, as we discussed in Chapter 12). These decisions, although generally less complex than the core physical design decisions, are certainly not trivial; again, they depend heavily on how we expect the stored data to be used.

Checklist: Locking and Concurrency.   Here are two important locking issues to consider during this phase:

1. Are any tables processes by applications that demand the *repeatable read* isolation level? What are the justification and potential for lock contention?
2. What locking options may affect the performance of small look-up tables, control tables, and code tables?

Design for the Data Volumes.   Key inputs to the design process are the volume of data and its growth projections during the *growth horizon*—the period of time for which our design is intended to be correct. Growth projections gathered early during development probably describe business entities, not database objects. It's the database designer's job to translate all such statistics into size and growth estimates for specific tables, rows, and indexes in the physical design.

Checklist: Data Volumes
1. Should we use data compression?
2. How much free space should we allocate to allow for expected growth, based on the need to keep stored data well organized, the likely pattern of database updates, and database reorganization frequency?

DBMS-Specific Handbooks

For detailed information on specific DBMS products, we recommend the following reference materials:

Oracle
Donald K. Burleson, *High Performance Oracle Database Applications* (Scottsdale, AZ: Coriolis Group Books, 1996).
Michael Corey, Michael Abbey, and Dan Dechichio, *Tuning Oracle* (Berkeley, CA: Oracle Press, 1995).

Mark Gurry and Peter Corrigan, *Oracle Performance Tuning* (Sebastapol, CA: O'Reilly & Associates, 2nd ed., 1996).

Eyal Oronoff, Kevin Loney, Noorali Sonawalla, *Advanced Oracle Tuning and Administration* (Berkeley, CA: Oracle Press, 1997).

Sybase

Brian Hitchcock, *Sybase Database Administrator's Handbook* (Upper Saddle River, NJ: Prentice Hall, 1996).

Jim Panttaja, Mary Panttaja, and Bruce Prendergast, *The Sybase SQL Server Survival Guide* (New York, NY: John Wiley & Sons, 1996).

Shaibal Roy and Marc Sugiyama, *Sybase Performance Tuning* (Upper Saddle River, NJ: Prentice Hall, 1996).

DB2

Blaine Lucik, *Advance Topics in DB2* (Reading, MA: Addison Wesley, 1993).

Craig S. Mullins, *DB2 Developer's Guide* (Indianapolis, IN: Sams Publishing, 1994).

Gabrielle Wiorkowski and David Kull, *DB2 Design and Development Guide* (Reading, MA: Addison Wesley, 3rd ed., 1992).

Informix

Joe Lumbley, *Informix Database Administrator's Survival Guide* (Upper Saddle River, NJ: Prentice Hall, 1995).

Robert D. Schneider, *Optimizing Informix Applications* (Upper Saddle River, NJ: Prentice Hall, 1995).

Elizabeth Suto, *Informix Performance Tuning* (Upper Saddle River, NJ: Prentice Hall, 1997).

Microsoft SQL Server

Jim Panttaja, Mary Panttaja, and Bruce Prendergast, *The Microsoft SQL Server Survival Guide* (New York, NY: John Wiley & Sons, 1996).

Ken England and Nigel Stanley, *The SQL Server Handbook* (Wobern, MA: Digital Press, 1996).

Ken England, *The SQL Server 6.5 Performance Optimization and Tuning Handbook* (Woburn, MA: Digital Press, 1997).

Using Data Replication

"Knowledge is what we get when an observer . . . provides us with a copy of reality that we can all recognize."

Christopher Lasch

In This Chapter . . .

What Is Data Replication
Why Replicate?
Replication Phases
Replication Products
Conclusion

Making copies of data for use on multiple processors at multiple sites is as old as the computer itself. Yet the technology that we discuss in this chapter can be considered to be in its infancy. In a 1996 analysis of the data replication market, International Data Corporation (IDC) indicated that prior to 1993, worldwide revenues for data replication were virtually nonexistent. In 1994 they were less than $40 million. By the end of the decade, however, these same revenues are expected to exceed $600 million.[1] Data replication is now considered an enabling technology. The types of things that it enables, such as mobile computing and data warehousing, will continue to motivate its growth. As of 1996, every major database vendor provided some type of data replication facility with its major DBMS product. There is little doubt that replication technology will be a major component of every enterprise-wide database system within the foreseeable future.

---

[1]Stephen D. Hendrick, "The Worldwide Market for Data Replication," *IDC Bulletin* (February 1996).

Most of the authors that deal with replication technology emphasize the integrity issues associated with replication. Indeed, these issues are formidable, but performance issues are formidable, too. As replication technology continues to gain popularity as an enabling technology, we can expect it to consume a greater portion of enterprise resources. Replication processes may cause performance degradation in transaction systems or unexpected surges in resource consumption. In this chapter, we focus on four of the performance principles that we introduced in earlier chapters:

▶ Efficiency Principle
▶ Locality Principle
▶ Parallelism Principle
▶ Workload Principle

What Is Data Replication?

To oversimplify a bit, *data replication* is the process of copying data from one site to another. It is an outgrowth of relational technology and the requirements for distributed databases. C. J. Date articulated these requirements in his 12 rules for distributed relational databases.[2] In these rules, Date advanced the idea that the database management system creates and maintains copies of entire tables or fragments of tables. The fragments can be either subsets of columns (that is, vertical fragments), subsets of rows (that is, horizontal fragments), or both. Ideally, the user never knows that the replica is a copy and can read or change the replica as if it were the original.

Replication strategies differ from one another in three ways: their **approach,** their **orientation,** and their **capture method.**

There are two approaches to replication. One approach is synchronous; it uses distributed transactions to send changes to remote databases. The second approach is based on "loose consistency" and employs asynchronous transfer of changes between sites.

Replication may be transaction-oriented or table-oriented. In a transaction-oriented strategy, a transaction is captured and transmitted to the replicated systems. In a table-oriented strategy, an entire table is transmitted.

Replication systems use one of three methods to detect and record changes:

---

[2]C. J. Date, "What Is a Distributed Database System," first published in two parts in *InfoDB* 2(2) (Summer 1987) and 2(3) (Fall 1987). Republished as Chapter 10 of C. J. Date, *Relational Database Writings 1985–1989* (Reading, MA: Addison-Wesley, 1990). A shorter version of the same paper also appeared as "Rules for Distributed Database Systems" in *Computerworld* (June 8, 1987).

▶ **Log-based replication.** The replication tool reads the recovery logs that contain the changes.

▶ **Trigger-based replication.** A special trigger is fired to capture changes to data.

▶ **Schedule-based replication.** A procedure detects changes or performs specific extracts according to a fixed schedule. This approach may also use a "Check-In"/"Check-Out" method to allow updates to replicated data.

Date's 12 Rules for Distributed Databases

Rule 1 Local Autonomy	Each site in a distributed database is independent of every other site.
Rule 2 No Reliance on Central Site	No single site is more important to the distributed database than any other.
Rule 3 Continuous Operation	The distributed database should not require shutdown for routine or emergency operations.
Rule 4 Data Location Independence	Entities accessing data will not know where it is stored.
Rule 5 Data Fragmentation Independence	A fragmented, distributed table must appear to be a single table to any entity accessing it.
Rule 6 Data Replication Independence	Copies of replicated data must be updatable.
Rule 7 Distributed Query Processing	Distributed database system will provide query optimization.
Rule 8 Distributed Transaction Management	Distributed database must provide transaction integrity.
Rule 9 Hardware Independence	Distributed database may not require specific hardware platforms.
Rule 10 Operating System Independence	Distributed database may not require specific operating systems.
Rule 11 Network Independence	Distributed database may not require specific network implementations or protocols.
Rule 12 DBMS Independence	Distributed database must support heterogeneous database management systems.

Some Requirements for a Replication Tool

Nigel Stokes, Vice President of DataMirror Corporation, suggests that every replication tool should have at least four basic properties:

▶ **Asynchronous.** The tool should not rely on two-phase commit during replication. Ideally, it should permit scheduling so that data propagation can take place outside of peak hours.

▶ **Selective.** The replication tool should capture incremental changes, and it should allow replication of fragments of tables. Ideally, the tool captures and propagates only the part of the row that changed, not the entire row.

▶ **Transformational.** The tool must support a large variety of transformations. These include data type changes as well as a variety of aggregations, string manipulation, and calculations.

▶ **Heterogeneous.** The tool must be able to extract and apply changes to a variety of potential platforms and data management systems. At the very least, the tool must be able to link legacy data sources and newer systems.

The strategy is built into the replication tool. Most tools are log-based (the method that has the least impact on the operational system) and use a transaction-oriented replication strategy, although a few tools allow the user to select between the two replication strategies. The important point to remember is that the tool determines the replication method; the method has a decisive effect on performance during the process of detecting and capturing changes in the operational system.

Synchronous versus Asynchronous Replication

Transactional or synchronous replication of changes occurs when a transaction changes data in the primary system. All remote databases that have copies of

Guideline 20.1	**Product selection is the most potent performance determinant for replication**

Once the replication tool is chosen, the replication method is chosen. Once the tool is chosen, the differences between trigger-based replication and log-based replication are academic.[3]

---

[3]Nagraj Alur, Principal Consultant, Database Associates, P.O. Box 310, Morgan Hill, CA, 95038. Telephone (408) 779-0436, or online at www.dbaint.com.

the changed information receive a copy of the change immediately. The change to all the databases occurs in the same unit of work as the change to the primary database. To make sure that the change is correctly applied to all the participating databases, the transaction must coordinate the commit across all the resource managers. This requires the use of two-phase commit.

Although synchronous replication has been successfully used with replication in high-performance systems such as Tandem's Remote Duplicate Database Facility and IBM's IMS Remote Site Recovery applications, which can replicate thousands of transactions per second, it is not well regarded when it comes to replicating changes in the client/server environment. As we concluded in Chapter 14, this type of replication imposes communication waits on the transaction and does not scale well. Considerable overhead is associated with synchronizing the commit states of multiple servers, which have variable communications and processing speeds and are susceptible to failure. Overall, synchronous replication is not used widely.

The impetus for asynchronous replication arose from a desire to replicate information without having to endure the problems associated with two-phase commit. But, to achieve this goal, we must treat the copy differently from the original; the copy can no longer be transparent. And, because the copy lags the source by some interval, it may not reflect the true state of affairs in the original.

Let's look at an example. Figure 20.1 shows a replicated database in which the customer table in Sacramento is replicated to San Jose, Los Angeles, and San Diego. This means that changes in Sacramento will be automatically propagated to the three replicated sites. Let's suppose that new entries in the master inventory table in Sacramento are sent to the replicated sites every 10 minutes. Because of this propagation delay, a customer calling the San Diego office

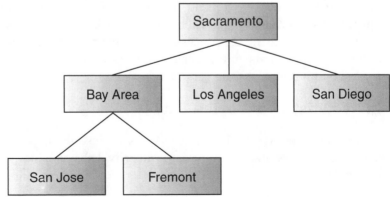

FIGURE 20.1   A replicated database structure.

would not be told about inventory changes made at Sacramento only a few minutes before.

Replication will soon bring the San Diego office up to date, but in the meantime, the "loose consistency" between the primary site and the replica may have caused the loss of a sale. Therefore, we must always consider the potential impact on both performance *and integrity* of any discrepancies between the origin and the replicated site.

There are trade-offs between the business and computing costs of consistency. When we substitute the loose consistency of asynchronous replication for the exact consistency provided by distributed transactions, we introduce some uncertainty into our business information, which may have an associated business cost. On the other hand, enforcing a higher degree of consistency among distributed databases lowers application performance and—because synchronous operations prevent us from using efficient batching techniques when propagating changes—increases the processing costs.

Guideline 20.2	**Asynchronous replication involves cost trade-offs**

Asynchronous replication lets us use efficient ways to process and propagate changes, but it introduces some uncertainty into our business information that may have an associated business cost. On the other hand, enforcing a higher degree of consistency among distributed databases usually increases processing costs and lowers application performance, which may itself have a business cost.

It's not always possible, however, to draw a simple and decisive line between synchronous and asynchronous replication. As G. Froemming points out, asynchronous replication may have some synchronous components.[4] Although freed from the overhead of the two-phase commit, some log-based replication systems maintain synchronous contact between the source and destination systems during the process of gathering replicated data and sending it to the destination. This may be acceptable if there are a few "low-volume" subscribers, but it does not scale very well as the number of subscribers increases.

Characteristics of Copied Data

We generally use five basic characteristics to describe copied data: **environment, time, access, data content,** and **integrity.** Let's consider each of these in more detail.

---

[4]G. Froemming, "Moving Forward with Replication, Part 2," *DBMS* (April 1996).

Environment.   **Environment** refers to the types of platforms, communication networks, operating systems, and database management systems that make up the enterprise. The environment defines replication's role. If the environment consists of heterogeneous databases and operating systems, replication may be needed to overcome inconsistencies among those systems. In a widely distributed system, replication may be used to enhance the efficiency of local access.

Time.   We can characterize copies as being:

▶ **Near real time.** The copy is slightly out-of-phase with the primary; this may mean a few seconds to a few minutes out-of-phase.

▶ **Event-driven.** A copy created "as of a particular time" is actually event-driven. Successful completion of a series of programs usually establishes a consistent state for a group of tables.

▶ **On demand.** The subscriber determines when to replicate the data.

Delay is designed into the replication process. We need to consider both the performance and the integrity aspect of delay. Even if a large replication delay is acceptable from an integrity viewpoint, performance considerations may demand a shorter latency period. Potential impact on the network may dictate the use of incremental replication, with relatively small latency to keep the network load within specified bounds.

We need to consider the following three performance dimensions when we're working with replication:

▶ The impact on the transaction system when changes are detected and captured for replication.
▶ The impact on network resources when the replicated changes are propagated to *all* of the target systems.
▶ The impact on the target system when the replicated changes are added.

As a general rule, long replication delay intervals minimize the impact on the source system but *increase* the impact on the network and receiving system. This is because the source system can schedule extract processing during relatively inactive periods, thereby avoiding overloading resources in the source system. But this strategy generally requires transferring more data across the network. The demand on network resources can be multiplied if there are multiple target sites. The time needed to process the data may also exceed any processing window that can be scheduled at the target.

> ### Guideline 20.3   Long replication delay can minimize impact on the operational system
>
> Long replication delay intervals typically minimize the impact on the source system because processes can be scheduled during nonpeak periods. But long delay intervals can also increase the impact on the network and receiving system by requiring a large volume to be sent.

Integrity is always compromised by unexpected delays that occur when a problem prevents replication from occurring. An unexpected delay means that the copy may be "stale." The data can be misleading. Applications or users should be able to tell whether a data element has become stale. In fact, this type of information may be required for most decision making. Unfortunately, none of the current replication products provides this type of information. If it is provided at all, the application supplies it.

When Is Information Current?

Nearly everyone associated with replication is tempted is to make sure that a replicated system is up-to-the-minute. Because everyone wants the copies to be correct, this temptation is understandable. Yielding to the temptation, however, can add unnecessary complexity and consume resources for no valid purpose. Surprisingly, there are many times when replicating data can overload the user with irrelevant and potentially misleading information.

In a data warehouse, the business defines what is current. If the business cycle is weekly, there generally is no need to replicate individual transaction changes to a data warehouse. Differences in business cycle allow the designer to select the best method for collecting, transforming, and propagating the changes. In many cases, scheduled extracts are a better method of replicating information than a near real-time method—both from the viewpoint of integrity and from that of performance.

Access.   Access is easily the most complex topic in replication. Replication technology allows any combination of read, update, and replication imaginable. But, all of these combinations resolve themselves into three basic access schemes: **consolidation, distribution,** and **peer-to-peer** or **bidirectional.** In consolidation, a single site receives changes from one or more sources, or "distributors." A distribution scheme is one where a source site distributes its changes to one or more target sites. Bidirectional replication allows every site to update and replicate its copies to any other site wishing to receive those changes. Bidirectional replication is difficult to manage and, for that reason, is often referred to as "chaos." Figure 20.2 illustrates these access schemes.

In reality, we don't use copied data in the same way at every site. How a site does use the data depends on its access rights to the replicated data. There are three basic rights: **ownership; update authority,** which includes the right to insert and delete rows; and **read-only** access. The simplest and most workable replication design restricts update access to the owner of the data. Every other site is limited to read-only access. Both the consolidation and the distribution schemes regulate ownership and update authority.

A receiving site can act as a distributor for other sites. This type of replication hierarchy is commonly used in mobile computing. The parent site receives replicated data, then replicates it to the mobile systems. Thus, the parent site acts as a focal point for the control of data on the mobile systems.

Applications like mobile computing often specify that multiple sites have the ability to update data. A mobile sales application would not be very useful if it did not allow the user to enter sales. These changes need to be consolidated into the parent system and replicated to other sites. A simple, single-site

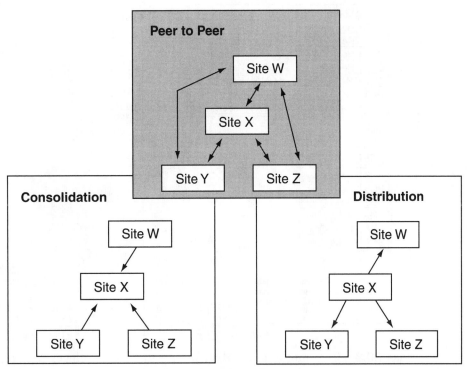

FIGURE 20.2   Three principle replication schemes.

owner replicating to read-only sites is not sufficient. Somehow, the authority to update tables must be delegated to some of the receiving sites without creating the type of chaos that usually results from bidirectional replication.

Two common methods are used to distribute ownership of data: data partitioning and rotating ownership. The two methods differ on which data is owned by the various sites. In the first case, a site owns only that part of table assigned to it. For example, it may own only the part of the sales catalog table pertaining to products sold from that site. In the second case, a site owns the entire table for a specific period of time. In each case, ownership is restricted to a single site. Updates are allowed only at that site; every other site is read-only.

As Figure 20.3 indicates, in partitioning, a logical table is divided—logically or physically—into fragments. If the fragments are physical, only the part of table owned by the site is located there; if the fragments are logical, the entire table is distributed to the site, but the site owns only a subset of the table. That site may change the data in this fragment and replicate those changes to other sites, but it can only read the remainder of the table. Both integrity and performance can benefit from partitioning. Partitioning improves integrity by

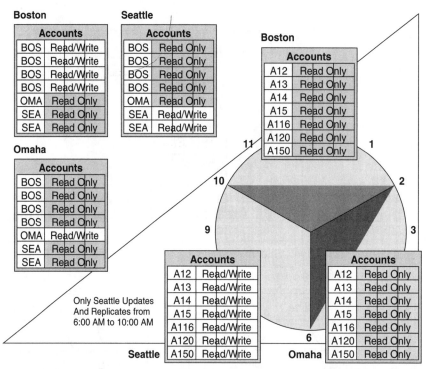

FIGURE 20.3 Two methods for distributing update privileges in a replicated environment.

restricting update of parts of the table to specific sites. Overall performance can improve if distribution of the fragments improves parallelism associated with reading and updating the table.

Guideline 20.4	**Partitioning tables can improve database performance**

Partitioning tables can improve overall database performance by increasing the total parallelism of update operations for a specific table.

The second method, rotating ownership, is like a time share. Ownership of the table changes according to a designated schedule. For example, as Figure 20.3 illustrates, Boston may own update rights to the table between noon and 3:00 P.M., while Seattle owns them between 6:00 A.M. and 10:00 A.M. During the time that the site owns the data, it may perform updates and replicate them to all subscribers. When the ownership period expires, a new site assumes ownership of the table, and the old site is restricted to read-only access.

In peer-to-peer or bidirectional replication, "update chaos" results when we eliminate single-site restrictions on update and allow every site to update its copy of the data. These changes are replicated to other sites, which may also be updating and replicating changes to the same table. Despite vendors' attempts to regulate the integrity issues, fully automatic bidirectional replication remains unworkable. Manual conflict resolution is always necessary.

Bidirectional replication also imposes a significant overhead on receiving systems because they must determine if the contents of one update arriving from a remote source conflicts with any other updates arriving from other sites. Finally, any delays during periods when data is unavailable because of manual conflict-resolution procedures are likely to be perceived as "poor performance" by users.

Data Content.   **Data content** refers to relationships between the copy and the original. Three aspects define this relationship:

▶ **Transformations** indicate the type of transformations that occur between the primary site and the copied data. Determining when the transformations occur is often a performance-based decision.

▶ **Representation** indicates whether the replica is a full copy of the table or a fragment of the table.

▶ **Replication method** indicates whether the replication copies an entire object or extracts only incremental changes. One important method involves continuous history, in which every event on the primary is replicated and inserted into the copy.

Integrity.   Asynchronous replication processes require constant attention to data integrity. But, integrity and performance often complement each other. For example, a fundamental rule of data integrity is that replicated data should be copied only after the data has been committed. From a performance viewpoint, this rule keeps replication from interfering with the transactional process. It also dispenses with any need to run resource-intensive compensating processes to back out uncommitted changes if the transaction rolls back its work.

The replication system must ensure that changes are always received by the target system. In the event of system outages, the changes must be kept until the target system receives them. This generally requires that additional storage resources be allocated in case the target is unavailable.

Many replication systems do not maintain complete transactional integrity at the target system (that is, the target site does not provide the same transactional guarantees as were provided at the primary site). An example may help to clarify this concept:

Suppose that at the source site, a single transaction debits the savings account by $100. In the same unit of work, it credits checking by $100. The system replicates copies of the savings and checking to a different location using asynchronous replication. The copy is "near real time."

As Figure 20.4 illustrates, replication can produce inconsistent results at the target site if transactional integrity is not supported. In the example, the savings account is updated in a different unit of work from the update of the checking account. Because the two updates may be performed in two independent, parallel paths, the outcome of the updates can't be predicted. It is possible that the savings account is debited by $100, but the update to the checking fails, leaving the database in error. To prevent this possibility, both the debit and the credit should occur in the same unit of work at the target, just as they did at the source.

Guideline 20.5	**Data integrity and replication performance go hand in hand**

Replicated data should be copied only after the data has been committed. This fundamental rule of data integrity is also beneficial to performance in that it separates the replication process from the transactional process and avoids the need for complex, resource-intensive compensating processes to back out uncommitted changes if the transaction rolls back its work.

Why Replicate?

Although performance enhancement was once the primary justification for replication, a number of additional reasons are emerging as organizations gain

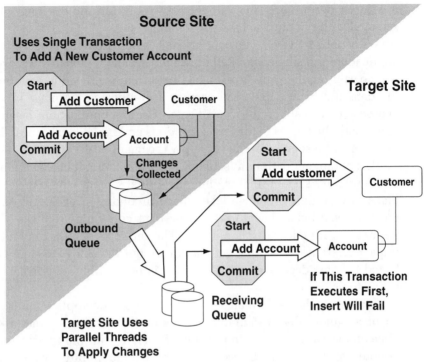

FIGURE 20.4   Transaction integrity requirements in replication.

experience with the technology. Today, the other major justifications for replication include:

▶ Data warehousing
▶ Mobility—distribution to a detached network
▶ Public information distribution
▶ Recoverability and availability
▶ Auditing
▶ Migration and coexistence

Performance Enhancement

Performance enhancement is still a major motivation for using replication. In Part III of the book, when discussing the SPE design principles, we referred several times to the role that data replication techniques can play in improving application performance. A well-designed data replication scheme can improve program performance by placing copies of data close to where the work is actually performed. This reduces network traffic and the long waits often associated with remote database processing.

We cannot, however, view performance solely from the perspective of a single application or a single site. Rather, we must view it globally. An overall performance gain requires an "investment" in system overhead to capture changes to the data and to distribute the changes to replicated systems. The investment overhead is typically in the form of enterprise communications resources needed to transmit the copies to the target locations and in the local processing and data management resources needed to apply the changes after they are received.

Part of the replication investment is the effect that it has on the performance of the primary system (that is, the operational system where the changes takes place). Every time a change takes place involving a replicated data object, it must be recorded and sent to all the systems containing replicas of that object. Replication functionality is not free. The replication tools may have minimal impact on transactions that activate them, but the source system is always affected to some degree, even if the effect is perceptible only to sensitive monitoring tools.

Evaluating the performance benefit for a specific application is more a matter of judgment than calculation. Is the cost of replicating data likely to produce an overall reduction in the cost of carrying out the transactions against a remote central server? The issue becomes even more intuitive when we view it from an enterprise vantage: Is the overall cost of replication justified by the performance enhancements for all applications employing it?

Data Warehousing

Although we discuss the performance issues surrounding data warehouses and data marts in Chapter 21, we would be remiss in not mentioning the topic here as well. Replication may be used to consolidate changes from operational databases or to propagate changes from the warehouse to distributed data marts. Existing data transformation limitations and control issues lead to controversy about the practicality of using replication for populating data warehouses. Because data is often extensively manipulated before it is used, these limitations can conceal important errors. In order to make sure that data is consistent and that subtle relationships are not lost, the warehouse needs to have data taken from the source when it is in an internally consistent state, and, as we shall see, replication cannot guarantee that consistency.

There is, however, general agreement that replication can be used productively in maintaining data marts. Replication is also widely used for operational data stores, which often just copy data from the transactional system with little transformation.

Mobile Computing

Replication may be the only practical method for delivering mobility to business computing applications. Mobile applications running on a portable system, such as a laptop, load data from a parent site, then detach from the network. Often, the portable system is given ownership of a unique subset of the replicated data so that the owner can perform whatever work is required. Later, the portable systems reconnect and, one by one, pass their changes to the parent site, which consolidates them. It is not unusual for the parent site to replicate the consolidated changes to a master site for further consolidation and distribution.

By their very nature, mobile applications "pull" updates from the source and "push" their changes back to the source. Thus, the source acts as both a distributor and a consolidator. The fact that replication can occur only when the mobile system is connected is a key performance issue for mobile systems.

It is important to note, however, that performance of the parent server is particularly vulnerable to sharp irregularities in its workload. Communication and replication services may show "spiking" if a large number of remote systems transfer changes back to the parent database at the same time. Similarly, replication resources are subject to strain when laptops pull changes from the outbound queues. This may also involve a significant amount of data transfer and processing if, in the interval since the previous connection, a large volume of changes have accumulated in the outbound queue.

For more discussion of middleware for mobile computing, see the capsule, *Offline Transaction Processing* in Chapter 15.

Recoverability and Availability

It is becoming increasingly common to use replication to create a "warm standby" for high-availability applications. This is a specialized form of replication that creates read-only replicas for use in the event the primary fails. There is normally no transformation of replicated data, and the target platform is nearly identical to the source platform. After all, a disaster plan for Oracle does not usually send its replication to Sybase. The target site is activated as the owner only if the primary fails.

Public Information Distribution and Auditing

Data replication is also an enabling technology for information publication, an increasingly popular application in which organizations make some types of corporate operational information available to the public through the Internet. In some cases, this type of information distribution provides a competitive edge for the enterprise supplying the information. Examples of publication include telephone directories, technical product information, and product ordering information. Security considerations mandate that this type of application replicate information from operational systems across the firewall.

Use of replication for auditing grows out of the ability to capture all the changes that occur in an operational database and use them to document accountability for the changes. Auditing employs a continuous history type of capture. If replication has been implemented for other reasons, then auditing requires very little additional performance overhead, but it is not a sufficient reason to implement replication.

Migration and Coexistence

Replication is also used for migration, copying data from a legacy system into the successor system. This occurs in two types of migration: "one time" and "coexistence."

The first type of migration—"one-time" migration—accesses the legacy system at a planned time. It transforms the data, then loads it to the successor system. Migrations from a file system to Gemstone, Oracle, or Sybase, for example, use "one-time" migration. Despite the need for extensive data scans and heavy processing loads, this technique involves only minimal performance consideration, at least as far as replication goes. The data must be moved, but it's only going to happen once.

The second type of migration—coexistence migration—is a far different issue. In this case, we are talking about maintaining a heterogeneous database environment in which we move data from one environment to another on a regular basis. This is a true replication environment in which the copies must be synchronized. From a performance perspective, replication for coexistence is no different from replication for any other purpose. Coexistence is a special name for a heterogeneous replication environment. Because it requires more transformation operations than some other types of replication applications, the performance interaction between the transformation and transport phases must be explicitly controlled.

Historically, these "coexistence solutions" never go away. New applications are often developed using the "legacy" systems. Replication performance concerns are no different for this environment than for any other. Depending on the number of target systems, it is usually more efficient to perform all of the transformations at the source, prior to the transport phase, rather than at the target.

Replication Phases

As Figure 20.5 illustrates, replication involves four distinct phases: **capture, transformation, transport,** and **apply,** each of which has its own performance concerns. Success in regulating overall replication performance is at least partially the result of regulating the performance of each phase.

Replication products differ in the way in which they implement these phases, and each implementation method involves a number of performance advantages and disadvantages. Since there is little (or no) chance of modifying a product's implementation method, it is important to select a replication product

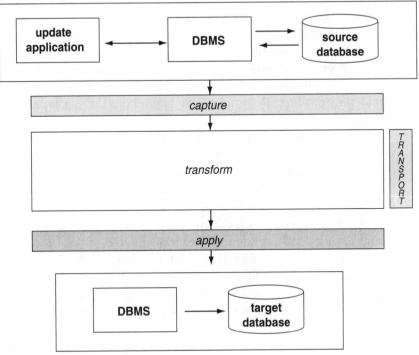

FIGURE 20.5   Mechanics of replication.

that is well suited to the task at hand and that fits into the overall system development scheme. And, if the replication product is going to be used with existing products, it should be able to take advantage of their strengths.

The Capture Phase

The capture phase detects changes occurring in the operational system. It may either store these changes or propagate them immediately. The capture phase always affects performance at the source in some way. Often, replication can be treated as a user of the operational system. Performance decisions in such cases are no different from performance decisions for any other application.

In a synchronous replication scheme, changes are transmitted immediately to the target system. A synchronous replication of a transactional change can impose overhead ranging anywhere from 300 percent to 1200 percent of the base throughput, depending on the complexity of the transaction.

Asynchronous replication moves changes into a holding area, usually called a stable queue, for later distribution. Major software products use one of three fundamental methods for asynchronous replication: triggers, "log sniffers," and scheduled extracts. Products using scheduled extracts may use triggers or they may read the log. But they use these facilities much differently than a "near-time" data capture replication method would use them. Scheduled replication processes do not try to capture changes as they occur; instead they use a technique that allows them to identify the changes at a later time. Products using scheduled extracts often use database facilities to detect changes after the fact, rather than trying to capture them as they occur. One replication product, Prism, for instance, reads the log tapes after they have been archived.

Trigger-based replication creates the most obvious source of additional overhead. For one thing, it uses a scarce resource, a trigger. More importantly, the resources required to load and fire the trigger need to be added to the overhead of the basic transaction. Log sniffers, on the other hand, do not add any overhead to the transaction itself. They rely on the fact that a DBMS already records all changes on its log, to provide for recovery from system failures. Log sniffers simply capture the changes from the DBMS log. They add processing overhead later, when the changes are taken from the log and written to the stable queue. Regardless of the method used, replication systems must all expend resources to determine if a particular change qualifies for capture. The resources involved in this process can become a bottleneck as the number of subscriptions grow.

Performance concerns during the capture phase need to focus on minimizing interference with the transactional system. Incremental replication requires configuring resources to ensure adequate capacity during the capture phase to support the subscribers to the system. For example, queues, whether files or tables, need to be of adequate size to ensure enough space for all changes being captured. If replication is log-based, providing an independent platform allows the replication tool to extract changes from the log in parallel with the transaction process making the changes.

The Transformation Phase

The transformation phase spans the other three phases. It can occur at the source database during the capture phase using views, joins, and standard SQL operators, or it can be performed at the source by means of special exits that employ either third-party routines or user-developed routines. Transformation processing can also be performed at the target using SQL operators, exits, or stored procedures. Table 20.1 shows some of the more common transformations.

There are, of course, many reasons for transforming data. For example, we may want to change it to conform to local standards or to summarize the information. Regardless of the reason for transforming the data, we need to address the question of where the transformation is going to take place; this can represent a major performance issue. Fortunately, some of the factors are relatively apparent. For example, if the workload at the source is sufficiently low, then the transformations can be performed there. And, if every receiving site is

Table 20.1 **Transformation Methods**

Method	Description
Joins	Changes to data in one table are joined to information from other table. Replicates join rows.
Aggregations	Process creates totals or summaries of changed data for replication.
Data type transformations	Data type of information is changed.
Default substitutions	A default is substituted for information associated with the change.
Concatenations	String manipulation operators create a new string in which part of information associated with the change is concatenated with other information. They may be used in conjunction with a join.
Table lookups	Names or descriptions are substituted for a foreign key.

going to have to perform the same transformation, the Efficiency Principle suggests that it is better to perform the transformation once, at the source. If the connection between source and target database is going to be synchronous, it is definitely better to transform as much of the data as possible either before or after the connection is established between the two databases. Trigger-based replication may affect transaction performance if we perform extensive transformation during the capture phase. It may be advisable to transform data at the destination, where it won't affect the transactional system.

Guideline 20.7	Consider the location for data transformation carefully

Data transformation decisions should be based on capacity and workload at the source, the number of targets receiving the same transformed data, and the impact on the transport phase.

Many transformations use SQL to change the data. These declarative transformations may need data objects at the source or at the target to function. In this situation, transforming the data at the site where the SQL will function is best. Of course, we can also perform data transformation at the beginning or end of the transport phase. Encryption and compression are examples of such transformations. Compression may improve transport performance by reducing the amount of data that we move through the network.

The Transport Phase

The function of the transport phase is to move replicated changes to the appropriate target sites. At its simplest, this phase is nothing more than a file transfer between two locations, but it can be much more involved. Reliability is all-important here. Each replicated object must receive a copy of every change made to the primary system. If the receiving server is unavailable, the changes must be held until it does become available. If there is a problem with the network, the replication system must use whatever means it can to guarantee that the changes are received by the target system. For example, some replication systems initiate a synchronous session between the source and target databases to ensure that the target database receives the changes.

As a general rule, in asynchronous replication, the tasks of the transport phase include gathering all the updates for a particular target site from an outbound queue, sending them to the target site, then purging the outbound queue of changes once it is determined that the target site has received the changes. In many cases, as we noted earlier, transformations take place as part of the transport phase, either immediately before the transfer or immediately afterward.

Performance during the transport phase is directly related to the amount of information that needs to be transferred. If a single column changes, the system can replicate either the entire row to the target or just the data that has changed. Performance is best in all four phases if the data to be copied is restricted to only that information that has changed (that is, the specific column and its keys). This requires the replication tool to extract a specific subset of columns whenever an individual data element changes, rather than the entire row whenever an individual data element changes.

Scheduling is probably the most potent influence on performance characteristics of the transport phase. Replication systems really need some type of intelligent scheduling mechanism analogous to cost-based optimization of data access. This is particularly true if they do not support explicit scheduling that allows the administrator to regulate the workload placed on network resources. Without this ability, an administrator working with a typical asynchronous replication tool must attempt to specify a replication interval that captures an optimal number of update operations to ensure optimal message length and an optimal number of sessions during peak periods. Table 20.2 summarizes some of these performance concerns.

Replication tools may employ either a "pull" architecture, a "push" architecture, or a "mixed" architecture. Many replication tool manufacturers prefer the push architecture because it interferes less with the operational system when it is associated with log-based capture. On the other hand, designers frequently prefer a pull architecture so that the receiving system can accept information during times when its resources are not stressed.

The advantages of pushing or pulling may not be obvious in a complex replication environment. For example, the push approach may not affect the

Table 20.2 **Transport Performance Concerns**

Issue	Performance Factors
Synchronous identification of changes when subscriber connects to receive changes	Low bandwidth for individual subscribers may cause performance degradation during transport phase. Increase in subscribers will cause degradation in performance. Transformations by subscriber can prolong connection?
When are changes actually moved from the log?	During connection, changes may introduce delay in transport. Periodically, changes may impact logging and purging of logs.

source system a great deal, but if the target system is a consolidator that receives replications from a large number of sources, its performance may be seriously affected. Further, it is not uncommon for multiple databases participating in a replication scheme to be "operational." For example, a sales database may receive copies of customer lists from a central database, but the receiving system is responsible for capturing all sales made to valid customers. The source database may actually generate a lower level of transaction activity than the target system.

The Apply Phase

The most important source of performance overhead in replication is the process of applying changes to the target system. During the apply phase, replicated data from the inbound stable queues modifies the data in the target system in some way. Any of the methods listed below can apply the changes to the target system. Each one may be very efficient under specific conditions, but they do differ in their basic efficiency. The list below orders these methods in terms of their basic efficiency in applying changes:

1. High-speed loading using a bulk load utility
2. Execution of a stored procedure
3. SQL UPDATE, DELETE, or INSERT
4. Use of ODBC for transparent access to target file system so that changes to a table in a DBMS can be applied to a "flat" file

The relative efficiency of each of these options depends on the specific objectives of the replication process and the environmental conditions in which the process operates. If replication requires application of a large volume of transactions during "off hours," then using a bulk-loading utility is far superior to any other method. On the other hand, using individual SQL statements or even stored procedures is better if replication sends a continuous stream of transactions to a target DBMS in order to maintain "near real-time" consistency. If the data has to be transformed during the apply phase, then the stored procedure may be the best practical method.

If we apply incremental updates, we can achieve a major performance benefit from using parallel write threads. But, the receiving system must allow multithreaded writes, and the replication and DBMS systems must provide a sufficient number of write threads to support parallel database operations. Parallelism also applies to the location of the server managing the inbound stable queue. If it is on a different platform than the database server, processing the stable queues can parallel the database update.

Guideline 20.8 Parallelism can improve replication performance significantly during the apply phase

Parallelism provides a significant performance enhancement during the apply phase. But, the replication system, must be correctly configured to achieve optimal benefits from parallel operation.

Bidirectional replication can disrupt performance during the apply phase. Changes to tables in any database can be replicated to all other participating databases. These changes, during the apply phase of an individual system, are taken from the inbound queue and tested to determine if they represent a valid update. The local system may have also made changes to its copy of the table. There may be multiple updates to the table waiting in the inbound queue. This update conflict is known as a "collision." The target system must detect and resolve these conflicts during the apply phase. In addition to the integrity exposure, bidirectional replication creates conditions for major performance degradation. Conflict detection involves significant overhead. Conflict detection must be a synchronous process; it must constantly monitor incoming transactions to determine if there is a potential "collision" needing resolution.

If any site can update and replicate its copy of a table, there is potential for two updates to be in conflict at a particular site, as we see in Figure 20.6. This type of conflict between updates can result in persistent errors that may or may not be detectable.

Ideally, we should avoid bidirectional replication and all of its inherent problems. This is possible only if we design the distributed database so that no two sites can update the same data at the same time.

Are There Conflicts That Cannot Be Detected and Resolved?

Most products that support bidirectional replication provide some means of conflict detection and automated resolution. Some conflicts, though, may not be detectable or resolvable without a major performance penalty. For example, comparing timestamps is one of the most common methods of resolving conflicts. Clocks from different systems need to be synchronized to compare their timestamps. Independent clocks are subject to differences in their initial synchronization and in the rate of "drift" with respect to one another. This type of clock error can make timestamp resolution invalid. If the replication delay is less than the clock error, then the timestamp is, for all practical purposes, useless for resolving conflicts between to replicated changes.

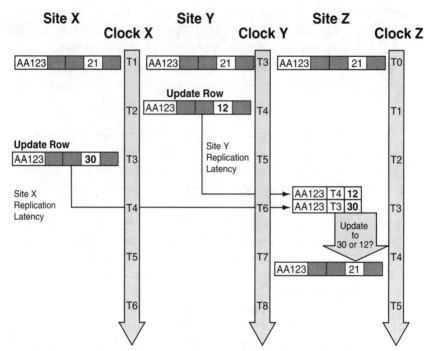

FIGURE 20.6   Conflict between updates to two replicated tables.

Replication Products

Every major DBMS vendor now supplies a replication tool that can work in a heterogeneous, multidatabase environment. In addition, a growing number of vendors are marketing specialized replication products. Many of these specialized products are specifically concerned with replicating data from operational databases to data warehouses or data marts.

Table 20.3 presents an alphabetical list of some of the vendors that currently offer replication tools.

Conclusion

Replication is a growing technology. It may or may not be the "killer app" of the '90s, as some have suggested, but it is likely to be an important force in enabling mobile computing and widespread public distribution of business information. Today, replication is already finding an important role in the growing requirements of the data warehouse/data mart environments.

Table 20.3   **Data Replication Vendors and Products**

Company and Product	Description
Data Mirror Corporation *Mirror/400*	AS/400 log-based replication tool. Supports bidirectional replication between AS/400, NT, and UNIX environments.
Evolutionary Technologies, Inc.	A UNIX-based system. Its main users are migrating data to new environments and maintaining data warehouses.
ETI	Operates across heterogeneous database environment.
IBM Corporation *Data Propagator*	Allows replication of read-only copies to IBM relational databases. Remote applications can only be "read-only." Supports incremental replication and periodic extracts. Allows scheduling of propagation of changes to target databases.
Informix, Inc. *Continuous Data Replicator*	A log-based replication system. Provides support for mobile computing and incremental and bidirectional replication.
Microsoft, Inc. *Microsoft SQL Server*	Provides log-based replication between Microsoft SQL Server and other environments. Uses ODBC drivers to replicate to heterogeneous targets, such as Oracle, Sysbase, and DB2.
Oracle, Inc. *Oracle7*	Provides trigger-based support for replication. Supports both read-only and bidirectional replication. Also supports remote applications and stored procedure replication. A separate product supports mobile computing. Oracle replication allows updates to be scheduled or performed on demand.
Praxis *Omnireplicator*	Provides log-based, bidirectional replication among the major database management systems.
Prism Solutions, Inc. *Prism Change Manager,* *Prism Warehouse Manager*	Offers two products to build and maintain data warehouses. Uses log tap to extract information for changes in the source system and generates a program to apply changes to the target system. Maintains technical metadata necessary for transformation and application of data to the target systems.
Sybase, Inc. Sybase replication products	Supports replication at the multiserver levels with an independent replication server. Also provides products that enable replication between servers and an API for writing applications using messaging protocols.

Performance engineering is a complex business when it comes to replication. It requires attention to the global concerns of the enterprise-wide distributed database system, as well as attention to requirements of individual tables. The possible variations in replication, along with permutations in ownership, contribute to this complexity. It is certainly not an environment where performance can be left to chance.

The replication system itself will frequently define what is possible as far as performance goes. Each tool allows a variable amount of parallelism, of scheduling, and of independence from the operational system. Selecting the system for data propagation often defines the level of replication performance that is possible.

Using Data Warehousing

"The sheer volume of information dissolves the information."

Günther Grass[1]

In This Chapter . . .

The Evolution of the Data Warehouse
Warehousing Concepts and Terminology
Data Warehouse Services
Analyzing Data in the Warehouse
Conclusion

Over the past 25 years corporate data-processing systems have evolved from batch processing magnetic tape files to online processing of central databases. Throughout this period, corporations have acquired enormous amounts of information about their operations, their customers, and their markets. In fact, in most organizations, the amount of data has outstripped the ability of the unaided mind to assimilate it. The data warehouse provides the means to use this information.

Over the years, various attempts have been made to provide business analysts and executives with ways to use this mass of corporate operational data to help them make tactical and strategic business decisions. Unfortunately, these attempts have generally not met expectations. This is one reason why so many end-user organizations purchased personal computers by the hundreds when they became available. The installation of these PCs, however, inevitably led to

---

[1]Günther Grass, Interview in *New Statesman and Society* (London, 22nd June, 1990); cited in *Microsoft Bookshelf*.

end users' needing the ability to download corporate operational data for further analysis and processing, causing data to be spread throughout an organization in an uncontrolled and *ad hoc* fashion. This, in turn, led to key business decisions being made using inconsistent and out-of-date data.

Two major drawbacks of giving end users direct access to operational data manifested themselves:

▶ Performance degradation occurred in the operational system, resulting from uncontrolled processing.
▶ Data was frequently not in the form the end user wanted.

Data warehousing addressed these problems by copying the data to a separate database and by reformatting it to fit end-user needs. This approach allows data to be integrated from multiple sources, reduces the impact of end-user computing on operational systems, and makes it much easier for the user to access and interpret data. Data warehousing also introduced controls to ensure that data is correct and that it provides information about when events occurred so as to avoid making decisions using invalid or inconsistent information.

The resulting data warehouse environment often contains large databases organized into subject areas. But the data it stores needs to be transformed and consolidated before it is useful. Transactional data is usually not in a form users find helpful for decision making. This transformation is normally carried out before the information is made available to the users.

Information retrieval and analysis are carried out by the client part of the data warehouse environment. Currently, much of these activities are done by a variety of first-generation retrieval, analysis, and presentation tools, which range widely in sophistication and power. To use these tools effectively, users generally need a considerable amount of knowledge about the sources of the information in the database. The more powerful tools locate the correct data objects based on the informational content of the analysis. These more powerful tools require extensive metadata support to be able to identify the source of the data and translate it from the form in which it is stored to the form in which it was captured.

As the data volume grows, the tools must also grow in sophistication, both in their ability to handle larger quantities of data and in their use of metadata. In its current incarnation, the data warehouse is already a resource-intensive environment, and it promises to become even more resource-intensive as complex analysis, data visualization, and metadata-driven access replace today's relatively simple data access methods. Yet, despite the complexity of the environment and the processes needed to operate it, performance concerns in the data warehouse are no different than they are for any other area of computing. The end user needs to obtain information as quickly as possible, and the expensive shared resources that comprise the data warehouse environment must deliver maximum throughput.

> **Guideline 21.1** **Data warehouse capacity planning is nonlinear**
>
> Provide memory, storage, and computing resources to accommodate sudden increases in data warehouse use brought about by new, qualitatively different demands. These demands will be produced by sudden shifts in information requests driven by changing business needs. They will also be driven by new types of information analysis, new types of specialized DBMSs, and a need to maintain a relatively constant response time to end-user information requests.

In the data warehousing environment, the challenges to good performance arise from increasing database sizes, the variety and complexity of the data analyses, and the need for sophisticated presentation of results. Addressing these challenges is the focus of this chapter.

The Evolution of the Data Warehouse

Changes in the business environment have led to a situation where organizations must react quickly to changes in the marketplace. Despite the demand for information created by this change, decision support and information analysis have evolved more slowly than transaction processing. When we examine why earlier attempts at providing end users with good business information were not successful, we find that:

1. IS organizations have been reluctant to give end users access to operational data because of the potential impact on the performance of operational systems and the possibility of unpredictable and uncontrollable demands on hardware resources.
2. End users are dissatisfied with operational data that is frequently not in the form they want. Business facts are distributed among many tables and are not easy to interpret. This situation is complicated by the fact that data needed for a specific informational purpose often resides in several different file systems and databases.

> ## Data Warehousing Information Online
>
> For more information about data warehousing, to find links to related sites, or to "chat" about data warehousing subjects, check out the data warehousing home page on the Internet at www.IDWA.org.

3. The query, reporting, and decision support tools available for end-user computing against centralized databases have been inadequate. The user is often faced with terminal-driven tools that are difficult and complex to use.

These observations spring from the fact that transaction processing and information analysis are fundamentally different functions. The following items illustrate the magnitude of their differences:

▶ The transaction usually involves a short interaction with database resources, often no more than a simple update of a single record. Information retrieval systems often require complex queries that can return large answer sets.
▶ The design of the two types of database also follow different principles. Transaction databases are highly normalized and employ a few carefully chosen indexes. Decision support databases are aggregated, denormalized, and very heavily indexed.
▶ In the transaction environment, access is usually carefully planned and tuned. Access for information retrieval applications, on the other hand, can be volatile, arising as a result of transient business circumstances.
▶ In the transaction environment, data is structured around the most efficient update process, and it is often structured around the requirements of a specific application. In the information retrieval environment, data often has to satisfy multiple purposes and multiple constituencies.

Segregation of the two types of databases is essential. Moving the data to specialized, read-only databases (that is, the data warehouse) separates the demands of information analysis from those of transactional processing.

A separate data warehouse has two main advantages:

▶ The warehouse data is organized for processing by business users rather than for processing by operational applications. Prebuilt summaries simplify access to data, and users do not need to be concerned about the intricacies of using data manipulation languages like SQL for joining multiple tables or using built-in functions.
▶ The data warehouse contains historical and summary data, and it consolidates information from many sources. Users do not have to search through multiple database systems to get important information.

The ability to present information is as important to the data warehouse as the data that it contains. The huge volume of data returned by many analyses makes understanding uninterpreted facts a very difficult task for business users. The data warehouse provides facilities to organize and interpret these facts meaningfully. Data visualization is one example of such a facility. Visualization allows relationships among thousands of facts to be represented as one or more images. Increasingly, data warehouses also support a host of complex processing capabilities as well as end-user environments allowing sophisticated analysis and presentation.

Guideline 21.2	Information presentation and consolidation are key characteristics of a data warehouse

A major goal of data warehousing is to present end users with meaningful information rather than raw facts. Regardless of the method used to deliver the information, the ability to consolidate and present information is as important to the data warehouse as the data that it contains.

The data warehouse is still in the process of evolving. Segregating the retrieval and analysis functions from transactional processing has served to liberate the data warehouse from the restrictions imposed by data collection facilities. Segregating the functions has also resulted in a new emphasis on specialized tools. The data warehouse is now becoming an information facility supporting more dynamic and innovative uses such as OLAP (online analytical processing) and data mining. As this evolution continues, future data warehouses will require more discipline in managing performance to deliver business value.

Warehousing Concepts and Terminology

Mercifully, data warehousing terminology has not kept pace with the proliferation of terms in the computer industry in general. In fact, the concepts associated with data warehousing are fairly straightforward—there are relatively few specialized phrases and acronyms. Figure 21.1 summarizes data warehousing concepts and terminology.

The Enterprise Data Warehouse

The enterprise data warehouse is not just a large database. It is an integrated system of databases, services, tools, and methods sharing one major purpose: to provide information for analysis.

As we discussed earlier in the chapter, data in the data warehouse differs in structure and purpose from data contained in operational systems. Bill Inmon summarizes these differences using a table similar to Table 21.1.[2]

We'll discuss performance requirements for data validation and transformation later in the chapter.

---

[2]Table 21.1 is adapted from an earlier version used by W. H. Inmon. A more comprehensive list appears as Figure 1.10 in W. H. Inmon, "*Building the Data Warehouse,*" (Wellesley, MA: QED Publishing Group, 1993), 18.

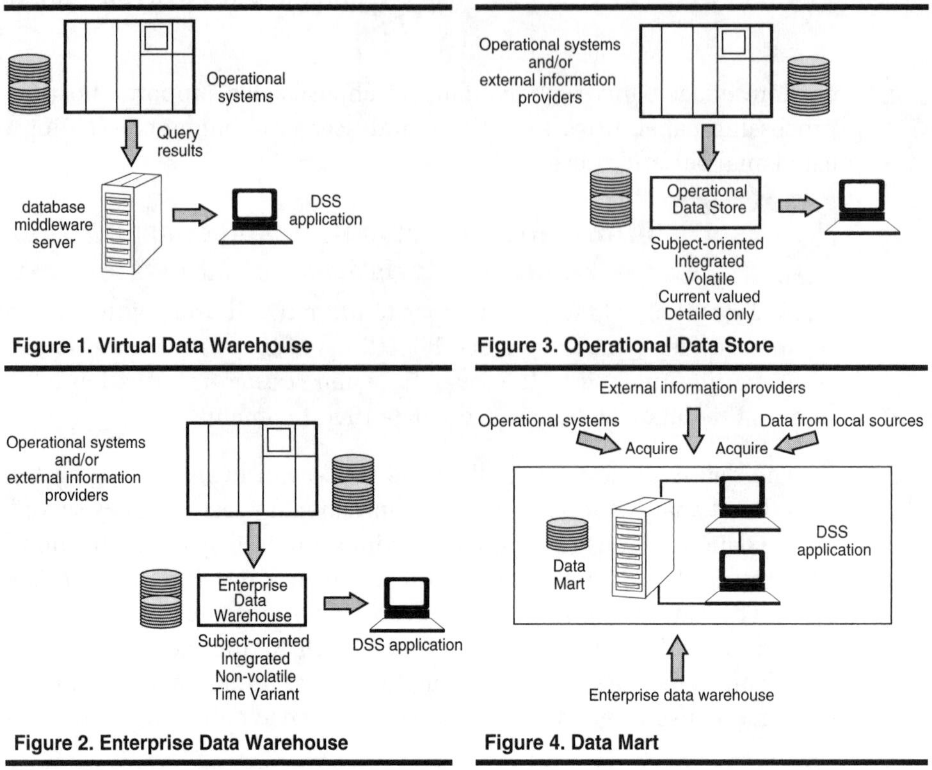

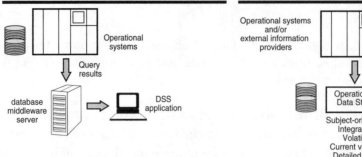

Figure 1. Virtual Data Warehouse

Figure 3. Operational Data Store

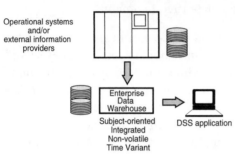

Figure 2. Enterprise Data Warehouse

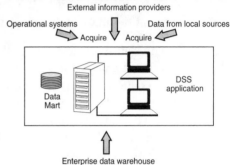

Figure 4. Data Mart

FIGURE 21.1 Data warehouse concepts.

Table 21.1 **Comparison of Characteristics of Operational and Decision Support Data**

Operational	Decision Support
► Detailed	► Detailed and summarized
► "Raw" data	► "Scrubbed" data
► Normalized tables	► Denormalized tables
► Application-oriented	► Subject-area-oriented
► Separate databases	► Merged databases
► Current	► Near-current and historical
► Volatile	► Mainly read-only
► Continuously updated	► Periodically refreshed
► Performance sensitive	► Less performance sensitive
► High availability	► High availability not essential
► Transaction processing	► Analysis-driven processing
► Critical to day-to-day business operations	► Analysis of business operations

The Virtual Data Warehouse.   The **virtual data warehouse** is an architecture that allows users direct access to operational data. It is often an organization's first attempt to create a data warehouse. Interference with the operational systems, along with inadequate analytical facilities, usually motivates the organization to create a segregated enterprise data warehouse.

Evolution from Two-Tier to Three-Tier Warehouses.   Organizations building dedicated data warehouses typically implement a central data warehouse containing data extracted from operational systems. Over time they often add smaller, so-called *second-tier* warehouse servers containing *slices,* and sometimes summaries, of the data in the central warehouse. End users access data from their local, second-tier server whenever possible, and they employ the central warehouse only when necessary.

As user demand increases, middleware facilities capable of handling security and navigation are needed to mediate data access, analysis, and presentation functions. As analyses become more complex, the three-tier architecture shown in Figure 21.2 becomes predominant.

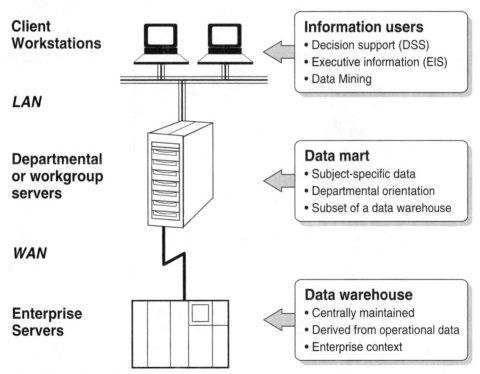

FIGURE 21.2   Three-tier data warehouse architecture.

Design a three-tier data warehouse architecture
Develop the design for a three-tier architecture for the data warehouse before implementing the first component. Increases in tool sophistication, metadata requirements, and database distribution mandate this architecture.

Operational Data Store

The Operational Data Store (ODS), illustrated in Figure 21.3, is a relatively recent addition to purely informational data resources. It has three main functions:

▶ It allows an integrated view of data across multiple applications.
▶ It allows analysis of current information without affecting the transactional systems.
▶ It often integrates data taken from different transactional systems and legacy systems employing different conventions and standards.

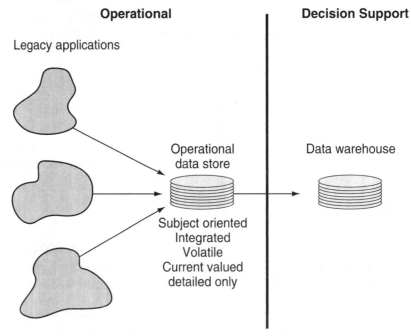

FIGURE 21.3   Operational data store.

The ODS represents a purely operational orientation; that is, it is concerned with current information, as opposed to the data warehouse, which contains historical information and provides a strategic perspective.

In some respects, the ODS resembles a data warehouse:

▶ ODS contents are organized into subject areas.
▶ ODS supports distribution of information to the enterprise.
▶ ODS integrates data from multiple transactional systems.
▶ ODS transforms data it receives to support the integration of information.

But, the ODS also differs from a data warehouse in a number of important characteristics:

▶ The ODS contains only current data.
▶ The ODS contains volatile data.
▶ The ODS contains only detail data.
▶ The ODS often acts as the system of record, or the official data source, for legacy data sources.

The differences between the two systems reflect the differences in their missions. The data warehouse provides an environment for strategic views of the enterprise, while the ODS provides an up-to-the-minute view of the enterprise's business activities. The ODS can also act as a staging area for the data warehouse.

> **Guideline 21.4** **Use the ODS as a consolidation environment**
> Use the ODS to consolidate legacy data with operational data to provide end users with a single conceptual view of current operations within the enterprise.

Data Marts

Data marts are subject-specific databases, allowing high-performance analysis of business information. They are usually designed to support a specific business situation.

As Figure 21.4 illustrates, data marts can be distributed to different organizations and installed on local servers. Data mart databases are also smaller than the central data warehouse. The combination of smaller size and local installation allows loading and refresh operations to be completed much more quickly than at the central warehouse. Queries and complex analyses are also performed more quickly in the data mart.

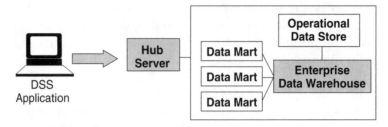

Figure 5. Multiuser data warehouse

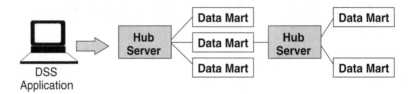

Figure 6. Distributed Data Marts

FIGURE **21.4**   Distributed data marts.

OLAP, ROLAP, and MDA

Analyzing business events to determine the causes of changes or to predict outcomes of plans is an important ability of the data warehouse. These analyses usually require construction of complex relationships such as trends, "clusters," or other types of transformations. Dimensional models capture the business process and may be stored in specialized multidimensional databases (MDD). When analyses are conducted across dimensions such as time, geographic location, or organization, they are known as multidimensional analyses (MDA).

Figure 21.5 shows the basic structure for a multidimensional model.

Online analytical processing (OLAP) refers to a combination of tools and databases used to perform MDA interactively. An analyst (a business user or a statistician) can perform analysis online in much the same way that data entry is done in OLTP.

OLAP comes in two major variations ROLAP, which refers to OLAP using a relational database, and MOLAP, which represents the flavor of OLAP used with multidimensional databases.

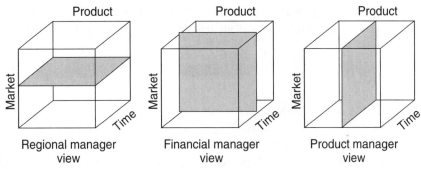

FIGURE 21.5   Multidimensional analysis.

Information on OLAP

The one newsgroup reference that is generally considered the "source" for OLAP discussion and current information is comp.databases.olap. The home page for the OLAP council is www.olapcouncil.org. In addition, nearly every OLAP vendor maintains a home page.

We discuss various aspects of OLAP performance later in the chapter.

Data Mining

Data mining, also known as database exploration or knowledge discovery, is a term used for a process of developing rules or process models from business data. It has proven to be extremely valuable to enterprises because it uses information gained from routine transactions to discover new ways to approach markets.

Data Warehouse Services

Warehouse services are concerned with managing data, retrieving and analyzing data, and allowing an end user to display analysis results in a meaningful manner.

These services arrange themselves into six basic groups:

- ▶ Acquire data
- ▶ Transport
- ▶ Map values and types
- ▶ Clean and validate
- ▶ Transform data
- ▶ Populate data warehouse

We'll use the architectural framework provided by DataBase Associates and illustrated in Figure 21.6 to structure our discussion of data warehousing performance issues.

Acquiring Data

The data warehouse copies information from transaction systems. Identifying, extracting, and transmitting the data from the source system to the consolidation database must not interfere with the transaction system. The process needs to make efficient use of the network resources as well. For example, we may capture and transmit incremental changes shortly after they occur in the transaction system so that we don't place a large amount of data on the network, or we may take a "snapshot" of the entire source table to avoid placing a burden on the workload of the transaction system. We discuss factors that influence decisions about types of extracts in Chapter 20, *Using Data Replication.*

Mapping, Cleaning: Data QA

Unfortunately, data arriving in a data warehouse from operational sources must always be presumed to be "dirty"; that is, it is polluted with inconsistencies and errors. This may sound like a strong statement, given the design efforts expended to ensure data integrity in the operational systems. The fact is that many factors can result in contaminated information. Not the least of these is

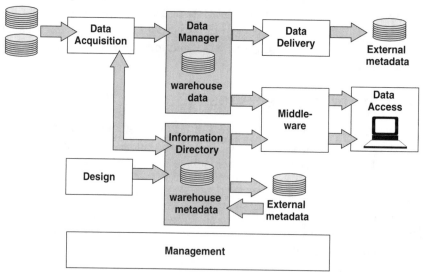

FIGURE 21.6   Data warehouse architecture.

the increasing tendency of enterprises to implement "autonomous" processing sites. These may employ naming variants and especially may allow conventions concerning data values to differ from those of other sites in the enterprise.

This problem is so pervasive in the industry that a 1991 MIT survey of 50 large corporations found that half the senior MIS executives believed their corporate information to be less than 95 percent accurate. Almost all said that "individual departmental databases were not good enough to be used for important decisions."[3] In 1992, 70 percent of respondents in an *Information Week* survey reported that business processes at their organizations had been delayed by corrupted data.[4]

The rapid growth of the DBMS market in recent years has only made the problem worse. Database servers are springing up everywhere, delivering data to networks of new workstation-based client/server applications. Extracts, summaries, and copies of data are scattered here, there, and everywhere. Past errors in the data get propagated into current data. New errors are introduced by errors in current software. In the future, still more errors will be introduced by software currently being created. It has been estimated that the typical corporation has eight versions of any piece of data somewhere in its computer files—but no one knows if those eight versions are the same!

Guideline 21.5   Data discrepancy impacts business performance

Reconcile discrepant data before making it available to users for analysis. Conflicting or erroneous data values will be passed directly into the decision-making and action processes of the business. This can produce the worst kind of performance degradation: degradation in business effectiveness.

Data warehousing aims to eliminate inconsistencies among the copies of data used in different parts of the corporation by managing the storage, copying, and distribution processes systematically.

To avoid building the data warehouse from discrepant data, the validity of information must be determined when it is received. This requires data processing resources. The actual resource requirement depends on the extent of "data cleansing" required. The QA operations may be restricted to tests for completeness, data typing, and referential integrity. The tests, however, may involve sets of rule-driven comparisons. Complete rule-based validation of data can be very expensive in terms of time and resources.

---

[3]Mark D. Hansen, "Zero Defect Data," Massachusetts Institute of Technology, Sloan School of Management, Thesis (M.S., 1991).
[4]Linda Wilson, "Devil in Your Data," *Information Week* (August 31, 1992).

The synopsis in Table 21.2 is based on Brackett's extensive discussion of data quality in *The Data Warehouse Challenge.*[5] It illustrates some of the complexity associated with data QA processing.

For many organizations, Table 21.2 may appear very "theoretical." But, the reality of these data quality components will become apparent as heterogeneous client/server systems and external data sources make data progressively

---

[5]M. H. Brackett, "The Data Warehouse Challenge: Taming Data Chaos," Chapter 7 in *Data Quality* (New York, NY: John Wiley & Sons, 1996).

Table 21.2   **Components of Data Quality**

Integrity Component	Data Elements
Data Integrity	
▶ Data value integrity	Includes data domains, use of default values, and application of business rules.
▶ Data structure integrity	Includes cardinality and referential integrity.
▶ Data retention integrity	Rules defining how long data is to be retained and what is to be done, purged, or changed.
▶ Data derivation integrity	Rules for derived data, the procedure, and the timing of the derivation.
▶ Redundant data integrity	Requirements if data occurrence is maintained redundantly throughout the enterprise. Often an issue with distributed systems. Closely aligned with data origin.
Data Accuracy	
▶ Tangible accuracy	Includes real-world characteristics such as scale, precision, and volatility. Specifies how well the data occurrence measures the event.
▶ Intangible accuracy	Confidence associated with the data source.
▶ Obsolescence	Involves data currency and/or indicates if the data has exceeded some time threshold making it irrelevant or perhaps misleading. This is an important issue in replication as well. See *When Is Information Current?* in Chapter 20.
▶ Origin	Often determines its correctness.
▶ Temporal accuracy	Definition of the time characteristics of the event.
▶ Data versions	The set of data values and structures that exist at a particular point in time.
Data Completeness	Concerned with whether all of the data elements needed to describe the business process are present and correct.

less reliable. Significantly more warehouse processing resources devoted to data QA will be needed to complete needed operations within reasonable timeframes. From a performance planning perspective, it is wise to be proactive and follow the principles that we elucidated in Chapter 5 and to define QA objectives very clearly. It is also wise to begin to invest in a data QA server with considerable power.

> **Guideline 21.6** **Plan for the processing costs to clean up data**
>
> Processing requirements for data QA will grow quickly. Define objectives for data cleansing and mapping to make best use of existing resources. Plan to increase processing to support this process and to provide an independent server for the purpose.

Transforming Data

Data usually requires a number of transformations before it is loaded into the data warehouse. Although these operations may be carried out during the extraction process at the source system, they are more commonly carried out in the data warehouse environment.

The capacity and the workload of the source and target processors are important in deciding where to perform the transformations. Often the data warehouse environment computing capacity is designed around the need to accommodate transformational processing. This is especially true when data is loaded into a multidimensional database and the results must be precomputed and stored in the MDD to facilitate performance during retrieval.

Considerations for locating transformation processing are identical to those in data replication that we address in Chapter 20 in the section, *The Transformation Phase.*

Populate the Data Warehouse: Storing the Data

Large host-based relational DBMSs often provide major data management resources for the *central data warehouse.* These tables are often very large because they contain the organization's history. The tables in the central warehouse are usually heavily indexed and partitioned to facilitate efficient loading and query processing.

Providing Access to Data

These services usually require sophisticated tools to provide display and analysis capabilities. Additionally, the end-user environment normally uses

The Cost-Effective Data Warehouse

"How much do the commandments cost?" asked Moses, skeptically. "They're free," said God. "In that case, I'll take ten," replied Moses.

Anonymous

Often data warehouses are exempted from the kind of cost-effective scrutiny applied to other systems resources. This is unfortunate. If anything, the relationship between the cost of data warehouse resources and the value delivered to the enterprise needs to be established more forcefully than in other systems areas. The cost of a data warehouse cannot exceed the value it returns to the enterprise. Sid Adelman, a consultant specializing in data warehouse implementation, notes that many companies are implementing databases in the terabyte range (1000 gigabytes) and that the business justification for this explosive growth is not being questioned by data warehouse administrators.[6]

The Consequences for Warehouse Performance

Large databases almost always cause some performance problems. They affect queries as well as data loads and updates.

▶ Smaller databases take less time to load or update. Long load/update times may result in the data warehouse being unavailable to users in a timely fashion.
▶ The query almost always takes longer with a large database, and users soon complain about poor response times.

Getting Growth under Control

If an organization is willing to take steps such as those listed next, it can reduce the uncontrolled growth of and improve its information warehouse services considerably.

---

[6]Sid Addleman can be reached via e-mail at *sidadelman@aol.com.*

mail services to distribute results of analysis and queries. Table 21.3 summarizes the types of services that commonly constitute end-user access.

As Table 21.3 indicates, there are many divergent methods for accessing and analyzing data in the data warehouse. Each has its own profile of resource consumption. Performance design depends on the distinct features of each method. We discuss the specific performance concerns of the most common access methods in the following sections.

1. Publicize the fact that size has a strongly negative effect on cost, performance, availability, risk, and management of the data warehouse.
2. Develop data standards on transformations, data replication, data ownership, and naming conventions.
3. Implement a cost-justification methodology for new warehouse storage capacity (its hard numbers can help management evaluate options).
4. Carefully consider the need to replicate data.
5. Give data administration the authority to determine data sources and the responsibility for populating metadata in a dictionary/repository.
6. Monitor data use and consider archiving data that is rarely accessed and archiving data that is never accessed. (*Murphy's corollary:* Purged data will be requested three weeks following deletion.)
7. Evaluate the necessity of keeping instance data as well as summarized data; older instance data may be archived while summarized data will probably be retained.
8. Review archiving schemes to determine how much historical data must be online and the response time requirements if historical data must be restored from less costly storage media.

If we do not find the most cost-effective methods of storage, we will undermine the ability of the data warehouse to add value to business processes. The trick is to know which data is necessary—the best warehouse is the one that contains the data users *really* need, but nothing that is irrelevant.

If we do not optimize the size of the warehouse, we will have to invest more time in optimizing the performance of queries and report programs that analyze the warehouse data. But, this effort, even if successful, is wasted. As Peter Drucker wrote in 1963, "*There is surely nothing so useless as doing with great efficiency what should not be done at all.*"[7]

---

[7]Peter Drucker, *The Practice of Management* (New York, NY: Harper & Row, 1963), 48.

Analyzing and Reporting Data

The entire purpose of a data warehouse architecture is to provide efficient data retrieval and analyses. The components are organized for this purpose, and there is often a very large amount of data. Retrieval is often unplanned, and analysis is intimately embedded in the retrieval operations. For example, locating the source of a profit problem may require one access to identify criteria, another to

Table 21.3   **Information Services**

Information visualization	Some type of visualization is always part of the end-user access. Visualization ranges from simple graphs of trends and distributions to display of tabular data to geographical systems and animations.
Ad hoc query access	A variety of query tools assist users in assembling a database query and return a tabular data display.
Personal data manager	Mobile computing is becoming increasingly important to the data warehouse environment. Tools often provide the means to simulate OLAP functions for data extracts.
Agent-based data access	This is probably the most exotic of the access methods associated with data warehousing. It certainly extends the domain of the data warehouse far beyond that of a single, large database. An agent is an event-based process that can "roam" through a network and that possesses a template for information required by the user. The process may be dispatched to search for conditions fulfilling the query. It may reside in a specific database or move to another network. When it encounters information matching a user's template, it routes that information to "home."

compute projected profits, and a third to identify organizations where projections meet problem criteria. These queries are often performed interdependently, rather than sequentially. Few methods currently are available to optimize performance since these queries may be spontaneous and unpredictable in nature.

Most warehouse access does not require complex analysis. Many queries are concerned with obtaining specific information on a well-defined topic and are performed repetitively. These monitoring types of access probably account for at least half the current warehouse operations. Performance management for these access types is a familiar process of tuning and optimizing, processes that we've discussed in a number of other contexts throughout the book.

Guideline 21.7	**Most data warehouse access is concerned with answering specific questions**

Plan for a data warehouse environment in which most access is concerned with answering specific questions about an ongoing business process. Precompute, store, and index summarizations and series (for example, time series) needed to resolve these specific questions to minimize use of computing resources.

Physical Database Design.   Physical database design is the process of selecting the optimal data structures for a database to best support the workload. Physical design has the most potent influence on performance during analysis and retrieval. Even though we discussed this general subject in some detail in Chapter 19, *Using DBMS Technology,* several aspects of database design apply specifically to data warehouse performance.

Three major decision points affect access:

▶ **Define data granularity.** The main data objects need to be built at a level of aggregation allowing sufficient detail to satisfy most of the queries against them without requiring additional analysis. Requiring data access at the level of an atomic transaction is normally not a good idea. This strategy imposes a requirement for aggregation on most analyses and increases the overhead on the retrieval process.

▶ **Aggregate data before or during the loading process.** Computing and storing key summarizations allows queries to navigate a series of predigested analyses, which will improve overall performance. Aggregate includes more than computing sums; it also includes computing any formula or series that will be accessed often.

▶ **Index generously.** Although the B-tree index once dominated the database, this general-purpose structure is being joined by a host of other auxiliary data stores intended to facilitate performance. DBMS vendors are racing to extend the variety and efficiency of indexing. A data warehouse usually devotes more space to indexes than it does to data. Refer to Chapter 19, *Using DBMS Technology* for more information on indexing in general and bitmap indexing in particular.

Data warehouse tables in relational databases are usually denormalized and are often designed to support dimensional retrieval and analysis. The star or snowflake schema, shown in Figure 21.7, is a relational implementation of a dimensional design. Many relational database vendors are beginning to provide optimizer support for these types of designs. For example, Oracle's optimizer recognizes the existence of a star schema from the tables involved in a complex join, and it provides an access path intended to optimize joins of dimensional tables with their fact table.

Other Data Warehouse Components

The other components represent parts of the data warehouse that do not yet exist, those that have performance considerations outside the scope of the book, or those we've discussed elsewhere in the book.

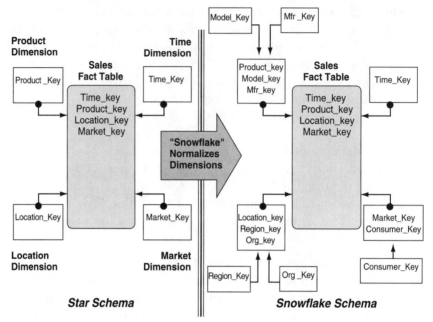

FIGURE 21.7   Star/snowflake schema.

Middleware Component.   This component allows access elements to access the various databases that comprise a distributed warehouse transparently. It is this component that allows transparent access to a variety of data warehouse components.

Design Component.   This is the component used by administrators and designers to modify the structure of the data warehouse. The design component is one of the "shoemaker's children." That is, the system designer generally neglects performance of these components in order to concentrate on the "paying customers," the end users.

Information Directory Component.   The metadata component of the data warehouse represents a major departure from other types of systems. Warehouse users can never know for sure where the best information about a subject is kept, nor can they know formats used to store that information. As a result, the information directory will become a central point for funneling all data access requests to the correct databases and then translating the results as they are returned to the user. As data warehouses grow in size and complexity, and as changes occur in the structure and values in the tables, only a metadata-driven process can find and retrieve information correctly.

The information directory is easily the best candidate for a future bottleneck. It is a good idea to keep this in mind as vendors increase their attempts to deliver powerful metadata products to support the data warehouse.

Management Component.   This component controls warehouse operations. It spans the other components and includes such things as authorization and authentication, backup and recovery, and performance monitoring and tuning. The management component can be implemented with differing levels of completeness. Archiving can be implemented at an atomic transaction level, at a subject level, or at a time fragment level. Authorization may be managed by establishing role-based groupings.

Data Delivery Component.   This component delivers the contents of the data warehouse to other warehouse components and to the end users. Delivery is yet another example of replication. The targets may range from individual spreadsheets to a specialized data warehouse.

Analyzing Data in the Warehouse

Analytic tools and techniques are in their infancy, yet they require considerable resources to deliver their results; we can reasonably expect their resource consumption to continue to grow. In the following sections, we describe some of the current analysis tools and the performance issues associated with them.

Response time during data access is very important to end users. And, despite the increasing amount of work required of data warehouse systems, users are unlikely to relax their response time requirements. Organizations increasingly are viewing slow response time to data access requests as an obstacle to efficient business processes. It makes no difference whether the access involves retrieving a single fact or completing a complex analysis. The user is coming to depend on efficient response times as well as correct results.

Guideline 3.14 in Chapter 3 introduces Nagraj's Law of Tuning Choices, but it may be useful here to summarize the specific means for regulating performance as implied by the guideline.

1. Do less work.
   ▶ Store less data overall by eliminating anything that's not needed.
   ▶ Provide useful subsets (data marts) and store them locally.
   ▶ Precompute aggregates and summaries; to do this, we must "know the user" and "monitor usage."
   ▶ Consider a "publish and subscribe" approach to the warehouse, as proferred by companies such as D2K with its Tapestry product and Virtual

The Performance Demand of Decision Support

The decision-support data warehouse represents a very real challenge for performance engineering. The reason for this is twofold: decision support applications generally need to access and analyze huge quantities of data, and they require large amounts of processing power and high I/O bandwidth for good performance. The processing requirements for large decision-support applications are expected to exceed 10,000–20,000 MIPS in the future, along with I/O bandwidths on the order of 100–200 MB per second. What does all this mean? For one thing, it means that it is very likely that the computing power required by data warehouse analyses will outstrip the ability of computers to deliver that power. Resource exhaustion is likely to appear without warning.

To ensure an information analysis environment that grows to meet the demand, the data warehouse architect must be alert for opportunities to embed proactive performance management in the data warehouse architecture. No opportunity should be neglected. If performance management is not integrated into the data warehouse architecture, performance can be expected to dwindle, then crash as greater tool sophistication places ever greater loads on system resources.[8]

---

[8]Colin White, "Supporting High-Performance DSS Applications," *InfoDB* (December 1994).

Information Technology (VIT) with its deliveryMANAGER and design-MANAGER products.

2. Make the best of what you have.
   - ► Optimize database design for read-only access by subject area (see Chapter 19).
   - ► Match workload to the capacity of the data warehouse server.
   - ► Use dedicated data warehouse servers.
   - ► Don't overload the data warehouse processor; refer back to our earlier discussions of sharing (Chapter 11 and 12), parallelism and load balancing (Chapter 13), and especially the importance of middleware that supports asynchronous processing (Chapter 15). Don't allow client-driven workload peaks to disrupt optimal data warehouse processing; queued requests smooth out workload at the server.
3. Steal from Peter to pay Paul and/or water down the requirements.
   - ► To leverage resources effectively, look at who is doing what and why. Are results needed in 1–2 seconds? In 10 minutes? In 2 hours or 24 hours? Match the method of information access to the business need.

▶ After you optimize the database design, look at the processing. If possible, support online real-time analyses with multithreaded background processing to handle complex computations.

▶ Use scheduled background processes for less urgent analysis. These processes can take advantages of lulls in demand.

▶ Again, consider using queued middleware to prioritize and load balance among request classes.

4. Throw money at the process.

▶ When all else fails, build capacity. Increase processor memory to allow bigger caches; use RAID disks, purchase larger SMP processors, or use MPP processors with a parallel-processing DBMS.

The Operational Data Store

The ODS probably comes the closest to classical OLTP performance tuning as does anything in the data warehouse environment. The data is closer in structure and in time to the operational database. More importantly, users' concerns are closely aligned with the concerns in a transactional system. Users often want to determine a simple fact about some aspect of the current business operation. Sometimes, the operating concerns are also similar. The ODS may have to be updated by transaction systems while query processing is active. Contention becomes a factor. It is an altogether familiar environment.

As we see in Figure 21.8, the ODS draws its information from transactional systems. The frequency with which this extract occurs determines both the cost and the complexity of the ODS environment. Inmon defines three classes of operational data stores. The classification is based on the latency with which changed data are extracted from the transaction systems. The Class I ODS, which is the most current form of ODS, is significantly more costly and difficult to maintain than either of the other two classes:

▶ **Class I.** The ODS is updated within 2–3 seconds of the change to the transactional system.

▶ **Class II.** The ODS is updated within 2–4 hours of the change to the transaction system.

▶ **Class III.** The ODS is updated every 24 hours (or longer) with changes from the transaction system.[9]

It should be emphasized that Inmon's classification refers to the latency between the end of the transaction and the extraction of the change for transmission

---

[9]William H. Inmon, "The Operational Data Store," *InfoDB,* 9(1) (February 1995), 21.

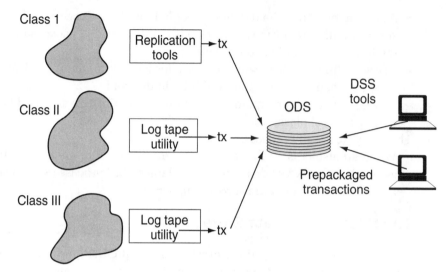

FIGURE 21.8   Operational transaction capture.

to the ODS, not the length of time required to complete the transaction. Many business processes can take several minutes to carry out, like placing an order while interacting with a customer, and then, before the conversation is over, confirming that the order will actually be filled from stock. In a Class I ODS, even though completing the business process may require a delay of "minutes," the system would extract the change within seconds of completion of the transactions and would transmit it to the ODS.

Although the ODS generally requires short query response time, it is a difficult requirement to satisfy. For one thing, the ODS must use dynamic summarization rather than precalculated summaries. This increases response times for complex queries. Fortunately, analysts and executives are often interested in seeing the changes to the same fact repeatedly throughout the day. For example, if inventory on hand is a critical piece of management information, a prepackaged query can be designed and optimized to deliver good performance.

The ODS database design is often tailored to a query environment, even at the cost of efficiency in database refresh operations. This is more easily supported in a Class II or Class III ODS, where updates can be limited to periods when the impact on query performance can be minimized. The Class II or Class III ODS allows use of scheduled background processes that can rebuild tables and indexes if necessary. In the Class I ODS, such options are not possible. The demands of the query operations will interfere with the demands of the refresh operations.

Guideline 21.8	**Use optimal access and refresh methods with the ODS**

Use of scheduled background processes with Class II and Class III ODS can reduce contention and improve resource utilization during refresh operations. Use of preplanned, stored queries can provide optimal data access for repetitive access.

As with nearly every aspect of the data warehouse, parallel data operations offer the main source of improvement for the ODS. If the DBMS supports parallel query operations, this can usually improve performance significantly.

Online Analytical Processing (OLAP)

E. F. Codd coined the term "OLAP" in a 1994 paper in which he attempted to establish guidelines for online analytic processing. Although Codd's original paper defined 12 Rules for OLAP, the list has since expanded to more than 50 rules, with additional entries supplied by vendors, industry watchers, and Codd himself. The original 12 rules helped to define some of the things that need to happen for online analysis to be a useful business tool. The proliferation of rules indicates that there really is no well-defined idea of what OLAP ought to do. Fifty or more "rules" don't provide much guidance. It is like the line from Nillson's album, *The Point,* ". . . a point in every direction is the same as having no point at all. . . ."[10]

OLAP is as important to the emerging field of data warehousing as online transaction processing, OLTP, is to traditional data processing. It represents a new ability for business users to determine what is happening in the organization and in the marketplace and to intervene proactively to improve business processes by correcting problems or by exploiting new opportunities. OLAP provides added value to justify storing the large amounts of data an enterprise collects.

OLAP needs to be distinguished from a simple query environment. Many, if not most, information requirements can probably be satisfied by a carefully designed query environment combining pretuned, stored queries with *ad hoc* capabilities. Most business situations are stable and well understood by the user. For this reason, many business information needs can be satisfied by a relatively stable set of data that answers a relatively well-defined business question.

---

[10]Harry Nilsson, "The Pointed Man" (narration), *The Point* recorded in 1971 by RCA Records, New York, NY.

Guideline 21.9	**OLAP is not a query tool**

Online analysis determines patterns from sets of data and presents them in a manner allowing the user to reorganize the outcomes of the analysis and begin a new one based on the previous outcome. A query returns information based on specific logical criteria.

By contrast, OLAP has its greatest value when information needs are unclear, when the data needed to resolve them cannot be precisely defined, or when the events producing the information are themselves volatile or ambiguous. An individual working within an OLAP environment may be searching for issues as well as searching for answers.

OLAP versus OLTP.   The differences between OLTP and OLAP are also worth mentioning because OLTP has guided much of our thinking in the area of performance. The performance demands of OLAP do not require new principles, but they do require a different mindset.

▶ Unlike OLTP, OLAP sessions cannot be planned accurately. OLTP is based on *repeating* a simple action thousands of times, whereas OLAP is often concerned with an *individual complex action that may never recur.*
▶ OLTP design is built on a single, clearly defined access to database objects; OLAP may involve a single query to a database object or a series of interdependent queries involving multiple large accesses.
▶ OLTP typically restricts database access to primary keys, whereas OLAP often requires its access to be driven by collateral data values.
▶ OLTP typically interacts with the database in extremely short sessions that are kept independent from interactions with the user OLAP frequently requires that connections with the database be maintained while the user interacts with the system.

OLAP is usually implemented by a set of client tools, which are often supported by dimensional database designs. These designs depart from the characteristic entity-relationship modeling and are usually dimensionally oriented. Performance design for online analysis must be mapped to the general types of analysis that are expected. The design needs to provide precomputed aggregations so that the OLAP tool can deliver good performance.

"Peak performance," when it comes to OLAP, is a relative term. Users in the OLAP environment are not more patient than any other users, but performance expectancy is more closely aligned with the difficulty of the task being undertaken. In OLTP, complexity in processing is hidden from the user; in

OLAP, the user generally creates the complexity of the analysis process. While immediate returns will never fail to cause delight, longer running analyses are tolerated so long as they are perceived to be proportional to the difficulty of the analysis.

OLAP workload often occurs during peak transactional periods and can interfere with transaction processing. In addition, OLAP can put a lot of data on the network, which can lead to degradation in transactional computing. Isolating OLAP environments to local subnetworks, or even individual LANs, can avoid this degradation. Isolation requires creating and distributing data marts to multiple locations. Local access reduces network load during complex analyses.

Data marts, or subject-specific databases, are frequently associated with OLAP. As we discussed earlier, there is a trade-off between the high-level performance a subject-specific data mart provides during analysis and the computing resources to extract, distribute, load, and precompute summaries for the data mart. If there are many data marts, this can amount to a great deal of investment in computing power. In general, the investment is worthwhile. The preparation of data marts can be scheduled during nonpeak processing times to regulate its impact on local system workload. Sometimes, data can even be precalculated before being distributed to receiving data marts, thereby helping reduce the total processing overhead.

Benchmarking OLAP Tools.   Benchmarks, which we discussed in Chapter 6, are extremely important to the warehouse operation, inasmuch as OLAP tools are supposed to scale gracefully. Until recently, however, no benchmarks were specifically concerned with performance of analysis in the online environment. The closest was the TPC-D benchmark, which attempts to assess decision-support performance against a high-availability database. TPC-D concentrates on data access performance associated with a group of business queries.

More recently, however, the OLAP Council has published a benchmark, called APB-1 (Analytical Processing Benchmark), that enables vendors to measure the effectiveness of OLAP tools The caution about benchmarks in the OLTP environment is worth mentioning in the world of OLAP as well. Like all benchmarks, the APB-1 benchmark serves to highlight important performance issues.

APB-1 is concerned with determining analytical throughput. It defines a metric, Analytical Query Time, as the ratio of the total server processing time to the number of queries processed. It measures throughput of analytical performance from the time the data is available until the final query is completed. The metric includes the time and resources required to load the data into the system.

The second aspect of the metric concerns defining the processes to be measured. Defining these processes has the effect of defining the most important OLAP operations. The operations being benchmarked by the OLAP Council are:

▶ Incremental loading of data from operational systems
▶ Aggregation of input level data along hierarchies
▶ Calculation of new data based on business models
▶ Time series analysis
▶ Drill down through hierarchies
▶ Ad hoc queries
▶ Multiple online sessions[11]

The APB-1 benchmark employs a sales and marketing system and incorporates a database structure composed of six dimensions, including time, and three aggregation dimensions (product, customer, and channel). The benchmark allows the database size to vary, but it stipulates minimum and maximum sizes for each dimension. Queries fall into categories according to the type of analysis being performed.

Data Mining

Describing performance concerns about data mining in a few paragraphs is a performance engineering feat in itself. **Knowledge discovery** is a relatively new area of computing combining the disciplines of artificial intelligence, very large database (VLDB) management, data warehousing, and business intelligence. Until recently, knowledge discovery has been an area of computing requiring knowledge of machine theorem-proving, statistics, and logic. This scope is changing quickly.

Data mining is another name for knowledge discovery, a process concerned with using machine learning to discover new information in existing databases. It is becoming important to the business operations in many industries. Data mining has already provided significant cost reduction in essential business processes. It has also discovered new sources of revenue from information contained in old sales records. Data mining promises to become an important business planning resource.

Data mining examines relationships among the records and fields that were collected during the course of doing business with existing customers with the

---

[11]OLAP Council Benchmark Specification, OLAP Council; online at *www.olapcouncil .org/*.

purpose of discovering new associations among facts—of discovering new predictive rules that will lead to new types of competitive advantage. Data mining requires a data warehouse to provide the historical data and a large body of stable, current data that has been subjected to careful "data cleansing."

Information visualization is important to data mining. Typically, data mining software will discover thousands of associations in the data. Presenting these associations is as important to the data-mining process as the process of discovery. The rules describing the associations are often visualized as decision trees or as density charts that show how closely the association relates the objects under study. Visualization allows the analyst to participate interactively in the process of discovering new associations or new rules.

Developing rules requires very large databases and significant computing resources. Because data-mining processes must examine a very large number of combinations, they are often carried out in the background. Usually, the database is divided into samples. The rule discovery process uses some of the samples to develop the set of rules and sets other samples aside. These other (that is, set-aside) samples provide data to test the newly derived rules. The number of columns determines how many times the process must be repeated.

Rule development is characterized by a large number of repetitive database accesses. Building and validating a model requires multiple traversals over the same tables and even the same rows to develop and discard associations, to develop a preliminary model, and to test it against previously unused data. Rule development may also involve repeated access to distributed databases.

Data mining often starts with a "triage" process in which an analyst tries to refine the subject area into a relatively well-defined problem statement that will guide the rule-building software. This phase uses simple, interactive SQL to provide crude identification of areas in which machine-learning components such as neural networks can work productively. This phase often develops simple descriptive statistics of likely samples. The idea is that these simple statistics provide "naive" predictions of associations. The rules created by the rule generator must improve on predictions generated by this initial set of associations. The preliminary "model" requires large numbers of SQL statements that create groupings and statistical summaries. These are expensive queries that need to be run interactively.

The triage process, however, offers an opportunity for performance management. It may be possible to consolidate required data into a data mart to gain some benefits from reducing the database size during early phases of model building. Temporary data marts can be developed using a variety of sampling techniques. The data mart can be used, then discarded. The rules that are developed can be tested against samples drawn from the full database in a scheduled, background process.

> ### Guideline 21.10 Use specialized data marts to improve data mining
>
> Consider creating temporary data marts to support online model building, especially in the first phase where dynamic SQL is used to create "naive" associations.

Data marts, although useful, do not provide the most important means for improving performance. Increasing parallelism in the system seems to be the most significant method for improving the performance of data mining. Parallel queries can speed database access. Parallel implementation of models can reduce the time needed to run the model against data. If data mining is going to occupy a significant place in the data-warehousing environment, then the enterprise needs to explore parallel technologies aggressively.

Conclusion

The data warehouse environment is only in its infancy in an industry that has, until very recently, been devoted to information capture. The performance concerns are no different from those of any other area of computing although aspects of the warehouse are more performance-intensive than a transaction environment. Business processes are becoming increasingly dependent on these large data repositories and the sophisticated processes necessary to predict business situations that cannot be detected by unaided perception. As this dependency grows, performance of retrieval and analysis will become more critical to the success of the warehouse.

Transaction Managers and Transaction Monitors

"Reality is that which, when you stop believing in it, doesn't go away."

Philip K. Dick

In This Chapter . . .

Transactions: An Overview
The Transaction Monitor
Transactional Performance Considerations
Conclusion

All business computing is concerned with the basic tasks of capturing, validating, storing, and using fundamental business information. Doing business requires many individuals to have nearly simultaneous access to shared information. Business computing requires that a great many individuals be able to add or change information whenever their responsibilities demand it. They need to make changes quickly and efficiently. Above all, however, they need to rely on the integrity of the information. Nothing can be allowed to distort the content of the changes made by the transactions.

Transaction processing is concerned with efficiency and with ensuring the integrity of changes to the data. It is a standard feature of the mainframe or host-centric environment and it is becoming increasingly important in the client/server environment. But transaction processing is a far more complex process in the distributed environment than it was in the host-centered environment. Transaction integrity must be preserved across a number of platforms

685

that differ in reliability and in the services they can provide. Transactions are now processed in an environment where a participant may "disappear" at a critical moment. Transactions may be broken into elements that are sent to different processors having different speeds and different resources, or they may be written to different databases that do not communicate with one another.

The transaction monitor, a standard feature of the mainframe, has been introduced into the distributed environment to deal with this complexity. The transaction monitor is a middleware facility that is supposed to integrate widely different data management resources and to improve the overall performance of shared resources within the enterprise.

Requirements for distributed transactional support in a wide variety of circumstances range from the classical "ATM" transactions familiar to mainframe programmers to an ability to interact transactionally with databases from the Web. And, of course, these transactional applications must be able to deliver their functions efficiently and quickly.

Transactions: An Overview

Because many texts are available on this subject, we've confined this overview to a description of the basic structure of transactions and a discussion of the effect of the structure on distributed processing environments. For more detailed background information, the reader is strongly encouraged to read any of the comprehensive works on the subject, especially *Transaction Processing: Concepts and Technique* by Gray and Reuter, the definitive work on transactions.[1]

What Is a Transaction?

Transactions are concerned with integrity. A simple transaction is defined by a starting point and a well-defined ending point. The requirements for transactional integrity have been formalized in the client/server environment and define what must happen to information when the transaction has been started, when it is explicitly ended, and when it fails without any notification at all.

Transactions are controlled interactions in which some resource—usually data—is accessed, and the correctness of the information that is changed is protected from distortion or loss. In transaction processing, the designer is usually concerned about interactions in which multiple individuals access and wish to change the same resource at the same time. The users may interfere with each other and/or compromise the validity of the information. Transactions must guarantee that the interchange captures, stores, and retrieves the information correctly.

---

[1] Jim Gray and Andreas Reuter, *Transaction Processing: Concepts and Techniques* (San Mateo, CA: Morgan Kaufmann, 1993).

> ### Guideline
> ## 22.1 A transaction is concerned with protecting the integrity of the data
>
> A transaction is an interaction that guarantees the integrity of the information, protecting it from distortion or loss as a result of change. The task is complicated in a client/server environment where transaction integrity must be preserved across a variety of platforms that differ in reliability and in the services they can provide.

"Integrity," in part, refers to the consistency of the contents of the resource. Suppose, for example, that an RDBMS has two tables, one of which is a set of employees working for a company, and the second a set of employee assignments. Then each entry in the second table (an assignment), must match an entry in the first (an employee). A transaction that deletes one of the employees must also remove that employee's assignments. If something fails, we expect to find either that the employee and all of the corresponding assignments were deleted successfully, or that neither the employee nor the assignments were deleted.

Integrity also refers to the correctness of data in a particular table when it is accessed by many users at the same time. The basic rule is that all concurrent transactions must be treated as if they were performed sequentially. That is, some database rule must apply the changes of one transaction while placing the changes of the second transaction "on hold." Thus, if one transaction changes an employee's salary and, at the same time, a second transaction tries to change the salary of the same employee to a different value, the second transaction must wait for the completion of the first.

As mentioned in Chapter 15, the atomic transaction is a simple transaction marked by a beginning and an end in which the data elements are guaranteed to meet four basic criteria: the ACID properties. Satisfying these ACID requirements has given transaction managers considerable significance in distributed processing.

Implementing support for transaction integrity means increasing the resources needed to process the transaction:

▶ Maintaining isolation requires some type of locking, which requires additional system overhead and which can create bottlenecks.

▶ Atomicity requires some process to guarantee that uncommitted changes can be removed, restoring the data to its starting values. Logging is the process implemented by most databases to accomplish this. It involves writing a record of changes to the disk before the actual changes are written to the database to support backing out the changes. A discussion of the types of logging is beyond the scope of this chapter, but it is worth noting that logging always contributes to overhead because of the additional I/O for the local database server.

▶ Achieving durability also requires logging but adds the further overhead of periodic checkpoints, to allow databases to be recovered to a recent point of consistency.

Also, if a transaction is going to be consistent across multiple databases, even more processes are required to synchronize all the participants in the transaction. All the participating databases need to make sure that they are consistent with every other database, and all the logs need to support this synchronization. Integrity requirements make distributed transactions high-overhead processes. Achieving the best performance requires applications that are carefully tailored to exploit the transaction-processing environment.

The Transaction Monitor

In the mainframe online environment, the transaction monitor usually managed key resources and provided display services. It was often tightly coupled with the operating system and existed in a "share everything" architecture. Applications executed within environmental boundaries defined and controlled by the transaction monitor.

The distributed transaction monitor is different. It is an application that coordinates resources that are provided by other services. These resources can include other transaction managers, database management systems, communications managers, or memory managers. In essence, the distributed transaction monitor coordinates any type of resource manager that a distributed environment can contain. But, like the older transaction monitor, it can regulate access to shared resources and it manages transactions. Figure 22.1 illustrates the flow of control between the transaction monitor, the transaction manager, and the application.

Transaction monitors have their greatest value in the complex, heterogeneous, **multidatabase** environment. **Resource manager** is a term denoting a program managing any kind of resource such as a database, memory, or even a communications port. Typically, however, it refers to a DBMS. In this environment, resource managers differ in the facilities they may possess to safeguard integrity. They also differ in their capacity and speed of response. Despite this discrepancy, all resource managers must act in a coordinated fashion to guarantee valid information. The transaction monitor provides this coordination.

A **transaction *manager*** is not the same as a **transaction *monitor.*** The transaction manager manages specific transactions. It is always associated with an

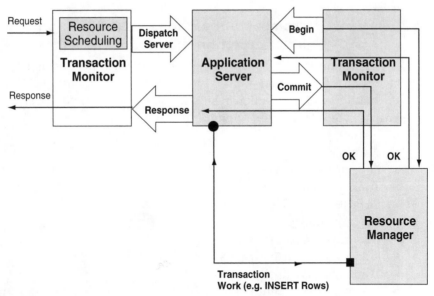

FIGURE 22.1   Transactions and the transaction monitor.

individual transaction and is normally tied to an individual resource manager during the scope of a particular transaction. The transaction manager makes sure that transactional guarantees are met for that resource.

A transaction monitor (often referred to as a TM), on the other hand, is a program that coordinates the activities of transaction managers and resource managers. It starts transactions and coordinates the commit across multiple transaction and resource managers. It is able to coordinate functions across widely divergent environments. The transaction monitor is designed to handle the most complex scenarios that can arise in the client/server environment.

The transaction monitor provides coordination among resource managers, which differ in their facilities for safeguarding integrity. This coordination enhances the recoverability of a database system beyond that which a single transaction manager can provide. In this respect, a transaction monitor can provide robust recovery across diverse database environments.

How the Transaction Monitor Works

The transaction monitor (TM) is a coordinator. It may operate in conjunction with database management systems, with memory managers, or with other transaction monitors. First and foremost, the goal of the TM is to guarantee the integrity of concurrent transactions. It guarantees that all participating servers synchronize

> ### Guideline 22.2 A transaction *manager* is not the same as a transaction *monitor*
>
> A transaction manager manages specific transactions and is always associated with an individual transaction. A transaction monitor (TM) coordinates the activities of transaction managers and resource managers. The services provided by a transaction *monitor* include:
>
> ▶ Administration
> ▶ Logging and recovery
> ▶ Tuning and load balancing
> ▶ Security
> ▶ Commit/rollback
> ▶ Coordination of failure recovery
> ▶ Registration of resource managers
> ▶ Transaction identification
> ▶ Language dependent libraries for calls to transaction monitor functions
> ▶ Deadlock/livelock detection

their activities, regardless of how compatible they may be with each other. The TM basically coordinates resources that are provided by other services.

As a performance tool, however, the TM regulates access to shared resources and facilitates system throughput. It acts to improve the parallelism available to servers and regulates workload across the servers and processors in the system. Table 22.1 summarizes the mechanisms the TM uses to achieve improved transaction performance.

The mechanisms shown in Table 22.1 also enable the transaction monitor to enhance the value of shared resources to the individual transactions making use of them. Coordinating shared resources allows the transaction monitor to improve performance of transaction processing in the enterprise by reducing the need for individual transactions to wait for specific resources and by dynamically providing additional computing resources when the processing volume requires it. From an enterprise perspective, the transaction monitor can improve performance as well as integrity.

The transaction monitor starts individual servers before they are needed. Prestarting processes is one of the sources of efficiency that a TM afford. Resource managers and servers are registered in the TM's execution environment at the time they are started. As the transaction load increases, the TM assigns incoming transactions to instances of a particular server based on its workload. If necessary, the TM can start new instances of a server to meet the demand. When the demand subsides, the TM can close the superfluous servers.

Table 22.1 **Four Mechanisms for Performance Optimization by Transaction Monitors**

Mechanism	Effect
Multiple prestarted services	TM starts multiple instances of a transaction service that are physically close to a resource manager. These processes are essentially on "active standby" and are waiting for work. The TM assigns requests to them as needed.
Load balancing	The process of assigning work to prestarted service so that each instance has a "fair share" of the incoming work. This ensures that the resources used by services are utilized to their fullest and that the likelihood of a resource becoming a bottleneck is reduced.
Scheduling functions	The ability of the TM to assign priorities to transaction requests, then to serialize execution of the requests. Scheduling priorities range from low priority, background tasks to very high-priority, system-level tasks.
Monitoring server status	Ensures that a server is available and responding to the service request. TM can detect deadlocking conditions and situations where the server has "disappeared" from the transaction.

Transaction Performance and the Transaction Monitor

The design of individual transactional applications must be structured appropriately to take advantage of the services offered by the transaction monitor. Applications that provide the TM with an array of services to manage, that partition their functionality to minimize messaging and data exchange, and that restrict conversational transactions to the absolute minimum will approach the optimal quickness of execution. If, in addition, the designer is attentive to system requirements and colocates application services with the resource manager or with replicated file services, then overall system efficiency is not taxed to pay for the speed of individual transactions.

A part of good performance requires that the transaction monitor and the services it uses have adequate hardware support. If there are adequate processing options, the load-balancing activities facilitate good performance:

▶ Use of parallel processors for the TM, as well as for the resource managers, improves enterprise-wide performance significantly.

The TP-Lite Alternative

"TP-Lite" is a term denoting circumstances when the management features of an individual resource manager are used in place of the full-function transaction monitor. The application doesn't even call the TM. This situation is possible when the full functions of a transaction monitor are not needed to guarantee that enterprise-wide integrity imposes overhead without reasonable justification. Most DBMS products guarantee transactional integrity, and all are fully recoverable. Indeed, most of the commercial DBMSs support load balancing across multiple processors. Why don't we let the resource manager manage the ACID characteristics and guarantee the correctness of our updates? Won't that work?

If there is no pressure for use of resources, it works perfectly. It fails if there are too many updates to the same RDBMS; the server will not be able to schedule itself properly, and we will have to wait for resources to become available. It also fails if there is a possibility of a deadlock for one resource managed by the DBMS and another managed by a different resource manager (memory, for example). Detecting and resolving that kind of deadlock (or worse, livelock) is beyond the ability of a DBMS. TP-Lite is often a good approach for quick updates.

In many cases, the presentation platform working with a DBMS can provide adequate guarantees for a simple transaction. If multiple servers need to be coordinated, or if multiple sites become involved, then TP-Lite breaks down. It also breaks down if concurrent access requirements increase beyond a few dozen users. The local resource manager simply lacks the facilities needed to regulate access to resources. Performance will decline until the transaction monitor is brought in to manage the higher-volume access.

▶ Local multiprocessors provide resource managers with an ability to distribute query processing and local integrity management processes (for example, logging) across processors at the local site.
▶ Providing servers at alternate sites lets the TM to distribute workload across multiple sites, allowing regulation of overall workload at a particular server.

Transactional Performance Considerations

The key measures used in assessing transactional performance are:

▶ Transaction service time
▶ Duration of transaction in the system
▶ Wait time

Planning the application and determining the effects it will have on service time and waiting time are subjects that we've addressed repeatedly in the book. Some of the specific deliverables may have a different name, but the principles governing them remain constant. Table 22.2 summarizes the basic deliverables, the activities required to produce them, and the principles they embody.

In this chapter, we focus primarily on the deliverables associated with the Locality and Parallelism Principles. That is to say, we focus on the deliverables associated with design activities. This does not imply that prediction and monitoring activities should be ignored. Proactive performance management requires good transaction models and an objective, well-planned program of measurement. There is also a need to discuss specific details of how to design those transactions to get the best performance from them.

Client/server designs create specialized groups of functions that are then organized into services and client processes. Assigning the functions to servers or to client processes is an important design decision. For example, all data management functions should be assigned to a server process, never to a client process.

Table 22.2 **Factors Affecting Key Performance Indicators**

Activity	Principle	Transaction Design Deliverable
Predict	Projection Principle	Transaction performance model
		Model of transactional load
		Communication load model
		Server blocking effects
Monitor	Monitoring Principle	Changes to transaction mix, processing volumes, and system growth
		Identify bottlenecks
		Monitor I/O
Design	Locality Principle	Data distribution
		Functional unity
		Server placement
		Partitioning of client/server/resource manager functionality
	Parallelism Principle	Potential server instances
		Serialized operations
		Data movement required to invoke parallel operations
		Limitations imposed by transactional locking or scheduling

Grouping functions, servers, and processes—both logically and physically—is another important design decision. For example, grouping services that depend on each other or that have similar operating characteristics will benefit performance.

This whole aspect of transaction design is more productive when we are diligent about applying the Locality Principle. One very important benefit of applying the Locality Principle effectively is that unnecessary messages between participants in a transaction are reduced or even eliminated. That is both a prime requirement for good performance in the distributed transaction environment and the reason why we repeatedly stress the concept of reducing messages between participants.

The Locality Principle is important to controlling transaction overhead. Typically, clusters of services perform a series of related tasks. These services are often grouped by functional characteristics and may be either bundled into a single server or separated. Clustering individual services within a server is a design decision that affects performance of the server.

Another potent performance consideration that must be incorporated into the design is the issue of how services are distributed geographically. In some respects, this consideration is even more important than exploiting the TM. Once again, we need to focus on reducing the number of messages between the participants. In distributing services geographically, we need to place the server so that the number of messages exchanged between the participants in a transaction are kept to a minimum. Because the overhead required to create, transmit, and decode a single message is significant, the number of messages is actually more significant than the message size.

The Parallelism Principle is the other principle to be stressed in distributed transaction design. As we discussed in Chapter 13 on the Parallelism Principle, applying this principle will usually improve performance. Transaction monitors, through their scheduling and load-balancing activities, provide an opportunity to improve parallelism in the system as a whole. The design of distributed transactions needs to exploit these activities to improve parallelism within the transactional application. The design may also improve parallelism in other ways, such as by designing multithreaded clients or by eliminating situations in which transactions need to be serialized. Resource locking, for example, is intended to serialize access to the resource. But, the use of transaction techniques such as optimistic locking, which we discuss later, can improve parallelism by postponing the locking until the last possible moment.

Distributed Database Design

Data distribution is probably first on any list of factors that affect performance. Performance almost always benefits from having all data in a single location, along with its associated service. As business requirements continue to expand and evolve, there is more and more need to distribute information. Local data access allows greater management control, and mobile computing requires distributed models that allow users to update detached databases that, in turn, update centralized structures.

It is important to note that the messages that must traverse between the participants in a transaction are the single greatest source of performance degradation in a distributed environment. Anything that we can do to reduce the amount of messaging between participants will improve the application's performance.

> **Guideline 22.3 Minimize messages**
>
> Communication overhead in a transaction is influenced more by the number of messages than the size of the messages. Therefore, the first goal of distributed transaction design is to reduce the number of messages among the participants.

The computing resources required to access data depend on the distribution of the data and the associated service. The distributed data design shown in Figure 22.2, for instance, may require very high overhead, or it may require minimal overhead depending on how the distribution of services corresponds to the distribution of data. If all access is to local data, then the process requires few resources. If, however, a service must update remote data, then local, network, and remote resources are needed. Overhead depends on the number of remote services and the number of remote data locations involved in the transaction because total overhead is directly proportional to the number of messages needed for data access. For example, a transaction accessing a remote service that then accesses a remote data resource manager generates a large number of messages. These include control messages, commands to services and resource managers, and transmission of data to servers and to the client.

The goal of minimizing messages in a transaction can be realized only if the database design and the distribution of application services are carefully coordinated. Chapter 18 offers a detailed discussion of using DBMS technology effectively, but it is worth mentioning here some distributed database design issues that are especially important to the design of distributed transactions:

▶ Very aggressive use of partitioning strategies to provide local copies of relevant data objects

▶ Colocating tables that belong to the same integrity constraint so as to eliminate messages needed to determine if a required dependency between tables is fulfilled

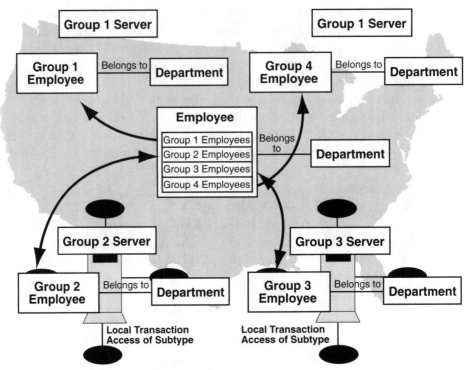

FIGURE 22.2   Distributed database design.

▶ Use of the same type of resource manager for data belonging to the same transaction groups

▶ Use of replicated file systems or replicated databases to supply local copies of reference data or slowly changing required information

The Logical Unit of Work

Earlier, in Guideline 22.1, we emphasized that a transaction protects information from loss or distortion during changes. The most important mechanism for providing this protection is the logical unit of work, or LUW. A transaction begins and ends an LUW. The changes made to data inside the LUW are private. They may not be shared with any other process until the transaction ends the LUW successfully and commits the changes to the database. All changes are concealed until that point because the transaction may elect to end the LUW and throw away all of the changes. But, the protection that the LUW provides imposes a heavy cost in overhead.

Given all of this, defining the logical unit of work for each group of database objects is easily the most important deliverable of the performance management plan. The transaction monitor regulates the consistency within individual LUWs. The LUW reflects requirements of the business transaction and the rules embedded in the data design. The fewer distributed messages the LUW requires, the faster it executes. Since we are primarily concerned with performance, the points in Table 22.3 are significant to distributed design.

Earlier in this chapter, when we discussed the need to separate the application function into client and server components, we mentioned that the database functions belong in the server. In Chapter 15 we also discussed partitioning the application to enhance performance. We need to apply the same principles to distributed transaction design.

Table 22.3　**Distributed Design Considerations**

	Single Data Object	**Multiple Data Objects**
Single location	Single objects should be the focus of an individual unit of work. A single object managed by a single resource manager provides the most efficiently performed update. There is also much less likelihood of other forms of degradation such as that introduced by locking.	If multiple objects are required, as they often are, they should be serviced by the same resource manager. The fact that they are colocated guarantees that the update is performed as quickly as possible. Multiple data objects may also be supported by declarative DBMS mechanisms that enhance the integrity.
Multiple locations	This is an instance of replication. See Chapter 20 for a detailed discussion of replication.	On rare occasions contingent updates need to be carried out in different locations. This is the worst case for performance. It is also a difficult situation for integrity. The TM must be employed in such cases. There is no possibility of TP-Lite or Loosley coupled transactions. At the very least, the resource managers should be of the same type. This ensures that the RMs employ the same isolation, commit, and recover methods.

Typically, client/server application designs partition functions into sets of subfunctions. These subfunctions can be assigned to client or server processes as required. They can be distributed to different platforms. A transaction design should try to benefit from this partitioning by colocating the application subfunctions requiring data with the database server that provides access to the data. This design will reduce the number of messages a transaction requires for the specific database operation.

In many cases, these functions may be implemented as stored procedures, which are managed by the DBMS. The stored procedures and the data they access are about as closely together as they can get. Sometimes, the stored procedure is implemented as a trigger that is automatically "fired" by changes made to specific database objects. Triggers are often used to implement a variety of cascading types of changes within a single server. They have the advantage of being a property of the data being changed rather than a property of the function changing the data—that advantage makes triggers independent of any specific application.

There is a down side to the use of triggers, though. They can produce performance problems by increasing the possibility of contention with other processes. The larger the number of changes occurring within a transaction, the greater the possibility that serious contention problems will be created by the locking that those changes require. A change to one object under the control of the transaction monitor that fires numerous triggers can produce multiple changes within the LUW. As we pointed out earlier, the LUW protects the changes from being seen by any other process. This means it will hold the locks until the LUW completes, even if the change involves changes to dozens of tables. So, the use of triggers must be designed and evaluated carefully.

Guideline 22.4   **Use triggers sparingly**

Don't use triggers indiscriminately when distributed update is possible. A remote update can encounter significant contention if it fires triggers that perform additional updates. If triggers act on remote data objects, the integrity and performance situation can be a real mess.

Grouping Transactions

The more work that a transactional client can send to a transaction monitor at one time, the better. Designing transactions so that they can be sent and processed in groups is one way in which this can be accomplished. The client needs to send groups of transactions to the server. The transaction design must also provide logic for the server to deal with multiple transactions. The server will have to manage multiple LUWs and handle a variety of outcomes. This practice allows the server to optimize the service time by executing a series of transactions without intervening communications waits, and it minimizes the messages exchanged between the transaction participants.

Guideline 22.5	Group transactions before sending them to the server

The transaction design needs to create groupings of transactions at the client before initiating a session with the server. This will serve to optimize service time at the server and will minimize messages exchanged.

A transaction also requires synchronization messages between the resource manager and the transaction monitor to coordinate the commit scope of the transaction. Predicting how many messages will be exchanged by the transaction monitor, the transaction manager, and the resource manager will require specific knowledge about the transaction.

If the initiator of the transaction is also remote from the resource manager, an exchange of messages occurs for each atomic transaction. This means additional overhead associated with the marshaling and unmarshaling of messages. It is assumed that every message is of optimal length. If not, most systems invoke a process like paging to write the overflow to temporary disk storage. In any event, creating and processing each message requires computing cycles as well as bandwidth. Once again, we emphasize the need to minimize messages in a distributed environment.

Transactions also need to be simple and short. They need to invoke as few data resources as possible, and they need to try to perform their work within a single commit. If a transaction can be carried out in less than 500ms, and if it can confine itself to updating a single table, it will probably perform well when hundreds of individuals are executing it at the same time.

Such simplicity however, is often not possible. Transaction requirements may demand an execution time far in excess of 500ms, and complex transactions using intermediate save points are often required. This is especially true when stored procedures are remotely invoked. We discuss the effects of longer, more complex transactions on performance, and especially on locking, in Chapter 15.

Specialized Performance Enhancing Techniques

Transaction monitors provide resources to safeguard integrity under the most adverse circumstances. Adverse circumstances occur only rarely, and transaction design can improve performance by "pushing the envelope" of integrity guarantees. An application can take advantage of conditions existing in specific, known situations to improve performance by circumventing these stringent safeguards. If the assessment is correct, the performance improvement will not be at the expense of integrity. If the assessment is incorrect, however, the integrity of the transaction can be compromised.

Judgment of the designer is all-important to the use of the following techniques.

Optimistic Update. Optimistic update is a well-known method for performing database updates. The procedure is based on the observation that two applications rarely update the same row at the same time. Of course, if the unusual happens, transaction integrity requires that the concurrent changes be prevented from interfering with each other.

Basically, optimistic update techniques apply an update to a row if the data in the row doesn't change. The technique requires two phases, a read phase and an update phase. The read phase obtains the baseline information, which is checked during the update phase. Figure 22.3 illustrates the process.

Optimistic update is an excellent technique to apply when RPCs are being used. It allows the client to operate relatively independently of the server. Most

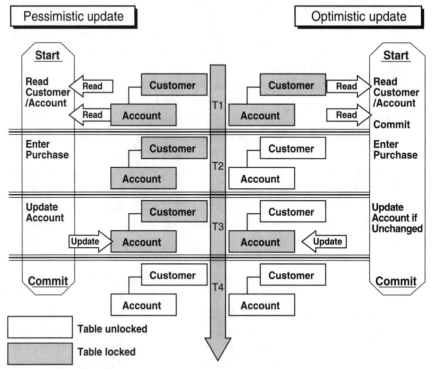

FIGURE 22.3 Optimistic update method.

of the time, the updates that are sent to the server are applied. Infrequently, additional messages need to be exchanged when a concurrent update from a different application violates the "optimistic" assumption.

Transaction Chopping.   Short, simple transactions are always more efficient than long, complex ones. Many times, however, a transaction needs to update multiple resources in a single unit of work. This creates a complex transaction that may perform badly and experience serious contention problems.

"Transaction chopping" refers to the process of implementing a single, long transaction as a series of smaller transactions. The problem is that the decomposition of the long transaction is not arbitrary. A transaction can be divided only if it does not lose its overall integrity. Will anyone be surprised to learn that transaction chopping is more difficult than the name implies? Dennis Shasha provides a detailed, formal analysis of the process so that the resulting subtransactions can be run in parallel, thereby improving performance and ensuring that integrity of the result is not compromised.[2]

Shasha also presents a rule of thumb. It basically states that if a transaction accesses two resources, it may be chopped into two transactions only if we are sure that every other possible transaction accesses no more than one of the resources. Transaction chopping can improve performance, but it may result in a loss of integrity as new, concurrent applications are added. It should be considered only when tables are owned by the application and when no new programs will violate essential requirements. This is the most important caveat associated with this process: No new transaction can access multiple resources within a single unit of work. If that happens, the "chopped" transaction becomes invalid.

Guideline 22.6   **Transaction chopping is temporary**
Use transaction chopping as a temporary measure to fix specific performance problems. Always document chopped transactions very visibly in case new applications invalidate the required update independence of participating tables.

Correctness of the transaction is all important. Performance improvement techniques should never compromise integrity to gain improvements in performance.

Relaxing Isolation.   Isolation is one of the four main transaction guarantees summarized by the ACID acronym. Isolation ensures that an individual is

_____
[2]Dennis E. Shasha, *Database Tuning: A Principled Approach* (Upper Saddle River, NJ: Prentice-Hall, 1992), 185–203.

working free from interference. It ensures that data that is being read is not being manipulated by some other process at the same time. It protects everyone in a multiuser environment from "trampling" each other. It also causes an untold number of headaches for developers who would like to develop efficient transactions to update a data object but learn that their carefully designed transaction never works quite right because it is being blocked by ". . . someone who is holding a lock on a required object and went out to lunch."

Locking, which we discussed extensively in Chapter 12, is the primary means of guaranteeing isolation. There are, however, other means of guaranteeing isolation, such as timestamp ordering, but transaction monitors and resource managers do not currently support timestamp ordering. Refer to Chapter 12 for a complete discussion on the impact of locking on performance and the standard classification of locking levels.

Basically, the resource manager issues a lock for an object before it allows access to the object itself. If the application cannot obtain the lock, it must wait until a lock becomes available before it can access the object. Most RDBMSs lock at the row or page level and employ more than one type of lock. Most file systems lock the entire file in an *exclusive* mode. It is important to realize that other resources, including queues, memory, and I/O devices, may also be locked. In fact, nearly any resource may be locked.

The problems that arise are that these resources may not be available when they are needed. An application has to wait—that is a problem. The application may have already locked one or more resources, thereby causing other applications to wait until those resources are released. And so on. **Deadlocks** occur when two applications each hold one resource the other needs. **Livelocks** occur when the same time-out situation occurs repeatedly. DBMSs and transaction monitors employ complex and sophisticated detection mechanisms to manage these contention situations. An application looking to improve its response time by using a loosely coupled transactional approach may find its performance suddenly deteriorating as the application volume grows and contention situations begin to arise that the resource manager cannot manage.

Guideline **22.7**	**Reduce the isolation level carefully**
	When reducing the isolation level, try to avoid situations where locking occurs outside of the control of a participating resource manager. This can lead to uncontrollable contention situations.

As we pointed out in Chapter 12, relaxing the isolation level is one of the most common performance measures available. Nearly every application, distributed or not, makes some use of the ability to relax the isolation level.

Segregating Informational and Transactional Processing

Mixing informational processing with transactional processing in a single transaction will result in poor performance. Transactions are dedicated to preserving data during changes, whereas informational processing is concerned with assembling a multitude of facts. Transactional databases are designed to make sure that every change is applied to one and only one data object, whereas informational processing duplicates information. Transactional applications restrict their access to a single remote server; informational applications assemble information from resources as far flung as the Internet.

But segregating informational and transaction processing has a more subtle aspect to it. Some type of query is required by almost every transaction. The application must determine if dependencies exist to process changes correctly. For example, the query must determine the bank balance before making a withdrawal, or it must ensure that an account exists before allowing a sale. These queries also constitute information processing; a high-performance transaction must also segregate the change component of the transaction from the information component.

Earlier in the chapter, we discussed "optimistic update," an example of segregating the information and change components within a transaction. In an independent database access, the client retrieves information. It is examined to determine if the requirements for an update are met. If the logic at the client concludes that the requirements are met, the transaction updates the database in a second independent transaction.

An even more efficient approach is to write the update statement in the transaction in such a way that the transaction does not have to read the table unless the update fails. For example, the transaction could invoke a database stored procedure similar to the following psuedocode:

```
START TRANSACTION
UPDATE ACCT BALANCE
SET CURR BAL = CURR BAL - :hv withdrawl
WHERE
   :hv withdrawl > CURR BAL
   AND ACCT ID = :hv myacct
IF SQLCODE = NOTFOUND
THEN
SELECT CURR BAL FROM ACC BALANCE
WHERE
   ACCT ID = :hv myacct
ELSE
COMMIT
```

One major advantage of either the optimistic approach or the alternative approach illustrated in the code example is that it takes advantage of an entirely subjective principle: **The Principle of the "Uphill Bicycle."** A bicyclist will never assume bad performance if a bicycle heading uphill goes slower and takes more effort than a bicycle headed downhill. If a user normally completes updates quickly, then is suddenly faced with a problem that is clearly labeled and that requires perceptible work, the user will usually conclude that the longer update time is due to the additional work needed to deal with the situation.

Incidentally, this principle relates to the external consequences of applying the Workload Principle correctly. If we take care not to burden the mainline path of an application with processing that's needed only for exception conditions, then the result will exhibit the kind of "optimistic" behavior we recommend here.

Guideline 22.8	**Use optimistic updating techniques**

Use optimistic update methods to segregate data retrieval aspects from change components of a transaction.

If a transactional program needs to read files or databases prior to updating them, the update should be done last in order to minimize the length of time that exclusive locks are held. The intent of locks is to serialize access to a data resource. If a transaction takes exclusive locks before it needs to, it prevents other applications from accessing the resource longer than necessary. Chapter 15 points out that locks should be retained for as little time as possible. For any transaction, this is best achieved by performing all read operations first, then performing updates immediately before the transaction ends.

Guideline 22.9	**Update the database at the end of the transaction**

If a single transaction must read and update the database, the update operation should always be performed last so that the most restrictive locks are held for the minimum amount of time.

Conclusion

Transaction monitors are becoming a key part of the distributed, client/server environment. They represent a class of middleware that leverages processing resources to service transaction requests efficiently. The transaction monitor provides services that optimize use of system resources to gain the greatest throughput and the highest integrity. To use the transaction monitor to its best advantage, the transactional application needs to be designed to exploit the transaction monitor's scheduling and load-balancing capabilities.

The transactional application must be built from simple, short applications wherever possible. Individual transactions should limit access of data objects to the least possible number, ideally no more than a half dozen. The client must be multithreaded so that communication waits do not necessarily prevent work from being completed in other areas. And, as much as possible, the number of messages in a transaction must be minimized.

The following design goals will help to ensure good performance in distributed transactions:

▶ Keep transactions short, less than 0.5 second if possible.
▶ Segregate informational and transactional functionality.
▶ Exploit existence of replicated services, especially file or data services.
▶ Group services by function, complexity, and frequency of execution.
▶ Separate longer-running servers from shorter-running ones.
▶ Don't wait.
▶ Do not use modal dialogs—they block other processes.
▶ Do not retrieve what you can compute.
▶ Do not combine processing with presentation.
▶ Do not combine direct access of a database with access managed by a transaction monitor.

These summarized points all help to develop independent processes that can be performed in parallel. They also help to design well-structured transactions that will guarantee integrity of the information.

Resources

A Performance-Oriented Glossary

Abstraction   A representation of a problem in a simplified general form, to eliminate irrelevant details. The basis for all types of modeling. (See Chapter 7.)

Access path (selection)   The process whereby the **Query optimizer** component of a DBMS selects an optimal sequence of low-level data manipulation actions (the *access path*) to satisfy one or more database queries, usually expressed as **SQL** statements. See also **Global optimization.**

ACID   The four key integrity properties of **Transaction processing**: **A**tomic, **C**onsistent, **I**solated and **D**urable. Applications adhering to these properties use *a combination* of systems software, application code, and business processes to enforce these properties of **OLTP** systems. See also **TRI-ACID.** (See Chapter 15.)

Aggregate   A static object structure created by grouping similar objects prior to execution time. For example, when performing repetitive UI tasks, a set of fixed windows, menus, and dialog boxes that require the minimum of navigation can significantly improve the **Perceived response time** of the application. (See Chapter 9.)

Analysis phase   Within the **SDLC,** the step in which we document the requirements for a particular business function or subject area. Analysis specifies *what* the system must do, not *how* it is to be done. Within **SPE,** identifying the users' most critical processing requirements that will determine many application and database design decisions. (See Chapter 4.)

Analytic modeling   A performance prediction technique normally done using a body of mathematical methods collectively referred to as **Queuing theory.** (See Chapter 6.)

API   *Application Programming Interface.* (See Chapter 3.)

Application design   In a database context, designing applications that will use the DBMS efficiently, including the best way to code (**SQL**) data manipulation statements. (See Chapter 19.)

Application load testing   Testing and verifying the performance of a server application under conditions that simulate the processing load that would be generated by a network of client workstations. (See Chapter 18.)

Application logic   Application functions that do not belong in the other **Layers**—the business logic and the flow of control among application components A layer of application software that manages communications between **Presentation logic** and **Data logic.** (See Chapter 2.)

Application middleware   A class of **Middleware** that permits two user-written application components communicate in any way that suits the application designer and developer. In contrast to **Presentation middleware** and **Database middleware,** application middleware allows the designer more flexibility to choose how the distributed components as an application will communicate. (See Chapter 15.)

Application partitioning   Distributing the processing components of applications for optimal performance given an existing geographical distribution of data. (See Chapter 19.)

Application performance profile   A collection of information about the performance characteristics of an application. Each row of an **Application-resource usage matrix** is a simple example of an application performance profile. (See Chapter 5.)

Application profiling   Monitoring and analyzing application behavior to determine how a particular program uses DBMS resources, or how a particular data manipulation request interacts with a particular database or set of databases—for example, by using an DBMS-supplied **Explain (or Showplan)** facility. Part of the process of developing an **Application performance profile.** (See Chapter 19.)

Application-resource usage matrix   A tabular depiction of applications mapped to logical and physical resources. Rows represent a *workload* A row of the matrix may be devoted to any application or group of *applications* having similar processing characteristics. Columns represent system *resources.* A column may be devoted to a *logical resource* like an object, a table, or a database, or to a *physical resource* like a processor, a disk device, or a network link. (See Chapter 3.)

APS   *Access Path Selection.* See **Access path, Query optimizer, Global optimization.** (See Chapter 19.)

Asynchronous application protocol   An **Application middleware** protocol in which the initiating process is **Unblocked**—it can continue processing after sending the request, possibly sending further messages to the same target process, or to others, in the meantime. Identifying asynchronous processes is the first step in creating high performance systems. Asynchronous processes minimize **Perceived response times,** and create opportunities to apply parallel processing and batching techniques. (See Chapter 15.)

Asynchronous events   Computer tasks or (secondary) conditions that can be handled independently of a (primary) task of interest, and therefore do not contribute to its response time. (See Chapter 3.)

Asynchronous replication   Replication of information without using a **Two-phase commit** protocol to maintain database integrity. The copy lags the source by some interval, called **Latency,** and so may not reflect the true state of affairs in the originating data source. The opposite of **Synchronous replication.** (See Chapter 20.)

Availability   The percentage of scheduled system time in which the computer is actually available to perform useful work. Often measured in terms of the Mean Time To Failure (**MTTF**). (See Chapter 3.)

Average job turnaround time   The interval between the instant that the computer system reads the batch program (or "job") and the instant that it completes program execution. See also **Elapsed time.** (See Chapter 3.)

Average service time   When any computing resource is shared among many processes, the average time a process takes to use the resource is known as its average *service time.* It is the sum of **Waiting time** and **Holding time.** (See Chapter 11.)

Average throughput   See **Throughput.** (See Chapter 3.)

Bandwidth (network)   *Bandwidth is the* capacity *of a network component to transmit data—in other words, its* **Throughput.** It is a function of the transmission medium (analogous to *the highway*) and protocol used (analogous to *the speed limit*). (See Chapter 11.)

Batch window   A period of time during which a job-stream must be started and finished. A collection of batch jobs that must run within an allotted amount of time. (See Chapter 3.)

Benchmark   A standard workload. The process of setting up, running, and measuring such a workload, for the purpose of comparing hardware or software performance. (See Chapter 3.)

Biasing techniques   Design techniques that favor a particular application or usage pattern. Often associated with **Grouping** techniques. Examples include database denormalization, which has the effect of biasing the storage structure in favor of one particular usage pattern, or customizing an Object Class within an ODBMS for a specific application. (See Chapter 9.)

Binding   The action of creating a static relationship between dissimilar components prior to program execution. (See Chapter 9.)

Bitmap indexes   An indexing method using a string of bits for each distinct key value. Within each string, the bits indicate which column values in the table match the particular key value. Bitmap indexes are particularly suited to columns with a low number of distinct values (i.e. low *cardinality*). (See Chapter 21.)

Block (or blocked) fetch   A DBMS server mechanism that transfers query result rows (the *result set* or *result table*) to the client requester in groups, rather than one row at a time. Also called *cursor record blocking.* (See Chapter 9.)

Blocked (interprocess communications)   See **Synchronous** communications. (See Chapter 15.)

Bottleneck device   The first device to saturate (i.e., to reach 100 percent of its capacity) as workload volumes increase. Also called the **Bottleneck server.** (See Chapter 3.)

Bottleneck server   See **Bottleneck device.** (See Chapter 3.)

Business drivers   See **Business factors.** (See Chapter 5.)

Business element drivers   See **Business factors.** (See Chapter 5.)

Business factors   The foundation upon which other key activities—setting objectives, designing, and predicting performance—are built, and the context for all SPE activities. *Key* business factors are the business quantities that most affect the processing load placed on the system. Also called **Business drivers, Business element drivers,** or **Natural forecasting units (NFUs).** (See Chapter 5.)

Business logic   See **Application logic.** (See Chapter 2.)

Cache   One of the most widely used techniques to improve software and hardware performance. It does this by retaining copies of frequently used data items—the cache—in a smaller but much faster device, and then searching the cache first for any requested data element. Since the cache is usually invisible to the requesting process, it gives the appearance of a reduced access time for the underlying device. (See Chapter 14.)

Cache hit-ratio (or hit-rate)   The metric by which we measure success of a **Cache.** (See Chapter 14.)

Cache hit/miss   Finding/not finding an element in a **Cache.** The **Cache hit-ratio** (or **hit-rate**) is the percentage of requests satisfied from a cache. (See Chapter 14.)

Centering principle   From a performance point of view, the act of focusing on those parts that will have the greatest impact on performance. (See Chapter 4.)

Checkpoint   A point of consistency that is recorded in persistent memory to allow for rapid restart in the case of an error. (See Chapter 9.)

Client application   That portion of a distributed application executing on an end-user's computer workstation within a 2*n* tier application (See Chapter 3.)

Client/server computing   A form of distributed computing in which an application is divided, or partitioned, into discrete processes, each of which typically executes on a different computing platform appropriate to the specific requirements of that process. (See Chapter 2.)

Cohesion   A term used in software design to describe the functional "strength" of a software *module,* in that the more help a module needs from its colleagues, the weaker it is. The concept of cohesion can obviously be generalized to apply in a similar way to other components like objects, data tables, and windows. (See Chapter 7.)

Committed read   A form of **Isolation level.** Applications may not read uncommitted, or dirty data, and will be prevented from overwriting another application's dirty data. (See Chapter 12.)

Compensating process   When any phase of a multiphase business process cannot complete, the appropriate set of compensating actions are taken to undo whatever partial progress has been made. In **Multitransaction workflows,** identifying an *updating* process usually triggers a requirement to design a compensating process. (See Chapter 17.)

Complete response time   All the time between the start of a task and the complete return of the response set. (See Chapter 3.)

Connection-oriented protocol   One in which the two parties first *connect,* exchange messages, and then *disconnect.* The exchange of messages may be **Synchronous** or **Asynchronous.** (See Chapter 15.)

Connectionless (application protocol)   One in which the initiator does not enter into a connection with the target process. The recipient of a message simply acts upon it—and if appropriate, responds—but retains no further relationship with the requester. (See Chapter 15.)

Construction phase   Within the **SDLC,** the step in which we write the necessary code to implement the **Technical design.** (See Chapter 4.)

Control logic   See **Application logic.** (See Chapter 2.)

Conversational (application communication protocol)   A **Connection-oriented** exchange of messages between two communicating processes, such that the two processes remain active throughout the exchange. Usually **Synchronous.** (See Chapter 15.)

CORBA   *Common **Object Request Broker** Architecture.* An architectural specification document released by the **OMG** that describes a messaging facility for *distributed objects* to provide a standard mechanism for objects to transparently invoke each other's services independently of OO languages, tools and platforms. An **Object Request Broker** that adheres to the specification is said to be *CORBA compliant.* (See Chapter 15.)

Coupling   The degree of interconnection or interdependence among the modules or data elements of a design. A good software design is one in which the degree of coupling is minimized and the types of coupling confined to the low end of the coupling spectrum. Essentially the inverse of **Cohesion.** (See Chapter 7.)

CRUD matrix   An array showing the **C**reate, **R**ead, **U**pdate, and **D**elete activity of a set of applications or programs mapped against a set of relational tables and/or columns. (See Chapter 3.)

Cursor record blocking   See **Block** (or **blocked**) **fetch.** (See Chapter 9.)

Cursor stability   A form of **Isolation level.** A row read by one application will not be changed by another application while it is being used. (See Chapter 12.)

Data analysis   The phase of database design concerned with identifying the logical structure of the information to be processed and stored. A necessary precursor to good relational and physical database design. (See Chapter 19.)

Data distribution   Determining the optimal scheme for distributing data among DBMSs situated at various locations in a distributed enterprise. (See Chapter 19.)

Data logic   One of the logical **Layers** of a distributed application containing all the logic that relates to the storage and retrieval of data, and enforcing business rules about data consistency. A component of the **Data management** functional area of the application. (See Chapter 2.)

Data management   A major grouping of the **Data logic** and database management **Layers** of an application. (See Chapter 2.)

Data mart   Subject-specific databases for departmental or workgroup use, usually designed to support a specific business situation. They may be created from the **Enterprise data warehouse,** or may be standalone databases in their own right, derived directly from operational data. (See Chapter 21.)

Data mining   A term used for a process of developing inferences from data and presenting them as rules or process models. Data mining examines the contents of a database with the purpose of discovering new associations among the facts recorded there. Also known as "database exploration" or "knowledge discovery." (See Chapter 21.)

Data replication   The process of copying data from one site to another. Replication strategies may be transactionally oriented or table-oriented. In a transaction-oriented strategy, a **Transaction** is captured and transmitted to the replica systems. In a table-oriented strategy, an entire table is transmitted. (See Chapter 20.)

Data transfer time (disk)   The time to read the data stored on the disk. Data transfer rates typically range from 1MB to 10MB per second. (See Chapter 3.)

Database design   One of the distinct DBMS-related design activities. Selecting among the logical and physical database structures offered by a particular DBMS, to meet application performance goals. (See Chapter 19.)

Database engine   Another term for a **DBMS,** a software product for managing information in databases.

Database gateway   A type of **Database middleware,** typically supporting an **ODBC API,** that provides remote database access. (See Chapter 19.)

Database middleware   Software (often supplied by a DBMS vendor) that ships **SQL** requests over a network to the DBMS, and returns any results to the application. See also **Database gateway.** (See Chapter 15.)

Database server   Strictly, the combination of a **DBMS** (software) and the computer (hardware) platform it resides on.

DBMS   *Database Management System.* Also called a **Database engine,** and sometimes a **Database server,** although the latter term normally includes both the hardware and the software.

DBMS tuning   Adjusting the many software options provided by a DBMS vendor to customize the behavior of a particular DBMS to best suit a particular mix of databases and application programs. (See Chapter 19.)

Deadlock   A situation in which two (or more) processes require a resource (usually a lock) held by the other. When deadlocks are common, application redesign is called for. (See Chapter 12.)

Declustering   See **Partitioning.** (See Chapter 13.)

Decoupled processes   Decoupling occurs when we can separate the different parts of a distributed system so that no one process ever needs to stop processing to wait for the other(s). The opposite of **Entangled components.** Along with **Multitransaction workflows,** one of the two key starting points for designing high-performance enterprise client/server systems. (See Chapter 15.)

Degree locality   Degree Locality refers to *closeness in capacity.* To ensure degree locality, we must match the data storage, transmission, and processing demands imposed by the business workload with the capacities of the hardware and software resources that make up the system. (See Chapter 10.)

Delay server   In a performance model, a delay server is used to represent a fixed delay imposed by a resource that is not being investigated by the model. (See Chapter 6.)

Deployment   Within the **SDLC,** the step in which we undertake the required steps to get the new system up and running in **Production** mode. Common tasks include loading old data to the new system, training users, and establishing a help desk. (See Chapter 4.)

Direct communication (application protocol)   A method of communication in which **Middleware** accepts a message from an initiating process and passes it directly to a target process. (See Chapter 15.)

Dirty read   A form of **Isolation level.** Applications may read data that has been updated but not yet committed to the database (*dirty data*), and that may never be committed if, for some reason, the updating application fails before it completes. (See Chapter 12.)

Distributed logic model   A form of **Distribution model,** such that we split the **Presentation logic** and **Data logic** components, with the Presentation manager and **Presentation logic** residing on the workstation and the **Data logic** and Data manager residing on the Server. The network link is placed between the presentation and data logic components. For most operational applications of a commercial nature, distributed logic is usually best, minimizing network traffic, whilst maximizing server database integrity. (See Chapter 2.)

Distributed transaction   See **Global transaction.** (See Chapter 15.)

Distributed Transaction Monitor   An evolution of traditional **OLTP Transaction Monitors,** which support *distributed* **Transaction processing** across multiple networks and platforms. DTMs manage transactions explicitly from inception to completion, providing the highest level of transaction processing reliability Contrast with **TP-Lite.** (See Chapter 15.)

Distribution model   In the design of distributed applications, a particular style that determines how logical **Layers** are assigned to physical tiers. Remote Presentation, Distributed Logic and Remote Data Access are three widely used distribution models. (See Chapter 2.)

DRDA *Distributed Relational Database Architecture.* IBM's protocol for exchanging SQL among its DB2 family of relational DBMSs, and the de-facto industry standard for interconnecting heterogeneous SQL database systems. (See Chapter 15.)

DSS *Decision Support System.* (See Chapter 9.)

DTC *Distributed Transaction Coordinator.* A product from Microsoft for its Windows platforms. The first stage appears in SQL Server 6.5, and supports distributed SQL Server transactions (the ability for client programs to initiate transactions across multiple SQL Server databases, irrespective of whether they are local or geographically dispersed). (See Chapter 15.)

Dynamic cache A **Cache** whose contents change according to its usage pattern, typically based on an **LRU** algorithm.

Dynamic compilation A form of **Binding,** in which an entire source module is compiled into machine language at execution time. The system may retain the compiled version temporarily in a cache for subsequent use, but does *not* retain a permanent copy of the compiled code. For example, see **Dynamic SQL.** (See Chapter 9.)

Dynamic Inheritance The successive loading of class definitions up the inheritance hierarchy, typically from disk, and if on a LAN, then remotely across the network to the server. A form of **Object Inheritance;** contrast with **Static inheritance.** (See Chapter 9.)

Dynamic lock escalation When a single process has acquired an excessive number of locks, the DBMS raises its lock level dynamically to *table* from *row* or *page,* lessening its impact on the system's shared memory resource. (See Chapter 12.)

Dynamic SQL The style of processing in which a DBMS receives an SQL statement at program execution time, evaluates various possible ways of processing that SQL request against the data, selects an *access path,* and then perform that access path. A form of **Dynamic compilation.** Contrast with **Static SQL.** (See Chapter 9.)

Effective response time The time that elapses before a user is free to interact with the system, even if the response to the initial request is not yet complete. This is often the metric by which the end-user evaluates the performance of an online system. (See Chapter 3.)

Effectual locality When we build enterprise information systems, achieving effectual locality means making sure that separate components work together smoothly to satisfy the user's needs. This can mean many things—dedicating physical resources to match the nature of the workload, building or selecting software components that mesh together, or picking software that suits the user's workload. (See Chapter 10.)

Efficiency principle The most efficient design is the one that maximizes the ratio of useful work to overhead. (See Chapter 9.)

EIS *Executive Information System.* (See Chapter 9.)

Elapsed time For a batch job, the amount of time that elapsed on the clock while the work was being processed. (See Chapter 3.)

Entangled components A system with high **Coupling,** or many interconnections among the components. This kind of design is the result of doing a poor job of **Grouping.** The opposite of **Decoupled processes.** (See Chapter 16.)

Enterprise computing The organizational perspective and the infrastructure needed to balance the concerns and perspectives of many constituencies (systems, applications, individual end-users, and departments). It takes a wider view, focusing on the costs and benefits of systems in the context of overall organizational goals, applying business priorities when making tradeoffs among individual perspectives. (See Chapter 3.)

Enterprise data warehouse   An integrated system of databases, services, tools and methods, whose data is typically derived from core subject areas of an enterprise's operational systems and possibly external data feeds for the purpose of cross-functional informational and analytical access (i.e., **DSS**). Often used by business analysts for the purposes of performing **OLAP** and **Data mining.** (See Chapter 19.)

Environment tuning   In the context of a database application, adjusting the hardware or software environment within which the DBMS and the applications operate. (See Chapter 19.)

Explain (or Showplan)   A DBMS design evaluation feature that depicts the database **Access path** selected by the **Query optimizer.** Typically used passively after completing the process of physical **Database design,** and so, of limited value as a robust design tool. See **APS.** (See Chapter 19.)

External response time   The response time delay imposed on a requester by a called component, also called **Minimum response time.** See also **Internal response time.** (See Chapter 3.)

Foreign code   Most of the instructions executed by any enterprise client/server application are not written by the programmer who coded the core application logic. They are supplied from outside ("foreign") sources such as a class library, a compiler, an application generator, or a DBMS. (See Chapter 8.)

Fragmentation   See **Partitioning.** (See Chapter 13.)

Function logic   See **Application logic.** (See Chapter 2.)

Function shipping   Sending the process ("function") to the server, as opposed to moving data across a network to the client for local processing. Can be implemented by **Stored procedures,** which have the additional advantage of batching all the requisite **SQL** function requests for a process within the DBMS itself. A good example of **Spatial locality.** (See Chapter 10.)

Generic development process   A general-purpose classification of the **SDLC** into seven generally accepted phases, without regard to a life-cycle model or methodology. The phases are **planning, analysis, schematic design, technical design, construction, deployment,** and **production.** (See Chapter 4.)

Global optimization   A technique used by a **Database gateway** to select the optimal access path for a query against a distributed database (See Chapter 9.)

Global transaction   A **Transaction** involving update activities at several nodes in a distributed system, and so requiring the participation of multiple **Transaction Managers** to coordinate the commit process. Also called a **Distributed transaction.** (See Chapter 15.)

Grouping   The appropriate location of functions or **Layers** within the distributed environment. Any situation in which connections are established between separate computing components (hardware or software, data or process) for the purpose of performing a task. The performance of any complex system will depend largely on the grouping choices and decisions made during the design of that system. (See Chapter 2.)

Holding time   The time a process takes to use a shared computing resource or device. See also **Scheduling time** and **Average service time.** (See Chapter 3.)

Hot spot   Excessive contention that occurs when too many concurrent applications need to lock the same data item, or the same small set of data items. (See Chapter 12.)

Internal response time   The response time viewed from *inside* a particular system component, from the time it receives a request until the time it returns the response. See also **External response time** and **Minimum response time.** (See Chapter 3.)

Interpretation   Using a separate *interpreter* program, proceeding instruction by instruction through the source code at execution time, reading the source code, and acting upon it. See also **Binding.** (See Chapter 9.)

Irrevocable process   An irrevocable process is one whose effects cannot be backed out by some kind of **Compensating process.** (See Chapter 16.)

Isolation level   A method of controlling the degree of data integrity enforcement in database applications. The type of insulation of database updates made by an application process from those made (or intended to be made) by another process. Common examples are **Cursor stability, Committed read, Dirty read,** and **Repeatable read.** (See Chapter 12.)

Just in time compilation   Proceeding through the source code instruction by instruction at execution time, converting the source code into machine code and then immediately executing the result, ideally retaining the converted instructions in case they are reused (in a program loop, for example). See also **Binding.** (See Chapter 9.)

Latency   The delay imposed by a computing device. In practice, *latency* is usually applied to devices other than the CPU—that is, memory and I/O devices—because they are slower than the CPU, and therefore they delay processing. (See Chapter 3.)

Layer   See **Layering.**

Layering   The subdivision of a system into a hierarchy of interconnected components. (See Chapter 16.)

Load Balancing   A re-distribution of a server workload by dynamically creating additional instances of a server application module to accommodate peaks in the distribution of work. An advanced feature typically incorporated in a well-configured **Distributed Transaction Monitor.** (See Chapter 15.)

Local transaction   When a complex **Global transaction** must update data at several nodes of a distributed system, it can often be decomposed into several smaller more granular (local) transactions. (See Chapter 15.)

Lock (database)   A locksize to prevent concurrent data manipulation activities, or changes to the structure of any table in the database (usually a named collection of tables). (See Chapter 12.)

Lock (page)   A locksize to protect all rows in a database or index page. (See Chapter 12.)

Lock (row)   A locksize to protect against concurrent manipulation of a single row or index entry. (See Chapter 12.)

Lock (table)   A locksize to prevent concurrent access to an entire table. (See Chapter 12.)

Logical design   An imprecise term; see **Schematic design.** In database design, *logical design* can mean either **Data Analysis,** or **Relational design,** or both. (See Chapter 4.)

Logical performance model   A performance **Model** that points out the amount of work the application needs to do—work that will make demands on whatever resources are ultimately involved—without taking into account the specific hardware and software on which the application runs. A logical performance model takes into account the **Business factors,** data structures and processes, and uses this information to estimate execution frequencies and the resulting *logical* I/O operations. (See Chapter 6.)

Lossless compression   *Lossless* methods preserve every bit of the original data, as is essential with most binary, numeric, and text data. (See Chapter 11.)

Lossy compression   A compression method where there can be a tradeoff between performance and the quality of the data delivered. (See Chapter 11.)

LRU   *Least Recently Used.* A common algorithm for dynamic **Cache** management. Elements of the **Cache** remain in storage in accordance with their relative utilization. As the demand for **Cache** elements diminishes over time, those elements will be progressively discarded from storage, being replaced by more heavily (and recently) accessed elements. (See Chapter 14.)

LUW   *Logical Unit of Work.* The interval within a business process (or **Transaction**) between the first update to a recoverable resource made by a **Resource manager,** and the ultimate disposition of the updates made by that process, as indicated by the decision to accept (commit) or reject (rollback) all updates to those resources. See also **ACID.** (See Chapter 22.)

MDA   *MultiDimensional Analysis.* A series of operations performed on data to resolve a specific analysis question, derived from the user's perception of data presented as specific business *dimensions.* Common dimensions are time, customer, product, geographic location or organization. These operations make up the great bulk of **OLAP,** and may employ the services of a **MDBMS** or **MOLAP** server. Contrast with **RDBMS** and **ROLAP** servers. Often used in conjunction with a **Star schema** design. (See Chapter 21.)

MDBMS   *MultiDimensional Database Management System.* See also **MDD** and **MOLAP.** (See Chapter 21.)

MDD   *MultiDimensional Database.* See **MDBMS.** (See Chapter 21.)

Message-oriented middleware   Commercial messaging middleware that supports application-to-application communication using a high-level messaging **API.** The messaging model may be direct (see **P2P**) or indirect (see **MQ**). The most well established **MQ** product is IBM's MQSeries. With messaging, each program has its own associated queue, and two programs communicate with each other by leaving a message on the message queue of the other application, at any location, and for any purpose. Messages may contain data, control information, or both. Programs may have an **Asynchronous** connection so that each can proceed at its own optimal pace. (See Chapter 15.)

Middleware   Software that enables inter-process communication. It provides an **API** that isolates the application code from the underlying network communication formats and protocols (FAPs). Also supplies intermediate system services (such as Security, Naming, Directory and Messaging). Following the three kinds of logic, we define three types of middleware: presentation, database and application (also called *distributed logic middleware*). The most sophisticated **Application middleware** implementations include **Message-oriented middleware, Distributed Transaction Monitors,** and **ORBs.** (See Chapter 15.)

Minimum response time   The time a requester is inactive between a component issuing a request and the return of the first character of the response to that; could also be referred to as the *observed* response time, or the **External response time** for a particular component. (See Chapter 3.)

Model   An **Abstraction** of a real system—a simplified representation that hides much of the real-world detail to reveal only those things that are important. During the **SDLC,** a model may be a formal or informal representation of *function* of the system under development, using text or diagrams, and providing a framework for development activities. In a performance model the focus is on system *resource usage.* (See Chapter 4.)

MOLAP   Multidimensional **OLAP** used either with a multidimensional DBMS (**MDBMS**) or a **MOLAP** server. (See Chapter 21.)

MOM   See **Message-oriented middleware.** (See Chapter 13.)

MPP   *Massively Parallel Processors.* A hardware implementation of the **Shared nothing** model. Each CPU or *node* in a shared nothing machine has its own allocation of memory and disks. Compare with **SMP.** (See Chapter 13.)

MQ   *Message Queuing.* A form of **Message-oriented middleware.** An application using **MQ** writes to a queue (or a *queue manager*) rather than directly to another application process. In a dialog between two programs, each program has its own associated queue, and they communicate with each other by leaving a *message* on the message queue of the other. The queue manager middleware takes care of moving messages between the queues. Because each process reads from and writes to a queue, rather than connecting directly to its partner, they can run independently, at different speeds and times, with or without a logical connection. (See Chapter 15.)

MTTF   *Mean Time To Failure.* We define a failure as any reason that the system is not available during normal operating hours. See also **Availability.** (See Chapter 3.)

Multithread measurement   Another term for a **Benchmark,** a controlled measurement of a known workload mix. (See Chapter 6.)

Multitransaction workflows   Often, we can split up the *business* transaction into a series of separate *computer* transactions. The result is a *multitransaction workflow.* Along with **Decoupled processes,** one of the two key starting points for designing high-performance enterprise client/server systems. (See Chapter 15.)

Multiprocessing   On a multiprocessor (a machine with multiple CPUs), the right operating system software can drive parallel processes, keeping multiple CPUs and even more disks busy Compare with **Multiprogramming.** (See Chapter 13.)

Multiprogramming   A long-established Operating System technique for running programs concurrently, creating the illusion of parallel processing, even though there may be only one **CPU.** Compare with **Multiprocessing.** (See Chapter 13.)

CPU   *Central Processing Unit.* The computer component that processes program instructions. See also **Multiprocessing, SMP,** and **MPP.**

Natural forecasting units (NFUs)   A term used by primarily by capacity planners to describe known **Business factors** that provide a convenient basis for forecasting future workload patterns (usually, but not necessarily, workload growth.). (See Chapter 5.)

Object   A computer *object* (in the object-oriented sense) is a representation of some real-world object, implemented as a collection of related properties of different types that, in some context, belong together. These properties may be static (data attributes) or dynamic (program modules, also called *object methods*). (See Chapter 10.)

Object Inheritance   A programming mechanism within the Object Technology paradigm that allows the properties (attributes and associated methods) of one object to be propagated to other objects, through the definition of a class hierarchy or inheritance hierarchy. (See Chapter 9.)

Observed response time   See **Minimum response time.** (See Chapter 3.)

ODBC   *Open Database Connectivity.* Microsoft's implementation of a generic interface (or **API**) permitting Windows-based applications to access a variety of diverse data sources. An example of a *call-level interface,* as specified by the SQL Access Group (SAG). Contrast with the *embedded* **SQL** interface found in IBM's DB2 family of products.

ODS   *Operational Data Store.* A database created for **DSS** applications but containing data with a purely *operational* orientation, concerned only with relatively current information about business transactions (as opposed to an **Enterprise data warehouse,** which typically also contains a lot of historical and aggregated data). Because an ODS accumulates current and recent data, it may act as a staging area between the operational systems and the **Enterprise data warehouse.** (See Chapter 21.)

OLAP   *Online Analytical Processing.* As distinct from more traditional Online Transaction Processing (**OLTP**), OLAP refers to a combination of tools and data used to discover trends and patterns in business events during interactive sessions. A business analyst can perform online **MDA** in much the same way that data entry is done in OLTP. (See Chapter 21.)

OLTP   *Online Transaction Processing.* The style of traditional, host-based enterprise computing supporting high volume, high performance mission-critical business applications. Typically implemented by a robust **Transaction Monitor,** guaranteeing support for the **ACID** properties of commercial **Transaction processing.** In the distributed environment, now supported by **Distributed Transaction Monitors.** Contrast with **OLAP.** (See Chapter 15.)

OMG   *Object Management Group.* An industry consortium responsible for creating the **CORBA** architectural specification.

Optimizer   A component of an **RDBMS** that analyzes an SQL statement and selects the **Access path** it considers likely to be the most efficient. (See Chapter 9.)

ORB   *Object Request Broker.* A form of **Application middleware** that arbitrates the interaction between *distributed objects.* (See Chapter 15.)

P2P   *Point-to-Point (messaging).* P2P **Middleware** relays a message between two or more partners who are connected and available. In other words, P2P middleware supports **Direct communication.** The most popular example of P2P middleware is PeerLogic's PIPES. (See Chapter 15.)

Paging (of memory)   The moving inactive parts of active processes to disk in order to reclaim some pages of physical (real) memory. (See Chapter 3.)

Parallelizing compiler   A type of compiler that can analyze large computationally intensive programs and identify instruction sequences that can be processed in parallel by a **Multiprocessing** computer. (See Chapter 13.)

Partition   The set of rows of a table that reside on a single node of a parallel processor. It can also be called a table *fragment.* (See Chapter 13.)

Partitioning   The process of distributing rows among **Partitions.** Also known as **Fragmentation,** or **Declustering** (because the rows are no longer clustered together on a single node). Not to be confused with **Application partitioning.** (See Chapter 13.)

Patch ("quick-fix")   A method of avoiding system design changes by writing new code that is typically inconsistent with system design. A short-sighted attempt to save money and, often, postpone the inevitable. (See Chapter 4.)

Perceived response time   The amount of time that a user *perceives* a task to take. It is disproportionately influenced by the longest response times. One rule of thumb is that the perceived value of average response time is the 90th percentile value of the response time distribution. (See Chapter 3.)

Physical design   See **Technical design.**

Physical performance model   A performance **Model** that adds performance measures for the specific hardware and software environment. (See Chapter 6.)

Planning phase   Within the **SDLC,** the step in which we identify the major functions of our business. We also identify *subject areas,* or broad areas of related business data, and correlate them with business functions (See Chapter 4.)

Presentation logic   One of the logical **Layers** of a distributed application containing all the logic needed to manage screen formats, the content of windows, and handle interaction with the user. A component of the User Interface functional area of the application. (See Chapter 2.)

Presentation management   A major grouping of the Graphic Layout and **Presentation logic Layers** of an application pertaining to user interface matters like managing menus, screen formats, and data validation. (See Chapter 2.)

Presentation middleware   *Screen-scrapers* or terminal emulation software that allows **Presentation logic** to execute at a location remote from business function logic. (See Chapter 15.)

Proactive performance management   Establishing performance *objectives* during planning and analysis, and comparing these with performance *predictions* made during design. During production, *monitoring* the system to verify that it meets our objectives. Seeking to identify problems before they occur. (See Chapter 4.)

Production   The daily operation of a computer system in support of routine business activity. The end goal of the **SDLC.** Within **SPE,** includes **proactive performance management.** (See Chapter 4.)

Pseudo-conversational (application communication protocol)   A method of mimicking **Conversational (application communication protocol)** using connectionless protocols, typically implemented by saving some context information, and then terminating the server process. Widely used in IBM's CICS and IMS/TM teleprocessing monitors. (See Chapter 15.)

Quantitative specification   How different parts of the processing will relate to business factors like the number of customers needing certain types of service, and the expected frequencies of those business activities. (See Chapter 8.)

Query optimizer   A crucial component of an **RDBMS** that maps the SQL query onto the physical data structures, and generates an **Access path**—a set of data access requests to lower level DBMS access methods. This process is called *automatic access path selection* (**APS**). A component that isolates the application developer or end-user from understanding the physical design characteristics of the database, and so implements the relational database model's feature of *physical database independence.* When based upon comparative evaluation of the relative cost of all reasonable access paths to the data, called a *cost-based* optimizer. The selected access path may be examined by an **Explain** (or **Showplan**) feature of the DBMS. (See Chapter 19.)

Query parallelism   Processing a single **SQL** statement using multiple parallel **Asynchronous** I/O streams and/or multiple process streams. (See Chapter 13.)

Queued (application protocol)   An **Application middleware** protocol in which the initiating process (or *queue manager* **Middleware**) places the message in a queue, from where the target process retrieves it later, at its convenience. A response, if required, flows back via a similar route. With queue management middleware, processes connect to a queue manager, rather than directly to their partners. A connection to a single queue manager can give the application access to multiple queues, and each of those queues can in turn be read by one or more partners. (See Chapter 15.)

Queuing theory   A body of mathematical methods used to perform **Analytic modeling.** Mathematical analysis of the type of data that is summarized in an **Application-resource usage matrix.** The mathematics first evaluate device utilization levels by accumulating the total impact of all processes on each resource, then compute the resultant delays each process experiences waiting for service. (See Chapter 6.)

Queuing time   Time spent waiting to be serviced by a shared resource. Also called **Waiting time,** or **Scheduling time.** (See Chapter 3.)

RAID   *Redundant Array of Inexpensive (or Independent) Disks.* Can provide faster data access to large blocks of data by using **Striping** the data and then reading from several disks in parallel. Most RAID devices also store some redundant control information that allows them to survive a disk failure without loosing the stored data. (See Chapter 3.)

RDBMS   *Relational Database Management System.* A Database Management System (DBMS) adhering to the principles of the Relational Model of data, first articulated by Dr. E. F. Codd in 1969. The prevailing DBMS in most current **Client/server computing** systems. (See Chapter 2.)

Relational design   The database design phase during which the output of a **Data Analysis** phase is converted into a set of relational tables, columns, and keys. Ideally, this design is DBMS-independent, but in practice, *Winsberg's Law of Logical Design* applies.

Remote data access model   A form of **Distribution model,** in which the Presentation Management and all **Data logic** resides on the client and only the Data Manager resides on the remote server. (See Chapter 2.)

Remote presentation model   A form of **Distribution model,** in which only the Presentation Manager function group resides on the client workstation; everything else (**Presentation logic, Data logic** and data manager) resides on the server. (See Chapter 2.)

Repeatable process   A repeatable process is one that does not change important and persistent business data. An inquiry can be repeated, but the update to a bank balance cannot. (See Chapter 17.)

Repeatable read   A form of **Isolation level** in which data items that have been read are locked until the application reaches a commit point, so that any data item, if re-read, will contain the same value as previously. (See Chapter 12.)

Resource manager   A program that manages any kind of resource such as a database, memory, or even a communications port. Typically, however, it refers to a DBMS. (See Chapter 22.)

Resource utilization   The average level of use of a particular system component over some period of time (because instantaneous device utilizations are usually either "*busy*" or "*idle*"). Often expressed as a percentage, for example, "CPU utilization is 85 percent". (See Chapter 3.)

Response time   In the **Transaction processing** or query environments, a measure of how long it takes to finish some task, often called a **Unit of work.** Typically understood as the time from the moment a user hits the *Enter* key until data is (first) returned to that user's workstation. In the batch processing environment, referred to as **Elapsed time.** See also **Complete response time, External response time, Internal response time,** and **Perceived response time.** (See Chapter 3.)

RID, ROWID   A *row identifier* in a B-tree index, which is used to locate a particular row in a particular database table. (See Chapter 19.)

ROLAP   Relational **OLAP** using a **RDBMS** as the *back-end.* A set of tools optimized for performing business analysis of events, trends and patterns. (See Chapter 21.)

Rotational delay (disk)   The time for the start of the data to rotate to the position of the read/write head. Typically, 4ms to 8ms. (See Chapter 3.)

RPC   *Remote Procedure Call.* **Middleware** that allows a program to call a remote program in the same fashion as a local one; typically employing naming and security servers to control access to remote programs. (See Chapter 13.)

Scalability   The capacity to perform more total work in the same **Elapsed time.** A system or machine would have linear or perfect scalability if increasing its compute power by some percentage had the effect of increasing its capacity to process work by the identical percentage. (See Chapter 13.)

Scheduling time   See **Queuing time.** (See Chapter 11.)

Schematic design   Within the **SDLC,** the step during which we develop the structure of the system at a high level, independent of the intended implementation platform(s) and technologies. Also called **Logical design.** (See Chapter 4.)

SDLC   *System (or Software) Development Life Cycle.* The collection of tasks and activities performed during the development of an information processing system, from initial inception through to **Production,** and beyond. May include a formal or informal development methodology, addressing the specification of phases, tasks/activities, critical success factors, deliverables, etc. (See Chapter 4.)

Seek time (disk)   The time for the read/write head to move laterally to the correct location on the magnetic surface. Typically about 10ms. (See Chapter 3.)

Sensitivity analysis   Using a (logical or physical) performance model to perform "what-if" analysis, and thereby identify the sensitivity of predicted performance to the implementation of proposed changes. (See Chapter 6.)

Service classes   Logical groupings of work that will receive a defined level of service. By supporting the service class concept, systems software allows an administrator to specify how shared computing resources should be allocated among competing workloads of differing sizes and priorities. (See Chapter 5.)

Service Level Agreement   A document that defines measures of performance, satisfactory performance levels, and individual roles and responsibilities. Typically the result of the agreement formulated by the team responsible for **Service level management.**

Service level management   The application of *matrix management* principles to the problem of performance, such that a *team* takes overall responsibility for performance. (See Chapter 4.)

Service level objectives   The agreed upon performance objectives, because they define organizational goals for the level of service to be provided to external or internal customers of the information systems. Typically documented and formalized in a service level agreement. (See Chapter 5.)

Service multiplier   The factor by which **Response time** is extended at various **Resource utilization** levels. (See Chapter 11.)

Shared disk   A Multiprocessor architecture that places the interconnect between the memory and the disks. Each processor has its own memory, but all the memories use the interconnect to satisfy the data access requests from all disks. All data stored on all disks is available to all processors via the memory. (See Chapter 13.)

Shared memory (or shared everything)   A **Multiprocessor** architecture in which the CPUs are all connected to the shared memory by the interconnect, with the memory being linked to all disks. Therefore the interconnect to the shared resource (memory) carries requests for that shared resource, or for data residing in that shared resource. (See Chapter 13.)

Shared nothing   A **Multiprocessor** architecture in which the interconnect links the processors only. Each processor has its own complement of memory and disks. (It is a slight misnomer to call this architecture *shared nothing,* because the interconnect itself is a shared resource). (See Chapter 13.)

Simulation Modeling   A performance prediction technique involving actually building a software **Model** of each device, a model of the queue for that device, model processes that use the devices, and a model of the clock in the real world. (See Chapter 6.)

Single-thread measurement   An application measurement made in a controlled environment, with no competing work. (See Chapter 6.)

Skimming effect   A phenomenon observed in multilevel caches, in which the first cache to receive an application's requests "skims off the cream" of frequently requested data items, passing only the cache misses through to the next level. (See Chapter 14.)

SLA   See **Service Level Agreement.** (See Chapter 4.)

SMP   *Symmetric Multiprocessors.* A hardware implementation of the **Shared memory** model. A single operating system manages all processes, handling I/O interrupts and scheduling CPU's to process work. The shared memory makes scheduling simple, because every CPU has access to the same data. (See Chapter 13.)

Snowflake schema   A more normalized variant of the **Star schema** design. (See Chapter 21.)

Soft skills   The non-technical requirements for successful **SPE (Software Performance Engineering).** For example, management skills, business awareness, good communication, negotiation and compromise. (See Chapter 4.)

Spatial locality   Closeness in distance. Spatial locality refers to the design issue of which components to collect together physically. A fundamental performance issues in the design of distributed systems. It suggests **Grouping** elements that will be used together. (See Chapter 10.)

SPE   *Software Performance Engineering.* Concise definition: *Software engineering with performance in mind.* (See Chapter 4.)

Full definition: *". . . a method for constructing software systems to meet performance objectives. The process begins early in the software life cycle and uses quantitative methods to identify sat-*

isfactory designs and to eliminate those that are likely to have unacceptable performance, before developers invest significant time in implementation. SPE continues through the detailed design, coding, and testing stages to predict and manage the performance of the evolving software and to monitor and report actual performance against specifications and predictions. SPE methods cover performance data collection, quantitative analysis techniques, prediction strategies, management of uncertainties, data presentation and tracking, model verification and validation, critical success factors, and performance design principles." C. U. Smith (1990)

SPEC   *Standard Performance Evaluation Corporation.* A consortium of RISC workstation manufacturers, and the collection of benchmarks they sponsor. (See Chapter 6.)

Speedup   The capacity of the system to perform a particular task in a shorter time. A system or processor would have linear speedup if increasing its compute power by some percentage had the effect of reducing the elapsed time for a task to the inverse percentage. (See Chapter 13.)

SQL   *Structured Query Language.* The data sublanguage generally accepted as the standard for definition, access and manipulation of data stored and managed by a **RDBMS.** (See Chapter 2.)

Standard applications   Programs whose behavior and workload are known. They can be used individually to investigate and isolate the location of performance problems. A suite of standard applications can be used to summarize system-wide **Response time** performance. (See Chapter 5.)

Star schema   Used in some Data Warehouse database designs, a design consisting of one or more large *fact* tables and several small *dimension* (or *reference*) tables. The fact tables contain the information of interest to the business, and the dimension tables are used to view this data across different dimensions, for example, time, product, or market. The key of a fact table is normally a combination of keys of the dimension tables. See also **OLAP, MOLAP, ROLAP,** and **MDA.** (See Chapter 13.)

Static cache   A **Cache** whose contents are fixed, regardless of usage patterns.

Static compilation   Compiling the entire source module into machine language once and storing a permanent copy of the executable version for repeated use later. One way of **Binding** source code instructions to the target processor. (See Chapter 9.)

Static inheritance   An object-oriented *compile and link* or *build* process; the logic from many separate source modules is combined into a single executable. A form of **Object Inheritance;** contrast with **Dynamic Inheritance.** (See Chapter 9.)

Static SQL   SQL that is compiled in advance of its execution by the DBMS, and its access path details stored in a DBMS catalog or directory for later use; contrast with **Dynamic SQL.** (See Chapter 9.)

Stepwise refinement   The systematic process of decomposition and elaboration, recursively developing new levels of detail as needed. It is the basis for the existence of the successive phases found in every **Model** of the **SDLC.** (See Chapter 7.)

Stored procedure   A collection of data processing statements co-located with the database(s) they manipulate (In that respect, they score high on **Spatial locality**). Stored database procedures eliminate the need to ship processing requests across the network, and may, if the procedures are pre-compiled into **Static SQL,** also eliminate the overheads of repeated compilation of those requests. (See Chapter 10.)

Striping (disk)   Spreading a sequence of data across a set of disks, so that every disk in the set can (when it makes sense for a particular data request) be read in parallel. (See Chapter 3.)

Synchronous (interprocess communications)   An **Application middleware** protocol in which the initiating process sends a message (typically called a *request*) and waits for a *response* before it can continue processing. Also called **Blocked.** The opposite of **Asynchronous** processing. (See Chapter 15.)

Synchronous replication   A style of data replication in which all remote copies of a database are notified immediately a change happens at the primary site. Moreover, the change to all copies occurs within the same unit of work as the change to the primary database. Requires use of the **Two-phase commit.** protocol. Also called **Transactional replication.** The opposite of **Asynchronous replication.** (See Chapter 20.)

Technical design   The **SDLC** phase in which we extend the work of schematic design for specific products. If we are using relational database technology, for example, we design for a specific relational product, such as DB2 or Oracle, and its unique characteristics. Also called **physical design.** (See Chapter 4.)

Temporal Locality   Temporal Locality refers to the performance benefits of completing a group of related actions at the same time, or sequentially without delay. (See Chapter 10.)

Thrashing   A situation that arises when **Paging** activity builds to the point at which the CPU is almost solely occupied with shuffling pages around with barely any time for useful work. (See Chapter 3.)

Three-tier architecture   An advance over the two-tier physical implementation of distributed computing in which a new **Layer** is introduced between the desktop client and the database server. Functions are embedded in the user interface, and business processes are captured in this middle layer that can also handle system services, while the information model is encapsulated in a data layer. Typically introduced to support the more stringent requirements of large, enterprise, distributed computing systems, such as high performance, **Scalability,** and security. We distinguish between the *logical layering* of function into **Presentation logic, Application logic, and Data logic,** and the *physical distribution* of function across client workstations, departmental servers, and enterprise servers. (See Chapter 2.)

Throughput   A measure of the amount of work a component or a system is performing as a whole, or a measure of the rate at which a particular workload (or subset) is being processed. Because it deals with system wide performance, in a client/server environment throughput is a measure of performance that is primarily used for *servers.* (See Chapter 3.)

Throughput chain   Similar to the concept of the critical path in project management, the throughput chain identifies all the devices involved in one application's interaction with a client/server computing environment. (See Chapter 11.)

TP-Lite   A limited form of support for **Transaction** processing provided by certain Client/ Server DBMS servers. (See Chapter 15.)

TPC   *Transaction Processing Council.* A consortium of DBMS vendors and other interested parties, and the collection of benchmarks they sponsor.

Transaction   An interaction that guarantees the integrity of updated information, protecting it from distortion or loss as a result of change. The task is complicated in a client/server environment where transaction integrity must be preserved across a variety of platforms and **Resource managers.** The basis of traditional **OLTP.** See also **ACID** and **LUW.** (See Chapter 22.)

Transaction Manager   Specialized software that manages specific **Transactions.** It is always associated with an individual transaction, and is normally tied to an individual **Resource manager** during the scope of a particular transaction. The transaction manager makes sure that transactional guarantees are met for that resource. Compare with **Transaction Monitor.** (See Chapter 22.)

Transaction Monitor   A standard feature of mainframe online processing for years, best typified by IBM's CICS/ESA and IMS/TM products In this environment, the transaction monitor usually manages key resources and provides display services; often tightly coupled with the operating system within a **Shared memory** architecture. In the distributed enterprise computing environment, evolving into the development of **Distributed Transaction Monitors.** (See Chapter 22.)

Transaction processing   A style of processing that is concerned with ensuring the integrity of changes to the data managed by one or more **Resource managers.** Also typically concerned with efficient processing of high volume workloads. Common in the mainframe or host-centric environment and increasingly important in the client/server environment in which **Transaction** integrity must be preserved across a number of platforms that differ in reliability and in the services they can provide. It supports the **ACID** attributes of transactions, and is managed by a **Transaction Manager,** or **Transaction Monitor.** In the distributed enterprise computing environment, supported by **Distributed Transaction Monitors.** (See Chapter 22.)

Transactional replication   See **Synchronous replication.** (See Chapter 20.)

TRI-ACID   A messaging implementation of the **Transaction processing ACID** properties in three separate steps. Involves recoverable message queues and guaranteed message delivery. (See Chapter 15.)

Two-phase commit   A method of coordinating a single **Transaction** across more than one DBMS (or other **Resource manager**). It guarantees data integrity by ensuring that transactional updates are committed in all of the participating databases, or are fully rolled back out of all of the databases, reverting to their states before commencement of the transaction. See also **Transaction processing, ACID,** and **LUW.** (See Chapter 12.)

Unblocked application protocol   See **Synchronous** communications. (See Chapter 15.)

Unit of work   In the context of the **Workload principle,** any software element whose size and scope is subject to design, but which, once created, is processed as a whole. Examples include routines, modules, **Transactions,** windows, messages, tables, and objects. Also known as a **LUW.** (See Chapter 8.)

User population   The set of users supported by a particular computer or software product. System performance is strongly influenced by user population attributes like *size, transaction rate,* or *response requirements.* (See Chapter 3.)

Virtual data warehouse   An architecture that allows direct access to operational databases and files from terminals or client workstations. Often leads to performance problems, because of *Inmon's Rule.* (See Chapter 21.)

VLDB   *Very Large Database.* A subjective term, but let us say, a database exceeding 500 gigabytes, and so presenting a distinct set of operational, performance and management challenges. It is expected that (multi) terabyte databases will soon be commonplace. (See Chapter 21.)

Waiting time   Time spent waiting to be serviced by a shared resource. Also called Wait time, **Queuing time** or **Scheduling time.** (See Chapter 3.)

Waiting time estimate   (processing time multiplied by utilization)/(100 minus utilization). Note the inverse (and exponential) relationship between waiting time and device utilization. (See Chapter 3.)

Wisconsin benchmark   A benchmark that measures relational DBMS performance, developed at the University of Wisconsin from 1981 onwards. Once the de facto standard, it has now been replaced in that role by the **TPC** benchmark(s). (See Chapter 3.)

Workload principle   To minimize total processing load for a workload composed of a number of separate components, minimize the sum across all workload components of *execution frequency* times *cost per execution.* (See Chapter 8.)

Index of Guidelines
by Subject Area

Index

A

abstraction, 709
access path, 274, 709
  Efficiency Principle, 278–280
accuracy, prediction, and detail considerations,
    performance prediction, 171, 172
ACID (atomic, consistent, isolated, durable), 709.
    See also transaction processing
  test, processing transactions, 485
  to TRI-ACID with MOM, 492–494
activity tracing and logging, 287, 288
Admahl's law, 387, 388
affinity analysis, 76
aggregate, 263, 709
analysis phase, 91, 709
analysis, simulation comparison, performance pre-
    diction, 182
  recommendations, 184–186
  what if . . ., impact of model changes, 182, 183
analytic modeling, 163, 164, 709
anticipatory buffering, 448
API (application programming interface), 21, 470,
    709
application
  area, 131
  context, 313
  design, 592, 709
    patterns, 520–526
  development tools, 572–576
  flow
    as performance factor, 14, 44
    designing, 538, 539
  -level protocols, middleware, 461–466
  load testing, 592, 709
  logic, 709
  middleware, 709, 710
    APIs, 473
    interoperates, 473–475
  partitioning, 238, 592, 710
  performance profiles, 130, 131, 710
    detailed, 131
    laws of, 132, 133
    workload characterization, 131
  profilers, 111
  profiling, 592, 710
  programming interface. *See* API
  -resource usage matrix, 75, 76, 331, 332, 710

  as SPE activity, 119, 120
    extending the matrix, 76–78
    using the matrix, 76
  tuning, 154–156
    Centering Principle and tuning, 156, 157
apply phase, data replication, 650–652
architectural patterns, 512–514
arrival distribution law, 338
associate, 264
asynchronous
  application protocol, 462, 710
  client/server communication, 478
  events, 52, 53, 710
  operations, batching of, 525
  patterns, 519
  replication, 710
  vs. synchronous replication, 632–634
atomicity, testing, 539, 540
availability, 710
  as measure of software quality, 60–62
  effect on performance, 46
average job turnaround time, 710. *See also* elapsed
    time
  batch processing and, 58
average service time, 710
average throughput. *See* throughput

B

bandwidth, 711
  availability, 73
  network delays, 352, 353
basic performance life-cycle, 97
batch
  processing, 47
    performance of, 58, 59
  vs. online transactions, 285, 286
  window, 711
batching, data integrity and, 537
benchmark, 711. *See also* benchmarking
  throughput, 59
  performance prediction, 163
benchmarking, performance prediction, 164, 165,
    186. *See also* benchmark
  complications in, 192–196
  deciding what to measure, 186, 187
  independent benchmarking organizations, 191,
    192

N